Lecture Notes in Computer Science 14674

Founding Editors

Gerhard Goos
Juris Hartmanis

The series Lecture Notes in Computer Science (LNCS), including its subseries Lecture Notes in Artificial Intelligence (LNAI) and Lecture Notes in Bioinformatics (LNBI), has established itself as a medium for the publication of new developments in computer science and information technology research, teaching, and education.

LNCS enjoys close cooperation with the computer science R & D community, the series counts many renowned academics among its volume editors and paper authors, and collaborates with prestigious societies. Its mission is to serve this international community by providing an invaluable service, mainly focused on the publication of conference and workshop proceedings and postproceedings. LNCS commenced publication in 1973.

José Manuel Ferrández Vicente ·
Mikel Val Calvo · Hojjat Adeli
Editors

Artificial Intelligence for Neuroscience and Emotional Systems

10th International Work-Conference on the Interplay
Between Natural and Artificial Computation, IWINAC 2024
Olhâo, Portugal, June 4–7, 2024
Proceedings, Part I

 Springer

Editors
José Manuel Ferrández Vicente
Universidad Politécnica de Cartagena
Cartagena, Spain

Mikel Val Calvo
Polytechnic University of Valencia
Valencia, Spain

Hojjat Adeli ⓘ
Ohio State University
Columbus, OH, USA

ISSN 0302-9743   ISSN 1611-3349 (electronic)
Lecture Notes in Computer Science
ISBN 978-3-031-61139-1   ISBN 978-3-031-61140-7 (eBook)
https://doi.org/10.1007/978-3-031-61140-7

This Springer imprint is published by the registered company Springer Nature Switzerland AG
The registered company address is: Gewerbestrasse 11, 6330 Cham, Switzerland

If disposing of this product, please recycle the paper.

Preface

The main topic of these IWINAC/ICINAC 2024 volumes is to study intelligent systems inspired by the natural world, in particular biology. Several algorithms and methods and their applications are discussed, including evolutionary algorithms. Bio-inspired intelligent systems have thousands of useful applications in fields as diverse as machine learning, biomedicine, control theory, telecommunications, and why not music and art. These volumes cover both the theory and practice of bio-inspired artificial intelligence, along with providing a bit of the basis and inspiration for the different approaches. This is a discipline that strives to develop new computing techniques through observing how naturally occurring phenomena behave to solve complex problems in various environmental situations. Brain-inspired computation is one of these techniques that covers multiple applications in very different fields. Through IWINAC/ICINAC we provide a forum in which research in different fields can converge to create new computational paradigms that are on the frontier between neural and biomedical sciences and information technologies.

As a multidisciplinary forum, IWINAC is open to any established institutions and research laboratories actively working in the field of natural or neural technologies. But beyond achieving co-operation between different research realms, we wish to actively encourage co-operation with the private sector, particularly SMEs, as a way of bridging the gap between frontier science and societal impact.

In this edition, four main themes outline the conference topics: Neuroscience, Affective Computing, Robotics, and Translational Systems.

1) Machine learning holds great promise in the development of new models and theories in the field of Neuroscience, in conjunction with classical statistical hypothesis testing. Machine learning algorithms have the potential to reveal interactions, hidden patterns of abnormal activity, brain structure and connectivity and physiological mechanisms of brain and behavior. In addition, several approaches for testing the significance of the machine learning outcomes have been successfully proposed to avoid "the dangers of spurious findings or explanations void of mechanism" by means of proper replication, validation, and hypothesis-driven confirmation. Therefore, machine learning can effectively provide relevant information to take great strides toward understanding how the brain works. The main goal of this field is to build a bridge between two scientific communities, the machine learning community, including lead scientists in deep learning and related areas within pattern recognition and artificial intelligence, and the neuroscience community. Artificial Intelligence has become the ultimate scale to test the limits of technological advances in dealing with Life Science challenges and needs. In this sense, the interplay between Natural and Artificial Computation is expected to play a most relevant role on the diagnosis, monitoring and treatment of Neurodegenerative Diseases, using the advanced computational solutions provided by Machine Learning and Data Science. This requires us to interchange new ideas, launch projects and contests, and eventually create an

inclusive knowledge-oriented network with the aim of empowering researchers, practitioners and users of technological solutions for daily life experience in the domains of Neuromotor and Linguistic competence functional evaluation, clinical explainability, and rehabilitation by interaction with humans, robots, and gaming avatars, not being strictly limited to only these, but inclusively open to others related. The use of Machine Learning-based Precision Medicine in monitoring daily life activity and providing well-being conditions to especially sensitive social sectors is one of the most relevant objectives. Case study descriptions involving neurodegenerative diseases (Alzheimer's disease, fronto-temporal dementia, cerebrovascular damage and stroke, autism, Parkinson's disease, amyotrophic lateral sclerosis, multiple sclerosis, Huntington's chorea, etc.) are included. Mild cognitive impairment (MCI) is considered the stage between the mental changes that are seen between normal ageing and early-stages of dementia. Indeed, MCI is one of the main indicators of incipient Alzheimer's disease (AD) among other neuropsychological diseases. The growth of these diseases is generating a great interest in the development of new effective methods for the early detection of MCI because, although no treatments are known to cure MCI, this early diagnosis would allow early intervention to delay the effects of the disease and accelerate progress towards effective treatment in its early stages. Although there have been many years of research, the early identification of cognitive impairment, as well as the differential diagnosis (to distinguish significant causes or typologies for its treatment), are problems that have been addressed from different angles, but are still far from being solved. Diverse types of tests have already been developed, such as biological markers, magnetic resonance imaging, and neuropsychological tests. While effective, biological markers and magnetic resonance imaging are economically expensive, invasive, and require time to get a result, making them unsuitable as a population screening method. On the other hand, neuropsychological tests have a reliability comparable to biomarker tests, and are cheaper and quicker to interpret.

2) Emotions are essential in human-human communication, cognition, learning and rational decision-making processes. However, human-machine interfaces (HMIs) are still not able to understand human sentiments and react accordingly. With the aim of endowing HMIs with the emotional intelligence they lack, Affective Computing focuses on the development of artificial intelligence by means of the analysis of affects and emotions, such that systems and devices could be able to recognize, interpret, process and simulate human sentiments.

Nowadays, the evaluation of electrophysiological signals plays a key role in the advancement towards that purpose since they are an objective representation of the emotional state of an individual. Hence, the interest in physiological variables like electroencephalogram, electrocardiogram, or electrodermal activity, among many others, has notably grown in the field of affective states detection. Furthermore, emotions have also been widely identified by means of the assessment of speech characteristics and facial gestures of people under different sentimental conditions. It is also worth noting that the development of algorithms for the classification of affective states in social media has experienced a notable increase in recent years. In this sense, the language of posts included in social networks, such as Facebook or Twitter, is evaluated with the aim of detecting sentiments of the users of those media tools.

Affective Computing and Sentiment Analysis is intended to be a meeting point for researchers who are interested in any of those areas of expertise related to sentiment analysis, and want to initiate their studies or are currently working on these topics. Hence, manuscripts introducing new proposals based on the analysis of physiological measures, facial recognition, speech recognition, or natural language processing in social media are examples of affective computing and sentiment analysis.

3) Over recent decades there has been an increasing interest in using machine learning, and in the last few years, deep learning methods, combined with other vision techniques, to create autonomous systems that solve vision problems in different fields. This special session is designed to serve researchers and developers to publish original, innovative and state-of-the art algorithms and architectures for real time applications in the areas of computer vision, image processing, biometrics, virtual and augmented reality, neural networks, intelligent interfaces and biomimetic object-vision recognition.

   This study provides a platform for academics, developers, and industry-related researchers belonging to the vast communities of Neural Networks, Computational Intelligence, Machine Learning, Deep Learning, Biometrics, Vision Systems, and Robotics, to discuss, share experience and explore traditional and new areas of computer vision, machine and deep learning combined to solve a range of problems. The objective of the workshop is to integrate the growing international community of researchers working on the application of Machine Learning and Deep Learning Methods in Vision and Robotics in a fruitful discussion on the evolution and the benefits of this technology to society.

4) Finally, Artificial Intelligence (AI) has become a catalyst for innovation in a wide variety of disciplines, playing a pivotal role in solving contemporary challenges. This session focuses on the translational applications of AI in multiple fields, highlighting how the technology is transforming key sectors in response to the needs of today's society. Grid and power infrastructure management is one of the domains where AI is revolutionizing efficiency and reliability. Through predictive analytics, optimization and proactive maintenance, AI enables a smarter and more resilient power grid, crucial in a world seeking decarbonization and the use of renewable energy. In agriculture, AI drives precision farming, improving agricultural production, water resource management and crop quality. In civil engineering, AI-assisted planning and design streamline construction projects and optimize infrastructure. Smart cities and urban planning benefit from AI to optimize transportation, waste management and the quality of life of inhabitants. In education, AI personalizes teaching and assessment, tailoring learning to the individual needs of students. In nutrition and food science, AI algorithms are used for creating healthy diets and detecting contaminants in food. This topic will explore how AI fosters innovation and transformation in these diverse areas, highlighting the solutions this technology offers to address current challenges and improve the quality of life in modern society. From smarter power grids to safer food, AI is paving the way to a more efficient and sustainable future in a variety of multidisciplinary fields.

The wider view of the computational paradigm gives us more elbow room to accommodate the results of the interplay between nature and computation. The

IWINAC/ICINAC forum thus becomes a methodological approximation (set of intentions, questions, experiments, models, algorithms, mechanisms, explanation procedures, and engineering and computational methods) to the natural and artificial perspectives of the mind embodiment problem, both in humans and in artifacts. This is the philosophy that continues in IWINAC meetings, the "interplay" movement between the natural and the artificial, facing this same problem every two years. This synergistic approach will permit us not only to build new computational systems based on the natural measurable phenomena, but also to understand many of the observable behaviors inherent to natural systems.

The difficulty of building bridges between natural and artificial computation was one of the main motivations for the organization of IWINAC 2024. The IWINAC/ICINAC 2024 proceedings contain the 99 works selected by the Scientific Committee from more than 193 submissions, after the refereeing process. The type of peer review used was single blind with an average number of reviews received per submission of 2.5, and an average number of papers per reviewer of 3 with external reviewers involved, outside the PC. The first volume, entitled Artificial Intelligence for Neuroscience and Emotional Systems and Health Applications, includes all the contributions mainly related to the new tools for analyzing neural data, or detecting emotional states, or interfacing with physical systems. The second volume, entitled Bioinspired Systems for Translational Applications: from Robotics to Social Engineering, contains the papers related to bioinspired programming strategies and all the contributions oriented to the computational solutions to engineering problems in different application domains, such as biomedical systems or big data solutions.

An event of the nature of IWINAC/ICINAC 2024 cannot be organized without the collaboration of a group of institutions and people who we would like to thank now, starting with Universidad de Granada and Universidad Politécnica de Cartagena. The collaboration of the Universidade do Algarve (UAlg), Nova University of Lisbon (NOVA) and Universidad Politécnica de Madrid (UPM), was crucial, as was the efficient work of the Local Organizing Committee, with Hugo Gamboa (NOVA), Joao de Sousa (UAlg), Pedro Gómez Vilda (UPM), Simao Souza (UAlg), Margarida Madeira (UAlg), Jaime Martins (UAlg), Carla Quintao (NOVA) and Luis Silva (NOVA). In addition to our universities, we received financial support from Red Nacional en Inteligencia Artificial para Neurociencia y Salud Mental (IA4NSM) and Apliquem Microones 21 s.l.

We want to express our gratitude to our invited speakers Hojjat Adeli, from Ohio State University (USA), Zidong Wang from Brunel University, London (UK), Nuno M. Garcia from Universidad de Lisboa (Portugal), and Asoke Nandi, from Brunel University, London (UK) for accepting our invitation and for their magnificent plenary talks.

We would also like to thank the authors for their interest in our call and the effort in preparing the papers, condition sine qua non for these proceedings. We thank the Scientific and Organizing Committees, in particular the members of these committees who acted as effective and efficient referees and as promoters and managers of pre-organized sessions on autonomous and relevant topics under the IWINAC/ICINAC global scope.

Our sincere gratitude goes also to Springer for their help and collaboration in all our joint editorial ventures.

Finally, we want to express our special thanks to BCD eventos, our technical secretariat, and to Ana María García, for making this meeting possible, and for arranging all the details that comprise the organization of this kind of event.

We want to dedicate these volumes of the IWINAC proceedings to Profs. Rodellar, Sánchez-Andrés and Mira.

June 2024

José Manuel Ferrández Vicente
Mikel Val Calvo
Hojjat Adeli

Organization

General Chair

José Manuel Ferrández Vicente   Universidad Politécnica de Cartagena, Spain

Organizing Committee

Mikel Val Calvo   Univ. Politécnica de Valencia, Spain

Honorary Chairs

Hojjat Adeli   Ohio State University, USA
Rodolfo Llinás   New York University, USA
Zhou Changjiu   Singapore Polytechnic, Singapore

Local Organizing Committee

Hugo Gamboa   Universidade NOVA de Lisboa, Portugal
Pedro Gómez-Vilda   Universidad Politécnica de Madrid, Spain
Joao de Sousa   Universidade de Algarve, Portugal
Simao Souza   Universidade de Algarve, Portugal
Margarida Madeira   Universidade de Algarve, Portugal
Jaime Martins   Universidade de Algarve, Portugal
Carla Quintao   Universidade NOVA de Lisboa, Portugal
Luis Silva   Universidade NOVA de Lisboa, Portugal

Invited Speakers

Hojjat Adeli   Ohio State University, USA
Zidong Wang   Brunel University, UK
Nuno M. Garcia   Universidad de Lisboa, Portugal
Asoke Nandi   Brunel University, UK

Field Editors

Sung-Bae Cho	Yonsei University, South Korea
Emilia Barakova	Eindhoven Univ. of Technology, Netherlands
Gema Benedicto	Universidad Politécnica de Cartagena, Spain
Diego Castillo-Barnes	Universidad de Granada, Spain
Enrique Dominguez	Universidad de Málaga, Spain
Félix de la Paz	Univ. Nacional de Educación a Distancia, Spain
Antonio Fernández-Caballero	Universidad Castilla-La Mancha, Spain
Jose García-Rodríguez	Universitat d'Alacant, Spain
Andrés Gómez-Rodellar	University of Edinburgh, UK
Pedro Gómez-Vilda	Universidad Politécnica de Madrid, Spain
Juan Manuel Górriz	Universidad de Granada, Spain
David Guijo-Rubio	Universidad de Córdoba, Spain
Marina Jodra	Universidad Complutense de Madrid, Spain
Vicente Julián-Inglada	Universitat Politècnica de València, Spain
Krzysztof Kutt	Jagiellonian University, Poland
Fco. Jesús Martínez Murcia	Universidad de Málaga, Spain
Rafael Martínez Tomás	Univ. Nacional de Educación a Distancia, Spain
Jiri Mekyska	Brno University of Technology, Czechia
Ramón Moreno	Grupo Antolin, Spain
Grzegorz J. Nalepa	Jagiellonian University, Poland
Andrés Ortiz	Universidad de Málaga, Spain
Daniel Palacios-Alonso	Universidad Rey Juan Carlos, Spain
José T. Palma	Universidad de Murcia, Spain
Jorge Pérez-Aracil	Universidad de Alcalá, Spain
Javier Ramírez	Universidad de Granada, Spain
Mariano Rincón Zamorano	Univ. Nacional de Educación a Distancia, Spain
Sancho Salcedo	Universidad de Alcalá, Spain
Jose Santos Reyes	Universidade da Coruña, Spain
Fermín Segovia	Universidad de Granada, Spain
Antonio Tallón	Universidad de Huelva, Spain
Ramiro Varela	Universidad de Oviedo, Spain

International Scientific Committee

Amparo Alonso Betanzos, Spain
Jose Ramon Álvarez-Sánchez, Spain
Margarita Bachiller Mayoral, Spain
Francisco Bellas, Spain
Emilia I. Barakova, Netherlands

Guido Bologna, Switzerland
Paula Bonomini, Argentina
Enrique J. Carmona Suárez, Spain
José Carlos Castillo, Spain
Germán Castellanos-Dominguez, Colombia

Contents – Part I

Machine Learning in Neuroscience

Morning Anxiety Detection Through Smartphone-Based
Photoplethysmography Signals Analysis Using Machine Learning Methods 3
   Masoud Sistaninezhad, Ali Jafarizadeh, Saman Rajebi,
   Siamak Pedrammehr, Roohallah Alizadehsani, and Juan M. Gorriz

Visualizing Brain Synchronization: An Explainable Representation
of Phase-Amplitude Coupling 14
   Andrés Ortiz, Nicolás J. Gallego-Molina, Diego Castillo-Barnes,
   Ignacio Rodríguez-Rodríguez, and Juan M. Górriz

Enhancing Neuronal Coupling Estimation by NIRS/EEG Integration 24
   Nicolás J. Gallego-Molina, Andrés Ortiz, Marco A. Formoso,
   Francisco J. Martínez-Murcia, and Wai Lok Woo

Causal Mechanisms of Dyslexia via Connectogram Modeling of Phase
Synchrony 34
   I. Rodríguez-Rodríguez, A. Ortiz, M. A. Formoso, N. J. Gallego-Molina,
   and J. L. Luque

Explainable Exploration of the Interplay Between HRV Features and EEG
Local Connectivity Patterns in Dyslexia 45
   Marco A. Formoso, Nicolás J. Gallego-Molina, A. Ortiz,
   Ignacio Rodríguez-Rodríguez, and Almudena Giménez

Enhancing Intensity Differences in EEG Cross-Frequency Coupling Maps
for Dyslexia Detection 55
   Diego Castillo-Barnes, Andrés Ortiz, Pietro Stabile,
   Nicolás J. Gallego-Molina, Patrícia Figueiredo, and Juan L. Luque

Improving Prediction of Mortality in ICU via Fusion of SelectKBest
with SMOTE Method and Extra Tree Classifier 68
   Mohammad Maftoun, Javad Hassannataj Joloudari, Omid Zare,
   Maryam Khademi, Alireza Atashi, Mohammad Ali Nematollahi,
   Roohallah Alizadehsani, and Juan M. Gorriz

A Cross-Modality Latent Representation for the Prediction of Clinical
Symptomatology in Parkinson's Disease 78
    Cristóbal Vázquez-García, F. J. Martinez-Murcia, Juan E. Arco,
    Ignacio A. Illán, Carmen Jiménez-Mesa, Javier Ramírez,
    and Juan M. Górriz

Zero-Shot Ensemble of Language Models for Fine-Grain Mental-Health
Topic Classification 88
    Cristina Luna-Jiménez, David Griol, and Zoraida Callejas

Enhancing Interpretability in Machine Learning: A Focus on Genetic
Network Programming, Its Variants, and Applications 98
    Mohamad Roshanzamir, Roohallah Alizadehsani,
    Seyed Vahid Moravvej, Javad Hassannataj Joloudari,
    Hamid Alinejad-Rokny, and Juan M. Gorriz

Enhancing Coronary Artery Disease Classification Using Optimized MLP
Based on Genetic Algorithm 108
    Mohammad Hashemi, Seyedeh Somayeh Salehi Komamardakhi,
    Mohammad Maftoun, Omid Zare, Javad Hassannataj Joloudari,
    Mohammad Ali Nematollahi, Roohallah Alizadehsani, Pietro Sala,
    and Juan M Gorriz

Extracting Heart Rate Variability from NIRS Signals for an Explainable
Detection of Learning Disorders 118
    Juan E. Arco, Nicolás J. Gallego-Molina, Pedro J. López-Pérez,
    Javier Ramírez, Juan M. Górriz, and Andrés Ortiz

Diagnosis of Parkinson Disease from EEG Signals Using a CNN-LSTM
Model and Explainable AI 128
    Mohammad Bdaqli, Afshin Shoeibi, Parisa Moridian,
    Delaram Sadeghi, Mozhde Firoozi Pouyani, Ahmad Shalbaf,
    and Juan M. Gorriz

Early Diagnosis of Schizophrenia in EEG Signals Using One Dimensional
Transformer Model 139
    Afshin Shoeibi, Mahboobeh Jafari, Delaram Sadeghi,
    Roohallah Alizadehsani, Hamid Alinejad-Rokny, Amin Beheshti,
    and Juan M. Gorriz

Diagnosis of Schizophrenia in EEG Signals Using dDTF Effective
Connectivity and New PreTrained CNN and Transformer Models 150
    Afshin Shoeibi, Marjane Khodatars, Hamid Alinejad-Rorky,
    Jonathan Heras, Sara Bagherzadeh, Amin Beheshti, and Juan M. Gorriz

A Survey on EEG Phase Amplitude Coupling to Speech Rhythm
for the Prediction of Dyslexia 161
    N. Gallego-Molina, F. J. Martinez-Murcia, M. A. Formoso,
    D. Castillo-Barnes, A. Ortiz, J. Ramírez, J. M. Górriz, P. J. Lopez-Perez,
    and J. L. Luque

Comprehensive Evaluation of Stroke Rehabilitation Dynamics: Integrating
Brain-Computer Interface with Robotized Orthesic Hand and Longitudinal
EEG Changes 171
    Yolanda Vales, Jose M. Catalan, Andrea Blanco-Ivorra, Juan A. Barios,
    and Nicolas Garcia-Aracil

PDBIGDATA: A New Database for Parkinsonism Research Focused
on Large Models 182
    R. López, F. J. Martinez-Murcia, J. Ramírez, T. Martín-Noguerol,
    F. Paulano-Godino, A. Luna, J. M. Górriz, and F. Segovia

A Comparative Study of Deep Learning Approaches for Cognitive
Impairment Diagnosis Based on the Clock-Drawing Test 191
    Carmen Jimenez-Mesa, Juan E. Arco, Meritxell Valenti-Soler,
    Belen Frades-Payo, Maria A. Zea-Sevilla, Andres Ortiz,
    Marina Avila-Villanueva, Javier Ramirez, Teodoro del Ser-Quijano,
    Cristobal Carnero-Pardo, and Juan M. Gorriz

Artificial Intelligence in Neurophysiology

Prediction of Burst Suppression Occurrence Under General Anaesthesia
Using Pre-operative EEG Signals 203
    Elif Yozkan, Enrique Hortal, Joël Karel, Marcus L. F. Janssen,
    Catherine J. Vossen, and Erik D. Gommer

Advances in Denoising Spikes Waveforms for Electrophysiological
Recordings 213
    Rocío López-Peco, Mikel Val-Calvo, Cristina Soto-Sánchez,
    and Eduardo Fernández

Analysis of Anxiety Caused by Fasting in Obesity Patients Using EEG
Signals 223
    Mariana Elizalde, Jesica Martínez, Mario Ortiz, Eduardo Iáñez,
    María Herranz-Lopez, Vicente Micol, and José M. Azorín

Evolution of EEG Fractal Dimension Along a Sequential Finger
Movement Task 233
    Sara Kamali, Fabiano Baroni, and Pablo Varona

Neuromotor and Cognitive Disorders

Stress Classification Model Using Speech: An Ambulatory Protocol-Based
Database Study 245
    Lara Eleonora Prado, Andrea Hongn, Patricia Pelle,
    and María Paula Bonomini

Exploring Spatial Cognition: Comparative Analysis of Agent-Based
Models in Dynamic and Static Environments 253
    Maria Luongo, Michela Ponticorvo, and Nicola Milano

Machine Learning for Personality Type Classification on Textual Data 261
    Igone Morais-Quilez, Manuel Graña, and Javier de Lope

Grad-CAM Applied to the Detection of Instruments Used in Facial
Presentation Attacks 270
    Irene García-Rubio, Roberto Gallardo-Cava, David Ortega-delCampo,
    Julio Guillen-Garcia, Daniel Palacios-Alonso, and Cristina Conde

Comparison of an Accelerated Garble Embedding Methodology
for Privacy Preserving in Biomedical Data Analytics 282
    Nikola Hristov-Kalamov, Raúl Fernández-Ruiz,
    Agustín álvarez-Marquina, Esther Núñez-Vidal,
    Francisco Domínguez-Mateos, and Daniel Palacios-Alonso

Unfolding Laryngeal Neuromotor Activity in Parkinson's Disease
by Phonation Inversion 300
    Pedro Gómez-Vilda, Andrés Gómez-Rodellar, Jiri Mekyska,
    Agustín Álvarez-Marquina, and Daniel Palacios-Alonso

Personalization of Child-Robot Interaction Through Reinforcement
Learning and User Classification 310
    Anniek Jansen, Konstantinos Tsiakas, and Emilia I. Barakova

EGG: AI-Based Interactive Design Object for Managing Post-operative
Pain in Children 322
    Jing Li, Kuankuan Chen, Liuyiyi Yang, Milou Mutsaers,
    and Emilia Barakova

Cepstral Space Projection on the Evaluation of Autistic Speech: A Pilot
Study 332
    Andrés Gómez-Rodellar, Marina Jodra-Chuan,
    José Manuel Ferrández-Vicente, and Pedro Gómez-Vilda

Unravelling the Robot Gestures Interpretation by Children with Autism
Spectrum Disorder During Human-Robot Interaction 342
    Gema Benedicto, Carlos G. Juan, Antonio Fernández-Caballero,
    Eduardo Fernandez, and Jose Manuel Ferrández

Real-Time Emotion Detection System's Impact on Pivotal Response
Training Protocol 356
    Gema Benedicto, Félix de la Paz, Antonio Fernández-Caballero,
    and Eduardo Fernandez

Intelligent Systems for Assessment, Treatment, and Assistance in Early Stages of Alzheimer's Disease and Other Dementias

Assessing the Interplay of Attributes in Dementia Prediction Through
the Integration of Graph Embeddings and Unsupervised Learning 371
    Pablo Zubasti, Antonio Berlanga, Miguel A. Patricio, and José M. Molina

Bayesian Network Structures for Early Diagnosis of MCI Using Semantic
Fluency Tests 381
    Alba Gómez-Valadés, Rafael Martínez-Tomás, and Mariano Rincón

Connectivity Patterns in Alzheimer Disease and Frontotemporal Dementia
Patients Using Graph Theory 390
    María Paula Bonomini, Eduardo Ghiglioni, and Noelia Belén Rios

Socio-Cognitive, Affective and Physiological Computing

Binary Classification Methods for Movement Analysis from Functional
Near-Infrared Spectroscopy Signals 401
    Daniel Sánchez-Reolid, Roberto Sánchez-Reolid,
    José L. Gómez-Sirvent, Alejandro L. Borja, José M. Ferrández,
    and Antonio Fernández-Caballero

Heart Attack Detection Using Body Posture and Facial Expression of Pain 411
    Gabriel Rojas-Albarracín, Antonio Fernández-Caballero,
    António Pereira, and María T. López

Non-intrusive and Easy-to-Use IOT Solution to Improve Elderly's Quality
of Life 421
    Luís Correia, Nuno Costa, Antonio Fernández-Caballero,
    and António Pereira

Human-Computer Interaction Approach with Empathic Conversational
Agent and Computer Vision 431
    Rafael Pereira, Carla Mendes, Nuno Costa, Luis Frazão,
    Antonio Fernández-Caballero, and António Pereira

Using Touch to Improve Emotion Recognition: Proposed System
and Expert Validation 441
    Luisa Merino Ramínez, José P. Molina, Álvaro Lanchas López,
    Félix de la Paz, Antonio Fernández-Caballero, and Arturo S. García

Affective Computing and Context Awareness in Ambient Intelligence

Human-in-the-Loop for Personality Dynamics: Proposal of a New
Research Approach 455
    Krzysztof Kutt, Marzena Kutt, Bartosz Kawa, and Grzegorz J. Nalepa

Emotion Prediction in Real-Life Scenarios: On the Way to the BIRAFFE3
Dataset 465
    Krzysztof Kutt and Grzegorz J. Nalepa

Towards Enhanced Emotional Interaction in the Metaverse 476
    J. A. Rincon, C. Marco-Detchart, and V. Julian

GOAP in Graph-Based Game Narrative Structures 486
    Iwona Grabska-Gradzińska, Ewa Grabska, Paweł Węgrzyn,
    and Leszek Nowak

A Framework for Explanation-Aware Visualization and Adjudication
in Object Detection: First Results and Perspectives 496
    Arnab Ghosh Chowdhury, David Massanés, Steffen Meinert,
    and Martin Atzmueller

Learning Tools to Lecture

Optimizing Didactic Sequences with Artificial Intelligence: Integrating
Bloom's Taxonomy and Emotion in the Selection of Educational
Technologies 509
    Pedro Salcedo-Lagos, Pedro Pinacho-Davidson,
    M. Angélica Pinninghoff J., Ricardo Contreras A.,
    Karina Fuentes-Riffo, and Miguel Friz Carrillo

Contrastive Learning of Multivariate Gaussian Distributions of Incremental
Classes for Continual Learning 518
    Hyung-Jun Moon and Sung-Bae Cho

Influence of Color on Academic Performance: A Studio with Auditory
Sustained Attention Within a Virtual Scenario 528
    Gabriel Ávila-Muñoz, Miguel A. López-Gordo,
    and Manuel Rodríguez-Álvarez

Author Index 539

Contents – Part II

Machine Learning in Computer Vision and Robotics

Unsupervised Detection of Incoming and Outgoing Traffic Flows in Video
Sequences 3
  Jose D. Fernández-Rodríguez, Pablo Carmona-Martínez,
  Rafaela Benítez-Rochel, Miguel A. Molina-Cabello,
  and Ezequiel López-Rubio

A Decentralized Collision Avoidance Algorithm for Individual
and Collaborative UAVs 13
  Julian Estevez, Daniel Caballero-Martin, Jose Manuel Lopez-Guede,
  and Manuel Graña

Improved Surface Defect Classification from a Simple Convolutional
Neural Network by Image Preprocessing and Data Augmentation 23
  Francisco López de la Rosa, Lucía Moreno-Salvador,
  José L. Gómez-Sirvent, Rafael Morales, Roberto Sánchez-Reolid,
  and Antonio Fernández-Caballero

Prediction of Optimal Locations for 5G Base Stations in Urban
Environments Using Neural Networks and Satellite Image Analysis 33
  Iván García-Aguilar, Jesús Galeano-Brajones, Francisco Luna-Valero,
  Javier Carmona-Murillo, Jose David Fernández-Rodríguez,
  and Rafael M. Luque-Baena

Enhanced Cellular Detection Using Convolutional Neural Networks
and Sliding Window Super-Resolution Inference 44
  Iván García-Aguilar, Rostyslav Zavoiko,
  Jose David Fernández-Rodríguez, Rafael Marcos Luque-Baena,
  and Ezequiel López-Rubio

Exploring Text-Driven Approaches for Online Action Detection 55
  Manuel Benavent-Lledo, David Mulero-Pérez, David Ortiz-Perez,
  Jose Garcia-Rodriguez, and Sergio Orts-Escolano

Deep Learning for Assistive Decision-Making in Robot-Aided
Rehabilitation Therapy 65
  David Martínez-Pascual, José. M. Catalán, Luis D. Lledó,
  Andrea Blanco-Ivorra, and Nicolás García-Aracil

Text-Driven Data Augmentation Tool for Synthetic Bird Behavioural
Generation 75
  David Mulero-Pérez, David Ortiz-Perez, Manuel Benavent-Lledo,
  Jose Garcia-Rodriguez, and Jorge Azorin-Lopez

Deep Learning for Enhanced Risk Assessment in Home Environments 85
  Javier Rodriguez-Juan, David Ortiz-Perez, Jose Garcia-Rodriguez,
  and David Tomás

Lightweight CNNs for Advanced Bird Species Recognition on the Edge 95
  Adrian Berenguer-Agullo, Javier Rodriguez-Juan, David Ortiz-Perez,
  and Jose Garcia-Rodriguez

Learning Adaptable Utility Models for Morphological Diversity 105
  Francella Campos-Alfaro, Carlos Jara, Alejandro Romero,
  Martín Naya-Varela, and Richard J. Duro

Deep Learning-Based Classification of Invasive Coronary Angiographies
with Different Patch-Generation Techniques 116
  Ariadna Jiménez-Partinen, Esteban J. Palomo, Karl Thurnhofer-Hemsi,
  Jorge Rodríguez-Capitán, and Ana I. Molina-Ramos

Bio-inspired Computing Approaches

Refinement of Protein Structures with a Memetic Algorithm. Examples
with SARS-CoV-2 Proteins 129
  Juan Luis Filgueiras and José Santos

Evolutionary Algorithms for Bin Packing Problem with Maximum
Lateness and Waste Minimization 140
  Jesús Quesada, Francisco J. Gil-Gala, Marko Đurasević,
  María R. Sierra, and Ramiro Varela

Stationary Wavelet Entropy and Cat Swarm Optimization to Detect
COVID-19 150
  Meng Wu, Shuwen Chen, Jiaji Wang, Shuihua Wang,
  Juan Manuel Gorriz, and Yudong Zhang

Private Inference on Layered Spiking Neural P Systems 163
  Mihail-Iulian Pleșa, Marian Gheoghe, and Florentin Ipate

Cooperative Multi-fitness Evolutionary Algorithm for Scientific
Workflows Scheduling 173
  Pablo Barredo and Jorge Puente

A Genetic Approach to Green Flexible Job Shop Problem Under
Uncertainty 183
    Sezin Afsar, Jorge Puente, Juan José Palacios,
    Inés González-Rodríguez, and Camino R. Vela

Social and Civil Engineering Through Human AI Translations

AI Emmbedded in Drone Control 195
    Daniel Caballero-Martin, Jose Manuel Lopez-Guede, Julian Estevez,
    and Manuel Graña

Dual-System Recommendation Architecture for Adaptive Reading
Intervention Platform for Dyslexic Learners 205
    J. Ignacio Mateo-Trujillo, Diego Castillo-Barnés,
    Ignacio Rodríguez-Rodríguez, Andrés Ortiz, Alberto Peinado,
    Juan L. Luque, and Auxiliadora Sánchez-Gómez

Accurate LiDAR-Based Semantic Classification for Powerline Inspection 215
    J. Luna-Santamaria, I. G. Rodríguez, J. R. Martínez-de Dios,
    and A. Ollero

RESISTO Project: Automatic Detection of Operation Temperature
Anomalies for Power Electric Transformers Using Thermal Imaging 225
    David López-García, Fermín Segovia, Jacob Rodríguez-Rivero,
    Javier Ramírez, David Pérez, Raúl Serrano, and Juan Manuel Górriz

RESISTO Project: Safeguarding the Power Grid from Meteorological
Phenomena 246
    Jacob Rodríguez-Rivero, David López-García, Fermín Segovia,
    Javier Ramírez, Juan Manuel Górriz, R. Serrano, D. Pérez,
    Ivan Maza, Anibal Ollero, Pol Paradell Solà, Albert Gili Selga,
    Jose Luis Domínguez-García, A. Romero, A. Berro, Rocío Domínguez,
    and Inmaculada Prieto

Multi-UAV System for Power-Line Failure Detection Within the RESISTO
Project 262
    Alvaro Poma, Francisco Javier Roman-Escorza, Miguel Gil,
    Alvaro Caballero, Ivan Maza, and Anibal Ollero

Smart Renewable Energies: Advancing AI Algorithms in the Renewable Energy Industry

Machine Learning Health Estimation for Lithium-Ion Batteries Under
Varied Conditions 275
    Gabriel M. C. Leite, Jorge Pérez-Aracil, Carolina Gil Marcelino,
    Gabriel García-Gutiérrez, Milan Prodanovic,
    Enrique García-Quismondo, Sergio Pinilla, Jesús Palma,
    Silvia Jiménez-Fernández, and Sancho Salcedo-Sanz

Energy Flux Prediction Using an Ordinal Soft Labelling Strategy 283
    Antonio M. Gómez-Orellana, Víctor M. Vargas, Pedro A. Gutiérrez,
    Jorge Pérez-Aracil, Sancho Salcedo-Sanz, César Hervás-Martínez,
    and David Guijo-Rubio

Medium- and Long-Term Wind Speed Prediction Using the Multi-task
Learning Paradigm 293
    Antonio M. Gómez-Orellana, Víctor M. Vargas, David Guijo-Rubio,
    Jorge Pérez-Aracil, Pedro A. Gutiérrez, Sancho Salcedo-Sanz,
    and César Hervás-Martínez

Data Augmentation Techniques for Extreme Wind Prediction Improvement 303
    Marta Vega-Bayo, Antonio Manuel Gómez-Orellana,
    Víctor Manuel Vargas Yun, David Guijo-Rubio, Laura Cornejo-Bueno,
    Jorge Pérez-Aracil, and Sancho Salcedo-Sanz

Autoencoder Framework for General Forecasting 314
    Dušan Fister, C. Peláez-Rodríguez, L. Cornejo-Bueno, J. Pérez-Aracil,
    and S. Salcedo-Sanz

Prediction of Extreme Wave Heights via a Fuzzy-Based Cascade Ensemble
Model 323
    C. Peláez-Rodríguez, L. Cornejo-Bueno, Dušan Fister, J. Pérez-Aracil,
    and S. Salcedo-Sanz

Machine Learning as Applied to Shape Parameterization of Submerged
Arch Structures 333
    Waldemar Hugo LLamosas-Mayca, Eugenio Lorente-Ramos,
    Jorge Pérez-Aracil, Alejandro M. Hernández-Díaz,
    Manuel Damián García-Román, and Sancho Salcedo-Sanz

Bioinspired Applications

Towards the Conformation of Constructive Political Discussion Groups.
A Computational Approach 347
  Pedro Pinacho-Davidson, Valentina Hernández, Ricardo Contreras,
  Pedro Salcedo, María Angélica Pinninghoff, and Karina Fuentes-Riffo

Topic Detection in COVID-19 Mortality Time Series 358
  Manuel Graña, Goizalde Badiola-Zabala, and Guillermo Cano-Escalera

Multicenter Prospective Blind External Validation of a Machine Learning
Model for Predicting Heart Failure Decompensation: A 3-Hospital
Validation Study 368
  Jon Kerexeta, Esperança Lladó Pascual, Cristina Martin,
  Nicola Goodfellow, Karina Anahi Ojanguren Carreira, Marco Manso,
  Barbara Guerra, Stanke Ladislav, Vohralík Tomáš, Esteban Fabello,
  Tatiana Silva, Michael Scott, Glenda Fleming, Andoni Beristain,
  and Manuel Graña

Fidex: An Algorithm for the Explainability of Ensembles and SVMs 378
  Guido Bologna, Jean-Marc Boutay, Quentin Leblanc,
  and Damian Boquete

Mitigating Class Imbalance in Time Series with Enhanced Diffusion
Models 389
  Ryan Sijstermans, Chang Sun, and Enrique Hortal

Measuring Spatial Behaviour and Cognition: A Method Based
on Trajectories Analysis and Supported by Technology and Artificial
Intelligence 400
  Michela Ponticorvo, Maria Luongo, Antonietta Argiuolo,
  and Onofrio Gigliotta

Clustering COVID-19 Mortality Time Series 410
  Murat Razi and Manuel Graña

Matrix Representation of Virus Machines 420
  Antonio Ramírez-de-Arellano, Francis George C. Cabarle,
  David Orellana-Martín, Mario J. Pérez-Jiménez, and Henry N. Adorna

Networks of Splicing Processors with Various Topologies 430
  Victor Mitrana, Mihaela Păun, and José Angel Sanchez Martín

Brainstorming on Dataset Reduction from an Heuristic Bioinspired Green
Computing Approach 441
    Ana Paula Aravena-Cifuentes, Lucia Porlan-Ferrando,
    J. David Nuñez-Gonzalez, and Manuel Graña

Diagnosis of Cervical Cancer Using a Deep Learning Explainable Fusion
Model 451
    Andrés Bueno-Crespo, Raquel Martínez-España, Juan Morales-García,
    Ana Ortíz-González, Baldomero Imbernón, José Martínez-Más,
    Daniel Rosique-Egea, and Mauricio A. Álvarez

Blockchain Framework Tailored for Agricultural IoTs 461
    Salaheddine Kably, Nabih Alaoui, Mounir Arioua, Khalid Chougdali,
    Samira Khoulji, and María Dolores Gómez-López

Enhancing Plant Disease Detection in Agriculture Through YOLOv6
Integration with Convolutional Block Attention Module 474
    Abdelilah Haijoub, Anas Hatim, Mounir Arioua, Ahmed Eloualkadi,
    and María Dolores Gómez-López

The Implementation of Artificial Intelligence Based Body Tracking
for the Assessment of Orientation and Mobility Skills in Visual Impaired
Individuals 485
    Roberto Morollón Ruiz, Joel Alejandro Cueva Garcés, Leili Soo,
    and Eduardo Fernández

Application of Graph Fourier Transform in the Diagnosis of Left Bundle
Branch Block from Electrocardiographic Signals 495
    Beatriz del Cisne Macas Ordóñez,
    Diego Vinicio Orellana Villavicencio, Marco Augusto Suing Ochoa,
    and María Paula Bonomini

Strict Left Bundle Branch Block Diagnose Through Explainable Artificial
Intelligence 504
    Beatriz del Cisne Macas Ordóñez, Javier Garrigos,
    Jose Javier Martinez, José Manuel Ferrández, Suraj Karki,
    and María Paula Bonomini

Cardiac Impulse Propagation in Left Bundle Branch Block 511
    Beatriz del Cisne Macas Ordóñez, Fernando Ingallina,
    Diego Vinicio Orellana Villavicencio, and María Paula Bonomini

Wearable Device Dataset for Stress Detection 518
Andrea Hongn, Lara Eleonora Prado, Facundo Bosch,
and María Paula Bonomini

Author Index 529

Machine Learning in Neuroscience

Morning Anxiety Detection Through Smartphone-Based Photoplethysmography Signals Analysis Using Machine Learning Methods

Masoud Sistaninezhad[1], Ali Jafarizadeh[2], Saman Rajebi[1],
Siamak Pedrammehr[3], Roohallah Alizadehsani[4(✉)], and Juan M. Gorriz[5]

[1] Department of Electrical Engineering, Seraj University, Tabriz, Iran
{b.sistaninejhad.ms,s.rajebi}@seraj.ac.ir
[2] Nikookari Eye Center, Tabriz University of Medical Sciences, Tabriz, Iran
[3] Faculty of Design, Tabriz Islamic Art University, Tabriz, Iran
s.pedrammehr@tabriziau.ac.ir
[4] Institute for Intelligent Systems Research and Innovation (IISRI) Deakin
University, Geelong, VIC, Australia
R.alizadehsani@deakin.edu.au
[5] Data Science and Computational Intelligence Institute, University of Granada,
Granada, Spain
gorriz@ugr.es

Abstract. Despite the absence of a standardized clinical definition, morning stress is widely recognized as the stress experienced upon waking. Given its established link to various diseases prevalent in modern society, the accurate measurement and effective management of stress are paramount for maintaining optimal health. In this study, we present a novel approach leveraging the sophisticated capabilities of smartphones to extract photoplethysmography (PPG) signals for immediate detection of morning stress. Data from 61 participants were meticulously collected and processed to extract PPG signals, subsequently employing 11 carefully selected features for stress detection. Through the utilization of the Support Vector Machine (SVM) for classification, we scrutinized the accuracy of our method against established benchmarks. Notably, by integrating the False Discovery Rate (FDR) formula and employing the Particle Swarm Optimization (PSO) algorithm, we achieved a significant enhancement in the classification rate, elevating it from 96% to an impressive 100%. These compelling results underscore the efficacy of our proposed methodology and illuminate the promising potential of smartphone-based morning stress detection as a viable tool for proactive health management.

Keywords: Morning stress · Photoplethysmography · smartphone · SVM · Machine learning · PSO

J. M. Ferrández Vicente et al. (Eds.): IWINAC 2024, LNCS 14674, pp. 3–13, 2024.
https://doi.org/10.1007/978-3-031-61140-7_1

1   Introduction

Biological signals are measurements of body processes that can be categorized into physical and physiological signals [11]. Physical signals include changes in body shape resulting from muscle activity, such as pupil size, eye movements, blinks, head movements, body and limb movements, breathing, facial expressions, body temperature, and tone of voice [7]. Physiological signals are closely related to essential body functions and include Electrocardiography (ECG), Blood Volume Pulse (BVP), Electroencephalography (EEG), Electrodermal activity (EDA), PPG signal, and Electromyography (EMG) [7]. The PPG signal is a non-invasive optical method used to measure blood volume changes. It can be recorded using a light detector and LED and consists of alternating currents (AC) and direct currents (DC) [2,6]. The AC part reflects heart rate, while the DC part is based on light scattered from blood vessels and tissue layers [5]. Parameters such as Pulse Rate (PR), Pulse Rate Variability (PRV), and blood oxygen saturation level (SPO2) can be derived from the PPG signal [14]. Image photoplethysmography (iPPG) or remote photoplethysmography (rPPG) allows the PPG signal to be recorded with a camera, such as a smartphone [16]. Smartphones with high-resolution cameras, processors, and LED flashes have facilitated direct measurement of vital characteristics like heart and breathing rates. This technique, similar to iPPG technology, enables smartphones to extract more features from the PPG signal waveform [12]. Smartphone-based PPG has been used for stress detection, achieving high classification accuracy and demonstrating potential for immediate stress diagnosis [3,17]. Various studies have explored different methods for smartphone-based PPG analysis, including analyzing the brightness of the captured frames and using specific color channels for signal extraction [9,10]. This study has employed machine learning algorithms such as SVM, KNN, MLP, and DT to improve classification accuracy for stress detection.

2   Methods

We present a method for measuring morning stress levels using PRV features from a video of people's fingertips. The process includes data collection, pulse wave extraction, PRV calculation, feature extraction, feature optimization, and stress level classification using SVM.

2.1   Data Collection

61 healthy adults (30 women, 31 men) aged 18-50 years participated in this study. They had no history of heart disease or mental disorders. The data was collected both in the morning and a few hours after waking up. 65% of participants had stressful jobs and 40% were students. The study used PsychoPy3 software to create tests with two stress levels. Rest periods were included between tests to eliminate previous stress effects. Measures were taken to increase stress, such as monitoring performance, limiting time to answer, and using stressful images.

Relaxing images included nature, flowers, and domestic animals. Stressful images included nature, wild animals, rocks, and fire. The Stroop effect is a psychological phenomenon that causes a delay in reaction time when dealing with incongruent stimuli compared to congruent ones. It involves presenting words that name a color, written in a different color than what the word denotes. When asked to identify the color of the word rather than reading the word itself, people take longer to respond if the ink color does not match the word's name. In the current study, the Stroop task was administered twice, the initial Stroop test referred to as Stroop 1, and the second stroop test denoted as Stroop 2.

2.2   Pulse Wave Extraction

According to previous studies [13,15], our method extracts the pulse wave by recording the subtle color changes related to the light absorption. The first step is forming the Decision Matrix, which includes the brightness of the pixels. Each frame of the recorded video had a brightness value in the red channel that was placed as rows of this matrix. Equation (1) illustrates the decision matrix.

$$X_{i,j} = \begin{bmatrix} x_{11} & x_{12} & \dots & x_{1n} \\ x_{21} & x_{22} & \dots & x_{2n} \\ \vdots & \vdots & \ddots & \vdots \\ x_{m1} & x_{m2} & \dots & x_{mn} \end{bmatrix} \tag{1}$$

The above matrix was normalized in the second step, and each element was named p_{ij}. In the third step, the entropy of each index E_j is calculated. Equation (3) is used to calculate the entropy, and k keeps the value between 0 and 1.

$$E_j = -k \sum_{i=1}^{m} p_{ij} \times \ln p_{ij} \qquad i = 1, 2, ..., m \tag{2}$$

The pulse wave can be calculated at a certain time t, as:

$$B_t(X) \equiv -H_t(X) = \sum_{(i,j)} p(x_{i,j}) \log_2 p(x_{i,j}) \tag{3}$$

where $x_{i,j}$ is the brightness of pixels i, j, and $p(x_{i,j})$ is the probability distribution function. The histogram of a digital image with brightness levels in the range [1-L,0] is a function that is calculated as the following:

$$h(r_k) = n_k \tag{4}$$

r_k is equal to the kth value of brightness and n_k is the number of image pixels with brightness r_k. If the histogram is considered a probability density function, we use:

$$p(r_k) = \frac{n_k}{MN} \tag{5}$$

where MN is the total number of pixels in the image. Figure 1 (a) shows the entropy signal of the red channel. Moving Average is a statistical technique used to analyze time series data. It is commonly used to smooth signals and reveal signal peaks. a 1-second moving average was used to smooth the signal. Figure 1 (b) shows the Smoothed PPG signal with signal peaks.

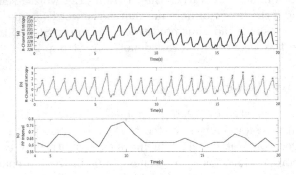

Fig. 1. (a) Shows the entropy signal of the red channel. (b) Smoothed PPG signal with signal peaks Smoothed PPG signal. (c) Shows an example of the estimated PRV. (Color figure online)

2.3   Feature Extraction

Feature extraction is a crucial stage in machine learning, and if the features are not extracted well, the decision-making algorithm cannot perform well, no matter how good it is. Thus, the best features should be provided to the decision-maker model. Various features can be extracted from the PPG signal, which can be divided into linear and non-linear features with a general view [1,8]. These linear features can be divided into frequency and time domains [4]. In this research, three features extracted from the time domain include a set of statistical features:

- SDNN: The standard deviation of PP intervals (ms) which can be obtained as:

$$\overline{PP} = \frac{1}{N} \sum_{i=1}^{N} PP \tag{6}$$

$$SDPP = \sqrt{\frac{1}{N} \sum_{i=1}^{N} (PP_i - \overline{PP})} \tag{7}$$

- RMSSD: The square root of the mean of the squares of the successive differences between adjacent PPs (ms) is as:

$$RMSSD = \sqrt{\frac{1}{N-1} \sum_{i=1}^{N-1} (PP_{i+1} - PP_i)^2} \tag{8}$$

- pPP50: The proportion of PP50 (the number of pairs of successive PPs that differ by more than 50 ms) is divided by the total number of PPs.

2.4   Stress Classification

Following the extraction of all features, they were utilized as input for learning systems trained to differentiate between stress and non-stress. SVM was employed for this purpose [4,9].

2.5   Fisher's Discriminant Ratio

In a scenario involving two classes, it is presumed that the data exhibit a Gaussian or quasi-Gaussian distribution to characterize the performance of FDR. FDR for data with two classes is as:

$$FDR = \frac{(\mu_1 - \mu_2)^2}{\sigma_1^2 - \sigma_2^2} \tag{9}$$

Weights in the form $a = [a_1, a_2, \ldots . a_n]$ are employed to modify the provided features. Subsequently, PSO algorithm is utilized to ascertain the values of these coefficients in a manner that maximizes the given FDR. The PSO algorithm is fundamentally designed to minimize the objective function, but in this case, the aim is to maximize the FDR. As a result, the fitness function of the PSO algorithm is defined as:

$$FitnessFunction = \frac{1}{FDR} \tag{10}$$

3   Results and Discussion

In order to train the classification algorithms, a total of 8 features from the volunteers, including (RMSSD, SDPP, pPP50, HF, LF, LF/HF, HR, SBP, DBP), were extracted from the PPG signal for immediate stress detection. Usually, the first step in machine learning studies is statistical data analysis. In order to obtain more accurate data, the experiment was carried out in several stages. In each stage, the volunteers reported their stress levels in all stages of relaxation, relaxing photos and songs, stressful photos and songs, Stroop1 and Stroop2. Table 1 shows the mean and standard deviation of the reported scales of stress level perceived by the participants in each stage.

Table 1. Statistical Characteristics of the Scales at each Progression Stage

Experiment stages	Number of Stages	Mean	SD
Rest	3	2.67	0.256
Relaxing photos and songs	3	2.86	0.340
Stroop1	3	4.33	0.236
Stroop2	2	6.45	0.157
Stressful photos and songs	3	7.90	0.277

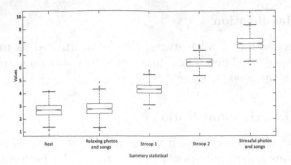

Fig. 2. Kruskal wallis of the distribution of reported scales.

Figure 2 shows the distribution of the reported scales of the perceived stress level after each test.

The results of the Kruskal Wallis analysis are shown in Table 2 and post-hoc comparisons are shown in Fig. 3.

Table 2. Kruskal-Wallis Anova analysis

Source	SS	df	MS	Chi-sq	Prob>Chi-sq
Columns	260.7	4	65.17	13.03	0.01
Error	19.3	10	1.9		
Total	280	14			

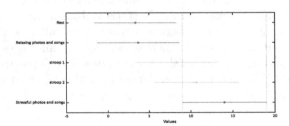

Fig. 3. post-hoc comparisons of reported scales

Based on the statistical significance level (P value) presented in Table 2 and a comparison of the reported values in Fig. 3, it can be inferred that there is a substantial difference between the reported values of 1 and 2 with 5 at a level of significance. The correlation between the reported scale and extracted characteristics was examined using Pearson's correlation coefficients to examine

Table 3. Correlation Coefficients Obtained from the Reported Scales and Extracted BVP Features

Characteristics	Pearson r	p
SBP	0.096	0.512
DBP	0.055	0.705
HR	0.122	0.402
SDPP	0.205	0.157
RMSSD	−0.142	0.331
pPP50	0.069	0.637
HF	−0.002	0.987
LF	−0.157	0.281
HF/LF	−0.065	0.657

the relationships between characteristics. The results of correlations shown in Table 3.

In order to better distinguish and identify the classes, the scales were clustered using the k-means algorithm. Low and medium stress values were placed in the no stress cluster, and high-stress values were placed in the stress cluster. In order to evaluate the performance, We utilized k-fold cross-validation with $k = 5$, and employed four distinct classifiers: multilayer perceptron neural network (MLP) with 10 neurons layers and Scaled Conjugate Gradient (SCG) optimization algorithm, SVM with box-constraint set to 80 and kernel-scale equal to 48, utilizing a linear kernel-function, K-Nearest Neighbor (KNN) with $k = 8$ and jaccard distance, and Decision Tree (DT) with min-leaf-size set to 1. To optimize the hyperparameters of all classification algorithms, we utilized bayesian optimization algorithm. Following clustering, MLP achieved an accuracy of 93.9%, with a sensitivity of 97.7% and a specificity of 66.6%. The SVM attained an accuracy of 91.8%, a sensitivity of 95.3%, and a specificity of 66.6%. Furthermore, the KNN model demonstrated an accuracy of 75.5%, a sensitivity of 86.1%, and a specificity of 0%. Lastly, the DT model achieved an accuracy of 91.8%, a sensitivity of 100%, and a specificity of 60%. The confusion matrix of the MLP, SVM, KNN, and DT classifiers utilizing BVP features is illustrated in Fig. 4.

Table 3 indicates a weak correlation between perceived stress levels and extracted characteristics, suggesting that the effectiveness of BVP measures as an independent feature in promptly diagnosing stress is limited. However, when combining the extracted features of the BVP signal with other factors such as age, gender, drug use, blood pressure, and heart rate, a new set of features was created to assess stress responses and cardiovascular activity. The results demonstrated a significant enhancement in the performance of machine learning algorithms. The combination of features led to an increase in MLP accuracy from 93.9% to 95.9%, sensitivity from 97.7% to 100%, and specificity from 66.6% to 66.7%. In the case of KNN, accuracy improved from 75.5% to 87.8%, and

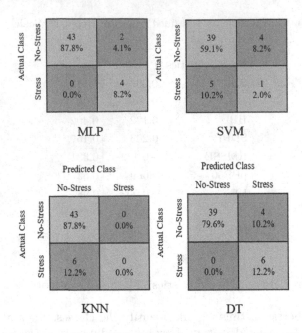

Fig. 4. Confusion matrix of MLP, SVM, KNN, and DT classifier with BVP features.

sensitivity increased from 86.1% to 87.8%, while specificity remained unchanged at 0% in both cases. In contrast, the accuracy of SVM decreased from 91.8% to 81.6%, sensitivity decreased from 95.3% to 90.6%, and specificity decreased from 66.6% to 20% when combining features. The accuracy of DT remained unchanged at 91.8%, with a sensitivity of 100% and a specificity of 60% in both cases. The confusion matrix of MLP, SVM, KNN, and DT with all features can be found in Fig. 5.

According to the mentioned results, the best performance belongs to MLP with all features and then DT. The comparative table illustrating the percentage of classification accuracy, sensitivity, and specificity in two distinct modes is shown in Table 4.

To achieve higher accuracy, FDR was used to weight the data. Figure 6 shows the weights obtained from FDR.

the accuracy of the SVM algorithm increased to 100% after applying the FDR coefficients obtained from the PSO algorithm. In general, it can be concluded that using clustering, extracting BVP features along with other features (age, gender, medication use, blood pressure and heart rate), applying optimal FDR coefficients, along with classification with SVM provides the highest accuracy and is effectively useful in early detection of stress.

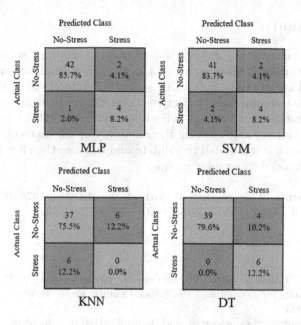

Fig. 5. Confusion matrix of MLP, SVM, KNN, and DT classifier with all features.

Table 4. Classification algorithm outcomes with all features and BVP features.

Model		Accuracy	Sensitivity	Specificity	MCC
MLP	with all features	95.9	100	66.7	0.8
	with BVP features	93.9	97.7	66.6	0.7
SVM	with all features	81.6	90.6	20	0.08
	with BVP features	91.8	95.3	66.6	0.62
KNN	with all features	87.8	87.8	0	0
	with BVP features	75.5	86.1	0	-0.14
DT	with all features	91.8	100	60	0.73
	with BVP features	91.8	100	60	0.73

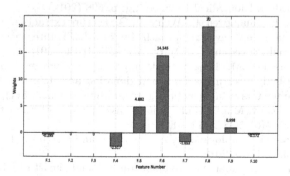

Fig. 6. The optimal weights derived through the FDR technique.

4   Conclusion

Our study presents a novel strategy for identifying morning stress by utilizing smartphone technology. Morning stress has significant implications for an individual's overall stress levels and health status. Therefore, our approach constitutes a valuable instrument for proactive stress management and the promotion of a healthy lifestyle. Our findings indicate a remarkable 100% accuracy in classifying morning stress, underscoring the reliability of our method. Nevertheless, additional research is warranted to validate and enhance the effectiveness of our approach in diverse demographic groups.

Acknowledgments. This research is part of the PID2022-137451OB-I00 project funded by the MCIN/AEI/10.13039/501100011033 and by FSE+.

References

1. Abdullah, S., Hafid, A., Folke, M., Lindén, M., Kristoffersson, A.: PPGfeat: a novel Matlab toolbox for extracting PPG fiducial points. Front. Bioeng. Biotechnol. **11**, 1199604 (2023)
2. Allen, J.: Photoplethysmography and its application in clinical physiological measurement. Physiol. Meas. **28**(3), R1 (2007)
3. Andarabi, S., Nobakht, A., Rajebi, S.: The study of various emotionally-sounding classification using KNN, Bayesian, neural network methods. In: 2020 International Conference on Electrical, Communication, and Computer Engineering (ICECCE), pp. 1–5. IEEE (2020)
4. Castaldo, R., Montesinos, L., Melillo, P., James, C., Pecchia, L.: Ultra-short term HRV features as surrogates of short term HRV: a case study on mental stress detection in real life. BMC Med. Inform. Decis. Mak. **19**(1), 1–13 (2019)
5. Castaneda, D., Esparza, A., Ghamari, M., Soltanpur, C., Nazeran, H.: A review on wearable photoplethysmography sensors and their potential future applications in health care. Int. J. Biosens. Bioelectron. **4**(4), 195 (2018)
6. Corazza, I., Zecchi, M., Corsini, A., Marcelli, E., Cercenelli, L.: Technologies for hemodynamic measurements: past, present and future. In: Advances in Cardiovascular Technology, pp. 515–566. Elsevier (2022)
7. Escabı, M.: Chapter 11-Biosignal processing. In: Introduction to Biomedical Engineering (3rd Edn.), Biomedical Engineering, p. 668 (2012)
8. Fan, P., Peiyu, H., Shangwen, L., Wenfeng, D.: Feature extraction of photoplethysmography signal using wavelet approach. In: 2015 IEEE International Conference on Digital Signal Processing (DSP), pp. 283–286. IEEE (2015)
9. Jafari, Z., Yousefi, A.M., Rajabi, S.: Using different types of neural networks in detection the body's readiness for blood donation and determining the value of each of its parameters using genetic algorithm. Innovaciencia **8**(1), 1–10 (2020)
10. Jonathan, E., Leahy, M.J.: Cellular phone-based photoplethysmographic imaging. J. Biophotonics **4**(5), 293–296 (2011)
11. Kasum, O., Perović, A., Jovanović, A.: Measures and metrics of biological signals. Front. Physiol. **9**, 1707 (2018)
12. van der Kooij, K.M., Naber, M.: An open-source remote heart rate imaging method with practical apparatus and algorithms. Behav. Res. Methods **51**, 2106–2119 (2019)

13. Li, D., Xu, Y., Gao, W.: Pulse wave signal modelling and feature extraction based on lognormal function from photoplethysmography in wireless body area networks. Biomed. Signal Process. Control **86**, 105156 (2023)
14. Maaoui, C., Bousefsaf, F., Pruski, A.: Automatic human stress detection based on webcam photoplethysmographic signals. J. Mech. Med. Biol. **16**(04), 1650039 (2016)
15. Park, J., Seok, H.S., Kim, S.S., Shin, H.: Photoplethysmogram analysis and applications: an integrative review. Front. Physiol. **12**, 808451 (2022)
16. Reguig, F.B.: Photoplethysmogram signal analysis for detecting vital physiological parameters: an evaluating study. In: 2016 International Symposium on Signal, Image, Video and Communications (ISIVC), pp. 167–173. IEEE (2016)
17. Sarabi, S., Asadnejad, M., Rajabi, S.: Using neural network for drowsiness detection based on EEG signals and optimization in the selection of its features using genetic algorithm. Innovaciencia **8**(1), 1–9 (2020)

Visualizing Brain Synchronization: An Explainable Representation of Phase-Amplitude Coupling

Andrés Ortiz[1,2(✉)], Nicolás J. Gallego-Molina[1,2], Diego Castillo-Barnes[1,2], Ignacio Rodríguez-Rodrguez[1,2], and Juan M. Górriz[3]

[1] Communications Engineering Department, University of Málaga, 29004 Málaga, Spain

[2] Andalusian Data Science and Computational Intelligence Institute (DaSCI), Granada, Spain

aortiz@ic.uma.es

[3] Department of Signal Theory, Networking and Communications, University of Granada, Granada, Spain

Abstract. In the realm of neuroscience, brain activity is often characterized by rhythmic oscillations at different frequency bands. These oscillations underlie various cognitive processes and constitutes the basis of communication between populations of neurons. Cross-frequency coupling (CFC) refers to techniques directed to study the interactions between oscillations at different frequencies, providing a more comprehensive view of neural dynamics than traditional measures of connectivity or based on the distribution of the power spectral density. In this paper, we propose a method to explore CFC local patterns in an explainable way, allowing to visualize them over time and to easily identify functional brain areas activated during a task development from the Phase-Amplitude Coupling (PAC) point of view.

Keywords: Cross-Frequency-Coupling · Phase-Amplitude Coupling · Brain connectivity · Dyslexia

1 Introduction

Cross-frequency coupling (CFC) [4] is a phenomenon observed in the brain where the oscillatory activity of neural signals at different frequency bands becomes coordinated or coupled. This intricate interaction provides valuable insights into the functional connectivity of different brain areas and constitutes a crucial aspect in the understanding of the complex dynamics of brain networks. In the field of neuroscience, the brain's activity is often characterized by rhythmic oscillations at different frequency bands (also called neural oscillations [4,7,11,14], such as delta, theta, alpha, beta, and gamma rhythms. These oscillations are thought to underlie various cognitive processes and are essential for communication between different brain regions. Phase-Amplitude coupling (PAC), which

J. M. Ferrández Vicente et al. (Eds.): IWINAC 2024, LNCS 14674, pp. 14–23, 2024.
https://doi.org/10.1007/978-3-031-61140-7_2

is a specific type of CFC, refers to the phenomenon where the phase or amplitude of the oscillations at one frequency is related to the phase or amplitude of oscillations at another frequency. Typically, PAC refers to the modulation of the higher bands amplitude (e.g. theta) by the phase of lower bands (e.g. gamma). One of the key advantages of studying brain connectivity by means of PAC coupling lies in its ability to unveil details of communication between neurons. This way, the synchronization of higher frequency oscillations in one area with lower frequency oscillations in another area may indicate effective communication between respective populations of neurons. On the other hand, since local neuronal oscillations at different bands imply the processing of different type of information, the long-range interaction between bands is associated to information integration between populations of neurons. As a consequence, PAC can uncover subtle and complex relationships that might be overlooked when only considering single-frequency or classical power-based analyses [10,18]. Other CFC measures related to PAC are those directed to measure phase consistency between two bands. This is the case of the Phase Locking Value (PLV) [5,16,18], which assesses how the phase of a signal (i.e.: lower frequency) is "locked" to the phase of another signal (i.e.: higher frequency) over time. Indeed, PLV allows studying phase synchronization or phase coherence between different brain regions or neuronal populations. Currently, different methods for acquiring functional information due to brain activity are available, such as Electroenphalography (EEG), magnetoencephalography (MEG), Near Infrarred Spectrography (NIRS) and Functional Magnetic Resonance Imaging (fMRI). Among these techniques, EEG and MEG are the used in the study of responses to stimuli that requires temporal or spatial resolution, respectively. Moreover, both techniques can be combined for precise source localization. However, the most popular technique due to its accesibility, low cost and non-invasive character is the Electroenphalography (EEG), that can be used to estimate functional connectivity by means of the frequency content of the signals acquired by each sensor.

In this work, we propose a method to extract to extract and study consistent local CFC patterns over time during the application of a stimulus. At the same time, the developed method provides the visualization of the patterns dealing with the explainability and facilitating the discovering of differential patterns among experimental conditions. Out method has been assessed using EEG data from the LEEDUCA database, consisting in controls and dyslexic children under an experiment of modified Auditory Steady-State Response (ASSR) where white noise has been modulated at different frequencies related to the production period of phonemes, syllabes and words in spanish. The experiments carried out demonstrated that the proposed method provides discriminant enough features to differentiate between controls and dyslexics, while showing the most relevant brain regions in which PAC is statistically significant. This, in turn, indicates information processing in these areas while the auditory stimulus is applied. The rest of the paper is organized as follows. Section 2 describes the database used in this work and the methods used to calculate and visualize the CFC patterns.

Section 4 shows the results and discussion. Finally, 5 draws the conclusions of this work.

2   Materials and Methods

2.1   The LEEDUCA Dataset

The data used in this work was obtained by the LEEDUCA research group at the University of Málaga (Spain) [1,15]. The LEEDUCA cohort follows more than 1400 children aged 4 to 8 years, applying cognitive and linguistic tasks directed to assess the reading skills [6]. The study was approved by the Medical Ethical Committee of the University of Málaga (05/02/2020 PND016/2020) and supported by the education office of the Junta de Andalucía (regional government) which granted permission to evaluate students at different public schools. The researchers selected an Electroencephalography (EEG) cohort composed of 48 subjects of age 7, 15 of which had clear reading deficit and 33 with no obvious impairment, after evaluation by expert clinicians. These groups had matching age and school-level socio-economic index (SEI). These students were presented an Auditory Steady-State Response (ASSR) stimulus whose amplitude is modulated at 16 Hz (average intra-syllabic rhythm in spanish) [13]. This stimuli was presented in 5 min sessions over different trials. EEG signals were acquired using Brainvision actiCHamp Plus (battery powered) with actiCAP electrodes (Brain Products GmbH, Germany) in a 32-channel 10–20 configuration optimized for auditory processing, sampled at 500 Hz.

2.2   Data Preprocessing

EEG preprocessing consisted in the following stages: 1) High-pass filtering using two-ways FIR filter in order to avoid phase distortion with cut-off frequency of 120 Hz. 2) 50 Hz Notch filter, 3) removal of ocular artifacts using Independent Component Analysis (ICA), 5) removal of other artifacts (manually), 6) channel-wise normalization to zero mean and unit variance and 7) baseline correction. In addition, all channels were referenced to Cz channel. This way, a filtered, multichannel signal $x_n(t)$ is composed, where t is the time sample and c is the channel for each stimulus. Since each stimulus is applied during 5 min, $x_c(t)$ have a total duration of 300 s. Subsequently, the signal $x_c(t)$ is split into 5 s, overlapped Hanning windows. Formally, we can express the windowed signal as

$$x_w(t) = x(t - t_k) \cdot w\left(\frac{t - t_k}{T} \cdot (M - 1)\right), \qquad t_k = \frac{k \cdot (1 - R) \cdot T}{K - 1} \qquad (1)$$

where t_k is the starting time of the window, and w is the Hanning window function, defined as

$$w(n) = 0.5 - 0.5\cos\left(\frac{2\pi n}{M - 1}\right), \quad n = \{0, 1, 2, ..., M - 1\} \qquad (2)$$

In the case of 5 min signal and 10 s windows with 0.5 overlapping rate, we have 30 overlapped windows. This window duration ensures the capture of Delta band.

2.3 Phase-Amplitude Coupling

As explained in the introduction section, PAC refers to the measure of coupling between lower and higher frequencies of a signal $x(t)$. Then, computing PAC requires band-pass filtering of the corresponding bands. This filtering is accomplished by 8-pole, two ways Finite Impulse Response (FIR) filter, since it is crucial to avoid phase distortion. Band-pass signals are then used to compute instantaneous phase $\phi(t)$ from its analytic version $z(t)$, which is obtained from the Hilbert transform as

$$z(t) = x(t) + jH[x(t)] \qquad (3)$$

where $H[x(t)]$ corresponds to the Hilbert transform (HT) of the signal $x(t)$

$$H[x(t)] = \frac{1}{\pi} \int_{-\infty}^{+\infty} \frac{x(t)}{t - \tau} d\tau \qquad (4)$$

The analytic signal, $z(t)$ allows us to estimate the instantaneous, unwrapped phase $\phi(t)$ as

$$\phi(t) = \angle z(t) = \tan^{-1} \frac{\Im(z(t))}{\Re(z(t))} \qquad (5)$$

Please note that we avoided the channel sub-index for the sake of clarity in the previous equations. As explained in the previous section, in this work we used PLV as a measure of neuronal synchronization, which has the advantage of immunity to false PAC estimation due to volume conduction. PLV is defined for each window as

$$\frac{1}{N} \sum_{n}^{M} |e^{\phi_1(n) - \phi_2(n)}| \qquad (6)$$

where $\phi(1)$ and $\phi(2)$ are the phase of low frequency and high frequency signals, respectively.

In order to avoid PLV values obtained by chance, a permutation test is performed [16]. This is addressed by generating *surrogates* of the lower frequency signal by shuffling all samples in the window. Using 200 permutations, we can compute the probability of obtaining higher PLV values (corresponding to higher levels of coupling) with the shuffled versions of the lower frequency signal than with the non-shuffled version. In other words, this allows to compute the p-value as a measure of significance of each PLV value.

2.4   Visualization of Local PAC Patterns

PAC is visualized by using a template composed by projecting the location of
the EEG electrodes from a 3-D space onto a 2-D surface. This is addressed by an
spherical projection which transform 3-D electrode locations into 2-D projected
locations as proposed by [3] (Fig. 1).

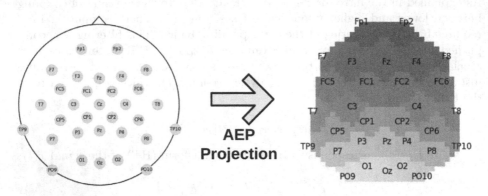

Fig. 1. Azimuthal Equidistant Projection (AEP) from topoplot electrode positions
(10–20 international system)

Specifically, we used the Azimuthal Equidistant Projection (AEP) [17] that is
widely extended in geographical map projection. This has the property that all
points on the map are at proportionally correct distances from the center point
(here, Cz), and all points on the map are at the correct azimuth (direction)
from the center point. Consequently, the projected positions of each electrode
are used as centers of a Voronoi tesellation, assigning areas of similar surface to
each electrode. Then, PAC values corresponding to each electrode are assigned
to the area covered according to the Voronoi set, and subsequently, the image is
interpolated to avoid hard transitions between areas. As a result, we obtain the
figures in Fig. 2.

This way, Figure shows the cumulative number of significant PLV values ($p <
0.05$) for each electrode, in order to identify the bands in which the interaction is
more statistically significant. As show in this figure, Delta-High Gamma, Theta-
High Gamma and Alpha-High Gamma are the pair of bands that can be selected
as most relevant.

3   Consistency of Temporal Patterns

As explained before, EEG channel data is split into overlapping windows. In
this work, the main aim is to use PAC patterns temporarly consistent, i.e. PAC
patterns that remains stable over time, which implies to perform a statistical validation for each signal considering all the time windows. This has been addressed

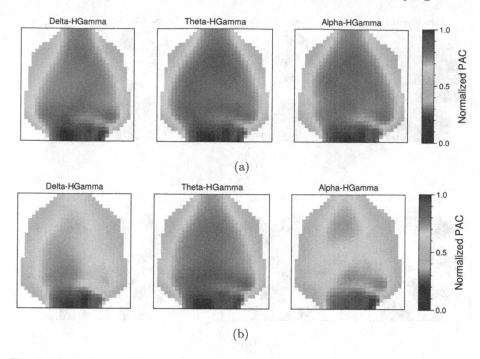

(a)

(b)

Fig. 2. Visualization of PAC patterns using the proposed method for (a) Controls and (b) Dyslexic subjects

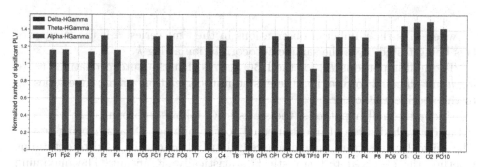

Fig. 3. Number of significant PLV values found at each electrode

by computing the autocorrelation of the signals for each channel at each time window.

In order to assess the statistical significance of the autocorrelations computed at different windows, we used the (LBQ) test [19], based on the Ljung-Box Q statistic, defined as:

$$Q = n(n + 2) \sum_{k=1}^{h} \frac{\hat{r}_k^2}{n - k} \tag{7}$$

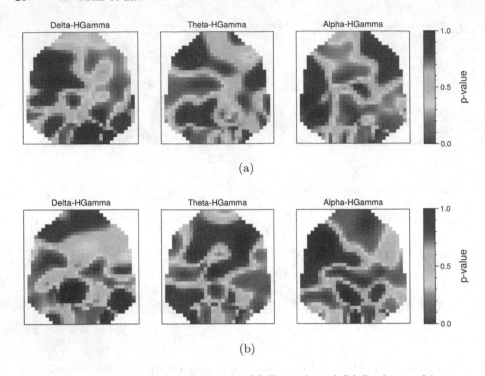

Fig. 4. Temporal significance Map for (a) Controls and (b) Dyslexic subjects

where n is the number of observations in the time series, h is the number of lags being tested, $\hat{r}_k$ is the sample autocorrelation at lag k.

The null hypothesis H_0 for the LBQ test is that the autocorrelations up to lag h are all equal to zero, i.e.: there is no autocorrelation among time series up to the specified lag order.

Under the null hypothesis, the statistic Q follows approximately a χ^2 distribution with degrees of freedom equal to the number of lags h being tested. The critical values from the chi-squared distribution can be used to determine whether the observed test statistic is statistically significant. The maximum number of lags involves a balance between capturing autocorrelation in the time series and avoiding overfitting, and was chosen as 50% ($n/2$ samples).

4   Results and Discussion

In this Section, we show results obtained using a 4.8 Hz ASSR stimulus. Firstly, the number of significant PLV values accounted for each phase-amplitude pair of bands have been accounted at each electrode. This way, Fig. 3 depicts the three pair of bands in which a larger number of significant values ($p < 0.05$) have been found. This shows that Theta (phase signal) - High Gamma (amplitude signal) is considerably significant than other bands. Language processing involves the integration of information over different timescales. Indeed, Theta-Gamma coupling may help in binding together relevant information that is distributed across various neuronal populations and processing stages. The theta phase can act as a temporal reference, enabling the synchronization of gamma oscillations during specific phases to enhance the processing of linguistic information. The presence of discriminant information in this PAC is consistent with the related literature [7,12], where EEG responses tracked phonetic features of speech provide evidences for impaired low-frequency cortical tracking to phonetic features during natural speech perception. Moreover [2] analyzes neurophysiological signals related to speech processing, focusing on the tracking of amplitude envelope of speech stimuli. According to this, theta-band exhibits greater modulation energy in a lower-frequency band. Additionally, this study also shows that coupling is present in delta and theta bands suggesting its role in the development of speech processing.

Discriminative capabilities of PLV patterns shown in Fig. 2 has been evaluated by feeding a gradient boosting classifier [9] in a *Pixels-as-Features* way, but using the temporal significance maps (Fig. 4) as a mask. The results obtained are graphically depicted in Fig. 5, where Theta-Gamma band exhibits the best area under ROC curve. These results have been assessed using k-folk cross validation scheme (k=5) (error bars in Fig. 5 indicates the standard deviation over the k-folds).

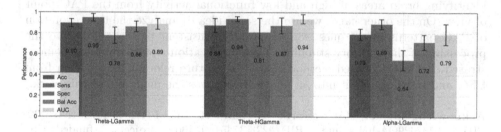

Fig. 5. Classification performance obtained for each PAC band

Since dimensionality of PAC images is considerably larger than the number of available samples [8], an experiment reducing the dimensionality by projecting the images into the 10 first principal components provided by Principal Component Analysis (PCA) has been carried out. These results are also detailed in Table 1.

Table 1. Classification results

Pixels-As-Features					
Bands	Acc	Sens 3	Spec	Bal ACC	AUC
Delta-HGamma	0.84±0.18	0.89±0.11	0.72±0.31	0.80±0.21	0.83±0.20
Theta-HGamma	0.86±0.11	0.91±0.09	0.73±0.25	0.82±0.16	0.83±0.16
Alpha-HGamma	0.85±0.05	0.92±0.07	0.73±0.16	0.83±0.07	0.89±0.14
PCA, 10 components					
Bands	Acc	Sens 3	Spec	Bal ACC	AUC
Delta-HGamma	0.85±0.08	0.88±0.06	0.77±0.24	0.82±0.14	0.92±0.06
Theta-HGamma	0.95±0.07	0.97±0.06	0.89±0.14	0.93±0.10	0.93±0.14
Alpha-HGamma	0.90±0.03	0.91±0.05	0.93±0.13	0.92±0.05	0.91±0.10

5   Conclusions

In this work, we proposed a method to transform Phase-Amplitude Coupling information from EEG signals into images. This provides an explainable view of the significant cross-frequency couplings found at each electrode, and demonstrates its usefulness when discriminating between controls and dyslexics from local PAC patterns. Indeed, it is possible to visually analyze these patterns, identifying brain areas of high and low functional activity from the PAC point of view. On the other hand, we use the same idea to analyze the time evolution of PAC patterns in the quest for temporally consistent patterns linked to the processing of the auditory stimulus. The classification results obtained demonstrated that the proposed method is able to capture relevant information from EEG and transforming it into an image, which was the main aim of this work.

Acknowledgements. This research is part of the PID2022-137461NB-C32, PID2022-137629OA-I00 and PID2022-137451OB-I00 projects, funded by MICIU/AEI/10.13039/501100011033 and by ERDF/EU, as well as UMA20-FEDERJA-086 (Consejería de Economía y Conocimiento, Junta de Andalucía) and by ERDF/EU. Work by D.C.B. is part of the grant FJC2021-048082-I funded by MICIU/AEI/10.13039/501100011033 and by European Union NextGenerationEU/PRTR. Work by I.R.-R. is funded by Plan Andaluz de Investigación, Desarrollo e Innovación (PAIDI), Junta de Andalucía.

References

1. Leeduca project. university of málaga. www.leeduca.uma.es. Accessed 20 Jan 2024
2. Attaheri, A., et al.: Delta- and theta-band cortical tracking and phase-amplitude coupling to sung speech by infants. bioRxiv p. 2020.10.12.329326, March 2021. https://doi.org/10.1101/2020.10.12.329326
3. Bashivan, P., Rish, I., Yeasin, M., Codella, N.: Learning Representations from EEG with Deep Recurrent-Convolutional Neural Networks, February 2016

4. Canolty, R.T., Knight, R.T.: The functional role of cross-frequency coupling. Trends Cogn. Sci. **14**(11), 506–515 (2010)
5. Cohen, M.X.: Analyzing Neural Time Series Data: Theory and Practice. MIT Press, Cambridge (2014)
6. De Vos, A., Vanvooren, S., Vanderauwera, J., Ghesquière, P., Wouters, J.: A longitudinal study investigating neural processing of speech envelope modulation rates in children with (a family risk for) dyslexia. Cortex **93**, 206–219 (2017)
7. Di Liberto, G.M., Peter, V., Kalashnikova, M., Goswami, U., Burnham, D., Lalor, E.C.: Atypical cortical entrainment to speech in the right hemisphere underpins phonemic deficits in dyslexia. NeuroImage **175**, 70–79 (2018). https://doi.org/10.1016/j.neuroimage.2018.03.072
8. Duin, R.P.: Classifiers in almost empty spaces. In: Proceedings 15th International Conference on Pattern Recognition. ICPR-2000, vol. 2, pp. 1–7. IEEE (2000)
9. Friedman, J.: Greedy function approximation: a gradient boosting machine. Ann. Statist. **29**, 1189–1232 (2000). https://doi.org/10.1214/aos/1013203451
10. Juan M. Górriz, et al.: Artificial intelligence within the interplay between natural and artificial computation: advances in data science, trends and applications. Neurocomputing **410**, 237–270 (2020). https://doi.org/10.1016/j.neucom.2020.05.078, https://www.sciencedirect.com/science/article/pii/S0925231220309292
11. Juan M. Górriz, et al.: Computational approaches to explainable artificial intelligence: advances in theory, applications and trends. Inf. Fusion **100**, 101945 (2023). https://doi.org/10.1016/j.inffus.2023.101945, https://www.sciencedirect.com/science/article/pii/S1566253523002610
12. Lizarazu, M., Carreiras, M., Molinaro, N.: Theta-gamma phase-amplitude coupling in auditory cortex is modulated by language proficiency. Human Brain Mapping **44**(7), 2862–2872 (2023). https://doi.org/10.1002/hbm.26250, https://onlinelibrary.wiley.com/doi/abs/10.1002/hbm.26250
13. Lizarazu, M., Lallier, M., Molinaro, N.: Phase-amplitude coupling between theta and gamma oscillations adapts to speech rate. Ann. N. Y. Acad. Sci. **1453**(1), 140–152 (2019)
14. Molinaro, N., Lizarazu, M., Lallier, M., Bourguignon, M., Carreiras, M.: Out-of-synchrony speech entrainment in developmental dyslexia. Human Brain Mapping **37**, 2767–2783 (2016)
15. Ortiz, A., López, P.J., Luque, J.L., Martínez-Murcia, F.J., Aquino-Britez, D.A., Ortega, J.: An anomaly detection approach for dyslexia diagnosis using EEG signals. In: Ferrández Vicente, J.M., Álvarez-Sánchez, J.R., de la Paz López, F., Toledo Moreo, J., Adeli, H. (eds.) IWINAC 2019. LNCS, vol. 11486, pp. 369–378. Springer, Cham (2019). https://doi.org/10.1007/978-3-030-19591-5_38
16. Penny, W., Duzel, E., Miller, K., Ojemann, J.: Testing for nested oscillation. J. Neurosci. Methods **174**(1), 50–61 (2008). https://doi.org/10.1016/j.jneumeth.2008.06.035, https://www.sciencedirect.com/science/article/pii/S0165027008003816
17. Snyder, J.P.: Map projections: a working manual. Technical report 1395, U.S. Government Printing Office (1987). https://doi.org/10.3133/pp1395
18. Tort, A.B.L., Komorowski, R., Eichenbaum, H., Kopell, N.: Measuring phase-amplitude coupling between neuronal oscillations of different frequencies. J. Neurophysiol. **104**(2), 1195–1210 (2010)
19. Upton, G., Cook, I.: A Dictionary of Statistics. Oxford University Press (2008). https://doi.org/10.1093/acref/9780199541454.001.0001

Enhancing Neuronal Coupling Estimation by NIRS/EEG Integration

Nicolás J. Gallego-Molina[1,2(✉)], Andrés Ortiz[1,2], Marco A. Formoso[1,2], Francisco J. Martínez-Murcia[2,3], and Wai Lok Woo[4]

[1] Communications Engineering Department, University of Málaga, 29004 Málaga, Spain
njgm@ic.uma.es
[2] Department of Signal Theory, Communications and Networking, University of Granada, 18060 Granada, Spain
[3] Andalusian Data Science and Computational Intelligence Institute (DaSCI), Granada, Spain
[4] Department of Computer and Information Sciences, Northumbria University, Newcastle Upon Tyne NE1 8ST, UK

Abstract. Neuroimaging techniques have had a major impact on medical science, allowing advances in the research of many neurological diseases and improving their diagnosis. In this context, multimodal neuroimaging approaches, based on the neurovascular coupling phenomenon, exploit their individual strengths to provide complementary information on the neural activity of the brain cortex. This work proposes a novel method for combining electroencephalography (EEG) and functional near–infrared spectroscopy (fNIRS) to explore the functional activity of the brain processes related to low-level language processing of skilled and dyslexic seven-year-old readers. We have transformed EEG signals into image sequences considering the interaction between different frequency bands by means of cross-frequency coupling (CFC), and applied an activation mask sequence obtained from the local functional brain activity inferred from simultaneously recorded fNIRS signals. Thus, the resulting image sequences preserve spatial and temporal information of the communication and interaction between different neural processes and provide discriminative information that enables differentiation between controls and dyslexic subjects.

Keywords: Multimodal Neuroimaging · Integrated EEG-fNIRS Analysis · Cross-Frequency Coupling · Functional Brain Activation · Dyslexia

1 Introduction

In the human brain, a vast number of neurons and their synapses work together to enable cognitive functions. This neural activity generates macroscopic brain

J. M. Ferrández Vicente et al. (Eds.): IWINAC 2024, LNCS 14674, pp. 24–33, 2024.
https://doi.org/10.1007/978-3-031-61140-7_3

signals by increasing the brain electrical activity, accompanied by a haemodynamic and metabolic response [4]. These direct and indirect effects of the running human brain can be measured and serve as sources for noninvasive neuroimaging techniques. Two of them are gaining popularity in the research community due to their low operating costs and ease of application: EEG and fNIRS. Having a high temporal resolution, EEG directly measures the neural electrical activities in the cerebral cortex by detecting the induced fluctuations over the scalp. However, EEG suffers from poor spatial resolution due to volume conduction. On the other hand, with good spatial but lower temporal resolution there is fNIRS. It is an optical technique that allows the study of haemodynamic responses in the brain by detecting changes in the concentration of oxygenated haemoglobin (HbO) and deoxygenated haemoglobin (HbR).

In this context, the combined use of two neuroimaging techniques is expected to surpass single-modality methods by complementing each other and exploiting their individual strengths [15,20]. This is especially emphasised when one technique relies on the haemodynamic principle and the other on the electrophysiological principle. In this way, EEG signals are associated with the neuronal electrical activity, while fNIRS signals are associated with the haemodynamic response. Thus, integrated EEG-fNIRS approaches provide more complete information on the functional activity of the brain. These advantages arise not only from their complementary technical properties, but are also based on a physiological phenomenon called neurovascular coupling [10]. This term refers to the spatial and temporal relationship between neural activity and the regulation of cerebral blood flow. In particular, the activation of neurons within a specific brain region produce an increase of blood flow to that region to meet the augmented demand of glucose and oxygen. This results in fluctuations of haemoglobin concentrations that can be detected by fNIRS.

Impairments of neurovacular coupling have been proposed in recent works as a sign for certain neurological diseases such as Alzheimer's disease and stroke [10,14]. Furthermore, building on the theoretical foundations of neurovascular coupling, the integration of fNIRS and EEG is attracting increasing interest in clinical and non-clinical topics [6]. In this work, we propose an integrated EEG-fNIRS approach applied to the diagnosis of Developmental Dyslexia (DD) with machine learning techniques [11,12]. This is a learning disability not related to mental age or inadequate schooling that impairs the learning processes of reading and spelling and affects 5–12% of the world's population [17]. We have explored the leverages of using local functional activation information from fNIRS signals to enhance the cross-frequency coupling (CFC) analysis performed on EEG signals from dyslexic and skilled readers. This approach aims to assess the presence of altered mechanisms of the neural oscillations that encode the speech signal behind the phonological deficit in DD [13] and it is based on concurrent EEG-fNIRS recordings during an experiment where participants were presented with non-interactive auditory stimuli consisting of amplitude modulated white noise at frequencies related to the core phonological units of Spanish. The rest of the paper is organised as follows. In Sect. 2, the database and methods used in this work are presented. Section 3 presents the principal results and Sect. 4, describes the conclusions and future work.

2   Materials and Methods

2.1   Dataset and Preprocessing

The data used in this work comes from a longitudinal study carried out by the LEEDUCA research group at the University of Málaga (Spain) [16], which consists of a cohort with more than 1400 children aged 4 to 8 years. It was approved by the Medical Ethical Committee of the University of Málaga (05/02/2020 PND016/2020) and with the permission of Education Office of the Junta de Andalucía to evaluate students at different public schools. Then, the quarterly application of a complete battery of cognitive and linguistic tasks to children allowed the selection of a sub-cohort for the subsequent concurrent EEG-fNIRS experiment. All selected participants are matched in age and socioeconomic index. The participants in the EEG-fNIRS sub-cohort, composed of 15 children with a clinical diagnosis of dyslexia and 29 with no obvious impairment, were presented with amplitude-modulated white noise at rates of 4.8, 16 and 40 Hz. These rates correspond to the average production rates for core speech units in the Spanish. Each participant underwent 15-minute sessions in which the stimuli were presented sequentially in ascending and descending order for 2.5 min each ($4.8 \rightarrow 16 \rightarrow 40 \mid 40 \rightarrow 16 \rightarrow 4.8\,Hz$).

EEG signals were acquired with the Brainvision actiCHamp Plus with acti-CAP (Brain Products GmbH, Germany). The sampling rate was $500\,Hz$ and its 32 electrodes follow a 10–20 configuration (auditory cortex montage). After the acquisition, the signals were baseline corrected and eye blinking artefacts were removed using blind source separation with Independent Component Analysis (ICA). Then, all channels are referenced to Cz electrode and normalised to zero mean and unit variance. In the case of fNIRS signals, the equipment used for the acquisitions was the NIRSport system with 16 optodes (eight sources and eight detectors) and a sampling frequency of 7.8125 Hz. A source-detector pair, separated by approximately 3 cm, makes up a channel; altogether we have 20 fNIRS channels per wavelength. Then, the preprocessing of the fNIRS signals has been done with the NIRSLAB software [1] including interpolation to address detector saturation, conversion of the intensity to optical density, artifact correction, transformation to haemoglobin concentration, and filtering with cutoff frequencies of 0.01 Hz and 0.09 Hz for removing artifacts of heart rate and breathing from the haemodynamic response. In addition, the placement of the electrodes, optodes and fNIRS channels over the language and auditory areas of the human brain in the EEG 10–20 system is depicted in Fig. 1.

2.2   CFS Image Sequences

The EEG signals were analysed using an CFC approach. This neural mechanism intervenes in the communication and interaction between different cogni-

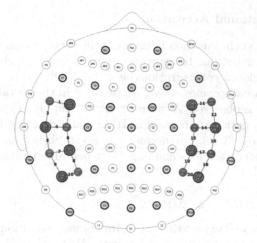

Fig. 1. Locations in the EEG 10–20 system of the EEG electrodes (grey circle with black edges), fNIRS optodes (red circles for sources and blue circles for detectors) and fNIRS channels, named from 1 to 20, are at the midpoint between a source-detector pair.

tive processes that take place in different frequency bands. In addition, the coupling between different brain rhythms is proposed to reveal the neural dynamics involved in healthy and pathological brain functions [5]. In particular, we explored the cross-frequency phase synchronisation (CFS). This is also known as cross-frequency phase-phase coupling and relies on assessing the constancy of the distribution of phase-angle differences between two frequency bands

$$CFS = \left| \frac{1}{n} \sum_{t=1}^{n} e^{i(\phi_A(t) - \phi_B(t))} \right| \tag{1}$$

where n is the number of time points, and $\phi_A(t)$ and $\phi_B(t)$ are the phase angles for the frequency bands A and B.

In order to explore the temporal evolution, we measured the CFS in segments of 5 s between pairs of frequency bands (Theta: 4–8 Hz, Alpha: 8–12 Hz; Beta: 12–30 Hz; and Gamma: 30–80 Hz) at each electrode. Thus, we have 31 CFS values in each of the 30 temporal segments for every combination of frequency bands. Additionally, here we propose an approach to transform CFC information into an image sequence with the aim of preserving the spatial information of EEG electrode locations while representing the temporal development of CFS during the experiment. For this, the locations of the EEG electrodes are projected from a 3-D space onto a 2-D surface [2]. Considering this 2-D surface, the CFS values computed at every segment are interpolated over a 32 × 32 mesh, resulting in 30 CFS images for each frequency band pair. Finally, we create three-channel CFS image sequences by combining the images obtained for three pairs of frequency bands.

2.3   fNIRS Functional Activation

Provided that the synchronisation between oscillatory processes corresponds to functional brain activity, due to neurovascular coupling, we should detect fluctuations of haemoglobin concentrations associated with this neural activation [4]. When a brain area becomes active, an increase in the metabolic demand for oxygen and glucose is observed. As a result, an oversupply of cerebral blood flow is produced and we notice an increase in HbO and a decrease in HbR in fNIRS signals from that area [3,18]. Furthermore, it is established that the changes in HbO and HbR concentrations stemming from neural activation are negatively correlated [8,19,21].

$$\Delta HbR = k_F \Delta HbO \qquad with \; -1 < k_F < 0 \qquad (2)$$

Therefore, we might well expect that when functional activation occurs we would measure a strong negative correlation between HbO and HbR in the haemodynamic response [7,22]. Taking this into account, we assessed functional activation during the experiment from the fNIRS signals by calculating the Spearman correlation coefficient between 25 s segments of HbO and HbR. This duration was selected to correspond to a typical haemodynamic response [3,18].

As we have used an fNIRS montage for the auditory cortex, this activation information only affects to the EEG electrodes placed in this area. Moreover, due to our source-detector separation, each fNIRS channel has a spatial resolution of approximately 3 cm. Thus, we can find which EEG electrodes are inside a sphere of radius 3 cm from the centre point of each fNIRS channel by finding the nearest neighbours (Table 1).

Then, we have created an activation mask sequence for each subject in a similar way than explained above for the CFS image sequences. In this case, for EEG electrodes in the auditory cortex, we seek the lowest Spearman correlation coefficient from the corresponding fNIRS channels. If this coefficient is lower than a threshold (-0.9) for that segment we consider the electrode activated and assign it a 1. In other case, the electrode is not activated and we assign it a 0. For the rest of the EEG electrodes as we do not have information from fNIRS we assign them a 1. In the creation of the activation mask sequence we consider the longer duration of the fNIRS segments. Therefore, one fNIRS segment correspond to five EEG segments. Finally, for each subject its own activation mask sequence is applied to its CFS image sequence.

2.4   Classification

At this point, we have an CFS image sequence with the functional activation over the auditory cortex from fNIRS for each subject. The RGB image in each frame (i.e. temporal segment) contains information from the CFS measured between the bands Theta-Gamma (R), Alpha-Beta (G) and Beta-Gamma (B). As a first approach, we used the average image over the frames for classification with pixel as feature. From each N_s samples in the LEEDUCA EEG-fNIRS dataset we get

Table 1. Nearest neighbours EEG electrodes.

fNIRS channel	Source-Detector	EEG electrodes	Hemisphere
1	S01-D01	FC5	Left
2	S01-D02	FC5	Left
3	S02-D01	T7	Left
4	S02-D02	FC5, T7	Left
5	S02-D03	T7	Left
6	S03-D02	CP5	Left
7	S03-D03	CP5	Left
8	S03-D04	CP5	Left
9	S04-D03	P7	Left
10	S04-D04	CP5, P7	Left
11	S05-D05	FC6	Right
12	S05-D06	T8	Right
13	S06-D05	FC6	Right
14	S06-D06	T8	Right
15	S06-D07	CP6	Right
16	S07-D06	T8	Right
17	S07-D07	CP6	Right
18	S07-D08	P8	Right
19	S08-D07	CP6	Right
20	S08-D08	P8	Right

an array that contains the $K = 3072$ features (32×32 *pixels* $\times 3$ *RGB channels*). For the classification method we selected a machine learning technique based on ensemble of weak prediction models known as gradient tree boosting [9]. The classification is performed in a stratified K-fold cross-validation scheme with k=5, and metrics such as the Area Under the Curve (AUC) for the Receiver Operating Characteristic (ROC) curves and the balanced accuracy (BAcc) are computed.

3   Results

We have work with the LEEDUCA dataset containing concurrent EEG-fNIRS signals from an experiment were children where exposed to amplitude-modulated white noise at rates of 4.8, 16 and 40 Hz. For this preliminary approach we present the results for the 4.8 Hz stimulus, as the syllable rate is expected to emphasise the impairments in neural mechanisms that occur in DD [13]. First, the EEG signals are transformed into CFS image sequences preserving the spatial information of EEG electrode location and containing the information about the temporal development of cross-frequency phase-phase coupling in the brain. An example of these sequences is depicted in Fig. 2.a for a control subject. In this figure (Fig. 2.a) the RGB images are represented for six temporal segments of the total sequence.

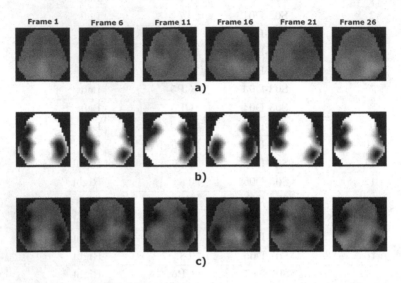

Fig. 2. Example of different image sequences for a representative control subject. a) CFS image sequence. b) fNIRS functional activation sequence. c) CFS-activation image sequence. Normalisation was performed to aid visualisation.

Then, the fNIRS activation mask is computed for each subject considering the proximity relation between fNIRS channels and EEG electrodes from Table 1. The fNIRS activation sequence for a control subject is shown in Fig. 2.b, where the darker pixels correspond to deactivated zones and the whiter pixels to activated areas. In the areas outside the auditory cortex the pixels are set to 1 as we do not have functional activation information from fNIRS. Each subject's functional activation mask is then applied to their CFS image sequence, resulting in the image sequence depicted in Fig. 2.c. In these images, the CFS over the auditory cortex from the EEG signals are modified in function of their activation inferred from the fNIRS signals. Thus, we started a new path for the development of a multimodal fNIRS-EEG integration analysis approach.

In the Table 2, we have included the classification results using gradient tree boosting considering pixels as features from the average image over the frames. In this first approach, the image sequences are extracted from the 4.8 Hz stimulus EEG and fNIRS signals and the outcomes are presented for the CFS image sequence both with and without the fNIRS functional activation mask applied. In each case, we show the average performance achieved in the five folds of cross-validation for the separated image channels and with the RGB images. Using the CFS image sequence corresponding to the channel B (which contains the information of the Beta-Gamma CFS), the classifier achieves better BAcc and AUC than combining the three channels (RGB image). However, after the application of the functional activation mask, the performance is improved for the average RGB image reaching a BAcc and AUC of 78.9%.

Table 2. Classification results with gradient tree boosting.

Average image used	Channel	BAcc	Sens	Spec	AUC
From CFS image sequence	R	0.553 ± 0.069	0.4 ± 0.226	0.706 ± 0.107	0.553 ± 0.069
	G	0.648 ± 0.175	0.467 ± 0.306	0.829 ± 0.139	0.648 ± 0.175
	B	0.747 ± 0.073	0.633 ± 0.067	0.861 ± 0.091	0.747 ± 0.073
	RGB	0.695 ± 0.139	0.567 ± 0.226	0.824 ± 0.143	0.695 ± 0.139
From CFS image sequence with activation mask	R	0.582 ± 0.068	0.367 ± 0.067	0.797 ± 0.112	0.582 ± 0.068
	G	0.673 ± 0.104	0.5 ± 0.183	0.847 ± 0.111	0.673 ± 0.104
	B	0.707 ± 0.184	0.567 ± 0.271	0.847 ± 0.111	0.707 ± 0.184
	RGB	$\mathbf{0.789 \pm 0.121}$	$\mathbf{0.733 \pm 0.17}$	$\mathbf{0.845 \pm 0.126}$	$\mathbf{0.789 \pm 0.121}$

Finally, we conducted permutation tests to assess the statistical significance of our findings. We have created a null distribution by shuffling the labels $N_{perm} = 1000$ times and in each permutation the classifier was re-trained using these shuffled label-data pairs. This was done in a five-fold cross-validation, where we evaluated the data-label link established by the classifier. Figure 3 shows a distribution of BAcc values obtained by the classifier with the random datasets and the p-value of the BAcc score with the original dataset. The p-value is calculated as the fraction of the observed results that are greater than or equal to performance achieved with the correct labels.

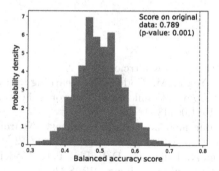

Fig. 3. Results of the permutation test. Null distribution is shown in blue. (Color figure online)

4   Conclusions and Future Work

In this work, we propose a novel approach for a multimodal EEG-fNIRS integration that aims to take advantage of the different characteristics of these two non-invasive neuroimaging techniques and provide more complete information on the functional activity of the brain. In order to achieve this, we rely on a concurrent EEG-fNIRS dataset arising from an experiment with non-interactive auditory stimuli presented to skilled and dyslexic seven-year-old readers. We have performed a transformation from time series data, EEG and fNIRS signals, to image sequences. Thus, preserving the information from the location of EEG electrodes and fNIRS channels and the temporal patterns of coordination of neuronal oscillations in brain functions. As a first step we have adopted an approach using pixels as features with a gradient tree boosting classifier, an efficient machine learning algorithm. Furthermore, through the application of the fNIRS functional activation masks obtained, we have improved the classification performance, reaching a BAcc of 78.9%.

The results obtained demonstrate the feasibility of the proposed method and provide the framework for further exploration of this line. Firstly, the integrated EEG-fNIRS analysis can be extended to the 16 and 40 Hz stimuli to account for other origins for the deficits found in DD. In addition, the method for deriving functional activation from fNIRS signals can be improved to better match the complexity of the haemodynamic response. Finally, it is needed the exploration of feature selection techniques to improve classification performance and other machine learning algorithms that benefit more from the spatial and temporal information contained in the image sequences.

Acknowledgments. This research is part of the PID2022-137461NB-C32, PID2022-137629OA-I00 and PID2022-137451OB-I00 projects, funded by the MICIU/AEI/ 10.13039/501100011033 and by European Union NextGenerationEU/PRTR, as well as TIC251-G-FEDER project, funded by ERDF/EU. Marco A. Formoso grant PRE2019-087350 funded by MICIU/AEI/10.13039/501100011033 by "ESF Investing in your future".

References

1. NITRC: Welcome. https://www.nitrc.org/
2. Bashivan, P., Rish, I., Yeasin, M., Codella, N.: Learning Representations from EEG with Deep Recurrent-Convolutional Neural Networks, February 2016. https://doi.org/10.48550/arXiv.1511.06448
3. Buxton, R.B.: Dynamic models of BOLD contrast. Neuroimage **62**(2), 953–961 (2012). https://doi.org/10.1016/j.neuroimage.2012.01.012
4. Buxton, R.B., Uludağ, K., Dubowitz, D.J., Liu, T.T.: Modeling the hemodynamic response to brain activation. Neuroimage **23**, S220–S233 (2004). https://doi.org/10.1016/j.neuroimage.2004.07.013
5. Canolty, R.T., Knight, R.T.: The functional role of cross-frequency coupling. Trends Cogn. Sci. **14**(11), 506–515 (2010). https://doi.org/10.1016/j.tics.2010.09.001
6. Chiarelli, A.M., Zappasodi, F., Pompeo, F.D., Merla, A.: Simultaneous functional near-infrared spectroscopy and electroencephalography for monitoring of human brain activity and oxygenation: a review. NPh **4**(4), 041411 (2017). https://doi.org/10.1117/1.NPh.4.4.041411

7. Cui, X., Bray, S., Reiss, A.L.: Functional near infrared spectroscopy (NIRS) signal improvement based on negative correlation between oxygenated and deoxygenated hemoglobin dynamics. Neuroimage **49**(4), 3039–3046 (2010). https://doi.org/10.1016/j.neuroimage.2009.11.050
8. Devor, A., Dunn, A.K., Andermann, M.L., et al.: Coupling of total hemoglobin concentration, oxygenation, and neural activity in rat somatosensory cortex. Neuron **39**(2), 353–359 (2003). https://doi.org/10.1016/S0896-6273(03)00403-3
9. Friedman, J.H.: Greedy function approximation: A gradient boosting machine. Ann. Stat. **29**(5), 1189–1232 (2001). https://doi.org/10.1214/aos/1013203451
10. Girouard, H., Iadecola, C.: Neurovascular coupling in the normal brain and in hypertension, stroke, and Alzheimer disease. J. Appl. Physiol. **100**(1), 328–335 (2006). https://doi.org/10.1152/japplphysiol.00966.2005
11. Górriz, J.M., et al.: Computational approaches to explainable artificial intelligence: advances in theory, applications and trends. Inf. Fusion **100**, 101945 (2023). https://doi.org/10.1016/j.inffus.2023.101945
12. Górriz, J.M., et al.: Artificial intelligence within the interplay between natural and artificial computation: advances in data science, trends and applications. Neurocomputing **410**, 237–270 (2020). https://doi.org/10.1016/j.neucom.2020.05.078
13. Goswami, U.: A temporal sampling framework for developmental dyslexia. Trends Cogn. Sci. **15**(1), 3–10 (2011). https://doi.org/10.1016/j.tics.2010.10.001
14. Li, R., Nguyen, T., Potter, T., Zhang, Y.: Dynamic cortical connectivity alterations associated with Alzheimer's disease: an EEG and fNIRS integration study. NeuroImage: Clinical **21**, 101622 (2019). https://doi.org/10.1016/j.nicl.2018.101622
15. Li, R., Yang, D., Fang, F., et al.: Concurrent fNIRS and EEG for brain function investigation: a systematic. Methodol. Focused Rev. Sens. (Basel) **22**(15), 5865 (2022). https://doi.org/10.3390/s22155865
16. Ortiz, A., Martinez-Murcia, F.J., Luque, J.L.: ohers: dyslexia diagnosis by EEG temporal and spectral descriptors: an anomaly detection approach. Int. J. Neur. Syst. **30**(07), 2050029 (2020). https://doi.org/10.1142/S012906572050029X
17. Peterson, R.L., Pennington, B.F.: Developmental Dyslexia, p. 27 (2015). https://doi.org/10.1146/annurev-clinpsy-032814-112842
18. Scholkmann, F., Kleiser, S., Metz, A.J., et al.: A review on continuous wave functional near-infrared spectroscopy and imaging instrumentation and methodology. Neuroimage **85**, 6–27 (2014). https://doi.org/10.1016/j.neuroimage.2013.05.004
19. Sheth, S.A., Nemoto, M., Guiou, M., et al.: Linear and nonlinear relationships between neuronal activity, oxygen metabolism, and hemodynamic responses. Neuron **42**(2), 347–355 (2004). https://doi.org/10.1016/S0896-6273(04)00221-1
20. Shibasaki, H.: Human brain mapping: hemodynamic response and electrophysiology. Clin. Neurophysiol. **119**(4), 731–743 (2008). https://doi.org/10.1016/j.clinph.2007.10.026
21. Tang, L., Avison, M.J., Gore, J.C.: Nonlinear blood oxygen level-dependent responses for transient activations and deactivations in V1 – insights into the hemodynamic response function with the balloon model. Magn. Reson. Imaging **27**(4), 449–459 (2009). https://doi.org/10.1016/j.mri.2008.07.017
22. Yamada, T., Umeyama, S., Matsuda, K.: Separation of fNIRS signals into functional and systemic components based on differences in hemodynamic modalities. PLoS ONE **7**(11), e50271 (2012). https://doi.org/10.1371/journal.pone.0050271

Causal Mechanisms of Dyslexia via Connectogram Modeling of Phase Synchrony

I. Rodríguez-Rodríguez[1,3]([✉]), A. Ortiz[1,3], M. A. Formoso[1,3],
N. J. Gallego-Molina[1,3], and J. L. Luque[2]

[1] Communications Engineering Department, University of Málaga,
29004 Málaga, Spain
[2] Department of Developmental and Educational Psychology, University of Málaga,
29004 Málaga, Spain
ignacio.rodriguez@ic.uma.es
[3] Andalusian Data Science and Computational Intelligence Institute (DaSCI),
Granada, Spain

Abstract. This paper introduces connectogram modeling of electroencephalography (EEG) signals as a novel approach to represent causal relationships and information flow between different brain regions. Connectograms are graphical representations that map the connectivity between neural nodes or EEG channels through lines and arrows of varying thickness and directionality. Here, inter-channel phase connectivity patterns were analyzed by computing Granger causality to quantify the magnitude and direction of causal effects. The resulting weighted, directed connectograms displayed differences in functional integration between individuals with developmental dyslexia versus fluent readers when processing 4.8 Hz amplitude-modulated noise, designed to elicit speech encoding mechanisms. Machine learning classification was subsequently implemented to distinguish participant groups based on characteristic connectivity fingerprints. The methodology integrates signal filtering, instantaneous phase analysis via Hilbert transform, Granger causality computation between all channel pairs, automated feature selection using novel mutual information filtering, construction of directed weighted connectograms, and Gradient Boosting classification. Classification analysis successfully discriminates connectivity patterns, directly implicating theta and gamma bands (AUC 0.929 and 0.911, respectively) resulting from rhythmic auditory stimulation. Results demonstrated altered cross-regional theta and gamma band oscillatory connectivity in dyslexia during foundational auditory processing, providing perspectives on multisensory and temporal encoding inefficiencies underlying language difficulties.

Keywords: EEG · connectograms · dyslexia · Granger causality · Hilbert · Gradient Boosting

© The Author(s), under exclusive license to Springer Nature Switzerland AG 2024
J. M. Ferrández Vicente et al. (Eds.): IWINAC 2024, LNCS 14674, pp. 34–44, 2024.
https://doi.org/10.1007/978-3-031-61140-7_4

1 Introduction

Developmental dyslexia (DD), affecting 5–12% of learners [15], is a prevalent learning disability causing reading and writing difficulties. However, traditional diagnosis based on behavioral tests can be subjective and vulnerable to external factors. Hence, objective techniques are imperative for accurate early detection, based on the latest techniques [5,9]. Connectivity analysis of brain signals is promising for revealing DD biomarkers.

Specifically, electroencephalography (EEG) enables noninvasive measurement of cortical activity with high temporal resolution. EEG studies have identified connectivity patterns related to neurological disorders and language faculties [19], elucidating coordination between regions during cognitive tasks [20]. Connectivity modeling can reveal directional relationships [24].

The theory proposes that phase synchronization deficits, impeding phonological development [6], may arise from atypical low-frequency neural speech encoding in DD. DD learner EEG studies have evidenced differential entrainment between frequency bands when processing speech [13]. Various methods have explored EEG spectral, statistical, and graphical features to analyze connectivity [4]. Further insight may arise by tools like Granger causality to probe oscillatory coordination [10].

We generate connectivity models by examining inter-channel phase Granger causality [7] relationships under prosodic auditory stimuli. Adopting a novel approach, directed weighted connectograms represent causal links between EEG channels. While connectograms effectively depict complex connectivity patterns from neuroimaging, we extend them to EEG classification through machine learning, addressing EEG signal intricacies. Specifically, we implement Gradient Boosting with the novel Mutually Informed Correlation Coefficient (MICC) filter for feature selection [8]. We seek to demonstrate distinct network connectivity fingerprints in DD learners during foundational auditory processing.

Our methodology trains models on an age-matched dataset [14] of DD and control learners. Preprocessing removes artifacts before bandpass filtering EEG channels into five frequency bands. Then, the Hilbert transform extracts phase components to compute Granger causality between all channel pairs, quantifying causal relationships to construct weighted directed connectograms displaying interplay polarity and strength. We classify groups using feature sets filtered for mutual information with DD labels and low inter-feature correlation.

This work introduces connectogram modeling of causal EEG dynamics for studying developmental disorders. By integrating signal processing, connectivity mapping, feature selection, and classification, the pipeline delivers enhanced EEG analytics. The approach expands the current understanding of brain network interactions in DD while demonstrating the feasibility of accurate automated screening. Findings could inform diagnostics and interventions for complex neurodevelopmental conditions.

2   Material and Methods

2.1   Data Acquisition

The EEG dataset was collected from 48 Spanish-speaking children aged 88–100 months, including 32 proficient readers and 16 children formally diagnosed with DD. Participants had normal or corrected vision without auditory issues. Prior to the experiment, guardians were informed and provided consent. The children were exposed to 15 min of white noise auditory stimulus modulated at 4.8 Hz to elicit foundational auditory processing patterns, informed by expertise on prosodic-syllabic frequencies in speech. EEG signals were captured using 32 electrode actiCAP per the 10–20 system, sampled at 500 Hz.

2.2   Preprocessing

The EEG signals underwent preprocessing to remove artifacts, including using independent component analysis to eliminate eye-blinking artifacts based on EOG channel observations and discarding segments with movement or impedance variations. Channels were then referenced to Cz. Next, signals passed through finite impulse response bandpass filters to obtain information within delta (1.5–4 Hz), theta (4–8 Hz), alpha (8–13 Hz), beta (13–30 Hz), and gamma (30–80 Hz) EEG bands without phase distortion that would occur with other filters. The two-way zero phase lag filtering compensates for phase lags. With the 80 Hz low-pass filtering, a 50 Hz notch filter was also applied during preprocessing to remove that frequency component.

2.3   Hilbert Transform

A Hilbert Transform (HT) can convert an actual signal into an analytic signal, a complex valued time series without negative frequency components. Performing a HT facilitates the computation of the time-varying amplitude, phase, and frequency of the analytic signal, termed the instantaneous amplitude, phase, and frequency.

The HT is mathematically defined for a signal $x(t)$, as shown in equation (1). By combining the original signal $x(t)$ with its HT, the analytic signal $z(t)$ can be obtained for signal $x(t)$ as shown in equation (2).

$$\mathcal{H}\left[x(t)\right] = \frac{1}{\pi} \int_{-\infty}^{+\infty} \frac{x(t)}{t-\tau} d\tau \tag{1}$$

$$z_i\left(t\right) = x_i\left(t\right) + j\mathcal{H}x_i\left(t\right) = a(t)e^{\left(j\phi(t)\right)} \tag{2}$$

From the analytic signal $z(t)$, it is straightforward to compute the instantaneous, unwrapped phase $\phi(t)$ can be obtained using the arctangent function on $z(t)$ as shown in equation (3).

$$\phi(t) = tan^{-1} \frac{im(z_i(t))}{re(z_i(t))} \tag{3}$$

Applying this HT provides the phase value for each time point. So, the phase component $\phi(t)$ facilitates a more nuanced analysis of oscillatory brain activities.

2.4   Granger Causality

Granger causality, first introduced by economist Clive Granger [7], is a statistical approach frequently used to assess causal interactions between continuous-valued time series. It is grounded in the premise that while the past and present may cause the future, the future cannot retroactively impact the past. More specifically, if x_t and y_t denote two stationary time series, then x_t is said to Granger-cause y_t if incorporating past values of x_t provides significantly improved prediction of future y_t compared to only using auto-regression based on past y_t values. Mathematically, let x_{t-k} and y_{t-k} represent the past k values of x_t and y_t, respectively. Granger causality can then be examined via the following two auto-regressive models:

$$\widehat{y}_{t1} = \sum_{k=1}^{l} a_k y_{t-k} + \varepsilon_t \tag{4}$$

$$\widehat{y}_{t2} = \sum_{k=1}^{l} a_k y_{t-k} + \sum_{k=1}^{w} b_k x_{t-k} + \eta_t \tag{5}$$

Here ε_t, η_t are white noise prediction errors, while a_k and b_k are least squares regression coefficient vectors fitted over l past x values and w past y values, respectively. Since real-world time series are finite, w is chosen significantly below the series length, optimized via the Akaike Information Criterion (AIC) [1]. If the F-test applied to (4) and (5) produces a p-value indicating significantly improved regression performance for (5), we conclude that x_t Granger causes y_t.

2.5   Feature Selection

The Mutually Informed Correlation Coefficient (MICC) [8] is a novel filter-based feature selection method to efficiently extract the most discriminative and relevant features from high-dimensional vectors for pattern classification problems. MICC scores each feature by combining mutual information (MI) and Pearson's correlation coefficient (PCC). MI measures the dependence between a feature and the class label. A higher MI indicates a more informative feature for classification. PCC quantifies the correlation between features. Higher PCC implies greater redundancy. The MICC score in equation (8) balances these components. $MI(i)$ calculates mutual information between feature i and class label C. $PCC(i,j)$ sums correlations of feature i with all other features. The parameter controls this trade-off. Features are ranked by MICC score for selection.

$$PCC(x,y) = \frac{1}{(n-1)} \sum_{i=1}^{n} \frac{(x_i - \bar{x})(y_i - \bar{y})}{(s_x s_y)} \qquad (6)$$

$$MI\,(A;B) = \sum_{x} \sum_{y} p(a,b) \log \frac{p(a,b)}{p(a)p(b)} \qquad (7)$$

$$score\,(i) = \alpha \times MI\,(i) - (1 - \alpha) \times \sum_{j=1}^{dim} PCC(i,j) \qquad (8)$$

As equation (6) shows, PCC determines a linear relationship between features x and y using means, standard deviations, and covariance. It ranges from -1 to 1, with 0 indicating no correlation. MI in equation (7) computes dependence between variables A and B using joint and marginal distributions. Higher MI values denote greater dependence.

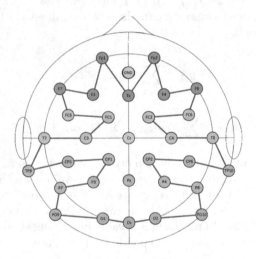

Fig. 1. Connectogram from the 10–20 system, 32 electrodes

2.6   Connectograms

Connectograms are invaluable neuroscientific tools to represent intricate brain connectivity patterns. Initially developed for magnetic resonance imaging (MRI), connectograms now also model electroencephalography (EEG) dynamics as networks of interconnected nodes and pathways mirroring neural connections and activities [3]. The spectrograms reflect a formation of 32 electrodes following the 10–20 system (Fig. 1).

Incorporating directionality and weighting further enhances EEG connectograms. Directed graphs account for asymmetric causality between nodes, unlike symmetric correlations. If electrode A influences B more than vice versa, connectograms can reveal such directional brain activity drivers [7]. Weighting via Granger causality numerically signifies causal influence strength be-tween EEG channels. Higher weights (lower Granger values) indicate greater certainty of one channel driving another, while lower weights suggest more ambiguous effects.

2.7   Machine Learning Classification

Ensemble methods amalgamate multiple diverse models via weighted major-ity voting to enhance prediction accuracy and stability beyond individual tech-niques. The critical concept involves synthesizing superior joint forecasts from the discrete outputs of component models.

Boosting initializes by weighting all training examples equally. However, weights are iteratively updated based on prediction accuracy from previous iter-ations. Incorrectly classified cases receive amplified emphasis in subsequent mod-els. Meanwhile, examples already predicted precisely endure attenuated signifi-cance. Thus, ensembles systematically stress overlooked nuances that no single model captures completely.

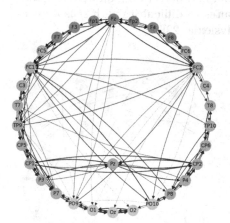

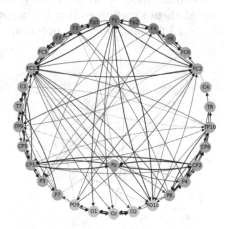

Fig. 2. Causality in control group, theta

Fig. 3. Causality in dyslexic group, theta

Gradient Boosting minimizes deviation or error metrics through iterative for-ward stagewise fitting of regression trees onto residuals. For binary classification, each iteration only fits one tree. By constructing additive models sequentially, Gradient Boosting concentrates new trees on minimizing the loss function gra-dient unexplained by previous iterations. The Mutually Informed Correlation Coefficient filter promises to improve performance while reducing complexity.

Extensive cross-validation across parameter grids optimizes tuning. Owing to ensemble diversity unlocking intricate patterns combined with exhaustive nonlinear residual fitting, Gradient Boosting excels at delivering accurate predictions across small, complex data where individual models falter.

3   Results

The direct preliminary representation of the Granger matrices in the control and dyslexia groups offers, at first glance, greater causal connectivity in the dyslexia group, as noted in [18]. Figure 3 (Connectogram of causality in dyslexic group) indicates this greater connection exemplified for the theta band than the control group (Fig. 2).

Features scores (FS) have been depicted in a bar graph (Fig. 4) and the respective connectogram (Fig. 5), and show differentiated functional connectivity between occipital and frontal brain regions (Oz-F8, O2-Fp1) in individuals with dyslexia when presented with a 4.8 Hz stimulus corresponding to the theta band. The occipital regions are involved in visual processing, while the frontal regions underpin executive functions like attention. As theta oscillations facilitate coordination between memory, attention, and perception, altered occipital-frontal theta synchronization likely contributes to difficulties with sensory context encoding and semantic processing in dyslexia [22].

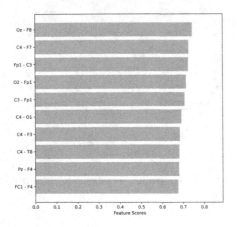

Fig. 4. Bar graph of FS, theta

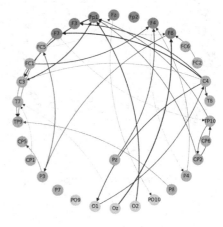

Fig. 5. Connectogram of FS, theta

Additionally, more significant frontal cortical activity is observed in people with dyslexia across frequency bands, suggesting compensation for deficiencies in early visual processing stages (C4-F7, Fp1-C3) [16]. However, reduced auditory network connectivity is seen in dyslexics' right hemispheres, specifically in the theta band. This highlights potential difficulties integrating visual and auditory information during prosodic processing due to impairments in temporal syllable integration and speech perception [16]. Given the role of theta band coherence between frontal and posterior regions in learning [22], these connectivity differences likely significantly impact language acquisition.

Continuing with altered causation between central and frontal regions (C4-F7, Fp1-C3). Central areas are involved in sensorimotor functions, while frontal regions support executive operations. fMRI evidence reveals atypical activations during reading in dyslexic children, potentially indicating attempted compensation for phonological processing weaknesses using alternative neural pathways [17]. Since central regions, including Broca's area, are integral for phonological encoding, and theta synchronization facilitates context encoding [22], differences in central-frontal connectivity could signify challenges coordinating sensory perception and motor output during speech production.

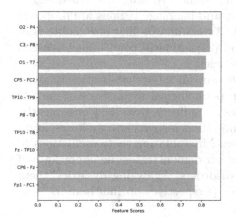

Fig. 6. Bar graph of FS, gamma

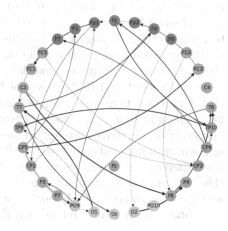

Fig. 7. Connectogram of FS, gamma

Regarding the gamma band, research has associated oscillations with integrating distributed neural information to facilitate perception, memory, and cognition [12]. Differences in gamma connectivity are observed between occipital and parietal (O2-P4), occipital and temporal (O1-T7) areas in people with dyslexia, as it is reflected in Figs. 6 and 7. As occipital regions mediate visual processing while temporal/parietal areas support speech and language integration, altered cross-talk between these domains aligns with theories that multi-sensory deficits in dyslexia stem from atypical interplay between vision and language functions [2]. Given gamma's role in binding neural networks through synchronized firing patterns, dyslexic connectivity differences likely signify less efficient audio-visual integration, which may complicate prosodic processing.

Furthermore, central-temporal/parietal gamma (O1-T7, C3-P8) alterations indicate problems coordinating auditory perception and articulatory movements

Table 1. Results of GB classifier

Band	Accuracy	AUC
Delta	0.855	0.857
Theta	0.896	0.929
Alpha	0.856	0.891
Beta	0.861	0.879
Gamma	0.865	0.911

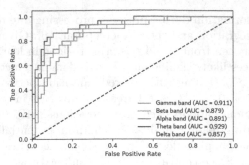

Fig. 8. ROC curves

for fluent reading. This theory is based on the importance of aligning senso-rimotor and sensory activity (CP5-Fc2) for skilled reading [23]. Rearranged dependencies between visual, speech-motor, and language regions are proposed to precipitate phonological deficits in DD. As gamma oscillations enable neural computations underlying comprehension [21], atypical connections between these areas may constitute network inefficiencies.

From Table 1 and ROC curves of Fig. 8, we can infer classification analysis that implicates theta and gamma bands in phonological weaknesses in the DD group due to rhythm processing inefficiencies in auditory areas [6]. Consequently, observing connectivity patterns in these bands offers insights into dyslexics' atypical sensorimotor and cognitive coordination. Manipulating theta oscillations to study impacts on speech processing [11] further demonstrates the importance of this frequency range for language and its disorders. Analyzing dyslexics' theta and gamma connectivity dynamics provides perspectives on multisensory, sensorimotor, and temporal integration deficits.

4   Conclusions

The methodology reveals network integration deficiencies in people with dyslexia within theta and gamma bands during foundational auditory processing. The automated pipeline integrating signaling processing, mapping, feature selection, and classification paves the way for innovative diagnostic screens and interventions for neurodevelopmental disorders.

Acknowledgments. This research is part of the PID2022-137461NB-C32, PID2022-137629OA-I00 and PID2022-137451OB-I00 projects, funded by the MICIU/AEI/10.13039/501100011033 and by ERDF/EU, as well as UMA20-FEDERJA-086 (Consejería de Economía y Conocimiento, Junta de Andalucía) and by European Regional Development Funds (ERDF). This research is part of the TIC251-G-FEDER project, funded by ERDF/EU. M.A.F. grant PRE2019-087350 funded by MICIU/AEI/10.13039/501100011033 by "ESF Investing in your future", I.R.-R. funded by Plan Andaluz de Investigación, Desarrollo e Innovación (PAIDI), Junta de Andalucía.

References

1. Akaike, H.: A new look at the statistical model identification. IEEE Trans. Autom. Control **19**(6), 716–723 (1974). https://doi.org/10.1007/978-1-4612-1694-0_16
2. Artoni, F., et al.: High gamma response tracks different syntactic structures in homophonous phrases. Sci. Rep. **10**(1), 7537 (2020). https://doi.org/10.1038/s41598-020-64375-9
3. Bullmore, E., Sporns, O.: Complex brain networks: graph theoretical analysis of structural and functional systems. Nat. Rev. Neurosci. **10**(3), 186–198 (2009). https://doi.org/10.1038/nrn2575
4. González, G.F., et al.: Graph analysis of EEG resting state functional networks in dyslexic readers. Clin. Neurophysiol. **127**(9), 3165–3175 (2016). https://doi.org/10.1016/j.clinph.2016.06.023
5. Górriz, J., et al.: Computational approaches to explainable artificial intelligence: advances in theory, applications and trends. Inf. Fusion **100**, 101945 (2023). https://doi.org/10.1016/j.inffus.2023.101945
6. Goswami, U.: A temporal sampling framework for developmental dyslexia. Trends Cogn. Sci. **15**(1), 3–10 (2011). https://doi.org/10.1016/j.tics.2010.10.001
7. Granger, C.W.: Investigating causal relations by econometric models and cross-spectral methods. Econometr. J. Economet. Soc. **37**(3), 424–438 (1969). https://doi.org/10.2307/1912791
8. Guha, R., Ghosh, K.K., Bhowmik, S., Sarkar, R.: Mutually informed correlation coefficient (MICC)-a new filter based feature selection method. In: 2020 IEEE Calcutta conference (CALCON), pp. 54–58. IEEE (2020). https://doi.org/10.1109/calcon49167.2020.9106516
9. Górriz, J.M., et al.: Artificial intelligence within the interplay between natural and artificial computation: advances in data science, trends and applications. Neurocomputing **410**, 237–270 (2020). https://doi.org/10.1016/j.neucom.2020.05.078
10. Hu, F., Wang, H., Wang, Q., Feng, N., Chen, J., Zhang, T.: Acrophobia quantified by EEG based on CNN incorporating granger causality. Int. J. Neural Syst. **31**(03), 2050069 (2021). https://doi.org/10.1088/1741-2552/abcdbd
11. Marko, M., Cimrová, B., Riečanský, I.: Neural theta oscillations support semantic memory retrieval. Sci. Rep. **9**(1), 17667 (2019). https://doi.org/10.1038/s41598-019-53813-y
12. Meeuwissen, E.B., Takashima, A., Fernández, G., Jensen, O.: Evidence for human Fronto-central gamma activity during long-term memory encoding of word sequences. PLoS ONE **6**(6), e21356 (2011). https://doi.org/10.1371/journal.pone.0021356
13. Molinaro, N., Lizarazu, M., Lallier, M., Bourguignon, M., Carreiras, M.: Out-of-synchrony speech entrainment in developmental dyslexia. Hum. Brain Mapp. **37**(8), 2767–2783 (2016). https://doi.org/10.1002/hbm.23206
14. Ortiz, A., Martinez-Murcia, F.J., Luque, J.L., Giménez, A., Morales-Ortega, R., Ortega, J.: Dyslexia diagnosis by EEG temporal and spectral descriptors: an anomaly detection approach. Int. J. Neural Syst. **30**(07), 2050029 (2020). https://doi.org/10.1142/s012906572050029x
15. Peterson, R.L., Pennington, B.F.: Developmental dyslexia. The Lancet **379**(9830), 1997–2007 (2012). https://doi.org/10.1016/s0140-6736(12)60198-6
16. Poeppel, D., Idsardi, W.J., Van Wassenhove, V.: Speech perception at the interface of neurobiology and linguistics. Philos. Trans. Royal Soc. B. Biol. Sci. **363**(1493), 1071–1086 (2008). https://doi.org/10.1093/oso/9780199561315.003.0011

17. Pugh, K.R., et al.: Functional neuroimaging studies of reading and reading disability (developmental dyslexia). Ment. Retard. Dev. Disabil. Res. Rev. **6**(3), 207–213 (2000). https://doi.org/10.1002/1098-2779(2000)
18. Rodríguez-Rodríguez, I., Ortiz, A., Gallego-Molina, N.J., Formoso, M., Woo, W.L.: Eeg interchannel causality to identify source/sink phase connectivity patterns in developmental dyslexia. Int. J. Neural Syst. **33**(04), 2350020 (2023). https://doi.org/10.1142/s012906572350020x
19. Romeo, R.R., Segaran, J., Leonard, J.A., Robinson, S.T., West, M.R., Mackey, A.P., Yendiki, A., Rowe, M.L., Gabrieli, J.D.: Language exposure relates to structural neural connectivity in childhood. J. Neurosci. **38**(36), 7870–7877 (2018). https://doi.org/10.1523/jneurosci.0484-18.2018
20. Schmidt, C., Piper, D., Pester, B., Mierau, A., Witte, H.: Tracking the reorganization of module structure in time-varying weighted brain functional connectivity networks. Int. J. Neural Syst. **28**(04), 1750051 (2018). https://doi.org/10.1142/s0129065717500514
21. Spironelli, C., Angrilli, A.: Developmental aspects of language lateralization in delta, theta, alpha and beta EEG bands. Biol. Psychol. **85**(2), 258–267 (2010). https://doi.org/10.1016/j.biopsycho.2010.07.011
22. Summerfield, C., Mangels, J.A.: Coherent theta-band EEG activity predicts item-context binding during encoding. Neuroimage **24**(3), 692–703 (2005). https://doi.org/10.1016/j.neuroimage.2004.09.012
23. Wang, L., Zhu, Z., Bastiaansen, M.: Integration or predictability? Further specification of the functional role of EEG gamma-band oscillations during language comprehension. Front. Psychol. **3**(187), 00187 (2012). https://doi.org/10.3389/fpsyg.2012.00187
24. Yaqub, M.A., Hong, K.S., Zafar, A., Kim, C.S.: Control of transcranial direct current stimulation duration by assessing functional connectivity of near-infrared spectroscopy signals. Int. J. Neural Syst. **32**(01), 2150050 (2022). https://doi.org/10.3390/bioengineering10070810

Explainable Exploration of the Interplay Between HRV Features and EEG Local Connectivity Patterns in Dyslexia

Marco A. Formoso[1,2]($\boxtimes$), Nicolás J. Gallego-Molina[1,2,3], A. Ortiz[1,2], Ignacio Rodríguez-Rodríguez[1,2], and Almudena Giménez[3]

[1] Communications Engineering Department, University of Málaga, 29004 Málaga, Spain
marco.a.formoso@uma.es

[2] Andalusian Data Science and Computational Intelligence Institute (DaSCI), Granada, Germany

[3] Department of Basic Psychology, University of Málaga, 29019 Málaga, Spain

Abstract. Heart Rate Variability (HRV) is a measure of the variation in time between successive heartbeats, reflecting the influence of the autonomic nervous system on the heart. It can provide insights into the balance between sympathetic and parasympathetic activity. The relationship between autonomic nervous system function, specifically parasympathetic activity, and certain learning disorders, including dyslexia, is currently under study. In this paper, we propose the use of explainable techniques to explore the relationships between HRV markers and local functional brain activity, estimated by cross-frequency coupling (CFC) from electroencephalography (EEG) signals recorded while auditory stimuli were applied to 7-year-old children. We analyze EEG data to examine the phase-to-phase brainwave coupling and use machine learning tools such as XGBoost and Shapley values to reveal brain regions that most contribute to different HRV features, with a focus on parasympathetic activity. Our findings suggest that HRV features related to stress can explain differential activations in the auditory cortex (Brodmann areas 39 and 40) during auditory stimulation in dyslexic children.

Keywords: EEG · NIRS · HRV markers · Explainable Artificial Intelligence · Dyslexia

1 Introduction

Nowadays, a large number of different measures are available to obtain physiological data. This means that we can obtain useful information from virtually any part of the body. Over the years, a number of tools have been developed and refined with great variability in what they can measure, from electrical signals to blood oxygen levels, temperature levels or internal body imaging through magnetic fields. In addition, the development of the artificial intelligence (AI) field

© The Author(s), under exclusive license to Springer Nature Switzerland AG 2024
J. M. Ferrández Vicente et al. (Eds.): IWINAC 2024, LNCS 14674, pp. 45–54, 2024.
https://doi.org/10.1007/978-3-031-61140-7_5

has opened the door to greatly improve the information that can be extracted from these measures and the relationship between them, leading to a deeper understanding of the human body [1,2]. In this paper, the focus is on two non-invasive techniques, electroencephalography (EEG) and functional near-infrared spectroscopy (fNIRS), both of which capturing brain activity.

EEG measures the electrical activity generated by the neurons. When they fired, they created small electrical currents, these currents are then recording by strategically placed electrodes in the scalp [3]. Several techniques have been developed to better understand what is happening in the brain. One of these involves calculating the synchrony of various brain waves, in the same brain region or in different ones, at what is known as coupling. In coupling, several values are obtained from the EEG; firstly decomposing it in several signals at different frequencies, the so-called brainwaves, and then computing some metric. This metric is obtained evaluating the coupling grade between signals, e.g., how the phase of one signal affects the amplitude of another one or how the phase of one signal affects the phase of another one. This is done in the so-called cross frequency coupling (CFC) methods [4].

fNIRS measures changes in blood oxygenation levels in the brain. This technique uses near-infrared light to estimate blood oxygenation levels, which occur in response to brain activity. This light can penetrate the scalp and skull, and it is absorbed by the hemoglobin [5]. From this measure, we can calculate the heart rate variability (HRV). In HRV the number of heart rate fluctuations is measured. This metric provides information about the sympathetic-parasympathetic balance status [6]. Several metrics have been developed either in the time domain or in the frequency domain in order to better study HRV. A review can be found in [7]. These metrics have been widely used in the study of illness and body behaviors. For example, its relation with stress is studied in the works of Kim et al. and Clays et al. [7,8]: Low parasympathetic activity, as indicated by a high variability in heart rate (HRV) variables, is related to a higher level of stress.

The integration of AI into the medical domain has significantly enhanced the evolution of diagnostic methods. In EEG analysis, approaches such as Formoso et al. and Ortiz et al. [9,10], leverage CFC measures and machine learning for dyslexia classification. Regarding HRV, Arco et al. [11] utilize machine learning algorithms to identify early dementia markers. While all this advances are compelling, it is crucial the comprehension of AI-driven decision-making processes to enhance the safety and reliability of these medical diagnostics and treatments. Techniques derived from game theory, such as Shapley values [12], help us in understanding the trade-offs between model characteristics and outcomes, facilitating the identification of features critical to medical challenges.

In this work, the focus is on the study of developmental dyslexia (DD) and its relation with stress markers provided by HRV and EEG. More specifically, how HRV stress markers like PNN20 or PNN50 suggest parasympathetic system activity when the subjects are exposed to auditory stimuli and its relation with certain brain areas that have been studied as closely related to DD. The rest of the work is structured as follows: section *Material and Methods* presents the methodology, including participant selection and data collection procedures as well as he data analysis techniques and machine learning models used. Then the *Results* and *Discussion* sections discuses the results and their implications. Finally, section *Conclusions* concludes the study with a summary of findings and suggestions for future research.

2   Materials and Methods

2.1   Database

The data was provided by the Leeduca research group at the University of Málaga, Spain. Carefully selected from a pool of 700 individuals across 20 primary schools in Andalucía, the participants were divided into control and experimental groups for a comprehensive evaluation that included the ATLAS family risk assessment and a detailed analysis at age 7. Table 1 shows the demographic of the subjects. Experiments complied with ethical standards, receiving approval from the Medical Ethical Committee of Málaga University (CEUMA 16-2020-H) and conducted according to the World Medical Association Declaration of Helsinki. They were also supported by the regional government of Andalusia's Education Office.

EEG signals were captured with a Brainvision actiCHamp Plus, featuring a 32-channel amplifier (500 Hz sampling rate). During fifteen-minute sessions, children were exposed to auditory stimuli in the form of white noise modulated at frequencies corresponding to phonological units in speech: 4.8 Hz, 16 Hz and 40 Hz. This non-interactive stimulus aimed to induce a semi-resting state for more accurate data capture.

Table 1. Demographics of the subjects included in the database.

Group	Male/Female	Mean Age (Months)
Control	17/15	94.1 ± 3.3
Dyslexia	7/9	95.6 ± 2.9

2.2   Cross Frequency Coupling with ISPC

The interplay between brain waves play a fundamental role in how we understand the brain activity. Fundamental cognitive process can be explained through this kind of interaction, where one signal modulates another one [13]. There are various ways to measure this coupling, being phase to phase or phase to amplitude the most common ones. In our work, a variation of a phase to phase one called Intersite Phase Clustering (ISPC) [14]. The first step to extract information using ISPC is to filter the different signals to extract the bands we will work on using a FIR filter. These bands are Theta $(4 - 8$ Hz), Alpha $(8 - 12$ Hz), Beta

(12 − 30 Hz) and Gamma (30 − 80 Hz). Since the instantaneous phase $\phi(t)$ is necessary to apply ISPC we extract it by means of Hilbert Transform 1:

$$z(t) = x(t) + j \cdot H[x(t)] \qquad \text{where} \qquad H[x(t)] = \frac{1}{\pi} \int_{-\infty}^{+\infty} \frac{x(t)}{t - \tau} d\tau \qquad (1)$$

$$\phi(t) = \angle z(t) = \tan^{-1} \frac{\Im(z(t))}{\Re(z(t))} \qquad (2)$$

Then the ISCP can be calculated with the next equation:

$$\text{CFS} = \left| \frac{1}{n} \sum_{t=1}^{n} e^{i(\phi_A(t) - \phi_B(t))} \right| \qquad (3)$$

where n is the number of time points, and $\phi_A(t)$ and $\phi_B(t)$ are the phase angles for the frequency bands A and B respectively. The combinations of bands where ISCP is applied are Theta-Gamma, Alpha-Beta and Beta-Gamma. These bands have been studied as being closely related to speech activity [9, 15–18].

2.3 Heart Rate Variability Descriptors

HRV features are a collection of statistics computed from the heart rate (HR). In this work, we extracted the heart rate from NIRS signals instead of using dedicate ECG acquisitions as is commonly done. The extraction of the HR from fNIRS follows several steps. Firstly, Temporal Derivative Distribution Repair (TDDR) method, as described by Fishburn et al. [19] is used. This method removes spike artifacts and baseline shifts. Then, the signals are filtered to fall in the range of 60–120 beats per minute, that is between 1 Hz and 2 Hz, a common heart rate in children. Then, the Hilbert Transform (1) is used, and its envelope calculated, obtaining the final heart rate signal.

Obtaining the HRV from a heart signal is a straightforward process. It involves a calculation of the distance (in ms) between consecutive signal peaks in what is called normal-to-normal intervals (NNI). Once obtained the NNIs, several metrics can be computed either in time-domain or frequency-domain. A depiction of some of the can be found in Table 2.

In this study, we concentrate on the PNN20 and PNN50 metrics. Both are the number of pairs of normal-to-normal (NN) intervals differing more than (20, 50) ms for the recording and divided by the total number of all NN intervals. The relationship between pNN20 or pNN50 and stress centers around the concept of autonomic nervous system balance, particularly the balance between the sympathetic nervous system ("fight or flight" response) and the parasympathetic nervous system ("rest and digest" response). High stress levels are associated with increased sympathetic activity and decreased parasympathetic activity. Since higher HRV (including higher pNN20 and pNN50 values) generally indicates greater parasympathetic activity and thus a more relaxed state, low pNN20 and pNN50 values can be indicative of stress or an overactive sympathetic nervous system [7, 8]. In simpler terms:

Table 2. HRV statistics overview

Variable	Units	Description
Time Domain		
SDNN	ms	Standard deviation of all NN intervals
SDANN	ms	Standard deviation of the averages of NN intervals in all 5-minute segments of the entire recording
RMSSD	ms	The square root of the mean of the sum of the squares of differences between adjacent NN intervals
NN50 count		Number of pairs of adjacent NN intervals differing by more than 50 ms
pNN50	%	NN50 count divided by the total number of all NN intervals
NN20 count		Number of pairs of adjacent NN intervals differing by more than 20 ms
pNN20	%	NN20 count divided by the total number of all NN intervals
Frequency Domain		
VLF	ms^2	Power in Very Low Frequency range
HF	ms^2	Power in High Frequency range
LF	ms^2	Power in Low Frequency range

- High pNN50/pNN20 values: These suggest a higher HRV, which is often associated with a healthier, more resilient heart. It may indicate a relaxed state where the body is able to adequately recover and respond to stress.
- Low pNN50/pNN20 values: These suggest a lower HRV, which could indicate stress, fatigue, or even potential heart-related issues. It reflects a state where the body's ability to adapt to stressors and recover might be compromised.

2.4   Explainable Regression Experiments

Gradient Boosting [20] and its upgrade XGBoost [21] are ensemble machine learning algorithms that could be used to perform classification or regression tasks. The base learned algorithms to construct the ensemble can be categorized in linear models, smooth models, and decision tree-based models (DT), being the last ones the most commonly used. It operates by constructing multiple models sequentially, with each new model being trained to correct the errors made by the previous ones.

It is simple to retrieve the valuable features through the trained model because of the structure of DT as the basic learner in the gradient boosting tree models. In particular, each node in a DT is a dataset splitting condition based on a single feature. However, this is not enough as it may not fully capture the multifaceted contributions of all features involved. Shapley values [12] offers a more nuanced and equitable understanding of feature contributions.

Shapley values have its origins in cooperative game theory are used to fairly distribute the payoff among players based on their contribution to the total payout. In the context of machine learning, they explain the contribution of each feature to the prediction of a particular instance. This is useful to gain insights of the model behaviour. The goal is to determine how much each feature contributes to the prediction, considering all possible combinations of features.

In our work, we use XGBoost python library [21] and SHAP python library [22]. The goal is to predict PNN50 and PNN20 using the CFS values previously described. Since the channels of the EEG are known and the correspond to certain brain regions, we can determine with the help of the SHAP values the relation between the activation of certain brain regions and its contribution to stress levels.

3   Results

As stated in the previous section the algorithm selected to perform the regression is XGBoost. This is framed inside a cross validation loop of 5 folds. The final dataset is composed of 58 control subjects and 30 dyslexic ones. Only the records for the 40 Hz stimuli have been used. For every band in the computed CFS(Theta-Gamma, Alpha-Beta, Beta-Gamma) there is a 30 segments x 31 channels matrix. These matrix of every subject are averaged segment-wise, thus for every subject we have three matrices, one for each band with 31 elements each. As mentioned above, the objective is to predict the PNN values from the CFS, to check which channels are the most efficient in discriminating the two groups. Several experiments have been performed, one using all the bands in order to predict PNN values, then again using each band individually. In Table 3 the final results are summarized showing the mean squared error (MSE) and mean absolute value (MAE) as well.

Table 3. PNNI Metrics Performance Comparison

PNN	Bands	MSE	MAE
PNN20	All bands	92.76	6.68
	Theta-Gamma	94.53	6.81
	Alpha-Beta	95.68	6.89
	Beta-Gamma	117.61	7.08
PNN50	All bands	107.41	7.40
	Theta-Gamma	139.11	7.92
	Alpha-Beta	109.01	7.83
	Beta-Gamma	151.02	8.46

As we can see, using all bands provides the best value errors of 6.68 and 7.40. The Shapley values for this both results are depicted in Figs. 1 and 2. The more discriminative channels appear in the top of the figures.

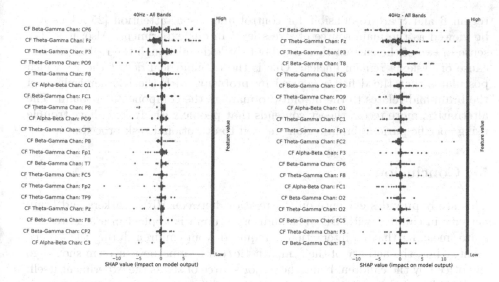

Fig. 1. Shapley values for PNN20

Fig. 2. Shapley values for PNN50

4   Discussion

The development of new tools and techniques and the incorporation of AI into the field of medicine have increased the possibilities for further study and understanding of the human brain. Brain coupling, either phase-to-phase of phase-to-amplitude, has been proven valuables assets. Fused with another source of information like fNIR and using novel AI techniques open the door to further increase the number and kind of experiments that can be performed.

In our work, several auditory at different frequencies were applied to children with and without diagnosed dyslexia. The goal is to stimulate the bran regions responsible for speech and auditory processing. Our theory is that this can also cause stress levels on dyslexic children even if it goes unnoticed by them. The association of the stress levels during the auditory experiment with the activity of certain brain regions shows that dyslexic children sympathetic/parasympathetic system behaves different that the ones on the control group.

Although the brain is all interconected we can separate the regions and functions of it at certain level. The most common is the Brodmann areas [23] which are commonly referenced in neuroscience and to describe the location of various cognitive functions. For example, Brodmann areas 39 and 40 are associated with parts of the parietal lobe involved in processes such as language and auditory processing. In our case, we can associate the electrodes with the closest Brodmann area. Thus, focusing of Figs. 1 and 2 the three most discriminant channels are: CP6, Fz, P3 and FC1. They correspond to the Brodmann areas 40, 08, 39 and 06 respectively. Among them, the ones that play a role in the language understanding and phonological processing are areas 40 and 39 [24] whereas region 6 and 8 are responsible for control and visual attention [25]. This can be viewed as the main source of stress level in our experiment. Also, it makes sense in two of the current theories about dyslexia, although the real origin and cause of dyslexia remain unclear. One is the phonological deficit theory, which postulates that the deficit is caused by problems with the left hemisphere of the brain and relates to the inability to manage the components of sound. The alternative, more recent theory contends that people with dyslexia have trouble using specific parietal brain regions related to attentional task procedures.

5   Conclusion

This study provides evidence on the relation between HRV markers and brain activity in children with DD. The auditory stimuli is applied in a semi-resting state, meaning that no interaction is required from children during the experiment. Thus, the activity of the sympathetic/parasympathetic system should go unnoticed by the children, being the major source of stress the experiment itself.

We identified important brain areas with different activity patterns associated with parasympathetic activity levels through machine learning methods, and interpreting the data using Shapley values. More precisely, Brodmann areas 40 and 39, which are important for language processing and phonological awareness.

We now have a more sophisticated knowledge of the role that each brain region plays in DD and the related parasympathetic reactions because to the application of machine learning techniques, especially gradient boosting methods in conjunction with Shapley values. Our research highlights the potential of using AI techniques in psychological and neurophysiological studies, opening the door to the creation of more sophisticated DD treatment plans and diagnostic instruments. More studies in this area may improve our understanding of the intricate relationship between stress and cognitive impairments, which could ultimately result in more individualized and successful interventions.

Although promising, additional research is required to completely understand the interactions between autonomic nervous system and brain activity linked to dyslexia.

Acknowledgements. This research is part of the PID2022-137461NB-C32, PID2022-137629OA-I00 and PID2022-137451OB-I00 projects, funded by the MICIU/AEI/10.13039/501100011033 and by ESF+ as well as UMA20-FEDERJA-086 (Consejería de Economía y Conocimiento, Junta de Andalucía) and by European Regional Development Funds (ERDF), as well as the BioSiP (TIC-251) research group and Univerisity of Málaga (UMA). This research is also part of the TIC251-G-FEDER project, funded by ERDF/EU. Marco A. Formoso grant PRE2019-087350 is funded by MICIU/AEI/10.13039/501100011033 by ESF Investing in your future. Ignacio Rodriguez-Rodríguez is funded by Plan Andaluz de Investigación, Desarrollo e Innovación (PAIDI), Junta de Andalucía.

References

1. Górriz, J.M., et al.: Artificial intelligence within the interplay between natural and artificial computation: advances in data science, trends and applications. Neurocomputing **410**, 237–270 (2020). https://doi.org/10.1016/j.neucom.2020.05.078
2. Górriz, J., et al.: Computational approaches to explainable artificial intelligence: advances in theory, applications and trends. Inf. Fusion **100**, 101945 (2023). https://doi.org/10.1016/j.inffus.2023.101945
3. Teplan, M., et al.: Fundamentals of EEG measurement. Measure. Sci. Rev. **2**(2), 1–11 (2002)
4. Hülsemann, M.J., Naumann, E., Rasch, B.: Quantification of phase-amplitude coupling in neuronal oscillations: comparison of phase-locking value, mean vector length, modulation index, and generalized-linear-modeling-cross-frequency-coupling. Front. Neurosci. **13**, 573 (2019)
5. Butler, L.K., Kiran, S., Tager-Flusberg, H.: Functional near-infrared spectroscopy in the study of speech and language impairment across the life span: a systematic review. Am. J. Speech Lang. Pathol. **29**(3), 1674–1701 (2020)
6. van Ravenswaaij-Arts, C.M., Kollee, L.A., Hopman, J.C., Stoelinga, G.B., van Geijn, H.P.: Heart rate variability. Ann. Intern. Med. **118**(6), 436–447 (1993)
7. Kim, H.-G., Cheon, E.-J., Bai, D.-S., Lee, Y.H., Koo, B.-H.: Stress and heart rate variability: a meta-analysis and review of the literature. Psychiatry Investig. **15**(3), 235 (2018)
8. Clays, E., et al.: The perception of work stressors is related to reduced parasympathetic activity. Int. Arch. Occup. Environ. Health **84**, 185–191 (2011)
9. Formoso, M.A., Ortiz, A., Martinez-Murcia, F.J., Gallego, N., Luque, J.L.: Detecting phase-synchrony connectivity anomalies in EEG signals. Application to dyslexia diagnosis. Sensors **21**(21), 7061 (2021)
10. Ortiz, A., Martínez-Murcia, F.J., Formoso, M.A., Luque, J.L., Sánchez, A.: Dyslexia detection from EEG signals using SSA component correlation and convolutional neural networks. In: de la Cal, E.A., Villar Flecha, J.R., Quintián, H., Corchado, E. (eds.) HAIS 2020. LNCS (LNAI), vol. 12344, pp. 655–664. Springer, Cham (2020). https://doi.org/10.1007/978-3-030-61705-9_54
11. Arco, J.E., Gallego-Molina, N.J., Ortiz, A., Arroyo-Alvis, K., López-Pérez, P.J.: Identifying HRV patterns in ECG signals as early markers of dementia. Expert Syst. Appl. **243**, 122934 (2024)
12. Shapley, L.S., et al.: A value for n-person games (1953)
13. Scheffer-Teixeira, R., Tort, A.B.: On cross-frequency phase-phase coupling between theta and gamma oscillations in the hippocampus. eLife **5**, e20515 (2016)
14. Cohen, M.X.: Analyzing Neural Time Series Data: Theory and Practice. MIT Press, Cambridge (2014)
15. Kimppa, L., Shtyrov, Y., Partanen, E., Kujala, T.: Impaired neural mechanism for online novel word acquisition in dyslexic children. Sci. Rep. **8**(1), 12779 (2018). https://doi.org/10.1038/s41598-018-31211-0
16. Thiede, A., Glerean, E., Kujala, T., Parkkonen, L.: Atypical meg inter-subject correlation during listening to continuous natural speech in dyslexia. Neuroimage **216**, 116799 (2020). https://doi.org/10.1016/j.neuroimage.2020.116799
17. Attaheri, et al.: Infant low-frequency EEG cortical power, cortical tracking and phase-amplitude coupling predicts language a year later (2022). https://doi.org/10.1101/2022.11.02.514963.

18. Gallego-Molina, N.J., Formoso, M., Ortiz, A., Martínez-Murcia, F.J., Luque, J.L.: Temporal EigenPAC for dyslexia diagnosis. In: Rojas, I., Joya, G., Català, A. (eds.) IWANN 2021. LNCS, vol. 12862, pp. 45–56. Springer, Cham (2021). https://doi.org/10.1007/978-3-030-85099-9_4

19. Fishburn, F.A., Ludlum, R.S., Vaidya, C.J., Medvedev, A.V.: Temporal derivative distribution repair (TDDR): a motion correction method for fNIRS. Neuroimage **184**, 171–179 (2019)

20. Friedman, J.H.: Greedy function approximation: a gradient boosting machine. Ann. Statist. **29**, 1189–1232 (2001)

21. Chen, T., Guestrin, C.: XGBoost: a scalable tree boosting system. In: Proceedings of the 22nd ACM SIGKDD International Conference on Knowledge Discovery and Data Mining, pp. 785–794 (2016)

22. Lundberg, S.M., Lee, S.-I.: A unified approach to interpreting model predictions. In: Advances in Neural Information Processing Systems, vol. 30, pp. 4765–4774. Curran Associates, Inc. (2017)

23. Brodmann, K.: Vergleichende Lokalisationslehre der Grosshirnrinde in ihren Prinzipien dargestellt auf Grund des Zellenbaues, Barth (1909)

24. Ardila, A., Bernal, B., Rosselli, M.: How localized are language brain areas? A review of Brodmann areas involvement in oral language. Arch. Clin. Neuropsychol. **31**(1), 112–122 (2016)

25. Tanaka, S., Honda, M., Sadato, N.: Modality-specific cognitive function of medial and lateral human Brodmann area 6. J. Neurosci. **25**(2), 496–501 (2005)

Enhancing Intensity Differences in EEG Cross-Frequency Coupling Maps for Dyslexia Detection

Diego Castillo-Barnes[1,2]($\boxtimes$), Andrés Ortiz[1,2], Pietro Stabile[3],
Nicolás J. Gallego-Molina[1,2], Patrícia Figueiredo[3], and Juan L. Luque[4]

[1] Communications Engineering Department, University of Málaga,
29004 Málaga, Spain
diegoc@uma.es
[2] Andalusian Data Science and Computational Intelligence Institute (DaSCI),
Granada, Spain
[3] Institute for Systems and Robotics (Lisboa/LARSyS) and Department of
Bioengineering, Instituto Superior Técnico, Universidade de Lisboa,
Av. Rovisco Pais 1, 1049-001 Lisboa, Portugal
[4] Department of Developmental and Educational Psychology, University of Málaga,
29004 Málaga, Spain

Abstract. In this study, we introduced and applied a novel histogram transformation technique to enhance the interpretability and discriminative power of Cross-Frequency Coupling (CFC) maps derived from EEG signals for dyslexia detection. Our approach addresses the challenge of subtle intensity differences in CFC maps, which can hinder the accurate identification of dyslexia-related patterns.

Through visual inspection and quantitative analysis, we demonstrated the effectiveness of the histogram transformation technique in amplifying intensity differences within CFC maps. Specifically, our results show significant improvements in the significance of CFC map pixels, particularly in the Alpha-Beta coupling band, post-transformation. This enhancement in discriminative power was further supported by the reduction in entropy and the identification of texture feature changes through Gray-Level Co-occurrence Matrix (GLCM) analysis.

Keywords: EEG · Cross-Frequency Coupling · Dyslexia · Image processing · Histogram transformation · Mann-Whitney-Wilcoxon · Cross-Entropy · GLCM · Interpretability

1 Introduction

Dyslexia, a neurodevelopmental disorder, influences learning abilities such as reading and linguistic skills. The early diagnosis of this disorder allows customized instruction for affected children, improving their academic success and self-esteem [31]. Diagnosing dyslexia often involves assessing a child's reading

© The Author(s), under exclusive license to Springer Nature Switzerland AG 2024
J. M. Ferrández Vicente et al. (Eds.): IWINAC 2024, LNCS 14674, pp. 55–67, 2024.
https://doi.org/10.1007/978-3-031-61140-7_6

accuracy, fluency, and understanding. However, traditional diagnosis methods may not capture the full spectrum of dyslexia symptoms due to the disorder's complex and diverse nature [24,26,34].

To address this challenge, novel techniques such as Cross-Frequency Coupling (CFC) from electroencephalogram (EEG) signals are increasingly being used to discern brain activity differences (even if they may be related with cognition or other behavioural aspects) in dyslexic individuals [3,6,30]. These techniques, analyzing either phase-amplitude and phase-phase coupling values, demonstrate effective detection of dyslexia-related networks in the brain, paving the way towards early intervention and improved therapeutic outcomes [17,19,21,22].

While artificial intelligence techniques analyzing EEG bands have been in the spotlight in recent years [18], yielding significant insights into dyslexia's biological underpinnings, works such as [4,13–16] present two main challenges: 1) the loss of interpretability, especially when applying techniques like Principal Component Analysis (PCA) and Holo-Hilbert Spectral Analysis (HHSA), and 2) the identification of intricate patterns that are especially crucial in the early stages of this disorder.

In this context, this work steers the spotlight towards the proposal and application of a novel histogram transformation technique to amplify intensity differences in the CFC maps between patients and controls. This unique approach aims to bridge the limitations observed in prior models by accentuating the edges of the regions of interest, thereby enabling easier discerning of controls and dyslexics. For that, our method takes the original CFC maps and transforms the activations of each pixel to their corresponding bin height in the histogram. This technique enhances the activation bounds within the CFC maps, especially in the absence of differentiated isolated activations, making it much easier for potential classifiers to distinguish dyslexic individuals from controls. Note that, done correctly, these new markers could offer deeper insights into dyslexia by accurately determining which brain areas are more related to developmental dyslexia, and revealing any potential associations between different brain regions.

In this work, we unravel our proposed histogram transformation model's strengths, unique features, and potential to drive more accurate early dyslexia detection. We hope that our novel contribution can inspire further research in this direction with a profound ripple effect on the futures of children with dyslexia.

2   Materials and Methods

2.1   Database

For this work we have made use of a dataset provided by the LEEDUCA research group at the University of Malaga (Spain) [25]. This dataset is the result of a comprehensive longitudinal study involving over 1400 children aged 4 to 8 years, all of whom underwent regular assessments involving cognitive and linguistic tasks. In this case, we randomly selected the EEG signals from a subset of 15 children diagnosed with dyslexia and a control group comprising 33 neurotypical children, all matched for age and socio-economic indices.

During the EEG acquisition, each child is exposed to auditory stimuli consisting of amplitude-modulated white noise presented at varying rates: 4.8 Hz, 16 Hz, and 40 Hz to encapsulate the core units of common language speech (Spanish). Each EEG recording session lasts 15 min (5 min for each frequency), during which the stimuli are presented continually and sequentially in a specific order: [4.8 → 16 → 40] Hz (ascending) and [40 → 16 → 4.8] Hz (descending). The EEG data were acquired using a Brainvision actiCHamp Plus system (www.brainproducts.com) with actiCAP electrodes configured to a 32-channel 10–20 layout and optimized specifically for auditory processing. Moreover, the EEG signals have been previously processed to remove artifacts induced by eye blinks, using an Independent Component Analysis (ICA); to normalize individual channels to zero mean and unit variance; to ensure a reference to the Cz electrode; and to undergo baseline correction.

Ethical approval for this study was obtained from the Medical Ethics Committee of the University of Malaga (CEUMA 16-2020-H), and written consent was obtained from the tutors in accordance with the Declaration of Helsinki of the World Medical Association. The research has the support of the *Consejería de Educación de la Junta de Andalucía* (Spain), facilitating its implementation in a number of public schools.

2.2   Generation of CFC Maps from EEG Signals

CFC measures in EEG signals help us to quantify the interactions (coordination) between different frequency bands in the brain. Although the most traditional approach consists of analyzing how the phase of one frequency band influences the amplitude of another frequency band, we have focused on evaluating phase-phase couplings since these kind of interactions play a crucial role in various cognitive processes such as memory, attention, and perception [27,30].

For CFC analysis, we have used a modification of the Intersite Phase Clustering (ISPC) method [9], termed CFS (Cross-Frequency phase Synchronization), focusing on the distribution of phase angle differences between frequency bands within the same electrode. The CFS measure is computed as the absolute mean phase difference between two frequency bands over time intervals Eq. (1):

$$\text{CFS}_{A,B} = \left| \frac{1}{n} \sum_{t=1}^{n} e^{i(\phi_A(t) - \phi_B(t))} \right| \qquad (1)$$

Here, $\phi_A(t)$ and $\phi_B(t)$ represent the phase angles for frequency bands A and B respectively, and n is the number of time points. We focus on Delta (0.5–4 Hz), Theta (4–8 Hz), Alpha (8–12 Hz), Beta (12–30 Hz), and Gamma (30–80 Hz) frequency bands. Filtered EEG signals are processed using Hilbert Transform to extract instantaneous phase, facilitating the computation of CFS values [11].

To visualize CFS maps, we project EEG electrode locations onto a 2D reference space using an Azimuthal Equidistant Projection method [5]. Interpolating CFS values between electrodes using Clough-Tocher interpolation [2], we generate maps representing spatial phase-phase coupling distributions between frequency bands. Figure 1 presents CFS maps derived from EEG signals of a randomly selected subject in the dataset, depicting spatial patterns of cross-frequency interactions.

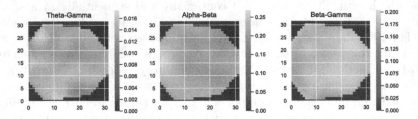

Fig. 1. CFS maps across the scalp for different coupling bands for our EEG analysis. Results obtained by averaging the data from a randomly selected subject in the LEEDUCA platform dataset. Exposure to a white noise auditory stimulus at 4.8 Hz.

2.3 Enhancing Differences in CFS Maps Through Histogram Transformation

While CFS maps can provide valuable insights, the differences in value are often subtle and challenging for visual interpretation and further image processing steps. In this context, there are many methods from which we could try to enhance the differences in CFS maps, such as Adaptive Histogram Equalization [29, 33], Contrast-Stretching [32], Gradient-Based Enhancement [8], Logarithmic-transformation [1], Contrast Enhancement using Discrete Wavelet Transform [10], Local Laplacian Filters [28], among others. However, when we analyze the CFS intensity maps in Fig. 1 and their associated histograms in Fig. 2, we realize that these histograms showcase narrow distributions because the intensity differences of the original images are relatively minor. This characteristic makes it challenging for any classifier to distinguish between controls and dyslexics based solely on these intensity values.

To mitigate this, we propose applying a simple but effective histogram transformation on the CFS maps. This technique consists of replacing the activations or intensity values of each pixel in CFS maps with the corresponding height of the bin in the histogram obtained from the map's original intensities. Since this height becomes our new intensity value, it intensifies the variation between different values, leading to enhanced differences and better visual separation of the features of interest in the histogram-equalized CFS maps whose subtle intensity differences might be clinically significant.

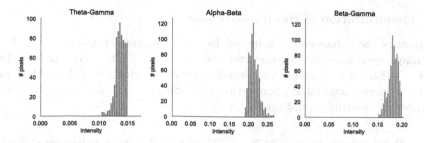

Fig. 2. Histograms illustrating the distribution of CFS intensity values for different coupling bands in the EEG analysis. Each histogram corresponds to a specific frequency band: Theta-Gamma, Alpha-Beta and Beta-Gamma.

Mathematically, this transformation can be described as follows:

– Let I_{orig} denote the original CFS map, then its histogram can be obtained as $H_{orig} = hist(I_{orig}, N_b)$, where $hist(.,.)$ is the histogram function and N_b is the number of bins.
– Let $h(i)$ be the height of bin i, where $i \in 1, ..., N_b$, then the histogram transformed CFS map, I_{trans} can be obtained as $I_{trans} = h(I_{orig})$ where $h(.)$ is the function that maps each intensity value in I_{orig} to its corresponding bin height in the histogram.

Following the application of this transformation to the CFS intensity maps depicted in Fig. 2, the resulting spatial distributions of intensity values, as illustrated in Fig. 3, reflect an accentuation of differences between regions, facilitated by the mapping of each intensity value to its corresponding bin height in the histogram.

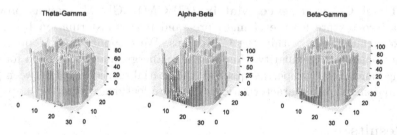

Fig. 3. Transformation of CFS intensity maps using histogram enhancement. Each subplot represents the spatial distribution of intensity values after applying the enhancement method to the CFS maps corresponding to different frequency coupling bands. The color of each voxel represents the height of the histogram bin associated with its intensity value, accentuating differences between regions.

2.4   Quantification of the Improvement

To quantify the enhancement achieved by the histogram transformation of the CFS maps, we employ two distinct metrics: the Mann-Whitney-Wilcoxon U-Test and Cross-Entropy analysis. Additionally, we assess changes in GLCM (Gray-Level Co-occurrence Matrix) properties pre- and post-transformation to understand texture feature alterations.

Mann-Whitney-Wilcoxon U-Test. The Mann-Whitney-Wilcoxon U-Test is a non-parametric statistical test used to determine whether there is a significant difference between two independent groups [12]. In our study, we utilize this test to compare the distributions of CFS map pixel values before and after histogram transformation for different band couplings. The null hypothesis is that the distributions of the two groups are equal, and a low $p-$value indicates a rejection of this hypothesis, suggesting a significant difference between the distributions.

Cross-Entropy. Cross-Entropy is a measure commonly used to assess the difference between two probability distributions. In our context, it allows us to quantify the change in entropy of coupling band distributions before and after histogram transformation. A decrease in cross-entropy indicates a reduction in uncertainty or disorder within the coupling, while an increase signifies greater uncertainty or disorder. The formula for cross-entropy is given by Eq. (2), where $p(i)$ and $q(i)$ represent the probability distributions before and after transformation, respectively.

$$H(p, q) = -\sum_{i} p(i) \log(q(i)) \tag{2}$$

Grey-Level Co-occurrence Matrix (GLCM). GLCM analysis provides insights into texture feature changes pre- and post-transformation by assessing pixel relationships within the CFS maps. We compute GLCM properties such as Contrast, Dissimilarity, Homogeneity, Energy, and Correlation for each coupling band. These properties quantify the spatial relationships between pixel values and enable the characterization of texture features within the maps [23].

3   Results

Visual inspection of the average CFS maps, derived from the 33 controls (top row) and 15 dyslexics children (bottom row) from the LEEDUCA subset, both before and after histogram transformation, reveals discernible differences in the intensity activations of CFS maps (Fig. 4 for Alpha-Beta coupling, Fig. 6 for Beta-Gamma coupling, and Fig. 7 for Theta-Gamma coupling).

Analysis of the negative logarithm of the p_{values}, arranged in descending order (Fig. 5), indicates a pronounced increase in the significance of CFS map

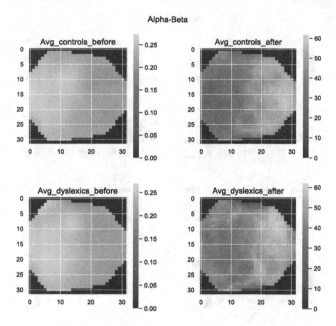

Fig. 4. Comparison of averaged CFS maps derived from control subjects and those with dyslexia for Alpha-Beta couplings before (left column) and after (right column) histogram transformation.

pixels in the alpha-beta band following histogram transformation. While some improvements are observed in other bands post-transformation, the differences between pre- and post-transformation curves are less prominent.

Cross-entropy analysis offers insights into the transformation's impact on coupling band entropy. For Theta-Gamma coupling, the initial cross-entropy of -1269.67 increased to -1419.57 post-transformation, indicating reduced entropy. Similarly, Alpha-Beta coupling exhibited a substantial increase in cross-entropy from -408.25 to -1338.35, suggesting decreased entropy. Surprisingly, Beta-Gamma coupling displayed a dramatic rise in entropy from -525.45 to 2165.82 after transformation, signifying increased disorder within the coupling.

Furthermore, GLCM properties were assessed to discern texture feature changes pre- and post-transformation. Before transformation, T-tests showed no significant differences in GLCM properties. However, post-transformation:

Theta-Gamma Coupling

– Contrast remained largely unchanged ($p_{\text{value}} = 0.1795$).
– Dissimilarity exhibited a significant decrease ($p_{\text{value}} = 0.0284$), indicating reduced heterogeneity.
– Homogeneity notably increased ($p_{\text{value}} = 0.0008$), suggesting greater uniformity in pixel value distributions.
– Energy showed no significant alteration ($p_{\text{value}} = 0.1688$).
– Correlation remained unchanged ($p_{\text{value}} = 0.8859$).

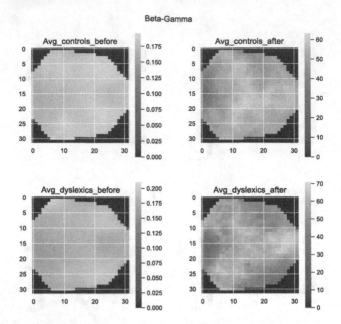

Fig. 5. Negative logarithm of p-values from Mann-Whitney-Wilcoxon U-Test for different band couplings before and after histogram transformation. The term 'Input Feature' denotes the pixels of the unraveled CFS maps, arranged in descending order based on their corresponding $-log(p_{value})$ values.

Alpha-Beta Coupling

- Contrast remained stable ($p_{value} = 0.8033$).
- Dissimilarity showed no substantial change ($p_{value} = 0.5292$).
- Homogeneity remained unchanged ($p_{value} = 0.2425$).
- Energy exhibited no significant difference ($p_{value} = 0.9627$).
- Correlation showed no significant change ($p_{value} = 0.9637$).

Beta-Gamma Coupling

- Contrast remained unchanged ($p_{value} = 0.6824$).
- Dissimilarity showed no substantial alteration ($p_{value} = 0.2325$).
- Homogeneity significantly increased ($p_{value} = 0.0119$), indicating greater uniformity.
- Energy remained unaffected ($p_{value} = 0.4984$).
- Correlation showed no significant change ($p_{value} = 0.7648$).

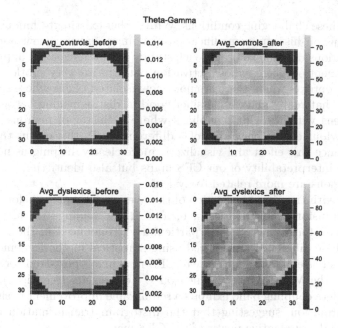

Fig. 6. Comparison of averaged CFS maps derived from control subjects and those with dyslexia for Beta-Gamma couplings before (left column) and after (right column) histogram transformation.

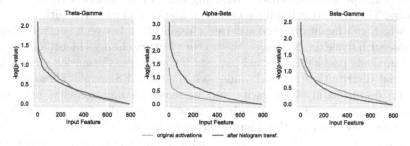

Fig. 7. Comparison of averaged CFS maps derived from control subjects and those with dyslexia for Theta-Gamma couplings before (left column) and after (right column) histogram transformation.

4   Discussion and Conclusions

EEG-based techniques have emerged as pivotal tools in unraveling the neurobiological underpinnings of dyslexia, as evidenced by studies conducted by Gallego Molina et al. [14,16] or Attaheri et al. [4] among others. In this context, our histogram transformation technique applied to the CFS maps presents a promising avenue for enhancing the detection of dyslexia as its application to narrow histograms or 'low-contrast' CFS maps can help to accentuate the differentiation between the pixels' intensity levels and raise classifiers' performance even under these challenging conditions. While other existing techniques, such as [1,7,20], focus on histogram modifications for image enhancement and normalization in various domains, our approach stands out for its specific application to the enhancement of images whose activation patterns are very subtle and homogeneous. In contexts where there are not a few isolated pixels whose sparse activations are what really make a classifier good at distinguishing between classes (as it happens with the CFC couplings where a cluster of neurons influences on the behaviour of another group of a different level), this means that we are able to enhance this effect and visualize it more clearly, helping us not only to improve the interpretability of our CFS maps but also identifying better which neuronal regions are more related to dyslexia.

Starting with the visual inspection of the average CFS maps before and after histogram transformation in Figs. 4, 6, and 7, our findings reveal discernible differences in intensity activations, particularly pronounced in the Alpha-Beta coupling. These differences, quantified using statistical methods, demonstrate a significant increase in the significance of CFS map pixels post-transformation, as indicated by the Mann-Whitney-Wilcoxon U-Test results (see Fig. 5). Notably, this Alpha-Beta coupling band exhibits a remarkable improvement in significance post-transformation, suggesting that the histogram transformation effectively enhances the discriminative power of the CFS maps.

The observed reduction in entropy for Theta-Gamma and Alpha-Beta couplings, as highlighted by the Cross-Entropy analysis, further supports the effectiveness of the proposed method in reducing uncertainty or disorder within these couplings. This reduction implies a clearer delineation of patterns within the CFS maps, which can facilitate more accurate classification between control subjects and those with dyslexia. Moreover, the texture feature changes identified through GLCM analysis provide additional insights into the transformation's impact on the spatial distribution of pixel values within the CFS maps. These changes, including decreases in dissimilarity and increases in homogeneity, underscore the transformation's role in promoting a more uniform distribution of intensity values, thereby enhancing the discriminative features of CFS maps.

In summary, our novel histogram transformation technique represents a significant advancement in dyslexia research using EEG-based analysis. By addressing the challenge of subtle intensity differences in CFC maps, our approach offers several key advantages. Firstly, it enhances the interpretability of CFC maps by facilitating clearer delineation of patterns, thereby aiding in the identification of dyslexia-related networks in the brain. This improvement in interpretability is crucial for gaining deeper insights into the neurobiological mechanisms underlying dyslexia. Secondly, our technique significantly boosts the discriminative power of CFC maps, potentially enhancing the accuracy of dyslexia detection algorithms. By improving the ability to differentiate between dyslexic individuals and controls, our method contributes to more reliable diagnostic outcomes, which is essential for effective intervention strategies. Lastly, our approach is computationally efficient and seamlessly integrates into existing CFC analysis pipelines, making it practical for real-time dyslexia detection systems. Its feasibility for deployment in clinical settings underscores its potential to impact dyslexia diagnosis and intervention on a broader scale.

Acknowledgments. This research is part of the TIC251-G-FEDER project, funded by ERDF/EU; part of the PID2022-137461NB-C32 funded by MICIU/AEI/10.13039/501100011033 and ERDF/EU as well as UMA20-FEDERJA-086 (Consejería de Economía y Conocimiento, Junta de Andalucía and by European Regional Development Funds (ERDF)). Work by D.C.-B. is part of the grant FJC2021-048082-I funded by MICIU/AEI/10.13039/501100011033 and by European Union NextGenerationEU/PRTR. LARSyS funding (DOI: 10.54499/LA/P/0083/2020, 10.54499/UIDP/50009/2020, and the 10.54499/UIDB/50009/2020).

References

1. Agaian, S.S., Silver, B., Panetta, K.A.: Transform coefficient histogram-based image enhancement algorithms using contrast entropy. IEEE Trans. Image Process. **16**(3), 741–758 (2007). https://doi.org/10.1109/tip.2006.888338

2. Alfeld, P.: A trivariate Clough-Tocher scheme for tetrahedral data. Comput. Aided Geom. Des. **1**(2), 169–181 (1984). https://doi.org/10.1016/0167-8396(84)90029-3

3. Aru, J., et al.: Untangling cross-frequency coupling in neuroscience. Curr. Opin. Neurobiol. **31**, 51–61 (2015). https://doi.org/10.1016/j.conb.2014.08.002

4. Attaheri, A., et al.: Infant low-frequency EEG cortical power, cortical tracking and phase-amplitude coupling predicts language a year later, November 2022. https://doi.org/10.1101/2022.11.02.514963

5. Bashivan, P., Rish, I., Yeasin, M., Codella, N.: Learning representations from EEG with deep recurrent-convolutional neural networks (2015). https://doi.org/10.48550/ARXIV.1511.06448

6. Canolty, R.T., Knight, R.T.: The functional role of cross-frequency coupling. Trends Cogn. Sci. **14**(11), 506–515 (2010). https://doi.org/10.1016/j.tics.2010.09.001

7. Chang, D.C., Wu, W.R.: Image contrast enhancement based on a histogram transformation of local standard deviation. IEEE Trans. Med. Imaging **17**(4), 518–531 (1998). https://doi.org/10.1109/42.730397

8. Chaple, G.N., Daruwala, R.D., Gofane, M.S.: Comparisions of Robert, Prewitt, Sobel operator based edge detection methods for real time uses on FPGA. In: 2015 International Conference on Technologies for Sustainable Development (ICTSD), February 2015. IEEE (2015). https://doi.org/10.1109/ictsd.2015.7095920

9. Cohen, M.: Analyzing Neural Time Series Data: Theory and Practice, January 2014. https://doi.org/10.7551/mitpress/9609.001.0001

10. Demirel, H., Ozcinar, C., Anbarjafari, G.: Satellite image contrast enhancement using discrete wavelet transform and singular value decomposition. IEEE Geosci. Remote Sens. Lett. **7**(2), 333–337 (2010). https://doi.org/10.1109/lgrs.2009.2034873

11. Dvorak, D., Fenton, A.A.: Toward a proper estimation of phase-amplitude coupling in neural oscillations. J. Neurosci. Meth. **225**, 42–56 (2014). https://doi.org/10.1016/j.jneumeth.2014.01.002

12. Fay, M.P., Proschan, M.A.: Wilcoxon-Mann-Whitney or t-test? On assumptions for hypothesis tests and multiple interpretations of decision rules. Stat. Surv. **4** (2010). https://doi.org/10.1214/09-ss051

13. Formoso, M.A., Ortiz, A., Martinez-Murcia, F.J., Gallego, N., Luque, J.L.: Detecting phase-synchrony connectivity anomalies in EEG signals. Application to dyslexia diagnosis. Sensors **21**(21), 7061 (2021). https://doi.org/10.3390/s21217061

14. Gallego-Molina, N.J., Formoso, M., Ortiz, A., Martínez-Murcia, F.J., Luque, J.L.: Temporal EigenPAC for dyslexia diagnosis. In: Rojas, I., Joya, G., Català, A. (eds.) IWANN 2021. LNCS, vol. 12862, pp. 45–56. Springer, Cham (2021). https://doi.org/10.1007/978-3-030-85099-9_4

15. Gallego-Molina, N.J., Ortiz, A., Martínez-Murcia, F.J., Formoso, M.A., Giménez, A.: Complex network modeling of EEG band coupling in dyslexia: an exploratory analysis of auditory processing and diagnosis. Knowl. Based Syst. **240**, 108098 (2022). https://doi.org/10.1016/j.knosys.2021.108098

16. Gallego-Molina, N.J., Ortiz, A., Martínez-Murcia, F.J., Rodríguez-Rodríguez, I.: Unraveling dyslexia-related connectivity patterns in EEG signals by Holo-Hilbert spectral analysis. In: Ferrández Vicente, J.M., Álvarez-Sánchez, J.R., de la Paz López, F., Adeli, H. (eds.) Artificial Intelligence in Neuroscience: Affective Analysis and Health Applications, pp. 43–52. Springer, Heidelberg (2022). https://doi.org/10.1007/978-3-031-06242-1_5

17. Giraud, A.L., Poeppel, D.: Cortical oscillations and speech processing: emerging computational principles and operations. Nat. Neurosci. **15**(4), 511–517 (2012). https://doi.org/10.1038/nn.3063

18. Górriz, J., et al.: Computational approaches to explainable artificial intelligence: advances in theory, applications and trends. Inf. Fus. **100**, 101945 (2023). https://doi.org/10.1016/j.inffus.2023.101945

19. Gross, J., et al.: Speech rhythms and multiplexed oscillatory sensory coding in the human brain. PLoS Biol. **11**(12), e1001752 (2013). https://doi.org/10.1371/journal.pbio.1001752

20. Kautsky, J., Nichols, N.K., Jupp, D.L.: Smoothed histogram modification for image processing. Comput. Vis. Graph. Image Process. **26**(3), 271–291 (1984). https://doi.org/10.1016/0734-189x(84)90213-5

21. Keitel, A., Gross, J., Kayser, C.: Perceptually relevant speech tracking in auditory and motor cortex reflects distinct linguistic features. PLoS Biol. **16**(3), e2004473 (2018). https://doi.org/10.1371/journal.pbio.2004473

22. Keshavarzi, M., et al.: Atypical beta-band effects in children with dyslexia in response to rhythmic audio-visual speech. Clin. Neurophysiol. **160**, 47–55 (2023). https://doi.org/10.1101/2023.03.29.534542

23. Mall, P.K., Singh, P.K., Yadav, D.: GLCM based feature extraction and medical X-ray image classification using machine learning techniques. In: 2019 IEEE Conference on Information and Communication Technology, December 2019. IEEE (2019). https://doi.org/10.1109/cict48419.2019.9066263

24. McArthur, G., et al.: Getting to grips with the heterogeneity of developmental dyslexia. Cogn. Neuropsychol. **30**(1), 1–24 (2013). https://doi.org/10.1080/02643294.2013.784192

25. Ortiz, A., Martinez-Murcia, F.J., Luque, J.L., Giménez, A., Morales-Ortega, R., Ortega, J.: Dyslexia diagnosis by EEG temporal and spectral descriptors: an anomaly detection approach. Int. J. Neural Syst. **30**(07), 2050029 (2020). https://doi.org/10.1142/s012906572050029x

26. Pacheco, A., Reis, A., Araújo, S., Inácio, F., Petersson, K.M., Faísca, L.: Dyslexia heterogeneity: cognitive profiling of Portuguese children with dyslexia. Read. Writ. **27**(9), 1529–1545 (2014). https://doi.org/10.1007/s11145-014-9504-5

27. Palva, J.M., Palva, S., Kaila, K.: Phase synchrony among neuronal oscillations in the human cortex. J. Neurosci. **25**(15), 3962–3972 (2005). https://doi.org/10. 1523/jneurosci.4250-04.2005
28. Paris, S., Hasinoff, S.W., Kautz, J.: Local Laplacian filters: edge-aware image processing with a Laplacian pyramid. Commun. ACM **58**(3), 81–91 (2015). https:// doi.org/10.1145/2723694
29. Pizer, S.M., et al.: Adaptive histogram equalization and its variations. Comput. Vis. Graph. Image Process. **39**(3), 355–368 (1987). https://doi.org/10.1016/s0734-189x(87)80186-x
30. Scheffer-Teixeira, R., Tort, A.B.: On cross-frequency phase-phase coupling between theta and gamma oscillations in the hippocampus. eLife **5** (2016). https://doi.org/ 10.7554/elife.20515
31. Snowling, M.J., Hulme, C., Nation, K.: Defining and understanding dyslexia: past, present and future. Oxf. Rev. Educ. **46**(4), 501–513 (2020). https://doi.org/10. 1080/03054985.2020.1765756
32. Yang, C.C.: Image enhancement by modified contrast-stretching manipulation. Opt. Laser Technol. **38**(3), 196–201 (2006). https://doi.org/10.1016/j.optlastec. 2004.11.009
33. Zhu, Y., Huang, C.: An adaptive histogram equalization algorithm on the image gray level mapping. Phys. Procedia **25**, 601–608 (2012). https://doi.org/10.1016/ j.phpro.2012.03.132
34. Zoubrinetzky, R., Bielle, F., Valdois, S.: New insights on developmental dyslexia subtypes: heterogeneity of mixed reading profiles. PLoS ONE **9**(6), e99337 (2014). https://doi.org/10.1371/journal.pone.0099337

Improving Prediction of Mortality in ICU via Fusion of SelectKBest with SMOTE Method and Extra Tree Classifier

Mohammad Maftoun[1], Javad Hassannataj Joloudari[2,3,4], Omid Zare[5], Maryam Khademi[6], Alireza Atashi[7], Mohammad Ali Nematollahi[8(✉)], Roohallah Alizadehsani[9], and Juan M. Gorriz[10]

[1] Department of Artificial Intelligence, Technical and Engineering Faculty, Islamic Azad University, South Tehran Branch, Tehran, Iran
st_m_maftoun@azad.ac.ir

[2] Department of Computer Engineering, Faculty of Engineering, University of Birjand, Birjand, Iran
javad.hassannataj@birjand.ac.ir

[3] Department of Computer Engineering, Islamic Azad University, Babol Branch, Babol, Iran

[4] Department of Computer Engineering, Technical and Vocational University (TVU), Tehran, Iran

[5] Department of Computer Science, University of Verona, Verona, Italy
omid.zare@univr.it

[6] Department of Applied Mathematics, Azad Islamic University, South Tehran Branch, Tehran, Iran
khademi@azad.ac.ir

[7] Department of Digital Health, Tehran University of Medical Sciences, Tehran, Iran
aratashi@sina.tums.ac.ir

[8] Department of Computer Sciences, Fasa University, Fasa, Iran
ma.nematollahi@fasau.ac.ir

[9] Institute for Intelligent Systems Research and Innovation (IISRI), Deakin University, Waurn Ponds, Australia
r.alizadehsani@deakin.edu.au

[10] Department of Signal Theory, Networking and Communications, Universidad de Granada, Granada, Spain
gorriz@ugr.es

Abstract. The healthcare system's increasing adoption of analytics and advanced computers demonstrates a growing tendency to develop a strong prognostication mechanism based on Artificial Intelligence (AI), utilizing technology to explore hidden relations between data and assessment in medical contexts. Hence, predicting the mortality of Intensive Care Unit (ICU) patients is a vital yet challenging task with significant implications for clinical decision-making in healthcare. This study aims to present an effective approach based on the AutoML framework for building Machine Learning (ML) models to predict mortality. PyCaret was applied as an AutoML framework in this study. ML

This research is part of the PID2022-137451OB-I00 project funded by the MCIN/AEI/10.13039/501100011033 and by FSE+.

© The Author(s), under exclusive license to Springer Nature Switzerland AG 2024
J. M. Ferrández Vicente et al. (Eds.): IWINAC 2024, LNCS 14674, pp. 68–77, 2024.
https://doi.org/10.1007/978-3-031-61140-7_7

approaches such as Extra Tree Classifier (ET), eXtreme Gradient Boosting (XGBoost), Random Forest (RF), Light Gradient Boosting Machine (LightGBM), Gradient Boosting Classifier (GBC), and Adaptive Boosting (AdaBoost), along with feature selection technique, SMOTE, and Auto Fine Tuned via Grid-Random search (GRS) by the assistance of PyCaret are employed to predict mortality. Results demonstrate that the hybrid (SelectKBest + SMOTE + ET) method achieves the highest AUROC of 93.54% for prediction, outperforming other models.

Keywords: Mortality prediction · ICU · SelectKBest · SMOTE · AutoML · Healthcare

1 Introduction

Artificial Intelligence (AI) systems have a high potential to be used in hospitals. In developing countries, most hospitals try to use the advantages of AI systems in different departments. In the healthcare sector of hospitals, the Intensive Care Unit (ICU) is a department that generally aids patients in recovering from serious ailments and conditions [3,8]. When it is obvious that an individual's health necessitates perpetual, thorough evaluation and adaptation, the patient will be relocated to an ICU. Upon hospital's ICU admission, extensive details of a patient's stay and treatment are recorded and stored for over a decade. These data are crucial for analysis, service improvement, disease research, and contributing to ongoing medical advancements [16]. Predicting the outcomes of ICUs based on these data facilitates timely interventions, staff allocation, and efficient equipment monitoring. In the domain of critical care studies, predicting mortality is one of the most significant responsibilities. According to the volatility of ICUs, even highly qualified personnel cannot be aware of the risk of patient mortality [23]. Machine learning (ML) as a subset of AI also provides a vital component in the world of medicine and healthcare, especially in identifying and predicting mortality. Due to the importance of ICU mortality prediction, employing supervised machine learning, encompassing classification algorithms is indispensable. The result of these learning algorithms could be different corresponding to various tasks in healthcare systems. Additionally, imperfect data may emanate from a variety of sources and include missing values, noise, imbalances in class, consistency, and inconsistencies. An important step before analysis and building machine learning models is data preparation to address these problems [12]. To improve overall model performance, the ultimate goal is to provide a refined dataset for further analysis using machine learning methods [19]. A recent advancement in ML termed AutoML attempts to extend the application of ML algorithms into other fields, such as healthcare. AutoML leads to improvement by automating the selection of models that effectively navigate the complexity-interpretability spectrum. As a result, model configurations are optimized for better performance, saving time and resources [9]. AutoML consists of two words: Automation and machine learning, which leads to greatly reducing tasks of data science specialists corresponding to statistical methods and machine learning [13]. Electronic Health Record (EHR) analysis has already benefited from the utilization of this novel technology. Even though the technology is still in its infancy, AutoML has the potential to improve and automate machine learning procedures for a wide range of healthcare applications [20].

This paper highlights the potential usage of the AutoML framework for presenting robust and accurate models for mortality prediction of ICU patients due to reducing time and simplifying the intricacy of interaction with machine learning models. The summarization of the main contribution in this paper is as follows:

1. Applying SelectKBest as a feature selection method to reduce computational costs
2. Addressing the class imbalance problem using SMOTE
3. Achieving state-of-the-art best results in AUC, accuracy, precision, Kappa, and MCC with values of 93.54%, 85.73%, 85.86%, 71.45%, and 71.56%.

In the rest of this paper, our study is outlined as follows. The literature review is discussed in Sect. 2. The main concepts and materials are presented in Sect. 3. The results of experiments and discussions are investigated in Sect. 4, and the conclusion and future works are found in Sect. 5.

2   Literature Review

In this section, we provide an overview of related studies utilizing machine/deep learning techniques. Wu et al. [4] have applied an enhanced machine learning model on the MIMIC-III database corresponding to heart failure to predict ICU mortality. Six general classifiers such as RF, Support Vector Machine (SVM), K Nearest Neighbor (KNN), Light Gradient Boosting Machine (LGBM), Bootstrap aggregating (Bagging), and Adaptive Boosting (AdaBoost) were used, and a stacking classifier based on ensemble learning played a vital role in this classification task. Oversampling techniques, including SMOTE, were also used to solve imbalanced data. Their study reported an accuracy of 95.25 In [21], Authors have introduced an optimal machine learning method based on a CatBoost-based model with disease-specific features that are highly tuned and effective in predicting patient mortality for mortality prediction of ICU patients. The dataset utilized originated from the recently published comprehensive electronic database comprising information from more than 200,000 ICU admissions from 208 hospitals in the United States to establish fine-tune and validate models. The best AUROC score of the proposed method was 91%, corresponding to mortality of the toxicology group patients. Mansouri et al. [18] have introduced a hybrid method based on Convolutional Neural Networks (CNNs) and eXtreme Gradient Boosting (XGBoost) for the prediction of early mortality in ICU. The preprocessing steps of their study were briefly as follows: Feature transformation, Solving class imbalance problem, CNNs and filtering strategy, and feature selection. Corresponding to ROC, the AUC of 0.863 was achieved in this paper.

In [17], Liu et al. were faced with high-dimensional big data of ICU patients which were imbalanced. They analyzed data and worked on preprocessing by feature extraction and data cleansing steps, which led to outliers being detected and removed in the other steps of preprocessing, data being normalized, and missing values being handled with imputation techniques. SVM was suggested as a classification algorithm and the parameters of SVM were optimized by chaos particle swarm optimization (CPSO). Their proposed method could achieve an AUC of 0.77 as an optimal performance in the testing set.

3   Materials and Methods

Identifying a patient's status in the ICU via machine learning techniques is the main purpose of this study. In the prepossessing step, the missing values in the dataset were filled using KNN imputation, and outlier data were normalized by the winsorization technique. The foremost step after preprocessing is to correct the dataset, including its features, to determine the extent to which one variable is dependent on other variables. To address this issue, we employed SelectKBest from Scikit-Learn, utilizing the Chi-Square test to reduce feature complexity and enhance analysis efficiency. After applying these processes, the dataset is ready to apply AutoML models. In this study, Pycaret's default configuration split the dataset into a 70% training set and a 30% testing set. To solve the class imbalance problem in the target variable, we also applied SMOTE during the Pycaret setting. Furthermore, for classification, six ML models were considered. The main steps of this study are presented in Fig. 1.

Fig. 1. The overview of the main steps in this study.

3.1   Dataset Used

The hospitals affiliated with Shahid Beheshti and Mashhad Universities of Medical Sciences and Health Services in Iran provided the manually gathered and documented data for this study between 2013 and 2019. This dataset represents the first 24 h of data obtained following the patient's entrance to the ICU [10]. As a result, the features are regarded to remain stable over the entirety of the investigation. There are 20 independent features and 1 dependent feature as a target and 2000 records in this dataset. Features are: Age, Sex (Gender), Body Temperature, Systolic Blood Pressure, Diastolic Blood Pressure, Pulse Rate, Respiratory Rate, HCO3, Blood PH, Na, K, Cr, Hct, WBCs, GCS, PTT, Ventilation, Addiction, Postoperative Patient, Diabetes, and Mortality Status.

3.2 Preprocessing

KNN imputation fills missing values in datasets by estimating values based on the mean/mode of nearby instances. It's effective when the data distribution is unknown, leveraging the k closest neighbors for prediction [5]. Any value that differs significantly from the rest of the data qualifies as an outlier. To solve this problem, the winsorization technique substitutes more centrally established representative values instead of extreme values [6,22]. Feature selection (FS) using a component of the scikit-learn library termed SelectKBest, leads to identifying the top k features with the highest scores. This process enables streamlining datasets and conducts model performance improvement and efficiency [7]. Reducing the stability and generalization performance of classifiers trained on unbalanced data sets would be disadvantageous as a main factor in machine learning problems, the Synthetic Minority Oversampling Technique (SMOTE) is employed to balance datasets with a significantly unequal ratio [14].

3.3 AutoML

AutoML, or "end-to-end machine learning process," is essentially an approach for streamlining the implementation and building machine learning models in real-world situations [11]. The main strength of *AutoML* is its automation and efficiency, even though human intervention is involved in just a small amount of this procedure [15].

We experimented with six widely-used ensemble classification models in this study. *LightGBM* improves memory and computational efficiency by using histogram-based tree growth and depth-limited leaf-wise tree construction. Friedman developed *XGBoost* in 2001, which combines weak classifiers to form a strong classifier by optimizing the loss function along the gradient direction. It uses second-order Taylor expansion for faster convergence and regularization to avoid overfitting. *RF* classifier trains decision trees using bootstrapping and bagging to provide robust generalization. *Gradient Boosting Classifier (GBC)* gradually incorporates weak models, primarily decision trees, to create a predictive model while avoiding overfitting. *AdaBoost* iteratively adjusts weights for misclassified data using one-level decision trees to transform weak classifiers into strong ones. *Extra Tree Classifier (ET)* employs non-correlated decision trees arranged in a forest, similar to a random forest, with separate tree-building techniques [1,2].

4 Result and Discussion

We employed Python programming language and the Pycaret library to implement AutoML models. AutoML's objective is to make machine learning accessible to individuals with limited experience. The results of AutoML's models are presented in this section. PyCaret also employed the stratified k-fold cross-validation (k = 10) technique to test these six classification models including RF, XGBoost, LightGBM, GBC, Adaboost, and ET utilizing seven performance metrics such as accuracy, recall, precision, F-measure, AUC, MCC and kappa were used to compare classification models. The proposed AutoML model's performance was evaluated based on the mentioned metrics. The values for these metrics were obtained using the confusion matrix, which reveals the classification algorithm's performance on input data by distinguishing various class types. Equations (1)–(7) were employed to calculate each metric, providing a comprehensive evaluation of the model's effectiveness which are as follows:

$$\text{Precision} = \frac{\text{TP}}{\text{TP} + \text{FP}} \tag{1}$$

$$\text{Recall} = \frac{\text{TP}}{\text{TP} + \text{FN}} \tag{2}$$

$$\text{F-measure} = \frac{2 \cdot \text{Precision} \cdot \text{Recall}}{\text{Precision} + \text{Recall}} \tag{3}$$

$$\text{Accuracy} = \frac{\text{TP} + \text{TN}}{\text{TP} + \text{TN} + \text{FP} + \text{FN}} \tag{4}$$

$$\text{AUC} = \int_0^1 t Pr(t) \, dt \tag{5}$$

$$\kappa = \frac{2 \cdot (\text{TP} \cdot \text{TN} - \text{FP} \cdot \text{FN})}{(\text{TP} + \text{FP}) \cdot (\text{TP} + \text{FN}) + (\text{TN} + \text{FP}) \cdot (\text{TN} + \text{FN})} \tag{6}$$

$$\text{MCC} = \frac{\text{TP} \cdot \text{TN} - \text{FP} \cdot \text{FN}}{\sqrt{(\text{TP} + \text{FP}) \cdot (\text{TP} + \text{FN}) \cdot (\text{TN} + \text{FP}) \cdot (\text{TN} + \text{FN})}} \tag{7}$$

The results of the model evaluation indicate the average estimated accuracy for each model. For instance, the RF model achieved an average accuracy of 84.47%, while XGBoost, LightGBM, GBC, Adaboost, and ET yielded accuracy values of 85.35%, 85.17%, 84%, 80.72%, and 85.73%, respectively.

In Table 1, the best result is obtained by considering FS, SMOTE, and extra tree classifier for improving performance and also the result of other models is provided in this table. These accuracy values provide insights into the models' predictive capabilities in the context of ICU patient mortality. Overall, the study showcases the application of AutoML techniques in a healthcare setting, emphasizing the accessibility and effectiveness of the proposed machine learning approach.

Table 1. The obtained results of AutoML models.

Model Name	AUC	Accuracy	Recall	Precision	F1 score	Kappa	MCC
FS + SMOTE + LightGBM	92.68%	85.17%	88.31%	83.21%	85.64%	70.33%	70.56%
FS + SMOTE + XGBoost	92.39%	85.35%	87.47%	83.75%	85.63%	70.71%	70.92%
FS + SMOTE + RF	92.56%	84.47%	87.75%	82.39%	84.96%	68.93%	69.13%
FS + SMOTE + GBC	91.36%	84%	85.41%	83.13%	84.20%	67.99%	68.11%
FS + SMOTE + AdaBoost	89.08%	80.72%	78.58%	82.15%	80.27%	61.44%	61.58%
FS + *SMOTE* + ET (Proposed method)	93.54%	85.73%	85.69%	85.86%	85.71%	71.45%	71.56%

In Table 2, hyperparameter's setting are also present using a combination of Grid-Random search. AutoML endured responsibilities like model selection and hyperparameter tuning, simplifying the complex machine learning process.

Table 2. Hyperparameters' setting.

Model Name	Parameters	Values
ET	n_estimators, criterion	100, gini
LightGBM	n_estimators, learning_rate, num_leaves	100, 0.1, 31
XGBoost	tree_method	auto
RF	n_estimators, criterion	100, gini
GBC	n_estimators, learning_rate, loss	100, 0.1, log_loss
AdaBoost	n_estimators, learning_rate	50, 1

We utilized the ROC analysis to evaluate the efficacy of our approach in predicting ICU mortality. Figure 2 showcases the ROC curve of our proposed method, illustrating its remarkable capability in distinguishing patients at risk of ICU mortality.

The outcomes of the 10-fold cross-validation demonstrate the adaptability of the proposed model in each fold. In Fig. 3, a full assessment of the model's effectiveness and opportunities for enhancement is provided by the comprehensive evaluation, which takes into account AUC, accuracy, precision, recall, F1-score, Kappa, and MCC.

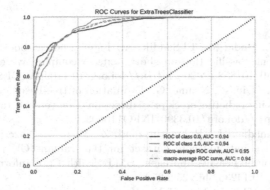

Fig. 2. The ROC of the proposed method.

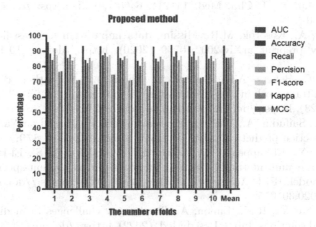

Fig. 3. The performance of the proposed method based on 10-fold cross-validation.

5   Conclusion

In this study, we utilized PyCaret as an AutoML framework to compare the effectiveness of machine learning models. The results highlight how well machine learning techniques work at identifying and classifying ICU patients' mortality. PyCaret is a useful tool that makes applying machine learning techniques for building and evaluating models easier. The results obtained validate the effectiveness of the approaches described. The Extra Tree Classifier was the best-performing model in the classification framework, with the highest accuracy (85.73%) and AUC (93.54%). Our forthcoming efforts will focus on incorporating deep learning techniques to enhance the accuracy of mortality prediction.

References

1. Al-Zamzami, F., Hoda, M., El-Saddik, A.: Light gradient boosting machine for general sentiment classification on short texts: a comparative evaluation. IEEE Access **8**, 101840–101858 (2020). https://doi.org/10.1109/ACCESS.2020.2997330
2. Ampomah, E.K., Qin, Z., Nyame, G.: Evaluation of tree-based ensemble machine learning models in predicting stock price direction of movement. Information **11**(6), 332 (2020). https://doi.org/10.3390/INFO11060332
3. Atashi, A., Ahmadian, L., Rahmatinezhad, Z., Miri, M., Nazeri, N., Eslami, S.: Development of a national core dataset for the Iranian ICU patients outcome prediction: a comprehensive approach. BMJ Health Care Inform. **25**(2) (2018). https://doi.org/10.14236/jhi.v25i2.953
4. Chiu, C.C., Wu, C.M., Chien, T.N., Kao, L.J., Li, C., Jiang, H.L.: Applying an improved stacking ensemble model to predict the mortality of ICU patients with heart failure. J. Clin. Med. **11**(21), 6460 (2022). https://doi.org/10.3390/jcm11216460
5. Choudhury, A., Kosorok, M.R.: Missing data imputation for classification problems. arXiv preprint arXiv:2002.10709 (2020). https://doi.org/10.48550/arXiv.2002.10709
6. Dash, C.S.K., Behera, A.K., Dehuri, S., Ghosh, A.: An outliers detection and elimination framework in classification task of data mining. Decis. Analytics J. **6**, 100164 (2023). https://doi.org/10.1016/j.dajour.2023.100164
7. Desyani, T., Saifudin, A., Yulianti, Y.: Feature selection based on Naive Bayes for caesarean section prediction. IOP Conf. Ser. Mater. Sci. Eng. **879**, 012091 (2020)
8. El-Rashidy, N., El-Sappagh, S., Abuhmed, T., Abdelrazek, S., El-Bakry, H.M.: Intensive care unit mortality prediction: an improved patient-specific stacking ensemble model. IEEE Access **8**, 133541–133564 (2020). https://doi.org/10.1109/ACCESS.2020.3010556
9. Ellis, R.J., Sander, R.M., Limon, A.: Twelve key challenges in medical machine learning and solutions. Intell. Based Med. (2022). https://doi.org/10.1016/j.ibmed.2022.100068
10. Ghorbani, R., Ghousi, R., Makui, A., Atashi, A.: A new hybrid predictive model to predict the early mortality risk in intensive care units on a highly imbalanced dataset. IEEE Access **8**, 141066–141079 (2020). https://doi.org/10.1109/ACCESS.2020.3013320
11. Górriz, J.M., et al.: Computational approaches to explainable artificial intelligence: advances in theory, applications and trends. Inf. Fus. **100**, 101945 (2023). https://doi.org/10.1016/j.inffus.2023.101945
12. Jain, V., Chatterjee, J.M. (eds.): Machine Learning with Health Care Perspective. LAIS, vol. 13, pp. 1–25. Springer, Cham (2020). https://doi.org/10.1007/978-3-030-40850-3
13. He, X., Zhao, K., Chu, X.: AutoML: a survey of the state-of-the-art. Knowl. Based Syst. **212**, 106622 (2021). https://doi.org/10.1016/j.knosys.2020.106622
14. Joloudari, J.H., Marefat, A., Nematollahi, M.A., Oyelere, S.S., Hussain, S.: Effective class-imbalance learning based on smote and convolutional neural networks. Appl. Sci. **13**(6), 4006 (2023). https://doi.org/10.3390/app13064006
15. Karmaker, S.K., Hassan, M.M., Smith, M.J., Xu, L., Zhai, C., Veeramachaneni, K.: AutoML to date and beyond: challenges and opportunities. ACM Comput. Surv. (CSUR) **54**(8), 1–36 (2021). https://doi.org/10.1145/3470918

16. Khope, S.R., Elias, S.: Strategies of predictive schemes and clinical diagnosis for prognosis using MIMIC-III: a systematic review. Healthcare **11**, 710 (2023). https://doi.org/10.3390/healthcare11050710

17. Liu, J., et al.: Mortality prediction based on imbalanced high-dimensional ICU big data. Comput. Ind. **98**, 218–225 (2018). https://doi.org/10.1016/j.compind.2018.01.017

18. Mansouri, A., Noei, M., Saniee Abadeh, M.: A hybrid machine learning approach for early mortality prediction of ICU patients. Prog. Arti. Intell. **11**(4), 333–347 (2022). https://doi.org/10.1007/s13748-022-00288-0

19. Misra, P., Yadav, A.S.: Impact of preprocessing methods on healthcare predictions. In: Proceedings of 2nd International Conference on Advanced Computing and Software Engineering (ICACSE) (2019). https://doi.org/10.2139/ssrn.3349586

20. Mustafa, A., Rahimi Azghadi, M.: Automated machine learning for healthcare and clinical notes analysis. Computers **10**(2), 24 (2021). https://doi.org/10.3390/computers10020024

21. Safaei, N., et al.: E-CatBoost: an efficient machine learning framework for predicting ICU mortality using the EICU collaborative research database. PLoS ONE **17**(5), e0262895 (2022). https://doi.org/10.1371/journal.pone.0262895

22. Sharma, S., Chatterjee, S.: Winsorization for robust Bayesian Neural Networks. Entropy **23**(11), 1546 (2021). https://doi.org/10.3390/e23111546

23. Sulaiman, R., Azeman, N.H., Mokhtar, M.H.H., Mobarak, N.N., Bakar, M.H.A., Bakar, A.A.A.: Hybrid ensemble-based machine learning model for predicting phosphorus concentrations in hydroponic solution. Spectrochim. Acta Part A Mol. Biomol. Spectrosc. **304**, 123327 (2024). https://doi.org/10.1016/j.saa.2023.123327

A Cross-Modality Latent Representation for the Prediction of Clinical Symptomatology in Parkinson's Disease

Cristóbal Vázquez-García, F. J. Martinez-Murcia[✉], Juan E. Arco,
Ignacio A. Illán, Carmen Jiménez-Mesa, Javier Ramírez, and Juan M. Górriz

Department of Signal Theory, Networking and Communications, Andalusian
Research Institute in Data Science and Computational Intelligence (DaSCI),
University of Granada, 18071 Granada, Spain
{cristobalvg,fjesusmartinez,jearco,illan,carmenj,javierrp,gorriz}@ugr.es

Abstract. Parkinson's disease (PD) is a neurodegenerative disorder
that affects millions of people worldwide. The diagnosis of PD is based
on clinical and neuroimaging data. This work proposes a novel approach
that jointly models several Variational Autoencoder (VAE) architectures
in order to maximize cross-modality prediction. We hypothesize that
123I-ioflupane SPECT could be related to motor symptomatology and
other dopaminergic deficits. We propose a joint modelling of several VAE
architectures for maximizing cross-modality prediction of the PD Clinical and Neuroimaging Data. The final model, with 5 common latents
and 2 neuroimaging and data specific latents achieve $R2$ values up to
0.8 for scores related to PD, including well known PD symptomatology
scales such as UPDRS ($R2 = 0.545$), at the same time that provides tools
for interpreting the results and the common latent distribution for both
clinical data and neuroimaging, paving the way for interpretable machine
learning tools in neurodegeneration.

1 Introduction

Computer Aided Diagnosis (CAD) of neurological diseases has been traditionally applied to neuroimaging data [4,5] under a supervised-learning paradigm.
Within this strategy, different machine learning pipelines were applied to the
neuroimaging data, including preprocessing, feature extraction, feature selection and model training, in order to predict discrete categories, either binary or
multi-class classification.

In recent years, unsupervised or self-supervised learning has gained ground
as a machine learning paradigm. This approach, sometimes in combination with
the supervised learning, has paved the way for an explainable machine learning
(XML), allowing both an interpretable feature extraction and high performance
classification. This has been successfully applied to neurological conditions such
as Alzheimer's Disease (AD) [11] or Parkinson's Disease (PD) [5]. Additionally,
these approaches allow to bridge the gap between multi-modal data sources in

J. M. Ferrández Vicente et al. (Eds.): IWINAC 2024, LNCS 14674, pp. 78–87, 2024.
https://doi.org/10.1007/978-3-031-61140-7_8

Table 1. Demographics (mean and standard deviation in brackets) of the PPMI subset used in this article.

Cohort	N	# Visits	Age	Family PD	UPDRS	STAI	GDS
PD Participant	846	2.34	62.47 [9.73]	2.43 [0.83]	33.62 [13.88]	65.28 [18.61]	2.48 [2.68]
Healthy Control	226	1.02	61.51 [11.47]	2.95 [0.22]	4.79 [4.24]	56.57 [14.91]	1.15 [1.9]
Prodromal	4	1.5	71.21 [5.6]	1.5 [1.0]	23.25 [8.85]	63.75 [13.2]	1.5 [1.73]

different domains for a unique purpose: providing a deeper understanding of neurodegeneration.

Latent variable models (LVMs) arise as the perfect match for this purpose. They provide the tools for estimating the latent distribution behind complex data, which is theoretically grounded at the manifold hypothesis [11]. A widely-used tool to estimate LVMs are Variational Auto-encoders (VAEs) [8]. VAEs are capable of estimating a latent distribution to any kind of data, and are the basis for many works that aim to discover new disease markers [1,7,9,11]. Specifically, the joint training of different deep learning architectures has been the subject of recent developments [1,9], and are behind state-of-the-art generative models such as Latent Diffusion [12]. They are, therefore, suitable for the next huge challenged in deep learning for medical data: bridging the gap between multiple data domains such as genetic, proteomic, neuroimaging and clinical symptomatology [3].

In this work we propose a joint modelling of several VAE architectures in order to maximize cross-modality prediction of PD clinical and neuroimaging data. We hypothesize that neuroimaging patterns found in 123I-ioflupane SPECT could be related to motor symptomatology and other symptoms related to dopaminergic deficit in PD. The contributions of this work involve: 1) the usage of structural reconstruction loss and alternative divergences based on Info-VAE; 2) the addition of specific constraint losses addressed at maximizing the cross-modality of the latent space, including common and modality-specific loss; and 3) the design of interpretable visualizations of the latent space in order to maximize explicability of the predictions.

2 Materials and Methods

2.1 Dataset and Preprocessing

Clinical data and its associated neuroimaging (123I-ioflupane) used in the preparation of this article were obtained on october 2023 from the Parkinson's Progression Markers Initiative (PPMI) database (http://www.ppmi-info.org/access-dataspecimens/download-data), RRID:SCR 006431. For up-to-date information on the study, visit www.ppmi-info.org. Data from the PPMI Public Curated Data Cut (revised in 2023) was crossed with those subjects and visits with available reconstructed 123I-Ioflupane imaging, to obtain a consolidated data subset with more than 2400 images from >1000 subjects. Demographics on the dataset can be found at Table 1.

58 features distributed in several categories were selected: cognitive, autonomy, motor and sum of scores; biomarkers, etc, including clinical scores (e.g. the unified Parkinson's disease rating scale -UPDRS-, Geriatric Depression Scale - GDS-,), cognitive status grading (e.g. Mini Mental State examination, Benton Judgment of Line Orientation Test -BJLOT- or Hopkins Verbal Learning Test -HVLT-), autonomy evaluation (different aspects of the SCales for Outcomes in PArkinson's disease -SCOPA- assessment), motor evaluation (tremor dominant -TD- or postural instability and gait difficulty -PIGD-) and others such as the Questionnaire for Impulsive-Compulsive Disorders in PD (QUIP).

Clinical data was standardized to the training set mean and standard deviation, and missing values were imputed using the median of each feature. Neuroimaging data was normalized [10] using the binding Potential (BP) $BP(v) = (I(v) - \mu_{bg})/\mu_{ns}$, where μ_{ns} is the mean intensity of non-specific regions. Additionally, a limiting function (tanh()) was applied to normalized data $BP(v)$ to confine the pixel values between 0 and 1, to prevent extreme values.

2.2 Multi-modal Joint Latent Variable Model

We propose a multi-modal joint self-supervised latent variable model, based on Variational Autoencoders (VAEs) [8]. The aim is to jointly model image volumes/tabular data pairs $\{i_i, d_i\}, i_i \in \mathcal{I}, d_i \in \mathcal{D}$ via a model that contains both common latent features $z_i^\odot \in \mathcal{Z}^\odot$, ensuring $z_i^{\odot ni} \approx z_i^{\odot td}$, and modality specific latents $z_i^{\ominus ni} \in \mathcal{Z}^{\ominus ni}$ and $z_i^{\ominus td} \in \mathcal{Z}^{\ominus td}$ for neuroimaging and tabular data respectively. VAEs use the evidence lower bound (ELBO) to optimize both the marginal likelihood of the data and the quality of the reconstruction:

$$\mathcal{L}_{ELBO}(x) = \mathbb{E}_{q_\phi(z|x)}[\log p_\theta(x|z)] - \lambda D(q_\phi(z|x) \| p(z)) \tag{1}$$

where D is any strict divergence [15]. Equation 1 can be decomposed in a reconstruction $\mathcal{L}_{recon}(x)$ and divergence $\mathcal{L}_{div}(z)$ terms. Many works use the Kullback-Leibler divergence to estimate $\mathcal{L}_{div}(z)$, including the original VAE paper [8]. However, it was shown that this approach usually converges to uninformative codes, especially where the differences in the dataset are minimal (such as our case) [2]. Zhao et al [15], generalized $\mathcal{L}_{div}(z)$ proposing a novel measure based on mutual information: the Maximum Mean Discrepancy (MDD):

$$\text{MMD}(p \| q) = \mathbb{E}_{p(z),p(z')}[k(z,z')] + \mathbb{E}_{q(z),q(z')}[k(z,z')] - 2\mathbb{E}_{p(z),q(z')}[k(z,z')] \tag{2}$$

where $k(z, z') = e^{-\frac{\|z-z'\|^2}{2\sigma^2}}$, a gaussian kernel.

We used the minimum square error (MSE) $\text{MSE}(x, x') = \frac{1}{N}\sum_n^N \| x - x' \|^2$ for $\mathcal{L}_{recon}(x)$ when dealing with tabular data in this work. Alternatively, we propose a neuroimaging-specific loss based on the Structural Similarity Index Measure (SSIM) [14]:

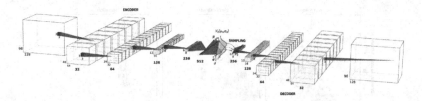

Fig. 1. Architecture of the proposed $VAE_{ni}(I)$, including the number of channels, filter size and output volume sizes for the encoder and decoder networks.

$$DSSIM(x, y) = 1 - SSIM(x, y) = 1 - \frac{(2\mu_x\mu_y + c_1)(2\sigma_{xy} + c_2)}{(\mu_x^2 + \mu_y^2 + c_1)(\sigma_x^2 + \sigma_y^2 + c_2)} \quad (3)$$

with c_1, c_2, two constants of values 0.01, 0.03, and the means and variances are computed on 3D image patches using a window size of (8, 8, 8).

This work jointly trains two VAEs: one VAE optimized for neuroimaging $i'_i = VAE_{ni}(i_i)$ and the second aimed at tabular data $d'_i = VAE_{td}(d_i)$. The imaging specific VAE is based on 3D convolutional layers, and uses a architecture already proven for neuroimaging decomposition [6] depicted at Fig. 1.

As for the tabular data VAE, $d'_i = VAE_{td}(d_i)$, it consist of a encoder $z_i = \phi_{td}(d_i)$, a multi-layer perceptron with F input neurons -corresponding to the specific number of input features, 58 in our case-, 512 hidden neurons in the hidden layer and Z latent features, and its inverse network $d'_i = \theta_{td}(z_i)$ of Z, 512 and F neurons respectively.

The multi-modal, joint training of the twin VAEs, focuses on: maximize similarity between the common latents $z_i^{\odot ni}$ and $z_i^{\odot td}$; maximize the specificity of the modality-specific latents $z_i^{\ominus ni}$ and $z_i^{\ominus td}$; and improve the cross-modality predictions. This is achieved by adding different regularization terms. The first of them is the common to specific ratio loss, minimised when the MSE between the common latents is small, and when the differences between the specific latents is large:

$$\mathcal{L}_{com/spec} = \frac{\mathcal{L}_{com}}{\mathcal{L}_{spec}} = \frac{\| z_i^{\odot ni} - z_i^{\odot td} \|^2}{\| z_i^{\ominus ni} - z_i^{\ominus td} \|^2} \quad (4)$$

Then, the reconstruction loss (either MSE or DSSIM) that already includes the same modality (SM) (e.g. $\mathcal{L}_{recon}(i_i'^{SM}, i_i)$) as in the original VAE, is also expanded using cross-modality (XM) reconstruction terms such as $\mathcal{L}_{recon}(i_i'^{XM}, i_i)$ from cross-modal predictions obtained as:

$$i_i'^{XM} = \theta_{ni}((z_i^{\odot td}, z_i^{\ominus ni})); \quad d_i'^{XM} = \theta_{td}((z_i^{\odot ni}, z_i^{\ominus td})) \quad (5)$$

2.3 Evaluation

The training, testing and evaluation sets is defined by the list of unique subjects, accounting respectively for 70%, 15% and 15% of the available subjects to

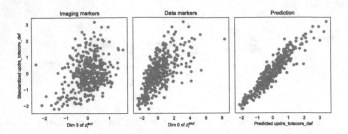

Fig. 2. Results for the prediction of UPDRS total score.

account for repeated measures in this longitudinal study, that amount to 1667, 363 and 390 image/data pairs. The performance of the model is evaluated via the Spearman's Correlation Coefficient (SCC) and its corresponding, multiple-comparisons corrected p-value, the coefficient of determination R2 and the MSE computed over the normalized features. The mutual information (MI) between the original data and the latent features is also non-parametrically estimated using the entropy estimation from k-nearest neighbors distances as in [13].

3   Results and Discussion

Table 2 shows that few features achieve a R2 larger than 0.4 in the test set. In general, the best scoring features are continuous variables (scores such as MDS-UPDRS, QUIP, HVLT-Delayed Recall, GDS, etc.), with a few bi or tri-modal distributed variables (any QUIP disorder, SCOPA-AUT Gastrointestinal). Highest SCC also correspond to similar features. It is worth noting that, during training, making differences in the preprocessing between continuous (clinical scores) and discrete variables (yes/no, or ordinal classification scales) hindered the training convergence and validity of the model, so the training is very sensitive to heterogeneity in the clinical features.

When looking at the prediction of the clinical score, we can see at Fig. 2 that the common latent account for large variability (high MI), especially in the third dimension; however, the outcomes of the model (right frame) are also corrected by the data-specific markers (middle frame) especially in the most extreme prediction (higher UPDRS values), which speaks of the ability of 123I-Ioflupane to account for severe PD symptomatology. This is confirmed in the interpretative image of the underlying common image manifold, shown at Fig. 3.

The visual distribution of the image manifold (Fig. 3) adds interpretability to the model. There, we can see that patterns typically linked to PD are clearly related to the distribution of the UPDRS predictions (in overimposed colormap). Larger, higher intensity striata are found in the top left corner of the image, which corresponds to the lowest UPDRS scores, whereas the UPDRS increases in the bottom-right direction at the same time that the intensity of the striata, its size and assymetry increase as well. This helps us analyse which neuroimaging patterns are associated to the prediction, contributing to XAI applied to PD.

Table 2. Cross-modality prediction results. Highest MI -if higher than 0.2-, SCC higher than 0.6, as well as R2 values higher than 0.4 are highlighted in bold. To facilitate reading of the results, the highest value in each column is emphasized.

Feature	Prediction			Common latents					Spec. latents	
	SCC	SCC p	R2	MI (0)	MI (1)	MI (2)	MI (3)	MI (4)	MI (0)	MI (1)
HVLT-False Alarms	0.223	0.000	-0.075	0.172	0.105	0.054	0.044	0.000	0.000	0.103
HVLT-Delayed Recognition	0.472	0.000	0.234	0.000	0.055	0.022	0.038	0.000	0.000	0.190
HVLT-Discrimination	0.481	0.000	0.096	0.096	0.047	0.004	0.000	0.000	0.041	**0.295**
HVLT-Delayed Recall	**0.731**	0.000	**0.543**	0.073	0.096	0.013	0.051	0.034	0.062	*0.551*
HVLT-Immediate/Total Recall	0.564	0.000	0.336	0.043	0.018	0.000	0.017	0.099	**0.229**	0.053
HVLT-Retention	0.567	0.000	0.359	0.023	0.036	0.000	0.101	0.002	0.101	0.174
HVLT-Animal subscore	0.324	0.000	0.061	0.000	0.022	0.000	0.053	0.037	0.080	0.133
Modified Schwab & England ADL	0.415	0.000	0.215	0.070	0.086	0.008	0.047	0.006	**0.230**	0.054
Symbol Digit Modalities Score	0.556	0.000	0.336	0.000	0.049	0.000	0.000	0.104	0.000	0.000
BJLOT	0.281	0.000	0.054	0.057	0.041	0.038	0.000	0.095	0.000	0.071
GDS	**0.614**	0.000	**0.477**	0.094	0.000	0.003	0.006	0.000	0.084	0.054
Letter Number Sequencing Score	0.380	0.000	0.163	0.000	0.000	0.001	0.065	0.095	**0.289**	0.028
MOCA Score (adjusted)	0.482	0.000	0.270	0.017	0.000	0.033	0.104	0.120	0.000	**0.236**
Epworth Sleepiness Scale	0.410	0.000	0.214	0.029	0.059	0.046	0.000	0.028	0.000	0.050
REM Sleep Behavior Disorder	0.317	0.000	0.024	0.049	0.004	0.017	0.048	0.019	0.028	**0.280**
QUIP Score	0.535	0.000	*0.844*	0.050	0.035	0.057	0.108	0.066	0.061	0.153
Any QUIP disorder	0.543	0.000	**0.722**	0.113	0.096	0.061	0.113	0.046	**0.211**	0.000
QUIP - Buying	0.052	0.322	0.331	0.001	0.017	0.000	0.014	0.000	0.137	**0.391**
QUIP - Eating	0.168	0.001	0.333	0.019	0.000	0.009	0.064	0.000	0.118	**0.337**
QUIP - Gambling	0.048	0.363	0.037	0.010	0.000	0.001	0.037	0.015	0.020	0.058
QUIP - Hobbies	0.221	0.000	0.177	0.035	0.059	0.016	0.059	0.020	0.005	0.081
QUIP - Punding	0.118	0.023	0.198	0.044	0.000	0.028	0.018	0.000	0.038	0.031
QUIP - Sex	0.073	0.166	0.176	0.018	0.030	0.000	0.048	0.037	0.003	0.105
QUIP - Walking or Driving	0.067	0.201	0.035	0.027	0.000	0.028	0.015	0.002	0.083	0.046
STAI Total Score	0.569	0.000	0.368	*0.182*	0.066	0.036	0.000	0.072	0.015	0.004
STAI State Sub-score	0.490	0.000	0.267	0.061	0.048	0.033	0.064	0.019	0.156	0.034
STAI Trait Sub-score	0.574	0.000	0.381	0.134	0.088	0.044	0.000	0.037	0.119	0.000
SCOPA-AUT Total	**0.609**	0.000	0.324	0.020	0.059	*0.256*	0.040	0.000	0.071	0.087
SCOPA-AUT Cardiovascular	0.332	0.000	0.172	0.000	0.000	0.113	0.010	0.000	0.000	0.000
SCOPA-AUT Gastrointestinal	**0.626**	0.000	**0.406**	0.042	0.027	0.019	0.000	0.012	0.177	0.000
SCOPA-AUT Pupillomotor	0.192	0.000	0.071	0.029	0.035	0.083	0.079	0.013	**0.371**	0.000
SCOPA-AUT Sexual Dysfunction	0.018	0.727	-0.271	0.018	0.074	0.076	0.072	0.025	0.163	0.004
SCOPA-AUT Thermoregulatory	0.411	0.000	0.207	0.020	0.016	0.072	0.000	0.026	**0.378**	0.067
SCOPA-AUT Urinary	0.340	0.000	0.034	0.000	0.000	0.073	0.000	0.000	0.094	0.010
UPDRS/P1 - Anxious Mood	0.397	0.000	0.259	0.000	0.000	0.045	0.000	0.000	**0.236**	0.049
UPDRS/P1 - Apathy	0.275	0.000	0.226	0.000	0.000	0.034	0.000	0.000	0.131	0.072
UPDRS/P1 - Cognitive Imp	0.336	0.000	0.149	0.000	0.000	0.008	0.077	0.000	0.059	0.022
UPDRS/P1 - Dopamine Disreg	0.098	0.061	0.127	0.000	0.000	0.000	0.000	0.000	0.100	0.008
UPDRS/P1 - Depressed Mood	0.311	0.000	0.285	0.031	0.000	0.007	0.043	0.000	0.029	0.050
UPDRS/P1 - Fatigue	0.490	0.000	0.240	0.045	0.039	0.011	0.061	0.000	0.155	0.000
UPDRS/P1 - Hallucinations	0.031	0.557	-0.020	0.000	0.078	0.000	0.023	0.000	0.179	0.000
MDS-UPDRS/P1 - Score	*0.776*	0.000	**0.675**	0.014	0.088	0.000	0.047	0.000	*0.569*	0.040
MDS-UPDRS/P2 - Score	0.674	0.000	**0.449**	0.030	*0.147*	0.013	0.101	0.060	**0.280**	0.083
MDS-UPDRS/P3 - Score	0.514	0.000	0.263	0.000	0.096	0.025	**0.236**	*0.137*	0.185	0.009
MDS-UPDRS - Total Score	**0.716**	0.000	**0.542**	0.014	0.077	0.051	0.242	0.120	**0.397**	0.026
TD - PIGD Score	0.162	0.002	-0.077	0.056	0.094	0.028	0.075	0.043	**0.269**	0.000
PIGD Score	0.523	0.000	0.231	0.000	0.074	0.000	0.117	0.012	0.126	0.000
HY Score	0.460	0.000	0.380	0.000	0.080	0.025	*0.275*	0.078	0.259	0.000
NHY Score	0.460	0.000	0.380	0.000	0.081	0.025	**0.274**	0.073	0.069	0.000

UPDRS Part 3, focusing on motor examination, is considered a more objective measure for motor impairment alongside the UPDRS Total Score. However, despite sharing a higher MI with common latents, it exhibits low predictive power ($R2 = 0.263$, $SCC = 0.514$). This discrepancy suggests that data-specific latents might exert a stronger influence on predictions due to subjective evaluation. Examination of the distribution over latent dimensions 3 and 4 (Fig. 4) reveals UPDRS Part 3's association with dopaminergic deficit patterns in the striata, confirming its link.

Other features with high R2 include SCOPA-AUT, which measures autonomic symptoms and shows an association with dimension 2 of the common latent. Figure 4 shows that the patterns associated to dimension 2 relate to asymmetry in the 123I-ioflupane uptake, especially with respect to the anterior/posterior part of the caudate nucleus, and therefore could be evidence of symptomatology arising for this pattern of neurodegeneration. Conversely, HVLT-Delayed Recall, dominated by dimension 1 of specific latents, lacks significant mutual information with common latents, indicating a spurious relationship likely influenced by head/brain size (Fig. 4).

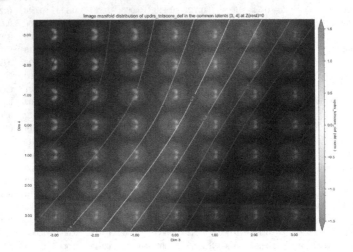

Fig. 3. Manifold distribution of the UPDRS total score and the ioflupane imaging over the dimensions 0 and 3 of the common latents.

As for the QUIP scale, it is an interesting case, since it achieved the highest R2 score (0.844), as well as the binomial "Any QUIP disorder", with $R2 = 0.722$. However, when looking at the MI between the common latents and the score, barely any component had a relevant MI with the feature (maybe the 3rd component); and just the data-specific components 0 (for any QUIP) and 1 (for the QUIP score) had a subtle relationship. This is even clearer when looking at the manifold distribution over the common latents at Fig. 4, where there is no obvious relation between the QUIP score and some imaging markers. To more

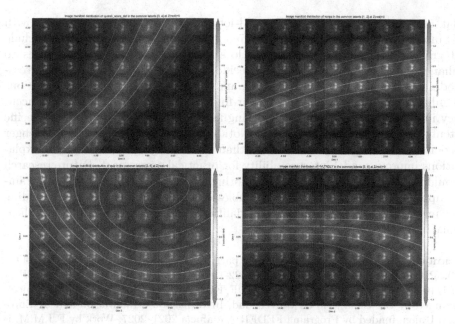

Fig. 4. Visualization of the distribution of the predicted features for 1) UPDRS-Part 3; 2) SCOPA-AUT Score; 3) QUIP and 4) HVLT-Delayed Recall and their corresponding image space over the common latent dimensions with higher MI.

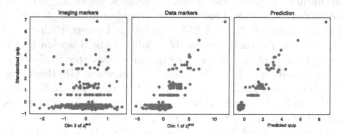

Fig. 5. Results for the prediction of the QUIP Score.

fully understand the contribution of the different common (neuroimaging) and specific (data) markers, we plot the relationship at Fig. 5. There, it can be seen that most of the variance is explained by the dimension 1 of the specific latents, however there exist residual information at dim 3 of the imaging markers that help refine the final prediction (right frame).

4   Conclusions

Our study introduces a novel approach that jointly models various Variational Autoencoder (VAE) architectures to optimize cross-modality prediction of Parkinson's disease (PD) clinical and neuroimaging data. We hypothesize that neuroimaging patterns from 123I-ioflupane SPECT scans correlate with PD motor symptoms and other dopaminergic deficits. Our contributions include integrating structural reconstruction loss and InfoVAE-based divergences to enhance model fidelity, introducing specific constraint losses to maximize cross-modality coherence in the latent space, and devising interpretable visualizations to enhance predictive explicability. Our findings demonstrate the model's accuracy in predicting PD motor scores using neuroimaging data, with data-specific latents refining predictive precision. Notably, cognitive scores show a stronger association with data-specific factors than neuroimaging latents. Visual explanations improve model interpretability for practical assessment. Future research should focus on refining the model, exploring alternative architectures, and training approaches to optimize latent-variable-score mutual information. Extending this methodology to other imaging modalities could broaden its clinical applicability.

Acknowledgements. This research is part of the projects PID2022-137629OA-I00, PID2022-137461NB-C32 and PID2022-137451OB-I00, funded by the MICIU/-AEI/10.13039/501100011033 and by "ERDF/EU", and the C-ING-183-UGR23 project, cofunded by the Consejería de Universidad, Investigación e Innovación and by European Union, funded by Programa FEDER Andalucía 2021–2027. Work by F.J.M.M. is part of the grant RYC2021-030875-I funded by MICIU/AEI/10.13039/501100011033 and by the "European Union NextGenerationEU/PRTR".

PPMI – a public-private partnership – is funded by the Michael J. Fox Foundation for Parkinson's Research and funding partners, including 4D Pharma, Abbvie, AcureX, Allergan, Amathus Therapeutics, Aligning Science Across Parkinson's, AskBio, Avid Radiopharmaceuticals, BIAL, BioArctic, Biogen, Biohaven, BioLegend, BlueRock Therapeutics, BristolMyers Squibb, Calico Labs, Capsida Biotherapeutics, Celgene, Cerevel Therapeutics, Coave Therapeutics, DaCapo Brainscience, Denali, Edmond J. Safra Foundation, Eli Lilly, Gain Therapeutics, GE HealthCare, Genentech, GSK, Golub Capital, Handl Therapeutics, Insitro, Janssen Neuroscience, Jazz Pharmaceuticals, Lundbeck, Merck, Meso Scale Discovery, Mission Therapeutics, Neurocrine Biosciences, Neuropore, Pfizer, Piramal, Prevail Therapeutics, Roche, Sanofi, Servier, Sun Pharma Advanced Research Company, Takeda, Teva, UCB, Vanqua Bio, Verily, Voyager Therapeutics, the Weston Family Foundation and Yumanity Therapeutics.

References

1. Arco, J.E., Ortiz, A., Castillo-Barnes, D., Górriz, J.M., Ramírez, J.: Ensembling shallow siamese architectures to assess functional asymmetry in Alzheimer's disease progression. Appl. Soft Comput. **134**, 109991 (2023). https://doi.org/10.1016/j.asoc.2023.109991
2. Bowman, S.R., Vilnis, L., Vinyals, O., Dai, A.M., Jozefowicz, R., Bengio, S.: Generating sentences from a continuous space. In: SIGNLL Conference on Computational Natural Language Learning (CONLL) (2016)
3. Duong, M.T., Rauschecker, A.M., Mohan, S.: Diverse applications of artificial intelligence in neuroradiology. Neuroimaging Clin. N. Am. **30**(4), 505–516 (2020). https://doi.org/10.1016/j.nic.2020.07.003

4. Górriz, J.M., et al.: Computational approaches to explainable artificial intelligence: advances in theory, applications and trends. Inf. Fus. **100**, 101945 (2023)
5. Górriz, J.M., et al.: Artificial intelligence within the interplay between natural and artificial computation: advances in data science, trends and applications. Neurocomputing **410**, 237–270 (2020)
6. Delgado de las Heras, E., et al.: Revealing patterns of symptomatology in Parkinson's disease: a latent space analysis with 3D convolutional autoencoders. In: Advances in Signal Processing and Artificial Intelligence: Proceedings of the 5th International Conference on Advances in Signal Processing and Artificial Intelligence, pp. 246–249 (2023)
7. Kim, M., Kim, J., Lee, S.H., Park, H.: Imaging genetics approach to Parkinson's disease and its correlation with clinical score. Sci. Rep. **7**(1) (2017). https://doi.org/10.1038/srep46700
8. Kingma, D.P., Welling, M.: Auto-encoding variational bayes. In: Proceedings of the International Conference on Learning Representations (ICLR) (2014)
9. Lei, B., et al.: Predicting clinical scores for Alzheimer's disease based on joint and deep learning. Exp. Syst. Appl. **187**, 115966 (2022). https://doi.org/10.1016/j.eswa.2021.115966
10. Martinez-Murcia, F., Górriz, J., Ramírez, J., Ortiz, A.: Convolutional neural networks for neuroimaging in Parkinson's disease: is preprocessing needed? Int. J. Neural Syst. **28**, 1850035 (2018)
11. Martinez-Murcia, F.J., Ortiz, A., Gorriz, J.M., Ramirez, J., Castillo-Barnes, D.: Studying the manifold structure of Alzheimer's disease: a deep learning approach using convolutional autoencoders. IEEE J. Biomed. Health Inf. **24**(1), 17–26 (2020). https://doi.org/10.1109/jbhi.2019.2914970
12. Podell, D., et al.: SDXL: improving latent diffusion models for high-resolution image synthesis (2023)
13. Ross, B.C.: Mutual Information between discrete and continuous data sets. PLoS ONE **9**(2), e87357 (2014). https://doi.org/10.1371/journal.pone.0087357
14. Wang, Z., Bovik, A., Sheikh, H., Simoncelli, E.: Image quality assessment: from error visibility to structural similarity. IEEE Trans. Image Process. **13**(4), 600–612 (2004). https://doi.org/10.1109/tip.2003.819861
15. Zhao, S., Song, J., Ermon, S.: InfoVAE: information maximizing variational autoencoders. arXiv preprint arXiv:1706.02262 (2017)

Zero-Shot Ensemble of Language Models for Fine-Grain Mental-Health Topic Classification

Cristina Luna-Jiménez(✉)📶, David Griol📶, and Zoraida Callejas📶

Departamento de Lenguajes y Sistemas Informáticos, E.T.S. de Ingenierías Informática y de Telecomunicación, Universidad de Granada, C/ Periodista Daniel Saucedo Aranda S/N, 18071 Granada, Spain
{cristina.lunaj,dgriol,zoraida}@ugr.es

Abstract. The apparition of Large Language Models has attracted the interest of the research community as well as the general public due to the impressive improvement of their communicative and comprehensive capacities in general conversations. Nevertheless, there are still many domains that require further evaluation, especially those related to sensitive data and users, such as mental health. In this article, we evaluate several ensemble approaches to combine the Zero-Shot predictions of several families of open-source Language Models, specifically, RoBERTa and LLama-2, in the task of mental-health topics classification under limited data and computational resource conditions. With this purpose, we employed two datasets containing realistic questions and answers, Counsel-Chat and 7Cups datasets labeled in 28 and 39 fine-grain unbalanced mental-health topics. The best ensembles of non-fine-tuned models with Zero-Shot approaches achieved an accuracy (ACC) of 43.29%, weighted-F1 (W-F1) of 41.32% and Macro-F1 (M-F1) of 31.79% in the 28 topics of Counsel-Chat; and 35.57% of ACC, 39.66% W-F1 and 28.12% of M-F1 in the 39 topics of 7Cups dataset. The error analysis reveals that models have difficulties in detecting less concrete topics (e.g. 'Social'), which suggests future lines to re-organize classes in topics and subtopics, or the incorporation into the ensemble of models adapted to these domains to compensate for these errors.

Keywords: AI & KE · Computational modeling of cognitive tasks · Knowledge modeling and formalization · Natural Language Processing · Large Language Models Ensemble · Fine-Grain Topic Classification

1 Introduction

The recent apparition of Large Language Models has implied a disruption in how people interact with conversational agents. However, there are still few studies that have evaluated their internal knowledge, neither whether they could be complementary in solving the same task, even though it could be a valuable resource to explain social behaviors since the massive data employed in their

J. M. Ferrández Vicente et al. (Eds.): IWINAC 2024, LNCS 14674, pp. 88–97, 2024.
https://doi.org/10.1007/978-3-031-61140-7_9

training will likely contain conversations comprising distinct profiles of society. In this regard, understanding their performance and capacities when dealing with delicate questions about mental health is key due to the vulnerable situation of this greater and greater group of population (the World Health Organization estimates that one in eight persons worldwide suffers from a mental illness [8]). Additionally, detecting limitations of certain models could help to propose others to complement and create ensembles of several Language Models to improve their performance and correct errors.

With this aim, and based on previous studies [1], we compared the performance of single Language Models against several ensemble versions in mental health topic classification. We evaluated these ensembles across two datasets, Counsel-Chat and 7Cups, containing samples of real-world questions (Q) and answers (A) posted by people likely suffering from a mental health disease. This Q and A were annotated in terms of 28 and 39 unbalanced topics, respectively. This large amount of topics, compared to classical two or three classes (according to [6] stress, suicide, and depression), emphasizes the complexity of the task, reporting scores in a broader span of scenarios to shed light on those applications in which these models could fail or work appropriately. In our study case, we ensembled the Zero-Shot predictions of RoBERTa and Llama-2 versions of models, evaluating their performance and inter-agreement rate in a scenario of limited data and computational resources.

The rest of the paper is organized as follows. Section 2 contextualizes previous works evaluating Large Language Models' capacities and publications in topic classification, especially related to the mental health domain. In Sect. 3, we detail the methods employed to distill and combine knowledge of several Language Models for performing mental-health topic classification, additionally, the setup is introduced. Then, in Sect. 4, we discuss the results obtained for our study case comparing single models with ensembles. Finally, in Sect. 5 we summarize the main conclusions and findings of this work and propose future research lines to investigate.

2   Related Works

Since the apparition of transformers [10], several modifications and updates have been investigated, leading to the current state-of-the-art Language Models, such as RoBERTa [7], Llama-2 [9], ChatGPT [3]. Despite their similarities, they also present differences that let organize them into several groups. First, BERT-derived families [4] (such as RoBERTa), are referred to as Masked Language Models (MLM), and they are frequently employed in classification tasks [5], being able to attend to bidirectional context to fill in the most suitable word for the 'mask' token. This group of models is only based on the encoder part of the transformers and returns a structured answer for the mask token. The second group is referred to as Causal Language Models (CLM), such as LLama-2 or ChatGPT. The architecture of these models is based on the decoder part of the original transformers and they are prepared to predict the next token based on previous information of the input sequence, being unidirectional. For this reason, these models are more suitable for conversations, although new versions have been fine-tuned for trying to solve classification tasks, such as mental-health disease detection [11]. However, contrary to MLM, one of the main limitations of employing these models in classification is that they generate non-structured responses, which makes it difficult to automatize and evaluate their performance in classification tasks on large datasets in Zero-Shot approaches. Luckily, recent investigations have proposed methods to change the output format to return one single predicted class in their outputs, this is the approach implemented in SBERT-InterpEVAL [1]. Based on this prior work, in this article, we propose employing this methodology to create ensembles of CLM and MLM models pre-trained on different domains with Zero-Shot strategies. This study also reports insights about the capacities of these models to extrapolate their knowledge to solve new tasks different from those initially intended.

Nevertheless, although Language Models are being employed in several domains, still some need further evaluations, this is for example the case of mental health. As stated in [6], they observed "a strong correlation between the scope of each study and the dataset employed"; however, if models are aimed to be employed in general real-world scenarios, they should be able to solve a broader span of tasks, especially in sensitive domains as mental health. For this reason, in our study, we selected two datasets with real-world questions posted by users potentially suffering from a mental-health disease, and answers given by experts in the area (e.g. therapists, contributors with expertise on a topic, etc.), for performing fine-grain mental health topic classification. We considered that this task is the minimum requirement that a model should fulfill to establish a conversation since it is necessary to distinguish a topic before starting to participate in the dialogue. In the ensembles, we combined models trained for open-domain and fine-tuned on mental health to study whether they could be complementary, as a possible solution to non-fine-tuning new models but just combining them following a maximum voting approach.

3   Methodology

Zero-Shot Approach. Although there exist several strategies to perform Zero-Shot or Few-Shots to evaluate Language Models, most of them are not easy to extrapolate to other families of models (e.g. BERT families versus Llama families). As was commented before, the reason is that different families of transformer-derived models could have variations in the structure of their outputs. Tables 1 and 2 illustrate differences in the responses of BERT-models in which a single token is used to predict the topic versus the response of LLama-2 models which is more elaborated and unstructured.

This difference made it difficult to combine the outputs of Zero-Shot approaches. However, recently SBERT-InterpEVAl approach [1] was proposed to compare models more fairly. This evaluation approach receives as input the outputs generated by Zero-Shot strategies of different models and projects these outputs into a common embedding space defined by SBERT. At the same time, the keywords of the labels to classify are also projected into the same embedding space. Having the embeddings of the key topics and the outputs of the Zero-Shot strategies, the predicted key topic is the one with maximum similarity with the embedding of the Zero-Shot output. As a result, unstructured outputs are transformed into a single-label prediction that can be exploited in ensemble approaches.

Table 1. Prompt template for classifying topics of Questions and answers with Llama-2 family models on Zero-Shot (before SBERT-InterpEVAL strategy).

Prompt:
Consider this post:
"It is not the case of being right or wrong, in my view. If you are asking
I believe you truly care for your boyfriend. It seems like he is having difficulties
in establishing trust in this relationship. The ideal would be to come closer
to his upsetness and to show him that you are there for him. I hope all goes well."
[Question: Which topic does the text belong to? Select one from the list: depression, anxiety, trauma, anger-management ...]

Response:
I would mark the topic as "relationships". The text is primarily focused on
the relationship between the speaker and their boyfriend, and offers
advice on how to support and care for him.

Table 2. Prompt template for classifying topics of Questions and Answers with RoBERTa-family models on Zero-Shot (before SBERT-InterpEVAL strategy).

Prompt:
"It is not the case of being right or wrong, in my view. If you are asking
I believe you truly care for your boyfriend. It seems like he is having difficulties
in establishing trust in this relationship. The ideal would be to come closer
to his upsetness and to show him that you are there for him. I hope all goes well."
The topic of the text is <mask>.

Response:
love

Ensemble of Language Models. The initial assumption in this article is that as the selected models differ in architecture, as well as the datasets employed to train them, they may contain complementary knowledge that could help to boost the performance of Zero-Shot approaches by combining their responses. Thus, wrong predictions of one model could be corrected by the others following a maximum voting approach, as happens in social democratic systems.

In our experiments, we compared several hard-voting combinations of the following models: RoBERTa, Llama-2, Mental-RoBERTa and MentaLlama. In all the strategies, the outputs of the SBERT-InterpEVAL methodology were considered since in previous works [1], they obtained higher scores in ACC; W-F1 and M-F1 compared to Zero-Shot strategies, providing also a single label. For all the approaches, we made combinations of three and four of the presented models, with one acting as 'president' in charge of deciding the predicted class in case of tie results.

Set-Up. As we commented before, we selected open-access and state-of-the-art models available in the HuggingFace library with different architectures derived from transformers and trained for open-domains tasks: RoBERTa ('roberta-base') and Llama-2 ('meta-llama/Llama-2-7b-chat-hf'); as well as their expert versions on mental-health domain, Mental-RoBERTa ('mental/mental-roberta-base') and MentalLlama ('klyang/MentaLlama-chat-7B').

The RoBERTa-Based models are the encoder-only variant of transformers with a total 124M of parameters, accepting 512 tokens of context as maximum. Unlike RoBERTa, Llama-2 families of models are a decoder-only variant of transformers, with the capacity to accept up to 4,000 tokens of context. During the experimentation, we employed the 7B option with the following bitsandbytes settings: double NF4 quantization, loaded in 4bits; and 16-bit floating point format for parameters during computation.

Regarding datasets, we employed the 'Counsel-Chat' dataset from Hugging-Face library[1] [2], which has 2,775 pairs of questions and answers extracted from 'www.counselchat.com' assigned to 30 different topics. Additionally, we also evaluated the presented approaches in the '7Cups' dataset, containing more than 136,000 pairs of questions and answers about topics related to mental health, with 6,270 unique questions on 39 different unbalanced topics.

We utilized the same filters and classes employed in [1]. After passing these filters, the Counsel-Chat dataset had 3,451 samples from 28 distinct themes; and 7cups had 142,230 samples from 39 different topics.

4   Experiments and Results

Tables 3 and 4 collect the results obtained after repeating **the Zero-Shot approaches** of previous works [1], and the scores obtained by the ensemble strategies for Counsel-Chat and 7Cups datasets, respectively.

As it can be observed, when the four models are stacked, metrics do not outperform the baseline of the unique top model, in the case of Counsel-Chat, this model is Llama-2; and in the case of 7Cups, the model that achieved the highest success rate is MentaLlama. The reason for this slight decay in rates when connecting the four models could be explained by the effect that the worse model exerts over the rest of the group. As we can see in Table 3, Mental-RoBERTa scores are 21.98 (ACC), 19.26 (W-F1), and 20.17 (M-F1) percentage points lower compared to the achieved by Llama-2, still the inclusion of this model into the group only decreases the rates in 0.72 (ACC), 0.95 (W-F1) and

---

[1] 'nbertagnolli/counsel-chat'.

1.62 (M-F1), which are not statistical significant differences which means that at least, the ensemble does not get worse than the single-model for Counsel-Chat dataset. For 7Cups, similar patterns can be observed comparing MentaLLama results with the ensembles R+MR+LL+MLL* and R+MR+LL*+MLL.

However, the top performance is achieved when only three models are combined: RoBERTa, LLama-2, and MentaLlama (R+LL+MLL). For Counsel-Chat, this combination of models achieves an increment of 1.10 (ACC), 0.86 (W-F1), and 0.58 (M-F1) percentage points from LLama-2 scores, when the 'president' of the ensemble is Llama-2. For 7Cups the increment is 1.07 (ACC), 0.96 (W-F1),

Table 3. Results of experiments on topic classification (28 topics) for the complete set (3,451 samples) of Counsel-Chat dataset for RoBERTa and Llama-2 models. The highest, the best. Acronyms: ACC = Accuracy, CI = Confidence Interval (95%), W-F1 = Weighted-F1, M-F1 = Macro-F1. (*) Indicates the model that acts as 'president' and decides in case of tie-in ensemble experiments.

Model(s)	Experiment	ACC ± CI	W-F1 ± CI	M-F1 ± CI
Zero-Rule	-	17.07 ± 1.25	4.98 ± 0.73	1.04 ± 0.34
RoBERTa (R)	SBERT-InterpEVAL	27.79 ± 1.49	24.91 ± 1.44	18.38 ± 1.29
Mental-RoBERTa (MR)	SBERT-InterpEVAL	19.62 ± 1.32	17.92 ± 1.28	11.04 ± 1.05
Llama-2 (LL)	SBERT-InterpEVAL	42.19 ± 1.65	40.46 ± 1.64	31.21 ± 1.55
MentaLlama (MLL)	SBERT-InterpEVAL	38.60 ± 1.62	37.18 ± 1.61	29.21 ± 1.52
R+MR+LL*+MLL	Ensemble	41.47 ± 1.64	39.51 ± 1.63	29.59 ± 1.52
R+MR+LL+MLL*	Ensemble	39.81 ± 1.63	38.00 ± 1.62	29.06 ± 1.51
R+LL*+MLL	Ensemble	**43.29 ± 1.65**	**41.32 ± 1.64**	**31.79 ± 1.55**
R+LL+MLL*	Ensemble	40.77 ± 1.64	39.50 ± 1.63	31.38 ± 1.55

Table 4. Results of experiments on topic classification (39 topics) for the complete set (142,230 samples) of 7Cups dataset for RoBERTa and Llama-2 models. The highest, the best. Acronyms: ACC = Accuracy, W-F1 = Weighted-F1, M-F1 = Macro-F1, CI = Confidence Interval (95%). (*) Indicates the model that acts as 'president' and decides in case of tie-in ensemble experiments.

Model(s)	Experiment	ACC ± CI	W-F1 ± CI	M-F1 ± CI
Zero-Rule	-	17.50 ± 0.20	5.21 ± 0.11	0.76 ± 0.05
RoBERTa (R)	SBERT-InterpEVAL	27.54 ± 0.23	28.52 ± 0.23	19.53 ± 0.21
Mental-RoBERTa (MR)	SBERT-InterpEVAL	16.39 ± 0.19	20.13 ± 0.21	13.91 ± 0.18
Llama-2 (LL)	SBERT-InterpEVAL	32.18 ± 0.24	37.80 ± 0.25	25.91 ± 0.23
MentaLlama (MLL)	SBERT-InterpEVAL	34.50 ± 0.25	38.70 ± 0.25	26.38 ± 0.23
R+MR+LL*+MLL	Ensemble	34.51 ± 0.25	38.50 ± 0.25	26.70 ± 0.23
R+MR+LL+MLL*	Ensemble	35.11 ± 0.25	38.37 ± 0.25	26.72 ± 0.23
R+LL*+MLL	Ensemble	34.89 ± 0.25	39.63 ± 0.25	27.85 ± 0.23
R+LL+MLL*	Ensemble	**35.57 ± 0.25**	**39.66 ± 0.25**	**28.12 ± 0.23**

and 1.74 (M-F1) percentage points from MentaLlama, which are statistically significant given the higher number of samples in this dataset.

To complement and conclude the comparison between ensembled models, we extracted **inter-rater agreements** between the predictions of the models. For two raters, Cohen's Kappas was calculated, whereas Fleiss' Kappas was used for measuring ensembles of 3 or more models since Cohen's Kappa is limited to two raters. Table 5 shows that RoBERTa and Mental-RoBERTa have a slight agreement for both datasets, which indicates that for the same samples, they do not usually agree which is interesting since a higher agreement was expected providing that mental-RoRBERTa was fine-tuned from RoBERTa. On the contrary, it is noticeable that this agreement is much higher when Llama-2 and MentaLlama are compared, reaching a Cohen's kappa higher than 0.4, this indicates that combining these two models is not going to provide as high variability in the final results as introducing other models, although still, their agreement is not that high as for discarding the idea of combining them since they achieve also the highest performance, as was reported in Tables 3 and 4. Finally, for 3 and 4 model combinations, Fleiss' kappa shows fair agreement, which implies that the knowledge of these models is not completely correlated; hence, they could be complementary. However, apart from being not that complimentary for reaching higher scores, they should have had high performance, which as we commented before, is not that high for RoBERTa and Mental-RoBERTa.

Table 5. Inter-Agreement kappas over the predictions of models.

Models	Kappa	
-	Counsel-Chat	7Cups
R - MR	0.237	0.226
LL-MLL	0.452	0.433
LL-R	0.231	0.288
MLL-R	0.221	0.320
LL-MLL-R	0.299	0.344
LL-MLL-R-MR	0.231	0.257

From the error analysis of the top ensembles displayed in Table 6, for Counsel-Chat the best-predicted class is 'trauma' with an F1-score of 65%, followed by 'anger-management' (62%), 'eating-disorders' (59%), 'anxiety' (56%), surpassing the random choice in more than 50% points ($1/28 = 3.58\%$). On the contrary, the R+LL*+MLL ensemble employed in Counsel-Chat presents difficulties for differentiating topics such as 'diagnosis', 'social relationships', or 'legal-regulatory'. Some of these errors could be occasioned by the similarity between certain topics, e.g. between 'social-relationships' and 'relationships', emphasizing the complexity of the task since some topics belong to non-disjoint sets. Regarding 7Cups, on the one hand, the best-predicted classes by the R+LL+MLL* ensemble are:

Table 6. F1 score per topic for the top ensemble models, R+LL*+MLL for Counsel-Chat; and R+LL+MLL*, for 7Cups.

	Counsel-Chat (3,451 samples)			7Cups (142,230 samples)		
	Topic	F1	Samples	Topic	F1	Samples
1	counseling fundamentals	0.55	272	Work	0.48	3,930
2	grief-and-loss	0.44	34	Bullying	0.55	6,340
3	anger management	0.62	71	ADHD	0.75	404
4	stress	0.38	16	Women's	0.02	89
5	intimacy	0.34	340	Eating	0.64	2,862
6	marriage	0.18	72	Weight	0.10	242
7	anxiety	0.56	446	Managing	0.03	8,733
8	domestic violence	0.34	37	Getting	0.00	910
9	family-conflict	0.18	198	PTSD	0.20	423
10	self-esteem	0.28	133	Self-Harm	0.70	7,677
11	substance abuse	0.51	50	Chronic	0.14	164
12	lgbtq	0.41	62	LGBTQ+	0.61	10,050
13	behavioral change	0.08	89	Disabilities	0.07	698
14	legal-regulatory	0.00	14	Alcohol-Drug	0.60	2,211
15	human-sexuality	0.06	8	Anxiety	0.52	18,551
16	workplace relationships	0.33	46	Spirituality	0.03	119
17	trauma	0.65	117	Grief	0.43	542
18	addiction	0.08	12	Borderline	0.40	64
19	diagnosis	0.00	23	Family	0.19	11,170
20	spirituality	0.41	53	Financial	0.25	47
21	eating-disorders	0.59	17	Breakups	0.23	22,736
22	depression	0.54	589	Social	0.02	494
23	relationship dissolution	0.07	125	Parenting	0.30	1,417
24	sleep-improvement	0.32	16	Bipolar	0.47	350
25	relationships	0.40	298	Sleeping	0.66	4,900
26	parenting	0.47	238	Depression	0.51	24,891
27	social-relationships	0.03	35	Autism	0.03	14
28	professional-ethics	0.08	40	Panic	0.09	3,638
29	-	-	-	Loneliness	0.28	1,638
30	-	-	-	Forgiveness	0.16	304
31	-	-	-	Relationship	0.12	2,844
32	-	-	-	Self-Esteem	0.04	311
33	-	-	-	Obsessive	0.67	398
34	-	-	-	Student	0.27	837
35	-	-	-	Recovery	0.01	19
36	-	-	-	Domestic	0.01	1,165
37	-	-	-	General	0.00	328
38	-	-	-	Sexual	0.01	16
39		-	-	Exercise	0.39	704

'ADHD' (Attention-deficit/hyperactivity disorder) with a 75% of F1, self-harm (70%), 'Obsessive' (67%), 'Sleeping' (66%) or 'Eating' (64%), again surpassing the random choice ($1/39 = 2.56\%$). On the other hand, the model struggles to detect the topics of the classes of 'General', 'Getting', 'Recovery' or 'Domestic', comparing this group with the successfully recognized, one of the possibilities of the limited performance in these classes could be due to the lack of concreteness of these classes. For illustration, many issues could fit in 'General' and models are opting instead for a more concrete label for these samples. In the future, special attention will be dedicated to passing these cases through a new annotation step to define better the concepts represented by these classes.

To conclude, this error analysis provides a clue about the expected coverage of these models when they are employed in mental-health domains without adapting them first. Additionally, they also indicate future steps and the characteristics of models to incorporate into the ensemble in order to increase the classification rates and reduce the errors committed in certain topics, e.g. models pre-trained in data related to the topic of 'legal-regulatory' for Counsel-Chat, or good at detecting 'autism' for 7Cups.

5   Conclusions

This study explores the combination of Large Language Models for fine-grain mental health topic classification. Compared with other approaches that require a larger amount of data and capacity for fine-tuning models, we evaluated the combination of the predictions of RoBERTa with Llama-2 models in Zero-Shot scenarios. Experiments reveal that the best ensembles improved the accuracy, weighted-F1, and macro-F1 scores of the single models of previous works [1] in two realistic datasets, Counsel-Chat and 7Cups, differentiating between 28 and 39 different topics. These results demonstrate the effectiveness of combining different families of Language Models architectures. In the future, we shall extend the study to other domains, as well as evaluate and integrate more models into the ensemble pipeline to discover a combination with lower inter-rater agreements that can allow higher performance for those scenarios in which data is scarce.

Acknowledgments. The research leading to these results has received funding from the 'CONVERSA: Effective and efficient resources and models for transformative conversational AI in Spanish and co-official languages' project with reference TED2021-132470B-I00, funded by MCIN/AEI/10.13039/501100011033 and by the European Union "NextGenerationEU/PRTR"; European Union's Horizon 2020 research and innovation program under grant agreement No. 823907 (MENHIR project: https://menhir-project.eu); and the Spanish R&D&i project GOMINOLA (PID2020-118112RB-C21 and PID2020-118112RB-C22) financed by MCIN/AEI/10.13039/501100011033.

Disclosure of Interests. The authors have no competing interests to declare that are relevant to the content of this article.

References

1. Anonymous: SBERT-InterprEVAL: SBERT for interpretability evaluation of transformer-derived architectures on mental-health topic classification (2024). Preprint at https://openreview.net/references/pdf?id=OuphQxftS9
2. Bertagnolli, N.: Counsel chat: bootstrapping high-quality therapy data (2020)
3. Brown, T., et al.: Language models are few-shot learners. In: Larochelle, H., Ranzato, M., Hadsell, R., Balcan, M., Lin, H. (eds.) Advances in Neural Information Processing Systems, vol. 33, pp. 1877–1901. Curran Associates, Inc. (2020)
4. Devlin, J., Chang, M.W., Lee, K., Toutanova, K.: BERT: pre-training of deep bidirectional transformers for language understanding. In: Proceedings of the 2019 Conference of the North American Chapter of the Association for Computational Linguistics: Human Language Technologies, Volume 1 (Long and Short Papers), Minneapolis, Minnesota, June 2019, pp. 4171–4186. Association for Computational Linguistics (2019). https://doi.org/10.18653/v1/N19-1423. https://aclanthology.org/N19-1423
5. Grootendorst, M.: BERTopic: neural topic modeling with a class-based TF-IDF procedure. arXiv preprint arXiv:2203.05794 (2022)
6. Hua, Y., et al.: Large language models in mental health care: a scoping review (2024)
7. Liu, Y., et al.: RoBERTa: a robustly optimized BERT pretraining approach (2019)
8. World Health Organization: World mental health report: transforming mental health for all (2022). https://iris.who.int/bitstream/handle/10665/356119/9789240049338-eng.pdf?isAllowed=y&sequence=1
9. Touvron, H., et al.: Llama 2: open foundation and fine-tuned chat models (2023)
10. Vaswani, A., et al.: Attention is all you need. In: Proceedings of the 31st International Conference on Neural Information Processing Systems, NIPS 2017, pp. 6000–6010. Curran Associates Inc., Red Hook, NY, USA (2017)
11. Yang, K., Zhang, T., Kuang, Z., Xie, Q., Ananiadou, S.: MentaLLaMA: interpretable mental health analysis on social media with large language models. arXiv preprint arXiv:2309.13567 (2023)

Enhancing Interpretability in Machine Learning: A Focus on Genetic Network Programming, Its Variants, and Applications

Mohamad Roshanzamir[1], Roohallah Alizadehsani[2(✉)], Seyed Vahid Moravvej[3], Javad Hassannataj Joloudari[4], Hamid Alinejad-Rokny[5], and Juan M. Gorriz[6]

[1] Department of Computer Engineering, Faculty of Engineering, Fasa University, Fasa, Iran
roshanzamir@fasau.ac.ir
[2] Institute for Intelligent Systems Research and Innovation (IISRI), Deakin University, Geelong, Australia
r.alizadehsani@deakin.edu.au
[3] Department of Electrical and Computer Engineering Isfahan University of Technology, Isfahan, Iran
sa.moravvej@alumni.iut.ac.ir
[4] Department of Computer Engineering, Technical and Vocational University (TVU), Tehran, Iran
javad.hassannataj@birjand.ac.ir
[5] BioMedical Machine Learning Lab, The Graduate School of Biomedical Engineering, UNSW Sydney, Sydney, NSW 2052, Australia
h.alinejad@unsw.edu.au
[6] Department of Signal Theory, Networking and Communications, Universidad de Granada, Granada, Spain
gorriz@ugr.es

Abstract. In current machine learning research, deep learning methodologies have become the prevalent approach across various domains, including decision-making processes. However, the interpretability of solutions generated by these algorithms remains a significant challenge, as these models do not inherently prioritize explainability. This lack of interpretability hampers the analysis of decision-making rationales. One potential remedy to this issue is the employment of Genetic Network Programming (GNP), a method within the evolutionary computing paradigm, known for its ability to generate more interpretable solutions. This study provides a concise overview of GNP, exploring its modifications and applications to demonstrate its utility in addressing the interpretability challenge in machine learning algorithms.

Keywords: Genetic Programming · Genetic Network Programming · Evolutionary Computing

© The Author(s), under exclusive license to Springer Nature Switzerland AG 2024
J. M. Ferrández Vicente et al. (Eds.): IWINAC 2024, LNCS 14674, pp. 98–107, 2024.
https://doi.org/10.1007/978-3-031-61140-7_10

1   Introduction

Artificial intelligence (AI) represents a broad field in computer science devoted to creating systems capable of performing tasks that would normally require human intelligence. This field of computer science has many diverse sub-disciplines, some of which, like neural networks and deep learning, act like a black box despite their very good performance and do not provide an explanation about the reasons for the decisions they make. In order to solve these types of challenges, sub-branches of artificial intelligence such as explainable artificial intelligence (XAI) [4] or some evolutionary computing algorithms such as Genetic Network Programming appear, which focus on making artificial intelligence systems more transparent and understandable for humans. Genetic Network Programming (GNP) is an evolutionary computing technique that extends the concepts of Genetic Algorithms (GAs) and Genetic Programming (GP). As shown in Fig. 1, unlike GP, which typically evolves tree structures to solve problems, GNP evolves network or graph structures. These networks consist of nodes and directed edges, forming a more flexible structure that can represent complex relationships and interactions more naturally in some cases.

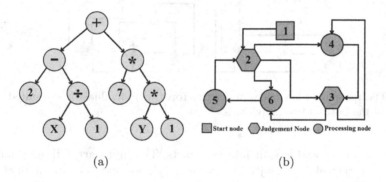

(a)   (b)

Fig. 1. a) tree structure of GP vs. b) graph structure of GNP.

As shown in Fig. 1.b, in GNP, each node in the network represents a start node, a judgment node, or an operation node. The edges define the flow of control or data between these nodes. This allows for the representation of various sequential and parallel processes, making GNP suitable for dynamic and complex problem-solving environments, such as control systems, optimization problems, and machine learning tasks. The genotype of the individual shown in Fig. 1.b is represented in Fig 2.

Figure 2 illustrates that each node is identified by a number i and consists of two main parts: the Node Gene and the Connection Gene. The Node Gene is divided into three smaller parts, where NTi represents the node's type, NFi indicates the function performed by the node, and di signifies the execution delay of the node's function. The Connection Gene, referred to as Bi, encompasses the

Page 100 — M. Roshanzamir et al.

Node 1	0	0	0	2 0		
Node 2	1	J_1	1	4 0	3 0	6 0
Node 3	1	J_2	1	6 0	4 0	
Node 4	2	P_1	5	3 0		
Node 5	2	P_2	5	2 0		
Node 6	2	P_1	5	5 0		

	Node Gene			Connection Gene (B_j)				
Node i	NT_i	NF_i	d_i	C_{i1}	d_{t1}	...	C_{in}	d_{in}

Fig. 2. Genotype structure of the individual shown in 1b.

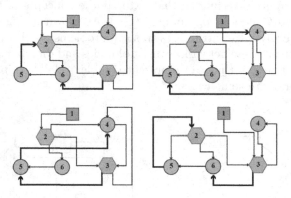

Fig. 3. The recombination operator on the top two individuals has resulted in the creation of the bottom two individuals.

branches of node i and is split into two parts. The first part, Cij, identifies the connection target of node i's jth branch, while the second part, dij, indicates the time delay for the transition of node i's jth branch.

The evolutionary process in GNP involves the generation of an initial population of network structures, evaluation of these structures based on a fitness function that measures their performance on the given task, and application of genetic operators such as selection, crossover, and mutation to evolve the pop-

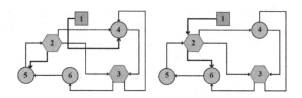

Fig. 4. The recombination operator on the left individual has resulted in the right individual creation.

ulation over successive generations. An example of the crossover and mutation operators of GNP is shown in Figs. 3 and 4 respectively. At crossover points, some randomly selected connections from the parent solutions are exchanged to create new offspring solutions. This exchange of genetic material facilitates exploration of the solution space and potentially leads to offspring solutions with better characteristics than their parents. The mechanism of mutation in GNP typically involves randomly changing some randomly selected connections of an individual in the population. The purpose of mutation is to introduce diversity into the population and explore new regions of the solution space that may lead to better solutions. Mutation allows for the exploration of novel solutions that may not have been present in the initial population or may have been overshadowed by more dominant solutions.

The overall goal of GNP algorithms is to evolve a network that maximizes or minimizes the fitness function, thereby solving the problem at hand.

GNP's network-based approach offers several advantages, including the ability to naturally represent iterative and recursive processes and maintain a balance between exploration and exploitation in the search space. It has been applied in various fields, including robotics, pattern recognition, and automated decision-making systems.

2   The Most Important Versions of GNP

GNP was presented for the first time in 2001 by Hirasawa et al. [5,6]. After that, different versions or variations of it were introduced, which tried to improve its efficiency by changing the structure defined for people or how the algorithm was implemented. This section introduces the most important articles published in this field.

GNP with Reinforcement Learning (GNP-RL) is a variation that integrates reinforcement learning principles with GNP, allowing the system to adapt and learn from interactions with the environment more effectively, leading to improved decision-making capabilities. In [15], the learning phase of GNP utilizes the SARSA algorithm, which combines characteristics of both Monte Carlo and Temporal Difference (TD) methods and uses eligibility traces to handle non-Markov tasks and long-delayed rewards. The SARSA algorithm is used to select the next current node based on the judgment result and execute the corresponding function. The proposed method in this paper allows for changing node functions in addition to node connections, making it a more general framework of GNP with RL. To use RL in GNP, some modifications were applied to the structure of individuals which is illustrated in Fig 5.

The same algorithm used in [1] allows for online learning, where programs can be changed incrementally based on rewards obtained during task execution. It also combines a diversified search of GNP and an intensified search of RL. It applies the proposed method to stock trading rules, specifically using technical analysis to determine the timing of buying and selling stocks based on technical indices such as the Relative Strength Index, MACD, Golden/Dead Cross, etc.

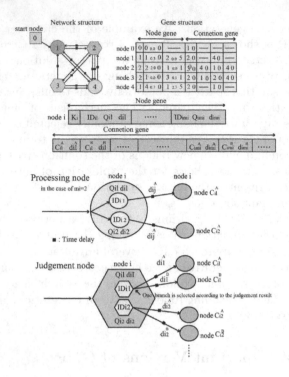

Fig. 5. Basic structure of individuals in GNP-RL [15].

The combination of GNP and RL in GNP-RL provides advantages such as online learning and a diversified search, allowing for efficient and effective stock trading rule creation.

Niching Genetic Network Programming (GNP-Niching) methods enable the GNP to maintain diversity among the solutions, which can prevent premature convergence and help in finding multiple optimal solutions in a multi-modal problem space. This method is used in [8]. In this paper, a Learning Classifier System (LCS) referred to as eXtended rule-based Genetic Network Programming (XrGNP) is introduced. According to the proposed method of this research, in contrast to the majority of existing LCSs, the rules are depicted and uncovered via a graph-based evolutionary algorithm known as GNP. Consequently, this approach possesses a remarkable capacity to model and advance the decision-making rules. The efficacy of XrGNP is demonstrated through experiments conducted on both benchmark and real-world multi-step problems. Niching genetic network programming was also used in [13]. A new LCS called niching genetic network programming with rule accumulation (nGNP-RA) was used in this research. This method distinguished itself by three key aspects. Firstly, it employed GNP as the rule generator, resulting in a higher ability to represent knowledge compared to traditional Genetic Algorithm (GA)-based LCSs. Secondly, GNP incorporates a novel niching mechanism to promote the discovery of diverse and high-quality rules. Lastly, a reinforcement learning (RL)-based mechanism is integrated to accurately assign credits to the discovered rules.

GNP with Estimation of Distribution Algorithms (GNP-EDA) combines GNP with Estimation of Distribution Algorithms, focusing on learning and exploiting the probabilistic model of promising solutions to guide the search process. Using this idea, in [12], a novel evolutionary paradigm was suggested and utilized for addressing traffic prediction issues by means of class association rule mining. In this research, a probabilistic model is built by estimating the probability distribution based on the selected elite individuals from the previous generation. This was done in order to replace the traditional genetic operators like crossover and mutation. The probabilistic model has the capability to enhance the evolution process and achieve the ultimate objective. This paper introduced two methods that were based on extracting the probabilistic information regarding the node connections and node transitions of GNP-EDAs for constructing the probabilistic model. Furthermore, a comparative study was conducted between the proposed paradigm and the conventional GNP in order to solve the traffic prediction problems using class association rule mining. A novel graph-based EDA, known as probabilistic model building genetic network programming (PMBGNP), was introduced by Li et al. [11]. By utilizing the graph structure of GNP, PMBGNP ensures a higher capability for expressing solutions compared to traditional EDAs when addressing specific problems. Additionally, a modified algorithm named reinforced PMBGNP has been proposed to integrate PMBGNP with reinforcement learning in order to enhance performance in terms of fitness values, search speed, and reliability. These algorithms are employed to solve the challenges associated with controlling agents' behavior. The same research was done in [10]. This paper presents a novel approach to utilizing the undesirable individuals by examining the substructures rather than the entire individual structures in order to solve RL problems, which typically decompose their complete solutions into sequences of state-action pairs. This investigation was conducted within the context of PMBGNP, which demonstrated successful RL problem-solving capabilities, in order to propose an expanded PMBGNP. The efficacy of this approach is substantiated through its application to an RL problem, specifically robot control. Li et al. [9] expanded the scope of PMBGNP from a discrete to a continuous search space. In addition to utilizing the conventional PMBGNP approach to evolve the node connections for optimal graph structures, the distribution of continuous variables of nodes is modeled using a Gaussian distribution. Similar to classical continuous Population-Based Incremental Learning (PBILc), the mean value and standard deviation were constructed accordingly. In this case, a reinforcement learning technique known as Actor-Critic (AC) was employed to update the mean and standard deviasion. The use of AC enables the calculation of the TD error, which serves as an evaluation metric for determining whether the selection of a continuous value is better or worse than expected. This scalar reinforcement signal plays a crucial role in determining whether the preference for selecting a particular continuous value should be enhanced or diminished, thereby allowing for the determination of the shape of the probability density functions of the Gaussian distribution. The proposed algorithm was applied to a specific reinforcement learning problem involving autonomous robot control, where the wheel speeds and sensor values of the robot are continuous variables. The experimental findings demonstrate the superiority of the proposed method when compared to conventional algorithms.

Adaptive Genetic Network Programming (Adaptive GNP) involves mechanisms that allow the GNP system to adjust its parameters or structure dynamically, enhancing its ability to cope with changing environments or problem requirements. In [7], an adaptive GNP approach is developed, which adjusts both the crossover and mutation probabilities of each search variable according to the prevailing circumstances. This adaptive mechanism facilitates the automatic modification of the evolution bias towards the frequently reused nodes found in high-quality individuals. The superiority of the adaptive GNP approach is then assessed through a comparative analysis with the traditional GNP method in a benchmark control testbed.

Parallel Genetic Network Programming (Parallel GNP) utilizes parallel computing techniques to improve the efficiency and scalability of GNP, making it suitable for solving large-scale and complex problems. In [19], parallel GNP has been put forward and implemented in functionally distributed systems comprised of multiple tasks. GNPs corresponding to these tasks in parallel GNP function autonomously and simultaneously, effectively addressing conflicts in task execution. Parallel GNP demonstrates quicker convergence and superior fitness outcomes compared to conventional GNP, as evidenced by simulations conducted on dynamic problems. The objective of [3] was to derive association rules from extensive and densely populated datasets utilizing GNP, while considering a real-world database that encompasses a substantial amount of attributes. A large database was partitioned into numerous small datasets, whereby each GNP addresses one dataset that contains attributes of an appropriate magnitude. These GNPs are subsequently processed in parallel. Furthermore, several novel genetic operations were introduced aimed at enhancing both the quantity and quality of the extracted rules.

These variations of GNP aim to enhance the algorithm's performance, adaptability, and applicability to a wide range of problems, from optimization to machine learning and control systems. Each version has been developed to address specific challenges or to leverage new computational paradigms, making GNP a versatile and powerful tool in the field of evolutionary computation.

2.1   Some Specific Applications of GNP Algorithm

The applications of GNP are diverse, reflecting its adaptability and the broad relevance of network-based modeling. In the field of robotics, GNP has been used to develop control systems that can adapt and learn from interactions with their environment, leading to more autonomous and efficient robots. In data mining and pattern recognition, GNP's ability to model complex relationships has been harnessed to uncover patterns and insights from large datasets, with applications ranging from financial market analysis to bioinformatics. Furthermore, GNP can be applied in traffic and transportation systems to optimize routing and scheduling, reducing congestion and improving efficiency. In the following, some applications of this algorithm are described briefly.

In recent years, intrusion detection has garnered significant attention from researchers as a technology utilized to monitor abnormal behavior and uphold network security. Among the various methods employed to construct intrusion detection systems (IDS), association rule mining stands as a prominent approach. Nevertheless, the existing association rule algorithms encounter challenges such as high false positive rates and low detection rates. Additionally, the abundance of rules may lead to an increase in uncertainty, which in turn affects the performance of IDS. To address these aforementioned issues, a modified GNP was proposed in [18] for class association rule mining. In this method, the incorporation of information gain into GNP node selection was suggested, taking advantage of the fact that node connections in the directed graph structure of GNP can be utilized to establish attribute associations. As a result, the most crucial attributes are selected and irrelevant attributes are eliminated before rule extraction. Consequently, not only is the uncertainty among class association rules alleviated, but also the time consumption is reduced. Moreover, the extracted rules can be applied to any classifier without compromising the detection performance.

In [2], the application of GNP for multiple nest foraging was examined by the researchers. Foraging is a complex area of study in swarm robotics, as it requires an aptitude for multiple rudimentary behaviors. This research introduced and assessed a modified version of GNP that incorporates the advantages of neural networks. The findings were compared to state-of-the-art foraging algorithms, such as the generic Neuro-evolution of Augmented Technologies and Novelty Search algorithms, as well as the more specific Multiple-Place Foraging Algorithm.

Madokoro et al. [16] put forth a technique for generating filters, which involves the modification of sensor signals through the utilization of GNP. The objective of this technique is to achieve automatic calibration in order to absorb individual differences. Essentially, this method involves the acquisition of knowledge pertaining to the topology and interconnections between input features and the signals used for teaching. Two types of classifiers were proposed in [14] utilizing class association rules. One of the classifiers is based on semisupervised learning, while the other one is based on a combination of supervised and semisupervised learning. The second method constructs multiple classifiers through the use of supervised learning and semisupervised learning, with the final decision being made by integrating the classification results of these classifiers. The paper utilizes the GNP method for association rule mining. One of the goals of this study is to expand the applicability of GNP to data mining that is based on semisupervised learning.

In [17], a comprehensive framework was employed, which included the GNP model, reinforcement learning, and a Multi-Layer Perceptron (MLP) neural network, for the purpose of data classification and stock return forecasting. Additionally, the GNP model's outcomes were utilized to predict the return by means of accumulation rules. The integration of these models was aimed at estimating the one-day return. The GNP model extracted an abundant number of rules based on 5 technical indicators with a 3 times period. The MLP network then classified the data and identified similarities between future and past data pertaining to a stock, considering a 5 sub-period. Subsequently, several conditions were established to select the best estimation between GNP-RL and ARMA. In comparison to the ARMA-GARCH model, which has been widely used for return estimation and risk measurement in previous research, the proposed GNP-ARMA model exhibited a superior forecasting capability, reducing the error by an average of 16.

3   Conclusion and Future Works

GNP has emerged as a powerful and versatile tool in evolutionary computation, with its various versions enhancing its adaptability and effectiveness across a wide range of applications. From robotics and data analysis to traffic management, GNP's ability to model and evolve complex network structures makes it a valuable approach for solving problems in dynamic and complex systems. As research continues and technology advances, it is anticipated that GNP will find new applications and undergo further refinements, continuing to contribute to advancements in artificial intelligence and computational modeling.

For future works, with the integration of deep learning techniques, GNP could enhance its capacity for pattern recognition and decision-making in more complex environments. Exploring hybrid models that combine the adaptability of GNP with the predictive power of neural networks could lead to breakthroughs in fields such as bioinformatics, autonomous systems, and smart grid management. Moreover, advancements in parallel computing and quantum computing offer promising avenues to significantly reduce the computational costs associated with GNP.

Acknowledgments. This research is part of the PID2022-137451OB-I00 project funded by the MCIN/AEI/10.13039/501100011033 and by FSE+.

References

1. Chen, Y., Mabu, S., Hirasawa, K.: Genetic network programming with reinforcement learning and its application to creating stock trading rules. In: Machine Learning. IntechOpen (2009)
2. Foss, F., Stenrud, T., Haddow, P.C.: Investigating genetic network programming for multiple nest foraging. In: 2021 IEEE Symposium Series on Computational Intelligence (SSCI), pp. 1–7. IEEE (2021)
3. Gonzales, E., Shimada, K., Mabu, S., Hirasawa, K., Hu, J.: Genetic network programming with parallel processing for association rule mining in large and dense databases. In: Proceedings of the 9th Annual Conference on Genetic and Evolutionary Computation, pp. 1512–1512 (2007)

4. Górriz, J.M., et al.: Computational approaches to explainable artificial intelligence: advances in theory, applications and trends. Inf. Fus. **100**, 101945 (2023)
5. Hirasawa, K., Okubo, M., Katagiri, H., Hu, J., Murata, J.: Comparison between genetic network programming (GNP) and genetic programming (GP). In: Proceedings of the 2001 Congress on Evolutionary Computation (IEEE Cat. No. 01TH8546), vol. 2, pp. 1276–1282. IEEE (2001)
6. Katagiri, H., Hirasawa, K., Hu, J., Murata, J.: Network structure oriented evolutionary model–genetic network programming–and its comparison with genetic programming. In: Proceedings of the 3rd Annual Conference on Genetic and Evolutionary Computation, pp. 179–179 (2001)
7. Li, X., He, W., Hirasawa, K.: Adaptive genetic network programming. In: 2014 IEEE Congress on Evolutionary Computation (CEC), pp. 1808–1815. IEEE (2014)
8. Li, X., Hirasawa, K.: A learning classifier system based on genetic network programming. In: 2013 IEEE International Conference on Systems, Man, and Cybernetics, pp. 1323–1328. IEEE (2013)
9. Li, X., Li, B., Mabu, S., Hirasawa, K.: A continuous estimation of distribution algorithm by evolving graph structures using reinforcement learning. In: 2012 IEEE Congress on Evolutionary Computation, pp. 1–8. IEEE (2012)
10. Li, X., Mabu, S., Hirasawa, K.: An extended probabilistic model building genetic network programming using both of good and bad individuals. IEEJ Trans. Electr. Electron. Eng. **8**(4), 339–347 (2013)
11. Li, X., Mabu, S., Hirasawa, K.: A novel graph-based estimation of the distribution algorithm and its extension using reinforcement learning. IEEE Trans. Evol. Comput. **18**(1), 98–113 (2013)
12. Li, X., Mabu, S., Zhou, H., Shimada, K., Hirasawa, K.: Genetic network programming with estimation of distribution algorithms for class association rule mining in traffic prediction. In: IEEE Congress on Evolutionary Computation, pp. 1–8. IEEE (2010)
13. Li, X., Yang, M., Wu, S.: Niching genetic network programming with rule accumulation for decision making: an evolutionary rule-based approach. Expert Syst. Appl. **114**, 374–387 (2018)
14. Mabu, S., Higuchi, T., Kuremoto, T.: Semisupervised learning for class association rule mining using genetic network programming. IEEJ Trans. Electr. Electron. Eng. **15**(5), 733–740 (2020)
15. Mabu, S., Hirasawa, K., Hu, J.: Genetic network programming with reinforcement learning and its performance evaluation. In: Deb, K. (ed.) GECCO 2004. LNCS, vol. 3103, pp. 710–711. Springer, Heidelberg (2004). https://doi.org/10.1007/978-3-540-24855-2_81
16. Madokoro, H., Nix, S., Sato, K.: Automatic calibration of piezoelectric bed-leaving sensor signals using genetic network programming algorithms. Algorithms **14**(4), 117 (2021)
17. Ramezanian, R., Peymanfar, A., Ebrahimi, S.B.: An integrated framework of genetic network programming and multi-layer perceptron neural network for prediction of daily stock return: an application in Tehran stock exchange market. Appl. Soft Comput. **82**, 105551 (2019)
18. Xu, Y., Sun, Y., Ma, Z., Zhao, H., Wang, Y., Lu, N.: Attribute selection based genetic network programming for intrusion detection system. J. Adv. Comput. Intell. Intell. Inform. **26**(5), 671–683 (2022)
19. Zhang, Y., Li, X., Yang, Y., Mabu, S., Jin, Y., Hirasawa, K.: Functionally distributed systems using parallel genetic network programming. In: Proceedings of SICE Annual Conference 2010, pp. 2626–2630. IEEE (2010)

Enhancing Coronary Artery Disease Classification Using Optimized MLP Based on Genetic Algorithm

Mohammad Hashemi[1], Seyedeh Somayeh Salehi Komamardakhi[1],
Mohammad Maftoun[2], Omid Zare[3], Javad Hassannataj Joloudari[1,4,5],
Mohammad Ali Nematollahi[6(✉)], Roohallah Alizadehsani[7], Pietro Sala[3],
and Juan M Gorriz[8]

[1] Department of Computer Engineering, Babol Branch, Islamic Azad University,
Babol, Iran
[2] Department of Artificial Intelligence, Technical and Engineering Faculty,
South Tehran Branch, Islamic Azad University, Tehran, Iran
st_m_maftoun@azad.ac.ir
[3] Department of Computer Science, University of Verona, Verona, Italy
{omid.zare,pietro.sala}@univr.it
[4] Department of Computer Engineering, Faculty of Engineering,
University of Birjand, Birjand, Iran
javad.hassannataj@birjand.ac.ir
[5] Department of Computer Engineering, Technical and Vocational University (TVU),
Tehran, Iran
[6] Department of Computer Sciences, Fasa University, Fasa, Iran
ma.nematollahi@fasau.ac.ir
[7] Institute for Intelligent Systems Research and Innovation (IISRI) Deakin
University, Waurn Ponds, Australia
r.alizadehsani@deakin.edu.au
[8] Department of Signal Theory, Networking and Communications,
Universidad de Granada, Granada, Spain
gorriz@ugr.es

Abstract. Heart disease is one of the most prevalent and serious health widespread issues affecting elderly and middle-aged individuals globally. Cardiovascular diseases (CVDs) impose considerable morbidity and mortality rates and entail considerable financial strain on global healthcare infrastructures. According to the report of the World Health (WHO) Organization, the mortality rate of heart disease will increase to 23 million cases by 2030. In healthcare, predicting diseases and analyzing electronic health records to derive useful patterns aid in early and accurate CAD diagnosis. Hence, in this paper, we worked on the Z-Alizadeh Sani dataset to demonstrate the strong ability of the machine learning technique in predicting CAD. We also applied the genetic algorithm to reduce dimension by finding the important features of the neural network. The results showcased that our proposed method could diagnose CAD by achieving the highest accuracy, sensitivity, and AUC of 94.71%, 96.29%, and 93.5%, respectively.

J. M. Ferrández Vicente et al. (Eds.): IWINAC 2024, LNCS 14674, pp. 108–117, 2024.
https://doi.org/10.1007/978-3-031-61140-7_11

Keywords: CAD Prediction · MLP · Feature Selection · Genetic Algorithm

1 Introduction

The biomedical system, one of the world's fastest-growing sectors, is primarily impacted by environmental deterioration, wildlife loss, and environmental contaminants, all of which contribute to pollution and ecosystem damage. These disruptions, combined with undesirable lifestyles, lead to a variety of life-threatening disorders that harm human health, among which cardiovascular disease stands out as a leading cause of mortality globally, particularly prevalent among middle-aged and elderly populations [1,3]. Coronary artery disease (CAD), in particular, is a major cardiovascular disease that causes high mortality [4]. The World Health Organization (WHO) predicts that by the year 2030, CAD will result in the demise of around 23 million cases [7]. Hence, implementing a healthcare application utilizing data mining and machine learning methods for automated coronary artery disease (CAD) diagnosis will aid cardiologists in promptly detecting the condition [11]. Different methods have been used to diagnose this disease until now, and data mining has a higher value in this field. One of the most common methods used to diagnose coronary disease is angiography, but its high costs are considered an important challenge in diagnosing this disease [5]. Among these methods have been proposed to replace angiography for coronary heart diagnosis, of which data mining and Machine Learning (ML) have been the most famous [12]. The science of data mining has a high scope to encourage researchers to use various techniques and algorithms to solve problems in various fields, in the field of disease diagnosis, various methods are used to pre-process data sets and build a strong model via ML techniques for more accurate disease diagnosis [1,11]. An important factor in model learning is the issue of feature selection, hence the feature selection stage is of great importance in data mining and its purpose is to remove unnecessary and sometimes destructive features [10]. There are different methods to select important features, the method used in this research is a hybrid method in which feature selection is done using a genetic algorithm which is an evolutionary optimization algorithm. This research aims to improve the accuracy of diagnosis of coronary heart disease using a method based on the combination of artificial neural networks and genetic algorithms. The neural network has been used as a suitable tool to build an accurate model to diagnose this disease, and to find the optimal solution, we have used the genetic algorithm, which is an evolutionary optimization algorithm. Obtaining the most suitable feature subset by a genetic algorithm that has the most optimal classification solution is another goal of this research. The rest of this paper is delineated as follows: Sect. 2 reviews related research on classifying the CAD datasets, while Sect. 3 discusses material and methods. Section 4 presents the experimental setup, evaluation criteria, and results. Section 5 concludes the study and suggests future research avenues.

2   Related Works

In this section, previous studies about the prediction of CAD using AI models will be investigated. Gupta et al. [2] presented DMHZ, a computational framework designed for diagnosing heart disease, validated with the Z-Alizadeh Sani dataset from the UCI repository. DMHZ operates principal component analysis (PCA) for extracting numeric features and multiple correspondence analysis (MCA) for categorical ones. Machine learning classifiers such as Logistic Regression (LR), Random Forest (RF), and Support Vector Machine (SVM) are trained within the DMHZ framework, and validation occurs through a holdout validation method with a 3:1 ratio. Results of experiments indicated that DMHZ outperforms several leading methods in terms of accuracy. KILIÇ and KELEŞ [6] enhanced and involved the Artificial Bee Colony (ABC) algorithm-based feature selection technique to the Z-Alizadeh Sani dataset. The adjusted method selected 16 features, improving accuracy and F-measure values to 89.4% and 89.4%, respectively, surpassing the performance of the original dataset. This approach showcased the efficacy of utilizing advanced algorithms for feature selection, contributing to improved predictive accuracy in heart disease diagnosis. In [8], the authors have enhanced coronary heart disease diagnosis by evaluating classification algorithms and proposing a hybrid feature selection method. They utilized CAD datasets to conduct detailed comparisons of accuracy, sensitivity, specificity, and other metrics. Experimenting with various classifiers, their study introduced a hybrid feature selection approach incorporating medical expertise. The results showcased promise, with accuracies of 81.84% and 87.12% in respective datasets, the methodology's efficacy in the improvement of the CAD diagnosis. Nandakumar and Narayan [9] described the Hamming distance feature selection approach for preprocessing and cleaning coronary artery disease datasets. Deep belief networks combined with the cuckoo search algorithm provided outstanding predictions. In the Z-Alizadeh Sani dataset, the highest accuracy was up to 89.7%.

3   Materials and Methods

In this study, an artificial neural network was employed to classify coronary artery disease. To improve classification accuracy, inappropriate features from the feature set needed to be eliminated; essentially, a feature selection process needed to be performed. For this purpose, a wrapper-based approach was utilized. As mentioned, the fitness function of the genetic algorithm in this study is the multilayer neural network. Therefore, for classification by the neural network, data were initially divided into three categories using a random-based partitioning function: training, validation, and testing sets. Evaluating the predictive model's performance involves assessing its results throughout the prediction process with validation and ultimately training data. In Fig. 1, all steps of this study are provided.

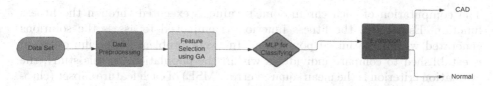

Fig. 1. The proposed flowchart of this study.

3.1 Dataset

The Z-Alizadeh Sani dataset was utilized, comprising information on 303 patients, of whom 216 were diagnosed with CAD. Fifty-five features were collected for each patient, including demographic characteristics, symptoms, results of physical examinations, electrocardiograms, echocardiograms, and laboratory tests.

3.2 Data Preprocessing

The Z-Alizade-Sani dataset comprised both numerical and string-based records. Data preprocessing aimed to normalize values within $[0, 1]$. Some features were binary (0 and 1) and required no changes, while others with values exceeding one were scaled using $(x - min)/(max - min)$. Post-normalization, numerical data were processed. String data were transformed to numerical values within $[0, 1]$, such as converting "female" and "male" to 0 and 1, respectively, for gender. This preprocessing ensured uniformity and compatibility for subsequent analysis, enhancing the dataset's usability and interpretability.

3.3 The Important Process of This Study

As the workflow of this study is based on the performance of the genetic algorithm, the description of the proposed method will be based on executing the phases of this algorithm. These phases include the steps detailed below: The body of the genetic algorithm requires an iterative loop to generate new generations, which is initiated after creating an initial population. The genetic algorithm begins by generating chromosomes representing solutions with diverse feature combinations. These initial solutions are formed randomly. The algorithm's objective is to find the best solution among them and enhance it. In this study, the genetic algorithm aims to identify the optimal subset of features from the dataset to improve the classification accuracy by the neural network, ultimately leading to better diagnosis of coronary artery disease. Chromosomes represent problem solutions. In this study, employing the wrapper method for feature selection, our solutions consist of different feature combinations, aiming for the best combination. Each chromosome is a vector equal to the number of features. With each element representing the presence (1) or absence (0) of a feature, each gene corresponds to a dataset feature. Since the dataset has 55 features, each chromosome comprises a vector with 55 genes, denoting feature presence or absence.

The computation of each chromosome's value is executed through the fitness function. Essentially, the fitness function is employed to assess the solutions generated within the initial population. In every problem, a specific criterion is established to compare individuals within the population. In this study, the evaluation criterion is the mean squared error (MSE) of each feature subset (chromosome). To ascertain the MSE for each chromosome, a multilayer perceptron (MLP) neural network has been utilized. In this study, a multilayer perceptron (MLP) neural network was employed for classification, featuring a hidden layer with four neurons using a sigmoid activation function and an output layer with a single neuron using a linear activation function. Initially, datasets with varying features were randomly assigned to each chromosome. Subsequently, each chromosome's designated dataset subset served as input to the neural network, while output data for "disease-free" and "diseased" classes were fed into the network's output. The neural network's MSE served as the fitness criterion for the genetic algorithm, reflecting performance across different feature subsets. The initial population of the genetic algorithm consists of chromosomes evaluated by the fitness function. Initially, the number of chromosomes is determined. Then, for each chromosome (representing subsets with different and random feature combinations), its fitness is calculated using the fitness function (in this study, the output of the multilayer perceptron neural network for classification). This fitness metric is utilized for comparing chromosomes. As an evaluation of the fitness performance in the genetic algorithm, the MSE criterion is used, which is the squared error score of the chromosome. This criterion is calculated by calculating the classification by the neural network of each data set with the features of each learner. In the following section, the results and evaluation metrics will be discussed to demonstrate the ability of our proposed method in the detection of CAD.

4 Results and Discussion

In this section, we evaluate a novel feature selection method using genetic algorithms and artificial neural networks (GANN) for coronary heart disease diagnosis. It compares the GANN method's performance against standard neural networks and combined GA-NN approaches from recent studies. We implement this AI system in MATLAB (2019a). Each run is characterized by the number of classes (in this case, 2 for binary classification), the number of iterations performed 100 times, the size of the population considered (15–25–30–40–50), the probability of a mutation occurring set to 0.2, the impact rate of mutation to 0.3, and the probability of crossover with the value of 0.8. These parameters were varied across runs to observe their effects on the algorithm's performance and results. By using the confusion matrix based on equations (1–4), we can analyze the performance of the corresponding algorithms. Providing specific evaluation metrics, the analysis reveals that the proposed method achieves significantly higher accuracy and reduces feature redundancy compared to other methods. The proposed method was evaluated using various metrics, including accuracy, MSE, sensitivity (TPR), and FPR with equations (5–8).

$$\text{True positive (TP): cases diagnosed correctly by the test.} \qquad (1)$$

$$\text{False positives (FP): cases diagnosed wrongly by the test.} \qquad (2)$$

$$\text{True negative (TN): cases diagnosed correctly as healthy by the test.} \qquad (3)$$

$$\text{False negative (FN): cases diagnosed wrongly as healthy by the test.} \qquad (4)$$

$$\text{Accuracy} = \frac{\text{TP} + \text{TN}}{\text{TP} + \text{FN} + \text{TN} + \text{FP}} \qquad (5)$$

$$\text{MSE} = \frac{1}{n} \sum_{i=1}^{n} (y_i - \hat{y}_i)^2 \qquad (6)$$

$$\text{Sensitivity} = \frac{\text{TP}}{\text{TP} + \text{FN}} \qquad (7)$$

$$\text{FPR} = \frac{\text{FP}}{\text{FP} + \text{TN}} \qquad (8)$$

These metrics assessed different aspects of the algorithm's performance, such as correctness, prediction accuracy, and the ability to identify positive instances. The results of all executions were provided in Table 1, providing insights into their strengths and weaknesses. This comprehensive evaluation aids in understanding the effectiveness of the proposed method.

Table 1. The results obtained from different executions of the algorithm.

Executions	MSE	Accuracy	Sensitivity	TPR	FPR
First	0.0233	92.73%	97%	0.97%	0.2%
Second	0.0193	93.72%	97%	0.97%	0.15%
Third	0.019	92.73%	95%	0.95%	0.18%
Fourth	0.0186	94.71%	96%	0.96%	0.1%
Fifth	0.019	93.39%	94%	0.94%	0.1%

Considering the problem type, a neural network tailored to the specific problem with its corresponding parameters should be created. These parameters remained constant across five runs, as determined in Table 2.

Table 2. Neural network parameters for 5 different runs

Type of Neural Network	Multi-layer Perceptron
Number of Neurons	2
Number of Hidden Layers	4
Training Set	70%
Validation Set	15%
Testing Set	15%

As observed in Table 1, the fourth run achieved the best result with an accuracy of 94.71%, selecting 24 features out of the 54 dataset features as the optimal features for coronary artery disease diagnosis. The set of features obtained from this run can be seen in Table 3.

Table 3. Selected features based on the best implementation of the proposed algorithm

Number of features	Selected features
24	Age, Weight, Sex, HTN, Ex-smoker, FH, Obesity, CRF
	CVA, Airway disease, CHF, BP, PR, Edema,
	Weak peripheral pulse, Diastolic murmur, Typical chest pain,
	Dyspnea, Function class, Exertional chest pain,
	ST elevation, T inversion, FBS, Cr, HB, VHD

The algorithm convergence diagram of the proposed method for the fourth implementation has been obtained according to Fig. 2. This graph is based on the number of iterations of the genetic algorithm and the amount of MSE obtained by the cost function for the best solution in each iteration. In Fig. 2, the algorithm reached its optimal solution with an MSE value of 0.0186 in the 37th iteration and concluded in the 100th iteration as per the stopping condition. The ROC curve in Fig. 3 shows an AUC value of 0.935, indicating the algorithm's accuracy in detecting the "disease-positive" class.

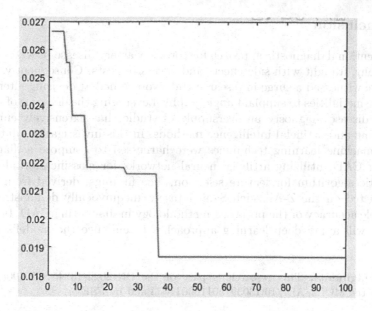

Fig. 2. Convergence diagram of the proposed method.

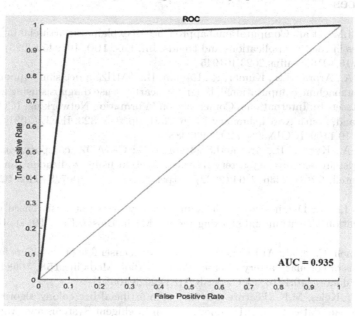

Fig. 3. The obtained ROC curve.

5   Conclusion

The conventional diagnostic approach for coronary artery disease (CAD) involves angiography, fraught with side effects and excessive costs. Consequently, recent years have witnessed a surge in research endeavors aimed at devising alternative diagnostic modalities to supplant angiography. Leveraging the domains of healthcare and disease diagnosis, an oversupply of studies has extensively employed data mining and artificial intelligence methods. In this investigation, data mining and machine learning techniques were harnessed to compose a diagnostic model for CAD, utilizing artificial neural networks for classification alongside the genetic algorithm for feature selection. The findings, derived from analysis conducted on the Z-Alizadeh Sani dataset, unequivocally demonstrate the remarkable accuracy of the proposed methodology in diagnosing CAD. In future work, we will apply deep learning approaches to enhance the model's performance.

Acknowledgments. This research is part of the PID2022-137451OB-I00 project funded by the MCIN/AEI/10.13039/501100011033 and by FSE+.

References

1. Górriz, J.M., et al.: Computational approaches to explainable artificial intelligence: advances in theory, applications and trends. Inf. Fus. **100**, 101945 (2023). https://doi.org/10.1016/j.inffus.2023.101945
2. Gupta, A., Arora, H.S., Kumar, R., Raman, B.: DMHZ: a decision support system based on machine computational design for heart disease diagnosis using z-alizadeh sani dataset. In: International Conference on Information Networking, ICOIN 2021, Jeju Island, South Korea, January 13-16, 2021, pp. 818–823. IEEE (2021). https://doi.org/10.1109/ICOIN50884.2021.9333884
3. Gupta, A., Kumar, R., Arora, H.S., Raman, B.: C-CADZ: computational intelligence system for coronary artery disease detection using z-alizadeh sani dataset. Appl. Intell. **52**(3), 2436–2464 (2022). https://doi.org/10.1007/S10489-021-02467-3
4. Jin, Z., Li, N.: Diagnosis of each main coronary artery stenosis based on whale optimization algorithm and stacking model. Math. Biosci. Eng. **19**(5), 4568–4591 (2022)
5. Khozeimeh, F., et al.: ALEC: active learning with ensemble of classifiers for clinical diagnosis of coronary artery disease. Comput. Biol. Medicine **158**, 106841 (2023). https://doi.org/10.1016/J.COMPBIOMED.2023.106841
6. Kiliç, Ü., Keleş, M.K.: Feature selection with artificial bee colony algorithm on z-alizadeh sani dataset. In: 2018 Innovations in Intelligent Systems and Applications Conference (ASYU), pp. 1–3. IEEE (2018)
7. Kolukisa, B., Bakir-Gungor, B.: Ensemble feature selection and classification methods for machine learning-based coronary artery disease diagnosis. Comput. Stand. Interfaces **84**, 103706 (2023). https://doi.org/10.1016/J.CSI.2022.103706
8. Kolukisa, B., Hacilar, H., Goy, G., Kus, M., Bakir-Gungor, B., Aral, A., Gungor, V.C.: Evaluation of classification algorithms, linear discriminant analysis and a new hybrid feature selection methodology for the diagnosis of coronary artery disease.

In: Abe, N., Liu, H., Pu, C., Hu, X., Ahmed, N.K., Qiao, M., Song, Y., Kossmann, D., Liu, B., Lee, K., Tang, J., He, J., Saltz, J.S. (eds.) IEEE International Conference on Big Data (IEEE BigData 2018), Seattle, WA, USA, December 10-13, 2018, pp. 2232–2238. IEEE (2018). https://doi.org/10.1109/BIGDATA.2018.8622609

9. Nandakumar, P., Narayan, S.: Cardiac disease detection using cuckoo search enabled deep belief network. Intell. Syst. Appl. **16**, 200131 (2022). https://doi.org/10.1016/J.ISWA.2022.200131

10. Shahid, A.H., Singh, M.P., Roy, B., Aadarsh, A.: Coronary artery disease diagnosis using feature selection based hybrid extreme learning machine. In: 3rd International Conference on Information and Computer Technologies, ICICT 2020, San Jose, CA, USA, March 9-12, 2020, pp. 341–346. IEEE (2020). https://doi.org/10.1109/ICICT50521.2020.00060

11. Velusamy, D., Ramasamy, K.: Ensemble of heterogeneous classifiers for diagnosis and prediction of coronary artery disease with reduced feature subset. Comput. Methods Programs Biomed. **198**, 105770 (2021). https://doi.org/10.1016/J.CMPB.2020.105770

12. Wiharto, Suryani, E., Setyawan, S., Putra, B.P.: The cost-based feature selection model for coronary heart disease diagnosis system using deep neural network. IEEE Access **10**, 29687–29697 (2022). https://doi.org/10.1109/ACCESS.2022.3158752

Extracting Heart Rate Variability from NIRS Signals for an Explainable Detection of Learning Disorders

Juan E. Arco[1,2,3]([⊠]), Nicolás J. Gallego-Molina[2,3], Pedro J. López-Pérez[4], Javier Ramírez[1,3], Juan M. Górriz[1,3], and Andrés Ortiz[2,3]

[1] Department of Signal Theory, Networking and Communications, University of Granada, 18010 Granada, Spain
[2] Department of Communications Engineering, University of Malaga, 29010 Malaga, Spain
[3] DaSCI Institute, University of Granada, Granada, Spain
jearco@ugr.es
[4] Department of Social Sciences, Universidad de la Costa, Barranquilla, Colombia

Abstract. Artificial Intelligence (AI) has improved our ability to process large amounts of data. These tools are particularly interesting in medical contexts because they evaluate the variables from patients' screening evaluation and disentangle the information that they contain. In this study, we propose a novel method for detecting developmental dyslexia by extracting heart signals from NIRS. Features in terms of different domains based on heart rate variability (HRV) are computed from the extracted signal, and dimensionality of the resulting data is reduced through Principal Component Analysis (PCA). To evaluate the discriminability of the information patterns associated with normal controls and dyslexic patients, the resulting components are entered into a linear classifier to evaluate the discriminability of the information patterns associated with normal controls and dyslexic patients, leading to an area under the ROC curve of 0.79. The explanatory nature of our framework, based on Shapley Additive Explanations (SHAP), yields a deeper understanding of the evaluated phenomenon, revealing the presence of behavioral variables highly correlated with the model's features. These findings demonstrate that heart information can be extracted from a different equipment than electrocardiogram tools, and that cardiac signal variables can be used to detect dyslexia in an early stage.

Keywords: Heart rate variability · NIRS · machine learning · signal processing · explicability · dyslexia

1 Introduction

The integration of artificial intelligence (AI) into healthcare has initiated a transformative era, revolutionizing medical research, diagnosis, treatment, and patient

J. M. Ferrández Vicente et al. (Eds.): IWINAC 2024, LNCS 14674, pp. 118–127, 2024.
https://doi.org/10.1007/978-3-031-61140-7_12

care. The applicability of AI in healthcare lies in its ability to analyze complex medical data at unprecedented speeds, identify patterns that may elude human perception, and customize interventions based on patient characteristics. Neurological pathologies are one of the contexts in which AI has been used, especially in the early detection of disorders such as Alzheimer's [5,7,18] or Parkinson's [2,4,16,17]. The applicability of AI for the identification of pulmonary affections has also been demonstrated in previous studies [3,6]. Most of these works rely on the application of intelligent solutions to Magnetic Resonance Imaging (MRI) or Positron Emission Tomography (PET), high-resolution techniques that allow the study of structural and functional changes. However, there are other interesting alternatives, such as near-infrared spectroscopy (NIRS), for studying the human brain. This technique provides a non-invasive way to study the physiological basis of neurovascular coupling, which describes the relationship between neuronal activity and localized changes in cerebral blood flow.

The integration of NIRS and machine learning has been explored in various domains. [13] examined the fractality of near-infrared spectroscopy signals, providing insights into the complexity and dynamics of NIRS data. Moreover, [9] compared classification methods used in machine learning for dysgraphia identification, highlighting the potential of machine learning in addressing writing difficulties and cognitive disabilities. Most importantly, NIRS enables the determination of the heart rate of a patient, which is very relevant given the need to understand the relationship between the brain and heart and how brain and cardiac conditions change in specific contexts. Heart rate variability (HRV), which refers to the fluctuation in the interval between successive heartbeats, is an important parameter. Variations in HRV have previously been linked to changes in the sympathetic and parasympathetic systems and can be used to detect anomalies associated with certain disorders that are not related to heart failure. Previous studies have demonstrated the potential of intelligent systems to extract vital information from HRV during different phases of epileptic seizures [19]. These systems operate on the assumption that seizures are preceded by changes in heart rate. In addition, alterations in HRV have manifested as a potential indicator of driver drowsiness [22] and can be used in the early detection of autonomic dysfunction in diabetes [12].

In the present study, we propose a method for evaluating the influence of heart rate on the early detection of developmental dyslexia (DD) from NIRS signals. Specifically, our approach provides a complete framework that covers the entire pipeline: preprocessing of the NIRS signal, extraction of heart rate responses, computation of features from HRV, supervised classification, and explanation of the results. Thus, the presented methodology covers several technical issues to provide an intelligent system that both identifies the pathology under study and determines the relationship between behavioral variables and this disorder. The rest of the paper is organized as follows. Section 2.1 contains a description of the dataset used in addition to how NIRS signals were acquired. Sections 2.3 and 2.4 detail the extraction of heart signal from NIRS, its preprocessing and the computation of the features from different domains.

The classification of the resulting data and how these variables are related to subjects' behavior are described in Sect. 2.5, whereas Sect. 3 and 4 summarize the results obtained and conclusions and future work, respectively.

2   Material and Methods

2.1   Participants

The LEEDUCA research group at the University of Málaga (Spain) provided the dataset used in this study [20], comprising 57 right-handed native Spanish-speaking seven-year-old children with no hearing impairment and normal or corrected-to-normal vision. We selected 40 skilled readers for the control group and 17 dyslexic readers for the experimental group in accordance with established standards [8]. The dyslexic children had received a formal diagnosis of dyslexia at school, whereas the skilled readers did not report any reading or spelling problems or a prior formal diagnosis of dyslexia. The legal guardians of the participants were fully informed about the study, were present throughout the experiment, and provided written consent.

2.2   NIRS Acquisition

NIRS acquisitions were conducted using the NIRSport system equipped with 16 optodes, comprising eight sources that emit light and eight detectors. Each source-detector pair, separated by approximately 3 cm, constitutes a channel, resulting in 20 NIRS channels per wavelength. The placement of the optodes over the language and auditory areas of the human brain is depicted in Fig. 1. During the NIRS recordings, signals were sampled at 7.8125 Hz while the participants were exposed to auditory stimuli comprising white noise amplitude modulated at 4.8, 16, and 40 Hz. Each stimulus had a duration of 2.5 min and was presented sequentially twice, first at 4.8 Hz, then 16 Hz, and finally 40 Hz, followed by a presentation at 40 Hz, then 16 Hz, and finally 4.8 Hz, resulting in a total duration of 15 min.

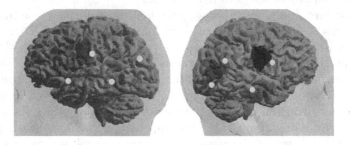

Fig. 1. NIRS optodes for left and right hemispheres. Sources are red and detectors yellow. Figure reproduced from [13] (Color figure online).

2.3 Extraction of Heart Signal from NIRS

The acquired raw signals were interpolated to address detector saturation, and the intensity was converted to the optical density. Motion artifacts in the optical density signal were corrected using the Temporal Derivative Distribution Repair (TDDR) method [10]. To ensure the presence of cardiac pulsation/heart signals, the quality of the corrected optical density signals was evaluated using the Scalp Coupling Index (SCI) introduced in [21]. Subsequently, the signals were bandpass filtered between 1 and 2 Hz. These cutoff frequencies correspond to the normal ranges of heart rate for seven-year-old children estimated in [11] using the 1st and 99th percentiles. Therefore, we isolated the heart signal in each NIRS channel and normalized them by dividing each signal by its envelope computed using the Hilbert transform. Each of these heart signals comes from an NIRS channel with an effective sampling frequency of 7.8125 Hz, whereas the NIRSport device has a sampling rate of 62.5 Hz that is shared among all sources.

The eight sources used sequentially are turned on during the recording. As each source contributes to four or six NIRS channels (2-3 source-detector pairs per wavelength), the illumination sequence of the sources follows an ascending order from source number 1 to number 8. The data points corresponding to a source were originally delayed $1/7.8125 = 0.128s$ relative to those from the previously activated source. However, the NIRSport device stores all data points from one illumination sequence on a single timestamp. We have 20 source-detector pairs and 2 wavelengths; therefore, we have 40 data samples that align in a straight line at each timestamp. Because cardiac pulsation is a systemic response, the heart signal is present in each NIRS channel. The correct time offset can be applied to each data sample from each source according to the illumination sequence to obtain a signal. We generated the final heart signal with a recovered sampling frequency of 62.5 Hz by averaging the data points at each timestamp and smoothing the waveform with a Savitzky-Golay filter with a 15-point window length.

2.4 Preprocessing

After the extraction of HR signals from NIRS, we focused on the analysis of HRV. The first step in quantifying HRV is to calculate the distances between consecutive peaks in the HR signal. When normal peaks are selectively considered by discarding those with abnormal measurements, the resulting intervals are known as Normal-to-Normal Intervals (NNI), as follows:

$$NNI_j = R_{j+1} - R_j \quad \text{for} \quad 0 \leq j \leq n-1 \tag{1}$$

where NNI_j denotes the NNI value at sample j, and R_j and R_{j+1} represent two consecutive peaks, with n denoting the total number of peaks. The first step of the automated process was to derive an estimated threshold from the time-varying distribution of the NNI series. The quartile deviation of the 90 surrounding beats for each heartbeat was computed to determine this threshold and then multiplied by a factor of 5.2. Assuming a normal distribution of the

NNI series, this amplified range encompasses 99.95% of all beats. This approach ensures the accurate detection of outliers and ectopic beats across a wide range of scenarios and effectively eliminates them from the signal. Different parameters were then computed to describe the information contained in the NNI. These values were obtained from time and frequency domains, in addition to non-linear measurements widely used in the field [1], to enhance the robustness of the procedure. This resulted in a total number of 31 parameters for each subject; however, a dimensionality reduction based on Principal Component Analysis (PCA) was performed. This technique projects data from its original space to a new space of lower dimensionality, where the eigenvectors define the direction of the axes and the eigenvalues derive the informativeness of each component. The mathematical expression for PCA involves determining the eigenvectors and eigenvalues of the data covariance matrix. Given a data matrix $\mathbf{X}$, where each column represents a different variable and each row represents a different observation, the covariance matrix σ is calculated as follows:

$$\Sigma = \frac{1}{n-1}\left((\mathbf{X} - \bar{\mathbf{x}})^T(\mathbf{X} - \bar{\mathbf{x}})\right) \tag{2}$$

where $\bar{\mathbf{x}}$ is the mean of vector $\mathbf{x}$: $\bar{\mathbf{x}} = \frac{1}{n}\sum_{i=1}^{n} x_i$, and each value of the vector represents the sample mean of a feature in the dataset. Thus, a new subset of 10 principal components was computed, but only the number of components that explained the 90% of the variance was used for subsequent stages of the pipeline.

2.5 Classification and Explainability

The resulting components were used to train a linear Support Vector Machine (SVM) classifier. A 5-fold cross-validation scheme was used to guarantee independence between the training and test subsets. Metrics derived from the confusion matrix were used to evaluate the system performance. Although high discrimination ability is desirable, it is also extremely important that the results can be interpretable to reveal the relationship between the inputs and outputs of a classification system. To do so, we used the SHapley Additive exPlanations (SHAP) method, which is a concept from cooperative game theory [15]. The Shapley value provides a consistent and locally accurate attribution approach for explaining the output of any machine learning model. Specifically, SHAP allows us to assess how a model's decision is influenced by the different features used during the training. This information is extremely relevant for understanding how a model works, in addition to identify the importance of each input variable.

We determined the relationship between the model derived from HRV features and behavioral data obtained during the database acquisition. This procedure was performed iteratively for each single behavioral variable. To do so, a 1D K-means clustering technique [23] was used to divide the cohort of patients into two different groups (controls and DD) based only on the behavioral variable under study. Next, the model was trained again, but not with the actual labels (the ones provided by clinicians), but with the new labels provided by this non-supervised process. The idea behind this procedure is that if the model replicates the labels extracted only from the behavioral data, there is a clear relationship between those variables and HRV features. Mathematically, the goal of the algorithm is to minimize the sum of the squared distances between the data points and the centroid of their assigned cluster. The objective function to minimize is the sum of the squared distances as follows:

$$J = \sum_{i=1}^{K} \sum_{j=1}^{N_i} \left\| x_j^{(i)} - \mu_i \right\|^2 \tag{3}$$

where K is the number of clusters, N_i is the number of data points in cluster i, $x_j^{(i)}$ is the j-th data point in cluster i and μ_i is the centroid of cluster i.

We adopted a non-parametric permutation test approach, as described in [14], to evaluate the statistical significance of the results. This technique involves shuffling the labels associated with each HR signal before classification. This process was iterated 10,000 times to construct an empirical accuracy distribution. The probability of a specific accuracy was obtained by comparing the resulting scores when the classifier was trained with correct labels and the empirical distribution. This probability is summarized by the p-value, as shown in Eq. 4.

$$p = \frac{n+1}{N+1} \tag{4}$$

where n represents the number of instances where the achieved precision exceeds the true precision, and N indicates the total number of permutations used to create the empirical distribution. A result is considered to be statistically significant if it falls below the predefined significance threshold, typically set at $p = 0.05$.

Table 1. Performance obtained for the different auditory stimuli. The baseline refers to modality in which no feature extraction was applied.

CTL *vs* DD	Bal Acc (%)	Sens (%)	Spec (%)	Prec (%)	AUC	F1-score (%)
			4.8 Hz stimulus			
Baseline	66.97±8.63	62.38±18.83	71.57±10.12	42.62±10.11	0.74±0.08	49.54 ±11.17
PCA	**72.21±6.36**	**70.95±8.30**	**73.48±6.11**	**47.65±6.70**	**0.78±0.04**	**56.88 ±6.98**
			16 Hz stimulus			
Baseline	71.40±9.73	71.43±15.65	71.38±8.43	46.03±8.05	0.78±0.10	55.60±9.95
PCA	**71.83±10.56**	**74.29±16.66**	69.38±10.13	45.65±9.06	**0.79±0.11**	**56.08±10.84**
			40 Hz stimulus			
Baseline	61.33±11.50	59.05±18.47	63.62±7.87	35.18±9.48	0.66±0.10	43.87±12.06
PCA	**67.81±7.33**	**68.10±13.43**	**63.71±6.77**	**38.61±5.49**	**0.71±0.10**	**48.96±6.91**

3   Results

Initially, we evaluated the ability of the classification framework to distinguish between CTL and DD patients. Our baseline approach uses the input features of different domains computed during the preprocessing of HRV signals. Once standardized and entered into an SVM classifier, the performance was evaluated for stimuli at three different frequencies: 4.8, 16, and 40 Hz. For the first one, we obtained an accuracy of 66.97%, in addition to an AUC of 0.74. These results changed when referring to the other stimuli, leading to an AUC of 0.78 and 0.66 for 16- and 40-Hz stimuli, respectively. Using PCA to reduce the dimensionality of the input features led to a gradual increase in performance in all cases, as shown in Table 1. These results demonstrate that data dimensionality plays a crucial role in the development of intelligent systems, especially when the number of samples and features is similar. Figure 2 represents the ROC curves for the three stimuli, demonstrating a similar performance for the 4.8- and 16-Hz stimuli and a slight decrease in the AUC for the 40-Hz stimulus. It should be noted that in all cases, the dimensionality reduction performed by PCA increased the performance. However, this improvement is particularly evident at 4.8- and 40-Hz stimuli.

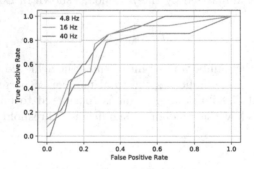

Fig. 2. ROC curves obtained for the three stimuli. The performance is similar for low frequencies (4.8 and 16 Hz), whereas it decays for the 40 Hz stimulus.

Figure 3 shows a violin representation of the most relevant SHAP values for the 4.8 Hz stimulus in the evaluation of three behavioral variables: RF_6, RV_7 and FL_7. These variables were selected because they are extremely relevant in the diagnosis of DD. As shown in Fig. 3, some HRV features are extremely important for the evaluation of these three variables. In terms of frequency-domain features, the power of very low frequency bands (VLF) and the entire frequency range have a positive and negative influence on the model output for the three scenarios evaluated. Moreover, variables such as CSI and, especially, SD2, also strongly influence the explainability of the model. With reference to the 16 Hz scenario, the PNNI20 feature has high importance in the first two scenarios, whereas the triangular index (in its regular and normalized version) is related to the first and third variables. The aforementioned variables are also important in the 16 Hz scenario. The TINN is just a normalized version of the TI, and the CVI is related to the SD2. Therefore, the PNNI20 is the only new variable that is revealed as important with the 16-Hz stimulus. The study of the 40-Hz stimulus leads to very similar results, with the number of NNIs greater than 20/50 ms and the minimum heart rate as the relevant features.

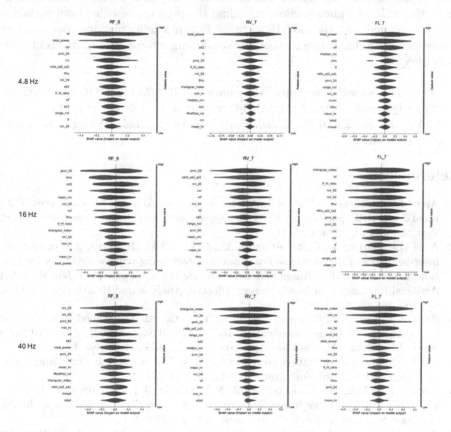

Fig. 3. SHAP values obtained for the three different stimuli (4.8, 16 and 40 Hz) in the evaluation of the relationship between HRV features and four behavioral variables: the reading of monosyllabic and disyllabic words in addition to pseudowords, and the reading speed.

4   Conclusions and Future Work

In this study, we propose a tool for detecting developmental dyslexia by extracting heart rate variability from NIRS signals. The first major contribution of this work is the novelty of studying heart rate without the use of electrocardiogram signals. This paves the way for several clinical studies in which ECG equipment is not available, demonstrating that heart information accessible through other techniques such as NIRS is highly valuable. Our second contribution is derived from the psychological implications of the results. The existence of meaningful patterns of information in HRV signals associated with dyslexia provides valuable insights for developing more effective diagnostic and therapeutic strategies. Finally, the explanatory nature of our framework yields a deeper understanding of the evaluated phenomenon, revealing the presence of behavioral variables highly correlated with the model's features. Future studies may improve this line of research as an innovative method for combining information in different data modalities.

Funding. The research was supported by projects PID2022-137451OB-I00, PID2022-137629OA-I00, and PID2022-137461NB-C32 funded by MICIU/AEI/10.13039/501 100011033 and by "ERDF/EU", and NextGenerationEU fund through "Margarita Salas" grant to JEA.

References

1. Arco, J.E., Gallego-Molina, N.J., Ortiz, A., Arroyo-Alvis, K., López-Pérez, P.J.: Identifying HRV patterns in ECG signals as early markers of dementia. Expert Syst. Appl. **243**, 122934 (2024)
2. Arco, J.E., Ortiz, A., Castillo-Barnes, D., Górriz, J.M., Ramírez, J.: Quantifying inter-hemispheric differences in Parkinson's disease using siamese networks. In: Ferrández Vicente, J.M., Álvarez-Sánchez, J.R., de la Paz López, F., Adeli, H. (eds.) Artificial Intelligence in Neuroscience: Affective Analysis and Health Applications, pp. 156–165 (2022)
3. Arco, J.E., Ortiz, A., Ramírez, J., Zhang, Y.D., Górriz, J.M.: Tiled sparse coding in eigenspaces for image classification. Int. J. Neural Syst. **32**(03), 2250007 (2022)
4. Arco, J.E., Ortiz, A., Castillo-Barnes, D., Górriz, J.M., Ramírez, J.: Ensembling shallow Siamese architectures to assess functional asymmetry in Alzheimer's disease progression. Appl. Soft Comput. **134**, 109991 (2023)
5. Arco, J.E., Ortiz, A., Gallego-Molina, N.J., Górriz, J.M., Ramírez, J.: Enhancing multimodal patterns in neuroimaging by Siamese neural networks with self-attention mechanism. Int. J. Neural Syst. **33**(4), 2350019 (2023)
6. Arco, J.E., et al.: Probabilistic combination of non-linear eigenprojections for ensemble classification. IEEE Trans. Emerg. Top. Comput. Intell. **7**, 1–11 (2022)
7. Arco, J.E., Ramírez, J., Puntonet, C.G., Górriz, J.M., Ruz, M.: Improving short-term prediction from MCI to AD by applying Searchlight analysis. In: 2016 IEEE 13th International Symposium on Biomedical Imaging (ISBI), pp. 10–13 (2016)
8. De Vos, A., Vanvooren, S., Vanderauwera, J., Ghesqui ère, P., Wouters, J.: A longitudinal study investigating neural processing of speech envelope modulation rates in children with (a family risk for) dyslexia. Cortex **93**, 206–219 (2017)
9. Dutt, S.: Comparison of classification methods used in machine learning for dysgraphia identification. Turk. J. Comput. Math. Educ. (Turcomat) **12**, 1886–1891 (2021)
10. Fishburn, F.A., Ludlum, R.S., Vaidya, C.J., Medvedev, A.V.: Temporal derivative distribution repair (TDDR): a motion correction method for FNIRS. Neuroimage **184**, 171–179 (2019)

11. Fleming, S., et al.: Normal ranges of heart rate and respiratory rate in children from birth to 18 years of age: a systematic review of observational studies. Lancet **377**(9770), 1011–1018 (2011)
12. Frattola, A., et al.: Time and frequency domain estimates of spontaneous baroreflex sensitivity provide early detection of autonomic dysfunction in diabetes mellitus. Diabetologia **40**, 1470–1475 (1997)
13. Gallego-Molina, N.J., Ortiz, A., Martínez-Murcia, F.J., Rodríguez-Rodríguez, I., Luque, J.L.: Assessing functional brain network dynamics in dyslexia from FNIRS data. Int. J. Neural Syst. **33**(04), 2350017 (2023)
14. Golland, P., Fischl, B.: Permutation tests for classification: towards statistical significance in image-based studies. In: Taylor, C., Noble, J.A. (eds.) IPMI 2003. LNCS, vol. 2732, pp. 330–341. Springer, Heidelberg (2003). https://doi.org/10.1007/978-3-540-45087-0_28
15. Graham, G., Csicsery, N., Stasiowski, E., Thouvenin, G., Mather, W.: Genome-scale transcriptional dynamics and environmental biosensing. Proc. Natl. Acad. Sci. **117**, 3301–3306 (2020)
16. Górriz, J., et al.: Computational approaches to explainable artificial intelligence: advances in theory, applications and trends. Inf. Fus. **100**, 101945 (2023)
17. Górriz, J.M., et al.: Artificial intelligence within the interplay between natural and artificial computation: advances in data science, trends and applications. Neurocomputing **410**, 237–270 (2020)
18. Jiménez-Mesa, C., Arco, J.E., Valentí-Soler, M., et al.: Using explainable artificial intelligence in the clock drawing test to reveal the cognitive impairment pattern. Int. J. Neural Syst. **33**(04), 2350015 (2023)
19. Lotufo, P., Valiengo, L., Benseñor, I., Brunoni, A.: A systematic review and meta-analysis of heart rate variability in epilepsy and antiepileptic drugs. Epilepsia **53**, 272–282 (2012)
20. Ortiz, A., Martinez-Murcia, F.J., Luque, J.L., Giménez, A., Morales-Ortega, R., Ortega, J.: Dyslexia diagnosis by EEG temporal and spectral descriptors: an anomaly detection approach. Int. J. Neural Syst. **30**(07), 2050029 (2020)
21. Pollonini, L., Olds, C., Abaya, H., Bortfeld, H., Beauchamp, M.S., Oghalai, J.S.: Auditory cortex activation to natural speech and simulated cochlear implant speech measured with functional near-infrared spectroscopy. Hear. Res. **309**, 84–93 (2014)
22. Sieciński, S., Kostka, P., Tkacz, E.: Heart rate variability analysis on electrocardiograms, seismocardiograms and gyrocardiograms on healthy volunteers. Sensors **20**, 4522 (2020)
23. Wu, X.: Optimal quantization by matrix searching. J. Algorithms **12**(4), 663–673 (1991)

Diagnosis of Parkinson Disease from EEG Signals Using a CNN-LSTM Model and Explainable AI

Mohammad Bdaqli[1] , Afshin Shoeibi[2]([envelope]) , Parisa Moridian[2] ,
Delaram Sadeghi[2] , Mozhde Firoozi Pouyani[1] , Ahmad Shalbaf[3] ,
and Juan M. Gorriz[2]

[1] Faculty of Electrical Engineering, K. N. Toosi University of Technology,
Tehran, Iran
[2] Data Science and Computational Intelligence Institute, University of Granada,
Granada, Spain
afshin.shoeibi@gmail.com
[3] Department of Biomedical Engineering and Medical Physics, School of Medicine,
Shahid Beheshti University of Medical Sciences, Tehran, Iran

Abstract. Parkinson's disease (PD), a complex and debilitating neurological disorder, often leads to progressive cognitive decline, including mild cognitive impairment (MCI) and dementia. Over the years, various methods have been developed to diagnose PD, with neuroimaging modalities, particularly electroencephalogram (EEG) recording, gaining significant traction among specialist doctors. This article presents a novel PD detection method employing deep learning (DL) techniques to analyze EEG signals. The proposed method utilizes the UC San Diego (UCSD) resting-state EEG dataset and involves a meticulous preprocessing phase encompassing filtering, channel selection, and EEG signal windowing. Subsequently, a novel 1D CNN-LSTM architecture is introduced for extracting salient features from EEG signals. In the classification stage, three algorithms, namely Softmax, support vector machine (SVM), and decision tree (DT), are employed and their performances compared. To assess the robustness of the classification models, k-fold cross-validation with k=10 is implemented. The results demonstrate that the SVM algorithm exhibits superior performance, achieving an impressive 99.51% accuracy for binary classification and 99.75% accuracy for multi-class classification tasks. To gain insights into the model's decision-making process and enhance interpretability, t-distributed Stochastic Neighbor Embedding (t-SNE) is utilized as an explainable artificial intelligence (XAI) method in the post-processing stage.

Keywords: Parkinson Disease · Diagnosis · EEG · CNN-CNN · Explainable Artificial Intelligence

J. M. Ferrández Vicente et al. (Eds.): IWINAC 2024, LNCS 14674, pp. 128–138, 2024.
https://doi.org/10.1007/978-3-031-61140-7_13

1   Introduction

Parkinson's disease (PD) is recognized as a significant progressive disorder of the nervous system that poses serious health risks to individuals worldwide [25]. This condition arises when there is an insufficient production of dopamine, a crucial chemical, in the nerve cells of the brain. The lack of dopamine production in these brain cells leads to a range of symptoms affecting both the motor and non-motor systems [5,12,18]. Motor problems commonly observed in PD patients include tremors, Bradykinesia, stiffness, and postural instability [5,12,25]. Additionally, non-motor symptoms, such as cognitive impairment, mood disorders, and autonomic dysfunction, are also prevalent in these patients [5,12]. While the exact cause of PD remains unclear, experts believe that a combination of genetic and environmental factors contribute significantly to the development of this disease [2,17,19,26].

Currently, there is no definitive test available for diagnosing PD, and in most cases, the expertise of neurologists and movement disorder specialists is required for accurate diagnosis [2,17,19,26]. However, several methods have been proposed for diagnosing PD, including medical history and physical examination, neurological evaluation, neuroimaging modalities, DaTscan, blood tests, and observation of the response to medication [12,18]. Among these methods, neuroimaging modalities, encompassing both functional and structural techniques, are widely favored by specialist doctors for the diagnosis of PD [5,12,18,25]. As PD is a brain disorder, researchers have demonstrated that functional neuroimaging modalities, particularly EEG signals, have shown promising results as a cost-effective tool for diagnosing this disease. EEG recording, as a non-invasive technique, provides valuable insights into brain function during PD [1,8,23].

However, the diagnosis of PD from EEG signals remains challenging for specialist doctors due to factors such as lack of specificity, limited spatial resolution, the need for expert interpretation, variability in results, and the presence of various noises. To address this challenge, researchers have conducted numerous studies in the field of computer-aided diagnosis systems (CADS) based on AI, aiming to assist in the diagnosis of PD using EEG signals [17,19,26]. These studies have employed various machine learning and DL models, leading to successful outcomes. For instance, Yang et al. [25] proposed a PD detection method that integrates machine learning and deep learning techniques. Their approach involved preprocessing steps such as filtering and segmentation on the EEG signals. Handcrafted features, including mean frequency, relative power, sample entropy, and multi-scale entropy, were combined with features extracted from a 1D-CNN architecture. This method achieved an accuracy of 97.54%.

This paper presents a novel CADS for PD detection from EEG signals using a 1D CNN-LSTM architecture. The efficiency of the proposed method is demonstrated using the UCSD dataset [18]. The pre-processing steps, including noise removal, channel selection, and segmentation, are performed using the EEGLAB toolbox [3,4]. The proposed 1D CNN-LSTM architecture for feature extraction from EEG signals is a key contribution of this work. Furthermore, various classification algorithms, such as Softmax [15], SVM [7], and DT [22], are tested and their results are compared in the subsequent step. Additionally, a post-processing stage is introduced in this paper, which aims to visualize the extracted feature space of the proposed deep learning model using the t-SNE technique [6]. The remaining sections of the article are organized as follows: Sect. 2 describes the proposed PD detection method and provides detailed steps. Statistical metrics and the evaluation method employed in this study are presented in another section. The results of the proposed method and Sect. 4 are reported, followed by a discussion, conclusion, and future work in Sect. 5.

2   Proposed Method

This section provides detailed information regarding the steps of the CADS based on the 1D CNN-LSTM architecture for PD diagnosis using EEG signals. The experiments in this section are conducted using the UCSD dataset [18]. In the initial step, pre-processing is performed, which involves noise removal, channel selection, and segmentation of the EEG signals. Next, the proposed 1D CNN-LSTM architecture is implemented to extract features from the EEG signals. Subsequently, various algorithms are utilized for feature classification. Finally, a post-processing step employing the t-SNE technique is employed to visualize the feature space. The block diagram in Fig. 1 provides a summary of the proposed method.

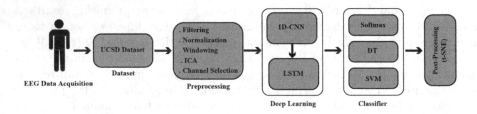

Fig. 1. The block diagram of proposed method.

2.1   Dataset

The simulations were performed using the UCSD resting-state EEG dataset [4]. This dataset includes EEG recordings from both healthy control (HC) subjects and individuals with Parkinson's disease (PD). The HC group comprises 16 people, and the PD group consists of 15 subjects [18]. EEG data from the HC subjects were collected once, while EEG recordings from PD patients were obtained on two separate days: one while they were taking medication and one while they were not [18]. All PD patients were diagnosed by a movement disorder specialist and are in the mild to moderate stages of the disease according to the Hoehn and Yahr scale [18]. The EEG signals were recorded using the

10–20 standard and the 40-channel BioSemi ActiveTwo system with a sampling frequency of 512 Hz. The average length of EEG recordings for each subject was 3.33 ± 0.32 min [18]. Figures 2 and 3 displays an example of EEG signals for HC and PD classes before and after drug injection.

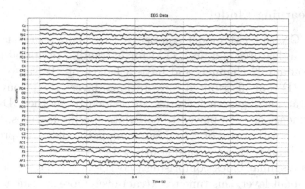

Fig. 2. EEG signal from a HC individual.

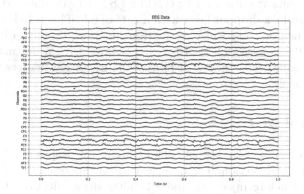

Fig. 3. EEG signal from an individual with PD.

2.2 Preprocessing

In this section, the pre-processing steps for the UCSD EEG dataset are presented. To pre-process the EEG signals, we utilized the EEGLAB toolbox [3,4] within the Matlab 2022b environment. Initially, the EEG signals were processed using the EEGLAB toolbox, resulting in the removal of 8 channels containing redundant information. Subsequently, a high-pass filter with a frequency of 0.5 Hz was applied to the EEG signals to eliminate artifacts from the data. The ICA method [3,4], available in EEGLAB, was employed to address issues such as city electricity noise, eye blinking, muscle interference, and bad channels. Following this, the EEG signals were segmented into 1-second intervals, as recommended in the references [14], to prepare them for use in the DL architecture.

2.3   Deep Learning Model

The proposed CNN-LSTM model comprises two main parts: a 1D-CNN for extracting spatial features and an LSTM for extracting temporal features. The EEG signals contain 32 channels and have a length of 512 samples, which are then fed into a 1D time distributed convolutional layer (1D-TConv) with 64 filters for the extraction of generic features. Subsequently, another 1D-TConv layer with similar dimensions is employed to calculate specific features, followed by a max-pooling layer with a size of 2 to down-sample the data. To prevent overfitting, a dropout layer with a 0.5 rate is utilized. The process is repeated in the next step, with a similar block comprising two 1D-TConv layers, a max-pooling layer, and a dropout layer, this time to extract even more specific features, using ReLU activation function for the 1D-TConv layers.

Recent research indicates that LSTM models are more effective in feature extraction from EEG signals compared to other RNN architectures [23–26]. Thus, the output features from the 1D-CNN architecture are fed into an LSTM layer with 140 units via a flatten layer. The LSTM layer then extracts spatial features, followed by a dropout layer with a rate of 0.5. This is followed by an FC layer with 140 neurons and ReLU activation function. Finally, a dropout layer with a rate of 0.5 is used, followed by an FC layer with a Softmax activation function for classification. Table 1 displayed the hyper parameters for proposed CNN-LSTM model.

3   Statistical Metrics

In this section, we present the statistical metrics for the proposed 1D CNN-LSTM architecture for PD detection. The dataset used in this research comprises three classes: HC, PD before injection, and PD after drug injection. Consequently, the evaluation parameters are calculated for a 3-class problem as well as several binary problems. In this work, we report the evaluation parameters, including accuracy (Acc), f1-score (F1), recall (Rec), and precision (Prec) [10,11,20,21], for the validation data. Additionally, we utilized the k-fold cross-validation method with k=10 (Tables 2 to 4).

4   Experiment Results

This section presents the results of the proposed method for diagnosing PD from EEG signals. All simulations were conducted using a hardware setup with 32 GB RAM, a Core i7 CPU, and NVidia GeForce 3090. Initially, the EEGLAB toolbox [3,4] was utilized in the Matlab 2022b environment to pre-process the UCSD

Table 1. Details for proposed 1D CNN-LSTM model.

Layers	Details	Filters	Kernel Size	Stride	Activation
1	Input	–	–	–	–
2	1D-TConv	64	3	1	ReLU
3	1D-TConv	64	3	1	ReLU
4	Max-Pooling	–	2	1	–
5	Dropout	–	–	–	Rate=0.5
6	1D-TConv	64	3	1	ReLU
7	1D-TConv	64	3	1	ReLU
8	Max-Pooling	–	2	1	–
9	Dropout	–	–	–	Rate=0.5
10	Flatten	–	–	–	–
11	LSTM	1	140	–	–
12	Dropout	–	–	–	Rate=0.5
13	Dense	140	–	–	ReLU
14	Dropout	–	–	–	Rate=0.5
15	Dense	2 or 3	–	–	Softmax

Table 2. Results multi-class classification problem in PD detection.

Classifier Method	Acc	Prec	Rec	F1
Softmax	99.497 (0.030)	99.416 (0.031)	99.851 (0.028)	99.498 (0.029)
SVM	99.514 (0.071)	99.514 (0.071)	99.514 (0.687)	99.514 (0.071)
DT	99.441 (0.034)	99.357 (0.028)	99.548 (0.027)	99.453 (0.033)

Table 3. Results HC-PDF classification problem in PD detection.

Classifier Method	Acc	Prec	Rec	F1
Softmax	99.687 (0.223)	99.676 (0.307)	99.707 (0.176)	99.691 (0.221)
SVM	99.752 (0.255)	99.819 (0.251)	99.689 (0.281)	99.754 (0.257)
DT	99.670 (0.241)	99.659 (0.293)	99.691 (0.248)	99.675 (0.239)

Table 4. Results HC-PDO classification problem in PD detection.

Classifier Method	Acc	Prec	Rec	F1
Softmax	99.324 (1.114)	99.370 (0.873)	99.279 (1.329)	99.324 (1.096)
SVM	99.422 (1.040)	99.426 (0.987)	99.426 (1.056)	99.426 (1.017)
DT	99.142 (1.321)	99.144 (1.269)	99.144 (1.336)	99.144 (1.289)

dataset [18]. Subsequently, the 1D CNN-LSTM architecture, classification algorithms, t-SNE method [6], and evaluation parameters were implemented using TensorFlow 2, Keras, and Scikit-learn toolboxes [16] in the Python environment. As mentioned earlier, the UCSD dataset [18] comprises HC, PDO, and PDF classes. The study addresses both a multi-class problem involving HC-PDF-PDO and two binary problems: HC-PDO and HC-PDF. The results of the proposed method for the various classification problems are presented in Tables 2 to 4.

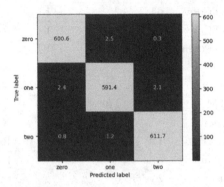

Fig. 4. Displaying confusion matrices for multi-class problem.

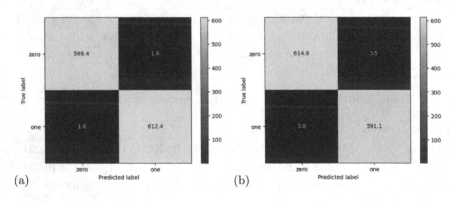

Fig. 5. Displaying confusion matrices for HC-PDF and HC-PDO problems problems: a) HC-PDF, b) HC-PDO.

According to Table 2 through 4, the Support Vector Machine (SVM) algorithm has outperformed other methods in multi-class classification. Additionally,
the SVM classification algorithm has shown promising results for HC-PDF and
HC-PDO classification problems compared to other methods. Figures 4 and 5
displays confusion matrices for SVM method for both multi-class and binary
classification problems. Based on the Figures 4 and 5, it can be seen that the
SVM method has been successful in diagnosing PD for multi-class and binary
classification problems.

In Fig. 6, the ROC curves for the proposed architecture are displayed for
binary and multiclass classification problems. As can be seen, the 1D CNN-
LSTM architecture has achieved successful results in PD diagnosis across various classification problems. Based on Figs. 6, the ROC curves for binary and
multi-class classification problems show 100%. DL models involve intricate mathematical operations that are challenging for humans to scrutinize, a particularly
significant issue when these networks are employed in medical contexts [6]. In
response to this challenge, XAI techniques have been developed to assist specialist doctors in interpreting and making accurate decisions about diseases [6]. In
this section, the t-SNE technique is utilized as one of the prominent XAI methods during post-processing, representing another novelty aspect of this paper.
Figure 7 displays the output of t-SNE for binary and multi-class classification
problems in PD diagnosis.

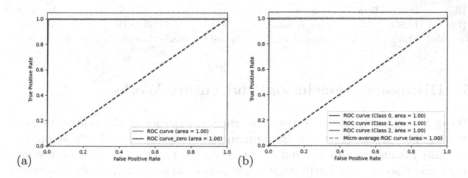

Fig. 6. Illustrating the ROC curves for proposed method: a) binary and b) multi-class
problem.

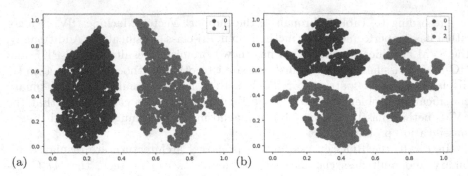

Fig. 7. t-SNE method as a post-processing step for the proposed model: a) binary classification, b) multi-class classification.

Table 5. A Comparison of the results presented in this article with those of other related studies.

Ref	Dataset	Preprocessing	Classifier	ACC (%)
[25]	Clinical	Feature Extraction	CNN	Acc=97.54
[5]	Iowa	PSD, DA	Bi-LSTM	Acc=97.92
[12]	Clinical	Different Methods	MVSAE	Acc=98.95
[18]	UCSD	CWT, Scalogram	2D-CNN	Acc=99.6
[15]	Clinical	Segmentation, Filtering	CNN	Acc=88.25
[17]	UNM, UCSD	Basic Preprocessing	2D-CNN	Acc=97.90
[2]	Different Datasets	Signal Decomposition	1D-CRNN-ELM	Acc=83.2
[14]	UCSD	Gabor Transform	DLB-LSTM	Acc=99.6
Our Work	UCSD	Normalization, ICA, Channel Selection	CNN-LSTM with SVM	Acc=99.75

5   Discussion, Conclusion, and Future Works

PD is a progressive, degenerative, and chronic disorder of the central nervous system that primarily affects the human motor system [5,25]. Its symptoms typically manifest gradually, and as the condition progresses, non-motor symptoms may also emerge. Early-stage symptoms include tremors, body movement stiffness, reduced range of motion, and difficulty walking [2,17,26]. Additionally, cognitive and behavioral symptoms such as depression, anxiety, and apathy can also occur. Furthermore, advanced stages of PD have been linked to other conditions, including dementia.

While there is no definitive method for diagnosing PD, various approaches have been explored, with EEG signals being particularly favored by specialists [5,12,18,25]. This paper introduces an enhanced method for detecting PD from EEG signals using a proposed 1D CNN-LSTM network and t-SNE. The primary novelties of this research in the feature extraction and post-processing methods. The 1D CNN-LSTM architecture, utilized for PD diagnosis for the first time, has yielded significant results in various classification problems. Additionally, t-SNE [6], employed as an XAI technique in the post-processing phase, represents a novel approach to detecting PD from EEG signals. In Table 5, we present the results of PD diagnosis papers and compare them with our proposed method. As observed, our proposed method in this paper has demonstrated significant results compared to other research. The CADS presented in this paper can serve as an effective tool to aid specialist doctors in early diagnosing PD from EEG signals in the future. Recently, researchers have used attention mechanism techniques in conjunction with CNN-RNN architectures to enhance the accuracy of diagnosis for various medical applications, yielding promising results. For future work, we can explore the use of CNN-RNN-attention mechanism architectures [13] to enhance PD diagnosis from EEG signals. Moreover, the application of transformer architectures [9] and attention-graph learning [24] can be considered for further research.

Acknowledgments. This research is part of the PID2022-137451OB-I00 project funded by the CIN/AEI/10.13039/501100011033 and by FSE+.

References

1. Arasteh, E., Mahdizadeh, A., Mirian, M.S., Lee, S., McKeown, M.J.: Deep transfer learning for Parkinson's disease monitoring by image-based representation of resting-state EEG using directional connectivity. Algorithms **15**(1), 5 (2021)
2. Dar, M.N., Akram, M.U., Yuvaraj, R., Khawaja, S.G., Murugappan, M.: EEG-based emotion charting for Parkinson's disease patients using convolutional recurrent neural networks and cross dataset learning. Comput. Biol. Med. **144**, 105327 (2022)
3. Delorme, A., Makeig, S.: EEGLAB: an open source toolbox for analysis of single-trial EEG dynamics including independent component analysis. J. Neurosci. Methods **134**(1), 9–21 (2004)
4. Delorme, A., et al.: EEGLAB, SIFT, NFT, BCILAB, and ERICA: new tools for advanced EEG processing. Comput. Intell. Neurosci. **2011**, 10–10 (2011)
5. Göker, H.: Automatic detection of Parkinson's disease from power spectral density of electroencephalography (EEG) signals using deep learning model. Phys. Eng. Sci. Med., 1–12 (2023)
6. Górriz, J.M., et al.: Computational approaches to explainable artificial intelligence: advances in theory, applications and trends. Inf. Fus. **100**, 101945 (2023)
7. Hearst, M.A., Dumais, S.T., Osuna, E., Platt, J., Scholkopf, B.: Support vector machines. IEEE Intell. Syst. Appl. **13**(4), 18–28 (1998)
8. Loh, H.W., et al.: GaborPDNet: Gabor transformation and deep neural network for Parkinson's disease detection using EEG signals. Electronics **10**(14), 1740 (2021)
9. Martín-Gutiérrez, D., Hernández-Peñaloza, G., Hernández, A.B., Lozano-Diez, A., Álvarez, F.: A deep learning approach for robust detection of bots in twitter using transformers. IEEE Access **9**, 54591–54601 (2021)
10. Mohammadpoor, M., Shoeibi, A., Shojaee, H., et al.: A hierarchical classification method for breast tumor detection. Iranian Journal of Medical Physics/Majallah-I Fīzīk-I Pizishkī-i Irān **13**(4) (2016)
11. Moridian, P., et al.: Automatic diagnosis of sleep apnea from biomedical signals using artificial intelligence techniques: methods, challenges, and future works. Wiley Interdisc. Rev.: Data Min. Knowl. Disc. **12**(6), e1478 (2022)

12. Nagasubramanian, G., Sankayya, M., Al-Turjman, F., Tsaramirsis, G.: Parkinson data analysis and prediction system using multi-variant stacked auto encoder. IEEE Access **8**, 127004–127013 (2020)

13. Niu, Z., Zhong, G., Yu, H.: A review on the attention mechanism of deep learning. Neurocomputing **452**, 48–62 (2021)

14. Obayya, M., Saeed, M.K., Maashi, M., Alotaibi, S.S., Salama, A.S., Hamza, M.A.: A novel automated Parkinson's disease identification approach using deep learning and EEG. PeerJ Comput. Sci. **9**, e1663 (2023)

15. Oh, S.L., et al.: A deep learning approach for Parkinson's disease diagnosis from EEG signals. Neural Comput. Appl. **32**, 10927–10933 (2020)

16. Pang, B., Nijkamp, E., Wu, Y.N.: Deep learning with tensorflow: a review. J. Educ. Behav. Stat. **45**(2), 227–248 (2020)

17. Rizvi, S.Q.A., Wang, G., Khan, A., Hasan, M.K., Ghazal, T.M., Khan, A.U.R.: Classifying Parkinson's disease using resting state electroencephalogram signals and u en-pdnet. IEEE Access (2023)

18. Shaban, M., Amara, A.W.: Resting-state electroencephalography based deep-learning for the detection of Parkinson's disease. PLoS ONE **17**(2), e0263159 (2022)

19. Shah, D., Gopan K, G., Sinha, N.: An investigation of the multi-dimensional (1d vs. 2d vs. 3d) analyses of EEG signals using traditional methods and deep learning-based methods. Front. Signal Process. **2**, 936790 (2022)

20. Shoeibi, A., et al.: Automatic diagnosis of schizophrenia and attention deficit hyperactivity disorder in RS-FMRI modality using convolutional autoencoder model and interval type-2 fuzzy regression. Cogn. Neurodyn. **17**(6), 1501–1523 (2023)

21. Shoeibi, A., Rezaei, M., Ghassemi, N., Namadchian, Z., Zare, A., Gorriz, J.M.: Automatic diagnosis of schizophrenia in EEG signals using functional connectivity features and CNN-LSTM model. In: International Work-Conference on the Interplay Between Natural and Artificial Computation, pp. 63–73. Springer (2022). https://doi.org/10.1007/978-3-031-06242-1_7

22. Song, Y.Y., Ying, L.: Decision tree methods: applications for classification and prediction. Shanghai Arch. Psychiatry **27**(2), 130 (2015)

23. Sugden, R.J., Diamandis, P.: Generalizable electroencephalographic classification of Parkinson's disease using deep learning. Inform. Med. Unlocked **42**, 101352 (2023)

24. Veličković, P., Cucurull, G., Casanova, A., Romero, A., Lio, P., Bengio, Y.: Graph attention networks. arXiv preprint arXiv:1710.10903 (2017)

25. Yang, C.Y., Huang, Y.Z.: Parkinson's disease classification using machine learning approaches and resting-state EEG. J. Med. Biol. Eng. **42**(2), 263–270 (2022)

26. Zhang, R., Jia, J., Zhang, R.: EEG analysis of Parkinson's disease using time-frequency analysis and deep learning. Biomed. Signal Process. Control **78**, 103883 (2022)

Early Diagnosis of Schizophrenia in EEG Signals Using One Dimensional Transformer Model

Afshin Shoeibi[1,2](✉) ⓘ, Mahboobeh Jafari[1] ⓘ, Delaram Sadeghi[1] ⓘ,
Roohallah Alizadehsani[3] ⓘ, Hamid Alinejad-Rokny[4] ⓘ, Amin Beheshti[5] ⓘ,
and Juan M. Gorriz[1] ⓘ

[1] Data Science and Computational Intelligence Institute, University of Granada,
Granada, Spain
afshin.shoeibi@gmail.com
[2] Internship in Health Data Analytics Program, AI-enabled Processes (AIP)
Research Centre, Macquarie University, Sydney, Australia
[3] Institute for Intelligent Systems Research and Innovation (IISRI),
Deakin University, Geelong, Australia
[4] UNSW BioMedical Machine Learning Lab, The Graduate School of Biomedical
Engineering, UNSW Sydney, Sydney, NSW 2052, Australia
[5] Data Science Lab, School of Computing, Macquarie University, Sydney,
NSW 2109, Australia

Abstract. Schizophrenia (SZ) is a complex mental disorder, hallmarked
by symptoms including delusions, hallucinations, disorganized speech,
cognitive impairments, and diminished motivation. Electroencephalography (EEG) recordings have become a critical tool for clinicians and
psychologists in diagnosing SZ. Nonetheless, interpreting EEG data to
diagnose SZ presents significant challenges for specialists, leading to
increased interest in leveraging artificial intelligence (AI) for early detection. This study introduces a novel approach for SZ detection from
EEG signals utilizing a transformer-based architecture. The methodology encompasses dataset selection, preprocessing, feature extraction, and
classification phases. The RepOD dataset was employed for all simulations. Preprocessing entails filtering, normalization, and segmenting into
time windows. Following this, a one-dimensional (1D) transformer architecture, incorporating various activation functions, is applied to extract
features from the preprocessed EEG signals. In the architecture's final
layer, the Softmax activation function is utilized for classifying the data.
The performance of the proposed model is assessed using a K-Fold cross-
validation strategy, with K set to 10. The proposed method achieved a
maximum accuracy of 97.62% in diagnosing schizophrenia (SZ), underscoring its potential efficacy in SZ diagnosis.

Keywords: Schizophrenia · Diagnosis · EEG Signals · Deep
Learning · Transformer

J. M. Ferrández Vicente et al. (Eds.): IWINAC 2024, LNCS 14674, pp. 139–149, 2024.
https://doi.org/10.1007/978-3-031-61140-7_14

1 Introduction

Schizophrenia (SZ) is one of the most common brain disorders that affect a person's thoughts, feelings, and behaviors [28]. About 20 million people worldwide have SZ, and they face various challenges in their daily activities [28]. The causes of SZ have not been discovered yet, but specialist doctors believe that a combination of genetic, chemical, and environmental factors play a role in the occurrence of this disease [27,28]. Some clinical research has shown that the structure and function of the brain cortex, as well as the connections of cortical regions, are changed in patients with SZ [1]. Symptoms of SZ, including hallucinations, delusions, lack of motivation, and lack of expression of emotions, typically appear from a young age [21]. SZ is more common in men than women, and people may develop long-term mental disabilities [27,28]. Clinical interviews, behavior observation, physical evaluations, DSM-5, and neuroimaging modalities are among the crucial methods of diagnosing SZ introduced by researchers and specialist doctors [22].

In recent years, neuroimaging modalities, including functional and structural methods, have been widely used in the diagnosis of SZ [22]. EEG is a non-invasive recording method that measures electrical fields in the brain [28]. This method is highly popular among specialist doctors and has been used in the diagnosis of brain disorders for about 90 years. EEG signals displayed nonlinear and chaotic behavior, which specialist doctors interpret experimentally [1,27,28]. EEG offers several advantages in the diagnosis of brain disorders, especially SZ, including non-invasiveness, portability, and high time and frequency resolution [22]. However, it also presents challenges such as different artifacts, lack of specificity, and limited spatial resolution [22]. Additionally, EEG recordings are long-term and have multiple channels, which can make interpretation difficult for specialist doctors and increase the risk of human error in correctly diagnosing SZ [22].

Researchers have shown that AI techniques are useful for improving and accelerating the process of diagnosing SZ from EEG signals [22,31]. In recent years, various conventional machine learning (ML) and deep learning (DL) techniques have been proposed for detecting SZ from EEG signals [22]. In the field of ML, feature extraction techniques from EEG signals include time, frequency, time-frequency, and nonlinear domains [2]. Some researchers have utilized characteristics of the time domain, such as statistical moments, in the diagnosis of SZ and have achieved favorable results [23]. Fast Fourier transform (FFT) is one of the most important feature extraction methods in the frequency domain [27]. Additionally, some researchers have utilized discrete wavelet transform (DWT) [14], empirical mode decomposition (EMD) [29], and short-time Fourier transform (STFT) [32] as time-frequency methods in SZ diagnosis research. Nonlinear features are crucial extraction methods in EEG signals and include entropies [25], fractal dimensions [25], synchronization likelihood [27], connectivity methods [25], etc.

DL networks are introduced to address the challenges of ML methods in various applications, particularly in medicine [3,11,13,26]. Feature learning, scalability, and hierarchical representation are some of the advantages of DL models compared to ML [11,26]. DL architectures can automatically extract important features from raw EEG data and are capable of processing and managing a large volume of EEG signals. Unlike ML methods, DL architectures can learn complex patterns and relationships from EEG data. Various DL models, such as 1D-CNNs [28], 2D-CNNs [24], RNNs [28], and CNN-RNNs [28], have been utilized to detect SZ from EEG signals. Furthermore, a new category of DL networks, known as attention mechanism models, has been recently introduced in medical applications, demonstrating high efficiency [16]. For instance, researchers in [7] have employed attention mechanism models in diagnosing SZ from EEG signals and have achieved significant results.

Compared to conventional DL methods, transformers have numerous advantages, including the attention mechanism, parallelization, handling of long-term dependencies, and scalability [22]. Additionally, their high performance in dealing with low input data is a crucial feature [22]. This paper proposes a transformer-based method for detecting SZ from EEG signals. Firstly, the proposed method was implemented using the RepOD dataset [27,28], and its EEG signals were preprocessed through normalization and windowing steps. Subsequently, a transformer architecture, along with various activation functions, was employed for feature extraction and classification from the EEG signals. This paper introduces a significant novelty in this field, as researchers have not previously utilized transformer models alongside various activation functions for diagnosing SZ. In the following, other parts of the paper are stated. The Sect. 2 introduces the proposed method based on transformers for detecting SZ. Section 3 presents the evaluation parameters. Section 4 reports the simulation details of the proposed method. Finally, the Sect. 5 presents the Conclusion, Discussion, and Future Works.

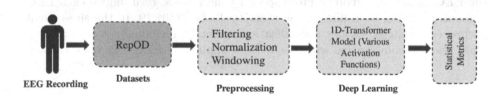

Fig. 1. The block diagram of proposed method.

2   Proposed Method

This section presents the details of the proposed method for SZ detection based on a transformer architecture. The block diagram, along with the steps of the proposed method, is shown in detail in Fig. 1. To demonstrate the effectiveness of the proposed method, the RepOD dataset [27,28] is utilized, which consists of two classes: HC and SZ, with 14 subjects available for each class. The EEG signals are preprocessed through normalization and windowing steps. Subsequently, a transformer architecture is tested, along with various activation functions, to extract features from the EEG signals. This section represents the most significant novelty of this paper. Finally, the Softmax activation function is employed for feature classification. The following sections provide further details regarding the steps of the proposed method.

2.1   Dataset

RepOD is a publicly available dataset for the diagnosis of SZ, which has been provided to researchers by [27,28]. This dataset consists of resting-state EEG signals categorized into two classes: SZ and HC. The EEG signals were recorded from 14 subjects with SZ, aged between 27.9 and 28.3 years [27,28]. Additionally, EEG signals were recorded from 14 HC subjects who shared the same age and gender characteristics as the SZ subjects [27,28]. The EEG signals in this dataset were sampled at a frequency of 250 Hz, and electrodes were placed on the scalp following the standard 10–20 system [27,28]. The researchers performed basic pre-processing steps on the EEG signals, including filtering and channel selection, resulting in the selection of 19 channels [27,28].

2.2   Preprocessing

The Preprocessing steps for the RepOD dataset [27,28] are discussed in this section. As mentioned in the previous section, initial preprocessing has already been performed by researchers [18] on the dataset. Subsequently, additional preprocessing steps, such as normalization and windowing, are applied to the dataset. The EEG signals in this dataset have a length of 25 s. In this section, the EEG signals are divided into 5-second time frames, resulting in each EEG segment changing from dimensions of 6250×19 to 1250×19. In the subsequent preprocessing steps, various normalization methods, including z-score and regularization in combination with z-score, are applied on EEG segments. [10,30].

2.3   Feature Extraction Based on Transformer

The general block diagram of a transformer architecture is illustrated in Fig. 2 [10,30]. According to Fig. 2, a transformer model comprises stacked self-attention, point-wise, and fully connected (FC) layers in both the encoder and decoder sections [10,30]. Self-attention (SA) is an attention mechanism model employed to capture inherent correlations [10,30]. Figure 3 illustrates the general block diagram of an SA network [10,30]. As depicted in Fig. 3, $X \in \mathbb{R}^{n \times c}$ the input is mapped into, $Q \in \mathbb{R}^{n \times d}$, $K \in \mathbb{R}^{n \times d}$ and $V \in \mathbb{R}^{n \times d}$ using the learnable parameters W^q, W^k, and W^v. The parameters Q, K, and V are defined as follows [10,30]:

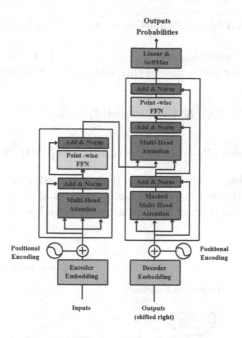

Fig. 2. A general block diagram for a transformer model [8,10]

$$Q = X \times W^q, W^q \in \mathbb{R}^{c \times d}$$
$$K = X \times W^k, W^k \in \mathbb{R}^{c \times d}$$
$$V = X \times W^v, W^v \in \mathbb{R}^{c \times d}$$

In the following, the normalization of the similarity and correlation between Q and K is denoted as $A \in \mathbb{R}^{n \times n}$, which represents the attention distribution [8]. The relationship of A is defined as follows [10,30]:

$$A(Q, K) = Softmax\left(\frac{Q \times K^T}{\sqrt{d}}\right)$$

Subsequently, the attention weight is applied to the value of V, and the resulting output relation $Z \in \mathbb{R}^{n \times d}$ is calculated as follows [10,30]:

$$Z = SA(Q, K, V) \qquad = A(Q, K) \times V = Softmax\left(\frac{Q \times K^T}{\sqrt{d}}\right)V$$

In the above equations, K represents an embedding matrix, while Q represents a look-up vector [10]. The attention matrix A is defined based on the interdependence between Q and K [10,30]. Furthermore, the output Z of the self-attention

(SA) layer is obtained by summing the values of V and weighting them by A [10, 30].

Based on Fig. 3, multiple head self-attention (MSA) blocks are utilized in parallel to generate output maps. In this section, the final relation is defined as follows [10, 30]:

$$Z(Q, K, V) = concat[Z_1, ..., Z_h]W^c$$

$$where Z_1 = Attention(QW_i^q, KW_i^k, VW_i^v)$$

In the above equation, h represents the number of attention heads, and $W^0 \in \mathbb{R}^{hd \times c}$ is a linear projection matrix that incorporates all attention heads [10, 30]. Additionally, the parameters of the i-th attention head are denoted as ,W_i^q ,W_i^k and W_i^v

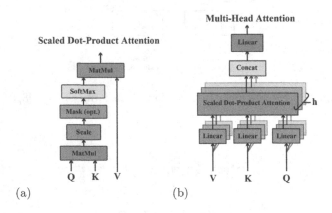

Fig. 3. The structure of the attention layer. a: Scaled Dot-Product Attention. b: Multi-Head Attention Mechanism [8, 10].

2.4　Classification

In the preceding section, the proposed transformer architecture was introduced for feature extraction from EEG signals. Researchers have utilized transformer models in diagnosing various diseases and have demonstrated the successful classification of input data using the Softmax function. Consequently, as depicted in Fig. 2, the Softmax activation function has been employed in this study to classify features for SZ detection.

3　Statistical Metrics

To demonstrate the effectiveness of the proposed method, several important evaluation parameters are calculated, including Accuracy (Acc), Specificity (Spec),

Precision (Prec), and AUC [27,28]. Furthermore, to ensure accurate evaluation of the proposed method, the k-fold cross-validation method with k=10 has been employed.

4   Experiment Results

The results of the proposed transformer-based method for detecting SZ from EEG signals are presented in this section. All simulations of the proposed method were conducted on a PC equipped with the following hardware resources: NVidia 3090 GPU, 32 GB RAM, and a Core i7 CPU. Preprocessing of the EEG signals was performed using Matlab 2019a software. To simulate the proposed transformer architecture and evaluate the performance using various parameters, PyTorch [30] and Scikit-Learn [19] toolboxes were employed in a Python environment, respectively. As discussed in the previous sections, this study utilizes a transformer architecture with various activation functions for SZ detection. It has been mentioned that different normalization techniques were employed to assess the effectiveness of the proposed transformer model with different activation functions. The simulation results for the transformer architecture, considering various activation functions and z-score normalization, are presented in Table 1. Based on Table 1, it is evident that the transformer network with the Gaussian Error Linear Unit (GeLU) activation function outperforms other activation functions in detecting SZ. GeLU is a linear activation function, whereas ReLU is piecewise linear and SeLU is piecewise non-linear. Previous research has demonstrated that GeLU exhibits superior performance on one-dimensional (1D) data compared to other activation functions [4,35].

Table 1. Results of proposed transformer with Z-score normalization.

Activation Functions	Acc	Prec	Spec	AUC
ReLU	93.347 (2.241)	91.915 (1.740)	94.835 (1.613)	98.552 (1.049)
SeLU	95.193 (1.192)	93.965 (1.853)	96.862 (1.132)	99.141 (1.108)
GeLU	95.678 (1.317)	92.036 (1.010)	95.254 (1.917)	99.158 (0.934)

Table 2. Results of proposed transformer model with Z-score normalization and l2 regularization.

Activation Functions	Acc	Prec	Spec	AUC
ReLU	95.272 (0.982)	92.360 (1.024)	96.988 (1.192)	98.961 (0.649)
SeLU	97.622 (0.814)	96.147 (1.121)	94.313 (1.170)	99.270 (0.956)
GeLU	96.348 (1.015)	93.359 (0.917)	96.865 (1.061)	98.214 (0.571)

The subsequent section presents the results of the proposed transformer architecture, considering various activation functions, as well as regularization and z-score [28] normalization techniques. Regularization methods are employed to mitigate overfitting and enhance the efficiency of deep learning architectures. In this section, the l2 regularization method [12] is utilized. The simulation results of this section [3] are reported in Table 2. As shown in Table 2, the combination of the l2 regularization method and the SeLU activation function has significantly improved the performance of the proposed transformer network for SZ detection. The l2 regularization controls computational complexity, while the SeLU activation function facilitates better training of the transformer architecture.

Table 3. The proposed method compared with related works in diagnosis of SZ.

Works	Preprocessing	DL Model	Classifier	Acc (%)
[15]	Handcrafted Features	LSTM	FC	Acc = 99.0
[24]	Filtering, CWT	PreTrained Models	SVM	Acc = 98.6
[17]	Segmentation	1D-CNN	FC	Acc = 98.07
[33]	Segmentation	Recurrent Auto-encoder (RAE)	FC	Acc = 81.81
[9]	ICA	1D-CNN	Softmax	Acc = 93
[6]	MSST Method	VGG16+Bi-LSTM	Softmax	Acc = 86.9
[20]	PCA	Proposed DL Model	Softmax	Acc = 98.65
[5]	Windowing	Hybridization of CNN	LR	Acc = 98.05
Our Work	Windowing, Segmentation	Transformer Model	Softmax	Acc = 97.62

5   Discussion, Conclusion, and Future Works

SZ is a cognitive disorder that significantly impacts a person's early brain development, thinking, emotions, perception, and behavior [22]. The onset of this disease can be gradual, with subtle changes in behavior and performance, or it can manifest suddenly with acute symptoms. Hallucinations, delusions, disordered thinking, and abnormal motor behavior are the primary symptoms associated with SZ [1,21]. Early diagnosis and prediction of this disease by specialized doctors are crucial to prevent its progression. Diagnosing SZ is challenging for specialists and psychologists due to the absence of a definitive medical test. Currently, doctors rely on evaluating clinical symptoms and neuroimaging data, particularly EEG signals, for diagnosis [22]. Given the challenges involved, there is a pressing need for a computer-aided diagnosis system (CADS) tool to assist in the diagnosis of this disease.

This paper presents a CADS for detecting SZ using a attention mechanism model called the transformer. The experiments are conducted on the RepOD dataset [27,28], which is chosen as the available dataset for evaluation. In the preprocessing step, several techniques including filtering, channel selection, normalization, and windowing are applied to enhance the efficiency of the CADS.

The key contribution of this paper lies in the utilization of a transformer architecture with various activation functions for feature extraction from EEG signals. This aspect is novel as transformer architectures with different activation functions have not been previously explored in SZ detection. The extracted features are then classified using the Softmax activation function. The experimental results demonstrate that the proposed transformer architecture, when combined with the SeLU activation function and Z-score normalization with l2 regularization, achieves a remarkable accuracy of 98.87% in SZ detection. This finding underscores the effectiveness of the proposed approach in accurately identifying SZ cases.

Table 3 compares the proposed method of this paper with other studies in the field. Based on Table 3, the proposed method in this work achieves higher accuracy compared to other approaches. This method can assist specialist doctors in the early diagnosis of SZ using EEG signals in medical centers. For future work, graph-attention mechanism networks can be explored for SZ detection from EEG signals. Recently, novel models based on attention mechanisms, such as spatial-temporal attention, and dual attention, have been introduced [34]. These models hold promise for future research in SZ diagnosis and can be considered for further investigation in this field.

Acknowledgments. This research is part of the PID2022-137451OB-I00 project funded by the CIN/AEI/10.13039/501100011033 and by FSE+.

References

1. Barros, C., Silva, C.A., Pinheiro, A.P.: Advanced EEG-based learning approaches to predict schizophrenia: promises and pitfalls. Artif. Intell. Med. **114**, 102039 (2021)
2. Boonyakitanont, P., Lek-Uthai, A., Chomtho, K., Songsiri, J.: A review of feature extraction and performance evaluation in epileptic seizure detection using EEG. Biomed. Signal Process. Control **57**, 101702 (2020)
3. Górriz, J.M., et al.: Computational approaches to explainable artificial intelligence: advances in theory, applications and trends. Inf. Fus. **100**, 101945 (2023)
4. Han, K., et al.: A survey on vision transformer. IEEE Trans. Pattern Anal. Mach. Intell. **45**(1), 87–110 (2022)
5. Hassan, F., Hussain, S.F., Qaisar, S.M.: Fusion of multivariate EEG signals for schizophrenia detection using CNN and machine learning techniques. Inf. Fus. **92**, 466–478 (2023)
6. Jindal, K., Upadhyay, R., Padhy, P.K., Longo, L.: BI-LSTM-deep CNN for schizophrenia detection using MSST-spectral images of EEG signals. In: Artificial Intelligence-Based Brain-Computer Interface, pp. 145–162. Elsevier (2022)
7. Karnati, M., Sahu, G., Gupta, A., Seal, A., Krejcar, O.: A pyramidal spatial-based feature attention network for schizophrenia detection using electroencephalography signals. IEEE Trans. Cogn. Dev. Syst. (2023)
8. Khan, S., Naseer, M., Hayat, M., Zamir, S.W., Khan, F.S., Shah, M.: Transformers in vision: a survey. ACM Comput. Surv. (CSUR) **54**(10s), 1–41 (2022)

9. Lillo, E., Mora, M., Lucero, B.: Automated diagnosis of schizophrenia using EEG microstates and deep convolutional neural network. Expert Syst. Appl. **209**, 118236 (2022)

10. Lin, T., Wang, Y., Liu, X., Qiu, X.: A survey of transformers. AI Open (2022)

11. Mohammadpoor, M., Shoeibi, A., Shojaee, H., et al.: A hierarchical classification method for breast tumor detection. Iranian J. Med. Phys. **13**(4), 261–268 (2016)

12. Moradi, R., Berangi, R., Minaei, B.: A survey of regularization strategies for deep models. Artif. Intell. Rev. **53**, 3947–3986 (2020)

13. Moridian, P., et al.: Automatic diagnosis of sleep apnea from biomedical signals using artificial intelligence techniques: methods, challenges, and future works. Wiley Interdisc. Rev.: Data Min. Knowl. Disc. **12**(6), e1478 (2022)

14. Najafzadeh, H., Esmaeili, M., Farhang, S., Sarbaz, Y., Rasta, S.H.: Automatic classification of schizophrenia patients using resting-state EEG signals. Phys. Eng. Sci. Med. **44**(3), 855–870 (2021)

15. Nikhil Chandran, A., Sreekumar, K., Subha, D.P.: EEG-based automated detection of schizophrenia using long short-term memory (LSTM) network. In: Patnaik, S., Yang, X.-S., Sethi, I.K. (eds.) Advances in Machine Learning and Computational Intelligence. AIS, pp. 229–236. Springer, Singapore (2021). https://doi.org/10.1007/978-981-15-5243-4_19

16. Niu, Z., Zhong, G., Yu, H.: A review on the attention mechanism of deep learning. Neurocomputing **452**, 48–62 (2021)

17. Oh, S.L., Vicnesh, J., Ciaccio, E.J., Yuvaraj, R., Acharya, U.R.: Deep convolutional neural network model for automated diagnosis of schizophrenia using EEG signals. Appl. Sci. **9**(14), 2870 (2019)

18. Olejarczyk, E., Jernajczyk, W.: Graph-based analysis of brain connectivity in schizophrenia. PLoS ONE **12**(11), e0188629 (2017)

19. Pedregosa, F., et al.: Scikit-Learn: machine learning in Python. J. Mach. Learn. Res. **12**, 2825–2830 (2011)

20. Prabhakar, S.K., Lee, S.W.: Improved sparse representation based robust hybrid feature extraction models with transfer and deep learning for eeg classification. Expert Syst. Appl. **198**, 116783 (2022)

21. Ranjan, R., Sahana, B.C., Bhandari, A.K.: Deep learning models for diagnosis of schizophrenia using EEG signals: emerging trends, challenges, and prospects. Arch. Comput. Methods Eng., 1–40 (2024)

22. Sadeghi, D., et al.: An overview of artificial intelligence techniques for diagnosis of schizophrenia based on magnetic resonance imaging modalities: methods, challenges, and future works. Comput. Biol. Med. **146**, 105554 (2022)

23. Sahu, P.K.: Artificial intelligence system for verification of schizophrenia via theta-EEG rhythm. Biomed. Signal Process. Control **81**, 104485 (2023)

24. Shalbaf, A., Bagherzadeh, S., Maghsoudi, A.: Transfer learning with deep convolutional neural network for automated detection of schizophrenia from EEG signals. Phys. Eng. Sci. Med. **43**, 1229–1239 (2020)

25. Shoeibi, A., et al.: A comprehensive comparison of handcrafted features and convolutional autoencoders for epileptic seizures detection in eeg signals. Expert Syst. Appl. **163**, 113788 (2021)

26. Shoeibi, A., et al.: Automatic diagnosis of schizophrenia and attention deficit hyperactivity disorder in RS-FMRI modality using convolutional autoencoder model and interval type-2 fuzzy regression. Cogn. Neurodyn. **17**(6), 1501–1523 (2023)

27. Shoeibi, A., Rezaei, M., Ghassemi, N., Namadchian, Z., Zare, A., Gorriz, J.M.: Automatic diagnosis of schizophrenia in EEG signals using functional connectivity

features and CNN-LSTM model. In: International Work-Conference on the Interplay Between Natural and Artificial Computation, pp. 63–73. Springer (2022). https://doi.org/10.1007/978-3-031-06242-1_7

28. Shoeibi, A., et al.: Automatic diagnosis of schizophrenia in EEG signals using CNN-LSTM models. Frontiers in Neuroinformatics **15** (2021)

29. Siuly, S., Khare, S.K., Bajaj, V., Wang, H., Zhang, Y.: A computerized method for automatic detection of schizophrenia using EEG signals. IEEE Trans. Neural Syst. Rehabil. Eng. **28**(11), 2390–2400 (2020)

30. Stevens, E., Antiga, L., Viehmann, T.: Deep learning with PyTorch. Manning Publications (2020)

31. Tyagi, A., Singh, V.P., Gore, M.M.: Towards artificial intelligence in mental health: a comprehensive survey on the detection of schizophrenia. Multimedia Tools Appl. **82**(13), 20343–20405 (2023)

32. WeiKoh, J.E., et al.: Application of local configuration pattern for automated detection of schizophrenia with electroencephalogram signals. Expert Syst., e12957 (2022)

33. Wu, Y., Xia, M., Wang, X., Zhang, Y.: Schizophrenia detection based on EEG using recurrent auto-encoder framework. In: International Conference on Neural Information Processing, pp. 62–73. Springer (2022). https://doi.org/10.1007/978-3-031-30108-7_6

34. Yan, C., Tu, Y., Wang, X., Zhang, Y., Hao, X., Zhang, Y., Dai, Q.: Stat: spatial-temporal attention mechanism for video captioning. IEEE Trans. Multimedia **22**(1), 229–241 (2019)

35. Zhang, H., Song, H., Li, S., Zhou, M., Song, D.: A survey of controllable text generation using transformer-based pre-trained language models. ACM Comput. Surv. **56**(3), 1–37 (2023)

Diagnosis of Schizophrenia in EEG Signals Using dDTF Effective Connectivity and New PreTrained CNN and Transformer Models

Afshin Shoeibi[1,2(✉)], Marjane Khodatars[1], Hamid Alinejad-Rorky[3], Jonathan Heras[4], Sara Bagherzadeh[5], Amin Beheshti[6], and Juan M. Gorriz[1]

[1] Data Science and Computational Intelligence Institute, University of Granada, Granada, Spain
afshin.shoeibi@gmail.com
[2] Internship in Health Data Analytics Program, AI-enabled Processes (AIP) Research Centre, Macquarie University, Sydney, Australia
[3] UNSW BioMedical Machine Learning Lab, The Graduate School of Biomedical Engineering, UNSW Sydney, Sydney, NSW 2052, Australia
[4] Department of Mathematics and Computer Science, University of La Rioja, La Rioja, Spain
[5] Department of Biomedical Engineering, Science and Research Branch, Islamic Azad University, Tehran, Iran
[6] Data Science Lab, School of Computing, Macquarie University, Sydney, NSW 2109, Australia

Abstract. Schizophrenia (SZ) is a multifaceted mental disorder that typically emerges in early adulthood, characterized by a spectrum of physiological and cognitive deficits. Electroencephalography (EEG) recordings are pivotal in SZ diagnosis, necessitating the expertise of specialist doctors and psychologists. However, the analysis of EEG signals is labor-intensive and susceptible to human error. This study introduces a deep learning (DL) pipeline for the early detection of SZ using EEG signals. The pipeline includes stages of dataset selection, preprocessing, feature extraction, and classification. For this study, the RepOD dataset, consisting of EEG recordings from 14 subjects with SZ and healthy controls (HC), was utilized. The preprocessing phase involves normalizing and segmenting the EEG data. Subsequently, the EEG signals are divided into various sub-bands via Discrete Wavelet Transform (DWT), and effective connectivity matrices are derived using the directed Directed Transfer Function (dDTF) technique. Following this, state-of-the-art pretrained DL models based on CNNs and transformers are applied to extract features and classify the 2D dDTF images obtained from different EEG sub-bands. Notably, the ConvNext-Tiny architecture demonstrated superior performance, achieving an accuracy of 96% in the beta sub-band. Furthermore, this model surpassed the performance of other DL models in terms of accuracy across additional EEG sub-bands.

J. M. Ferrández Vicente et al. (Eds.): IWINAC 2024, LNCS 14674, pp. 150–160, 2024.
https://doi.org/10.1007/978-3-031-61140-7_15

Keywords: Schizophrenia · EEG · Detection · DWT · dDTF · Transformers

1   Introduction

Schizophrenia is a severe psychiatric disorder with a complex and heterogeneous neurological genetic background, which profoundly affects the early development of the brain, as well as a person's thinking, emotions, perception, and behavior [18]. According to a report by the World Health Organization (WHO), approximately 25 million individuals are affected by SZ, although it is less prevalent compared to other neurological disorders [18]. The symptoms of this disorder typically emerge between the ages of 20 and 30, and they are more frequently observed in men than in women [18,23]. The primary symptoms of SZ include hallucinations, delusions, disordered thinking, and abnormal motor behavior. It is important to note that SZ may exhibit symptoms that are similar to other brain disorders such as bipolar disorder, attention deficit hyperactivity disorder (ADHD), and temporal lobe epilepsy [1].

Diagnosing SZ is consistently challenging for specialist doctors due to the absence of a specific medical test. Instead, doctors typically rely on evaluating clinical symptoms and interpreting neuroimaging modalities, particularly EEG signals, for diagnostic purposes [18,23]. EEG recording offers a cost-effective, non-invasive, and easily set-up method with high temporal and frequency resolution. In hospital settings, specialist doctors visually analyze EEG signals to diagnose SZ, which can be a time-consuming process [24]. Additionally, EEG signals often contain various artifacts, further complicating accurate diagnosis for specialists [23]. Moreover, EEG signals provide complex information about brain function during SZ, making direct analysis by specialists difficult. In response, researchers have introduced various AI-based techniques aimed at extracting important features from EEG signals.

Feature extraction techniques for EEG signals can generally be classified into two categories: machine learning (ML) and deep learning (DL) methods [8,9,15,22]. ML-based feature extraction methods encompass four domains: time, frequency, time-frequency, and nonlinear. Given the non-linear nature of EEG signals, researchers have introduced various non-linear feature extraction methods for this domain. Non-linear techniques include connectivity methods, entropies, fractal dimensions, and the largest Lyapunov exponent [2,9]. Connectivity methods, in particular, play a crucial role as they offer valuable insights into functional interactions and networks within the brain [19]. These methods enable the analysis of neural interactions at different levels, including frequency-specific connectivity, directional connectivity, and non-linear interactions [19]. On the other hand, DL techniques, such as convolutional neural networks (CNNs) and recurrent neural networks (RNNs), represent a newer category of AI techniques that have gained prominence in the feature extraction and classification of EEG signals [8]. DL models excel at extracting complex relationships between EEG signals in an unsupervised manner, enabling them to capture intricate patterns and representations within the data [8].

This paper presents a novel method for SZ detection using an effective connectivity method and pretrained models. Initially, the EEG signals from the RepOD dataset [23] undergo preprocessing steps, including normalization and windowing. Subsequently, the EEG signals are decomposed into delta, theta, alpha, beta, and gamma sub-bands using the DWT method [21]. The next step involves the extraction of effective connectivity matrices for each segment of the EEG sub-bands using the dDTF method [4]. Moving forward, 2D images based on the dDTF method are fed into the input of DL models. At this stage, various DL architectures, namely ConvNext-Tiny [12], RegNetx [29], MobileViT [13], MNasNet [26], and MobileVit-V2 [14], are employed for feature extraction and classification of the EEG signals. The second novelty of this paper lies in the utilization of different new DL models (based on CNNs and transformers) and the comparative analysis of their results. Next, the subsequent sections of the paper are introduced. The proposed method of this paper, along with the details of its sections, is outlined in Sect. 2. Section 3 presents the results of the proposed method. Finally, Sect. 4 encompasses the Conclusion, Discussion, and Future Works.

2   Proposed Method

This section presents the steps involved in the proposed SZ detection method utilizing pretrained DL models. Figure 1 illustrates the stages of the method outlined in this article, which include dataset selection, preprocessing, feature extraction, and classification. All simulations are conducted on the available RepOD dataset [23], consisting of two classes: SZ and HC, with 14 subjects in each class. The preprocessing step encompasses both low-level and high-level processes. The low-level preprocessing involves normalization and windowing steps, while the high-level step comprises signal decomposition and the calculation of effective connectivity matrices using the dDTF method. Subsequently, DL architectures are employed for feature extraction and classification from EEG signals, and their results are compared. The following sections provide detailed information on each component of the proposed method.

2.1   Dataset

The RepOD dataset, initially introduced by [27], has been utilized in SZ diagnosis research. This dataset comprises EEG signal recordings in the resting state from 14 subjects in the HC class and 14 subjects in the SZ class. The subjects in both classes fall within an age range of 27.9 to 28.3 years and have similar gender distributions. The EEG signals were recorded following the 10–20 standard with a sampling frequency of 250 Hz. Initially, some preliminary pre-processing steps, such as filtering and channel selection, were applied to this dataset. Subsequently,

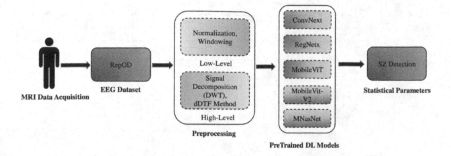

Fig. 1. Block diagram of the proposed method.

19 EEG channels were selected for each subject for further processing. Figures 2 and 3 showcases a sample of the EEG signals from subjects diagnosed with SZ and HC.

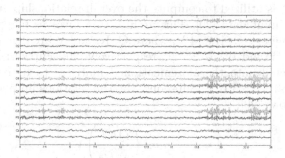

Fig. 2. EEG signal from an individual with SZ.

2.2   Preprocessing

In this section, we provide a detailed explanation of the RepOD dataset [23] preprocessing step, which consists of both low-level and high-level steps. The low-level preprocessing involves the normalization and windowing of EEG signals. Specifically, the EEG signals are segmented into 5-second intervals, resulting in 19 channels for each frame. In high-level preprocessing step, the EEG signals are first decomposed into delta, theta, alpha, beta, and gamma sub-bands using the DWT [21]. Subsequently, the dDTF method is applied to extract connectivity matrices for each EEG sub-band. Figure 4 displays samples of dDTF images for sub-bands from SZ subjects. This aspect of the section represents the first innovation of this paper, as dDTF images have not previously been extracted from sub-bands of EEG signals for SZ diagnosis.

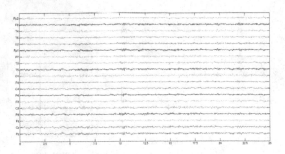

Fig. 3. EEG signal from a healthy control individual.

2.3   Feature Extraction and Classification

Transformer architectures represent one of the most recent attention mechanism models, initially introduced by Vaswani et al. [20]. These networks are composed of primary components such as self-attention (SA) and multi-head self-attention (MHSA) [20]. SA is utilized to compute the overall relationship among different segments of the input data [20]. This architecture involves mapping the input X to three parameters: Q, K,and V, where Q, K, and V are denoted as , $W^Q \in \mathbb{R}^{d \times d_q}$, $W^k \in \mathbb{R}^{d \times d_k}$ and $W^v \in \mathbb{R}^{d \times d_v}$, respectively [20]. Furthermore, the input data X is projected onto the aforementioned matrices to derive $Q = XW^Q$,$K = XW^K$, and $V = XW^V$. Subsequently, the relationship pertaining to SA is defined as follows [20]:

$$A = Softmax \left(\frac{QK^T}{\sqrt{D_q}} \right) V$$

MHSA comprises multiple SA (head) blocks designed to capture intricate dependencies within the input data. Within MHSA,$W^{Q_i}, W^{K_i}, W^{V_i}$ represents learnable weight matrices for each head [20]. Generally, the MHSA relationship is defined as follows [20]:

$$MHSA(Q, K, V) = [Z_0, Z_1, ..., Z_{h-1}]W^0$$

In the above equation, h represents all heads in the MHSA section. Additionally,$W^0 \in \mathbb{R}^{h.D_v}$ performs the linear transformation of heads, andZ_i can be expressed as [20]:

$$Z_i = Softmax \left(\frac{QW^{Q_i} \left(KW^{K_i} \right)^T}{\sqrt{\frac{D_q}{h}}} \right) VW^{v_i}$$

In the field of medicine, limited access to extensive datasets poses a significant challenge [22]. However, transformer architectures have proven effective in overcoming this challenge in medical domains. In this section, pretrained transformer

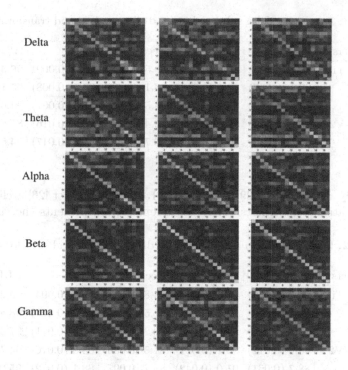

Fig. 4. dDTF images samples for EEG sub-bands.

models, specifically MobileViT [13], and MobileVit-V2 [14] are employed for SZ
detection from EEG signals. Each of these networks is applied to dDTF images
generated from EEG sub-band frequencies, and their results are compared. This
section represents the most significant novelty of this paper since previous studies
have not utilized pretrained transformer models for SZ diagnosis.

3   Experiment Results

In this section, we present the results of the proposed method. The simulations
were conducted on a hardware system equipped with an NVidia 2080 GPU,
16 GB RAM, and a Core i7 CPU. The pre-processing step of the EEG signals
was carried out using Matlab 2021b software. The calculation of dDTF effective connectivity utilized the SIFT library in the EEGLAB toolbox [3] as well
as Matlab 2021b software. Pretrained transformer models were implemented
using the PyTorch library [25]. Furthermore, the Scikit-Learn library [16] was
employed to compute statistical metrics. This paper explores the implementation of various transformer architectures for SZ detection from EEG signals.
Table 1 displays the simulation results of pretrained transformer models using
dDTF [4] based on the delta sub-band. It is evident that the ConvNext-Tiny
architecture [12] attains the highest accuracy compared to other architectures.

Table 1. Results for delta sub-band using dDTF method and transformers.

Transformers	Acc	Prec	Rec	F1	AUROC
ConvNext-Tiny	89.6 (0.013)	88.2 (0.021)	91.5 (0.011)	89.8 (0.009)	96.3 (0.002)
RegNetx	87.7 (0.007)	87.4 (0.012)	88.1 (0.022)	87.8 (0.008)	95.1 (0.007)
MobileViT	85.9 (0.007)	85.6 (0.019)	86.5 (0.023)	86.0 (0.007)	94.0 (0.005)
MobileVit-V2	78.0 (0.010)	81.3 (0.039)	73.4 (0.058)	76.9 (0.016)	87.9 (0.012)
MNasNet	86.8 (0.016)	87.0 (0.012)	86.7 (0.029)	86.8 (0.017)	94.5 (0.011)

Additionally, the RegNetx [29], MobileViT [13], and MNasNet [26] architectures also yield satisfactory results. The subsequent section presents the simulation

Table 2. Results for theta sub-band using dDTF method and transformers.

Transformers	Acc	Prec	Rec	F1	AUROC
ConvNext-Tiny	95.7 (0.040)	96.5 (0.040)	94.8 (0.008)	95.6 (0.004)	99.2 (0.001)
RegNetx	94.1 (0.012)	96.6 (0.004)	91.5 (0.024)	93.9 (0.011)	98.8 (0.002)
MobileViT	91.6 (0.011)	94.6 (0.008)	88.2 (0.024)	91.3 (0.011)	97.3 (0.007)
MobileVit-V2	86.5 (0.012)	90.7 (0.011)	81.5 (0.036)	85.8 (0.016)	94.4 (0.006)
MNasNet	88.7 (0.061)	91.0 (0.042)	85.7 (0.097)	88.1 (0.072)	95.2 (0.048)

results for dDTF [4] utilizing the theta sub-band with transformer models, which are displayed in Table 2. It is evident that the ConvNext-Tiny architecture [12] achieves the highest accuracy compared to other models. Additionally, the Reg-Netx [29], MobileViT [13], and MobileVit-V2 [14] architectures also demonstrate successful SZ detection. Furthermore, upon comparing Tables 1 and 2, it becomes apparent that transformer networks generally achieve better results in the theta sub-band compared to the delta sub-band. Table 3 presents the results of

Table 3. Results for alpha sub-band using dDTF method and transformers.

Transformers	Acc	Prec	Rec	F1	AUROC
ConvNext-Tiny	92.5 (0.014)	90.9 (0.025)	94.5 (0.014)	92.7 (0.012)	97.6 (0.005)
RegNetx	91.1 (0.011)	91.5 (0.017)	90.6 (0.025)	91.2 (0.012)	96.8 (0.003)
MobileViT	89.0 (0.007)	88.3 (0.016)	90.4 (0.028)	89.1 (0.008)	96.1 (0.005)
MobileVit-V2	83.2 (0.011)	83.5 (0.015)	82.2 (0.046)	82.8 (0.017)	91.2 (0.009)
MNasNet	88.5 (0.014)	88.9 (0.018)	88.1 (0.033)	88.5 (0.015)	95.6 (0.009)

transformer architectures on the alpha sub-band. It is evident that the ConvNext-Tiny architecture [12] yields the best results in the alpha sub-band.

Additionally, the RegNetx architecture [29], as one of the newer DL architectures, also achieves significant outcomes. Moving on, Table 4 displays the results of transformer models for dDTF [4] based on the beta sub-band. Similar to the previous tables, the ConvNext-Tiny and RegNetx architectures demonstrate success in feature extraction and classification of 2D images based on the dDTF [4] in the beta sub-band. Finally, Table 5 presents the results of dDTF [4] based on the

Table 4. Results for beta sub-band using dDTF method and transformers.

Transformers	Acc	Prec	Rec	F1	AUROC
ConvNext-Tiny	96.0 (0.006)	94.1 (0.007)	94.1 (0.011)	94.1 (0.006)	98.5 (0.004)
RegNetx	93.5 (0.014)	95.6 (0.013)	91.8 (0.023)	93.3 (0.014)	98.1 (0.005)
MobileViT	91.4 (0.017)	92.6 (0.019)	90.1 (0.018)	91.3 (0.017)	97.4 (0.007)
MobileVit-V2	86.1 (0.011)	87.1 (0.018)	84.7 (0.027)	85.9 (0.013)	93.9 (0.009)
MNasNet	91.8 (0.018)	91.7 (0.021)	92.01 (0.03)	91.8 (0.018)	97.5 (0.006)

gamma sub-band for SZ diagnosis. Similar to Tables 1 to 4, the ConvNext-Tiny network [12] achieves the highest accuracy for the gamma sub-band compared to other models. Based on Tables 1 to 5, it is evident that the beta sub-band yields the best results among other sub-bands. This can be attributed to the fact that SZ is commonly observed in late adolescence to young adulthood, and there is a direct correlation between SZ and the beta band of the human brain. By comparing the results of Tables 1 to 5 with the findings of clinical research, it is evident that the proposed method presented in this article has achieved reliable results in the diagnosis of SZ.

Table 5. Results for gamma sub-band using dDTF method and transformers.

Transformers	Acc	Prec	Rec	F1	AUROC
ConvNext-Tiny	92.1 (0.006)	92.9 (0.016)	91.3 (0.016)	92.3 (0.006)	97.4 (0.005)
RegNetx	91.5 (0.008)	92.4 (0.014)	89.7 (0.024)	91.7 (0.011)	97.1 (0.005)
MobileViT	89.6 (0.014)	91.6 (0.022)	87.4 (0.031)	89.4 (0.015)	96.5 (0.007)
MobileVit-V2	86.3 (0.018)	86.2 (0.026)	86.5 (0.018)	86.3 (0.009)	94.6 (0.006)
MNasNet	89.8 (0.009)	93.3 (0.012)	85.9 (0.015)	89.4 (0.009)	96.3 (0.005)

4   Discussion, Conclusion, and Future Works

This paper presents a method for SZ detection using the dDTF effective connectivity method [4] and pretrained transformer models. The proposed method consists of four main sections: dataset selection, pre-processing, feature extraction, and classification. First, the RepOD dataset [23] is chosen for implementing the proposed method in this study. In the pre-processing stage, several steps are performed, including normalization, windowing, data decomposition, and calculation of effective connectivity matrices. In this step, EEG signals are decomposed into different frequency sub-bands, and the dDTF method [4] is applied to each sub-band. This investigation into the impact of EEG sub-bands on the accurate diagnosis of SZ constitutes the first novelty of this paper. Next, pretrained DL models, namely ConvNext-Tiny [12], RegNetx [29], MobileViT [13], MNasNet [26], and MobileVit-V2 [14], are compared to extract features and classify the input data. The use of these pretrained DL architectures in SZ diagnosis is a novel aspect of this paper, as it has not been explored before. The results from the proposed

Table 6. Comparison of the results presented in this article with other related works.

Works	Preprocessing	Feature Extraction	Classifier	Acc (%)
[28]	Filtering	SpEn, InEn, ShEn, HFD, KOL, ApEn	SVM	Acc = 88.5
[17]	ICA	DFA, HE, RQA, FD, KOL, LZC, LLE	SVM	Acc = 92.17
[11]	Segmentation	Microstate Features	SVM	Acc=90.93
[7]	Segmentation	Microstate and CNN Features	SVM	Acc=75.64
[30]	Segmentation	RAE	Softmax	Acc=81.81
[10]	MSST Method	VGG16+Bi-LSTM	Softmax	Acc=86.9
Our Work	Segmentation, Normalization, DWT, dDTF	Transformer Models	Softmax	Acc=96.00

method in Sect. 4 demonstrate that the ConvNext-Tiny architecture [12] outperforms other transformer techniques in SZ detection. Furthermore, the findings indicate that the beta sub-band is particularly effective in diagnosing SZ compared to other sub-bands. This observation aligns with the fact that SZ typically manifests during adolescence and young adulthood, as supported by our study results. Table 6 presents a comparison between the results of this article and related works in the field of SZ diagnosis using EEG signals and AI techniques. According to the table, the proposed method in this paper has achieved significant results compared to other related studies. Explainable Artificial Intelligence (XAI) is a burgeoning field in medicine, and for future research, methods like t-SNE can be employed to enhance SZ diagnosis [6]. Additionally, graph-transformer [31] and dual mechanism models [5] could be explored in future works to improve SZ diagnosis.

Acknowledgments. This research is part of the PID2022-137451OB-I00 project funded by the CIN/AEI/10.13039/501100011033 and by FSE+.

References

1. Barros, C., Silva, C.A., Pinheiro, A.P.: Advanced EEG-based learning approaches to predict schizophrenia: promises and pitfalls. Artif. Intell. Med. **114**, 102039 (2021)
2. Boonyakitanont, P., Lek-Uthai, A., Chomtho, K., Songsiri, J.: A review of feature extraction and performance evaluation in epileptic seizure detection using EEG. Biomed. Signal Process. Control **57**, 101702 (2020)
3. Delorme, A., Makeig, S.: EEGLAB: an open source toolbox for analysis of single-trial EEG dynamics including independent component analysis. J. Neurosci. Methods **134**(1), 9–21 (2004)
4. Franaszczuk, P.J., Bergey, G.K., Kamiński, M.J.: Analysis of mesial temporal seizure onset and propagation using the directed transfer function method. Electroencephalogr. Clin. Neurophysiol. **91**(6), 413–427 (1994)
5. Fu, J., Liu, J., Tian, H., Li, Y., Bao, Y., Fang, Z., Lu, H.: Dual attention network for scene segmentation. In: Proceedings of the IEEE/CVF Conference on Computer Vision and Pattern Recognition, pp. 3146–3154 (2019)
6. Górriz, J.M., et al.: Computational approaches to explainable artificial intelligence: advances in theory, applications and trends. Inf. Fus. **100**, 101945 (2023)
7. Hassan, F., Hussain, S.F., Qaisar, S.M.: Fusion of multivariate EEG signals for schizophrenia detection using CNN and machine learning techniques. Inf. Fus. **92**, 466–478 (2023)
8. Jafari, M., et al.: Empowering precision medicine: Ai-driven schizophrenia diagnosis via EEG signals: a comprehensive review from 2002–2023. Appl. Intell. **54**(1), 35–79 (2024)
9. Jafari, M., et al.: Emotion recognition in EEG signals using deep learning methods: a review. Comput. Biol. Med., 107450 (2023)
10. Jindal, K., Upadhyay, R., Padhy, P.K., Longo, L.: Bi-LSTM-deep CNN for schizophrenia detection using MSST-spectral images of EEG signals. In: Artificial Intelligence-Based Brain-Computer Interface, pp. 145–162. Elsevier (2022)
11. Keihani, A., Sajadi, S.S., Hasani, M., Ferrarelli, F.: Bayesian optimization of machine learning classification of resting-state EEG microstates in schizophrenia: a proof-of-concept preliminary study based on secondary analysis. Brain Sci. **12**(11), 1497 (2022)
12. Li, J., Wang, C., Huang, B., Zhou, Z.: ConvNeXt-backbone HoVerNet for nuclei segmentation and classification. arXiv preprint arXiv:2202.13560 (2022)
13. Mehta, S., Rastegari, M.: MobileViT: light-weight, general-purpose, and mobile-friendly vision transformer. arXiv preprint arXiv:2110.02178 (2021)
14. Mehta, S., Rastegari, M.: Separable self-attention for mobile vision transformers. arXiv preprint arXiv:2206.02680 (2022)
15. Moridian, P., et al.: Automatic diagnosis of sleep apnea from biomedical signals using artificial intelligence techniques: methods, challenges, and future works. Wiley Interdisc. Rev.: Data Min. Knowl. Disc. **12**(6), e1478 (2022)
16. Pedregosa, F., et al.: Scikit-Learn: machine learning in Python. J. Mach. Learn. Res. **12**, 2825–2830 (2011)
17. Prabhakar, S.K., Rajaguru, H., Lee, S.W.: A framework for schizophrenia EEG signal classification with nature inspired optimization algorithms. IEEE Access **8**, 39875–39897 (2020)
18. Sadeghi, D., et al.: An overview of artificial intelligence techniques for diagnosis of schizophrenia based on magnetic resonance imaging modalities: Methods, challenges, and future works. Comput. Biol. Med. **146**, 105554 (2022)

19. Sakkalis, V.: Review of advanced techniques for the estimation of brain connectivity measured with EEG/MEG. Comput. Biol. Med. **41**(12), 1110–1117 (2011)
20. Shamshad, F., et al.: Transformers in medical imaging: a survey. Med. Image Anal., 102802 (2023)
21. Shensa, M.J., et al.: The discrete wavelet transform: wedding the a trous and mallat algorithms. IEEE Trans. Signal Process. **40**(10), 2464–2482 (1992)
22. Shoeibi, A., et al.: Automatic diagnosis of schizophrenia and attention deficit hyperactivity disorder in RS-FMRI modality using convolutional autoencoder model and interval type-2 fuzzy regression. Cogn. Neurodyn. **17**(6), 1501–1523 (2023)
23. Shoeibi, A., Rezaei, M., Ghassemi, N., Namadchian, Z., Zare, A., Gorriz, J.M.: Automatic diagnosis of schizophrenia in EEG signals using functional connectivity features and CNN-LSTM model. In: International Work-Conference on the Interplay Between Natural and Artificial Computation, pp. 63–73. Springer (2022). https://doi.org/10.1007/978-3-031-06242-1_7
24. Shoeibi, A., et al.: Automatic diagnosis of schizophrenia in EEG signals using CNN-LSTM models. Front. Neuroinform. **15**, 777977 (2021)
25. Stevens, E., Antiga, L., Viehmann, T.: Deep learning with PyTorch. Manning Publications (2020)
26. Tan, M., Chen, B., Pang, R., Vasudevan, V., Sandler, M., Howard, A., Le, Q.V.: MnasNet: platform-aware neural architecture search for mobile. In: Proceedings of the IEEE/CVF Conference on Computer Vision and Pattern Recognition, pp. 2820–2828 (2019)
27. Tan, M., Chen, B., Pang, R., Vasudevan, V., Sandler, M., Howard, A., Le, Q.V.: MnasNet: platform-aware neural architecture search for mobile. In: Proceedings of the IEEE/CVF Conference on Computer Vision and Pattern Recognition, pp. 2820–2828 (2019)
28. Thilakvathi, B., Devi, S.S., Bhanu, K., Malaippan, M.: EEG signal complexity analysis for schizophrenia during rest and mental activity. Biomed. Res.-India **28**(1), 1–9 (2017)
29. Vu, N.T., Huynh, V.T., Nguyen, T.N., Kim, S.H.: Ensemble spatial and temporal vision transformer for action units detection. In: Proceedings of the IEEE/CVF Conference on Computer Vision and Pattern Recognition, pp. 5769–5775 (2023)
30. Wu, Y., Xia, M., Wang, X., Zhang, Y.: Schizophrenia detection based on EEG using recurrent auto-encoder framework. In: International Conference on Neural Information Processing, pp. 62–73. Springer (2022). https://doi.org/10.1007/978-3-031-30108-7_6
31. Yun, S., Jeong, M., Kim, R., Kang, J., Kim, H.J.: Graph transformer networks. In: Advances in Neural Information Processing Systems, vol. 32 (2019)

A Survey on EEG Phase Amplitude Coupling to Speech Rhythm for the Prediction of Dyslexia

N. Gallego-Molina[1,3], F. J. Martinez-Murcia[2,3]([✉]), M. A. Formoso[1,3],
D. Castillo-Barnes[1,3], A. Ortiz[1,3], J. Ramírez[2,3], J. M. Górriz[2,3],
P. J. Lopez-Perez[4], and J. L. Luque[5]

[1] Department of Communications Engineering, University of Malaga,
29071 Málaga, Spain
[2] Department of Signal Theory, Networking and Communications,
University of Granada, 18071 Granada, Spain
fjesusmartinez@ugr.es
[3] Andalusian Institute on Data Science and Computational Intelligence,
18071 Granada, Spain
[4] Department of Social Sciences, Universidad de la Costa,
080001 Barranquilla, Colombia
[5] Department of Developmental and Educational Psychology, University of Malaga,
29071 Málaga, Spain

Abstract. Developmental dyslexia (DLX) hinders the reading learning process of 5%–12% of the world's population. Those affected by DLX show difficulties in oral phonological tasks, the biological underpinnings of which are still hotly debated. Current research has shown abnormal brain oscillatory coupling to speech rhythms, a procedure known as 'entrainment', key to encode phonological representations of speech units. Therefore, brain entrainment to speech rhythms could be used as features in an automatic diagnostic system. This work explores the use of Phase amplitude coupling (PAC) measures to quantify the entrainment between auditory rhythmic stimuli and Electroencephalography (EEG) signals. PAC features are used to train an interpretable machine learning system for predicting DLX in children, achieving accuracy over 90% for the entrainment between the 40 Hz stimulus and the Gamma band using Heights Ratio PAC. Analysis of the classification model reveal differences in the entrainment at regions typically associated to language, paving the way for an accurate and interpretable DLX diagnosis methodology.

1 Introduction

Developmental dyslexia (DLX) is a condition that hinders the learning of reading and spelling in 5%–12% of the world's population [21]. DLX is manifested by a phonological deficit; a set of difficulties in oral tasks such as rhyme judgment, syllable counting or stress pattern classification. DLX's phonological deficits could be better understood within the framework of current theory of language [11]. In these theories, the encoding of audio information into words is achieved at a

© The Author(s), under exclusive license to Springer Nature Switzerland AG 2024
J. M. Ferrández Vicente et al. (Eds.): IWINAC 2024, LNCS 14674, pp. 161–170, 2024.
https://doi.org/10.1007/978-3-031-61140-7_16

neural level by a distributed network oscillating at temporal rates. This process is frequently known as "entrainment" [18], and has been proven using techniques such as Magnetoencephalography (MEG) or electroencephalography (EEG) in subjects under a wide variety of stimuli [11,18].

DLX differences in entrainment to speech were assessed by estimating the coupling between brain rhythms and specific speech units [11], including impaired entrainment to delta band of natural speech [18] or impaired delta entrainment to natural speech in children [5]. Abnormal patterns were also found in the low gamma (25–35 Hz) bands in [15]. These works prove that entrainment to speech rhythm is a potential marker for the detection of dyslexia.

Phase amplitude coupling (PAC) is the preferred option for estimating entrainment in many works with both children and adults [5,15,18]. PAC assesses whether the phase of low-frequency oscillations modulates the amplitude envelope of high frequency oscillations. In the brain, PAC has been shown to measure effective communication during cognitive processes [14], revealing a hierarchical structure of the EEG data. It has also been used to model the connectivity of brain regions in which theta oscillation triggers high gamma power [1]. Measures such as Heights Ratio (HR) [14], the Modulation Index (MI) [23], Mean Vector Length (MVL) [1], Gaussian Copula PAC (gcPAC) [13] or Phase Locking Value (PLV) [11,19].

Previous approaches of applying machine learning (ML) to the diagnosis of developmental dyslexia include using the Event Related Potential (ERP) of the EEG channels or temporal and spectral features of subjects under non-speech auditory stimuli [6,9,10,17,20]. These works show that there are relevant differences between children with dyslexia and normal readers, and even relating some of these associations to indicators of Phonological Awareness (PA).

In this work, we have extensively explored this possibility. We synthesized amplitude modulated (AM) white-noise at different rates related to speech units of the Spanish language: a theta stimulus at 4.8 Hz, a beta - 16 Hz, and a gamma - 40 Hz for phonemes. Quantifying the entrainment of the brain to these synthetic signals may allow us to investigate whether there is a non-linguistic, impaired entrainment to acoustic rhythms. We performed the study on 48 7-year-old children, 15 of whom were diagnosed with DLX, and recorded the EEG signals while listening to the stimulus. We then measured the entrainment between the stimulus and the EEG using five different PAC measures. These features were later aggregated per EEG band and used to generate features for a Support Vector Machine classifier (SVC).

2   Methods

2.1   Data Acquisition and Preprocessing

The data used in this work were obtained by the LEEDUCA research group at the University of Málaga (Spain) [6,17,20]. The researchers selected an EEG cohort consisting of 48 subjects aged 7 years: 15 with a clear reading deficit and 33 with no obvious impairment (CTL). These groups had matching age

Table 1. Demographics and test results of the EEG cohort.

Group	N	Age (months)	SCI	PA	RAN	VSTM
CTL	33	94.1 [3.3]	5.091 [2.53]	0.616 [0.17]	0.517 [0.22]	0.468 [0.19]
DLX	15	95.6 [2.9]	4.533 [2.07]	0.275 [0.19]	0.378 [0.15]	0.389 [0.26]

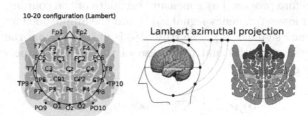

Fig. 1. 10–20 EEG electrode layout in the Lambert azimuthal representation used in this article (left) and explanation of the projection (right).

and school-level socio-economic index (SCI) measured in a scale 1–10. Table 1 shows the demographic details and neuropsychological results, including PA, rapid automatized naming (RAN) and Verbal Short-Term Memory (VSTM) of this cohort.

Students were presented with AM white noise stimuli at a theta - 4.8 Hz (θ-stim), a beta - 16 Hz stimulus (β-stim), and a gamma - 40 Hz stimulus (γ-stim). Stimuli were presented in sequential ascending and descending order (4.8–16 - 40–40 - 16–4.8 Hz) for 2.5 min each, for a total acquisition time of 15 min. EEG signal acquisition was performed using a 10–20 configuration optimized for auditory processing (see Fig. 1 for electrode localization and a brief explanation of the Lambert azimuthal projection). EEG data underwent preprocessing in Brainvision Analyzer: referencing, bandpass filtering (0.1–150 Hz), notch filtering (45–55 Hz), and ocular correction. Segments were created on artifact-free markers, followed by baseline correction (−100 to 0 ms mean subtraction). Depending on the EEG data, we obtained a different number of segments per subject and stimulus. Subsequent processing of each 31-channel segment is performed individually, and the different PAC measures are then aggregated as described in Sect. 2.3.

2.2 Cross-Frequency Coupling

Cross-Frequency Coupling (CFC) techniques have played a major role in EEG research in recent years [18]. With a solid theoretical basis, cross-frequency PAC has been linked to communication between brain areas involved in perception, cognition, and action [2]. To define PAC we use the analytic signal $z(t) = x(t) + j\mathcal{H}\{x(t)\}$, where $\mathcal{H}[x(t)]$ is the Hilbert Transform of $x(t)$

The analytic signal $z(t)$ allows us to estimate the instantaneous amplitude envelope $a(t)$ and phase $\phi(t)$ of $z(t)$ as:

$$a(t) = |z(t)| = \sqrt{\Re(z(t))^2 + \Im(z(t))^2}, \quad \phi(t) = \angle z(t) = \tan^{-1} \frac{im(z(t))}{re(z(t))} \quad (1)$$

PAC is therefore proposed as a measure estimate of the coupling between the phase $\phi_1(t)$ of a lower-frequency signal $x_1(t)$ and the amplitude envelope $a_2(t)$ of a higher frequency signal $x_2(t)$. The PLV [19] is obtained from the phase of the lower-frequency signal $\phi_1(t)$ and the phase of the higher-frequency amplitude envelope signal $\angle a_2(t)$ as:

$$PLV = \frac{1}{N} \sum_{t=0}^{N-1} \left| e^{-j\angle a_2(t)} e^{-j\phi_1(t)} \right| \quad (2)$$

where N is the length of the signals for $t \in 1 \dots N$.

For the HR and the MI [23], a vector quantization is applied on $a_2(t)$ with respect to the phase signal $\phi_1(t)$. To do so, the range of phases $[-\pi, \pi]$ is divided onto J quantiles, and therefore, a counting vector p_j is defined for the jth quantile of phases in the instantaneous phase vector $\phi_1(t)$:

$$p_j = \frac{1}{M} \sum_{t \in T_j} a_2(t) \quad \text{and} \quad T_j = \{t | \phi_1(t) \in j^{th} \text{quant.}\} \quad (3)$$

where M is the number of elements in the set T_j.

In one of the first approaches to compute MI, we define the quantized vector $\mathbf{p} = [p_0, \dots p_{J-1}]$. Afterwards, $\mathbf{p}$ is normalized so that it sums up to 1, so that its elements P_j can be interpreted as the probability of the jth phase bin. MI is computed as the Kullback-Leibler divergence of P with respect to the uniform distribution:

$$MI = 1 + \frac{1}{\log(J)} \sum_{j=0}^{J-1} P_j \log(P_j) \quad (4)$$

A simpler approach was the HR, defined in [23] from $\mathbf{p}$:

$$HR = \frac{\max(\mathbf{p}) - \min(\mathbf{p})}{\max(\mathbf{p})} \quad (5)$$

gcPAC [13] is a continuous approach to compute MI on EEG signals. In [13] it was proven that the MI between two continuous variables X and Y is equal to the negative entropy of their statistical copula. The method uses the entropy of the joint distribution over X and Y equals the marginal entropy plus the entropy of the copula function. Therefore, the copula can be obtained as:

$$H(C) = H(X, Y) - H(X) - H(Y) \quad (6)$$

The last method tested in this work is usually preferred for high-quality segments, the MVL [2]. It is defined as the magnitude of a signal whose amplitude is the envelope of the high-frequency signal $a_2(t)$ and its phase is the phase of the low-frequency modulating signal $\phi_1(t)$:

$$MVL = \frac{1}{N} \sum_{t=0}^{N-1} \left| a_2(t) e^{j\phi_1(t)} \right| \tag{7}$$

PAC values can be produced by chance. To rule out this possibility we use permutation testing to generate Z-scores as in [23] by generating surrogate versions $a_s(t)$ of the amplitude signal by barrel-switching the amplitude signal $a(t)$ at different levels. Surrogate PAC measures are computed for each $a_s(t)$, generating a surrogate PAC distribution from which Z-scores for the observed PAC_o can be computed as:

$$Z = \frac{\text{PAC}_o - \mu_{\text{PAC}_s}}{\sigma_{\text{PAC}_s}} \tag{8}$$

with μ_{PAC_s} and σ_{PAC_s} the mean and standard deviation of the surrogate PAC distribution. In this work, 200 surrogates are generated for computing the PAC Z-score between the phase of the stimuli and the amplitude of EEG signals at different frequencies using the TensorPAC 6.5 python package [4]. This Z-score will be considered henceforth as the PAC measure.

2.3 Feature Aggregation and Classification

We estimated a single PAC Z-score that measures the interaction between a synchronized stimulus $\phi(t)$ and a narrowband filtered EEG signal at each electrode, $a(t)$. $a(t)$ was filtered at 49 frequency points f_b ranging from f_s, the frequency of the stimulus, to 200 Hz on a logarithmic scale. This results in an array of 31×49 PAC values per EEG segment, one for each combination of EEG channel and center frequency of the bandpass applied to obtain $a(t)$. Spectral features are usually aggregated into frequency bands [5,15,18]: Delta (from 0.5 to 4 Hz), Theta (from 4 to 8 Hz), Alpha (from 8 to 12 Hz), Beta (from 12 to 25 Hz) and the Gamma band is divided into two, namely Gamma (from 25 to 80 Hz), and Epsilon (from 80 to 200 Hz) [18].

For each frequency band, a set of PAC values (in Z-score) is built $\text{PAC}_{band} = \{\text{PAC}_{f_b}, \ldots\}$ for all $f_b \in (f_{ini}, f_{end})$, where f_{ini} and f_{end} are the frequency extrema of the bands. The final PAC for band B is the number of PAC values in the set PAC_{band} above a threshold $Z_{th} = 1.65$, which corresponds to the Z-score for that PAC_{f_b}. Afterwards, this number can be normalized using the total number of elements in PAC_{band}. The PAC_{band} for each subject is then obtained as the average of the PAC calculated for each 5-s segment.

2.4 Evaluation and Interpretability

Differences in PAC to rhythmic stimuli were assessed via classification accuracy of a linear Support Vector Machine classifier (SVC) [16] with different parameters and distance metrics. SVCs have been shown to maintain a high statistical

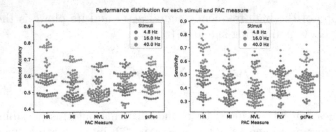

Fig. 2. Comparison of performance measures in experiments for each stimulus and PAC estimation method. Each point represents the cross-validated balanced-accuracy/sensitivity for a SVC with a different combination of EEG band, parameter C and SVC penalty using all 31 EEG channels. See Sect. 2.4 for more details on the performance evaluation of the PAC features.

power to detect moderate-to-large effect sizes with small samples, even in scenarios with a significant class imbalance. In their basic, linear form, it is possible to observe the classification weights, allowing a deeper interpretation of the "relevance" of the input features. L1 and L2 norms, as well as different regularization parameters $C = 10^i$, $\forall i \in [-4, 5]$ have been tested. We used the python 3.8 implementation of LIBSVM in sklearn [3]. A repeated (10 times) stratified 5-fold CV is used to estimate the performance of the classification task. In each CV fold, four performance measures were obtained: accuracy, sensitivity, specificity and, given the imbalance of our data, balanced accuracy.

A nonparametric framework based on a permutation test is proposed for the statistical analysis of the results [8]. Since neuroimaging experiments typically involve high-dimensional databases with small sample sizes, where central limit approximations tend to be poor, this procedure is preferred over parametric inference. Permutation testing is performed independently at each CV fold, estimating the null distribution with 200 permutations of the train and test label vectors, and retraining a SVC with the same parameters. To estimate a p-value, the proportion of events where the surrogate performance score was higher than the actual performance was estimated. Additionally, the SVC coefficients are used to assess interpretability. The SVM linear discriminative model learns a model $\mathbf{y} = \mathbf{wx}$, and thus a coefficient vector $\mathbf{w}$ for the input data. In this work, the input data are the aggregated PAC Z-measures B for each electrode and band, as commented before. Therefore, the coefficient should be interpreted as positive when the contribution of B tilts the balance of the classifier towards predicting DLX subject, and negative when this contribution is towards CTL.

3   Results and Discussion

3.1   Best Performing Stimuli and PAC Measures

Our classification analysis reveals that HR is by far the best PAC measure for the stimuli and segments, achieving up to 90% accuracy for the HR and 40 Hz stimulus (mean accuracy and [standard deviation] over all CV folds in the best case:

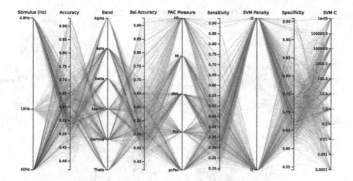

Fig. 3. Parallel coordinates plot of the stimulus, PAC measure, the SVC parameters (penalty and C) and their respective performance. Color is linked to the specific stimulus. The highest performance is linked to the HR PAC between the γ-stim (40 Hz) and Gamma/Epsilon EEG.

0.929 [0.08], $p = 0.0069$). Figure 2 shows the distribution of the performance achieved by each PAC measure, as estimated by balanced accuracy (trade off between sensitivity and specificity) and sensitivity. Each point represents a performance estimate with a different combination of EEG band, parameter C of SVC and SVC penalty using all 31 EEG channels. This allows the estimation of the best performing measures and stimuli in discriminating subjects with and without DLX.

While the γ-stim (40 Hz) is the best performing one, when measured with the Heights Ratio, the 16 Hz β-stim also achieves high performance with HR (around 80%, best acc. 0.830 [0.11], $p = 0.0225$), and slightly less with MI (around 70% sensitivity and balanced accuracy). It is no coincidence that they depend on the quantization of the phases of the instantaneous phase vector, as defined in Eq. 3. HR is particularly better at detecting large differences in the quantized amplitude vector, as it can be seen from Eq. 5. Larger differences imply a larger modulation index, which in our case is better captured by the simpler HR measure. As for the 4.8 Hz θ-stim, all PAC measures achieve similar -and worse- sensitivity, but specificity is slightly higher in the case of PLV and MVL. The higher resolution of the phase stimulation (over 100 points per cycle vs. about 12 points per cycle for the 40 Hz stimulation at $F_s = 500$) is probably one of the reasons. The best accuracy in this case is not significant (0.738 [0.13], $p = 0.0945$).

3.2   Effect of Classification Hyperparameters

All combinations of stimuli, PAC measures and classifier parameters are displayed at a parallel coordinates plot at Fig. 3. A parallel coordinates plot is a useful data visualization strategy for displaying and comparing multivariate data. It consists of a set of parallel lines or axes, each representing a different variable, and the data points are plotted as lines connecting each of the

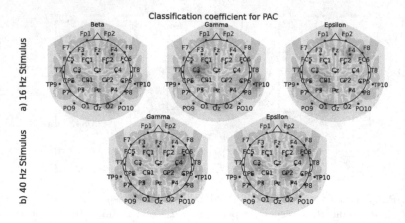

Fig. 4. Classification weights of the linear SVC trained for discriminating between DLX and CTL subjects using the HR entrainment between the stimuli (16 and 40 Hz) and different bands.

corresponding variable axes. In this particular case, each line represents a combination of hyperparameters and performance, and the color is related to the specific PAC measure. Here we can observe that the performance of the SVC is hardly dependent on the parameter C (used for regularization). However, the type of penalty used (l2 and l1) does have a moderate impact, with the l2 norm achieving higher performance in both accuracy and sensitivity. The L2 norm is particularly advantageous in terms of performance with the β-stim.

3.3   Assymetric Differences Between DLX and CTL

Regarding the combination of stimulus and band, the entrainment between the γ-stim and the gamma band, with HR is the most discriminative. Large separation is achieved by the β-stim - Gamma entrainment, and also by γ-stim - Epsilon and 16 Hz - Epsilon, all with the HR measure. To dig deeper into this performance, we depict the SVC coefficients -weights- for these two stimuli and the different bands, measured by HR in Fig. 4.

First, the contribution of the electrodes in the two hemispheres is not symmetrical for any of the β-stim and γ-stim Hz entrainment with beta, gamma and epsilon bands. As for the best performing combinations (β-stim and γ-stim with gamma), we observe differences and similarities. For the β-stim (16 Hz), the largest positive coefficients are found at C3 and TP10, and negative for the region around CP5, P4 and C4. For the γ-stim (40 Hz), the largest contributions are along the line formed by CP2-C4-FC6, and there are large negative coefficients in electrodes around key areas in language: P3, FC1 and F3. A similar pattern is found along all Beta, Gamma and Epsilon bands. In general, key areas of the left hemisphere involved in normal reading [7] showed higher gamma entrainment with the phoneme stimuli. In contrast, right hemisphere areas (CP2, FC6) were more activated in dyslexics and negatively correlated with reading performance. This is consistent with recent evidence suggesting that language performance in DLX is compensated by neural mechanisms in the right hemisphere in both adults [22] and adolescents [12].

4 Conclusions

Impaired phase-amplitude (PA) coupling in dyslexia (DLX) may stem from deficient entrainment to speech rhythms. We investigated 48 7-year-olds' EEG responses to non-speech stimuli, finding high accuracy (up to 90%) in DLX diagnosis using support vector classification (SVC) with PAC features, particularly in gamma band entrainment at 40 Hz. SVC weights highlighted brain entrainment differences in language-associated regions, suggesting a promising, interpretable diagnostic tool for DLX.

Acknowledgements. This research is part of the projects PID2022-137629OA-I00, PID2022-137461NB-C32 and PID2022-137451OB-I00, funded by the MICIU/AEI/10. 13039/501100011033 and by "ERDF/EU", and the C-ING-183-UGR23 project, cofunded by the Consejería de Universidad, Investigación e Innovación and by European Union, funded by Programa FEDER Andalucía 2021-2027. Work by F.J.M.M. is part of the grant RYC2021-030875-I funded by MICIU/AEI/10.13039/501100011033 and by the "European Union NextGenerationEU/PRTR".

References

1. Canolty, R.T., et al.: High gamma power is phase-locked to theta oscillations in human neocortex. Science **313**(5793), 1626–1628 (2006)
2. Canolty, R.T., Knight, R.T.: The functional role of cross-frequency coupling. Trends Cogn. Sci. **14**(11), 506–515 (2010)
3. Chang, C.C., Lin, C.J.: LIBSVM: a library for support vector machines. ACM Trans. Intell. Syst. Technol. **2**(3), 1–27 (2011)
4. Combrisson, E., Nest, T., Brovelli, A., Ince, R.A.A., Soto, J.L.P., Guillot, A., Jerbi, K.: Tensorpac: an open-source Python toolbox for tensor-based phase-amplitude coupling measurement in electrophysiological brain signals. PLoS Comput. Biol. **16**(10), e1008302 (2020)
5. Di Liberto, G., Peter, V., Kalashnikova, M., Goswami, U., Burnham, D., Lalor, E.: Atypical cortical entrainment to speech in the right hemisphere underpins phonemic deficits in dyslexia. NeuroImage **175**, 70–79 (2018)
6. Formoso, M.A., Ortiz, A., Martinez-Murcia, F.J., Gallego, N., Luque, J.L.: Detecting phase-synchrony connectivity anomalies in EEG signals: application to dyslexia diagnosis. Sensors **21**(21), 7061 (2021)
7. Friederici, A.D., Gierhan, S.M.: The language network. Curr. Opin. Neurobiol. **23**(2), 250–254 (2013)
8. Golland, P., Fischl, B.: Permutation tests for classification: towards statistical significance in image-based studies. In: Taylor, C., Noble, J.A. (eds.) IPMI 2003. LNCS, vol. 2732, pp. 330–341. Springer, Heidelberg (2003). https://doi.org/10.1007/978-3-540-45087-0_28

9. Górriz, J.M., et al.: Computational approaches to explainable artificial intelligence: advances in theory, applications and trends. Inf. Fusion **100**, 101945 (2023)
10. Górriz, J.M., et al.: Artificial intelligence within the interplay between natural and artificial computation: advances in data science, trends and applications. Neurocomputing **410**, 237–270 (2020)
11. Goswami, U.: Speech rhythm and language acquisition: an amplitude modulation phase hierarchy perspective. Ann. New York Acad. Sci. **1453**, 67–78 (2019)
12. Hoeft, F., et al.: Neural systems predicting long-term outcome in dyslexia. Proc. Natl. Acad. Sci. **108**(1), 361–366 (2011)
13. Ince, R.A., Giordano, B.L., Kayser, C., Rousselet, G.A., Gross, J., Schyns, P.G.: A statistical framework for neuroimaging data analysis based on mutual information estimated via a gaussian copula. Hum. Brain Mapp. **38**(3), 1541–1573 (2017)
14. Lakatos, P., Shah, A.S., Knuth, K.H., Ulbert, I., Karmos, G., Schroeder, C.E.: An oscillatory hierarchy controlling neuronal excitability and stimulus processing in the auditory cortex. J. Neurophysiol. **94**(3), 1904–1911 (2005)
15. Lehongre, K., Ramus, F., Villiermet, N., Schwartz, D., Giraud, A.L.: Altered low-gamma sampling in auditory cortex accounts for the three main facets of dyslexia. Neuron **72**(6), 1080–1090 (2011)
16. Martinez-Murcia, F.J., Ortiz, A., Gorriz, J.M., Ramirez, J., Castillo-Barnes, D.: Studying the manifold structure of Alzheimer's disease: a deep learning approach using convolutional autoencoders. IEEE J. Biomed. Health Inf. **24**(1), 17–26 (2020)
17. Martinez-Murcia, F.J., et al.: EEG connectivity analysis using denoising autoencoders for the detection of dyslexia. Int. J. Neural Syst. **30**(07), 2050037 (2020)
18. Molinaro, N., Lizarazu, M., Lallier, M., Bourguignon, M., Carreiras, M.: Out-of-synchrony speech entrainment in developmental dyslexia. Hum. Brain Mapp. **37**(8), 2767–2783 (2016)
19. Mormann, F., Fell, J., Axmacher, N., Weber, B., Lehnertz, K., Elger, C.E., Fernández, G.: Phase/amplitude reset and theta-gamma interaction in the human medial temporal lobe during a continuous word recognition memory task. Hippocampus **15**(7), 890–900 (2005)
20. Ortiz, A., Martinez-Murcia, F.J., Luque, J.L., Giménez, A., Morales-Ortega, R., Ortega, J.: Dyslexia diagnosis by EEG temporal and spectral descriptors: an anomaly detection approach. Int. J. Neural Syst. **30**(07), 2050029 (2020)
21. Peterson, R., Pennington, B.: Developmental dyslexia. Lancet **379**, 1997–2007 (2012)
22. Shaywitz, S.E., et al.: Neural systems for compensation and persistence: young adult outcome of childhood reading disability. Biol. Psychiat. **54**(1), 25–33 (2003)
23. Tort, A.B., Komorowski, R., Eichenbaum, H., Kopell, N.: Measuring phase-amplitude coupling between neuronal oscillations of different frequencies. J. Neurophysiol. **104**(2), 1195–1210 (2010)

Comprehensive Evaluation of Stroke Rehabilitation Dynamics: Integrating Brain-Computer Interface with Robotized Orthesic Hand and Longitudinal EEG Changes

Yolanda Vales[1]([✉]) [iD], Jose M. Catalan[1] [iD], Andrea Blanco-Ivorra[1] [iD],
Juan A. Barios[1,2] [iD], and Nicolas Garcia-Aracil[1] [iD]

[1] Robotics and Artificial Intelligence Group, Miguel Hernández University,
Avda. de la Universidad s/n, 03202 Elche, Spain
{yvales,jcatalan,ablanco,nicolas.garcia}@umh.es,
juanantonio.barios@grupohla.com
[2] Neuroscience Unit, HLA Vistahermosa Hospital, Alicante, Spain

Abstract. Stroke-induced motor deficits need personalized rehabilitation therapies to maximize motor recovery. Integrating Brain-Computer Interface (BCI) technology with robotized exoskeletons, enabling a closed-loop proprioceptive feedback loop to the injured brain, represents a promising approach for enhancing rehabilitation outcomes. However, understanding the longitudinal impact of this integrated approach on stroke recovery is paramount importance. Monitoring through electroencephalography (EEG) patterns holds promise in providing valuable insights into the neurophysiological adaptations occurring during rehabilitation, thereby providing valuable data for personalized treatment strategies and therefore, for optimizing the recovery process.

A longitudinal study was conducted to assess the effect of integrating a BCI-robotized orthesic hand in stroke rehabilitation, leveraging clinical evaluation and quantitative EEG analysis for monitoring. This study aims to elucidate neural mechanisms underlying rehabilitation and optimize treatment strategies to enhance stroke recovery, with EEG changes serving as valuable indicators of neuroplasticity.

Keywords: BCI · stroke · EEG · exoskeleton

Abbreviations

ATH	Atherotrombotic
BCI	Brain-Computer Interface

This work was supported by the Ministry of Science and Innovation, belonging to the Agencia Estatal de Innovación (AEI) through the projects PLEC2022-009424 and PID2022-139957OB-I00, and by the Conselleria de Innovación, Universidades, Ciencia y Sociedad Digital, through the project CIPROM/2022/12.

J. M. Ferrández Vicente et al. (Eds.): IWINAC 2024, LNCS 14674, pp. 171–181, 2024.
https://doi.org/10.1007/978-3-031-61140-7_17

EEG	Electroencephalography
ERD	Event-related desynchronization
ERP	Event-related potencial
ERS	Event-related synchronization
FMA-UE	Fugl-Meyer Assessment for upper extremity
MCA	Middle Cerebral Artery
MRC	Medical Research Council
MRI	Magnetic Resonance Imaging
PCA	Posterior Cerebral Artery

1 Introduction

Stroke is a leading cause of long-term disability worldwide, with motor deficits representing a significant challenge in post-stroke rehabilitation efforts. Despite advancements in rehabilitation techniques, maximizing recovery potential remains a complex endeavor, demanding tailored approaches to address the diverse needs of stroke survivors. In recent years, the integration of innovative technologies has emerged as a promising avenue to enhance rehabilitation outcomes.

One such technological advancement is the integration of Brain-Computer Interface (BCI) technology with robotized exoskeletons. This integration allows for a closed-loop proprioceptive feedback loop to the injured brain, potentially facilitating motor function restoration and recovery. By establishing direct communication between the brain and external devices, BCI systems enable stroke survivors to control robotic orthesic through neural signals, thus bypassing damaged neural pathways and promoting motor relearning.

Furthermore, longitudinal monitoring of neurophysiological changes through quantitative Electroencephalography (EEG) analysis offers valuable insights into the underlying mechanisms of stroke recovery. EEG-based biomarkers of neuroplasticity can provide objective measures of cortical reorganization and adaptive changes in brain networks following stroke. This information is crucial for understanding individual variations in recovery trajectories and tailoring rehabilitation interventions to optimize outcomes.

Despite the potential benefits of integrating BCI technology with robotized orthesic hands and leveraging longitudinal EEG monitoring in stroke rehabilitation, there remains a need for comprehensive evaluation and validation of these approaches. Understanding the longitudinal impact of this integrated system on stroke recovery outcomes is essential for informing evidence-based rehabilitation practices and optimizing treatment strategies.

Current studies aiming to employ EEG as a functional biomarker in chronic stroke patients face several challenges. Integrating EEG recordings within BCI tasks could significantly enhance the diagnostic potential of EEG in stroke patients. Secondly, EEG signals undergo substantial modifications following hemispheric strokes, posing challenges in effectively controlling BCI systems. Although previous studies have shown promising outcomes by utilizing signals from both affected and unaffected hemispheres in stroke rehabilitation, there remains a need for further research to evaluate EEG signals specifically in stroke patients. Thirdly, stroke patients with severe motor impairments are often excluded from studies requiring voluntary movement, limiting the applicability of findings. By incorporating robotic devices into research protocols, it becomes feasible to explore brain responses to passive movements, even in patients with severe motor deficits, thus facilitating studies within this population.

In this context, we present a longitudinal study aimed at comprehensively evaluating the integration of BCI technology with robotized orthesic hands in stroke rehabilitation. By leveraging quantitative EEG analysis, we seek to monitor neurophysiological changes over time and identify biomarkers of neuroplasticity associated with motor recovery. The findings of this study are expected to contribute to a deeper understanding of the neural mechanisms underlying stroke rehabilitation and inform the development of personalized treatment approaches to optimize recovery outcomes for stroke survivors.

2   Material and Methods

2.1   Participants

The study was performed at IMED Hospital (Benidorm, Spain), with patients who suffered a stroke. The patients were referred by the physicians of the rehabilitation area of the hospital according to the established inclusion criteria. The protocol of this study complies with the Research Ethics Committee. All patients were properly informed and they signed the informed consent before the experiment.

The inclusion criteria comprised adult stroke survivors in the subacute or chronic stage, presenting hemiplegia in one of the upper limbs, capable of cooperating and comprehending task instructions, as well as understanding all pertinent information related to the study. The study included 7 stroke patients

Table 1. Clinical characteristics of the patients.

ID	Sx	Age	Stroke	Side	Time	Severity	FMA-UE	MRC
1	M	64	Lacunar stroke	Right	1 year	severe	47/66	2/5
2	F	47	Hemorrhage in MCA - PCA	Left	2 years	severe	28/66	1/5
3	F	70	Stroke MCA protuberance	Right	4 months	severe	20/66	2/5
4	F	31	Ischemic stroke	Left	1 year	severe	20/66	2/5
5	F	83	ATH ischemic stroke	Left	7 months	moderate	53/66	4/5
6	F	47	ATH ischemic stroke in MCA	Right	11 months	severe	28/66	1/5
7	F	76	Carotid ischemic stroke	Left	1 year	moderate	59/66	4/5

Note. **MCA**, Middle Cerebral Artery; **PCA**, Posterior Cerebral Artery; **ATH**, Atherotrombotic; **FMA-UE**, Fugl-Meyer Assessment for upper extremity [6], **MRC**, Medical Research Council [9].

(6 women, mean age 59, 71 ± 18, 61 years and 9 healthy participants (2 women; mean age 27, 22 ± 3, 80 years).

The participants were categorized into three distinct groups based on their health status and severity of stroke: Control (n = 9), composed of healthy individuals; Moderate (n = 2), consisting of stroke patients with a Medical Research Council (MRC) [9] score of 3 or higher; and Severe (n = 5), comprising stroke patients with a MRC score of 2 or lower (Table 1).

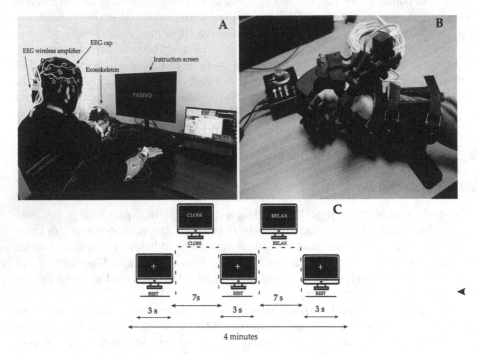

Fig. 1. Experimental setup. **A.** EEG cap used according to the International 10/20 system. **B.** Modular hand exoskeleton designed in our group. **C.** Experimental timeline design of PASSIVE and CLOSE tasks. Duration of movement lasts 4 s separated by an inter-trial-intervals of 5.5 s.

2.2   Description of the Experimentation

Sessions. During each session, participants were involved in a structured activity comprising three distinct tasks, with each task consisting of 24 randomly presented repetitions, as illustrated in Fig. 1:

- **Passive Task**: Participants experienced continuous passive slow closing and opening movements of a hand exoskeleton without exerting any intentional effort. The exoskeleton, is commercialized and distributed by the spin-off iDRhA [3,7], is illustrated in the Fig. 1B. This task commenced with a visual cue displaying the word 'Passive'.

- **Active Task**: Participants were instructed to actively open and close their hand continuously. This task was introduced through a visual cue displaying the word 'Move'.
- **Relaxation Task**: Participants were instructed to imagine engaging in an activity without physical movements, such as contemplating a landscape or focusing on a point on the screen. This task was presented using a visual cue featuring the word 'Relax'.

Throughout the trials, participants were instructed to maintain fixation on a designated point on the screen, identified by a white cross. Within each trial, participants completed 12 Relaxation tasks, which were interspersed randomly with another 12 tasks, either Passive or Active. It's noteworthy that participants exclusively performed either Passive or Active tasks within a single trial, while Relaxation tasks were consistently included in every trial throughout the session. Moreover, participants were advised to avoid blinking and making eye movements during the task, reserving these actions for the inter-trial interval. Each task was conducted across two successive trials: initially with participants using their non-paretic or non-dominant hand, followed by the use of their paretic or dominant hand.

The hand exoskeleton utilized for passive mobilization of the hand (Fig. 1A) is commercialized by the spin-off iDRhA [7]. This device enables individual movement of the index and middle fingers, as well as the pair formed by the ring and little finger, while the thumb remains stationary [4,5].

Longitudinal Evaluation. Participants underwent an intensive upper limb rehabilitation program at the IMED International Center Hospital. This comprehensive program involved multiple sessions per week led by a dedicated multidisciplinary team of rehabilitation specialists, including physiotherapists, occupational therapists, and rehabilitation physicians, targeted to the improvement of motor function and dexterity in the affected upper limb following a stroke. To monitor progress, participants underwent thorough EEG evaluation following every 10 rehabilitation sessions.

2.3 EEG Data Analysis

Data Acquisition: The BCI2000 software, a versatile standard platform [10], served as the framework for EEG data acquisition during experimental tasks. Electrodes were positioned based on the 10–20 system, with additional electrodes added as necessary. EEG data were captured using a non-invasive commercial EEG wireless amplifier, the BrainVision® Liveamp. Participants were directed to execute the described motor tasks while EEG signals were recorded.

Data Preprocessing: Recorded EEG data underwent several preprocessing steps to ensure data quality and remove artifacts. EEGLAB toolbox (version 14.1.1) [2] and custom scripts developed in Matlab® R2018b were employed for signal processing. First, EEG signals were high-pass filtered at 0.5 Hz and low-pass filtered at 40 Hz using a finite impulse response filter. Subsequently, the data were resampled to a uniform sampling rate of 128 Hz to facilitate further analysis. Event-related segments, centered around task cues, were extracted from the continuous EEG data, including a 3-s baseline period before the cue onset and 4-s periods during and 2.5 s after the task execution. Baseline correction was applied to these epochs to remove any baseline drift. In instances where patients exhibited ischemic lesions in the right hemisphere, EEG recordings underwent mirroring across the sagittal plane. This approach was employed to enhance the comparability of their EEG patterns with those of other participants, as documented in previous studies [11]. To analyze the left and right hemispheres, electrodes outside the midline were averaged.

Independent Component Analysis (ICA) and Artifact Rejection: Visual inspection was used to identify and reject trials contaminated by muscle activity, eye movement, blinks, or single-channel noise. ICA decomposition, implemented in the EEGLAB toolbox using the extended Infomax algorithm, was employed to separate EEG signals into statistically independent components, aiming to identify and remove artifacts. ICLabel scores were computed to assess the likelihood of each component representing artifact sources, and components exceeding predefined rejection thresholds were removed from the data. Components associated with eye movements, muscle activity, or other non-brain-related sources were identified and excluded from further analysis. This process ensured the removal of artifacts while preserving neural signals of interest [8].

Data Analysis: Following artifact rejection, EEG epochs corresponding to specific experimental conditions were selected for further analysis. Trials were categorized based on the type of task cue presented, and only epochs meeting predefined criteria were retained. After preprocessing, the data underwent segmentation into epochs lasting for 11 s each: 3 s preceding the visual cue indicating the task onset, 4 s encompassing the task execution, and 4 s following the task's completion. The epoch zero was aligned with the task onset, yielding epoch durations spanning from −3 to 8 s. This approach ensured comprehensive coverage of the targeted phenomena for analysis. The preprocessed EEG data were subjected to further analysis to investigate neural correlates of motor or cognitive tasks. Time-frequency analysis, event-related potential (ERP) analysis, and connectivity measures will be employed to examine task-related neural dynamics and functional brain networks. Statistical analyses were conducted to assess the significance of observed effects and evaluate group differences.

3 Results

3.1 Time Frequency

We conducted an analysis of the averaged time-frequency representation of EEG recordings. Our findings revealed the expected power event-related desynchronization (ERD) within the 8–12 Hz (alpha band) and 13–30 Hz (beta band) frequency ranges, demonstrating consistency across both stroke and control

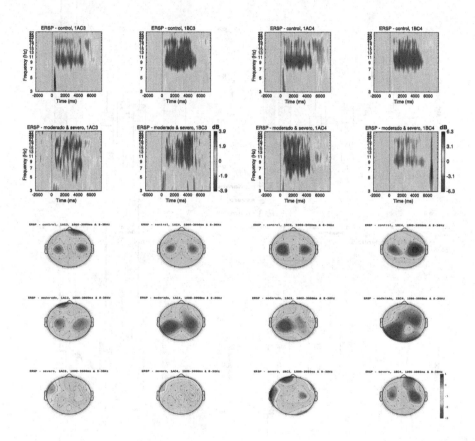

Fig. 2. A. Time-frequency analysis of EEG activity over the ipsilesional (left side of the figure) and contralesional (right side) hemisphere during contralateral hand movement. The upper row displays data from the CONTROL group, while the lower row presents data from the STROKE group. Each row shows the grand average of subjects within the respective group, with signals recorded from electrodes C3 and C4 (stroke lesion in the left hemisphere). **B.** Topographic maps illustrating EEG amplitudes in the 8–30 Hz frequency range, analyzed during the stable part of movement task (time-range 1000–3000 ms), for the CONTROL (upper), MODERATE (middle), and SEVERE (lower) groups. The left part of each panel represents the PASSIVE task, while the right part depicts the ACTIVE task.

groups (Fig. 2A). Additionally, we observed a reduction of contralesional event-related synchronization (ERS) in the beta band among moderately affected stroke patients during passive movement, with a complete absence noted in the severe group. Particularly noteworthy was the more pronounced presence of ERS during the exoskeleton-based task (PASSIVE).

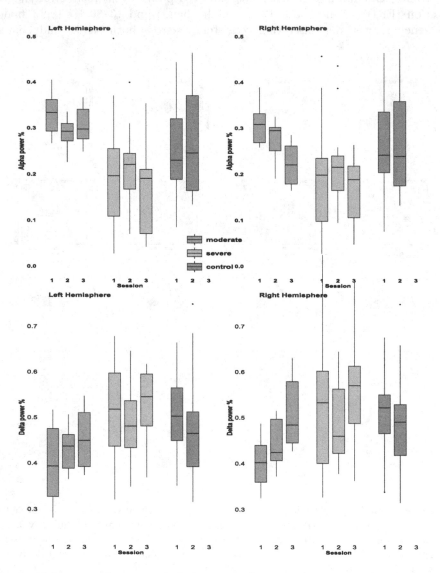

Fig. 3. Alpha power (upper row), Delta power (lower row) evolution along sessions.

3.2   Topographic Maps

During the stable phase of the movement task (time range 1000–3000 ms), we conducted an analysis of topographic maps depicting EEG amplitudes within the 8–30 Hz frequency range (Fig. 2B). Clear differences were discerned between the groups, consistent with previous findings reported in [1]. Control participants demonstrated bilateral activation during both passive and active tasks. In contrast, the moderate group displayed an expanded area of ERD activation, while the severe group exhibited a marked reduction compared to controls.

3.3   Power Bands

We conducted an analysis of delta and alpha power over time in participants both with and without stroke (Fig. 3). Among stroke patients, we noted a significant difference in alpha power, with moderately affected individuals exhibiting higher levels compared to those with severe impairment, whereas the opposite trend was observed in delta power. Particularly noteworthy was the observation that the progression of these changes was more pronounced in the right hemisphere (non-affected) among stroke participants.

4   Discussion, Study Limitations and Future Work

In this study, we present preliminary results about the exploration of cortical oscillations during passive hand movements facilitated by an exoskeleton, utilizing a non-invasive EEG acquisition system. Expanding on our prior exploration of the ERD/ERS phenomenon [1], the current results focus on time evolution of power bands.

The study is subject to several limitations that merit brief consideration. One notable limitation is the absence of structural Magnetic Resonance Imaging (MRI) data, which precluded the correlation of individual anatomical information with EEG analysis. Incorporating structural MRI data in future studies could provide valuable insights into the relationship between brain structure and neurophysiological changes observed during rehabilitation.

Additionally, the relatively small sample size may limit the generalizability of the findings. Future research endeavors, currently in progress, should aim to increase size and diversity of our cohort to validate and extend the current findings.

Furthermore, the study focused primarily on the chronic phase of stroke rehabilitation. Long-term follow-up assessments are essential to evaluate the durability of the observed neurophysiological changes and their impact on functional outcomes over time. However, it is also crucial to recommend further investigation into the acute phase of stroke rehabilitation to elucidate the immediate effects of the integrated BCI-robotized orthesic hand system on neurophysiological adaptations and functional recovery.

Lastly, while the integrated BCI-robotized orthesic hand system shows promise for stroke rehabilitation, its efficacy may vary depending on individual patient characteristics and rehabilitation settings. Future studies should explore factors influencing treatment response and consider implementing personalized rehabilitation protocols tailored to each patient's needs and capabilities.

Addressing these limitations and pursuing future research directions will contribute to a deeper understanding of stroke rehabilitation dynamics and facilitate the development of more effective and personalized treatment strategies.

5   Conclusion

The current findings of this pilot study expand upon our earlier research [1]. We evaluated the EEG changes along the study in patients with severe stroke. For this purpose, we showed our preliminary results, finding significant differences between moderate and severe groups in evolution of power bands. These findings underscore the distinct patterns of brain electrical activity in individuals affected by stroke and underscore the importance of understanding the impact of brain injury on neural activity.

Ethics Approval and Consent to Participate. This work involved human subjects in its research. Approval of all ethical and experimental procedures and protocols was granted by the Miguel Hernandez University's Ethical Committee under Application No. 2017.32.E.OEP.

Disclosure of Interests. The authors have no competing interests to declare that are relevant to the content of this article.

Availability of Data and Materials. The datasets generated and/or analyzed during the current study are available from the corresponding author upon reasonable request.

References

1. Barios, J.A., et al.: Movement-related EEG oscillations of contralesional hemisphere discloses compensation mechanisms of severely affected motor chronic stroke patients. Int. J. Neural Syst. **31**(12), 2150053 (2021)
2. Delorme, A., Makeig, S.: Eeglab: an open source toolbox for analysis of single-trial EEG dynamics including independent component analysis. J. Neurosci. Methods **134**(1), 9–21 (2004)
3. Díez, J.A., Blanco, A., Catalán, J.M., Bertomeu-Motos, A., Badesa, F.J., García-Aracil, N.: Mechanical design of a novel hand exoskeleton driven by linear actuators. In: Ollero, A., Sanfeliu, A., Montano, L., Lau, N., Cardeira, C. (eds.) ROBOT 2017, vol. 694, pp. 557–568. Springer, Heidelberg (2017). https://doi.org/10.1007/978-3-319-70836-2_
4. Diez, J.A., Blanco, A., Catalan, J.M., Badesa, F.J., Lledo, L.D., Garcia-Aracil, N.: Hand exoskeleton for rehabilitation therapies with integrated optical force sensor. Adv. Mech. Eng. **10**(2), 1–11 (2018)

5. Díez, J.A., Catalán, J.M., Blanco, A., García-Perez, J.V., Badesa, F.J., Gacía-Aracil, N.: Customizable optical force sensor for fast prototyping and cost-effective applications. Sensors **18**(2) (2018). https://doi.org/10.3390/s18020493. https://www.mdpi.com/1424-8220/18/2/493

6. Fugl-Meyer, A.R., Jääskö, L., Leyman, I., Olsson, S., Steglind, S.: The post-stroke hemiplegic patient. 1. a method for evaluation of physical performance. Scand. J. Rehabil. Med. **7**(1), 13–31 (1975)

7. iDRhA: Innovative Devices for Rehabilitation & Assistance (2019). https://idrha.es/. Accessed 28 Feb 2024

8. Mognon, A., Jovicich, J., Bruzzone, L., Buiatti, M.: Adjust: an automatic EEG artifact detector based on the joint use of spatial and temporal features. Psychophysiology **48**(2), 229–240 (2011)

9. Paternostro-Sluga, T., et al.: Reliability and validity of the medical research council (MRC) scale and a modified scale for testing muscle strength in patients with radial palsy. J. Rehabil. Med. **40**(8), 665–671 (2008)

10. Schalk, G., McFarland, D.J., Hinterberger, T., Birbaumer, N., Wolpaw, J.R.: BCI 2000: a general-purpose brain-computer interface (BCI) system. IEEE Trans. Biomed. Eng. **51**(6), 1034–1043 (2004)

11. Wu, J., et al.: Connectivity measures are robust biomarkers of cortical function and plasticity after stroke. Brain **138**(8), 2359–2369 (2015)

PDBIGDATA: A New Database for Parkinsonism Research Focused on Large Models

R. López[1], F. J. Martinez-Murcia[1], J. Ramírez[1], T. Martín-Noguerol[2], F. Paulano-Godino[2], A. Luna[2], J. M. Górriz[1], and F. Segovia[1(✉)]

[1] Department of Signal Theory, Networking and Communications, University of Granada, Granada, Spain
fsegovia@ugr.es
[2] MRI Unit, Radiology Department, HT Medica, Madrid, Spain

Abstract. Medical imaging plays a pivotal role in understanding neurodegenerative diseases like Parkinson's, aiding in early diagnosis and treatment monitoring. Despite its importance, obtaining comprehensive imaging datasets remains challenging. In response, we introduce a new database comprising brain images from Parkinson's patients and healthy controls, addressing the scarcity of such resources in the field. The database currently houses around 3000 subjects, offering a diverse and extensive collection for research purposes. Leveraging this dataset, we conduct experiments employing classical models to delineate neuroanatomical disparities between Parkinson's patients and controls. Our findings not only underscore the potential of this database in advancing Parkinson's research but also highlight its significance in facilitating the translation of findings into clinical practice, ultimately enhancing patient care and outcomes.

Keywords: Parkinson's disease · Magnetic Resonance Imaging · multivariate analysis

1 Introduction

Medical imaging has become an integral part of diagnosing and treating neurodegenerative diseases, including Parkinson's disease. As our understanding of these conditions deepens, the role of imaging techniques has expanded, providing valuable insights into disease progression, early detection, and treatment monitoring. In recent decades, medical imaging has transitioned from a specialized tool to a routine practice in clinical settings. Physicians and researchers rely on various imaging modalities to visualize brain structures, assess functional changes, and identify abnormalities. For Parkinson's disease, in particular, medical imaging plays a crucial role in understanding the underlying pathophysiology and tracking disease progression.

Despite the increasing demand for medical imaging data, researchers face significant challenges in obtaining large and diverse datasets. Initiatives like the

J. M. Ferrández Vicente et al. (Eds.): IWINAC 2024, LNCS 14674, pp. 182–190, 2024.
https://doi.org/10.1007/978-3-031-61140-7_18

Alzheimer's Disease Neuroimaging Initiative (ADNI) and the Parkinson's Progression Markers Initiative (PPMI) have made substantial efforts to collect and share imaging data [8]. However, the scarcity of comprehensive datasets remains a bottleneck for advancing research, hindering the translation of research into clinical practice. In addition, the great variability of formats and modalities coming from different scanner, along with the difficulties in extracting such images from a clinical environment complicates the creation of a database even further.

Parkinson's disease, characterized by dopaminergic dysfunction and progressive motor and non-motor symptoms, presents a compelling case for advanced imaging exploration. Over recent decades, various imaging modalities have been scrutinized, with nuclear imaging taking center stage [3]. Radiotracers targeting dopaminergic activity have offered valuable insights into the pathophysiology and progression of PD, augmenting diagnostic accuracy and therapeutic stratification [12].

In the field of image analysis, the dichotomy between univariate and multivariate approaches has long prevailed [6]. Univariate methods, led by statistical parametric mapping (SPM), have allowed finding localized alterations in brain structure and function. However, the growing interest in multivariate techniques, driven by advances in deep learning, has revolutionized the landscape of neuroimaging analysis [11]. Deep learning models excel at searching for intricate patterns within vast datasets, promising greater diagnostic accuracy and prognostic efficacy [9]. Despite the rise of multivariate methodologies, their effectiveness depends on the availability of large and diverse image repositories. Unfortunately, the limited availability of adequately sized datasets makes it difficult to fully exploit the potential of these sophisticated analytical paradigms. Consequently, the imperative to build, share and maintain comprehensive imaging datasets, spanning diverse demographic and clinical cohorts, takes on critical importance in driving neuroimaging research to new advances that improve the diagnosis and treatment of the most prevalent diseases. And, what is even more important, being able to obtain procedures and models adapted to the great diversity present in real clinic environment [14].

In this article we describe the database we are developing, which currently contains more than 3000 patients. In order to demonstrate its potential, we show some experiments based on classical models.

2   Database Description

All the data used for the creation of this database have been provided by "HT médica". They are, therefore, real data, generated in a real clinical environment. Figure 1 shows some graphs representing the number of studies of different modalities, areas and anatomical regions present in the company.

Due to the amount of information, the need to be able to access the data in the shortest possible time (speed) and the variability present in the raw data, the database has been designed as a Data Lake [4,10]. A Data Lake is a storage repository that allows storing large amounts of data in its raw and unprocessed

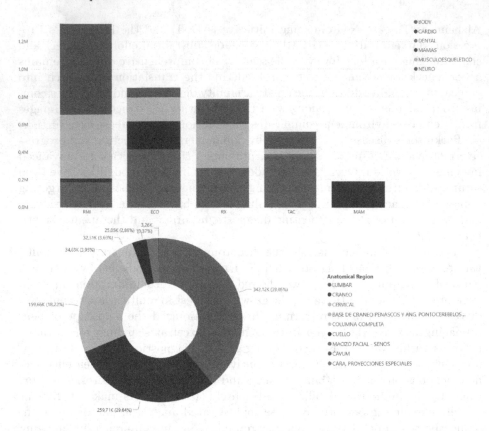

Fig. 1. *Top*: Number of studies by imaging modality and anatomical area. *Bottom*: Number of neurological structural magnetic resonance studies by anatomical region.

form, sourced from various origins and in a wide variety of formats. Unlike traditional storage systems, which require data to be structured and organized before storage, a Data Lake enables the capture of data swiftly and without imposing a rigid structure. This means that data can be stored quickly and cost-effectively, with the flexibility to be processed and analyzed later according to specific user needs. Data lakes are used in a variety of fields, including big data analytics, business intelligence, and scientific research, among others. Their ability to efficiently store large volumes of data makes them a valuable tool for those seeking to harness the wealth of information in the digital age (Figs. 2 and 3).

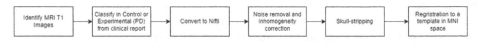

Fig. 2. Outline of the process to remove noise and correct inhomogeneities in images.

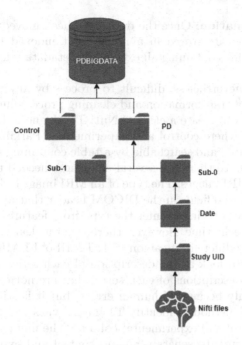

Fig. 3. Outline of the data loading process.

The process followed to create this Data Lake consisted of classical Extraction Transformation and Load (ETL) steps:

- **Data Extraction:** Radiological image data are usually stored in a Picture Archiving and Communication System (PACS) server while radiological reports and clinical information are stored in an Radiological Information System (RIS) database. A PACS is usually an on-premise server that can only be accessed within the clinical environment via DICOM protocol [2]. A Python application that implements the DICOM protocol was implemented to extract the data. It consists of a Python code along with a database to log and monitor every interaction with PACS server and the RIS database.
  The application is divided into two main processes that communicates asynchronously by using a message broker. The first part of the application,the DICOM Extractor, retrieves batches of radiological images from the PACS server, radiological reports from the RIS database, and save them in a temporary local storage. It uses a date, a modality and an anatomical zone to filter images. Then the Accession Numbers that link radiological images with radiological reports and clinical information is obtained.
  The second process takes batches of data extracted from the first part of the application and apply some basic steps before moving them out of the clinical environment such as anonymization and extraction of relevant DICOM fields contained in the header of the images.

- **Data Transformation:** Once the data have been moved out of the clinical environment, they are stored in a raw format indexed by Study Instance UID. Also, a csv file containing all extracted metadata information per study is created.

  These data are, nevertheless, difficult to process by any neuroimaging software. Therefore, a transformation and cleaning process must be applied. The aim of this step is to create a cleaned Nifti T1 Magnetic Resonance Imaging (MRI) database, where control and experimental (Parkinson disease) group are clearly separated and searchable by a table containing all metadata information per study. To that end, several challenges needed to be faced:

  - Identify T1 MRI images: The type of an MRI image is difficult to obtained since there are no fields in the DICOM header that allow that identification. One way is trying to infer the type from features like the repetition time and the echo time. However, there is not a clear pattern in these features to really differentiate among T1, T2, IR of FLAIR image types. The other way is to look at the description of each series. These are manual radiologist's descriptions of each series that are not completely accurate though, mainly because of human errors, but it is still the quickest and more reliable method to identify T1 image types.

  - Identify control and experimental cohorts: The more solid way to obtain the ground truth to separate among control and experimental cohorts, consists of labeling images by an experienced psychiatrist. However, this method is unfeasible. Firstly, because it is cost and time consuming and secondly, because of the difficulty associated with the diagnosis of Parkinson. Therefore, any developed procedure to analyze Parkinson disease will always have to cope with errors. A less reliable but a cheaper and faster method involves extracting the diagnosis from the clinical reports. In this work, control and experimental cohorts have been identified by examining clinical information and radiological reports.

  - Clean images: In order to analyze and extract conclusions from images, they all have to be in the same format and with the same alignment. To achieve this, all DICOM images were first transformed into Nifti format. Then a process to remove noise and correct inhomogeneities was carried out. Finally, the skull was removed and the images were registered to a template so that all of them were moved into the MNI (Montreal Neurological Institute) space. The whole preprocess pipeline, that can be seen in 2, was carried out by using SPM software [7].

- **Data Loading:** The Data Lake were finally created by loading data and structure them as in 3. A table containing all metadata has also been created in order to access files in the shortest possible time.

The final Data Lake consists of 2714 control subjects and 244 experimental subjects.

3 Experiments and Results

Several experiments were conducted in order to evaluate the potential of the database for group comparison analyses, including assisted diagnosis of Parkinson's disease.

We first selected a subset of 503 patients, of whom 244 are diagnosed with Parkinsonism and the remaining 259 are considered neurologically healthy controls. From each of them an MRI image was taken and segmented for this study, using the segmentation algorithm implemented in SPM [1], and resulting in different tissues per patient in MNI space. All except gray matter were discarded for this first analysis.

After data segmentation and preprocessing, we performed an analysis based on a 2-sample t-test to compare the populations of controls and PD patients in a univariate approach. This analysis was performed using SPM. The null hypothesis was set to assume lower intensity in PD patient images and the result was corrected to compensate for false positives due to multiple comparisons (0.05, FWE). The result is shown in Fig. 4 (left).

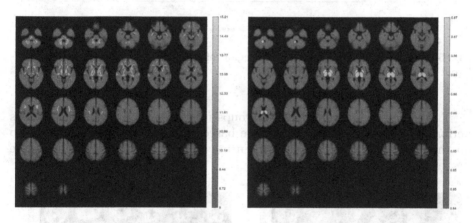

Fig. 4. *Left:* Areas with significant differences ($p < 0.05$, FWE) between control and PD patients according to a univariate t-test analysis. The color scale codifies the t-statistic values. *Right:* Regions that allow the separation of controls and PD patients with a hit rate greater than 50% (after discounting the upper bound of the classification error) using a statistical classifier.

A comparison between groups was also performed using different multivariate approaches. In this approach, we proceeded first with an analysis based on Statistical Agnostic Mapping [5], an agnostic approach that does not assume any model in the data and allows us to generate a map with the brain regions that, using a linear statistical classifier, provide a precision higher than 50% once the upper bound of error in the estimation of this measure is subtracted. The result is shown in Fig. 4 (right).

SAM divides the brain into 116 regions (those defined in the AAL atlas) [13] and calculates the accuracy of a linear classifier in each of them individually. This analysis shows a result closer to the expected one, where only the palladium and the thalamus are indicated as regions with significant differences. Although the analysis also identified a subregion of the cerebellum, it is possibly a false positive and does not appear on the map due to its size and location. The accuracy achieved by each region and the upper bound of the error are shown in Fig. 5.

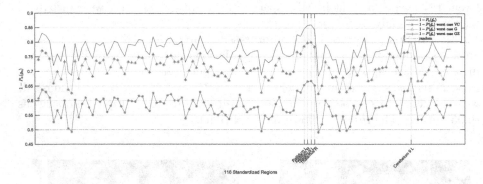

Fig. 5. Classification of each individual region of controls and PD patients using different upper bounds.

The second comparison between groups using a multivariate approach was performed using a classification scheme based on support vector machines. To do this end, we trained the classifier using 80% of the images and used the

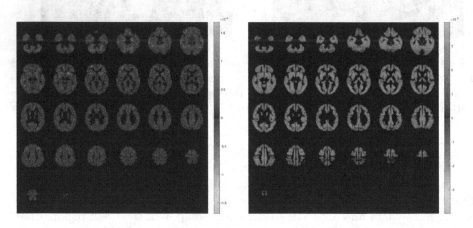

Fig. 6. *Left:* Map with the weights of a SVM classifier trained to separate controls and PD patients. *Right:* First PCA coefficient remodeled to the shape of a brain volume. The main axial slices are shown.

remaining 20% to evaluate the trained model. The evaluation process yielded an accuracy of 87% in the separation of controls and PD patients. Since the classifier was trained using all voxels as features, it is possible to obtain a map of the importance of each voxel in the separation by looking at the weight matrix of the trained model. The result is shown in Fig. 6 (left).

The last multivariate approach carried out consisted of applying a transformation to the data using Principal Component Analysis (PCA) [7]. This transformation allows us to determine the regions of space in which the images show the highest variance. Figure 6 (right) shows the map obtained after modeling the first PCA coefficient (the one that concentrates most of the variance) remodeled in the form of brain volume.

4 Conclusions

Our study introduced a novel database of brain images encompassing Parkinson's patients and healthy controls, addressing a critical gap in neuroimaging research. The database, which housed over 3000 patients, provided a valuable resource for investigating the pathophysiology of Parkinson's and improving diagnostic accuracy. Through experiments utilizing classical models, we demonstrated the utility of this resource in delineating neuroanatomical disparities between Parkinson's patients and controls. These findings underscored the significance of large-scale, diverse imaging datasets in driving advancements in neuroimaging analysis and clinical practice.

Furthermore, our study highlighted the importance of adapting analytical paradigms to real clinical environments, emphasizing the need for procedures and models tailored to the diverse settings encountered in clinical practice. As the field increasingly embraces multivariate methodologies, the demand for comprehensive imaging datasets becomes ever more pressing. Initiatives like ours aimed to bridge this gap, fostering collaborative efforts to build, share, and maintain expansive repositories of imaging data. Such endeavors are crucial for unlocking the full potential of advanced analytical techniques, ultimately improving the diagnosis and treatment of neurodegenerative diseases. Moving forward, continued investment in data infrastructure and collaborative initiatives will be essential for driving neuroimaging research towards impactful clinical applications.

Acknowledgment. This research is part of the PID2022-137629OA-I00, PID2022-137461NB-C32 and PID2022-137451OB-I00 projects, funded by the MICIU/AEI /10.13039/501100011033 and by "ERDF/EU", and the C-ING-183-UGR23 project, cofunded by the Consejería de Universidad, Investigación e Innovación and by European Union, funded by Programa FEDER Andalucía 2021–2027.

References

1. Ashburner, J., Friston, K.J.: Unified segmentation. Neuroimage **26**(3), 839–851 (2005). https://doi.org/10.1016/j.neuroimage.2005.02.018
2. Bidgood, W.D., Jr., Horii, S.C., Prior, F.W., Van Syckle, D.E.: Understanding and using DICOM, the data interchange standard for biomedical imaging. J. Am. Med. Inf. Assoc. **4**(3), 199–212 (1997). https://doi.org/10.1136/jamia.1997.0040199
3. Castillo-Barnes, D., et al.: Nonlinear weighting ensemble learning model to diagnose parkinson's disease using multimodal data. Int. J. Neural Syst. **33**(08), 2350041 (2023). https://doi.org/10.1142/S0129065723500417
4. Gentner, T., Neitzel, T., Schulze, J., Gerschner, F., Theissler, A.: Data lakes in healthcare: applications and benefits from the perspective of data sources and players. Procedia Comput. Sci. **225**, 1302–1311 (2023). https://doi.org/10.1016/j.procs.2023.10.118
5. Gorriz, J.M., et al.: Statistical agnostic mapping: a framework in neuroimaging based on concentration inequalities. Inf. Fusion **66**, 198–212 (2021). https://doi.org/10.1016/j.inffus.2020.09.008
6. Gorriz, J.M., Suckling, J., Ramirez, J., Jimenez-Mesa, C., Segovia, F.: A connection between pattern classification by machine learning and statistical inference with the General Linear Model. IEEE J. Biomed. Health Inf. **26**, 5332–5343 (2021). https://doi.org/10.1109/JBHI.2021.3101662
7. Khedher, L., Ramírez, J., Górriz, J.M., Brahim, A., Segovia, F.: Early diagnosis of Alzheimer's disease based on partial least squares, principal component analysis and support vector machine using segmented MRI images. Neurocomputing **151**(Part 1), 139–150 (2015). https://doi.org/10.1016/j.neucom.2014.09.072
8. Marek, K., et al.: The Parkinson's progression markers initiative (PPMI) - establishing a PD biomarker cohort. Ann. Clin. Transl. Neurol. **5**(12), 1460–1477 (2018). https://doi.org/10.1002/acn3.644
9. Martinez-Murcia, F.J., et al.: Assessing mild cognitive impairment progression using a spherical brain mapping of magnetic resonance imaging. J. Alzheimer's Dis. **65**(3), 713–729 (2018). https://doi.org/10.3233/JAD-170403
10. Muratov, S.Y., Muravyov, S.B.: Framework architecture of a secure big data lake. Procedia Comput. Sci. **229**, 39–46 (2023). https://doi.org/10.1016/j.procs.2023.12.005
11. Segovia, F., et al.: Multivariate analysis of dual-point amyloid PET intended to assist the diagnosis of Alzheimer's disease. Neurocomputing **417**, 1–9 (2020). https://doi.org/10.1016/j.neucom.2020.06.081
12. Segovia, F., et al.: Multivariate analysis of 18F-DMFP PET data to assist the diagnosis of parkinsonism. Front. Neuroinf. **11**, 1–9 (2017). https://doi.org/10.3389/fninf.2017.00023
13. Tzourio-Mazoyer, N., et al.: Automated anatomical labeling of activations in SPM using a macroscopic anatomical parcellation of the MNI MRI single-subject brain. Neuroimage **15**(1), 273–289 (2002). https://doi.org/10.1006/nimg.2001.0978
14. Wang, Y., Kung, L., Byrd, T.A.: Big data analytics: understanding its capabilities and potential benefits for healthcare organizations. Technol. Forecast. Soc. Chang. **126**, 3–13 (2018). https://doi.org/10.1016/j.techfore.2015.12.019

A Comparative Study of Deep Learning Approaches for Cognitive Impairment Diagnosis Based on the Clock-Drawing Test

Carmen Jimenez-Mesa[1,2](✉)(iD), Juan E. Arco[1,2](iD), Meritxell Valenti-Soler[4], Belen Frades-Payo[4](iD), Maria A. Zea-Sevilla[4], Andres Ortiz[1,3](iD), Marina Avila-Villanueva[5], Javier Ramirez[1,2], Teodoro del Ser-Quijano[4], Cristobal Carnero-Pardo[6], and Juan M. Gorriz[1,2](iD)

[1] Data Science and Computational Intelligence (DASCI) Institute, University of Granada, Granada, Spain
carmenj@ugr.es
[2] Department of Signal Theory, Networking and Communications, University of Granada, 18010 Granada, Spain
[3] Department of Communications Engineering, University of Malaga, 29010 Málaga, Spain
[4] Alzheimer Disease Research Unit, CIEN Foundation, Carlos III Institute of Health, Queen Sofía Foundation Alzheimer Center, Madrid, Spain
[5] Department of Biological and Health Psychology, Autonomous University of Madrid, 28049 Madrid, Spain
[6] FIDYAN Neurocenter, Granada, Spain

Abstract. The global prevalence of dementia is on the rise, posing a challenge to healthcare systems worldwide. The disease leads to irreversible deterioration of cognitive function, which underlines the importance of early detection to mitigate its impact. The Clock Drawing Test (CDT) is a widely used tool in cognitive assessment, as it involves manually drawing a clock on a piece of paper. Despite its widespread use, CDT scoring methods often rely on subjective expert assessments. Thus, machine learning and deep learning-based models are recently being proposed for the automated evaluation of CDT drawings. In this study, we compare two state-of-the-art models, a simple CNN and API-Net, as cognitive state classification systems. Two databases were used, one from Spanish clinical centers (7009 samples) and the other from a hospital in Thailand (3108 samples). The obtained results align with expected accuracy rates in such scenarios (around 80%) and are similar in both models. Specifically, the accuracy rates obtained with the Spanish database are 75.65% and 72.42%, and with the Thai database, 86.42% and 86.90%. This reflects that the implementation of an excessively complex model is not necessary given the available sample size and the binary classification scenario. Therefore, although both models could be useful in the clinical domain, opting for models with lower computational costs is advisable to make them more cost-effective and easily accessible.

© The Author(s), under exclusive license to Springer Nature Switzerland AG 2024
J. M. Ferrández Vicente et al. (Eds.): IWINAC 2024, LNCS 14674, pp. 191–200, 2024.
https://doi.org/10.1007/978-3-031-61140-7_19

Keywords: Alzheimer's Disease · Attentive pairwise interaction · Clock Drawing Test · Cognitive impairment · Deep Learning · Image processing

1   Introduction

Dementia, which is most frequently caused by Alzheimer's disease (AD), ranks among the most prevalent neurological syndromes globally [12]. Its diagnostic process begins with the administration of cognitive assessment tools to evaluate the cognitive status of individuals. Since millions worldwide are impacted by dementia, early identification becomes crucial to slow the advancement of the disease, especially in the absence of curative treatments. Two standard neuropsychological screening tests for early detection are the Mini-Mental State Examination (MMSE) [5] and the Montreal Cognitive Assessment (MoCA) [13].

The Clock Drawing Test (CDT) is another widely-used screening tool that assesses cognitive changes, including visuospatial functions, frontal lobe execution, and memory [6]. It is included in MoCA, but can be used independently. In this test, patients draw a clock with the numbers from 1 to 12 and specific clock hands positioning (ten past eleven). The resulting drawing is evaluated by a physician, who assigns a score reflecting the patient's cognitive status, aiding in the detection of potential cognitive impairment (CI).

While the CDT is widely used due to its simplicity and high sensitivity [16], the manual, time-consuming, and subjective nature of the physician-performed scoring task poses challenges. Fortunately, recent years have witnessed the rise of machine learning (ML) and deep learning (DL) techniques [7], offering automated solutions for the evaluation of this test [2].

In this study, we will conduct a comparative analysis of the use of a simple convolutional neural network (CNN) proposed by Jimenez-Mesa et al. [10] and an attentive pairwise interaction network (API-Net) implemented by Raksasat et al. [14] for the evaluation and scoring of CDT drawings. To achieve this, the databases from both studies will be employed with both DL models in a binary case-control experiment.

2   Materials and Methods

2.1   CDT Databases

Two databases are employed in this study. We presented the first one in [10], which comprises a total of 7009 CDT drawings. Among these, 5368 were contributed by individuals with normal cognitive function (healthy controls, HC), while 1641 were drawn by individuals with CI, including mild cognitive impairment or dementia. The drawings were sourced from volunteers at the Multidisciplinary Unit of the CIEN Foundation in Madrid, Spain, and the Department of Neurology of FIDYAN Neurocenter in Granada and Malaga, Spain. All participants providing clinical information and CDT drawings gave informed consent for the use of their data in clinical research. The Vallecas Project, serving as the framework for this study, received approval from the Ethics Committee of the Spanish Carlos III Institute of Health. The cognitive status of each participant was diagnosed through the consensus of a team comprising experienced neurologists and neuropsychologists, considering various factors such as age, clinical data, cognitive tests, and more. The average age of the participants is 73.30 years, with the CI group having an average age of 74.36 and the HC group an average age of 72.98. The ratio between females and males is 1.49.

The second dataset was introduced by Raksasat et al. [14], who made this database publicly accessible at https://github.com/cccnlab/CDT-API-Network. It comprises CDT images gathered during MoCA assessments conducted at the King Chulalongkorn Memorial Hospital in Bangkok, Thailand,covering the years 2019 to 2021. Ethical approval for the data collection was obtained from the institutional committee (0926/64). The average age of the participants in this database is 67 years, with a female-to-male ratio of 3:1. Each CDT drawing in this database was evaluated using the Shulman scoring rubric [16], resulting in categorisation into six groups. Specifically, score 0 (13 drawings) indicates no reasonable depiction of a clock, score 1 (20 drawings) represents severe visuo-spatial deficits, score 2 (53 drawings) denotes moderate visuo-spatial deficits, score 3 (352 drawings) signifies incorrect representation of the correct time, score 4 (1047 drawings) suggests minor visuo-spatial deficits, and score 5 (1623 drawings) indicates a normal depiction. Given the focus of our study on CI vs. HC, we adopted the criterion of considering drawings with a score of 3 or lower as samples indicating cognitive impairment (a total of 438), while scores 4 and 5 were categorized as healthy controls (a total of 2670). This classification aligns with the understanding that Shulman clock scores of less than 4 correspond to severe cognitive disorders [17], and this criterion has been consistently applied in the state of the art [3,14].

2.2   Image Preprocessing

The preprocessing process for the Spanish database was previously detailed in [9,10]. In summary, the drawing sheets were scanned, followed by the application of a clock detection algorithm to remove other elements, centre the image on the clock, binarise it, and resize it to 224×224. Examples from both categories, HC and CI, are depicted in the first two columns of Fig. 1. The Thai database was obtained in a preprocessed state, with scans anonymised and cropped to include only the clock. Examples of these processed images are illustrated in the last two columns of Fig. 1. For compatibility with our CNN model, these images were converted to greyscale and adjusted to a size of 224×224.

For usage in API-Net, images from both databases were resized to 256×256 and normalised using the mean and standard deviation from the Imaginet Dataset [4]. No data augmentation was applied to maintain a study focused on real images, enhancing its clinical utility in addition to reducing computational costs. Due to imbalances in both databases, we opted to randomly downsample

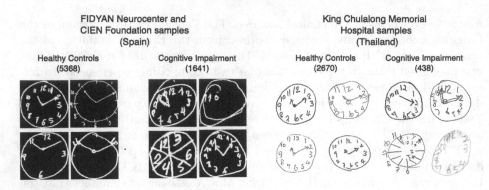

Fig. 1. Examples of preprocessed CDT drawings from the two different datasets analysed in the study. On the left, labelled images from FYDIAN Neurocenter and CIEN Foundation (Spain). On the right, images from King Chulalongkorn Memorial Hospital (Thailand) labelled according to Shulman scores. Specifically, control images are associated with scores five and four, while samples of cognitive impairment are associated with scores three and below.

the HC category in both databases to match the sample size of their respective CI categories.

2.3   Convolutional Neural Network

In a previous work, we proposed a simple CNN as a classification model for CDT drawings [10]. This network consists of a set of convolutional layers associated with pattern extraction and a set of linear layers used for classification. The architecture of this CNN model is illustrated in Fig. 2. The architecture comprises four 2D convolutional blocks, each consisting of a convolutional layer, batch normalization, rectified linear (ReLU) activation function, and a max pooling layer. The classification layers consist of three fully-connected layers. To prevent overfitting, dropout [18] was applied in conjunction with the linear layers. The model is finalized with a softmax layer to predict the probability of each sample belonging to the two analyzed classes, CI and Healthy Controls (HC).

Model Settings. The loss function chosen for this model was binary cross-entropy, and the optimisation process employed the Adam optimiser [11] with a learning rate of 0.001. The number of epochs applied for training was 70, using a batch size of 1. Whereas a dropout probability of 0.3 was applied in the fully-connected layers.

2.4   Attentive Pairwise Interaction Network

API-Net is a proposed architecture for fine-grained classification task [19], i.e. when images in different categories are highly similar.The idea is inspired by the

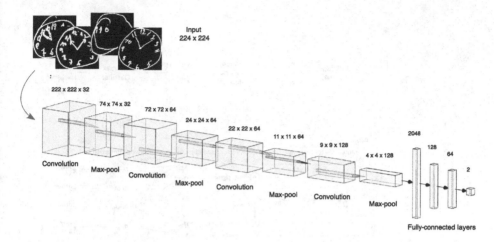

Fig. 2. Implemented convolutional neural network. The convolutional layers can be clustered into four convolutional blocks (convolutional layer, batch normalisation, ReLU activation and MaxPooling layer). A dropout of 0.3 is applied before the classification layers, where linear layers with sigmoid activation are implemented. The output is the class-related probability of the sample.

way humans compare similar images or objects, looking at both to find subtle differences [1]. It consist on three modules: a backbone, the API module and a softmax classifier, which are illustrated in Fig. 3.

The backbone is a feature extractor to generate embedding feature vectors from the images. It could be implemented using s any CNN without classification layers. It is feed with two fine-grained images and it generates two embedding vectors, $\mathbf{x}_1$ and $\mathbf{x}_2$ for each image. These vectors are introduced in the API module so that it learns to distinguish the two images contrastively. This module is the core of the architecture and is divided into three sub-modules: mutual vector learning, gate vector generation and pairwise interaction.

The submodule of mutual vector learning consists of generating a mutual vector, $\mathbf{x}_m$, from $\mathbf{x}_1$ and $\mathbf{x}_2$ by means of a mapping function:

$$\mathbf{x}_m = f_m\left([\mathbf{x}_1, \mathbf{x}_2]\right) \tag{1}$$

The authors [19] proposed the use of a multilayer perceptron (MLP) network of type encoding-decoding with a dropout layer in between to be fed with the concatenation of x_1 and x_2. This mutual vector tends to capture contrastive clues from the two fine-grained images. Next, the gate vector generation submodule aims to generate distinct features from the perspective of each individual image. To do this, $\mathbf{x}_m$ and $\mathbf{x}_i$ interact as follow to generate a gate vector:

$$\mathbf{g}_i = sigmoid\left(\mathbf{x}_m \odot \mathbf{x}_i\right), \quad i \in \{1, 2\} \tag{2}$$

where $\odot$ is the Hadamard product (channel-wise product is applied). Finally, a pairwise interaction is perform to obtained four attentive feature vectors by

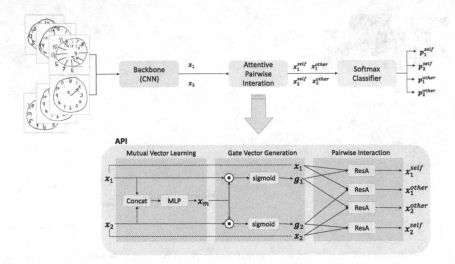

Fig. 3. API-Net's framework. The architecture consists of three parts. The backbone is in charge of generating the reduced vectors for each image. The attentive Pairwise Interaction (API) component provides the pairwise interaction between fine-grained images to improve the learning of the network. The API consists of three modules: creation of a mutual vector from the embeddings, generation of the gate vectors, and application of an interaction mechanism applying residual attention to obtain the four attentive feature vectors. Finally, a softmax classifier is applied to obtain the probabilities of belonging to each class and to calculate the loss function together with a score-ranking regularisation term.

means of interaction mechanisms using residual attention:

$$\mathbf{x}_1^{self} = \mathbf{x}_1 + \mathbf{x}_1 \odot \mathbf{g}_1 \tag{3}$$

$$\mathbf{x}_2^{self} = \mathbf{x}_2 + \mathbf{x}_2 \odot \mathbf{g}_2 \tag{4}$$

$$\mathbf{x}_1^{other} = \mathbf{x}_1 + \mathbf{x}_1 \odot \mathbf{g}_2 \tag{5}$$

$$\mathbf{x}_2^{other} = \mathbf{x}_2 + \mathbf{x}_2 \odot \mathbf{g}_1 \tag{6}$$

With this mechanism, each embedding vector $\mathbf{x}_i$ generates two attentive feature vectors, $\mathbf{x}_i^{self}$ and $\mathbf{x}_i^{other}$, by considering its own gate vector and the gate vector of the other image, respectively. This enhances the discriminative clues from both images.

The attentive feature vectors are entered into the last module of the architecture, the softmax classifier. In this step, the probability of belonging to each class of these attentive feature vectors is estimated as follows:

$$\mathbf{p}_i^j = softmax\left(\mathbf{W}\mathbf{x}_i^j + \mathbf{b}\right) \tag{7}$$

where $\{\mathbf{W}, \mathbf{b}\}$ are the parameter set of the classifier, $i \in \{1, 2\}$ and $j \in \{self, other\}$. To train the API-Net architecture, the loss function proposed to optimise the parameters of the model is as follows:

$$\mathcal{L} = \mathcal{L}_{ce} + \lambda \mathcal{L}_{rk} \tag{8}$$

where $\mathcal{L}_{ce}$ is the cross entropy loss, $\mathcal{L}_{rk}$ is the score ranking loss and λ is a regularisation coefficient to balance both losses. Therefore, the cross entropy loss could be seen as the one to be regularised by the score ranking loss. The mathematical terms of the two losses are:

$$\mathcal{L}_{ce} = -\sum_{i \in \{1,2\}} \sum_{j \in \{self, other\}} \mathbf{y}_i^\top \log\left(\mathbf{p}_i^j\right) \tag{9}$$

$$\mathcal{L}_{rk} = \sum_{i \in \{1,2\}} \max\left(0, \mathbf{p}_i^{other}(c_i) - \mathbf{p}_i^{self}(c_i) + \epsilon\right) \tag{10}$$

where $\mathbf{y}$ is the one-hot encoded label vector of image i, $\top$ represents the transpose of a matrix, c_i is the index related to the ground-truth label of image i, and ϵ is the score-ranking-loss margin. The score ranking loss is implemented to guide the model in favoring $\mathbf{x}_i^{self}$ over $\mathbf{x}_i^{other}$, as $\mathbf{x}_i^{self}$ is activated by its own gate vector, i.e. it should be more discriminatory.

It should be noted that, during training, the entire API-Net network is adjusted. However, for prediction, the API module is excluded, and the output from the backbone is directly passed to the softmax classifier.

Model Settings. With the aim of comparing the results with the study by Raksasat et al. [14], their code was used as a basis (https://github.com/cccnlab/CDT-API-Network), and model's parameter values were applied as in their work. The main change is that their aim was to classify based on Shulman score (multiclass experiment), while in this study, a binary classification is performed (HC vs. CI). In the embedding pairwise batch construction, the criteria were maintained to create the image pairs. Both intra-class image pair and inter-class image pair were considered. For each image m_i of the batch, the most dissimilar one is chosen as the intra-class pair, while the most similar one is chosen as the inter-class pair. This similarity is measured by Euclidean distance. Pretrained convolutional layers of ResNet152 [8] were implemented as backbone. The images' size (input size) was 256×256 pixels, the number of epochs was 100, the optimizer was Adam with a learning rate of 5×10^{-5}. Moreover, λ was established as 1, ϵ was set to 0.005, and the batch size was 4.

3   Experiments and Results

Four different experiments were conducted, combining the implementation of the CNN and API-Net with the use of both databases (Spanish and Thai). In all experiments, K-fold cross-validation with K = 5 was established as the framework to obtain the relevant metrics (balanced accuracy, precision, and sensitivity). Additionally, the area under the curve (AUC) value for the ROC curve was estimated.

Table 1 summarises the classification results obtained in each of the experiments. Similar performance metrics were achieved using the Thai database for both models, CNN and API-Net, with balanced accuracies exceeding 86% and AUC values of 0.93 and 0.92, respectively. Conversely, results obtained with the Spanish database are also comparable, albeit to a slightly lesser extent, for both models. Notably, in the case of API-Net, a higher standard deviation was observed compared to the CNN model.

Table 1. Classification results obtained using CNN and API-Net with the Spanish and Thai databases.

Experiment	CNN		API-Net	
Database	Spanish	Thai	Spanish	Thai
Acc (%)	75.65 ± 1.10	86.42 ± 0.90	72.42 ± 3.25	86.90 ± 1.91
Spec (%)	77.82 ± 2.13	85.16 ± 3.00	66.01 ± 12.47	85.18 ± 7.44
Sens (%)	73.49 ± 2.98	87.67 ± 3.32	78.83 ± 7.48	88.61 ± 5.52
AUC	0.83 ± 0.01	0.93 ± 0.01	0.81 ± 0.02	0.92 ± 0.02

4   Discussion

This study presents a comparative analysis between our proposed CNN and API-Net within the context of classifying CDT drawings for cognitive diagnostic assessment, i.e. a case-control classification scenario. Both models demonstrate satisfactory classification performance on paper-and-pencil drawings without the face clock preprint [2]. The metrics, detailed in Table 1, reveal that, at least for the given sample sizes, API-Net does not exhibit significantly superior results. For instance, an average accuracy of 86.42% and 86.90% is achieved using the Thai database in the CNN and API-Net, respectively. However, API-Net may prove valuable for more intricate tasks, such as scoring classification scenarios, as outlined in [14], where selecting a specific Shulman score for the drawing poses a challenging undertaking.

The difference in accuracy rates with both databases (75.65% and 72.42% with the Spanish dataset and 86.42% and 86.90% with the Thai dataset) derives from the fact that the Thai database was divided based on the Shulman scores, considering scores 4 and 5 as a normal cognitive state, while the rest (0–3) are associated with CI. In contrast, the Spanish database is more independent of the participant's drawing score (standard criteria from 0 to 7) [15], as we have the clinical diagnosis of each patient. This can lead to healthy subjects drawing the clock inaccurately and still being diagnosed as healthy. The observed decrease in accuracy with the Spanish database in API-Net (72.42%) may be attributed to its binary image nature, as opposed to RGB or grayscale, aligning more with the pre-trained parameters of ResNet-152.

In future studies, we could reevaluate API-Net's performance by exploring the impact of data augmentation, processing the Spanish database without binarization or using our CNN as backbone. Additionally, it would be valuable to investigate its suitability for scoring classification rather than diagnostic scenarios. Overall, it is evident that the state-of-the-art proposed networks for CDT classification have the potential to be used in the clinical domain. Nevertheless, it is advisable to prioritise models that are more accessible and cost-effective for practical clinical applications.

5 Conclusion

In this study, we compare two previously validated models, a CNN and API-Net, designed for CDT image classification in a cognitive state classification context (HC vs. CI). Both models exhibit similar performance, suggesting that, given the database size, the application of complex networks (API-Net) may be unnecessary, as comparable results can be achieved with a CNN of significantly lower computational cost. These findings highlight the utility of DL models in cognitive studies.

Acknowledgments. This research is part of the PID2022-137629OA-I00, PID2022-137461NB-C32 and PID2022-137451OB-I00 projects, funded by the MICIU/AEI/ 10.13039/and by "ERDF/EU", and the C-ING-183-UGR23 project, cofunded by the Consejería de Universidad, Investigación e Innovación and by European Union, funded by Programa FEDER Andalucía 2021–2027.

Disclosure of Interests. The authors have no competing interests to declare that are relevant to the content of this article.

References

1. Bruner, J.: A Study of Thinking. Routledge, Abingdon (2017)
2. Chan, J.Y.C., et al.: Evaluation of digital drawing tests and paper-and-pencil drawing tests for the screening of mild cognitive impairment and dementia: a systematic review and meta-analysis of diagnostic studies. Neuropsychol. Rev. 1 11 (2021). https://doi.org/10.1007/s11065-021-09523-2
3. Chen, S., Stromer, D., Alabdalrahim, H.A., Schwab, S., Weih, M., Maier, A.: Automatic dementia screening and scoring by applying deep learning on clock-drawing tests. Sci. Rep. **10**(1) (2020). https://doi.org/10.1038/s41598-020-74710-9
4. Deng, J., Dong, W., Socher, R., Li, L.J., Li, K., Fei-Fei, L.: Imagenet: a large-scale hierarchical image database. In: 2009 IEEE Conference on Computer Vision and Pattern Recognition, pp. 248–255. IEEE (2009)
5. Folstein, M.F., Folstein, S.E., McHugh, P.R.: Mini-mental state: a practical method for grading the cognitive state of patients for the clinician. J. Psychiatr. Res. **12**(3), 189–198 (1975)
6. Freedman, M., Leach, L., Kaplan, E., Winocur, G., Shulman, K., Delis, D.C.: Clock Drawing: A Neuropsychological Analysis. Oxford University Press, New York (1994)

7. Górriz, J., Álvarez Illán, I., Álvarez Marquina, A., et al.: Computational approaches to explainable artificial intelligence: advances in theory, applications and trends. Inf. Fusion **100**, 101945 (2023). https://doi.org/10.1016/j.inffus.2023.101945

8. He, K., Zhang, X., Ren, S., Sun, J.: Deep residual learning for image recognition. In: Proceedings of the IEEE Conference on Computer Vision and Pattern Recognition, pp. 770–778 (2016)

9. Jiménez-Mesa, C., et al.: Automatic classification system for diagnosis of cognitive impairment based on the clock-drawing test. In: IWINAC 2022, pp. 34–42. Springer, Heidelberg (2022). https://doi.org/10.1007/978-3-031-06242-1_4

10. Jiménez-Mesa, C., et al.: Using explainable artificial intelligence in the clock drawing test to reveal the cognitive impairment pattern. Int. J. Neural Syst. **33**(04) (2023). https://doi.org/10.1142/s0129065723500156

11. Kingma, D.P., Ba, J.: Adam: a method for stochastic optimization. arXiv preprint arXiv:1412.6980 (2014)

12. Knopman, D.S., et al.: Alzheimer disease. Nat. Rev. Dis. Primers **7**(1) (2021). https://doi.org/10.1038/s41572-021-00269-y

13. Nasreddine, Z.S., et al.: The montreal cognitive assessment, moCA: a brief screening tool for mild cognitive impairment. J. Am. Geriat. Soc. **53**(4), 695–699 (2005)

14. Raksasat, R., et al.: Attentive pairwise interaction network for AI-assisted clock drawing test assessment of early visuospatial deficits. Sci. Rep. **13**(1) (2023). https://doi.org/10.1038/s41598-023-44723-1

15. Seetha, J., Raja, S.S.: Brain tumor classification using convolutional neural networks. Biomed. Pharmacol. J. **11**(3), 1457 (2018)

16. Shulman, K.I.: Clock-drawing: is it the ideal cognitive screening test? Int. J. Geriatr. Psychiat. **15**(6), 548–561 (2000)

17. Shulman, K.I., Shedletsky, R., Silver, I.L.: The challenge of time: clock-drawing and cognitive function in the elderly. Int. J. Geriatr. Psychiat. **1**(2), 135–140 (1986)

18. Srivastava, N., Hinton, G., Krizhevsky, A., Sutskever, I., Salakhutdinov, R.: Dropout: a simple way to prevent neural networks from overfitting. J. Mach. Learn. Res. **15**(1), 1929–1958 (2014)

19. Zhuang, P., Wang, Y., Qiao, Y.: Learning attentive pairwise interaction for fine-grained classification. In: AAAI, pp. 13130–13137 (2020)

Artificial Intelligence
in Neurophysiology

Prediction of Burst Suppression Occurrence Under General Anaesthesia Using Pre-operative EEG Signals

Elif Yozkan[1], Enrique Hortal[1]([✉]) [iD], Joël Karel[1] [iD], Marcus L. F. Janssen[2] [iD], Catherine J. Vossen[3] [iD], and Erik D. Gommer[2] [iD]

[1] Department of Advanced Computing Sciences, Maastricht University, Maastricht, The Netherlands
enrique.hortal@maastrichtuniversity.nl
[2] Department of Clinical Neurophysiology, Maastricht University Medical Center, Maastricht, The Netherlands
[3] Department of Anesthesiology and Pain Medicine, Maastricht University Medical Center, Maastricht, The Netherlands

Abstract. Intraoperative burst suppression (BS) is associated with postoperative neurocognitive disorders, which could lead to increased mortality, morbidity and longer hospitalisation. The main objective of this study is to build a machine learning model capable of predicting the BS pattern between the phases of induction and incision, based on EEG and patient characteristics acquired preoperatively. To this end, several models, namely decision trees, random forest, XGBoost, SVM and logistic regression, were trained on the data with varying window sizes. The performance of the trained models is evaluated using stratified 5-fold cross-validation and a $5 \times 2cv$ t-test was applied to test significance. The main objective is to study, among other factors, the potential impact of the anaesthetic dosage on BS occurrence with the aim of personalising this process. The results obtained indicate that a Logistic Regression approach trained on the data epoched into 7-s windows can achieve a precision score of 0.63 and an ROC-AUC score of 0.61 while predicting future BS occurences. Furthermore, the explanations of the feature importance obtained from the SHapley Additive exPlanations (SHAP) demonstrate that the mean absolute power delta and alpha bands contribute the most to the predictions as well as the dosage of the anaesthetic agent propofol.

Keywords: Burst Suppression · Anaesthesia · EEG · SHapley Additive exPlanations

1 Introduction

Administration of anaesthesia entails gradual alterations in the EEG wave patterns as the patient enters the state of unconsciousness [3]. When anaesthesia

J. M. Ferrández Vicente et al. (Eds.): IWINAC 2024, LNCS 14674, pp. 203–212, 2024.
https://doi.org/10.1007/978-3-031-61140-7_20

is overly deep, due to the administration of excessive anaesthetic doses, a specific pattern called burst suppression (BS) is observed in the EEG recordings. These burst suppression patterns involve an alternating pattern of bursts, high frequency and high amplitude waves (75–250 μV), which are interrupted by low-amplitude suppressions which have a longer duration [17].

The occurrence of burst suppression during a surgical procedure is undesired since there is evidence that its emergence is associated with postoperative complications. These could involve a longer recovery process and have adverse post-operative outcomes such as postoperative neurocognitive disorders (PNDs) [7] and Postoperative Delirium (POD) [13], although this is still under debate. Analyzing and predicting EEG BS patterns can be highly effective for offering insights into the characteristics and causes of this phenomenon to enhance understanding and prevention. A preliminary study by Maastricht University and MUMC+ (Maastricht University Medical Centre+), employing descriptive statistics and backward selection logistic regression to examine EEG BS, revealed a correlation between lower band frequencies in preoperative EEG and the emergence of BS post-induction [15].

The detection of BS, along with its relationship with the depth of the anaesthesia, has been extensively studied in different contexts and using varying methods including both supervised and unsupervised machine learning pipelines. For instance, [14] analyzed the intraoperative EEG data of the patients who are undergoing cardiopulmonary bypass surgery, using multitaper spectral estimation methods, to automatically detect BS patterns and their duration. Their study demonstrates an association between the decreased power in the alpha and beta ranges and the susceptibility to BS. Similarly, [5] used band-wise power and spectral analysis in their study on classifying propofol-induced unconsciousness. Their approach, including the implementation of PCA trained support vector machine classifier, provided promising results as it reached a precision of 0.86 while maintaining an AUC of 0.94. Moreover, along with a time-frequency approach, the analysis of stationarity of EEG signals was taken as a baseline in the study of neonatal EEG BS patterns in [2]. Their framework, which utilizes Singular Value Decomposition of the time-frequency domain and Renyl Entropy as its main features achieves almost perfect performance as they obtain a total accuracy of 99.6% from their classification process.

The bispectral index (BIS), which combines multiple EEG features into a single parameter, is also studied in this context. In [4], an insight is provided into the association among the extracted BIS values with the BS rate. Their method involves a regression, based on different doses of anesthesia administered to 10 different patients. Their results showed a linear correlation between the BIS and BS pattern especially when the suppression ratio is greater than 40%.

In contrast to the approaches which adopt supervised learning, [12] proposes a novel unsupervised algorithm which detects burst suppression per minute to monitor the sedation level in patients who are in the intensive care unit. The algorithm uses a certain set of predetermined rules such as the duration of bursts, the distance and the similarity between the formed covariance matrices. Their approach provides a more personalized framework, which does not need fine-tuning of the algorithm, unlike the supervised counterparts.

This study aims to develop a predictive model to foresee the occurrence of EEG burst suppression patterns during general anaesthesia using author's preliminary work [15] as a foundational reference. It also seeks to investigate the potential contribution of not only various preoperative EEG parameters but also patient characteristics and drugs administered, to the prediction process through diverse machine learning techniques. There is evidence that Mild Cognitive Impairment EEG signatures can be found in the resting state EEG [11]. We investigated whether a combination of patient characteristics, anaesthetics and pre-surgery EEG features yields a good predictive power. By adding explainability in the form of SHAP values, it is investigated whether these additional features contribute to the model compared to relying on EEG features alone.

2 Methods

2.1 Data

In this retrospective study[1], 378 patients (72.1 ± 8.54, 75.2% male) who underwent carotid artery endarterectomy between January 2015 and December 2020 with continuous 20-channel EEG monitoring were included. Patients were selected if a preoperative baseline EEG of more than 20 s with eyes closed was available. The perioperative EEG signals were annotated by technicians of the Department of Clinical Neurophysiology of the MUMC+, indicating whether or not BS occurred after induction. Out of these 378 patients, 137 (around 35%) exhibited BS episodes.

In this study, only four frontal channels (Fp1, Fp2, F7 and F8), filtered between 0.5–45 Hz, were considered, in line with available tools on the market such as the BIS monitoring frontal sensors. Moreover, the underlying mechanism of loss of consciousness is the anteriorization of alpha rhythm due to propofol [20]. Anonymized data from each participant was collected at various stages of the surgical procedure, including the preoperative, induction, incision, and final phases. However, for this study, only data from the preoperative phase is utilized for model training, labelled as whether there was BS after induction. As seen in Fig. 1, in the preoperative phase, the EEG signals were recorded both while eyes were open as well as when closed for many consecutive times. The induction phase is the period where anaesthesia is administrated to the patient. We used the period between induction and the start of the surgery to investigate the relationship with BS pattern occurrence.

In addition to the EEG signal information, the given data encompasses 155 variables which contain personal and additional information about the medical history of patients as well as the information regarding the process of the surgery such as the dosage of different anesthetics administered to each patient.

---

[1] Approval was obtained from the Medical Ethical Board of the Maastricht University Medical Centre (METC 2023–2543) on the 15th of June 2021 for this retrospective study.

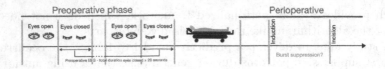

Fig. 1. Different phases of a surgical operation.

2.2 Pre-processing

Artifact and Noise Removal. To eliminate artefacts in the EEG signals, Individual Component Analysis (ICA), particularly FastICA from the MNE Python's ICA module [8], is applied.

Extracting Frequency Domain Features from EEG Signals. Each signal is transformed into the frequency domain using Welch's method, calculating Power Spectrum Density (PSD) by averaging overlapping signal segments with a Hanning window. This approach minimizes noise while maintaining a balance between spectral smoothness and resolution [19]. To analyze signal characteristics in the frequency domain, the mean absolute power of key frequency bands (delta (1–3.9 Hz), theta (4–7.9 Hz), alpha (8–12.9 Hz), beta (13–30.9 Hz), and gamma (30–45 Hz)) was calculated. This involved computing and averaging the area under the PSD curve for each channel within these spectral ranges [16].

Data Windowing. To assess the impact of dividing data into equal-sized windows on classification algorithm performance, EEG data was segmented into epochs of 2, 5, 7, and 10 s, each with a 0.5-s overlap between successive windows.

Feature Selection. In the analysis of BS patterns, patient data, including personal/medical history and pre-surgery medications, was filtered to identify key variables. Variables missing over 20% of data and non-essential variables, such as ICU stay duration and systole/diastole levels, were excluded. A correlation filter using Point Bi-Serial Correlation, suitable for linking numeric variables with binary outcomes [9] eliminated highly correlated pairs to reduce redundancy while significant variables, including propofol and remifentanil dosages with correlation coefficients of 0.33 and 0.31 and $p < 0.05$, were retained for training. Finally, data standardization was applied to meet classification algorithm requirements. Following the aforementioned process, the resultant feature set used in this study comprises: *mean_delta, mean_theta, mean_alpha, mean_beta, mean_gamma, dosage_propfol, dosage_remifentanil,* and *age.*

2.3 Training

For the training process, inherently explainable supervised classification algorithms like decision tree, random forest, and XGBoost were chosen, in addition to support vector machines and logistic regression approaches. The ground truth for these models is the occurrence of BS after induction as annotated by the technicians.

2.4 Models Evaluation

To evaluate classification model performance, for non-windowed data, stratified K-fold cross-validation with $K = 5$ was utilized, addressing the dataset's imbalance (25% BS prevalence) to preserve the class ratio in each fold. For windowed data, ensuring no patient overlap between training and test folds, stratified group K-fold cross-validation was applied. Model reliability and performance were assessed using *Precision*, *F1-Score*, and *ROC-AUC* metrics.

Furthermore, to verify the statistical significance of the predictive performance differences among the employed methods, a 5×2cv t-test was conducted. This test involves five replications of two-fold cross-validation [1]. The test statistic is computed as follows:

$$ t = \frac{p_1^{(1)}}{\sqrt{\frac{1}{5} \sum_{i=5}^{5} S_i^2}} \tag{1} $$

where p_1^1 denotes the difference in scores of the models for the first fold of the initial iteration, and S_i^2 is the sample variance in the score differences in the ith iteration.

2.5 Generating Explanations with SHAP

Beyond standard evaluation metrics, Shapley values, as derived from the SHAP (SHapley Additive exPlanations) method [10], were utilized to understand the impact of each feature on the trained models. The SHAP method interprets model predictions by computing the contribution of individual features.

3 Experiments

The baseline approach involved using the pre-processed original data (without windowing) to evaluate the efficacy of the chosen models in predicting BS occurrence. Then, the influence of segmenting the data into windows is investigated by evaluating the predictive performances of the methods for both windowed (data segmented into 2, 5, 7 and 10-second windows) and non-windowed data. To test whether the differences observed in the results of the evaluation metrics are indeed significant, a 5×2cv t-test was performed for both windowed and non-windowed data sets. We trained the models using different settings, and we included in the results the best performances from each model based on their top hyperparameter combinations.

Table 1. Mean Evaluation scores for non-windowed and windowed data. Best and second-best results per column are highlighted in bold and in italics, respectively.

Classifier	Non-Windowed			Windowed (7-s)		
	Precision	F1-Score	ROC-AUC	Precision	F1-Score	ROC-AUC
Logistic Regression	*0.39*	*0.39*	**0.57**	**0.63**	**0.55**	**0.61**
Decision Tree	**0.48**	**0.47**	*0.56*	0.20	*0.21*	*0.51*
Random Forest	0.33	0.33	0.52	0.19	0.20	0.50
XGB	0.31	0.35	0.53	0.2	0.19	0.50
SVM	0.18	0.23	0.51	*0.21*	*0.21*	0.42

4   Results and Discussion

4.1   Models Evaluation

Table 1 and Fig. 2 present the outcomes of each model. For readability purposes, only the data with the best-performing window size (7 s) is included in the windowed data analysis. Regarding the baseline model (non-windowed), while overall scores are modest, decision trees achieved the highest precision (0.48) and ROC-AUC (0.56). A comparison between Table 1 (left) and the box-whisker plots in Fig. 2 (left) reveals its performance is comparable to logistic regression. This fact is also supported by the $5 \times 2cv$ t-test shown in Table 2, suggesting that the decision tree classifier's performance on non-windowed data is not statistically significant, as all p-values exceed 0.05. Additionally, it is important to note the considerable variation in the precision scores of this model.

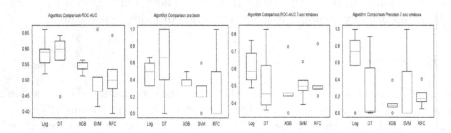

Fig. 2. Box-whisker comparison of the algorithm scores for the original (left) and the windowed data (right).

Upon thorough assessment of various windowing sizes, the 7-s window emerged as the most effective, yielding the best scores among all considered sizes. A 2-s window produced lower precision and ROC-AUC scores compared to other options. On the other hand, while the 10-s windowed data exhibited

Table 2. Results of the 5 × 2cv t-test between Decision Tree Classifier and the others for non-windowed data

Algorithms	test-statistic	p-value
DT-LOG	−0.148	0.88
DT-RFC	0.381	0.719
DT-XGB	0.440	0.678
DT-SVM	−0.237	0.7

Table 3. Results of the 5 × 2cv t-test between Logistic Regression and the other classifiers for the windowed data

Algorithms	test-statistic	p-value
LOG-DT	−6.468	0.001
LOG-RFC	−8.340	0.0002
LOG-XGB	−8.660	0.020
LOG-SVM	5.10	0.0001

a marginally higher precision score in comparison to the 7-s window, the latter demonstrated a more balanced trade-off between precision and ROC-AUC scores.

After selecting this window size, the box-plot comparison of classification algorithms in Fig. 2 (right) shows the logistic regression model as the superior performer, with a narrower spread of scores compared to decision trees. Table 1 (right), detailing the mean evaluation scores for models trained on windowed data, highlights that the logistic regression achieves an ROC-AUC of 0.61 and a precision score of 0.63. The primary factor contributing to its superior performance, particularly in comparison to tree-based classifiers, could be attributed to the abundance of numerical features incorporated into the model. Moreover, the 5 × 2cv t-test corroborates this comparison. As indicated in Table 3, logistic regression demonstrated a significant difference in predictive performance in comparison with the other models.

Comparing the performance of the logistic regression model trained on both non-windowed and the best-performing windowing strategy (7 s, see Table 1), it is evident that the model trained on the windowed data outperforms, particularly in terms of precision, achieving a mean precision exceeding 60% and consequently, a higher ROC-AUC score.

The primary advantage of the windowing method lies in its ability to expand the sample space, a critical factor in enhancing model performance. The incorporation of overlapping windows further extends the sample size while mitigating the loss of information caused by data segmentation. On the other hand, although the duration of the BS pattern lacks precise characterization, numerous studies have indicated that the combined duration of burst and suppression typically falls within the range of 3 to 5 s [6]. Consequently, excessively small window sizes often fail to furnish sufficient information regarding the burst suppression pattern.

4.2 Explainability Analysis

With the logistic regression model trained on 7-second windowed data achieving the highest prediction scores, SHAP explanations were only provided for this model. The SHAP summary plot in Fig. 3 reveals that the mean power of *delta*

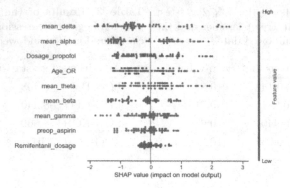

Fig. 3. SHAP global explanations for Logistic Regression trained on 7-sec windowed data.

and *alpha* bands significantly influences the model's predictions. The frequency activities of the bursts are predominantly concentrated in the frequency ranges of 0–4 Hz and 4–7 Hz, as indicated in previous research [13]. Additionally, a prior study on the same dataset established a strong correlation between lower frequency bands and the burst suppression pattern [15]. The SHAP explanations provided here reinforce these findings. Notably, while lower delta power values occasionally show positive contributions, higher delta power values generally exhibit a stronger positive impact. Hence, the substantial contribution of the delta band to the model's predictions is unsurprising. Furthermore, a low frontal alpha band power often signifies a higher likelihood of experiencing burst suppression [13, 18]. The prevalence of data points with low alpha power on the positive side aligns with previous research findings.

The results also illustrate that increased dosages of the anaesthetic agent propofol are associated with a higher probability of experiencing burst suppression. This observation is reasonable since higher administration of anaesthetic agents elevates the likelihood of the BS pattern occurring in patients [21]. A similar association is noted for remifentanil dosage.

4.3   Limitations and Future Work

In retrospect, higher precision and ROC-AUC scores would enhance the reliability of the experiment results. The main limitations were the limited samples and a lack of detailed variables about burst suppression occurrence. Breaking down annotations into bursts and suppressions separately could improve predictive power, considering the complex nature of BS, which involves interruptions by low-amplitude and low-frequency suppressions with varying durations. The absence of information on burst and suppression duration in the signal is another limitation, suggesting the need for larger window sizes in specific instances.

The study highlights challenges, including the need to investigate the influence of channels beyond the four frontal ones for compatibility with commercial systems. The scarcity of short-duration preoperative resting-state EEG data is a limitation, and enriching the dataset with neurocognitive evaluations like MoCA or MMSE could be beneficial. In that line, incorporating a broader range of EEG signatures, such as theta-to-alpha ratios could also be valuable. Additionally, investigating other opioids, which are underrepresented in the retrospective dataset, is necessary for comprehensive information about anaesthetic agents. Finally, while this study focused on prediction, in practical scenarios like operating rooms, providing a numerical output indicating the likelihood of burst suppression occurrence may be advantageous for implementing appropriate precautions based on the BS rate.

5 Conclusion

This study aimed to develop a prediction model for EEG burst suppression patterns between the induction and incision phases of surgical procedures using preoperative data from the Maastricht University Medical Center (MUMC+), building on a previous study on the same dataset. Despite some limitations, our models demonstrated reasonable predictive capabilities being the logistic regression model trained on windowed data the most promising approach, supported by $5 \times 2cv$ t-test results. Analysis revealed that delta and alpha bands' mean absolute power significantly contributed to prediction. Windowing methods, particularly with 7-s window size, yielded higher precision and ROC-AUC scores compared to non-windowed data. These findings align with a previous study emphasizing the importance of lower frequency bands in detecting burst suppression. It is noteworthy that, while promising results have been demonstrated in the detection of burst suppression in previous works [2,5], to the best of the authors' knowledge, this study represents the first instance of utilizing exclusively preoperative EEG and opioid information for predicting future occurrences of BS.

In practical terms, the applications of this study consider the early detection of burst suppression before the induction phase of surgery. This approach establishes the basis for predicting the likelihood of future burst suppression occurrences based on preoperative data, enabling experts to adjust the dosage of anaesthetic agents accordingly, providing a personalized procedure. Additionally, explainability, a must-have in the medical domain, provides insights for domain experts to investigate factors influencing pattern occurrence, laying the groundwork for further research and enhancements.

References

1. Alpaydm, E.: Combined 5×2 cv F test for comparing supervised classification learning algorithms. Neural Comput. **11**(8), 1885–1892 (1999)
2. Awal, M.A., Colditz, P.B., Boashash, B., Azemi, G.: Detection of neonatal EEG burst-suppression using a time-frequency approach, pp. 1–6 (2014)

3. Brown, E.N., Lydic, R., Schiff, N.D.: General anesthesia, sleep, and coma. N. Engl. J. Med. **363**(27), 2638–2650 (2010)
4. Bruhn, J., Bouillon, T.W., Shafer, S.L.: Bispectral index (BIS) and burst suppression: revealing a part of the bis algorithm. J. Clin. Monit. Comput. **16**, 593–596 (2000)
5. De Faria, W., Schamberg, G., Brown, E.N.: Classifying EEG of propofol-induced unconsciousness in the presence of burst suppression, pp. 1–5 (2020)
6. Dumermuth, G., Molinari, L.: Spectral analysis of the EEG - some fundamentals revisited and some open problems. Neuropsychobiology **17**(1–2), 85–99 (1987)
7. Evered, L., et al.: Recommendations for the nomenclature of cognitive change associated with anaesthesia and surgery-2018. Anesthesiology **129**(5), 872–879 (2018)
8. Gramfort, A., et al.: MEG and EEG data analysis with MNE-Python. Front. Neurosci. **7**(267), 1 (2013)
9. Gupta, S.D.: Point biserial correlation coefficient and its generalization. Psychometrika **25**(4), 393–408 (1960)
10. Lundberg, S.M., Lee, S.I.: A unified approach to interpreting model predictions. Adv. Neural Inf. Process. Syst. **30**, 1–10 (2017)
11. Meghdadi, A.H., et al.: Resting state EEG biomarkers of cognitive decline associated with Alzheimer's disease and mild cognitive impairment. PloS One **16**(2), e0244180 (2021)
12. Narula, G., Haeberlin, M., Balsiger, J., Strässle, C., Imbach, L., Keller, E.: Detection of EEG burst-suppression in neurocritical care patients using an unsupervised machine learning algorithm. Clin. Neurophysiol. **132**(10), 2485–2492 (2021)
13. Pawar, N., Barreto Chang, O.L.: Burst suppression during general anesthesia and postoperative outcomes: mini review. Front. Syst. Neurosci. **15**, 767489 (2022)
14. Plummer, G.S., et al.: Electroencephalogram dynamics during general anesthesia predict the later incidence and duration of burst-suppression during cardiopulmonary bypass. Clin. Neurophysiol. **130**(1), 55–60 (2019)
15. den Ridder, T., Mess, W., Hortal, E., et. al.: Can baseline EEG predict burst suppression after induction of anesthesia in patients undergoing carotid artery surgery? preliminary results of a retrospective analysis. In: Abstract Dutch Association of Anesthesiology (2022)
16. Saby, J.N., Marshall, P.J.: The utility of EEG band power analysis in the study of infancy and early childhood. Dev. Neuropsychol. **37**(3), 253–273 (2012)
17. Särkelä, M., Mustola, S., Seppänen, T., Koskinen, M., Lepola, P., Suominen, K., et al.: Automatic analysis and monitoring of burst suppression in anesthesia. J. Clin. Monit. Comput. **17**, 125–134 (2002)
18. Shao, Y.R., et al.: Low frontal alpha power is associated with the propensity for burst suppression: an electroencephalogram phenotype for a "vulnerable brain". Anesth. Analg. **131**(5), 1529 (2020)
19. Solomon, O.M., Jr.: PSD computations using welch's method. NASA STI/Recon Technical Report N **92**, 23584 (1991)
20. Weiner, V.S., et al.: Propofol disrupts alpha dynamics in functionally distinct thalamocortical networks during loss of consciousness. Proc. Natl. Acad. Sci. **120**(11), e2207831120 (2023)
21. Yoshitani, K., Kawaguchi, M., Takahashi, M., Kitaguchi, K., Furuya, H.: Plasma propofol concentration and EEG burst suppression ratio during normothermic cardiopulmonary bypass. Br. J. Anaesth. **90**(2), 122–126 (2003)

Advances in Denoising Spikes Waveforms for Electrophysiological Recordings

Rocío López-Peco[1](✉) ⓘ, Mikel Val-Calvo[2] ⓘ, Cristina Soto-Sánchez[1] ⓘ,
and Eduardo Fernández[1,3] ⓘ

[1] Instituto de Bioingeniería, Universidad Miguel Hernández, Elche, Spain
`rocio.lopezp@umh.com`
[2] Research Institute for Human Centered Technology, Polytechnic University of Valencia, Valencia, Spain
[3] CIBER-BBN, Madrid, Spain

Abstract. The processing of neural signals faces significant challenges, particularly within the framework of electrophysiological recordings involving electrical stimulation. Extensive efforts have been dedicated to automating this analysis, but several aspects, such as artifact removal, still require further improvements. To address some of these challenges, we have devised a novel strategy based on waveform clustering, spike detection, artifact template matching, and advanced filtering techniques. This approach facilitates an automated workflow for neural denoising and sorting, thereby diminishing human bias and enabling automatic processing within a reasonable timeframe. To assess the efficacy of our algorithms, we conducted tests on electrophysiological recordings acquired during experiments involving electrical stimulation of the human visual cortex. The results demonstrate a strong overall performance, as evidenced by robust F1 scores. These newly developed tools are available as open source on *Github*.

Keywords: Spike denoising · Spike sorting · Machine learning

1 Introduction

Intracortical stimulation and electrophysiological recording methodologies are pivotal in neuroscientific research, providing deep insights into the brain's complex functions [1]. These techniques involve the direct application of electrical impulses to specific brain regions and the capture of neuronal electrical signals. The analysis of neuronal signals offer a comprehensive view of both spontaneous and stimulated brain activities and play a crucial role in understanding the relationships between neural activity and aspects of plasticity, perception, action, and behavior [2].

In this context, modern probes capture signals from a multitude of neurons. Among the various approaches to understanding neuronal dynamics and behaviour, analysis of the activity patterns of individual neurons is the only

© The Author(s), under exclusive license to Springer Nature Switzerland AG 2024
J. M. Ferrández Vicente et al. (Eds.): IWINAC 2024, LNCS 14674, pp. 213–222, 2024.
https://doi.org/10.1007/978-3-031-61140-7_21

way to characterise the specific behaviour of neurons in response to any stimulus [3]. As a result, understanding a circuit's properties necessitates the precise identification of neurons and their interactions, and to do so, we need to identify the single neurons as individual units, a process called *spike sorting* [4]. To extract single neuron activity information from the recorded data, computational methods require the use of software algorithms to exclude the artefacts and to identify which component of the signal belongs to which neuron. Classically, neuronal spikes are clustered based on parameters such as their waveform to infer their source neuron [3]. This has typically involved supervised clustering algorithms.

Analyzing signals from electrophysiological recordings of cortical activity, especially where electrical micro-stimulation is applied, presents complex challenges [5] being labor-intensive and often inefficient for the analysis of large datasets prevalent in contemporary research [6].

Consequently, software with different approaches have been developed to deal with the problems of noise, artefacts and difficult signal classification. Although the quality of the analysis has improved, it is still a challenge to work with electrophysiological signals and often the choice of the most appropriate software for each data set is also difficult. [7]. This process has led to the existence of different signal processing and spike sorting algorithms where comparison between them and standardisation becomes difficult. As a consequence of the unification request, many of these algorithms were compiled in the *SpikeInterface* project. [8].

SpikeInterface is a Python framework that consolidated multiple spike sorting technologies to streamline the processing, comparison, and validation of neural data from extracellular recordings. This framework addresses most of the processing stages needed in neuroscience research, from data extractors, preprocessing, sorting and comparison methods. Additionally, it calculates metrics such as firing rates and amplitude distributions.

However, one of its weaknesses is the handling of stimulation artefact. The noise removal tools are focused on general filtering and correction techniques [9] but does not have a precise development for specific removal of artefact shapes.

The aim of this article is to develop an automatic signal denoising process and to include this step in the analysis pipeline. Computational algorithms, machine learning methods and automated data analysis techniques will be used to address the challenges of scalable and efficient analysis of the complex neural datasets. Finally, we want to make our methodology accessible on *GitHub*.[1]

2   Methods

A comprehensive analysis pipeline designed for the processing of neural spike data is presented in Fig. 1 and described below in the methodology sections.

---

[1] https://github.com/rociolopeth/AI-SpikeScope.

This pipeline integrates several critical stages organized in two main steps: Neural denoising and Spike sorting. High-pass filtering, amplitude threshold analysis, neural waveforms denoising and spike sorting are some of the most critical aspects used in this methodology. Our approach is encapsulated in a Python-based framework, employing custom-built modules for each processing step.

The final workflow process is designed to be fully automatic, requiring minimal manual intervention, which significantly reduces the processing time and potential for human error.

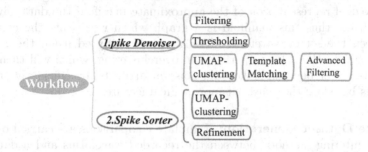

Fig. 1. Neural spike processing pipeline. Workflow with two main components and subcomponents.

2.1 Acquisition System and Dataset

The neural signals were recorded in humans visual cortex using *Trellis* software 1.14.4.41 version [10] from *Ripple Neuro*. Stimulation protocols were configured with proprietary software to design custom protocols and delivered through the *Summit* stimulation system *(Ripple, Salt Lake City, UT)*. An intracortical microelectrode *Utah* array consisting of *96* electrodes was used. Electrophysiological data acquisition was carried out at a 30000 Hz sampling frequency. Data is collected in *NSX* and *NEV* format from the *Blackrock Multichannel System* [11]. The dataset used for this study comprehends two distinct sources:

1. Spontaneous activity recordings.
2. Stimulation activity recordings: Balanced square biphasic trains of 50 pulses at 300 Hz; phase duration 170 μs/phase; interphase duration 60 μs. Delivered currents range between 1 to 100 μA in 10 μA steps.

2.2 Neural Signal Denoising

Data Preparation and Initial Processing: The pipeline begins high-pass filtering the raw signal between 250–7,500 Hz using a *Butterworth filter* order = 3, with a sampling frequency set at 30000 Hz. Then amplitude threshold analysis is performed, wherein neural spike waveforms are evaluated against predefined minimum and maximum amplitude thresholds. Waveforms are extracted using an amplitude threshold of six standard deviations relative to the *Signal-to-Noise Ratio(SNR)*. This step ensures that waveforms falling outside the specified amplitude range are excluded, reducing noise and irrelevant data early in the analysis.

Topological Representation Clustering: The denoising strategy core methodology is designed to process neural spike waveforms through a series of analytical steps. Utilizing a *Uniform Manifold Approximation and Projection (UMAP)* manifold representation. *UMAP* works by constructing an intermediate topological representation of the approximate manifold the data have been sampled from, thus this manifold is a graph which represents the connectivity between the set of waveforms. The graph is analyzed using the *Louvain-Communities* method [12] to perform an overclustering, which will then allows us to better filter between spikes and noise or artifacts, by efficiently grouping waveforms based on their distinct morfological features.

Template Dataset Generation: Template comparisons are carried out with advanced filtering methods between the recorded waveforms and a dataset of noise and neural waveform templates. These templates serve as benchmarks for identifying authentic neural spikes and differentiating them from noise or artifacts. A collection of templates—extracted from spontaneous and stimulation recordings— was previously created that allowed us to differentiate spikes from artefacts based on their similarity. The dataset comprises 248 spike templates and 43 artifact templates, which were obtained from custom and predefined datasets through the manually curation with *NeuroSorter Interface*[2]. It is important to note that the *NeuroSorter Interface* serves exclusively as a software tool for visualization and manual curation, without engaging in the processing of signals. This software loads spike waveforms directly from *.NEV* file formats. These files store only waveforms, between 250–7500 Hz at 30000 Hz, with a *SNR* above 4.8–6 (adjusted according to spike amplitude). The manual curation process was guided by a specific rationale: to include only those waveforms with an amplitude exceeding six times the standard deviation relative to the *SNR* [13]. This criterion ensured the inclusion of waveforms from neurons in close proximity to the electrode. To mitigate individual bias, manual curation was conducted by three independent experts.

Template Matching: The computing of a set of statistical metrics on the representative waveform and the templates are performed to search for valid neural spikes while minimizing the inclusion of artifacts. The statistical metrics used in this process are described below and an example from 2 different clusters with the advanced filtering process is shown in Fig. 2.

1. **Z-Score Normalization:** The average waveform pattern for each cluster is represented through z-score normalization, standardizing the waveform data.

---

[2] https://github.com/mikelval82/NeuroSorter-Interface.

2. **Correlation Analysis:** Spearman correlation coefficient [14] between the average waveform and predefined spike and artifact templates to identify the best-matching templates for each unit.

  (a) **Artefacts rejection:** Units with a higher correlation to an artifact template than the best-matching spike template, exceeding a Spearman correlation threshold of 0.9, are considered noise and filtered out.

The non-rejected waveforms continue to be further evaluated in step 3, 4 and 5 where advanced filtering features will be extracted.

3. **Linear Regression:** A linear regression analysis is conducted to evaluate the trend of the average waveform.

4. **DTW:** the method is computed to measure the distance between the phase space representations of the mean waveform and its best-matching spike template, where a low distance indicates strong similarity.

5. **Variability Quantification:** The variability within each cluster is quantified using a normalized standard deviation criterion to assist in distinguishing true spikes from noise.

6. **Comprehensive Decision Making:** The final decision to accept or reject units is based on a collective assessment of noise identification from metrics extracted in previous steps; correlation with templates spikecorr¿0.7; waveform trend in degrees with respect to the x axis $-15° < \theta < 15°$; DTW distance < 0.6 μV; and intracluster variability < 0.6(Std). Units satisfying all criteria are accepted as true spikes.

Detailed steps of the full algorithm are explained in Algorithm 1.

Collectively, with these techniques we work in retaining neural spikes, while artifacts and noise are expected to be removed.

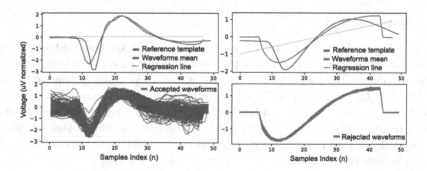

Fig. 2. Template matching for 2 clusters. Top subplots: normalized voltage of mean spike waveforms (blue), reference templates overlaid (green), regression lines (pink dashed lines). Bottom left subplot: overlaped waveforms classified as spikes, matching the reference template (*Spearman* corr = 0.95, p = 0.0006). Bottom right subplot: rejected waveforms (*Spearman* corr = 0.92, p = 0.05). (Color figure online)

Algorithm 1. Neural Waveforms Denoising Algorithm:

1: **for** each cluster **do**
2:      Calculate z-score normalized mean to represent average waveform pattern.
3:      Compute correlation between average waveform and predefined spike templates.
4:      Compute correlation between average waveform and artifact templates.
5:      Determine best-matching spike template using Spearman correlation coefficient.
6:      Evaluate best-matching artifact template.
7:      **if** correlation with any artifact template > correlation with best-matching spike template AND Spearman correlation > 0.9 **then**
8:          Mark unit as noise and filter out.
9:      **end if**
10:     Perform linear regression to evaluate trend of average waveform.
11:     Compute DTW distance between phase space representations of mean waveform and its best-matching spike template.
12:     Quantify variability within each cluster using normalized standard deviation criterion.
13:     Make final decision based on:
        - Noise determination
        - Correlation with spike and artifact templates
        - Trend of average waveform
        - DTW distance
        - Variability within the cluster
14:     **if** unit meets all criteria **then**
15:         Mark as accepted.
16:     **else**
17:         Mark as rejected.
18:     **end if**
19: **end for**

2.3   Spike Sorting

Sorting Procedure: The denoised spike waveforms are then subjected to a stage that categorizes the spikes into distinct units based on their waveform shape properties. A graph representation of the spike data is generated with *UMAP*. The *Louvain* method for community detection effectively group spikes into clusters based on their similarity. Here, unlike the earlier denoising phase which utilizes overclustering to distinguish between spikes and noise or artifacts, the focus shifts towards identifying the best set of clusters, thus a refinement process is performed to merge those clusters that are similar.

Refinement of Spike Clusters: After the denoised spike waveforms clustering in the previous step, the algorithm revisits the clusters to detect and merge similar units. The similarity between the mean waveforms of different clusters is computed, identifying clusters that are sufficiently similar based on the *DTW* similarity metric. Following the calculation of *DTW* similarity, the resultant value is compared against a dynamically determined threshold. This threshold is derived by inversely relating it to the mean number of spikes per cluster,

adjusted by a predefined margin. A similarity measure falling below this calculated threshold indicates a significant degree of resemblance between the time
series. As a way to reduce the likelihood of over-segmentation similar clusters
are merged into single units. This means that spikes with comparable waveform
morphologies are classified under the same unit.

2.4 Implementation Details

The full pipeline was implemented in *Python*, using libraries such as *NumPy* for
numerical operation, UMAP for the manifold representation and dimensionality reduction, *NetworkX* for graph construction, *Community-Louvain* for cluster
detection and *similarity measures* to compute DTW metrics. *Spearman correlation* was computed using *scipy*.

2.5 Software Testing

Quality metrics were carried out also in python code for the neural denoising
in a stimulation dataset—made up two recordings. Manual cleaning process in
the software *NeuroSorter Interface* to remove artifacts was performed in both
recordings to compare with the automatic method .

Regarding the metrics used, *Precision* measures the proportion of true positive results in all positive predictions, indicating the model's accuracy in identifying relevant instances. *Recall*, or *sensitivity*, assesses the model's ability to detect
all actual positives. *Precision* and *Recall* are combined into a single metric—*f1-
score*—, providing a balanced measure of the model's performance. *f1-score* was
obtained for the template-matching classification as well as for the waveforms
one. The formula for the *f1-score* is given by:

$$F1 = 2 \times \frac{\text{precision} \times \text{recall}}{\text{precision} + \text{recall}}$$

Additionally, a confusion matrix was used to visually represent the denosing
model predictions across different classes in the stimulation subset, allowing to
identify any biases or weaknesses in class-specific performance.

3 Results

3.1 Denoising and Spike Extraction Quality Measurement

The application of the Denoising Algorithm—*detailed in Algorithm 1*—on the
two recordings stimulation dataset, has yielded outcomes shown in Table 1. The
algorithm demonstrated a high precision in identifying spikes (0.87) and artefacts (0.99), with a recall of 0.99 for spikes and 0.87 for artefacts as shown in
the confusion matrix in the Fig. 3. These metrics indicate a strong ability of
the algorithm to correctly identify true positive cases for both spikes and artefacts. The F1-score, which is a harmonic mean of precision and recall, stood at

Table 1. Classification Report 1: denoising algorithm's performance

	Precision	Recall	F1-Score	Support
Spikes	0.87	0.99	0.92	2025
Artefact	0.99	0.87	0.92	2371
Accuracy			0.92	4396
Macro Avg	0.93	0.93	0.92	4396
Weighted Avg	0.93	0.92	0.92	4396

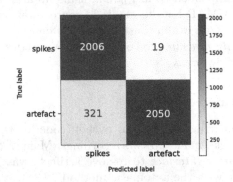

Fig. 3. Confusion matrix: algorithm's classification performance. The majority of spike and artifact instances are correctly identified, with 2,006 true positive spikes and 2,050 true positive artifacts. Misclassifications are minimal, 19 spikes mislabeled as artifacts and 321 artifacts mislabeled as spikes.

0.92 for both categories, underscoring the balanced accuracy of the algorithm in classifying neural waveforms.

Furthermore, the overall accuracy of the algorithm was measured at 0.92 across a total of 4,396 waveform instances. This high level of accuracy demonstrates the algorithm's efficacy in waveform denoising. The macro-average and weighted-average values for precision, recall, and F1-score were consistently above 0.92, further reinforcing the robustness of the algorithm in dealing with both prevalent and rare waveform classes within the dataset. The support values, which indicate the number of true instances in each class, confirm a relatively even distribution across classes.

The execution time for the denoising process was just 20.09 s, which is considerably less than the time required for manual denoising.

These results collectively highlight the algorithm's capability to retain critical neural spike information while effectively removing artefacts and noise.

4   Discussion

Artifact removal is a complex process that can be tackled in a variety of ways, from hardware processing to software processing. It can be performed on-line or off-line, but each strategy comes with its own limitations. For the hardware perspective, JW Gnadt et al. [15] proposed a method based on adaptive filters for real-time cancellation of stimulation artifacts, which offers versatility among stimulation patterns and significantly improves the quality of the neural recording, but its complexity requires specific hardware and software. From the software perspective, Okreghe et al. [16] proposed a deep neural network-based spike classification with improved channel selection and artifact removal, but it faces problems of applicability to real-world data, possible overfitting, and dependence on diverse and high-quality training data. In case of readapting the dataset for retraining or fine tuning the model to better fit other scenarios, both hardware requirements and expertise are required. The automatic neural denoising method proposed in this paper aims to address these problems for offline processing without specific hardware requirements, open source and modular to be scalable, which also allows for easy adaptation to alternative scenarios through the modification of the templates dataset.

In the context of existing spike sorting and cleaning solutions, our software enters the field with distinct advantages and areas for growth. Established *MAT-LAB* based tools like *IronClust* or *HDSort* face licensing restrictions. Python-based tools such as *Kilosort* and *SpykingCircus2* offer more accessibility but often come with high computational demands, requiring resources like *CUDA* or *Numba* for efficient processing [8] and the need for GPU computing resources. Our software is designed to provide an accessible, less resource-intensive alternative tailored to human cortex data analysis, but easily scalable by generating new templates from new databases. However we recognize its limitations compared to the specialized functionality of some established tools.

5   Conclusions

Our method eliminates a potential day to day human bias that can affect the extraction of action potentials and artefacts from electrophysiological data, making our approach a more reliable and objective strategy while significantly reducing the human cost. We believe that our tool will be beneficial to the scientific community.

Acknowledgements. This research was funded in part by grants DTS19/00175 and PDC2022-133952-100 from the Spanish *"Ministerio de Ciencia, Innovación y Universidades"* and by the European Union's *Horizon 2020* Research and Innovation Programme under Grant Agreement No. 899287 *NeuraViPeR*.

References

1. Zhao, S., et al.: Tracking neural activity from the same cells during the entire adult life of mice. Nat. Neurosci. **26**(4), 696–710 (2023)
2. Wang, Y., et al.: Implantable intracortical microelectrodes: reviewing the present with a focus on the future. Microsyst. Nanoeng. **9**(1), 7 (2023)
3. Roth, R.H., Ding, J.B.: From neurons to cognition: technologies for precise recording of neural activity underlying behavior. BME Front. **2020**, 7190517 (2020)
4. Li, J., Chen, X., Li, Z.: Spike detection and spike sorting with a hidden Markov model improves offline decoding of motor cortical recordings. J. Neural Eng. **16**, 016014 (2018)
5. Panskus, R, et al.: On the stimulation artifact reduction during electrophysiological recording of compound nerve action potentials. In: 45th Annual International Conference of the IEEE Engineering in Medicine & Biology Society (EMBC), pp. 1–5. IEEE (2023)
6. Bongard, M., Micol, D., Fernández, E.: Nev2lkit: a new open source tool for handling neuronal event files from multi-electrode recordings. Int. J. Neural Syst. **24**(4), 1450009(2014)
7. Pachitariu, M., et al.: Fast and accurate spike sorting of high-channel count probes with KiloSort. In: Lee, D., et al. (eds.) Advances in Neural Information Processing Systems, vol. 29. Curran Associates, Inc. (2016)
8. Buccino, A.P., et al.: SpikeInterface, a unified framework for spike sorting. eLife **9**, e61834 (2020)
9. Preprocessing module – SpikeInterface Documentation. https://spikeinterface.readthedocs.io/en/latest/modules/preprocessing.html
10. Neuro, R.: Trellis EEG & ERP Acquisition Software. https://rippleneuro.com/support/software-downloads-updates/
11. Blackrock Neurotech Software (2024). https://blackrockneurotech.com/products/software/
12. Blondel, V.D., et al.: Fast unfolding of communities in large networks. J. Stat. Mech. Theory Exp. **2008**(10), P10008 (2008)
13. Nordhausen, C.T., Maynard, E.M., Normann, R.A.: Single unit recording capabilities of a 100 microelectrode array. Brain Res. **726**(1–2), 129–140 (1996)
14. Spearman, C.: The proof and measurement of association between two things. Am. J. Psychol. **15**(1), 72–101 (1904)
15. Gnadt, J.W., et al.: Spectral cancellation of microstimulation artifact for simultaneous neural recording in situ. IEEE Trans. Biomed. Eng. **50**(10), 1129–1135 (2003)
16. Okreghe, C.O., Zamani, M., Demosthenous, A.: A deep neural network-based spike sorting with improved channel selection and artefact removal. IEEE Access **11**, 15131–15143 (2023)

Analysis of Anxiety Caused by Fasting in Obesity Patients Using EEG Signals

Mariana Elizalde[1,2(✉)], Jesica Martínez[2], Mario Ortiz[1,3], Eduardo Iáñez[1,3], María Herranz-Lopez[2], Vicente Micol[2], and José M. Azorín[1,3,4]

[1] Brain-Machine Interface System Lab, Miguel Hernández University of Elche, 03202 Elche, Spain
{melizalde,mortiz,eianez,jm.azorin}@umh.es
[2] Institute for Research, Development and Innovation in Health Biotechnology of Elche, Miguel Hernández University of Elche, 03202, Elche, Spain
{jesica.martinezg,mherranz,vmicol}@umh.es
[3] Engineering Research Institute of Elche-I3E, Miguel Hernández University of Elche, 03202 Elche, Spain
[4] Valencian Graduated School and Research Network of Artificial Intelligence-ValGRAI, 46022 Valencia, Spain

Abstract. This paper investigates the neural aspects of obesity, shifting from a focus on isolated brain structures to dynamic neural network interactions. Exploring substance-related and addictive disorders as a foundation, it extends this understanding to alterations in functional integration within reward brain areas, particularly fronto-parietal and temporal regions, in individuals with BMI between 29.6 and 36.6.

Obesity, a global health concern impacting 39% of the population, is associated with diverse brain activity patterns in regions governing intake regulation, satiety, self-control, and impulsivity. Shared neural irregularities between obese individuals and drug addicts suggest common mechanisms fueling reward-seeking behaviors.

Utilizing advanced signal processing technologies, our EEG study involving four participants, explores the interplay of brain function and obesity. Collaborating with a nutritionist underscores the role of dietary considerations in this complex relationship. EEG recordings during fasting and postprandial states proof significant alterations in beta and gamma frequency bands, highlighting FC2, FC4, and F6 as critical electrodes.

This exploration into neural changes during different physiological states provides valuable insights into the intricate relationship between brain function and obesity. The integration of electroencephalographic features offers a nuanced understanding, paving the way for future research and interventions in the intersection of obesity and neuroscience.

Keywords: Obesity · Overweight · EEG · Electrodes · dlPFC

1 Introduction

In reconsidering the brain as a highly integrated and dynamic system, researchers have shifted their perspective on reward-related behaviors and addictive

© The Author(s), under exclusive license to Springer Nature Switzerland AG 2024
J. M. Ferrández Vicente et al. (Eds.): IWINAC 2024, LNCS 14674, pp. 223–232, 2024.
https://doi.org/10.1007/978-3-031-61140-7_22

disorders. [3]. Instead of attributing them solely to single brain structures, there is a growing acknowledgment that these phenomena may emerge from the dynamic activity of extensive neural networks. The brain, being highly susceptible to physical changes, plays a pivotal role in this intricate interplay [4].

Recent neuroscience studies focusing on substance-related and addictive disorders reveal noteworthy alterations in the functional integration between reward brain areas, particularly among fronto-parietal and temporal regions [7].

Building on these insights, prior investigations into functional connectivity in overweight and obese individuals have uncovered changes in various brain networks, particularly in fronto-parietal areas, when compared to lean counterparts [3].

The abnormal accumulation of fat, commonly referred to as obesity or overweight, is categorized by the World Health Organization (WHO) based on Body Mass Index (BMI). WHO distinguishes values equal to or exceeding 25 as overweight and values equal to or exceeding 30 as obesity [11]. This global health concern has reached pandemic proportions, affecting around 39% of the world's population, with an annual mortality rate exceeding 2.8 million individuals due to the complications associated with excess weight or obesity [10].

Understanding human eating behaviors involves recognizing the interplay between physiological hunger and the rewarding properties of food. Recent studies underscore alterations in the brain's response to food stimuli, affecting critical aspects such as intake regulation, satiety, self-control, and impulsivity. Individuals with obesity exhibit varied activity levels in key brain areas, including the amygdala, hippocampus, hypothalamus, insula, and dorsolateral prefrontal cortex (dlPFC), all associated with sensorimotor processing, memory, emotions, and the reward system [1].

The hypothalamus, a crucial region for appetite and food intake regulation, exhibits a slower decrease in its overall neuronal firing rate activity among individuals with obesity, delaying the feeling of satiety during food consumption [6]. Moreover, alterations in the brain's reward circuit, governing self-control and impulsivity, result in reduced activity in the left dorsolateral prefrontal cortex and left anterior cingulate cortex. This reduction in activity leads individuals with obesity to require a greater quantity of food stimuli for equivalent satisfaction compared to their healthier counterparts [1].

Remarkably, similarities in neural irregularities between obese individuals and drug addicts, such as a heightened anticipated pleasure response to rewards but a blunted pleasure response upon reward attainment, contribute to the perpetuation of reward-seeking behaviors [9].

To comprehend the genesis of obesity, it becomes imperative to delve into the neural changes occurring in overweight individuals. The increased availability of neuroimaging technologies, including functional magnetic resonance imaging (fMRI), positron emission tomography (PET), and electroencephalography (EEG), has sparked a surge in studies comparing brain responses in these weight categories. Unlike traditional behavioral studies, which often yield conflicting results, neuroimaging research consistently unveils notable differences in brain regions associated with eating behavior [2].

This transition towards leveraging neuroimaging technologies underscores their potential to offer clarity where traditional studies may fall short. The integration of these advanced tools significantly enhances our comprehension of the neural underpinnings of weight-related behaviors [5]. Therefore, our paper outlines the methodology employed in our EEG study, discusses the findings of significant electrodes, and explores the implications for future research and interventions in the realm of obesity and neuroscience.

2 Materials and Methods

For the execution of brain activity recordings, the wireless 32-channel EEG system from Brain Products, based on the LIVEAMP amplifier, was utilized. Additionally, for the analysis of the obtained EEG records, Matlab R2022b software was employed.

2.1 Subjects

Four subjects participated in this study, comprising two men and two women, aged between 30 and 51; with BMI between 29.6 and 36.6. Each volunteer received information about the study and signed a consent form approved by the ethics committee of the Miguel Hernández University of Elche.

2.2 Procedure

For the execution of this study, the participation of a nutritionist from Nutrievidence SND, located at the Scientific Park of Miguel Hernández University of Elche, was enlisted. This collaboration played a pivotal role in facilitating the collection of demographic data, blood pressure measurements, anthropometric analyses, blood analyses, and the administration of questionnaires to assess the anxiety levels, well-being, and physical activity of the volunteers. The inclusion of a nutritionist in our research team not only ensures comprehensive data acquisition, but also emphasizes the critical role of dietary considerations in the intricate relationship between brain function and obesity.

As we navigate through the intricate web of neural interactions, it becomes increasingly apparent that the significance of involving a balanced and healthful diet extends beyond its physiological implications. It is worth noting that, while the dietary intervention is not focused on the current study, it is planned for future investigations. The collaboration with the nutritionist lays the groundwork for the application and analysis of dietary strategies, providing a comprehensive understanding of their potential impact on the neurological aspects of individuals grappling with obesity.

Following the data collection by the nutritionist, the subjects proceeded to the recording of electroencephalographic signals. For this purpose, they were instructed to arrive in a fasting state, without hair gel or spray, and with washed but dry hair. Additionally, it was confirmed that they had no contraindications for the recording, such as epilepsy, schizophrenia, or other conditions.

Nutrition Consultation Protocol: The nutrition consultation protocol involved standard procedures, including informing participants about the project, obtaining informed consent, collecting demographic and health data, measuring blood pressure, completing the IPAQ questionnaire for physical activity assessment, gathering anthropometric data, and explaining the STAI questionnaire for anxiety assessment. Additionally, participants were asked to provide dietary recall information. The nutritionist then summarized the outcomes, including results from the dietary recall and questionnaires, along with blood analysis results.

Protocol for EEG Signal Recording: To conduct this segment of the study, the volunteer was briefed on the procedure for the brain activity recording, and permission was sought for the capture of photographs and videos during the test. To this end, the informed consent form was provided for signature. Additionally, the volunteer was asked to complete the VAS questionnaire while fasting.

During the execution of this study segment, three blood extractions were performed on the subjects with the intention that this information could be analyzed in a future study to examine correlations with electroencephalography records and biochemical markers.

Hence, the protocol was executed as depicted in Fig. 1, divided into three periods: fasting, during breakfast, and postprandial. For the fasting period, an initial blood sample was drawn, followed by the first recording session (Register 1). This session lasted for 2 min and 45 s, during which the participant was instructed to relax with closed eyes and refrain from making any movements (visualizing themselves on a beach, lying down, and listening to the sound of the waves). The initial 15 s of this period were allocated for signal stabilization, followed by 30 s of rest. Subsequently, the second recording session (Register 2) was conducted in a similar manner, involving another 2 min and 45 s of relaxation with closed eyes and without movements, with the initial 15 s dedicated to signal stabilization. Another 30 s of rest followed.

The fasting period concluded with Register 3, followed by the breakfast period (Register 4). These two, along with Register 7 (the final postprandial recording), were omitted from this study to mitigate potential artifacts. However, they are planned for use in future studies.

The postprandial period was conducted in a manner similar to the fasting period, starting with Register 5. This recording, lasting for 2 min and 45 s, involved the subject relaxing with closed eyes and without making movements (visualizing themselves on the beach, lying down, and listening to the sound of the waves). The first 15 s were dedicated to signal stabilization, followed by a 30-s rest. Subsequently, Register 6 was initiated, lasting for another 2 min and 45 s, where the subject was once again instructed to relax with closed eyes and without making movements, with the initial 15 s allocated for signal stabilization. Another 30 s of rest followed.

To conclude the protocol, a third and final blood extraction was performed, and the subject was asked to complete the VAS questionnaire once again. The whole session lasted around 109 min.

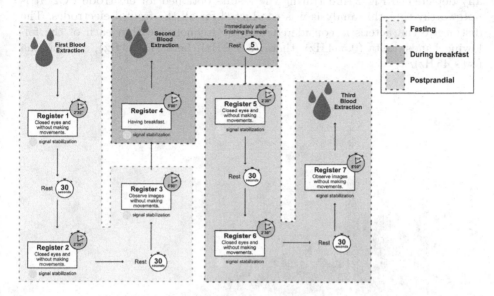

Fig. 1. Diagram of the protocol followed for the acquisition of brain activity with EEG and blood sample collection. Only closed eyes registers were used for this research.

2.3   Data Processing

With the analysis of the data obtained from EEG registers, the objective was to determine which region of the brain undergoes a change in its activity during fasting and postprandial periods, identifying the electrodes that indicate a significant alteration. To achieve this, the decision was made to analyze the registers where subjects had their eyes closed, aiming to minimize the possibility of artifacts. Therefore, four EEG recordings were selected for analysis, two corresponding to fasting (register 1 and 2) and two corresponding to postprandial (register 5 and 6).

To achieve this, the following procedure was carried out for each of the subjects:

Partition by Epochs: For the four registers with closed eyes to be analyzed (R1-2 and R5-6), a total time of 2 min and 30 s was taken (excluding signal stabilization time). Then, these periods were segmented into 5-s duration epochs with a 1-second displacement. The choice of these specific parameters aims to capture the dynamic variations in electroencephalographic signals during the closed-eye condition.

Compute the Spectrum: For every epoch, the spectrum was computed at each frontal electrode. This approach is justified by the localization of the reward system-associated region in the dlPFC [1]. The corresponding analysis is visually depicted in Fig. 2, illustrating the results obtained for electrode FC2. It is noteworthy that this analysis was conducted for all the frontal electrodes. The distinctive characteristic considered was the frequency within each of the following bands: delta (0.5–4 Hz), theta (3.9–8 Hz), beta (13–30 Hz), and gamma (30 - 45 Hz).

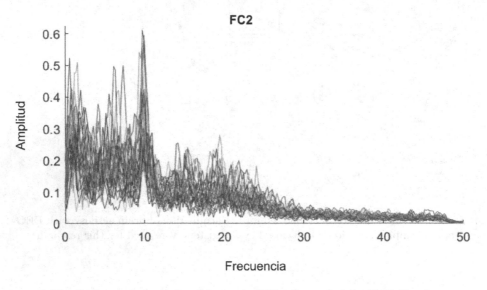

Fig. 2. Spectral Analysis of electrode FC2 - Computed for Each Epoch

Remove Out-of-range Spectra: The mean spectra for each electrode by averaging the spectra across the epochs was calculated, and a range of ± 2.5 times the standard deviation was applied to exclude spectra falling outside of this range. Subsequently, the mean was recalculated using the remaining spectra. This process ensures that only relevant and statistically consistent spectra contribute to the final analyses.

Compute the Root Mean Squared Error (RMSE) for the Mean Spectrum of the Epochs per Electrode Between Registers: With the new means, the root mean square error (RMSE) was calculated for the following combinations: the first fasting record (R1) with the second fasting record (R2), the first postprandial record (R5) with the second postprandial record (R6), the first fasting record with the first postprandial record, the first fasting record with the second postprandial record, the second fasting record with the first postprandial record, and the second fasting record with the second postprandial record.

Considering that both fasting and both postprandial records were taken with a short time difference, the hypothesis was formulated (Fig. 3) that the two records taken during the fasting period (R1 and R2) and the two records taken during the postprandial period (R5 and R6) should have their RMSE values almost close to zero since they were taken with a minimal time difference between each other. Therefore, it was decided to average their values in a first column. Based on this same hypothesis, the RMSE value of the combined records between fasting and postprandial periods should be higher as they are combining different periods. Consequently, in a second column, the following combinations were averaged: R1 with R5, R1 with R6, R2 with R5, and R2 with R6.

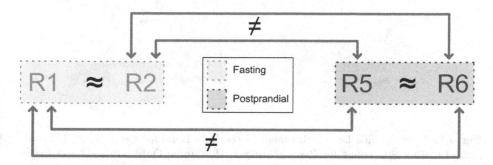

Fig. 3. Diagram illustrating the hypothesis that the RMSE values between two fasting records (R1 and R2) should be almost equal and close to zero, as well as for the two postprandial records (R5 and R6), while the combination of both periods, fasting and postprandial, should be different and higher.

Determine the Significant Electrodes: Once both columns of RMSE values were obtained, the next step involved determining the most significant electrodes through a Wilcoxon rank sum test. To achieve this, electrodes were selected based on the hypothesis that the first column should exhibit values lower than those in the second column.

While this procedure was applied to all mentioned frequency bands, particular attention was given to choosing electrodes within the beta and gamma frequency bands. This focus stems from the alterations observed in these bands due to anxiety and satiety levels [7].

3   Results and Discussion

The analysis of EEG spectral data revealed distinct patterns of neural activity across various frequency bands, particularly in the beta and gamma bands, which have been previously associated with anxiety and satiety levels. Following the removal of out-of-range spectra, as illustrated in Fig. 4 for the Beta band, only statistically consistent spectra contributed to the subsequent analyses.

Subsequent electrode significance testing identified specific electrodes that exhibited significant differences in root mean square error (RMSE) values between experimental conditions, providing insight into the modulation of anxiety and satiety responses at the neural level.

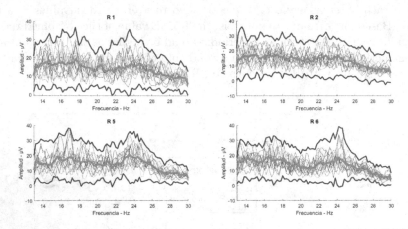

Fig. 4. Subject-Specific Data Refinement in the Beta Band for electrode FC2: Exclusion of Outlier Spectrums for Precise Analysis (Retaining Only Subject's Spectrums within Mean ± 2.5 Standard Deviations). Average amplitude in bolded green and upper and lower limits for ± 2.5 std. in bolded blue. The individual spectrum for 30 epochs are shown in thinned lines. (Color figure online)

In Table 1, the results of the significant electrodes in both bands are provided. The electrodes meeting the criteria outlined in the preceding section, spanning both the beta frequency band (13–30 Hz) and the gamma frequency band (30–45 Hz), exhibited variability among subjects (refer to Table 1). The notation "Y" in the table signifies the presence of significance in that frequency band, while "N" indicates the absence. Double letters, such as "Y, Y," correspond to significance in both the beta and gamma bands, respectively.

Table 1. Significant Electrodes in Beta and Gamma Frequency Bands Across Subjects

	F1	F2	FC1	FC2	FC3	FC4	F5	F6	AF3	AF4	FCZ	FT7
Frequency band	β	β	β	β,γ	γ	β,γ	γ	β,γ	γ	β	β	γ
Subject 1	Y	Y	Y	Y,Y	Y	Y,Y	Y	Y,Y	Y	N	Y	Y
Subject 2	Y	Y	Y	Y,Y	Y	Y,Y	Y	N,Y	Y	Y	Y	Y
Subject 3	Y	Y	Y	Y,Y	Y	Y,Y	Y	Y,Y	Y	Y	Y	Y
Subject 4	Y	N	Y	Y,Y	Y	Y,N	N	N,Y	N	Y	N	Y

These criteria guided the determination of significant electrodes when aligning with the majority of subjects in both frequency bands. Consequently, FC2, FC4, and F6 emerged as the identified significant electrodes.

This finding aligns with the observations presented by Stein et al., emphasizing that individuals with certain anxiety levels may display an imbalance in the dorsolateral prefrontal cortex (dlPFC), characterized by hypoactivity on the left side and hyperactivity on the right side [8].

4   Conclusions

In conclusion, our EEG study has revealed crucial insights into the neural intricacies of obesity, identifying critical electrodes like FC2, FC4, and F6. Moving forward, our research will delve into two key areas. Firstly, we aim to assess changes in critical electrode dynamics post-dietary interventions, unraveling the impact of dietary choices on neural correlates. Secondly, we plan to explore the effects of neurostimulation on these critical electrodes, paving the way for innovative therapeutic strategies. This study not only enhances our understanding of obesity's neurological dimensions but also charts a course for future investigations, blending neuroscience and intervention approaches for effective management of metabolic disorders.

Acknowledgments. This work is part of the OBRAINSITY project - Novel therapeutic approaches to metabolic diseases: modulation of food intake and energy balance through nutraceuticals and neurotechnology, funded by the Department of Innovation, Universities, Science, and Digital Society of the Generalitat Valenciana (PROMETEO/2021/059).

Disclosure of Interests. The authors have no competing interests to declare that are relevant to the content of this article.

References

1. Carnell, S., Gibson, C., Benson, L., Ochner, C.N., Geliebter, A.: Neuroimaging and obesity: current knowledge and future directions. Obesity Rev. **13**, 43–56 (2012). https://doi.org/10.1111/j.1467-789X.2011.00927.x
2. Crosson, B., Ford, A., McGregor, K.M., Meinzer, M., Cheshkov, S., Li, X., Walker-Batson, D., Briggs, R.W.: Functional imaging and related techniques: an introduction for rehabilitation researchers. J. Rehabil. Res. Dev. **47**, vii (2010). https://doi.org/10.1682/JRRD.2010.02.0017
3. Imperatori, C., et al.: Modification of EEG functional connectivity and EEG power spectra in overweight and obese patients with food addiction: an eloreta study. Brain Imaging Behav. **9**, 703–716 (2015). https://doi.org/10.1007/s11682-014-9324-x
4. Khemapathumak, P., Lookhanumanchao, S., Sittiprapaporn, P.: EEG power spectra during stroop color word task training in obese patients, pp. 30–33. IEEE (2017). https://doi.org/10.1109/ECTICon.2017.8096165

5. Lowe, M.R., van Steenburgh, J., Ochner, C., Coletta, M.: Neural correlates of individual differences related to appetite. Physiol. Behav. **97**, 561–571 (2009). https://doi.org/10.1016/j.physbeh.2009.04.001
6. Matsuda, M., et al.: Altered hypothalamic function in response to glucose ingestion in obese humans. Diabetes **48**, 1801–1806 (1999). https://doi.org/10.2337/diabetes.48.9.1801
7. Ridder, D.D., et al.: The brain, obesity and addiction: an EEG neuroimaging study. Sci. Rep. **6**, 34122 (2016). https://doi.org/10.1038/srep34122
8. Stein, D.J., Medeiros, L.F., Caumo, W., Torres, I.L.: Transcranial direct current stimulation in patients with anxiety: current perspectives. Neuropsychiat. Dis. Treat. **16**, 161–169 (2020). https://doi.org/10.2147/NDT.S195840
9. Volkow, N.D., Wang, G., Tomasi, D., Baler, R.D.: Obesity and addiction: neurobiological overlaps. Obesity Rev. **14**, 2–18 (2013). https://doi.org/10.1111/j.1467-789X.2012.01031.x
10. WHO: Obesity (2021). https://www.who.int/news-room/facts-in-pictures/detail/6-facts-on-obesity
11. WHO: Obesity and overweight (2021). https://www.who.int/news-room/fact-sheets/detail/obesity-and-overweight

Evolution of EEG Fractal Dimension Along a Sequential Finger Movement Task

Sara Kamali[✉][iD], Fabiano Baroni[iD], and Pablo Varona[iD]

GNB. Dpto. de Ingenieria Informatica. Escuela Politecnica Superior,
Autonomous University of Madrid, 28049 Madrid, Spain
{sara.kamali,fabiano.baroni,pablo.varona}@uam.es

Abstract. We used dual EEG and EMG recordings to assess the neural dynamics of motor activity during a stereotyped sequential finger movement. We analyzed the evolution of EEG complexity, assessed using Katz fractal dimension (KFD), in three brain regions involved in the task (multisensory association (MA), sensory and left and right motor areas) and its relation with response time, defined by EMG onset. The KFD was calculated for multiple time windows, defined with respect to the go cue or the EMG onset. We observed a positive correlation between the KFD and the EMG onset latency in various time windows in all the areas. This relationship reversed for trials with a late EMG onset. While all the areas manifested a similar pattern of correlations, the motor area showed the lowest, and the MA area the highest, complexity values between these four brain regions. The KFD tended to decrease as the task progressed, consistently with previous observations of reduced neural variability with task engagement.

Keywords: Simultaneous EEG and EMG analysis · sequential finger movement · Katz fractal dimension

1 Introduction: Fractal Dimension and its Application on EEG Signals Analysis

The relationship between brain dynamics and behavior has been a long yet unresolved quest in neuroscience research. The difficulty of assessing this relationship lies in the partial observability of the brain with current neurotechnologies and, thus, the lack of clear links between recorded neural activity and behavioral patterns. This problem can be better studied in motor tasks, where time references and stereotyped patterns in motor nervous signals enable the identification of key elements in the dynamics of neural activity.

In this context, several works have addressed the study of dual electroencephalographic (EEG) and electromyographic (EMG) recordings, e.g. see [1,2]. Electromyographic recordings provide information about muscle motion in the form of time series that can be compared with simultaneous EEG recordings of brain activity.

J. M. Ferrández Vicente et al. (Eds.): IWINAC 2024, LNCS 14674, pp. 233–242, 2024.
https://doi.org/10.1007/978-3-031-61140-7_23

In this research, we analyzed dual EEG and EMG recordings to characterize brain dynamics during a sequential finger movement task. The non-stationary and complex nature of EEG signals makes it a challenging problem even when the motor task is highly stereotyped. Nonlinear analysis methods, i.e., the calculation of Lyapunov exponents, correlation dimension, delay embedding and entropy, are among the useful quantitative methods in evaluating the state and characteristics of brain waveforms [13,15]. The analysis of fractal dimension is also another nonlinear approach used in the study of EEG time series for classification and evaluation of the complexity of brain states [12]. Our research question was whether there is a pattern in the evolution of fractal dimension when the state of the brain changes during the different phases of a movement task. In the next sections, we explain the EEG and EMG preprocessing steps and our method for calculating the fractal dimension, and then we report the results of the analysis. We hypothesized that the shift from the resting state to performing a movement should change the dimensionality of the signals reflecting the motor coordination, and we showed that the dynamics display a characteristic evolution as illustrated by the evolution of the fractal dimension.

2   Materials and Methods

2.1   Dataset and Motor Task

In this study, we used a hand movement dataset recorded with a common reference 64-channel Biosemi EEG device, with 512 Hz sampling rate [3]. The subjects were asked to perform a sequential finger movement with 20 trials on each hand. The motor task was a simple repetitive action: tapping the thumb against each finger, starting from the index finger and progressing sequentially to the little finger, once in each trial (Fig. 1). This results in 40 trials of executive hand movement for each subject. Our motivation in this study was to investigate the evolution of the complexity of the recorded EEG signals during the trials and its relation with the movement onset. The hypothesis was that there is a correlation between the complexity of the brain activity and the latency of the subject's response to the go cue.

2.2   EEG Signals Preprocessing

We first analyzed the independent components of the EEG signals. We chose to apply the adaptive mixture of independent component analyzers (AMICA) [14] for removing the artifacts and accessing the source of EEG signals. Several works show that AMICA gives the best results for this purpose among other available independent component (IC) decomposition algorithms. Leutheuser and et al. showed that in several measures AMICA outperforms Infomax which is another strong tool in decomposing the signals into its components [9]. Also, Stergiadis and et al. compared five common IC analysis (ICA) methods and reported AMICA as the best algorithm in source separation, considering entropy, correlation, and mutual information reduction of the components [16].

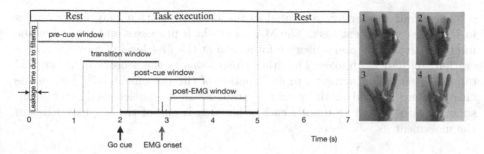

Fig. 1. The top left panel shows the timeline of each motor task trial. The four panels on the right show the sequence of finger movements in this task. The duration of each trial was 7 s. A monitor was used to present the stimulus (go cue). The first 2 s corresponded to the waiting time when the monitor screen was black. At the time $t = 2$ s, the word 'left' or 'right' appeared on the monitor in random order for three seconds. Subjects were instructed to perform the sequential finger movement, on the requested hand, only once, during these 3 s. Then the monitor screen turned black and there was a random rest time (4.1 to 4.8 s) which was cut into 2 s in the final shared dataset. The four intervals shown with the labels clarify the location of the windows that were used for fractal dimension calculation, discussed in Sect. 2.5. The leakage time, $t = 210$ ms in the timeline, is due to wavelet decomposition.

We used EEGlab commands and extensions to preprocess the data [4] with the following steps: 1. High pass finite impulse response (FIR) filtering with filtfilt at 1 Hz. 2. Removal of line nose with the EEGlab cleanline extension. 3. Rectification of problematic segments of the signals and removal of the bad channels with the EEGlab Artifact Subspace Reconstruction extension. The standard deviation limit was set to 4. 4. Average referencing of the data. 5. Segmenting the continuous signals into the trials. 6. Removal of bad trials. 7. Decomposing the time series with the AMICA plugin. 8. Extracting the dipoles of the ICs with the pop-dipfit-settings extension. 9. Automatic labeling of ICs with the pop-iclabel function. After preprocessing, we had the ICs, their dipole's location and the IC labels, i.e., whether an IC had a brain source or it was noise, artifact, or a combination of them. Out of 38 subjects, we excluded 6 subjects because they had less than two ICs labeled as brain components with a probability higher than 60%, or the residual variance of their dipole fitting was more than 15%.

Clustering the Dipoles. To study the data at the group level, we clustered the brain ICs. This was done based on the location of the dipoles. First, we removed the dipoles which did not correspond to brain components. We created a study in Matlab and used EEGlab for this task. The clustering was performed on the brain ICs of all subjects. The clustering was performed based on the location of the dipoles, their event-related synchronization perturbation (ERSP) [11] and the scalp maps. This yielded four clusters with more than 50% of the subjects in each (Fig. 2). We kept only one IC from each subject in each cluster. Not all the subjects had an IC in every cluster.

These four clusters were located in the brain areas that play integral roles in the finger movement task. The MA area, which processes and integrates the interpretative visual and sensory information at the first level of movement generation [10] had 23 dipoles. The other cluster was in the sensory area, with 24 dipoles. This region activates in anticipation of the movement [17]. Two of the clusters were located in the primary motor areas at the left and right hemispheres, with 21 and 18 dipoles each. This area is one of the key executives of the movement [6].

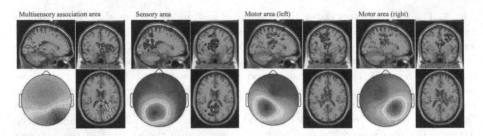

Fig. 2. Dipoles and scalpmaps of the selected clusters: the four plots at the left, in green show the 23 dipoles of the MA, at the sagittal, coronal, and top plane. The scalp map shows the topography of the average potential distribution for all the dipoles at this cluster. The warmer colors show higher positive values and the colder ones show smaller negative values. The second set shows the same plates and maps for the 24 dipoles of the sensory area and the last two sets in magenta and red, with 21 and 18 dipoles, respectively belonging to the motor areas at the left and right hemispheres. (Color figure online)

2.3   EMG Signals Preprocessing

We extracted the EMG onset times as a reference time to investigate the changes in the complexity of the activity of dipoles regarding the movement. In conjunction with this neural data, we had simultaneous recordings of EMG data obtained from a 4-channel setup, with two sensors placed on each side of each arm. The pitfall of the current dataset is the lack of a recording of the exact times of finger tapping. We could only extract the first time the activity of the EMG passed the threshold for detection of the movement. Extraction of the onset of movement for the other fingers was not possible from the EMG recordings.

The first three steps of EMG preprocessing were the same as for the EEG signals. Then we performed a low-pass filtering at 200 Hz, subtracting the two signals from the same hand to get the bipolar signal and remove the cardio signals. After this, we applied a moving average window with a length of 15 samples, equal to 29.3 ms, and found the maximum of the signals for each trial, during the hand movement execution and set its 20% as the threshold. The first time after the go cue that the signal passed this threshold was set as the EMG onset time, indicating the movement related to the tapping of the thumb and the index finger, the first move in the task (Fig. 1). If the standard deviation at the pre-cue interval of a trial was higher than 1/3 the standard deviation of the execution interval, we labeled it as a bad trial and removed it. After extracting the onset time of all the trials for each subject, we removed the outlier trials. Since the only instruction for the execution of the movement was to do it during the 3 s time window after the go cue, we were flexible with setting the upper and lower limits for outlier selection. We set the lower threshold at $(Q_1 - 2\text{IQR})$ and upper threshold at $(Q_3 + 2\text{IQR})$, where IQR stands for the interquartile range. After applying these steps and criteria, if a subject had more than 50% of its trials labeled as bad trials, we removed that subject from the study. This resulted in the rejection of 6 subjects. Only one of these subjects was in the 32 subjects included in the clustering (Fig. 3).

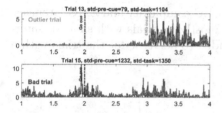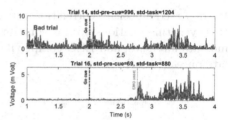

Fig. 3. The bipolar EMG of the left-hand movement for four representative single trials. The trials with high standard deviations before the go cue were marked as 'bad trials' and removed. The outlier trials were removed after the detection of the EMG onset.

2.4 Katz Fractal Dimension

We used Katz fractal dimension (KFD) [8] to compute the complexity of the signals since, among the other fractal dimension calculation algorithms, it achieves the best accuracy and most consistent results for EEG signal analysis and classification [5]. If the data point P_i has the Cartesian coordinates (x_i, y_i), the algorithm starts with the computation of the Euclidean distance between consecutive data points, for all N points in the time series:

1. $\text{Dist}(Pi, P_{i+1})$: $l_i = \sqrt{(x_{i+1} - x_i)^2 + (y_{i+1} - y_i)^2}$; $i = 1, ..., N - 1$
2. The sum of these distances is computed as: $L = \sum_{i=1}^{N-1} l_i$
3. Then the maximum distance between the first data point and any other point in the series is found: $D_{\max} = \max(\text{Dist}(P_1, P_i)_{i=2,...,N})$
4. Finally, the Katz dimension is computed as:

$$\text{KFD} = \frac{\log_{10}(N - 1)}{(\log_{10}(D_{max}/L) + \log_{10}(N - 1))} \tag{1}$$

2.5   KFD Time Windows

To follow the changes in the complexity of the signal, we extracted four time intervals over each trial, using the go cue and the first EMG onset as the reference events. These intervals are shown in Fig. 1, as pre-cue, the transition from pre-cue to the post-cue, post-cue and post-EMG onset. The lengths of all the windows were equal to 1.5 s. There was a 50% overlap between consecutive windows. This changed in the case of the last two windows and the overlap could be slightly more or less, depending on the latency of the EMG onset at each trial. We used the wavelet decomposition to extract the average power in the range of 8 to 40 Hz, with the EEGlab *pop_newtimef* command. Then the KFD, Eq. (1), was computed over each window, for each trial.

3   Results

We observed a positive correlation between EEG complexity and EMG latencies. However, this relationship was contributed mostly by trials with short or intermediate latencies, and EEG complexity tended to decrease for the trials with a late onset (Fig. 4).

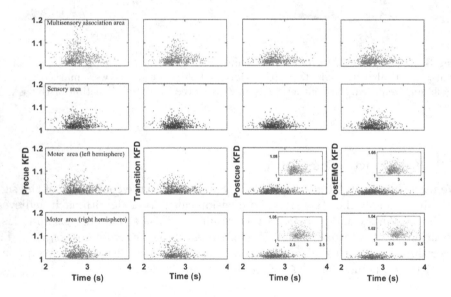

Fig. 4. The relation of KFD with EMG onset is shown for each of the four brain areas considered (MA, sensory and left and right motor areas, varying along rows) and each time window for KFD estimation (Precue, Transition, Postcue, PostEMG, varying along columns). Insets at the bottom right panels show a zoom-in of the plots on top of the empty regions.

The variability of KFD values was larger for trials with intermediate latencies and smaller for trials with very short or very long latencies. The plots on the top row show that the relation between complexity and EMG onset had less variation in range over different phases of the task for the MA area compared to the three other regions. All the areas showed a decrease in the KFD range as subjects were involved with the task, in the post-cue window. This window had the lowest range of KFD values for the MA and the sensory area. At the two bottom rows, the KFD of the motor areas showed smaller values of KFD in the last windows, belonging to the post-EMG interval. Here, we observed a clear decreasing trend as the KFD window moved from the pre-cue window toward the movement interval. A dense area in the intermediate latencies during the execution is observable. The motor areas at the left and right hemispheres had the smallest range of KFD during the execution phase.

Table 1 shows a significant positive correlation between the KFD and the EMG onset time at all intervals at the MA and sensory areas. Both motor areas show significant correlations in the execution windows. However, none of the correlation values are high, with the highest correlation reaching 0.232 for the transition window for the MA area. The pattern of the distribution of data points in Fig. 4, initially shows a positive trend in the KFD values as EMG increases. The majority of the data points are in this region. However, the KFD values show a decreasing trend for the high EMG onset times. This nonlinear trend in the relation between the KFD and latencies can explain the low correlation values.

Table 1. Spearman's correlation values and corresponding p-values between EMG onset time and KFD. All the p-values for the MA area are smaller than 10^{-6}. The correlations with non-significant p-values are marked as *n.s.*.

KFD interval	Association	Sensory	Motor, left	Motor, right
Pre-cue	0.199	0.075, 0.029	*n.s.*	*n.s.*
Transition	0.232	0.073, 0.033	*n.s.*	*n.s.*
Post-cue	0.165	0.083, 0.016	$0.135, 2.6 \times 10^{-4}$	$0.136, 6.8 \times 10^{-4}$
Post-EMG	0.173	0.078, 0.023	0.113, 0.002	$0.165, 3.4 \times 10^{-5}$

Figure 5 shows the evolution of KFD along the trial phases, plotting the KFD of consecutive intervals (illustrated in Fig. 1) against each other. All four brain areas showed a highly correlated relation between the consecutive intervals. This implies that the change in the complexity of the signal was not abrupt. Also, the MA and sensory areas kept a relatively similar range of KFD over the four selected windows. The range of the KFD was smaller for the motor area compared to the two other regions during the execution (Fig. 5, last two columns of the second and third rows). In the four brain areas, and especially in the motor areas, KFD variability was reduced during the motor execution phase. The relation between KFD in consecutive windows showed more convergence toward the identity line when comparing the post-EMG versus the post-cue windows (last row in Fig. 5) with the previous transitions (first two rows), for all the areas.

This result is compatible with previous reports that show a reduction in the variability of the neural activity during the task engagement [7]. The correlation values between KFD estimates for each pair of consecutive time windows are reported in Table 2. For all of the areas and time window pairs, the correlation values are high and extremely significant.

Table 2. Spearman's correlation for the KFDs at consecutive time windows, all the p-values are $< 10^{-6}$.

KFD interval	Association	Sensory	Motor, left	Motor, right
Pre-cue and transition	0.784	0.807	0.861	0.799
Transition and post-cue	0.729	0.774	0.754	0.751
Post-cue and post-EMG	0.829	0.860	0.813	0.766

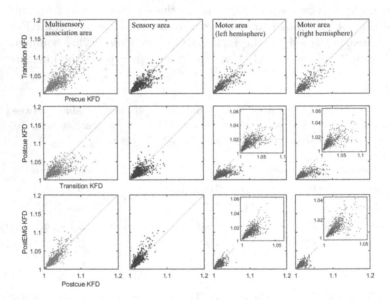

Fig. 5. Katz fractal dimension of consecutive windows. The first row shows the KFD of the transition from rest to the post-cue against the KFD of the rest time before the cue onset. The second row shows the KFD after the onset of the cue against the KFD of the transition from the pre- to the post-cue. The third row depicts the KFD of the post-EMG onset window against the post-cue KFD.

4   Conclusion

A simple sequential finger movement task provides an adequate experimental paradigm to characterize neural dynamics in relationship to time references of motor activity. In this paper, we have studied the relation between the KFD as a measure of the complexity of the activity of four brain areas that play key roles in finger movement tasks. The simultaneous recording of EMG signals made it possible to extract the EMG onset timings, which provided another time reference (in addition to the go cue) to segment the EEG traces according to the sequential structure of the task. This enabled the characterization of KFD along the different phases of each trial. The KFD in the left and right motor areas showed the lowest range of values compared to the other two regions. Also, there was a clear decreasing trend in KFD in these areas as the task moved forward, reflecting the motor task engagement.

We observed significant, albeit low, correlations between EMG onset and KFD in multiple task phases. A closer inspection suggests a nonlinear relationship between these two variables in all brain areas. Where the KFD increases with EMG onset at low and intermediate latencies and decreases for long latencies.

The EMG recordings in the experimental database used in this study do not reflect the details of the sequential motor task, e.g., clear events when the fingers touch in a stereotyped sequence. However, we have shown that known time references for the motor onset allow the quantification of the fractal dimension at different stages in the evolution of the neural activity. Experiments, where additional time references for the motor task are available, could yield a more detailed characterization of the neural dynamics. Such analyses can be used in novel methodologies for disease biomarker design and to develop performance metrics for neuro-rehabilitation tasks.

Acknowledgements. We thank Scott Makeig and Seyed Yahya Shirazi, from the Swartz Center for Computational Neuroscience, Institute for Neural Computation, UCSD, for their supervision and advice on the preprocessing of the EEG dataset.

This research was supported by grant PID2021-1223 47NB-100 (funded by MCIN-AEI/ 10.13039/501100011033 and ERDF - "A way of making Europe").

References

1. Babiloni, C., et al.: Simultaneous recording of electroencephalographic data in musicians playing in ensemble. Cortex **47**(9), 1082–1090 (2011). https://doi.org/ 10.1016/j.cortex.2011.05.006
2. Bulea, T.C., Kilicarslan, A., Ozdemir, R., Paloski, W.H., Contreras-Vidal, J.L.: Simultaneous scalp electroencephalography (EEG), electromyography (EMG), and whole-body segmental inertial recording for multi-modal neural decoding. JoVE (77), e50602 (2013). https://doi.org/10.3791/50602
3. Cho, H., Ahn, M., Ahn, S., Kwon, M., Jun, S.C.: EEG datasets for motor imagery brain-computer interface. GigaScience **6**(7), gix034 (2017). https://doi.org/10. 1093/gigascience/gix034
4. Delorme, A., Makeig, S.: EEGLAB: an open source toolbox for analysis of single-trial EEG dynamics including independent component analysis. J. Neurosci. Methods **134**(1), 9–21 (2004). https://doi.org/10.1016/j.jneumeth.2003.10.009

5. Esteller, R., Vachtsevanos, G., Echauz, J., Litt, B.: A comparison of waveform fractal dimension algorithms. IEEE Trans. Circ. Syst. I: Fund. Theory Appl. **48**(2), 177–183 (2001). https://doi.org/10.1109/81.904882

6. Indovina, I., Sanes, J.N.: On somatotopic representation centers for finger movements in human primary motor cortex and supplementary motor area. Neuroimage **13**(6), 1027–1034 (2001). https://doi.org/10.1006/nimg.2001.0776

7. Ito, T., et al.: Task-evoked activity quenches neural correlations and variability across cortical areas. PLoS Comput. Biol. **16**(8), e1007983 (2020). https://doi.org/10.1371/journal.pcbi.1007983

8. Katz, M.J.: Fractals and the analysis of waveforms. Comput. Biol. Med. **18**(3), 145–156 (1988). https://doi.org/10.1016/0010-4825(88)90041-8

9. Leutheuser, H., Gabsteiger, F., Hebenstreit, F., Reis, P., Lochmann, M., Eskofier, B.: Comparison of the AMICA and the InfoMax algorithm for the reduction of electromyogenic artifacts in EEG data. In: 2013 35th Annual International Conference of the IEEE Engineering in Medicine and Biology Society (EMBC), pp. 6804–6807 (2013). https://doi.org/10.1109/EMBC.2013.6611119

10. Machado, S., et al.: Sensorimotor integration: basic concepts, abnormalities related to movement disorders and sensorimotor training-induced cortical reorganization. Rev. Neurol. **51**(7), 427–436 (2010). https://doi.org/10.33588/rn.5107.2010228

11. Makeig, S., Debener, S., Onton, J., Delorme, A.: Mining event-related brain dynamics. Trends Cogn. Sci. **8**(5), 204–210 (2004). https://doi.org/10.1016/j.tics.2004.03.008

12. Namazi, H., Ala, T.S.: Decoding of simple and compound limb motor imagery movements by fractal analysis of Electroencephalogram (EEG) signal. Fractals **27**(03), 1950041 (2019). https://doi.org/10.1142/S0218348X19500415

13. Natarajan, K., Acharya, U.R., Alias, F., Tiboleng, T., Puthusserypady, S.K.: Nonlinear analysis of EEG signals at different mental states. Biomed. Eng. Online **3**, 1–11 (2004). https://doi.org/10.1186/1475-925X-3-7

14. Palmer, J.A., Kreutz-Delgado, K., Makeig, S.: Amica: an adaptive mixture of independent component analyzers with shared components. Swartz Center for Computatonal Neursoscience, University of California San Diego, Technical Report (2012)

15. Rodriguez-Bermudez, G., Garcia-Laencina, P.J.: Analysis of EEG signals using nonlinear dynamics and chaos: a review. Appl. Math. Inf. Sci. **9**(5), 2309 (2015). https://doi.org/10.12785/amis/090512

16. Stergiadis, C., Kostaridou, V.D., Klados, M.A.: Which BSS method separates better the EEG signals? a comparison of five different algorithms. Biomed. Signal Process. Control **72**, 103292 (2022). https://doi.org/10.1016/j.bspc.2021.103292

17. Sun, H., et al.: Sequential activation of premotor, primary somatosensory and primary motor areas in humans during cued finger movements. Clin. Neurophysiol. **126**(11), 2150–2161 (2015). https://doi.org/10.1016/j.clinph.2015.01.005

Neuromotor and Cognitive Disorders

Stress Classification Model Using Speech: An Ambulatory Protocol-Based Database Study

Lara Eleonora Prado[1(✉)], Andrea Hongn[2], Patricia Pelle[3],
and María Paula Bonomini[1,2,4]

[1] Departamento de Ciencias de la Vida, Instituto Tecnológico de Buenos Aires
(ITBA), Ciudad Autónoma de Buenos Aires, Argentina
lprado@itba.edu
[2] CONICET, Instituto Argentino de Matemática "Alberto P. Calderón" (IAM),
Buenos Aires, Argentina
[3] Universidad de Buenos Aires, Facultad de Ingeniería, Instituto de Ingeniería
Biomédica (IIBM), Buenos Aires, Argentina
[4] Departamento de Electrónica, Tecnología de Computadoras y Proyectos,
Universidad Politécnica de Cartagena, Cartagena, Spain

Abstract. Chronic stress poses a significant risk to health, potentially
leading to long-term diseases such as cancer and diabetes. Analyzing
stress through speech presents a promising avenue, as it offers accessibility and scalability using only a microphone and processor. This study
focuses on quantifying stress through speech analysis and its potential
implications for disease prevention and treatment.

A speech database was obtained from 36 subjects who participated
in a stress induction protocol. Acoustic features, including Pitch and
Mel-Frequency Cepstral Coefficients (MFCCs), were extracted from the
audio recordings. Supervised parametric classifications were conducted
using XGBoost, with feature sets defined based on correlation analysis
and feature importance. The classification results were validated using
leave-one-out validation.

Key findings include the development of a speech database for stress
detection in laboratory settings, optimization of feature sets for the
model, resulting in a classification accuracy of 82%. These results highlight the feasibility of speech-based stress analysis and its potential
impact on healthcare strategies.

Keywords: Stress · voice · Speech · XGBoost · Machine Learning

1 Introduction

Stress is the body's response to any event that demands attention or action,
affecting homeostasis. Prolonged exposure to stressors can lead to a phase of
exhaustion, disrupting the release of stress hormones and contributing to various health issues, including cardiovascular, gastrointestinal, and inflammatory

J. M. Ferrández Vicente et al. (Eds.): IWINAC 2024, LNCS 14674, pp. 245–252, 2024.
https://doi.org/10.1007/978-3-031-61140-7_24

diseases, as well as cancer and diabetes [1–4]. Detecting and quantifying stress within clinical practice, alongside integrating stress management into treatments, holds significant potential for preventing and managing diseases [5,6].

Voice serves as a primary communication mechanism for humans, with its production involving both the central nervous system (CNS) and the autonomic nervous system (ANS). Consequently, changes in speech under stress have been the focus of research for decades [7]. Various approaches, including detection systems based on acoustic features and machine learning classification models, have been developed. These systems offer the possibility of creating simple and computationally low-cost classification models. For instance, in [8], an accuracy of 88% was achieved using statistical classifiers based on phonetic acoustic features from real emergency call audio databases. Similarly, [9] applied component-wise gradient boosting to a database of vocal features from adult helpline audio recordings, resulting in an accuracy of 97.39%.

This research proposes the construction of a simple and fast classification model, using a database comprising neutral and stress blocks defined in healthy patients. The aim is to develop a reproducible and scalable protocol for stress classification, with a system of low computational cost.

2   Methods

2.1   Database

Suspects aged 18 to 30 years old, without pre-existing chronic illnesses, were recruited. They underwent an stress induction protocol in person initially, and virtually in a second phase. Audio recordings and physiological signals (EDA, BVP, HR, and temperature) were collected during the interviews using the Empatica E4 wristband. The audio recordings were captured using the built-in internal microphones of computers, with a sampling frequency of 44.8 kHz, and the Audacity software.

The protocol was conducted sequentially in neutral, stress induction, and rest stages, as illustrated in Fig. 1. The baseline questions stage involved inquiries about the date, weather, and age of the participants. During the counting task, participants were instructed to count from 0 to 10, alternating with the word 'pum'. The TMCT block required subjects to perform arithmetic calculations within a time limit and respond orally. The opinion stage consisted of two parts: participants were asked to develop their opinion on a selected topic within 30 s, followed by developing the opposite opinion on the same topic within another 30 s. The topic is selected beforehand by the interviewer based on a questionnaire where participants rate their level of agreement on various topics. Finally, in the subtraction block, participants had to consecutively subtract the number 13 starting from the number 1022.

2.2   Feature Extraction

Signal processing was performed in Python and the specialized audio library librosa was employed for the extraction of acoustic features. The extracted

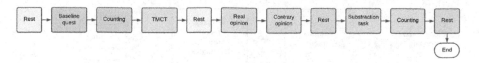

Fig. 1. Interview block diagram. Blocks with oral responses are marked in color, red for those classified as stressful and blue as neutral. (Color figure online)

features included Pitch, Spectral Centroid, High-Frequency Ratio (HFR), and Mel-Frequency Cepstral Coefficients (MFCCs). These attributes, except for the HFR, are time-domain signals. Therefore, statistics were computed for each feature to obtain a single value per feature, aiming to create a static database. Table 1 defines the characteristics considered for the classification model. After defining the static features for the entire database, the data were normalized for subsequent stages.

Table 1. Features on consideration for model training

Main feature	Derived Statistics	Total features	Main feature method
Pitch	mean, std, range, min and max	5	librosa.pyin
Spectral centroid	mean, std, range, min and max	5	librosa.feature.spectral_centroid
High Frequency ratio	–	1	librosa.stft
Mel Frequency cepstral coefficients (MFCC)	mean	13	librosa.feature.mfcc
Total acoustic features		24	

2.3 Supervised Classification

Figure 2 illustrates a diagram outlining the stages of the classification model development. Once the features were obtained, the database was organized into blocks, with each subject presenting multiple occurrences of stress and neutral states. The classification criteria utilized the protocol's classification: neutral blocks denoted neutral occurrences, while stress-inducing blocks represented stressful occurrences. Following feature extraction, the correlation matrix of the feature set was generated using pandas, with a correlation threshold set at 0.4.

Next, a supervised classification model using XGBoost was implemented. This algorithm employs the gradient boosting method and utilizes a set of weak decision trees as initial classifiers. In each trial, subjects were divided between training and testing sets to ensure that the same participant did not appear in both sets. Due to the protocol containing a greater number of stress-induced blocks, the data were imbalanced, leading to oversampling and undersampling of the database using the imbalanced-learn library. Undersampling randomly removed occurrences of the majority class, while oversampling randomly duplicated occurrences of the minority class to achieve a 0.5 proportion between classes.

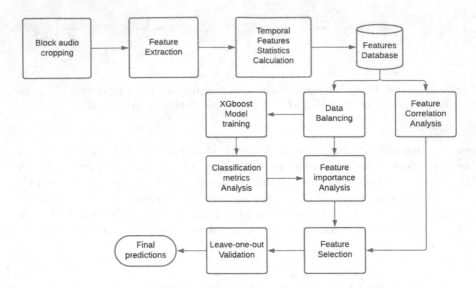

Fig. 2. Methodology block diagram

To define the model and optimize the results, feature selection was performed using the *feature_importance* functionality of XGBoost, complemented by correlation analysis. The algorithm was trained with all features and sets of similar features (Pitch, Spectral Centroid, and MFCCs). Features with the highest weight in the overall set and the specific set were selected based on this analysis. Different combinations were considered, taking into account the established correlation criterion, and classification metrics were obtained for these sets with and without balancing.

Finally, a leave-one-out validation was conducted based on the subjects. For each feature set, the model was trained with occurrences from all subjects except one. This process was repeated for all subjects, and the results obtained for the same set were averaged to compare the performance of each set.

3   Results

The distribution of the database between males and females and audio classified as stress and neutral states is shown in Table 2. The proportion of female audio recordings is 0.47, while the proportion of audio recordings in a neutral state is 0.34. The raw database consists of 253 occurrences per 24 characteristics, exhibiting an imbalance in classification. Balancing through oversampling increases the database to 366 occurrences, while undersampling reduces it to 140 occurrences.

Figure 3 illustrates the feature importance for a model trained with all features. Initially, the top 11 attributes were selected, which consistently ranked highly even when the model was trained with specific feature sets. Subsequently,

Table 2. Characterization of participants and the database

Sex	Quantity	Age	Blocks		
			Stress	Neutral	Total
Women	17	25 ± 4	76	32	108
Men	19	20.7 ± 2.2	107	38	145
Total	36	22.5 ± 3.6	183	70	254

20 combinations of attributes were formulated, and models were trained using each set with various balancing techniques.

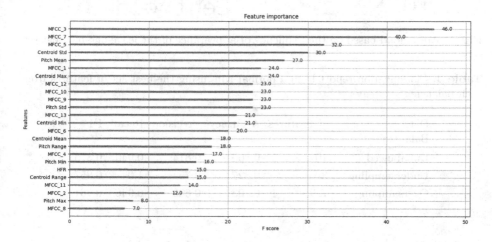

Fig. 3. Feature importance ranking

Leave-one-out validation was conducted using these 20 combinations, and the best feature sets were identified by selecting only those yielding results above the third quartile of accuracy. Table 3 showcases the metrics of the best-performing models from leave-one-out validation. The frequency of appearance of features in these selected sets is visualized in Figure 4. Additionally, Table 4 presents the classification report from the best feature set chosen for each data balancing

Table 3. Leave-one-out classification metrics statistics from the best sets of features

Data Balancing	Third Quartile	Accuracy	Precision	Recall	F1
Unbalanced	0.749	0.760	0.819	0.874	0.823
Undersampling	0.753	0.795	0.701	0.717	0.684
Oversampling	0.691	0.717	0.741	0.847	0.749

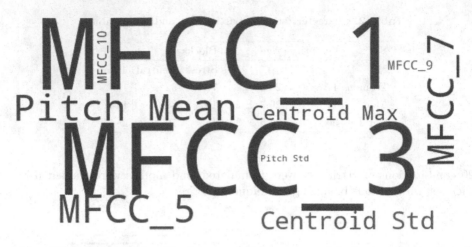

Fig. 4. Word cloud based on the frequency of appearance of the leave-one-out selected sets

Table 4. Classification report from a normal run, using the best set of features from each balancing strategy

Data Balancing	# Features	Accuracy	Precision	Recall	F1
Unbalanced	10	0.804	0.814	0.946	0.875
Undersampling	8	0.827	0.75	1.0	0.857
Oversampling	7	0.703	0.636	0.946	0.761

strategy. These results were obtained using a standard model training approach with a training proportion of 0.8.

4   Discussion

Artificial intelligence has proven to be useful in a wide range of bioengineering solutions [10]. Findings on this moderately small database supports the latter. In Table 2, it can be observed that the obtained database exhibits considerable imbalance, requiring the implementation of balancing techniques. However, undersampling may render the model more susceptible to overfitting by significantly reducing the number of occurrences. Conversely, oversampling entails randomly duplicating occurrences of the minority state, which could exacerbate the risk of overfitting and introduce biases, potentially degrading data quality.

Regarding feature selection, a notable emphasis on Mel-Frequency Cepstral Coefficients (MFCCs) is observed, consistent with previous literature [11–13]. The most efficient coefficients are of a lower order, which is associated with phonetic information. Additionally, pitch, a prominent acoustic feature in speech studies, has also been selected, although there is no consensus on its expected behavior [14]. Cross-validation reveals that integrating these features enhances the model's performance, though specific improvements warrant further clarification. A model for voice and effort (MoVE) is presented in [7], where different types of mental stress are contemplated, and each one has its own feature tendencies. Integration of multiple features could help create a model capable of detecting these complex tendencies.

Tables 3 and 4 delineate the capability of the obtained audio database to classify between neutral and psychological stress states. This underscores the functionality of the developed stress induction protocol. One of the challenges with laboratory stress and emotion-induced speech databases is that they are inferior at manifesting stress and emotion compared to natural situations [15]. Despite this limitation, the results obtained from the database (82% in the best scenario) are comparable with those of real stress speech databases. For instance, in [8], an accuracy of 88% was achieved using real emergency calls, while 97.39% accuracy was reported in [9] using audios from a helpline. Moreover, the feasibility of classifying speech audios using static acoustic characteristics holds significant promise due to its low computational cost and potential algorithm explainability.

Finally, considering the results obtained for each balancing strategy, oversampling demonstrates inferior performance, while undersampling and the unbalanced case yield similar and superior outcomes.

5   Conclusion

The research has successfully achieved its initial goal of developing a low-cost stress classification system based on a simple and reproducible protocol. The audio recordings obtained from interviews using different computers were used to generate a database of static features, which was successfully classified using XGBoost.

While these results provide a promising outlook on the use of speech to detect stress, several limitations should be considered for future research. Firstly, the database's imbalance highlights the need for incorporating more neutral stages when replicating the protocol. Secondly, the classification of blocks should be complemented with physiological validation to enhance the reliability of the results. Additionally, expanding the variety of acoustic features beyond temporal characteristics could improve the model's performance. Lastly, further validation of the model in natural speech settings is warranted.

In summary, while this research represents a significant step forward in stress detection from speech, addressing these limitations will be crucial for advancing the field and realizing the full potential of speech-based stress detection systems.

References

1. Yaribeygi, H., Pahani, Y., Sahraei, H., Johnson, T., Sahebkar, A.: The impact of stress on body function: a review. EXCIL J. **16**, 1057–1072 (2017)
2. Dimsdale, J.E.: Ashtary-Larky: psychological stress and cardiovascular disease. Int. J. Endocrinol. Metab. (2019). https://doi.org/10.1016/j.jacc.2007.12.024
3. Black, J., et al.: Systematic review: the role of psychological stress in inflammatory bowel disease. Aliment. Pharmacol. Ther. **56**(8), 1235–1249 (2022). https://doi.org/10.1111/apt.17202
4. Afrisham, R., Paknejad, M., Soliemanifar, O., Sadegh-Nejadi, S., Meshkani, R., Ashtary-Larky, D.: The influence of psychological stress on the initiation and progression of diabetes and cancer. J. Am. Coll. Cardiol. **51**(13) (2008). https://doi.org/10.5812/ijem.67400
5. Claar, R.L., Blumenthal, J.A.: The value of stress-management interventions in life-threatening medical conditions. Curr. Dir. Psychol. Sci. **12**(4), 133–137 (2003). https://doi.org/10.1111/1467-8721.01248
6. Antoni, M.H., Dhabhar, F.S.: The impact of psychosocial stress and stress management on immune responses in patients with cancer. Cancer **125**(9), 1417–1431 (2019). https://doi.org/10.1002/cncr.31943
7. Van Puyvelde, M., Neyt, X., McGlone, F., Pattyn, N.: Voice stress analysis: a new framework for voice and effort in human performance. Front. Psychol. **9**, 1994 (2018). https://doi.org/10.3389/fpsyg.2018.01994
8. Tavi, L.: Classifying females' stressed and neutral voices using acoustic-phonetic analysis of vowels: An exploratory investigation with emergency calls. Int. J. Speech Technol. **22**(3), 511–520 (2018). https://doi.org/10.1007/s10772-018-09574-6
9. Iyer, R., Nedeljkovic, M., Meyer, D.: Using vocal characteristics to classify psychological distress in adult helpline callers: retrospective observational study. JMIR Formative Res. **6**(12), e42249 (2022). https://doi.org/10.2196/42249
10. Górriz, J., et al.: Computational approaches to explainable artificial intelligence: advances in theory, applications and trends. Info. Fusion **100**, 101945 (2023)
11. Rodellar-Biarge, V., Palacios-Alonso, D., Nieto-Lluis, V., Gomez-Vilda, P.: Speech parameter selection for emotional stress characterization in women. In: 3rd IEEE International Work-Conference on Bioinspired Intelligence (2014). https://doi.org/10.1109/iwobi.2014.6913932
12. Lu, H., et al.: StressSense: detecting stress in unconstrained acoustic environments using smartphones. In: Proceedings of the 2012 ACM Conference on Ubiquitous Computing (2012). https://doi.org/10.1145/2370216.2370270
13. Iliev, A.I., Scordilis, M.S., Papa, J.P., Falcão, A.X.: Spoken emotion recognition through optimum-path forest classification using glottal features. Comput. Speech Lang. **24**(3), 445–460 (2010). https://doi.org/10.1016/j.csl.2009.02.005
14. Pisanski, K., et al.: Multimodal Stress Detection: testing for covariation in vocal, hormonal and physiological responses to trier social stress test. Horm. Behav. **106**, 52–61 (2018). https://doi.org/10.1016/j.yhbeh.2018.08.014
15. Ruiz, R., Absil, E., Harmegnies, B., Legros, C., Poch, D.: Time- and spectrum-related variabilities in stressed speech under laboratory and real conditions. Speech Commun. **20**(1–2), 111–129 (1996). https://doi.org/10.1016/s0167-6393(96)00048-9
16. Vaikole, S., Mulajkar, S., More, A., Jayaswal, P., Dhas, S.: Stress detection through speech analysis using machine learning. In: IJCRT, vol. 8 (2020)

Exploring Spatial Cognition: Comparative Analysis of Agent-Based Models in Dynamic and Static Environments

Maria Luongo[✉], Michela Ponticorvo, and Nicola Milano

NAC Lab Orazio Miglino, Department of Humanistic Studies,
University of Naples "Federico II", Naples, Italy
maria.luongo@unina.it

Abstract. The adoption of agent-based modeling represents a transformative approach in the study of spatial cognition, providing a dynamic and flexible framework to explore and enhance navigational behaviors across varied environmental landscapes.

In our study, we crafted and analyzed two specialized agent-based models, each designed for a unique set of conditions: one focuses on navigation in a static environment, while the other is geared towards adaptation in a dynamic setting, both employing mobile agents. Our comparative analysis reveals that agents trained in dynamic settings adapt better when tested in static environments, showing enhanced performance. This improvement highlights the robust adaptability of agents to varied contexts, especially when transitioning from complex, changing environments to simpler, static ones.

However, agents trained in static environments struggle to achieve similar gains in dynamic settings, indicating a challenge in adapting to increased complexity. This asymmetry underscores the importance of dynamic training for developing versatile and effective navigational strategies.

Keywords: Spatial cognition · spatial behaviour · agent-based models · behavioural task

1 Introduction

Spatial cognition is a fundamental aspect of survival and interaction for both biological agents, like mammals, and synthetic autonomous agents operating within expansive environments [8–10]. This cognitive function is essential for encoding, storing, recognizing, and recalling spatial information about one's surroundings. It involves understanding the placement and relevance of objects such as nutrients or other agents, which is critical for an agent's adaptive decision-making and behavior. In scientific research, modeling these agents has become an indispensable method to probe into and comprehend complex spatial phenomena, particularly in space exploration and navigation. Their application is particularly notable in simulating and analyzing agents' exploration abilities in diverse

J. M. Ferrández Vicente et al. (Eds.): IWINAC 2024, LNCS 14674, pp. 253–260, 2024.
https://doi.org/10.1007/978-3-031-61140-7_25

and heterogeneous environments [13]. This is pivotal for fields like robotics, artificial intelligence, and cognitive sciences, where understanding spatial navigation is key. Moreover, autonomous agents face the significant challenge of developing effective strategies for orientation, obstacle avoidance, and goal achievement in dynamic and often unpredictable scenarios [2,4,7]. Agent models enable a thorough examination of how these entities make decisions in response to different sensory inputs - visual, auditory, or tactile - integrating this information to adapt to evolving spatial conditions [14]. Our research utilizes simulations across varied environmental setups to shed light on the subtleties of an agent's exploratory behavior. Therefore, it endeavors to deepen the understanding of spatial cognition by investigating how autonomous agents navigate and adapt to complex environments, by employing sophisticated modeling techniques and simulations across diverse environmental setups. Moreover, through our study, we seek to elucidate the factors influencing exploratory effectiveness and identify strategies for enhancing autonomous systems' navigational capabilities. Ultimately, our work contributes to the broader field of spatial cognition research, offering valuable insights into both biological and artificial systems' navigational abilities and advancing the development of intelligent technologies for various applications, including robotics, artificial intelligence, and cognitive sciences.

2   Methodology

In our modeling project, we drew inspiration from the "WaterWorld" task, a prominent example within the EvoJAX framework (Fig. 1) [18]. Regarding the "WaterWorld" task, an agent is engaged in an environment where his main objective is to collect as many items defined as "food" as possible, while at the same time avoiding items classified as "poisons". This task requires the agent to intelligently navigate the environment, making strategic decisions to maximize its score through food acquisition and minimizing exposure to poisons.

2.1   EvoJAX

EvoJAX is a versatile software framework designed to advance research and development in neuroevolution and reinforcement learning, integrating elements of neuroevolution, where neural networks are optimized using evolutionary algorithms, with deep learning and reinforcement learning techniques [16]. Built for efficiency and scalability, EvoJAX leverages modern hardware, especially GPUs, for high-performance computations and large-scale simulations [3].

The framework utilizes JAX, a library for high-performance numerical computing, which enables auto-differentiation and optimized Python function compilation, crucial for neural network training. Indeed, EvoJAX comes with several simulation environments, like WaterWorld, to test and evaluate the performance of evolved agents, offering insights into how agents learn and behave in different scenarios. It's designed for flexibility, allowing users to define their environments, neural networks, and evolutionary algorithms, making it a versatile tool for AI

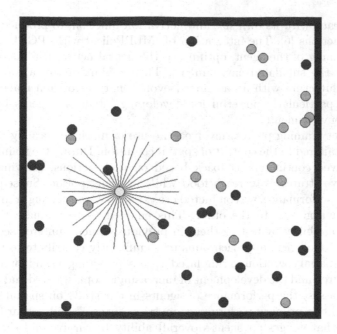

Fig. 1. The image depicts the WaterWorld task from EvoJAX. The light gray bubble represents the agent, while the black bubble symbolizes poison, and the gray bubbles denote food. (Color figure online)

research and development, particularly appealing to researchers and developers focused on neural network evolution and reinforcement learning. Therefore, EvoJAX thus facilitates the exploration of new ideas and approaches in artificial evolution and machine learning.

2.2 Materials and Method

To conduct our study on spatial cognition in simulated agents, we designed and implemented two distinct simulated environments: one where the agent was mobile and the food and poison were static, and a second where the agent was mobile while food and poison moved randomly. Two key components are utilized for agent training process: 'PGPE' (Policy Gradients with Parameter-based Exploration) and 'MLPPolicy' (Multi-Layer Perceptron Policy). 'PGPE' is an evolutionary algorithm used for optimizing the parameters of a neural network [15, 17]. This approach stands out for its effective exploration of the parameter space, leveraging policy gradients to guide evolution. Unlike relying on reward-based gradient estimates, 'PGPE' exploits direct variation of parameters to find optimal configurations. On the other hand, 'MLPPolicy' represents the neural network architecture used by the agent. It is a multi-layer feedforward neural network, commonly employed for approximating complex functions [19]. In 'MLPPolicy', inputs from the environment are transformed through various hidden layers, each with its own size and activation function, to produce an action or a set of actions [6]. The integration of 'MLPPolicy' with 'PGPE' allows for effective training of the agent, optimizing the neural network to maximize performance in the simulated environment. This combination of a robust neural network architecture with an advanced evolutionary algorithm makes training in EvoJAX particularly powerful for developing intelligent agents in complex simulation environments.

The agent training process involved the use of machine learning algorithms specifically tailored to the context of spatial cognition. During the training phase, agents received continuous feedback based on their actions, allowing them to learn effective strategies to reach food while avoiding poison. Subsequently, to assess agent performance, we conducted cross-tests by transferring trained agents from one environment to the other. This enabled us to evaluate the agents' generalization ability by testing them in previously unencountered scenarios.

Our methodological approach aims to significantly contribute to the understanding of spatial cognition in simulated agents, providing a solid foundation for further research and the development of increasingly sophisticated and adaptable models. To assess the performance of agents in our study on spatial cognition, we employed two primary performance metrics: "fitness" and "reward." Fitness is a metric that gauges an agent's overall ability to survive and thrive in the simulated environment [1]. Fitness provides a comprehensive assessment of the agent's abilities in achieving predefined objectives. Reward, on the other hand, is a specific measure used in the context of machine learning. During the training process, agents receive rewards or penalties based on their actions. For instance, reaching food yields a positive reward, while coming into contact with poison result in a negative penalty. Therefore, the reward is designed to incentivize agents to develop optimal strategies for maximizing their success in completing the mission. The combined use of fitness and reward offers a comprehensive evaluation of agent capabilities, considering both overall performance in the simulated environment (fitness) and the specific learning process during training (reward). Together, these metrics have enabled us to derive scores for the agent in both training and testing across the simulated environments, resulting in a holistic performance index of the agent's effectiveness.

2.3   Results

Figure 2 illustrates the performance of a model trained in a static environment, where food and poison are placed in fixed positions, and subsequently tested in a dynamic environment where food and poison move over time.

During training in the static environment, the agent's average scores show a steady increase with the number of iterations. This suggests effective learning of score maximization in an environment with fixed food and poison positions.

However, when tested in the dynamic environment where food and poison are in motion, the agent's average scores are comparatively lower than those in the static environment, albeit demonstrating a consistent upward trend.

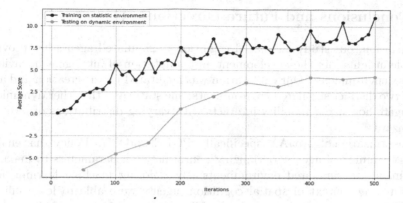

Fig. 2. This graph depicts the performance of agents trained in a static environment, and then tested in a dynamic environment. The x-axis represents the number of iterations during training, and the y-axis indicates the average score achieved by the agents.

Figure 3 depicts the performance outcomes of a model initially trained within a dynamic environment, characterized by the shifting positions of food and poison, and later tested in a static setting, where these locations are stationary.

During its training phase in the dynamic environment, the model exhibits fluctuating average scores as iterations progress. This fluctuation underlines the complexity of adapting to continually changing conditions, requiring ongoing strategy refinement by the model. Upon testing in a static environment, with unchanging food and poison placements, the model's performance markedly improves, evidenced by a notable upward trajectory in average scores, surpassing the scores observed during its training in the dynamic context.

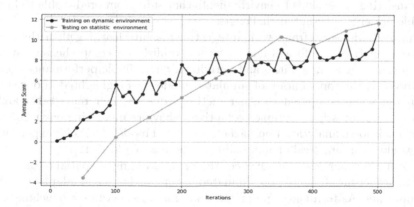

Fig. 3. This graph illustrates the performance of agents trained in a dynamic environment, and subsequently tested in a static environment. The x-axis represents the number of iterations during training, while the y-axis indicates the average score achieved by the agents.

3   Conclusions and Future Directions

In conclusion, our study on spatial cognition in simulated agents has provided valuable insights into the development and adaptation of intelligent behavior in complex environments. Our exploration was facilitated by the creation and analysis of two distinct simulated environments, one static and the other dynamic, to investigate how agent mobility interacts with varying distributions of resources and hazards.

The utilization of EvoJAX, specifically 'PGPE' and 'MLPPolicy', has enabled effective training of agents, optimizing neural network parameters to maximize performance in simulated environments. By tailoring machine learning algorithms to the context of spatial cognition, agents were able to learn efficient strategies for navigating towards food while avoiding poison, demonstrating the adaptability of their decision-making processes. Our research highlights a complex panorama of adaptability and learning among the agents. Those trained within dynamic settings showcased a remarkable capacity for generalization, adeptly applying their learned strategies to novel, static environments. This adaptability was evident in their testing phase within a static environment, where they not only matched but exceeded the performance levels seen during their training phase in dynamic settings, indicating that training under variable conditions equips agents with the versatility needed to adapt to simpler.

Conversely, agents trained in static settings exhibited a different trajectory of learning. While these agents scored well during their initial training in static environments, their subsequent testing in dynamic conditions revealed struggles to adjust to the new, more unpredictable settings, initially resulting in considerably lower scores. Although there was an improvement in performance, it did not reach the levels seen during their training phase. This suggests that while learning in dynamic environments lays a foundational framework for adaptability, translating those skills to environments that shift from predictable to highly variable presents substantial challenges.

Our methodological framework, integrating machine learning algorithms with evaluative metrics like fitness and reward, establishes a comprehensive system for analyzing agent capabilities and deriving a quantifiable performance score.

Moreover, the contribution of simulated models, as highlighted in our study, stands out when compared to other methods due to their remarkable ability to mimic and investigate complex adaptive behaviors in varying environments. Unlike traditional analytical approaches, simulated models facilitate experiments that would be impractical or impossible in the real world [5, 12].

In summary, our research advances the understanding of spatial cognition by offering deeper insights into how simulated agents navigate and adapt to varying environments. As technology progresses, our findings serve as a benchmark for designing and implementing intelligent systems capable of functioning effectively across diverse spatial contexts, as well as highlighting the limitations of agents in adapting to new environments.

References

1. Adami, C., Ofria, C., Collier, T.C.: Evolution of biological complexity. Proc. Natl. Acad. Sci. **97**(9), 4463–4468 (2000)
2. Alonso-Mora, J., DeCastro, J.A., Raman, V., Rus, D., Kress-Gazit, H.: Reactive mission and motion planning with deadlock resolution avoiding dynamic obstacles. Auton. Robot. **42**, 801–824 (2018)
3. Bradbury, J., et al.: JAX: composable transformations of Python+NumPy programs (2018). http://github.com/google/jax
4. Dhakan, P., Merrick, K., Rañó, I., Siddique, N.: Intrinsic rewards for maintenance, approach, avoidance, and achievement goal types. Front. Neurorobotics **12**, 63 (2018)
5. Durán, J.M.: What is a simulation model? Mind. Mach. **30**(3), 301–323 (2020)
6. Lange, R., et al.: Discovering attention-based genetic algorithms via meta-blackbox optimization. In: Proceedings of the Genetic and Evolutionary Computation Conference, pp. 929–937 (2023)
7. Maes, P.: Situated agents can have goals. Robot. Auton. Syst. **6**(1–2), 49–70 (1990)
8. Ponticorvo, M., Coccorese, M., Gigliotta, O., Bartolomeo, P., Marocco, D.: Artificial intelligence applied to spatial cognition assessment. In: Ferrández Vicente, J.M., Álvarez-Sánchez, J.R., de la Paz López, F., Adeli, H. (eds.) Artificial Intelligence in Neuroscience: Affective Analysis and Health Applications. IWINAC 2022. LNCS, vol. 13258. Springer, Cham (2022). https://doi.org/10.1007/978-3-031-06242-1_40
9. Ponticorvo, M., Miglino, O.: Encoding geometric and non-geometric information: a study with evolved agents. Anim. Cogn. **13**, 157–174 (2010)
10. Ponticorvo, M., Walker, R., Miglino, O.: Evolutionary robotics as a tool to investigate spatial cognition in artificial and natural systems. In Artificial Cognition Systems, pp. 210–237. IGI Global (2007)
11. Ponticorvo, M., Miglino, O.: IS LANGUAGE NECESSARY TO MERGE GEOMETRIC AND NON-GEOMETRIC SPATIAL CUES? THE CASE OF THE "BLUE-WALL TASK". In: Modeling Language, Cognition And Action, pp. 209-213 (2005)
12. Roberts, N., Anderson, D., Deal, R., Garet, M., Shaffer, W.: Introduction to computer simulation-a system dynamics modeling approach. J. Oper. Res. Soc. **48**(11), 1145–1145 (1997)
13. Shook, E., Wang, S.: Investigating the influence of spatial and temporal granularities on agent-based modeling. Geogr. Anal. **47**(4), 321–348 (2015)
14. Schillaci, G., Hafner, V.V., Lara, B.: Exploration behaviors, body representations, and simulation processes for the development of cognition in artificial agents. Front. Robot. AI **3**, 39 (2016)
15. Sehnke, F., et al.: Parameter-exploring policy gradients. Neural Netw. **23**(4), 551–559 (2010)
16. Tang, Y., Tian, Y., Ha, D.: EvoJAX: hardware-accelerated neuroevolution. In: Proceedings of the Genetic and Evolutionary Computation Conference Companion, pp. 308–311 (2022)
17. Toklu,N.H., et al.: ClipUp: a simple and powerful optimizer for distribution-based policy evolution. In: International Conference on Parallel Problem Solving from Nature, pp. 515–527 (2020)

18. Karpathy, A.: REINFORCEjs (2015). https://cs.stanford.edu/people/karpathy/reinforcejs/waterworld.html
19. Kern, F.: Using the multi-level perspective on socio-technical transitions to assess innovation policy. Technol. Forecast. Soc. Chang. **79**(2), 298–310 (2012)

Machine Learning for Personality Type Classification on Textual Data

Igone Morais-Quilez[1], Manuel Graña[1(✉)], and Javier de Lope[2]

[1] Computational Intelligence Group, University of the Basque Country, UPV/EHU, San Sebastian, Spain
manuel.grana@ehu.eus

[2] Department of Artificial Intelligence, Polytechnic University of Madrid (UPM), Madrid, Spain

Abstract. The Myers-Briggs Type Indicator (MBTI) is typifies personality on the basis of four basic dichotomy traits. It has been used by psychologists with diverse applications in real life and clinical settings. Recently there are attempts to carry out MBTI indexing by Machine Learning (ML) techniques applied to several kinds of signals among them textual data extracted from interactions in social networks. In this paper we apply a battery of well known ML approaches to the prediction of MBTI categories based on features extracted by natural language processing (NLP) techniques from textual data extracted from a social network devoted to personality evaluation. The results are in agreement with the literature, showing that prediction of MBTI personality indicator is highly reproducible.

1 Introduction

In the field of natural language processing (NLP), Sentiment Analysis is a technique used to determine the sentiment of opinion expressed in published texts. It involves analyzing the text data to classify it as Positive, Negative or Neutral based on the underlying sentiment conveyed by the words and phrases used [10]. The analysis of personality can be also involved in the analysis of opinions from text mining, which could allow to predict reactions and the involvement of the user in social networks [1]. Also personality analysis can allow to drive the user to specific desired directions [7]. There have been a number of attempts to predict the personality category from textual data [3] which have found that some personality traits are more difficult to predict than others.

This paper aims to the reanalysis of a dataset of textual information focusing on an specific personality indicator, the Myers-Briggs Type Indicator (MBTI) [2,11] which has become rather popular in social network sentiment analysis. The paper proposes a battery of machine learning algorithms over frequential features extracted from the textual data by a well stablished NLP pipeline. The contents of the paper is as follows: Sect. 2 provides some motivation and background information. Section 3 describes the materials and methods. Section 4 gives the results of the computational experiments. Finally, Sect. 5 provides the conclusions of the paper.

© The Author(s), under exclusive license to Springer Nature Switzerland AG 2024
J. M. Ferrández Vicente et al. (Eds.): IWINAC 2024, LNCS 14674, pp. 261–269, 2024.
https://doi.org/10.1007/978-3-031-61140-7_26

2   Background

Fig. 1. A synoptic view of Myers-Briggs Type Indicator (MBTI) elements.

In the field of Sentiment Analysis, it is common to use some Personality types [4,5,8,9] as a way of categorizing and understanding different patterns of behavior, thoughts, and emotions that individuals exhibit consistently over time. They provide a framework for understanding individual differences and can be valuable for personal development, relationship-building, and achieving success in various aspects of life. One of the most well-known frameworks for understanding personality types is the Myers-Briggs Type Indicator (MBTI) [2,11], which categorizes individuals into 16 different personality types based on four dichotomies, illustrated in Fig. 1:

1. Extraversion (E) vs. Introversion (I): Describes how individuals interact with their environment. Extraverts tend to be outgoing, social, and energized by interactions with others, while introverts are more reserved, reflective, and energized by solitary activities.
2. Sensing (S) vs. Intuition (N): Describes how individuals gather information. Sensors rely on their five senses and focus on concrete, factual information, while intuitives rely on patterns, connections, and possibilities, often focusing on abstract concepts.
3. Thinking (T) vs. Feeling (F): Describes how individuals make decisions. Thinkers tend to prioritize logic, objectivity, and consistency in decision-making, while feelers prioritize empathy, harmony, and personal values.
4. Judging (J) vs. Perceiving (P): Describes how individuals approach the outside world. Judgers prefer structure, organization, and planning, and are decisive and goal-oriented, while perceivers prefer flexibility, spontaneity, and adaptability, and are open-ended and exploratory.

Personality analysis plays a significant role in various fields due to its ability to provide insights into individual differences, behaviors, preferences, and motivations. Here's a brief explanation of its relevance in several fields:

1. Psychology: Personality analysis is fundamental in psychology as it helps psychologists understand and explain human behavior, cognition, and emotion. It provides a framework for studying personality traits, disorders, development, and dynamics within individuals and across populations.
2. Human Resources and Management: In the business world, personality analysis is used extensively in human resources and management. It helps in recruitment and selection by identifying candidates whose personalities align with job requirements and organizational culture. Personality assessments also aid in team building, leadership development, conflict resolution, and performance management.
3. Education: Personality analysis in education helps teachers understand students' learning styles, preferences, and strengths. It enables educators to tailor teaching methods, curriculum, and classroom environments to meet the diverse needs of students, leading to more effective learning outcomes.
4. Clinical Psychology and Psychiatry: Personality analysis is crucial in clinical settings for diagnosing and treating mental health disorders. Psychologists and psychiatrists use personality assessments to assess symptoms, identify personality disorders, develop treatment plans, and monitor progress over time.
5. Counseling and Therapy: In counseling and therapy, personality analysis facilitates the therapeutic process by fostering self-awareness, insight, and personal growth. Therapists use personality assessments to understand clients' perspectives, motivations, coping mechanisms, and interpersonal patterns, helping them address issues, overcome challenges, and improve their overall well-being.
6. Marketing and Consumer Behavior: Personality analysis is utilized in marketing and consumer behavior research to understand consumer preferences, attitudes, and purchasing decisions. Marketers use personality insights to develop targeted advertising campaigns, product designs, and branding strategies that resonate with specific personality types and demographic segments.
7. Sports and Performance Psychology: In sports psychology, personality analysis helps coaches and athletes optimize performance, enhance motivation, and manage stress. By understanding athletes' personalities, psychologists can tailor training programs, mental skills training, and performance strategies to match individual needs and goals.

3 Materials and Methods

3.1 Data Collection:

The (MBTI) Myers-Briggs Personality Type Dataset is a Kaggle dataset that contains over 8600 rows of data, on each row is a persons:

- Type (This person's 4 letter MBTI code/type)
- A section of each of the last 50 things they have posted (Each entry separated by "|||" (3 pipe characters))

This data was collected through the PersonalityCafe forum, which provides a large selection of people and their MBTI personality type, as well as what they have written.

3.2   Feature Extraction

For this personality analysis problem, we extracted features from text data for the last 50 posts of each person in the PersonalityCafe forum to predict and classify their personality types. For feature extraction we follow these steps:

- First We obtain the **Word Frequencies** which involve counting the occurrences of specific words or phrases in a text corpus. These features capture the language patterns and vocabulary used, which can be indicative of their personality traits. For example, individuals high in extraversion may use more social words, whiles those high in neuroticsm may use more negative or emotional words.
- Next, we obtain the **Word Embeddings**, which represent words as dense, low-dimensional vectors in a continuous vector space. These vectors capture semantic relationships between words based on their context in the text corpus. Word embeddings can be used to represent the semantic meaning of words and phrases, allowing machine learning models to capture subtle nuances in language use related to personality traits.
- The next step is to obtain the **Part-of-Speech Tags**, which classify words in a text corpus into categories such as nouns, verbs, adjectives, and adverbs. These tags provide information about the grammatical structure and syntax of sentences, which can be relevant for personality analysis. For example, individuals with high openness to experience may use more adjectives to describe novel concepts or ideas.
- The numerical features are defined by the term frequency inverse document frequencies (TF-IDF) which provide the relative probability of appearance of terms as a probabilistic vector extensively used in context based retrieval and recommendation systems [12].
- We can also obtain the **Sentiment Analysis** to classify text data into positive, negative, or neutral sentiment categories. These features capture the emotional tone and sentiment expressed in the text, which can be indicative of personality traits such as neuroticism or agreeableness. For example, individuals high in neuroticism may express more negative sentiments in their writing,

3.3   Target Classes

In this paper we opted to classify the data into the different 16 codes for personality in the first experiment and into the four binary variables (Extraversion - Introversion, Sensing - Intuition, Thinking - Feeling and judging - Perceiving)

3.4 Classification Models

We have applied the battery of models that can be found in the Matlab classifier design application with a 10-fold cross validation approach. Such models are standard tools for the AI practitioners [6]. Performance reported are the average results on the test folds of the cross validation process. The available models include several flavors of Support Vector Machines (SVM) with linear, quadratic, cubic, and Gaussian kernels, which are preconfigured with fine, medium and coarse hyperparameters. Analogous variation of K-Nearest Neighbor approaches (KNN), trees, and ensambles of trees are provided. Additionally, Linear and Quadratic Discriminants, Logistic Regression (LR), Gaussian and Kernel Naive Bayes (GNB), and some variations of Multi-layer Perceptrons (MLP) generically named Neural Networks are provided. Table 1 contains the full collection of classifiers.

3.5 Performance Evaluation Metrics

We report the classification accuracy, which is the ratio of the number of correct predictions to the total number of input samples, and the Area Under Curve (AUC) of the Receiver Operating Characteristic (ROC) curve which is a robust metric used to evaluate the performance of binary classification models. For multiclass problems, the AUC is often computed for each class considering the remaining classes as a single class, thus compressing the confusion matrix. The ROC curve is a graphical representation of the trade-off between the true positive rate (sensitivity) and the false positive rate (1 - specificity) across different threshold values.

Here's a complete definition of the AUC-ROC metric computation:

1. True Positive Rate (TPR) or Sensitivity: TPR measures the proportion of positive instances that are correctly identified by the model. It is calculated as: $TPR = \frac{TP}{TP+FN}$ where: TP is the number of true positives (correctly predicted positive instances), and FN is the number of false negatives (positive instances incorrectly predicted as negative).
2. False Positive Rate (FPR) or $1 - Specificity$: FPR measures the proportion of negative instances that are incorrectly classified as positive by the model. It is calculated as: $FPR = \frac{FP}{FP+TN}$ where FP is the number of false positives (negative instances incorrectly predicted as positive), and TN is the number of true negatives (correctly predicted negative instances).
3. ROC Curve: The ROC curve is created by plotting the TPR against the FPR for different threshold values. Each point on the curve represents a specific threshold value.
4. Area Under Curve (AUC): AUC is the area under the ROC curve. The AUC can be calculated using various methods, such as the trapezoidal rule or the Wilcoxon-Mann-Whitney statistic $AUC = \int_0^1 TPR(FPR)d(FPR)$. It quantifies the overall performance of the classification model. A higher AUC value indicates better discrimination between positive and negative instances by the model. The AUC value ranges from 0 to 1, when AUC = 0.5 or below implies

that the model has no discrimination ability (equivalent to random guessing). An AUC = 1 implies perfect discrimination, where the model perfectly separates positive and negative instances, i.e.

4   Results

Table 1. Performance metrics achieved by the classifiers in the multicategory formulation of the problem (16 categories).

Classifier	Accuracy%	AUC
Fine Tree (FT)	52.4	0.66
Medium Tree MT)	49.7	0.64
Coarse Tree (CT)	41.8	0.60
Linear Discriminant (LD)	65.2	0.77
Quadratic Discriminant (QD)	Failed	Failed
Logistic Regression (LR)	26.5	0.51
Gaussian Naive Bayes (GNB)	51.2	0.72
Kernel Naive Bayes (KNB)	46.6	0.60
Linear SVM (LSVM)	59.4	0.85
Quadratic SVM (QSM)	60.9	0.84
Cubic SVM (CSVM)	60.3	0.84
Fine Gaussian SVM (FGSVM)	21.1	0.49
Medium Gaussian SVM (MGSVM)	55.8	0.85
Coarse Gaussian SVM (CGSVM)	38.4	0.82
Fine KNN (FKNN)	6.0	0.50
Medium KNN (MKNN)	23.0	0.66
Coarse KNN (CKNN)	23.4	0.78
Cosine KNN (CosKNN)	33.4	0.73
Cubic KNN (CuKNN)	26.3	0.69
Weighted KNN (WKNN)	22.9	0.69
Ensemble Boosted Trees (EBT)	54.2	0.72
Ensemble Bagged Trees (EBaT)	53.3	0.70
Ensemble Subspace Discriminant (ESD)	65.5	0.79
Ensemble Subspace KNN (ESKNN)	12.7	0.59
Ensemble RUSBoosted Trees (ERT)	47.9	0.68
Narrow Neural Network (NNN)	44.6	0.58
Medium Neural Network (MNN)	48.3	0.62
Wide Neural Network (WNN)	55.7	0.69
Bilayered Neural Network (BNN)	41.7	0.63
Trilayered Neural Network (TNN)	38.3	0.64

Table 2. Performance in cross-validation experiments of the classifiers tackling binary pairs. EI Extraversion vs. Introversion, SI Sensisng vs Intuition, TF Thinking vs Feeling, JP Judging va Perceiving. Classifier acronyms are defined in Table 1.

Classifier	EI Acc.%	AUC	SI Acc. %	AUC	TF Acc. %	AUC	JP Acc. %	AUC
FT	83.0	0.69	82.6	0.74	74.9	0.78	74.8	0.80
MT	83.4	0.73	82.8	0.74	73.2	0.78	73.9	0.80
CT	81.0	0.67	81.7	0.72	69.4	0.68	67.6	0.73
LD	85.0	0.87	84.8	0.86	77.2	0.84	80.6	0.88
QD	79.2	0.53	77.5	0.54	66.5	0.70	73.3	0.80
LR	84.5	0.86	83.9	0.85	**77.7**	**0.84**	80.5	0.88
GNB	75.0	0.79	74.4	0.78	71.1	0.77	75.9	0.83
KNB	78.9	0.56	44.6	0.53	55.6	0.50	55.1	0.55
LSVM	84.7	0.87	84.6	0.87	77.5	0.84	81.1	0.88
QSVM	85.4	0.87	84.8	0.86	77.6	0.85	**81.5**	**0.89**
CSVM	85.5	0.87	84.7	0.86	77.6	0.84	81.0	0.88
FGSVM	78.9	0.52	77.0	0.52	59.2	0.51	55.0	0.51
MGSVM	83.9	0.87	83.7	0.87	76.6	0.84	80.8	0.88
CGSVM	79.1	0.87	78.8	0.87	71.6	0.84	80.4	0.88
FKNN	26.5	0.51	76.8	0.50	42.9	0.50	46.5	0.50
MKNN	73.3	0.69	78.1	0.69	60.5	0.61	61.1	0.64
CKNN	78.9	0.74	77.0	0.77	64.7	0.69	55.6	0.76
CosKNN	80.0	0.71	78.4	0.70	63.3	0.65	68.3	0.74
CuKNN	79.7	0.70	78.5	0.72	64.6	0.66	65.1	0.70
WKNN	76.6	0.70	78.0	0.69	59.4	0.61	59.2	0.65
EBT	**85.5**	**0.88**	**85.0**	**0.87**	77.7	0.85	79.1	0.87
EBaT	82.2	0.84	80.8	0.83	74.4	0.82	77.1	0.84
ESD	84.1	0.87	83.9	0.87	77.0	0.85	81.2	0.89
ESKNN	73.0	0.71	79.3	0.75	58.8	0.68	67.4	0.73
ERT	79.8	0.83	80.4	0.84	73.3	0.81	74.8	0.82
NNN	81.0	0.79	80.1	0.79	72.2	0.77	75.7	0.82
MNN	81.9	0.78	80.6	0.80	73.2	0.77	77.2	0.83
WNN	83.3	0.84	82.4	0.83	75.3	0.82	78.5	0.86
BNN	80.7	0.76	79.1	0.75	71.2	0.74	74.8	0.79
TNN	80.4	0.76	78.8	0.74	71.1	0.74	74.8	0.79

The first set of results regard the multi-class classification of text features into MBTI categories given by all possible combinations of dychotomic factors. The results are provided in Table 1. The accuracy corresponds to the averago accuracy for all classes, while the AUC corresponds to higher value for all categories. This difference explain the high variations between tow values. Accuracy values are very low and change widely from one model to other. Best results are obtained by ensambles of classifiers, specifically by the ensemble of subspace discriminant classifiers. SVM classifiers also provide a relative average performance. The attempts to apply Principal Component Analysis (PCA) in order to reduce dimensions were fruitless. The TF-IDF features are almost orthogonal, therefore preserving a high percentage of the total variance result in very little dimension reduction, while performance does not improve in all cases test.

The second set of results correspond to the binary classification problems for each dichotomic MBTI factor, shown in Table 2. The highest performance for each problem is highlighted in bold fonts. Overall results improve in this formulation of the problem. The accuracy results for each binary classification problem are over 80% in many classifier models. The most difficult problem is the Thinking versus Feeling dichotomy, contrary to results reported by other works which find that the Judging versus Perceiving dichotomy is the most difficult to predict [3]. However, the Thinking versus Feeling dichotomy imbalance is greater than the Judging versus Perceiving dichotomy, which can explain the increased difficulty of prediction. The Extraversion versus Introversion and the Sensing versus Intuition dychotomies report the best results, both using the same Ensemble of Boosted Trees.

5   Conclusions

This paper examines the feasibility of predicted the personality type indicated by the MBFI categories from textual data using machine learning approaches over textrual features extracted by NLP methods. We have considered two ways of formulating the problem, one as a multi-class problem, where we have sixteen categories given by all possible combinations of the MBTI dychotomic factors. This problem is rather difficult due to the high class imabalance, so results of machine learning approaches are very poor. The second formulation treats each MBTI binary factor independently, thus posing four independent binary classification problems. In this case, results are very good for some classifier models. Overall, the response of the models evaluated on this data extremely variable, suggesting that the problem is inherently difficult and classifier models can be unstable.

References

1. Adamopoulos, P., Ghose, A., Todri, V.: The impact of user personality traits on word of mouth: text-mining social media platforms. Inf. Syst. Res. **29**(3), 612–640 (2018)
2. Bharadwaj, S., Sridhar, S., Choudhary, R., Srinath, R.: Persona traits identification based on Myers-Briggs type indicator (MBTI)-a text classification approach. In: 2018 International Conference on Advances in Computing, Communications and Informatics (ICACCI), pp. 1076–1082. IEEE (2018)

3. En Jun Choong and Kasturi Dewi Varathan: Predicting judging-perceiving of Myers-Briggs type indicator (MBTI) in online social forum. PeerJ **9**, e11382 (2021)
4. Ezpeleta, E., Garitano, I., Arenaza-Nuño, I., Hidalgo, J.M.G., Zurutuza, U.: Novel comment spam filtering method on Youtube: sentiment analysis and personality recognition. In: Garrigós, I., Wimmer, M. (eds.) ICWE 2017. LNCS, vol. 10544, pp. 228–240. Springer, Cham (2018). https://doi.org/10.1007/978-3-319-74433-9_21
5. Genina, A., Gawich, M., Hegazy, A.: An approach for sentiment analysis and personality prediction using Myers Briggs type indicator. In: Hassanien, A.E., Slowik, A., Snášel, V., El-Deeb, H., Tolba, F.M. (eds.) AISI 2020. AISC, vol. 1261, pp. 179–186. Springer, Cham (2021). https://doi.org/10.1007/978-3-030-58669-0_16
6. Górriz, J.M., Álvarez-Illán, I., Álvarez-Marquina, A., et al.: Computational approaches to explainable artificial intelligence: advances in theory, applications and trends. Inf. Fusion **100**, 101945 (2023)
7. Jaysundara, A., De Silva, D., Kumarawadu, P.: Personality prediction of social network users using LSTM based sentiment analysis. In: 2022 International Conference on Smart Technologies and Systems for Next Generation Computing (ICSTSN), pp. 1–6. IEEE (2022)
8. Komisin, M.C., Guinn, C.: Identifying personality types using document classification methods. PhD thesis, University of North Carolina Wilmington Wilmington (2011)
9. Lin, J., Mao, W., Zeng, D.D.: Personality-based refinement for sentiment classification in microblog. Knowl.-Based Syst. **132**, 204–214 (2017)
10. Liu, B.: Sentiment analysis and opinion mining. Springer Nature (2022)
11. Quenk, N.L.: Essentials of Myers-Briggs Type Indicator Assessment. Wiley, Hoboken (2009)
12. Wu, H.C., Luk, R.W.P., Wong, K.F., Kwok, K.L.: Interpreting TF-IDF term weights as making relevance decisions. ACM Trans. Inf. Syst. **26**(3), 1–37 (2008)

Grad-CAM Applied to the Detection of Instruments Used in Facial Presentation Attacks

Irene García-Rubio⬤, Roberto Gallardo-Cava⬤, David Ortega-delCampo⬤, Julio Guillen-Garcia⬤, Daniel Palacios-Alonso(✉)⬤, and Cristina Conde⬤

Universidad Rey Juan Carlos, C/ Tulipán S/N, 28933 Móstoles, Madrid, Spain
{irene.garciar,roberto.gallardo,david.ortega.delcampo,julio.guillen,
daniel.palacios,cristina.conde}@urjc.es
https://blogs.etsii.urjc.es/frav/

Abstract. Biometric recognition, especially facial recognition, has achieved significant success, but it faces challenges like counterfeiting biometric data. This paper proposes a Facial Presentation Attack Detection (PAD) system that incorporates contextual information to identify and discard attacks involving detectable Presentation Attack Instruments (PAIs). The aim is to streamline computational efforts and enhance the subsequent PAD system's analysis of facial features. The PAD system yields excellent results, achieving a 99% accuracy rate. This high performance is confirmed through the application of a Explainable Artificial Intelligence (XAI) technique, Grad-CAM.

Keywords: Computer Vision · eXplainability Artificial Intelligence · Facial Presentation Attack Detection System · Convolutional Neural Network · Grad-CAM

1 Introduction

Biometric recognition systems, particularly facial recognition, have gained widespread popularity in recent decades, becoming integral in user-driven applications. The digitization era has further emphasized their role in authentication tools [2], sparking increased research interest [15]. These systems, leveraging unique human attributes like facial features and fingerprints, offer exceptional security, precision, and user-friendliness compared to conventional methods [13]. Facial recognition technology is extensively applied in various fields, including forensics, law enforcement, healthcare, banking, residential security, and smartphone access.

However, facial recognition systems face challenges, especially concerning Presentation Attack Instruments (PAI), which involve attempts to deceive the system with counterfeit biometric data [16]. To counteract this vulnerability, Facial Presentation Attack Detection (PAD) techniques [7] have been developed to fortify the security of facial recognition systems.

J. M. Ferrández Vicente et al. (Eds.): IWINAC 2024, LNCS 14674, pp. 270–281, 2024.
https://doi.org/10.1007/978-3-031-61140-7_27

Within the literature, one frequently encounters various proposals for PAD systems, each aiming to address novel challenges or improve the robustness of existing solutions. Nevertheless, a common trend is observed: all these systems crop the facial image before feeding it into the network, both during training and testing phases. While this practice ensures that the network learns specific facial characteristics and patterns associated with authentic faces, it also results in the omission of pertinent information about the artifacts and instruments employed in the attack. This data could potentially simplify the differentiation between genuine and deceptive faces.

Hence, this paper suggests developing a facial PAD system that, alongside the facial image, incorporates contextual information to identify and discard attacks involving easily detectable PAIs. This approach aims to streamline computational efforts for the subsequent PAD system, which is responsible for conducting a more intricate analysis of the facial features.

In the pursuit of improved understanding and effectiveness of the proposed model, the concept of 'explainability' (XAI) becomes invaluable. XAI methods play a crucial role in addressing ethical and legal considerations in AI systems. By identifying biases and ensuring transparency, XAI helps to enhance system fairness and accountability, feature selection and extraction, refines model training processes, and strengthens defenses against facial presentation attacks. In biometrics, the systems are connected with reality, as their decisions can have significant effects on people. Therefore, explanations must be provided to ensure accountability and transparency in decision-making processes [3]. Additionally, by enabling an understanding of the decision-making process of the facial PAD system, XAI techniques highlight the importance and usefulness of contextual information.

2   Related Work and Background

2.1   PAD Techniques

In the realm of facial PAD, the period from 2000 to 2014 was marked by the dominance of hardware-based solutions, followed by software-based methods using hand-crafted features during 2005–2015. However, since 2014, the field has transitioned towards modern feature-based models, particularly those based on deep learning [16].

In software-based techniques, features are extracted from high-resolution facial images captured by cameras, and these features are used to differentiate between genuine and fake images [5].

There are different software-based techniques, with Deep Learning being one of them. These facial PAD methods have made substantial progress, outperforming traditional detectors that rely on handcrafted features. They utilize deep CNNs to automatically learn hierarchical feature representations with superior discriminative capabilities. This paper will use this approach for the implementation of a facial PAD system.

2.2   XAI Techniques

In recent years, the field of eXplainable Artificial Intelligence has witnessed significant advancements. To gain a comprehensive perspective on XAI, it's valuable to consider different approaches and methods used in this domain. Ras et al. [10] introduce an intriguing approach by organizing XAI methods within a three-dimensional space, the axes of which are Model Distillation, Intrinsic Methods and Visualization Methods, offering a structured framework to navigate and comprehend this critical field.

The Visualization methods provide explanations by highlighting the input data features that strongly influence the neural network's output. It comprises two methods, Perturbation-Based Methods and Backpropagation-Based Methods.

This last method identify input features to highlight based on the evaluation of gradient signals that flow from the output to the input during network training [4,18]. Grad-CAM, the method used in this paper, falls under this category [12].

3   Methods and Materials

3.1   Design and Implementation

To handle the large database, image preprocessing involves two key steps: rescaling and normalization. Normalization is crucial to prevent gradient explosion during neural network training, adjusting pixel values from [0, 255] to [0, 1] for improved computation and faster convergence. This normalization also ensures fair comparisons and analysis in texture and data acquisition methods. Rescaling transforms images to 576p width and 324p height, as indicated in Table 1.

The CNN is trained with Adam optimizer, known for its adaptive learning rates, efficient convergence, and robustness with noisy data.

The loss function is Categorical Cross-Entropy, optimal for multiclass classification. It aligns predicted probabilities with true labels, aids gradient-based optimization, and penalizes confident incorrect predictions for well-calibrated distributions.

The model proposed in this project is a sequential model that incorporates the layers presented in Table 1.

3.2   eXpainable Artificial Intelligence Grad-CAM

Gradient-weighted Class Activation Mapping (Grad-CAM) is a backpropagation-based technique designed to enhance the interpretability of CNN models by highlighting regions within input data that are considered to be crucial for making predictions [12].

Grad-CAM has certain advantages, e.g., unlike Guided Backpropagation, Grad-CAM provides precise spatial localization of influential regions within an image, making it invaluable for understanding where key features lie. Additionally, it overcomes the limitations of CAM, ensuring its broader utility in

Table 1. This table show the structure of the model used.

Layer (Type)	Output (Shape)	Param #
conv2d (Conv2D)	(None, 324, 576, 32)	896
batch_normalization (batchNorm)	(None, 324, 576, 32)	128
conv2d_1 (Conv2D)	(None, 324, 576, 32)	9248
batch_normalization_1 (batchNorm)	(None, 324, 576, 32)	128
max_pooling2d (MaxPooling2D)	(None, 162, 288, 32)	0
dropout (Dropout)	(None, 162, 288, 32)	0
conv2d_2 (Conv2D)	(None, 162, 288, 64)	18496
batch_normalization_2 (batchNorm)	(None, 162, 288, 64)	256
max_pooling2d_1 (MaxPooling2D)	(None, 81, 144, 64)	0
dropout_1 (Dropout)	(None, 81, 144, 64)	0
conv2d_3 (Conv2D)	(None, 81, 144, 128)	73856
batch_normalization_3 (batchNorm)	(None, 81, 144, 128)	512
max_pooling2d_2 (MaxPooling2D)	(None, 40, 72, 128)	0
activation (Activation)	(None, 40, 72, 128)	0
dropout_2 (Dropout)	(None, 40, 72, 128)	0
flatten (Flatten)	(None, 368640)	0
dense (Dense)	(None, 128)	47186048
batch_normalization_4 (batchNorm)	(None, 128)	512
dropout_3 (Dropout)	(None, 128)	0
dense_1 (Dense)	(None, 5)	645

Total params: 47,290,725

Trainable params: 47,289,957

Non-Trainable params: 768

interpreting diverse CNN structures and enhancing the discrimination between classes. In Grad-CAM, the last convolution layer preserves spatial location information lost in fully-connected layers, allowing neurons to identify specific parts of a class.

3.3   Procediment

Utilizing a 20-layer deep model with 47 million parameters, the convolutional layers transform input images through convolutional filters for feature extraction. Pooling layers reduce dimensionality and generalize features, enhancing spatial-agnostic recognition [17]. To combat overfitting, dropout layers deactivate nodes probabilistically [1]. Batch normalization standardizes inputs within mini-batches, reducing statistical noise impact [11]. An isolated ReLU activation layer (see in Table 1) is included for future Grad-CAM explainability. Grad-CAM elucidates the CNN's decision-making process, promoting transparency, trust, and optimization in artificial intelligence systems.

3.4 Statistical Analysis

The CNN-model was evaluated using various metrics, including accuracy, the confusion matrix, precision, recall, F-score, APCER and BPCER.

Confusion Matrix provides a structured representation of a model's performance by tabulating the TP, TN, FP and FN predictions. This matrix serves as the basis for calculating several evaluation metrics that measure the accuracy, precision, recall, and overall effectiveness of a classification model [9]. Where TP, TN, FP and FN respectively denote "True Positive", "True Negative", "False Positive" and "False Negative" decisions.

Accuracy, Precision, Recall, and F-Score have been computed following the methodology outlined in the referenced article [8].

APCER. The Attack Presentation Classification Error Rate assesses a system's accuracy in distinguishing genuine presentations from attacks (see Equation 1), preventing unauthorized access and minimizing the risk of falsely identifying legitimate users as attackers in biometric authentication systems.

BPCER. The Bonafide Presentation Classification Error Rate assesses a system's accuracy in correctly identifying legitimate presentations and minimizing the chances of misclassifying genuine users as attackers (see Equation 2), preventing unnecessary disruptions.

$$\text{APCER} = \frac{\sum_{i=1}^{N_{PAIS}} (1 - RES_i)}{N_{PAIS}} \quad (1) \quad \text{BPCER} = \frac{\sum_{i=1}^{N_{BF}} (RES_i)}{N_{BF}} \quad (2)$$

Where N_{PAIS} represents the total number of attacks, N_{BF} denotes the count of bona fide instances, and RES_i is assigned a value of 1 if the image is classified as an attack or 0 if it is classified as bona fide.

3.5 Database

The study utilizes the FRAV_RS_RGB dataset from the Face Recognition & Artificial Vision Group (FRAV) at Rey Juan Carlos University. This dataset comprises high-quality 192×1080 pixel images of diverse individuals captured with an RGB camera. It includes 32,952 images from 185 users, categorized by gender and age. The images are classified into five groups representing different image types: presentation attacks using printed photographs, masks, eyeless masks, and video player devices, along with a fifth group containing genuine faces.

To train and evaluate the CNN, the dataset is split into two sets, with 80% (26,361 images) used for training and the remaining 20% (6,591 images) for performance assessment [6]. The primary objective is to classify images based on whether they depict genuine facial identities or instruments used in presentation attacks.

4   Results

Accuracy. Utilizing the proposed model in Sect. 3.1, and after 30 training epochs with a batch size of 64, a success rate of 99.40% is attained in the test set.

Confusion Matrix. Table 2 shows the five confusion matrices per class resulting from the test phase. The elements represent True Positives (TP), True Negatives (TN), False Positives (FP), and False Negatives (FN). The labels are categorized into the target class and the remaining classes. The remaining classes are combined into one group, 'rest', to assess the model's recognition of the observed class.

Table 2. Confusion Matrices of the implemented system.

			Predicted Labels	
			Attack	Rest
True Labels	Printed Photographs Attacks	Attack	1062	18
		Rest	14	5497
	Mask Attacks	Attack	1173	0
		Rest	1	5417
	Eyeless Mask Attacks	Attack	1203	1
		Rest	0	5387
	Video Player Devices Attacks	Attack	922	0
		Rest	0	5669
			Bona Fide	Rest
True Labels	Bona Fide	Bona Fide	2198	14
		Rest	18	4361

Precision, Recall and F-Score. The results of the model for each attack can be seen in Table 3.

Table 3. Performance of the Facial PAD System: Precision, Recall and F-Score.

Metric	Class	Percentage
Precision	Printed Photographs Attack	98.6%
	Masks Attack	99.9%
	Eyeless Masks Attack	100%
	Video Player Devices Attack	100%
	Bona Fide	99.1%
Recall	Printed Photographs Attack	98.3%
	Masks Attack	100%
	Eyeless Masks Attack	99.9%
	Video Player Devices Attack	100%
	Bona Fide	99.3%
F-Score	Printed Photographs Attack	98.5%
	Masks Attack	99.9%
	Eyeless Masks Attack	99.9%
	Video Player Devices Attack	100%
	Bona Fide	99.2%

APCER. To calculate this metric, the four different types of attacks, as well as the sum of all of them, have been taken into account. The results can be seen in Table 4.

BPCER. To calculate this metric, the images have been divided into two sets: attacks and bona fides. The result can be seen in Table 4.

Table 4. Performance of the Facial PAD System: APCER and BPCER.

Metric	Class	Value
APCER	Printed Photographs Attack	0.016666
	Masks Attack	0.0
	Eyeless Masks Attack	0.000830
	Video Player Devices Attack	0.0
	Total Attack Images	0.004338
BPCER	Bona Fide VS Total Attack Images	0.006329

5   Discussion

The model boasts an impressive 99% accuracy, with precision exceeding 98% and high recall, showcasing its ability to identify positive samples effectively.

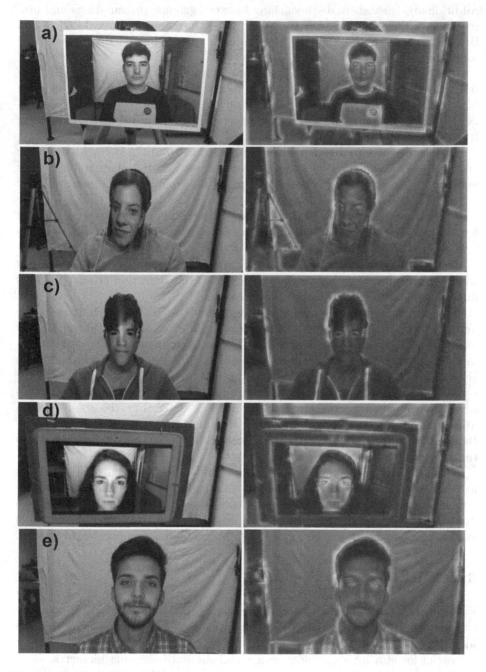

Fig. 1. a) Grad-CAM heatmap of a Printed Photograph Attack. b) Grad-CAM heatmap of a Mask Attack. c) Grad-CAM heatmap of an Eyeless Mask Attack. d) Grad-CAM heatmap of a Video Player Device Attack. e) Heatmap of a Genuine Face.

Additionally, it excels in distinguishing between genuine presentations and presentation attacks, evident in its exceptional performance in both APCER and BPCER. These results highlight the system's robust and reliable Facial PAD solution.

The application of Grad-CAM provides interpretable heatmaps, visually representing the network's attention during facial attack classification and genuine face verification. Overlaying them onto input images confirms the network's proficiency in distinguishing between attack types and genuine faces, enhancing transparency and result reliability.

In the case of a **printed photograph** attack, Grad-CAM reveals that the network relies on identifying specific elements, such as the photograph's edges and supporting tripod, as well as scrutinizing the contours of the person in the image (Fig. 1 a).

For a **mask attack**, Grad-CAM shows that the network focuses on distinct facial attributes, directing attention to mask textures, edges, and nuances of the eyes where the mask might terminate (Fig. 1 b).

In the case of an **eyeless mask attack**, Grad-CAM reveals a similar strategy with heightened attention to facial texture and edge detection around the eyes due to potential occlusion within the mask (Fig. 1 c).

For an attack involving a **video player device**, Grad-CAM illustrates the network's priority on the edges of the playback device (e.g., a Tablet) and its attachment, facilitating the identification of device components. The corresponding heatmaps underscore the network's resilience against such attack modalities (Fig. 1 d).

In discriminating between **genuine faces** and attacks, Grad-CAM reveals a reverse engineering process where the network determines the absence of an attack based on textures and elements. Heatmaps indicate activations consistent with a real face, empowering the network to make precise determinations regarding face authenticity (Fig. 1 e).

Grad-CAM's heatmaps reveal the network's proficiency in distinguishing attack types with contextual information. Analyzing elements like photo frames enables accurate presentation attack classification, highlighting the crucial role of contextual information in swift identification and mitigation. This enhances system efficiency, reducing false positives and alleviating computational burden.

6   Conclusion

Facial PAD systems play a vital role in ensuring facial recognition technology's integrity and reliability by effectively detecting presentation attacks, preventing identity theft, fraud, and unauthorized access. Their continuous advancement is crucial for staying ahead of evolving threats and bolstering biometric security measures across various domains. The presented PAD system offers diverse applications, from enhancing security in biometric systems to fortifying against counterfeit data for fraud prevention in access control, financial transactions, and identity verification. Additionally, integrating contextual data optimizes resource allocation, enhancing security in airports, secure facilities, and fostering trust in financial and e-commerce transactions.

On the other hand, XAI is essential for ensuring transparency, accountability, and trustworthiness in AI systems, providing insights into decision-making processes and mitigating biases in critical applications such as healthcare and finance.

Together, these technologies promote ethical AI development and responsible decision-making.

Currently, there is a lack of standards in the development of explainable techniques, posing a significant challenge in fields such as artificial intelligence and machine learning. Works like this one offer significant advances by providing some insights towards standardization in this area. However, due to the absence of clear guidelines and regulations, these efforts encounter limitations in their scope and applicability. Although these works shed light on the path towards greater explainability in artificial intelligence systems, much remains to be done to establish solid and widely accepted standards in this constantly evolving field.

Due to the use of a proprietary database and limited access to databases, comparisons with existing literature have become difficult. However, a similar study has been found [14]. There are significant differences compared to this study such as the use of cropped face images and the fact that all faces belong to only 20 individuals, with 5 individuals reserved for testing. Regarding the results, it is noteworthy that, while the printed photograph attack has been the most challenging to detect for the implemented network, it generalizes very well in this other study. Nevertheless, the results produced by the presented network are superior for all attacks, once again demonstrating the effectiveness of utilizing contextual information.

Limitations arise from the training database, featuring controlled lighting and lacking diversity in age and ethnicity, potentially biasing the system's performance. Future directions include expanding the database with diverse images and implementing a facial information-based attack detection system. Research focuses on refining the Grad-CAM technique through *Guided backpropagation*, introducing *Guided Grad-CAM*, and exploring complementary methods for a more comprehensive understanding of the network's reasoning.

In summary, the results suggest the potential effectiveness of utilizing contextual information, that may reduce the workload of systems by enabling the rapid identification of attacks involving instruments. Further investigation could shed more light about the potential of these kind of design.

Acknowledgements. This work was supported in part by Spanish Ministerio de Ciencia e Innovación under Grant PID2021-124176OB-I00, in part by Universidad Rey Juan Carlos, and in part by the Spanish General Directorate of Police. Additionally, the work was guided and supported by all members of the FRAV group: High-performance research group in Facial Recognition and Artificial Vision of Universidad Rey Juan Carlos, who provided the database used for the experiments.

References

1. Baldi, P., Sadowski, P.J.: Understanding dropout. In: Advances in Neural Information Processing Systems, vol. 26 (2013)
2. Bolle, R., Pankanti, S., Ratha, N.: Evaluation techniques for biometrics-based authentication systems (FRR). In: Proceedings 15th International Conference on Pattern Recognition. ICPR-2000. vol. 2, pp. 831–837 (2000). https://doi.org/10.1109/ICPR.2000.906204
3. Confalonieri, R., Coba, L., Wagner, B., Besold, T.R.: A historical perspective of explainable artificial intelligence. WIREs Data Min. Knowl. Discovery **11**(1), e1391 (2021)
4. Erhan, D., Bengio, Y., Courville, A., Vincent, P.: Visualizing higher-layer features of a deep network. Technical Report, Univeristé de Montréal (2009)
5. Galbally, J., Marcel, S., Fierrez, J.: Image quality assessment for fake biometric detection: Application to iris, fingerprint, and face recognition. IEEE Trans. Image Process. **23**(2), 710–724 (2013)
6. Gholamy, A., Kreinovich, V., Kosheleva, O.: Why 70/30 or 80/20 relation between training and testing sets: a pedagogical explanation. Int. J. Intell. Technol. Appl. Stat. **11**(2), 105–111 (2018)
7. ISO/IEC JTC 1/SC 37: Iso/iec 30107-1:2023 information technology - biometric presentation attack detection. Technical report, International Organization for Standardization (2023). https://www.iso.org/obp/ui/#iso:std:iso-iec:30107:-1:ed-2:v1:en
8. ISO/IEC JTC 1/SC 37: Iso/iec 5725-1:2023 accuracy (trueness and precision) of measurement methods and results part 1: General principles and definitions. Technical report, International Organization for Standardization (2023). https://www.iso.org/obp/ui/#iso:std:iso:5725:-1:ed-2:v1:en
9. Luque, A., Carrasco, A., Martín, A., de Las Heras, A.: The impact of class imbalance in classification performance metrics based on the binary confusion matrix. Pattern Recogn. **91**, 216–231 (2019)
10. Ras, G., Xie, N., van Gerven, M., Doran, D.: Explainable deep learning: a field guide for the uninitiated. J. Artif. Int. Res. **73**, 68 (2022). https://doi.org/10.1613/jair.1.13200
11. Santurkar, S., Tsipras, D., Ilyas, A., Madry, A.: How does batch normalization help optimization? In: Bengio, S., Wallach, H., Larochelle, H., Grauman, K., Cesa-Bianchi, N., Garnett, R. (eds.) Advances in Neural Information Processing Systems. vol. 31. Curran Associates, Inc. (2018). https://proceedings.neurips.cc/paper/2018/file/905056c1ac1dad141560467e0a99e1cf-Paper.pdf
12. Selvaraju, R.R., Cogswell, M., Das, A., Vedantam, R., Parikh, D., Batra, D.: Grad-CAM visual explanations from deep networks via gradient-based localization. Int. J. Comput. Vis. **128**(2), 336–359 (2019). https://doi.org/10.1007/s11263-019-01228-7
13. Selwal, A., Gupta, S.K., Kumar, S.: A scheme for template security at feature fusion level in multimodal biometric system. Adv. Sci. Technol. Res. J. **10**(31), 23–30 (2016)
14. Sequeira, A.F., Silva, W., Pinto, J.R., Gonçalves, T., Cardoso, J.S.: Interpretable biometrics: should we rethink how presentation attack detection is evaluated? In: 2020 8th International Workshop on Biometrics and Forensics (IWBF), pp. 1–6. IEEE (2020)

15. Sharma, D., Selwal, A.: FinPAD: state-of-the-art of fingerprint presentation attack detection mechanisms, taxonomy and future perspectives. Pattern Recogn. Lett. **152**, 225–252 (2021)
16. Sharma, D., Selwal, A.: A survey on face presentation attack detection mechanisms: hitherto and future perspectives. Multimedia Syst. **29**(3), 1–51 (2023). https:// link.springer.com/article/10.1007/s00530-023-01070-5
17. Sun, M., Song, Z., Jiang, X., Pan, J., Pang, Y.: Learning pooling for convolutional neural network. Neurocomputing **224**, 96–104 (2017)
18. Zeiler, M.D., Fergus, R.: Visualizing and understanding convolutional networks. arXiv preprint arXiv:1311.2901 (2013). https://doi.org/10.48550/arXiv.1311.2901

Comparison of an Accelerated Garble Embedding Methodology for Privacy Preserving in Biomedical Data Analytics

Nikola Hristov-Kalamov[1], Raúl Fernández-Ruiz[1],
Agustín álvarez-Marquina[2], Esther Núñez-Vidal[1],
Francisco Domínguez-Mateos[1], and Daniel Palacios-Alonso[1,2]

[1] Escuela Técnica Superior de Ingeniería Informática, Universidad Rey Juan Carlos,
Tulipán S/N, Móstoles 28933, Spain
{nikola.hristov,raul.fruiz,francisco.dominguez,daniel.palacios}@urjc.es,
e.nunezv.2021@alumnos.urjc.es
[2] Center for Biomedical Technology, Universidad Politécnica de Madrid,
Madrid 28220, Spain
aalvarez@fi.upm.es

Abstract. This research work proposes a novel, encryption-based method for comparing embeddings generated by neural networks on various information types (text, images, videos, audio, etc.). This approach prioritizes real-world applications dealing with sensitive or private data, particularly in biomedical and biometric analysis, where even minor information leaks can be highly detrimental. To address this concern, the method performs all necessary calculations within a highly secure and efficient encryption layer. Notably, this work introduces practical solutions applicable to real-world biomedical data scenarios.

Keywords: Biomedical Data Analytics · Deep Learning · Embedding distance · Cryptography · Oblivious Transfer · Garbled Circuits · Homomorphic Encryption

1 Introduction

Machine learning has become a powerful tool for processing and analyzing various types of information, especially biometric and biomedical data, in the current digital era. These data are used for applications such as smartphone unlocking, identity verification, border control, and clinical data management. However, these systems often deal with sensitive personal information that can pose serious security risks if misused. Several publications and frameworks have proposed solutions to address this issue, such as [25], which outlines the "Privacy

This work was supported in part by Spanish Ministerio de Ciencia e Innovación under Grant PID2021-124176OB-I00, in part by Universidad Rey Juan Carlos, and in part by the Spanish General Directorate of Police.

J. M. Ferrández Vicente et al. (Eds.): IWINAC 2024, LNCS 14674, pp. 282–299, 2024.
https://doi.org/10.1007/978-3-031-61140-7_28

by Design" approach, and [8], which provides a framework for the secure handling of biometric and biomedical data. These solutions aim to not only prevent unauthorized access and identity theft, but also ensure that individuals retain control over their most personal identifiers in a highly connected world.

However, removing obvious identifiers such as names and addresses is not enough to protect data from re-identification, as previous attacks have shown [22,30]. There are laws and regulations, such as HIPAA [24] and GDPR [27], that offer guidance, and user-friendly data anonymization tools that are emerging. However, robust artificial intelligence methods for protecting privacy are still scarce in practice.

This paper presents a method to compare data with deep learning (DL) under an encryption layer that ensures its privacy. DL is a subfield of machine learning that uses many computational units to perform predictions based on large amounts of data. It has gained popularity in recent years for classification and pattern recognition tasks.

Encryption of deep learning layers is also an emerging research topic. For instance, homomorphic encryption (HE) allows training a neural network over encrypted data. A learnable image encryption scheme is one example of this approach [38]. Our work explores the opposite scenario, using pre-trained models to obtain results from encrypted inputs. This is similar to previous works such as [3,17,19,20].

In summary, the combination of DL and encryption is a promising research area that could improve data privacy and security. As DL models become more complex and use larger datasets, the demand for effective encryption methods will increase.

1.1 State of the Art

This section consists of two parts. First, we summarize the privacy issues in biometrical data analysis and the key challenges associated with privacy protection. Second, we provide a technical overview of encrypted data comparison methods.

Privacy in biometrical data analysis is addressed by three manuscripts. In [21], the authors examine the perspectives and recent advances in protecting patient privacy in the dynamic healthcare landscape. They emphasize the importance of safeguarding patient information as a core principle in healthcare. They also identify the following concerns arising from the increased complexity and diversity of healthcare and biomedical data and the methods used in data collection. Eicher et al. [12] discuss the challenges of protecting data privacy in data-driven environments, especially in the context of building and evaluating privacy-preserving prediction models. They present a comprehensive tool for building and evaluating these models, which is available as open-source software. Xiang and Cai [33] explain the key challenges associated with privacy protection and the secondary use of health data. Some of these challenges are:

1. **Balancing Privacy and Utility**: There is a trade-off between the need for privacy protection and the utility and value that can be derived from the secondary use of health data.

2. **Risk of Privacy Breach**: Storing protected health information (PHI) in health data poses a high risk of privacy breach, while excessively de-identifying data can lead to loss of meaningful information and low data quality.
3. **Regulatory Compliance**: Complying with privacy laws and regulations, such as the Health Insurance Portability and Accountability Act (HIPAA) in the US, adds complexity to the secondary use of health data.
4. **Reidentification Risk**: There is a concern about the potential reidentification of individuals from supposedly de-identified health data, which can compromise privacy.
5. **Data Sharing Challenges**: Ensuring secure and controlled data sharing among different entities while safeguarding privacy is a significant challenge in the context of health data.
6. **Consumer Trust**: Maintaining consumer trust in healthcare institutions and experts while handling their sensitive health data is crucial for successful secondary use initiatives.

Among these publications, [12,33] are noteworthy, as they specifically mention privacy-preserving models (and explicitly homomorphic encryption) as potential solutions.

Technical overview of encrypted data comparison methods, more specifically, encrypted embedding comparisons, is given by five papers. Kim et al. [17] discuss computing the similarity of text embeddings using a privacy-preserving homomorphic solution and highlight its advantages and limitations. Lee et al. [20] present a similar solution and offer a Homomorphic Encryption based scheme for text classification. Chen et al. [9] introduce THE-X, an approximation approach for transformers that enables privacy-preserving inference of pre-trained models and discuss the pros and cons of using Homomorphic Encryption in this field. Yu et al. [36] propose a novel approach for privacy-preserving document similarity using latent semantic analysis (LSA) and highlight its advantages over existing protocols. Nautsch et al. [23] explain the importance of protecting biometric templates and vendor model parameters in speaker recognition systems to comply with European data privacy regulations. They suggest, once again, the use of Homomorphic Encryption to ensure data privacy demands without compromising recognition accuracy.

Each of these papers uses different Homomorphic Encryption models to achieve varying results. The most recent publications use a bootstrapped Somewhat Homomorphic Encryption approach, using the CKKS [10] variant specifically to accommodate the operations with decimal values present in distance calculation between embeddings. Full or Somewhat Homomorphic Encryption is usually the first choice for these kinds of operations but it can be very computationally slow, and require enormous data exchange and initialization times.

Our research work is mainly based on oblivious transfer, garbled circuits and partial homomorphic encryption. All these techniques require less computation between parties and a lighter information exchange but have their limitations such as their one-use-per-generation nature and some overhead in the number of communications necessary.

It is also important to mention technical publications that aim to compute entire encrypted neural networks. Here two papers are of note. Garbled Neural Networks are Practical [3]. In this paper, the authors take advantage of the significant arithmetic operations required to evaluate neural networks and use optimization for Garbled Circuits specifically made for this type of calculation. They evaluate a wide range of neural networks and show that the proposed approach is up to 100 times more efficient than direct boolean masking and approximately 40% more efficient than a recent circuit masking approach for neural networks.

Our work takes a different approach, evaluating neural networks locally without any cryptography and only comparing encrypted embeddings. This allows much faster computation but is reserved for problems based on data comparison. Additionally, since embedding comparison also requires significant arithmetic computation, this work also compares its algorithms to an alternative using the same Garbled Circuit optimization, namely Garbling Gadgets for Boolean and Arithmetic Circuits [4], obtaining faster results.

Another paper is: Tabula: Efficiently Computing Nonlinear Activation Functions for Secure Neural Network Inference [19]. Their approach precomputes secure lookup tables for the non-linear activation gates during an offline phase, reducing communication, storage, and runtime costs. This enables a practical online phase with minimal communication costs. Once more our work only requires the final step of neural network evaluation and is therefore computationally faster. However, this publication is still of note as it significantly reduces computation times of pure Garbled Circuits and Homomorphic Encryption techniques.

The paper is organized as follows: Sect. 2 describes an overview of the theoretical framework needed for this solution. Section 3 summarizes the algorithm design and implementation. Section 4 states key experimental outcomes obtained from profiling this implementation. Section 5 discusses said outcomes and presents a use case for this framework. Section 6 presents conclusions and future lines of research.

2 Theoretical Framework

2.1 Information Comparison

Information comparison is the process of measuring how similar or different pieces of data (such as images, text, videos, audio, etc.) are based on their content. A common and popular technique for this is to use neural networks, especially convolutional neural networks (CNNs), to capture patterns and features from a piece of data. These networks convert the inputs into vectors of multiple elements called embeddings. Each embedding reflects the distinctive attributes of its corresponding input. By comparing these embeddings in a high-dimensional space, similarities can be accurately calculated.

2.2   Cryptography

Four cryptographic concepts are used for garbled embedding comparison:

Oblivious Transfer (OT). More specifically 1-out-of-2 OT, is a fundamental cryptographic primitive that allows a receiver to select one out of 2 messages from a sender without revealing which one was selected or learning anything about the other. This is an important building block in many cryptographic algorithms, such as Garbled Circuits (described in 2.2).

As pointed out in [14], OT requires some amount of asymmetric encryption and can't be entirely based on cheap symmetric cryptography. However, a base number of OTs can be generated "asymmetrically" and stretched via different OT extension methods. Some of these methods are described in [7,15,26,34]. This concept is of special note as it provides a large number of OTs with minimal computation and communication.

Oblivious Linear Evaluation (OLE). Another cryptografic primitive that allows two parties to obtain correlated outputs. More specifically, the first party (A) inputs a value a, the second party (B) inputs two values b_1, b_2, and as an output, A obtains $c = b_1 \cdot a + b_2$.

OLE can be seen as the arithmetic counterpart to OT and is also a building block for many cryptographic techniques. It is important to mention **Vector OLE (VOLE)** [1], a generalization of OLE for vector inputs, where A inputs a scalar a, B inputs two vectors $\overline{b_1}, \overline{b_2}$ and as an output, A obtains $\overline{c} = \overline{b_1} \cdot a + \overline{b_2}$

Garbled Circuits (GCs). These constructs allow the evaluation of an arbitrary function that requires inputs from two parties while preserving the secrecy of said inputs. The function mentioned above is implemented at the logic gate level with each gate input bit and output bit substituted with randomly chosen labels. See Yao's original implementation for the general idea [35].

The two parties are divided into a generator and an evaluator. The generator prepares the GC and the evaluator computes its results. For GC evaluation, one OT is required for every evaluator input bit. Additionally, for each operation between two bits, without any optimizations, four messages must be encrypted using a symmetric cipher (most commonly AES) and subsequently 1 of the four results must be de-garbled by the evaluator using once more symmetric encryption. A very basic AND gate evaluation with a GC can be seen in Fig. 1.

In this image, A is the generator and B is the evaluator. During generation, A will create four labels w_{A0}, w_{A1}, w_{B0} and w_{B1}. Following this, a 1-out-of-2 OT is performed where B obtains their corresponding w_B label. After that, A will generate the GC (as seen in the table of the figure), permute the resulting output rows and send them to B with its corresponding input label w_A. Finally, B knowing it's own input label and A's input label, will only be able to properly de-garble one of the four outputs and obtain a result bit or another label for a subsequent garbled gate.

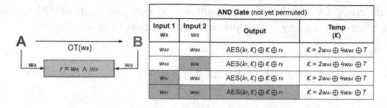

		AND Gate (not yet permuted)	
Input 1 w_A	Input 2 w_B	Output	Temp (K)
w_{A0}	w_{B0}	$AES(k_f, K) \oplus K \oplus r_0$	$K = 2w_{A0} \oplus 4w_{B0} \oplus T$
w_{A0}	w_{B1}	$AES(k_f, K) \oplus K \oplus r_0$	$K = 2w_{A0} \oplus 4w_{B1} \oplus T$
w_{A1}	w_{B0}	$AES(k_f, K) \oplus K \oplus r_0$	$K = 2w_{A1} \oplus 4w_{B0} \oplus T$
w_{A1}	w_{B1}	$AES(k_f, K) \oplus K \oplus r_1$	$K = 2w_{A1} \oplus 4w_{B1} \oplus T$

Fig. 1. GC AND gate using the fixed cipher optimization (described in [6]), where k_f is a fixed key used for all circuits, K is a temporary auxiliary value and T is a tweaked number unique to every garbled gate.

Depending on the function, either party or both parties may receive some final output. If the generator requires an output, the evaluator may share the result or the two parties may repeat the functionality with switched roles.

GCs have the advantage of being able to compute any arbitrary finite function between two parties but the longer the function, the more computation and data exchange is required. More specifically, a linear dependency is maintained between the length of the function and the circuit cost. Several techniques have been used to address this issue, such as [6,31,37], etc.

Homomorphic One-Time Pad (HOTP). A One-Time Pad (OTP) is a single-use encryption method that maps a message to a cipher with information-theoretic security. Any OTP must have some essential properties:

1. The construct must be used once for a single message and then discarded.
2. The key of the OTP must be generated randomly.
3. The key space K and resulting ciphertext space C must be equal to or greater than the message space M.
4. Every possible key must map each distinct message to a distinct ciphertext.

There are many variants of OTPs and some have certain homomorphic properties. In this paper, modular addition with a random key is used.

Let m be a message selected from M. Let k be a key randomly selected from the set $\{k \in \mathbb{N}, k \leq n\}$ where $n \geq |M|$. Lastly, let c be the resulting ciphertext. Encryption and decryption are done using modular addition and subtraction:

$$c = (m + k) \bmod n$$
$$m = (c - k) \bmod n \tag{1}$$

Note that, this construct is additively homomorphic modulo n when adding a constant a to the ciphertext:

$$(c + a) \bmod n = ((m + k) \bmod n + a) \bmod n = (m + k + a) \bmod n \tag{2}$$

Additionally, with some key adjustments, additive homomorphism modulo n with another ciphertext can be achieved:

$$c_3 = (c_1 + c_2) \bmod n = (m_1 + m_2 + k_1 + k_2) \bmod n \tag{3}$$

In this case, for the homomorphism to be complete, an additional step is required where a new key is composed from the two previous ones:

$$k_3 = (k_1 + k_2) \bmod n$$
$$c_3 = (m_1 + m_2 + k_1 + k_2) \bmod n = ((m_1 + m_2) + k_3) \bmod n \tag{4}$$

3   Design and Implementation

The scenario is as follows: Two parties, A and B, want to compare two images by measuring the distance between their embeddings, which are obtained with a neural network that both parties know. However, A and B do not want to share their images or embeddings with each other. The algorithm we propose can work with any type of embeddings (such as image, text, video, audio, etc.), as explained in Sect. 5.

To evaluate our algorithm, we first compare random embeddings using a standard method and an encrypted method. Then we compare real embeddings from a *"proof of concept"* neural network trained on the "Fashion MNIST" dataset. We provide two images of clothing items, and the network generates an embedding for each one and determines if they belong to the same category. We use a fully connected neural network and extract 128 embedding elements. This is a simple setup, but it demonstrates that our algorithm is effective and can be applied to larger networks, embeddings, and problems.

In practice, after each party extracts their image embedding locally, they compute the distance between them using one of two functions:

1. **Cosine distance.**

$$similarity = \frac{\bar{x} \cdot \bar{y}}{|x| \cdot |y|} = \left(\frac{x_0}{|x|} \cdot \frac{y_0}{|y|} \right) + \left(\frac{x_1}{|x|} \cdot \frac{y_1}{|y|} \right) + \left(\frac{x_2}{|x|} \cdot \frac{y_2}{|y|} \right) + \dots \tag{5}$$

As can be seen, the conventional cosine distance can be broken down into a sum of products.

2. **Euclidean distance.**

$$similarity^2 = (y_0 - x_0)^2 + (y_1 - x_1)^2 + (y_2 - x_2)^2 + \dots =$$
$$(y_0^2 + x_0^2 - 2y_0x_0) + (y_1^2 + x_1^2 - 2y_1x_1) + (y_2^2 + x_2^2 - 2y_2x_2) + \dots \tag{6}$$

Similarly, the squared result of the conventional Euclidean formula can be broken down into a sum of products and squared terms.

The baseline process uses these functions without encrypting any inputs. The output is then matched with the output from the encrypted method to measure the accuracy of the algorithm.

Optionally, the output can be compared with some thresholds to determine if the images are in the same category, different categories, or indeterminate. This step enhances privacy as a **discrete output** (one of three choices) can thwart attempts to reconstruct the hidden inputs from the output.

3.1   Fixed Precision Decimal Values

This research work addresses decimal values using a fixed-precision binary app-roach. Instead of using floating-point representation, it treats decimal numbers as whole numbers and allocates dedicated bit groups for the integer and frac-tional parts. When operands have differing bit allocations, the study employs shifting to achieve alignment before performing operations.

Focusing on three core operations - comparison, addition, and multiplication - it can be seen that comparison and addition results maintain the same bit pre-cision as their inputs. However, multiplication presents a challenge: the outcome requires twice the number of bits compared to the inputs. To mitigate this, the study opts for a trade-off by halving the bit fields of the operands before mul-tiplication. While this optimizes bit usage, it also comes at the cost of reduced precision in the final result.

3.2   Initial Solution only Using GCs

As a naive first step, the entire embedding comparison can be evaluated inside GCs (as mentioned in 2.2, these allow any arbitrary operation and function to be computed). The first party (A) can be the generator and the other party (B) the evaluator. This approach, however, becomes **extremely costly** when examining the required computation and data exchange. Note that, both the cosine and Euclidean distances are comprised of sums and products (as shown previously) which require expensive circuits. For the following cost analysis, λ represents the security parameter of the GCs (usually 128 bits), u_e represents the number of values in each embedding to be compared and u_b represents the number of bits (or bit precision) for each value. Additionally, GC-friendly circuits are used, such as the one presented in [18].

Addition. For the cosine distance a total of $(u_e - 1) \cdot u_b \cdot 2 \cdot \lambda$ bits need to be exchanged and $(u_e - 1) \cdot u_b \cdot 2$ AES encryptions must be performed by both parties. For the Euclidean distance, the number of bit exchanges and AES computations are doubled.

Multiplication by a Known Constant. For both distance functions, $u_b - 1$ additions are required. Consequently, a total of $u_e \cdot (\sum_{i=u_b+1}^{2 \cdot u_b} i \cdot 2 \cdot \lambda)$ bits need to be exchanged and $u_e \cdot (\sum_{i=u_b+1}^{2 \cdot u_b} i \cdot 2)$ AES encryptions must be performed by the generator and evaluator.

Comparison. If three discrete answers are required, a singular circuit with two separate comparisons is prepared. Consequently, a total of $2 \cdot u_b \cdot 2 \cdot \lambda$ bits need to be exchanged and $2 \cdot u_b \cdot 2$ AES encryptions must be performed by both parties.

When using larger embeddings, a different approach is necessary. Intuitively, GC performance is adequate for the comparison but another method is required for the arithmetic operations. In this research work, two alternatives are presented for the most costly operation, namely the product by a known constant. The first one is an original construct based on OT we referred to as **OT fractional multiplication** and the second one is based on OLE transformation.

3.3   OT Fractional Multiplication

This method (see Algorithm 1) allows the evaluator (B) to compute the encrypted result of a binary multiplication between an unknown value x and a known value y.

Algorithm 1. OT Integer Multiplication

Input A: $x \in \mathbb{Z}_2^{u_b}$ and **Input B**: $y \in \mathbb{Z}_2^{u_b}$

for $(i = 0;\ i < u_b;\ i{+}{+})$ do

    Part A:

    $w_{0i} = rnd(0, 2^{2u_b})$ ▷ random number from 0 and $2^{2u_b} - 1$

    $w_{1i} = (w_{0i} + (x{<}{<}i)) \mod (2^{2u_b})$ ▷ The "$<<$" represents a left bit shift

    $k = (k + w_{0i}) \mod (2^{2u_b})$

    Part B:

    $c = (c + w_{y[i]i}) \mod (2^{2u_b})$ ▷ B's OT label depends on the i-th bit of y $(y[i])$

Output A: $k \in \mathbb{Z}_2^{2u_b}$ and **Output B**: $c \in \mathbb{Z}_2^{2u_b}$ such that $c - k \equiv x \cdot y \mod (2^{2u_b})$

When considering values with decimal parts, the fixed precision approach described in 3.1 is taken (also using the mentioned optimization). The result is provided in Algorithm 2.

Algorithm 2. OT Fractional Multiplication

Input A: $x \in \mathbb{Z}_2^{u_b/2}$ and **Input B**: $y \in \mathbb{Z}_2^{u_b/2}$

for $(i = 0;\ i < u_b;\ i{+}{+})$ do

    Part A:

    $w_{0i} = rnd(0, 2^{u_b})$ ▷ random number from 0 and $2^{u_b} - 1$

    $w_{1i} = (w_{0i} + (x{<}{<}i)) \mod (2^{u_b})$ ▷ The "$<<$" represents a left bit shift

    $k = (k + w_{0i}) \mod (2^{u_b})$

    Part B:

    $c = (c + w_{y[i]i}) \mod (2^{u_b})$ ▷ B's OT label depends on the i-th bit of y $(y[i])$

Output A: $k \in \mathbb{Z}_2^{u_b}$ and **Output B**: $c \in \mathbb{Z}_2^{u_b}$ such that $c - k \equiv x \cdot y \mod (2^{u_b})$

Note that for this optimized algorithm, $u_b/2$ OTs are needed, each u_b bits long and both additively correlated ($w_{1i} = w_{0i} + x{<}{<}i$). Typically base OT or OT extension methods produce OTs with different sizes and correlations. Normally labels are λ (128) bits long and usually, the two labels for each bit are either not correlated or have an XOR correlation with a value delta (COTs). To

---

Algorithm 3. OT Transformation

Input A: w_{0i}, w_{1i} and **Input B:** w_{Bi}
for $(i = 0; i < u_b/2; i{+}{+})$ **do**
   Part A:
   $w'_{0i} = w_{0i}[0 : u_b]$
   $w'_{1i} = (w'_{0i} + x{<}{<}i) \mod (2^{u_b})$
   $aux = (w'_{0i} + x{<}{<}i - w_{1i}[0 : u_b]) \mod (2^{u_b})$
   Part B: ▷ A sends the aux variable to B
   if the i-th choice bit is 0 **then**
      $w'_{Bi} = w_{Bi}[0 : u_b]$
   else if the i-th choice bit is 1 **then**
      $w'_{Bi} = (aux + w_{Bi}[0 : u_b]) \mod (2^{u_b})$
Output A: w'_{0i}, w'_{1i} and **Output B:** w'_{Bi}

---

transform any OTs (w_{0i}, w_{1i}, w_{Bi}), regardless of length or correlation, into the desired form (w'_{0i}, w'_{1i}, w'_{Bi}), the following process is utilized (Algorithm 3):

Where $[0 : u_b]$ represents taking the first u_b bits of a number. This process is based on the OT transformation methods presented in [5] and later optimized in [2]. For each transformation, a communication of u_b bits is required.

As a final observation, note that the result of **OT fractional multiplication** is equivalent to the same HOTP described in Subsect. 2.2. The product is encrypted by adding a random key k modulo n, thus creating a ciphertext c that has the same additive homomorphic properties.

3.4 Multiplication Based on OLE Transformation

This method allows the evaluator (B) to compute the encrypted result of a multiplication between an unknown value x and a known value y. A pre-established OLE where the roles of A and B are swapped is utilized. The notation is therefore adjusted from $c = b_1 \cdot a + b_2$ to $c = a_1 \cdot b + a_2$. A transformation algorithm may be used to obtain a HOTP (identical to the one described in 2.2), where the encrypted message is $x \cdot y$. The process is shown in Algorithm 4.

Algorithm 4. OLE Transformation

Input A: $a_1, a_2, x \in \mathbb{Z}_2^{u_b}$ and **Input B:** $c, b, y \in \mathbb{Z}_2^{u_b}$
A sends value: $aux_A = (a_1 + x) \mod (2^{u_b})$
B sends value: $aux_B = (b + y) \mod (2^{u_b})$
A computes: $(k_{OUT} = a_2 + aux_B \cdot x) \mod (2^{u_b})$
B computes: $(c_{OUT} = c - aux_A \cdot b) \mod (2^{u_b})$
Output A: $k_{OUT} \in \mathbb{Z}_2^{u_b}$ and **Output B:** $c_{OUT} \in \mathbb{Z}_2^{u_b}$
Such that $(c_{OUT} - k_{OUT}) \mod (2^{u_b}) = x \cdot y$

This process is very similar to OT transformation scheme presented in [5]. For each transformation, a communication of $2 \cdot u_b$ bits is required for the auxiliary messages. When considering values with decimal parts, the fixed precision approach described in 3.1 is taken (also using the mentioned optimization).

Sometimes pre-established OLEs have different bit lengths than needed. As long as the said length is higher than u_b, the least significant u_b bits can be taken from each value a_1, a_2, c and b. The resulting constructs will still have the needed arithmetic correlation.

There are various ways to pre-compute OLEs, but this algorithm does not work with the quickest one, which is VOLE generation. As Sect. 2.2 illustrates, a VOLE is equivalent to multiple OLEs that have a common scalar (a) in their pairs. This scalar repetition prevents the algorithm from applying the masking and transformation methods described in Algorithm 4.

VOLE generation is an efficient way to pre-compute OLEs, but this algorithm cannot use it. Without this option, pre-establishing OLEs becomes more costly in terms of computation, data transfer, and algorithm complexity. Hence, these limitations should be considered when selecting a multiplication method.

3.5   Solution Using Custom Multiplication, HOTP and GCs

Using either multiplication method and distance function, the arithmetic sections may be calculated with a reduced computational complexity framework as shown in Algorithm 5.

Algorithm 5. Encrypted Distance

Input A: $mult(x,y), dist, \overline{e_x}$ and **Input B**: $mult(x,y), dist, \overline{e_y}$

for $i = 0$; $i < u_e$; $i{+}{+}$ do

$\quad c, k = mult(\overline{e_x}[i], \overline{e_y}[i])$

$\quad$ if $dist ==$ cosine then

$\quad\quad$ **Part A**:

$\quad\quad\quad s_k = (s_k + k) \mod (2^{u_b})$

$\quad\quad$ **Part B**:

$\quad\quad\quad s_c = (s_c + c) \mod (2^{u_b})$

$\quad$ else if $dist ==$ euclidean then

$\quad\quad$ **Part A**:

$\quad\quad\quad s_k = (s_k - (\overline{e_x}[i])^2 + 2 \cdot k) \mod (2^{u_b})$

$\quad\quad$ **Part B**:

$\quad\quad\quad s_c = (s_c + (\overline{e_y}[i])^2 + 2 \cdot c) \mod (2^{u_b})$

Output A: s_c and **Output B**: s_k

Where $mult(x,y)$ represents the approach chosen for computing the product and $dist$ is the distance function.

On the one hand, using the **cosine distance**, it may be seen that s_c (the encrypted similarity value) is the sum of the ciphertexts of OT multiplication for each pair of embedding values. Whereas, s_k (the key to the encrypted similarity value s_c) is the sum of the keys outputted by the same OT multiplications. In essence, this method creates one giant ciphertext with one giant mega-key. On the other hand, using the **Euclidean distance**, the process is very similar with two main differences. The squared value known to the evaluator $(\overline{e_y}[i]^2)$ is added to the ciphertext, taking advantage of the additive homomorphism. Additionally, the squared value unknown to the evaluator $(\overline{e_x}[i]^2)$ is subtracted from the key. When decrypting, said key will be subtracted from the ciphertext and the aforementioned squared value $(\overline{e_x}[i]^2)$ will be added to the result. Once more, taking advantage of the additive homomorphism, one giant ciphertext is created (s_c) and one giant mega-key (s_k).

As a final step, regardless of the distance algorithm chosen, the output may be decrypted by having the generator share the mega-key. Optionally, a discrete answer can be provided indicating whether two embeddings come from the same category, a different one or the algorithm couldn't determine with enough accuracy. To achieve this a GC is used.

A GC is prepared that takes as an argument the mega-key (s_k) from the generator and the similarity ciphertext (s_c) from the evaluator. The GC then performs the following steps:

1. The similarity value is obtained. $s_v = (s_c - s_k) \mod (2^{u_b})$.
2. The similarity value is compared to a "same information" threshold. $s_v > t_1$. When using Euclidean distance $s_v > (t_1)^2$.
3. The similarity value is compared to a "different information" threshold. $s_v < t_2$. When using Euclidean distance $s_v < (t_2)^2$.
4. Two bits representing each comparison are outputted, such that:
   - 00: Couldn't determine with enough accuracy.
   - 01: The embeddings are different.
   - 10: The embeddings are similar or the same.
   - 11: Internal error (something went wrong).

All parts of this new approach are analyzed using once more the λ, u_e and u_b parameters.

If using OT multiplication, each product requires $u_b/2$ OT transformations and $u_b \cdot u_b/2$ bits, for a total of $u_e \cdot u_b \cdot u_b/2$ bits in data exchange. Furthermore, the computation is trivial, especially if the upper bound is $2^{16}, 2^{32}$ or 2^{64}, as these values correspond to the lengths of pre-built data types in most programming languages (unsigned shorts, integers or longs) and don't require applying the modulo operation (allowing bit overflow creates the same effect).

If using OLE transformation, each product requires $2 \cdot u_b$ bits, for a total of $u_e \cdot 2 \cdot u_b$ bits in data exchange. Additionally, the computation is also trivial for the same aforementioned reasons.

Finally, the comparison GC is bigger as it needs to decrypt the similarity ciphertext and therefore requires an additional subtraction. Consequently, the total data exchange needed is $3 \cdot u_b \cdot 2 \cdot \lambda$ bits. In terms of computation, $3 \cdot u_b \cdot 2$ AES encryptions must be performed by the generator and evaluator. More concrete results are shown in Sect. 4.

4   Results

Four different techniques for arithmetic calculations are compared based on their data exchange requirements, as shown in Table 1. The first approach uses only garbled circuits (GCs). The second approach utilizes optimized GCs for arithmetic circuits from a previous work [4]. The last two techniques implement the algorithm proposed in this paper, employing two distinct multiplication methods: OT fractional multiplication and OLE transformation.

A security parameter, λ, of 128 bits is assumed, and three embedding sizes are examined. Each embedding element initially starts as a float or double but is converted to a fixed-precision 32-bit value ($u_b = 32$). For the remaining techniques, the integer part's bit length is set to 0, as the chosen neural network outputs embeddings between 0 and 1. Values of exactly 1 are converted to 0.99999999. Lastly, the results for the arithmetically optimized GCs is taken [4].

Table 1. Data exchange requirements (kB).

Embedding Length (#)	Naive Approach (kB)	Arithmetic GCs (kB)	OT_frac_mult & HOTP (kB)	OLE_trans & HOTP (kB)
128	6335	258	**8.5**	**1.5**
1024	50687	2064	**68**	**12**
4096	202751	82560	**272**	**48**

Table 1 displays the data exchange requirements in kilobytes (kB). Embedding length has no impact on the discrete step. The naive approach requires 1 kB of data exchange, while the other techniques necessitate 3 kB.

Furthermore, total computation times for arithmetic calculations, presented in Table 2, are measured. The focus is on the last two techniques due to their significantly faster performance. A single-core AMD Ryzen 9 5900X processor is used, and SIMD instructions with 128-bit registers are employed for the GC to accelerate AES encryptions and other label operations.

Table 2 displays the computation times in microseconds (μs) for various embedding lengths and distance functions. The discrete step is also independent of the embedding length. Both the generator (A) and evaluator (B) require a constant time of **23** μs and **20** μs, respectively.

Lastly, the algorithm's precision is assessed by comparing it to a baseline distance evaluation where no inputs are hidden. Both OT fractional multiplication and OLE transformation achieve very high precision, exceeding **99.98%** for cosine distance and **99.998%** for Euclidean distance.

Table 2. Computation times of arithmetic calculations (µs). The time measurements are obtained by averaging multiple executions of the same algorithm.

Embedding Length (#)	Distance Function (Cos/Euc)	OT_frac_mult & HOTP (µs)		OLE_trans & HOTP (µs)	
		Generator (A)	Evaluator (B)	Generator (A)	Evaluator (B)
128	Cos	1	1	≤ 1	≤ 1
	Euc	1	1	≤ 1	≤ 1
1024	Cos	10	12	1	1
	Euc	10	12	1	1
4096	Cos	50	52	6	6
	Euc	51	52	7	6

5 Discussion

From the first table (Table 1), two things can be noted. Firstly, the two custom multiplication methods achieve an exponential improvement in data exchange over the naive approach and a substantial improvement over the arithmetically optimized GCs. Secondly, approximately 4 to 5 times less data exchange is required by the OLE transformation scheme, compared to OT multiplication. However, it is important to note that OT extension and OLE generation data are not taken into account by these results. These amounts will heavily depend on the algorithms chosen but as a general rule, greater exchange is required by OLE generation.

Concerning Table 2, two main aspects can be observed. First of all, a linear dependency with embedding size is shown by both schemes but 9 to 10 times faster measurements are obtained by the OLE transformation-based products. However, it is important to note once more that far more computation will be necessary for OLE generation than OT generation (something not reflected in this table). Secondly, roughly the same time is taken by the generator and evaluator to perform their respective computation. Additionally, as with the data exchange sizes, the discrete step is constant and of equal duration between the two parties.

The precision of the algorithms is analyzed and near-perfect accuracy is achieved regardless of the multiplication method or distance function. This reinforces the claim that the presented schemes are practical in real-world scenarios.

The strengths, weaknesses and use cases of this work are worth discussing. As already seen, the main advantage of this scheme is its speed. Very little data exchange and even less computation are required by the proposed algorithms. Additionally, these methods scale well with embedding size, maintaining a linear dependency with information transition and computation. This work is therefore very apt in cases where speed is of the essence or where very large embeddings are utilized. Furthermore, as any kind of embedding can be compared, no special considerations are needed when training models for embedding extraction.

Already trained neural networks can be utilized without modification. Lastly, malicious security is somewhat easy to establish as extensive research on the topic is available for OT extension, OLE generation, GC generation and GC evaluation.

The main disadvantage of this scheme is the one-time use of all its cryptography. Every construct (OT, OLE, GCs...) must be discarded when used and generated again on subsequent operations. This problem is not presented by other methods, such as ones based on Full or Somewhat Homomorphic Encryption. Another weakness is the need for an active channel between the two parties to perform the discrete step. Even if the required data exchange is very low, this is not a fully asynchronous method and therefore some communication is required in between calculations.

Broadly speaking, the use of artificial intelligence for health data requires large datasets that can be obtained by sharing data across different institutions. It poses privacy challenges that can be partly solved by distributed learning, which uses cryptographic methods to avoid data transfer [11,16], and [28]. However, privacy protection also needs to consider the output level where the prediction models should not reveal any personal information [29]. Anonymized data is one way to achieve this goal and thus reduce privacy risks while preserving the usefulness and accessibility of the data [13,32]. In this article, the authors describe an ongoing work to bridge this gap by incorporating encryption approaches into biomedical data analysis.

6   Conclusion

The privacy of biomedical data (or other private information) is crucial to be preserved by encryption techniques nowadays. A novel, agile and powerful option for the transfer and computation of encrypted information is provided in this article. Additionally, the new emerging field intersecting deep learning and cryptography is of great interest today. However, proper implementation, human intervention or the intelligibility of results are complicated by its morphology. Further research is needed in this area to supplement this study and other similar solutions.

Regarding the technical aspect, the distance between two neural network embeddings (representing images, sound files, text, video, etc.) under a layer of cryptography is aimed to be computed by this research work. Alternatives for two distance functions (cosine and Euclidean) and two algorithms based on OT and OLE are presented. Very promising outcomes, especially in terms of computational speed and the amount of communication required, are provided by these methods.

High precision for both distances (cosine and Euclidean) is attained, obtaining 99.98% and 99.998%, respectively. Additionally, low assessment times are achieved regardless of embedding length, accomplishing full functionality in a few microseconds. Likewise, data exchange appears to be linearly correlated with embedding length. However, some remaining concerns remain such as the one-time use of cryptography. Comparison of the performance with other research works and the study of privacy-preserving explainable approaches are necessary aspects to be explored.

References

1. Applebaum, B., Damgård, I., Ishai, Y., Nielsen, M., Zichron, L.: Secure arithmetic computation with constant computational overhead. Cryptology ePrint Archive, Paper 2017/617 (2017)
2. Asharov, G., Lindell, Y., Schneider, T., Zohner, M.: More efficient oblivious transfer and extensions for faster secure computation. In: Proceedings of the 2013 ACM SIGSAC Conference on Computer & Communications Security, pp. 535–548. CCS '13, Association for Computing Machinery, New York, NY, USA (2013). https://doi.org/10.1145/2508859.2516738
3. Ball, M., Carmer, B., Malkin, T., Rosulek, M., Schimanski, N.: Garbled neural networks are practical. IACR Cryptol. ePrint Arch. p. 338 (2019)
4. Ball, M., Malkin, T., Rosulek, M.: Garbling gadgets for Boolean and arithmetic circuits. In: Proceedings of the 2016 ACM SIGSAC Conference on Computer and Communications Security, pp. 565–577. CCS '16, Association for Computing Machinery, New York, NY, USA (2016). https://doi.org/10.1145/2976749.2978410
5. Beaver, D.: Precomputing oblivious transfer. In: Coppersmith, D. (ed.) CRYPTO 1995. LNCS, vol. 963, pp. 97–109. Springer, Heidelberg (1995). https://doi.org/10.1007/3-540-44750-4_8
6. Bellare, M., Hoang, V., Keelveedhi, S., Rogaway, P.: Efficient garbling from a fixed-key blockcipher. In: 2012 IEEE Symposium on Security and Privacy, pp. 478–492. IEEE Computer Society, Los Alamitos, CA, USA (2013). https://doi.org/10.1109/SP.2013.39
7. Boyle, E., et al.: Efficient two-round OT extension and silent non-interactive secure computation. In: Proceedings of the 2019 ACM SIGSAC Conference on Computer and Communications Security, pp. 291–308. CCS '19, Association for Computing Machinery, New York, NY, USA (2019). https://doi.org/10.1145/3319535.3354255
8. Breebaart, J., Busch, C., Grave, J., Kindt, E.: A reference architecture for biometric template protection based on pseudo identities. In: ASDFASD, pp. 25–38 (2008)
9. Chen, T., et al.: THE-X: privacy-preserving transformer inference with homomorphic encryption. In: Muresan, S., Nakov, P., Villavicencio, A. (eds.) Findings of the Association for Computational Linguistics: ACL 2022, pp. 3510–3520. Association for Computational Linguistics, Dublin, Ireland (2022). https://doi.org/10.18653/v1/2022.findings-acl.277
10. Cheon, J.H., Kim, A., Kim, M., Song, Y.: Homomorphic encryption for arithmetic of approximate numbers. In: Takagi, T., Peyrin, T. (eds.) ASIACRYPT 2017. LNCS, vol. 10624, pp. 409–437. Springer, Cham (2017). https://doi.org/10.1007/978-3-319-70694-8_15
11. Dankar, F.K., Madathil, N., Dankar, S.K., Boughorbel, S.: Privacy-preserving analysis of distributed biomedical data: designing efficient and secure multiparty computations using distributed statistical learning theory. JMIR Med. Inform. $7(2)$, e12702 (2019)
12. Eicher, J., Bild, R., Spengler, H., Kuhn, K.A., Prasser, F.: A comprehensive tool for creating and evaluating privacy-preserving biomedical prediction models. BMC Med. Inform. Decis. Mak. $20(1)$, 1–14 (2020)

13. El Emam, K., Arbuckle, L.: Anonymizing health data: case studies and methods to get you started. O'Reilly Media, Inc. (2013)
14. Impagliazzo, R., Rudich, S.: Limits on the provable consequences of one-way permutations. In: Goldwasser, S. (ed.) CRYPTO 1988. LNCS, vol. 403, pp. 8–26. Springer, New York (1990). https://doi.org/10.1007/0-387-34799-2_2
15. Ishai, Y., Kilian, J., Nissim, K., Petrank, E.: Extending oblivious transfers efficiently. In: Boneh, D. (ed.) CRYPTO 2003. LNCS, vol. 2729, pp. 145–161. Springer, Heidelberg (2003). https://doi.org/10.1007/978-3-540-45146-4_9
16. Jordan, M.I., Mitchell, T.M.: Machine learning: trends, perspectives, and prospects. Science **349**(6245), 255–260 (2015)
17. Kim, D., Lee, G., Oh, S.: Toward privacy-preserving text embedding similarity with homomorphic encryption. In: Chen, C.C., Huang, H.H., Takamura, H., Chen, H.H. (eds.) Proceedings of the Fourth Workshop on Financial Technology and Natural Language Processing (FinNLP), pp. 25–36. Association for Computational Linguistics, Abu Dhabi, United Arab Emirates (Hybrid) (2022). https://doi.org/10.18653/v1/2022.finnlp-1.4
18. Kolesnikov, V., Sadeghi, A.-R., Schneider, T.: Improved garbled circuit building blocks and applications to auctions and computing minima. In: Garay, J.A., Miyaji, A., Otsuka, A. (eds.) CANS 2009. LNCS, vol. 5888, pp. 1–20. Springer, Heidelberg (2009). https://doi.org/10.1007/978-3-642-10433-6_1
19. Lam, M., Mitzenmacher, M., Reddi, V.J., Wei, G.Y., Brooks, D.: Tabula: Efficiently computing nonlinear activation functions for secure neural network inference (2022)
20. Lee, G., Kim, M., Park, J.H., Hwang, S.W., Cheon, J.H.: Privacy-preserving text classification on BERT embeddings with homomorphic encryption. In: Carpuat, M., de Marneffe, M.C., Meza Ruiz, I.V. (eds.) Proceedings of the 2022 Conference of the North American Chapter of the Association for Computational Linguistics: Human Language Technologies, pp. 3169–3175. Association for Computational Linguistics, Seattle, United States (2022). https://doi.org/10.18653/v1/2022.naacl-main.231
21. Malin, B.A., Emam, K.E., O'Keefe, C.M.: Biomedical data privacy: problems, perspectives, and recent advances. J. Am. Med. Inform. Assoc. **20**(1), 2–6 (2013)
22. Narayanan, A., Shmatikov, V.: Robust de-anonymization of large sparse datasets. In: 2008 IEEE Symposium on Security and Privacy (2008), pp. 111–125. IEEE (2008)
23. Nautsch, A., Isadskiy, S., Kolberg, J., Gomez-Barrero, M., Busch, C.: Homomorphic Encryption for speaker recognition: protection of biometric templates and vendor model parameters. In: Proceedings the Speaker and Language Recognition Workshop (2018), pp. 16–23 (2018). https://doi.org/10.21437/Odyssey.2018-3
24. O'herrin, J.K., Fost, N., Kudsk, K.A.: Health insurance portability accountability act (HIPAA) regulations: effect on medical record research. Ann. Surg. **239**(6), 772 (2004)
25. Palacios-Alonso, D., et al.: Privacidad por diseño, clave para la buena gobernanza. Derecom, pp. 215–223 (2021)
26. Raghuraman, S., Rindal, P., Tanguy, T.: Expand-convolute codes for pseudorandom correlation generators from LPN. In: Handschuh, H., Lysyanskaya, A. (eds.) Advances in Cryptology - CRYPTO 2023, pp. 602–632. Springer Nature Switzerland, Cham (2023). https://doi.org/10.1007/978-3-031-38551-3_19
27. Regulation, P.: General data protection regulation. Intouch **25**, 1–5 (2018)
28. Shokri, R., Shmatikov, V.: Privacy-preserving deep learning. In: Proceedings of the 22nd ACM SIGSAC Conference on Computer and Communications Security, pp. 1310–1321 (2015)

29. Shokri, R., Stronati, M., Song, C., Shmatikov, V.: Membership inference attacks against machine learning models. In: 2017 IEEE Symposium on Security and Privacy (SP), pp. 3–18. IEEE (2017)
30. Sweeney, L.: Computational disclosure control: A primer on data privacy protection. Ph.D. thesis, Massachusetts Institute of Technology (2001)
31. Vladimir Kolesnikov, T.S.: Improved garbled circuit: free XOR gates and applications. In: ICALP '08: Proceedings of the 35th International Colloquium on Automata, Languages and Programming, Part II, pp. 486–498 (2008)
32. Xia, W., Heatherly, R., Ding, X., Li, J., Malin, B.A.: Ru policy frontiers for health data de-identification. J. Am. Med. Inform. Assoc. **22**(5), 1029–1041 (2015)
33. Xiang, D., Cai, W., et al.: Privacy protection and secondary use of health data: strategies and methods. BioMed Res. Int. **2021**, 6967166 (2021)
34. Yang, K., Weng, C., Lan, X., Zhang, J., Wang, X.: Ferret: fast extension for correlated OT with small communication. In: Proceedings of the 2020 ACM SIGSAC Conference on Computer and Communications Security, pp. 1607–1626. CCS '20, Association for Computing Machinery, New York, NY, USA (2020). https://doi.org/10.1145/3372297.3417276
35. Yao, A.C.C.: How to generate and exchange secrets. In: 27th Annual Symposium on Foundations of Computer Science (SFCS 1986), pp. 162–167 (1986). https://doi.org/10.1109/SFCS.1986.25
36. Yu, X., Chen, X., Shi, J.: Vector based privacy-preserving document similarity with LSA. In: 2017 IEEE 9th International Conference on Communication Software and Networks (ICCSN), pp. 1383–1387 (2017). https://doi.org/10.1109/ICCSN.2017.8230336
37. Zahur, S., Rosulek, M., Evans, D.: Two halves make a whole: Reducing data transfer in garbled circuits using half gates. Cryptology ePrint Archive, Paper 2014/756 (2014)
38. Zhou, J., Li, J., Panaousis, E., Liang, K.: Deep binarized convolutional neural network inferences over encrypted data. In: 2020 7th IEEE International Conference on Cyber Security and Cloud Computing (CSCloud)/2020 6th IEEE International Conference on Edge Computing and Scalable Cloud (EdgeCom), pp. 160–167 (2020). https://doi.org/10.1109/CSCloud-EdgeCom49738.2020.00035

Unfolding Laryngeal Neuromotor Activity in Parkinson's Disease by Phonation Inversion

Pedro Gómez-Vilda[1](✉) [ID], Andrés Gómez-Rodellar[2] [ID], Jiri Mekyska[3] [ID],
Agustín Álvarez-Marquina[1] [ID], and Daniel Palacios-Alonso[4] [ID]

[1] NeuSpeLab, CTB, Universidad Politécnica de Madrid, 28220 Pozuelo de Alarcón,
Madrid, Spain
{pedro.gomezv,agustin.alvarez}@upm.es
[2] Usher Institute, Faculty of Medicine, University of Edinburgh, Edinburgh, UK
a.gomezrodellar@ed.ac.uk
[3] Department of Telecommunications, Brno University of Technology, Brno,
Czech Republic
mekyska@vut.cz
[4] Escuela Técnica Superior de Ingeniería Informática, Universidad Rey Juan Carlos,
Campus de Móstoles, Tulipán, s/n, 28933, Móstoles, Madrid, Spain
daniel.palacios@urjc.es

Abstract. Neuromotor disorders are a group of neurodegenerative alterations involving the neuromuscular system. Among them, Parkinson's disease (PD) is the one with fastest growing rates. Speech is one of the activities affected by PD, producing strong negative impact on the personal wellbeing of affected people. The present study aimed to characterize PD speech by using a neuromechanical model of phonation by speech inversion methods to estimate the differential activity of the thyroarytenoid and cricothyroid articulations (dNA) under the control of two independent direct neuromotor pathways. The dNA amplitude distributions from persons with PD and age-matched healthy control subjects (HCs) were compared with respect to a mid-age normative database (RSPs). Results show that for the male group 75% of PD and 100% of HC participants were labelled as misaligned to normative. Within the female group misalignments with respect to normative were of 75% in both cases. Regarding the normative participants, 12.5% (males) and 25% (females) were misaligned with respect to their average distributions. This methodology could help in characterizing and explaining neurodegenerative phonation alterations.

Keywords: neurodegenerative diseases · Parkinson's disease ·
phonation · speech processing · laryngeal neuromotor activity

This research received funding from grants of the Czech Ministry of Health no. NU20-04-00294, and EU - Next Generation EU (project no. LX22NPO5107 (MEYS)), and a doctoral scholarship under grant number: MR/N013166/1, funded by the MRC and CMVM, U. of Edinburgh.

J. M. Ferrández Vicente et al. (Eds.): IWINAC 2024, LNCS 14674, pp. 300–309, 2024.
https://doi.org/10.1007/978-3-031-61140-7_29

1 Introduction

The movement disorder first described by Dr. James Parkinson as shaking palsy known since on as Parkinson's disease (PD), is the second most prevalent one among neurodegenerative diseases. The number of PD cases has doubled in the past 25 years [1]. Global estimates in 2019 showed over 8.5 million individuals with PD, an increase of 81% with respect to 2000, having caused 329,000 deaths, an increase of over 100% since 2000 [2]. PD manifests itself as a progressive deterioration condition of motor and non-motor symptoms developing along many years before clear manifestations become evident, according to Bloem, Okun & Klein [3]. The general symptoms associated with PD are bradykinesia, rigidity, freezing of gait, frozen facial mask (hypomimia), postural sway, and distal limb resting tremor, among others [4]. According to Tsanas & Arora [5] "speech as an item within comprehensive PD clinical scales has been previously shown to be very strongly associated with overall PD symptom severity as assessed using standardized clinical metrics". An alteration of speech known as hypokinetic dysarthria is one of the motor symptoms of PD [6], affecting respiration, phonation, articulation, prosody, and fluency [7]. Phonation symptoms, such as *musculus vocalis* hypotonia, vocal fold imbalance, and tremor in voice (altered neuromotor feedback) are some manifestations of PD-related neurodegeneration on speech [8]. Precise knowledge of the neural processes and models regulating the respiratory and phonation systems in the body is essential to explain the effects of PD on speech in terms of neurological circuit modeling [9]. In these past years, the field of statistical machine learning of speech for biomedical applications has experienced an important expansion [10]. However, these studies do not provide the same level of insight that mechanistic models can provide, i.e., models that build on the physical principles of voice production to characterize the underlying mechanisms in PD-related pathology [6]. The present study aims to describe phonation based on a neuromechanical model in terms of amplitude distributions of laryngeal tensor and relaxer neuromotor activity of the vocal folds during the emission of a sustained vowel [aː]. To achieve this, differentiated estimations of the vocal fold body stress (VFBS) are propsed as potential predictors of dysarthric behavior from participants with PD and healthy control subjects. The paper is structured as follows: Sect. 2 is devoted to describe the neuromechanical fundamentals, neuromotor activity estimation, methodology of comparison, and experiment evaluation; Sect. 3 presents the results, which are commented and discussed in Sect. 4, as well as exposing conclusions, contributions, findings, and insights.

2 Materials and Methods

The brain areas involved in the control of neuromotor pathways related to phonation considered in the present study proceed from the primary motor cortex vocalization area (PCVA) are those directly implied in activating the larynx muscles by phonatory motoneurons (direct activation pathway) ([6,11]). Other circuits providing neuromotor control feedback (indirect pathways) will not be taken into consideration. Under this scope, the PVCA include the laryngeal motor cortex [12], premotor cortex, supplementary motor area, and cerebellar lobule VI. There is consensus in that as far as vocalization is concerned, the direct pathway is mainly controlled by the ventromedial central sulcus peak (VmCSP) corresponding to Broadmann area 4p, and the dorsolateral peak (DsP) in area 6, both on the precentral gyrus next to articulator control areas [13]. In the case under study, the agonist-antagonist direct neuromechanical activity of the *musculus vocalis* is known to be controlled by the vocal fold tensor (crycothyroid) and the relaxer (thyroarytenoid). Rödel et al. [14] reported selective stimulation of the vocal fold tensor (cricothyroid muscle: CTM) or relaxer (thyroarytenoid muscle: TAM). Brown et al. [12] suggested that both muscular systems are innervated differently, specifically by the external superior laryngeal nerve (SLN) and the recurrent laryngeal nerve (RLN). The differential neuromotor activity (dNA) may be defined as the separated agonist-antagonist activity of neuromotor pathways controlling phonation. The working assumption in the present study will consider that the dNA projected to the lower neuromotor units through the direct activation pathway of the LBMS is mainly related to VmCSP and DsP activity, as far as the phonation of a sustained vowel [a:] is involved. Therefore, for the present study the role of secondary areas (indirect activation pathway) is of minor relevance. The above-mentioned structures, and their role in phonation control are summarized in Fig. 1. The cricothyroid joint, schematically represented in Fig. 1 allows the external elongation of the vocal folds by the stretching and activation of the cricothyroid muscle compatible with an increase of VFBS [15]. The external branch of the SLN innervates the CTM, which is the only tensor of the TAM. The RLN innervates the TAM, which combined with the arytenoid muscles (lateral and oblique) contribute to adduction, abduction, and relaxation of the vocal folds. The primary objective of the study is to evaluate the existence of strong relationships between VFBS and dNA on the brain areas responsible for premotor and motor control because the laryngeal motor activity is transferred by larynx muscles, inducing the contraction of the TAM, measured by the unbiased VFBS transforming neural discharges into muscle contraction. The modeling of these relationships would allow system inversion, provided that adequate operators could be designed based on system identification methodologies. Therefore, it would be possible to advance in the projection of the neuromotor activity estimated from phonation biomechanics towards the brain area activity, described as electroencephalographic EEG frequency bands. The estimation of the amplitude distributions of dNA on the tensor (RLN) and relaxer (SLN) pathways depends on the VFBS, as:

$$ASVF \rightarrow [LPI] \rightarrow GS \rightarrow [VFBMI] \rightarrow VFBS \rightarrow$$
$$\rightarrow [D2WR] \rightarrow dNA_{ct,ta} \rightarrow [PDFB] \rightarrow p_{ct,ta} \tag{1}$$

where projection functions are distinguished from signals by being enclosed between brackets [•], and the following acronyms apply: ASVF: acoustic signal of vowel phonation; LPI: linear predictive inversion; GS: glottal source; VFBMI:

vocal fold biomechanical model inversion; D2WR: derivation and double wave rectifier; $dNA_{ct,ta}$: dynamic neuromotor activity (cricothyroid, thyroarytenoid); PDFB: probability distribution estimation; pct,ta: amplitude probability distributions of $dNA_{ct,ta}$.

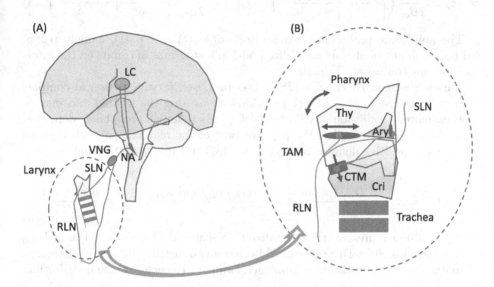

Fig. 1. Schematic representation of the cricothyroid joint and associated neuromuscular structures. (A) Cortico-bulbar-laryngeal direct neuromotor pathways. LC: laryngeal cortex. NA: nucleus ambiguous in medulla oblongata. VNG: extracranial vagus nerve ganglia. SLN: superior laryngeal nerve. RLN: retrolaryngeal nerve. (B) Detailed view of the thyroarytenoid joint: Thy: thyroid cartilage. Ary: arytenoid cartilages. Cri: cricoid cartilage. TAM: thyroarytenoid muscle. CTM: cricothyroid muscle. The agonist-antagonist role that CTM and TAM will play in the cricothyroid joint is represented by the curved double-arrow line.

The estimation of the VFBS from the ASVF consisted in the following steps: a 24-pole inverse lattice-ladder filter based on the iterative adaptive inverse filtering (IAIF) algorithm [16] was used to reconstruct the VFBS on segments of four-seconds long at a sampling frequency of 16 kHz. A description of the inversion filter details can be found in [17]. The VFBS given in $N.m^{-1}$ was estimated adjusting a 2-mass model of the vocal fold biomechanics [17], and detrended. The estimation of the $dNA_{ct,ta}$ is based on the VFBS ξ_b as composed of a basal quiescent (quasi-constant) value $\xi_{b0} > 0$ and a dynamic (variable) component ξ_{bd}:

$$\xi_b(t) = \xi_{b0}(t) + \xi_{bd}(t) \tag{2}$$

This model shows that ξ_{bd} is a zero-mean variable, which can be decomposed on the two components (cricothyroid and thyroarytenoid) by double wave rectification. Therefore, except for the scale factor, the $dNA_{ct,ta}$ ($s_{ta}(t)$ and $s_{ct}(t)$) may be obtained by double-wave rectification of the vocal fold stiffness derivative:

$$s_{ct}(t) = \frac{1}{2B_{ct}} \left(\left| \frac{\delta\xi_{bd}(t)}{\delta t} \right| - \frac{\delta\xi_{bd}(t)}{\delta t} \right); \ s_{ta}(t) = \frac{1}{2B_{ta}} \left(\left| \frac{\delta\xi_{bd}(t)}{\delta t} \right| + \frac{\delta\xi_{bd}(t)}{\delta t} \right) \quad (3)$$

The amplitude probability distributions of $s_{ct}(t)$ and $s_{ta}(t)$, namely $\mathbf{p}_{ct}(x)$ and $\mathbf{p}_{ta}(x)$ are estimated as normalized 50-bin histograms of counts on the interval 0–50 pps (pulses per second).

Jensen-Shannon Divergence (JSD) was proposed for the statistical comparisons of these probability density functions, measuring the mutual information between paired amplitude distributions of $dNAs$ taken as probability densities, i.e. $p(x)$ and $q(x)$, defined in the positive part of the real axis ($x \geq 0$), because $dNA(x)$ is a positive definite variable. The JSD [18] may be estimated as:

$$D_{JS}(p(x)|q(x)) = \frac{D_{KL}(p(x)|m(x)) + D_{KL}(q(x)|m(x))}{2}; m(x) = \frac{p(x) + q(x)}{2} \quad (4)$$

where variable x represents the normalized dNA amplitude ($0 \leq x \leq 1$) and D_{KL} is the Kulback-Leibler Divergence [18] between two distributions. The alignment estimation is based on the JSD from each sample i to each average distribution:

$$D_{i|MRS} = D_{JS}(p_i(x)|\bar{p}_{MRS}(x)); \ D_{i|FRS} = D_{JS}(p_i(x)|\bar{p}_{MFRS}(x));$$
$$D_{i|MHC} = D_{JS}(p_i(x)|\bar{p}_{MHC}(x)); \ D_{i|FHC} = D_{JS}(p_i(x)|\bar{p}_{FHC}(x)); \quad (5)$$
$$D_{i|MPD} = D_{JS}(p_i(x)|\bar{p}_{MPD}(x)); \ D_{i|FPD} = D_{JS}(p_i(x)|\bar{p}_{FPD}(x))$$

where $\bar{p}_{MRS}(x)$, $\bar{p}_{MHC}(x)$, $\bar{p}_{MPD}(x)$, $\bar{p}_{FRS}(x)$, $\bar{p}_{FHC}(x)$, and $\bar{p}_{FPD}(x)$ are the respective distribution averages from 50 bin histograms on the amplitude interval [0,50] pps (pulses per second). $D_{i|MRS}$, $D_{i|MHC}$, and $D_{i|MPD}$ are the distances of each sample i dNA amplitude distribution to each average dNA amplitude distribution of the male datasets. $D_{i|FRS}$, $D_{i|FHC}$, and $D_{i|FPD}$ are the respective distances to the female datasets. A naïve bisector criterion ($BiCr$), will classify a subject i as reference-aligned if the following condition holds, and as reference-misaligned otherwise:

$$D_{i|MPD} > D_{i|MRS} \text{ for male subsets;}$$
$$D_{i|FPD} > D_{i|FRS} \text{ for female subsets;}$$
$$\quad (6)$$

The target speech database (PARCZ) was collected at St. Anne's University Hospital in Brno (Czech Republic), containing recordings of sustained emisions of [a:] produced by PD patients of both genders (subsets MPD from males, and FPD from females), and similar recordings from age-matched healthy control subjects (MHC from males, and FHC from females). The reference database containing recordings from normative middle-aged participants was collected at Hospital Universitario Gregorio Marañón of Madrid, Spain (HUGMM). The data subsets used in the study corresponded to recordings from eight male and eight female PD participants, selected from the PARCZ database, as well as from eight male and eight female HC participants. Recordings from eight male and eight female participants from the HUGMM database were also used (MRS and FRS). FPD patients were labelled as P1xxx, MPD as P2xxx, FHC as C1xxx, MHC as C2xxx, MRS as N10xx and FRS as N11xx.

3 Results

The estimation process summarized in (1) is exemplified in Fig. 2 for a 4 s long phonation sample of [a:] from a male PD patient.

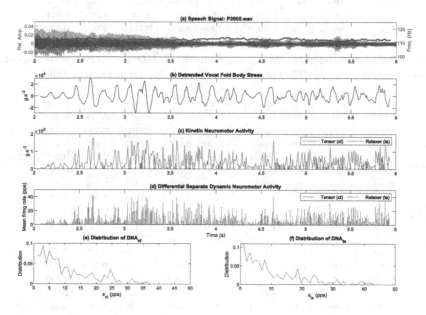

Fig. 2. Results from applying the inverse modelling process to a 4 s long phonation segment: a) Speech signal (blue) and f_0 (red); b) Detrended VFBS; c) Kinetic neuromotor activity from VFBS (blue: ct, red: ta); d) Estimations of dNA_{ct} and dNA_{ta}; e) and f) Their respective amplitude distributions.

The amplitude distributions of dNA_{ct} and dNA_{ta} represented in (e) and (f) behave as first-order χ^2 ones. The comparisons listed in (5) are given in Tables 1 (dNA_{ct}) and 2 (dNA_{ta}). For each sample, a position in a 2D-plane may be estimated by triangulation, for which the distances between the average dataset

Table 1. JSD estimations on the dNA_{ct} from the MPD and MHC with respect to the average MRS and MHC. The cases contrary to (6) are printed in bold.

$P_{i|MPD}$	$\bar{p}_{MRS}$	$\bar{p}_{MHC}$	$P_{i|MHC}$	$\bar{p}_{MRS}$	$\bar{p}_{MHC}$	$P_{i|MRS}$	$\bar{p}_{MHC}$	$\bar{p}_{MRS}$
P2005	0.541	0.389	C2001	0.381	0.171	R1005	0.154	0.471
P2009	0.464	0.193	C2002	0.428	0.152	**R1018**	**0.244**	**0.230**
P2010	**0.101**	**0.412**	C2008	0.312	0.098	R1027	0.213	0.219
P2012	0.285	0.111	C2009	0.260	0.200	R1028	0.162	0.331
P2017	**0.148**	**0.233**	C2010	0.512	0.323	R1030	0.102	0.397
P2018	0.460	0.249	C2011	0.302	0.193	R1032	0.125	0.483
P2019	0.409	0.164	C2013	0.393	0.095	R1033	0.366	0.523
P2023	0.460	0.229	C2014	0.400	0.123	R1034	0.119	0.315
$P_{i|FPD}$	$\bar{p}_{FRS}$	$\bar{p}_{FHC}$	$P_{i|FHC}$	$\bar{p}_{FRS}$	$\bar{p}_{FHC}$	$P_{i|FRS}$	$\bar{p}_{FHC}$	$\bar{p}_{FRS}$
P1006	0.491	0.288	C1003	0.386	0.133	R1105	0.220	0.360
P1007	0.414	0.167	C1004	0.338	0.086	R1108	0.255	0.402
P1008	0.469	0.185	C1005	0.320	0.092	**R1112**	**0.251**	**0.224**
P1020	**0.066**	**0.353]**	**C1006**	**0.106**	**0.303**	R1116	0.267	0.501
P1021	0.404	0.147	C1007	0.437	0.263	R1117	0.090	0.356
P1022	**0.168**	**0.429**	C1012	0.470	0.215	R1120	0.162	0.369
P1025	0.495	0.325	C1017	0.520	0.233	R1121	0.233	0.544
P1026	0.392	0.105	**C1018**	**0.145**	**0.238**	**R1125**	**0.304**	**0.173**

Table 2. JSD estimations on the dNA_{ta} from the MPD and MHC with respect to the average MRS and MHC. The cases contrary to (6) are printed in bold.

$P_{i|MPD}$	$\bar{p}_{MRS}$	$\bar{p}_{MHC}$	$P_{i|MHC}$	$\bar{p}_{MRS}$	$\bar{p}_{MHC}$	$P_{i|MRS}$	$\bar{p}_{MHC}$	$\bar{p}_{MRS}$
P2005	0.518	0.396	C2001	0.397	0.146	R1005	0.124	0.530
P2009	0.472	0.191	C2002	0.446	0.200	**R1018**	**0.282**	**0.194**
P2010	**0.094**	**0.409**	C2008	0.353	0.119	R1027	0.179	0.211
P2012	0.298	0.159	C2009	0.246	0.205	R1028	0.108	0.261
P2017	**0.099**	**0.268**	C2010	0.523	0.307	R1030	0.064	0.389
P2018	0.465	0.226	C2011	0.293	0.133	R1032	0.084	0.390
P2019	0.375	0.122	C2013	0.399	0.115	R1033	0.300	0.547
P2023	0.458	0.177	C2014	0.326	0.110	R1034	0.112	0.338
$P_{i|FPD}$	$\bar{p}_{FRS}$	$\bar{p}_{FHC}$	$P_{i|FHC}$	$\bar{p}_{FRS}$	$\bar{p}_{FHC}$	$P_{i|FRS}$	$\bar{p}_{FHC}$	$\bar{p}_{FRS}$
P1006	0.544	0.321	C1003	0.390	0.150	R1105	0.085	0.265
P1007	0.411	0.170	C1004	0.355	0.082	R1108	0.238	0.497
P1008	0.440	0.194	C1005	0.370	0.084	**R1112**	**0.285**	**0.210**
P1020	**0.106**	**0.328**	**C1006**	**0.122**	**0.366**	R1116	0.229	0.490
P1021	0.457	0.218	C1007	0.453	0.248	R1117	0.123	0.331
P1022	**0.098**	**0.330**	C1012	0.466	0.241	R1120	0.137	0.345
P1025	0.522	0.358	C1017	0.504	0.259	R1121	0.240	0.514
P1026	0.314	0.118	**C1018**	**0.239**	**0.292**	**R1125**	**0.340**	**0.132**

distributions given in Table 1 and 2 have to be considered with respect to their reference bases $\mathbf{D}_{JS}(\bar{\mathbf{p}}_{MHC}|\bar{\mathbf{p}}_{MRS})$ and $\mathbf{D}_{JS}(\bar{\mathbf{p}}_{FHC}|\bar{\mathbf{p}}_{FRS})$, as shown in Fig. 3. The bisector line expresses the alignment limit according to (6).

Figure 3 shows a similar behavior of the neuromotor activity in the cricothyroid and thyroarytenoid distributions $dNAct$ and $dNAta$. The results in Tables 1 and 2, and in Fig. 3 are summarized in Table 3.

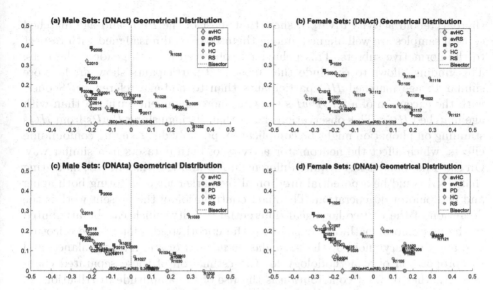

Fig. 3. Three-band plot of PD and HC distributions referred to RS participants: cricothyroid dNA_{ct} and thyroarytenoid dNA_{ta} from males (a, c)) and females (b, d). The bisector is the locus where $D_{i|MPD} = D_{i|MRS}$ or $D_{i|FPD} = D_{i|FRS}$.

Table 3. Alignment/misalignment with respect to reference datasets.

Subset	MPD	MHC	MRS	FPD	FHC	FRS
dNA_{ct}	2/6	0/8	7/1	2/6	2/6	6/2
dNA_{ta}	2/6	0/8	7/1	2/6	2/6	6/2

4 Discussion and Conclusions

The potential of estimating laryngeal pathways' neuromotor activity from neuromechanical inversion of sustained vowel phonations in PD has been presented. The results in Table 1 and Fig. 3 (a and b), corresponding to the cricothyroid activity dNA_{ct}), show that six out of eight MPD participant samples were more aligned to the age-matched MHC set than to the reference MRS, with the exception of (P2010 and P2017). All the eight MHC samples were more aligned with themselves than with respect to MRS reference participants. One MRS participant (R1018) was more aligned with MHC than with its own dataset. Regarding the female datasets, the situation is quite similar. Two out of eight FDP participants (P1020 and P1022) were more aligned with the reference dataset FRS than with the age-matched one FHC. Two out of eight FHC participants (C1006 and C1018) were more aligned with FRS than with their own dataset. Within the reference dataset FRS two out of eight participants (R1112 and R1125) were more aligned to FHC participants than to their own dataset. Similarly, the results in Table 2 and Fig. 3 (c and d), corresponding to the thyroarytenoid activity dNA_{ta}), show that most of the PwP and age matched control samples are well aligned among themselves, and misaligned with respect to the normative subsets. This behavior is observed in both genders' datasets. This finding allows to conclude that most PD participants show $dNAs$ more similar to age matched HC participants than to mid-age reference RS ones, with the exception of a few $PwPs$ showing more alignment with RS than with age matched HCs. This observation shows that distinguishing $PwPs$ from HCs standing on phonation might be complicated, possibly due to aging confounding effects, which affect the neuromotor activity of both datasets in a similar way. On the other hand, dNA is quite different in PD and HC than in RS, indicating that dNA could be a potential prodromal biomarker for monitoring both aging and neuromotor degeneration. The main contribution of the present work is the definition of the cortico-laryngeal differential activity which can be attributed to the neuromotor pathways controlling the cricothyroid joint by the cricothyroid and thyroarytenoid by the *musculus vocalis* tensor and relaxer balance, and the proposition of a methodology for the estimation of these separated channels. Another relevant contribution is the use of the amplitude distributions of each differential channel in the characterization of aging and neurodegenerative phonation. This methodology could be of utility in neurologic disorder assessment, monitoring, and rehabilitation, as well as in clinical neurolinguistics.

References

1. Tysnes, B., Storstein, A.: Epidemiology of Parkinson's disease. J. Neural Transm. **124**, 901–905 (2017). https://doi.org/10.1007/s00702-017-1686-y
2. World Health Organization (2023) Parkinson disease. https://www.who.int/newsroom/fact-sheets/detail/parkinson-disease (visited 2023.03.16)
3. Bloem, B.R., Okun, M.S., Klein C.: Parkinson's disease. Lancet **397**(10291), 284–2303 (2021). https://doi.org/10.1016/S0140-6736(21)00218-X
4. Bhat, A., Acharya, U.R., Dadmehr, N., Adeli, H.: Parkinson's Disease: cause factors, measurable indicators, and early diagnosis. Comput. Biol. Med. **102**, 234–241 (2018). https://doi.org/10.1016/j.compbiomed.2018.09.008
5. Tsanas, A., Arora, S.: Data-driven subtyping of Parkinson's using acoustic analysis of sustained vowels and cluster analysis: findings in the Parkinson's voice initiative study. Springer Nat. Comput. Sci. **3**, 232 (2022). https://doi.org/10.1007/s42979-022-01123-y
6. Duffy, J.R.: Motor Speech Disorders: Substrates, Differential Diagnosis, and Management, 3rd edn., Elsevier (2013)
7. Mekyska, J., et al.: Robust and complex approach of pathological speech signal analysis. Neurocomputing **167** 94–111 (2015). https://doi.org/10.1016/j.neucom.2015.02.085
8. Sapir, S., Ramig, L.O., Spielman, J.L., Fox, C.: Formant centralization ratio: a proposal for a new acoustic measure of dysarthric speech. J. Speech Lang. Hear. Res. **53**, 114–125 (2010). https://doi.org/10.1044/1092-4388(2009/08-0184)
9. Schulz, G.M., Varga, M., Jeffries, K., Ludlow, C.L., Braun, A.R.: Functional neuroanatomy of human vocalization: an H215O PET study. Cereb. Cortex **15** 1835–1847 (2005). https://doi.org/10.1093/cercor/bhi061

10. Amato, F., Saggio, G., Cesarini, V., Olmo, G., Costantini, G.: Machine learning-and statistical-based voice analysis of Parkinson's disease patients: a survey. Expert Syst. Appl. **219**, 119651 (2023). https://doi.org/10.1016/j.eswa.2023.119651
11. Rektorová, I., Mikl, M., Barrett, J., Marecek, R., Rektor, I., Paus, T.: Functional neuroanatomy of vocalization in patients with Parkinson's disease. J. Neurol. Sci. **313**(1-2), 7–12 (2012). https://doi.org/10.1093/cercor/bhi06
12. Brown, S., Laird, A.R., Pfordresher, P.Q., Thelen, S.M., Turkeltaub, P., Liotti, M.: The somatotopy of speech: phonation and articulation in the human motor cortex. Brain Cogn. **70**(1), 31–41 (2009). https://doi.org/10.1016/j.bandc.2008.12.006
13. Dietrich, M., Andreatta, R.D., Jiang, Y., Stemple, J.C.: Limbic and cortical control of phonation for speech in response to a public speech preparation stressor. Brain Imaging Behav. **14**, 1696–1713 (2020). https://doi.org/10.1007/s11682-019-00102-x
14. Rödel, R.M., et al.: Human cortical motor representation of the larynx as assessed by transcranial magnetic stimulation (TMS). Laryngoscope **114**(5), 918–922 (2004). https://doi.org/10.1097/00005537-200405000-00026
15. Hammer, G.P., Windisch, G., Prodinger, P.M., Anderhuber, F., Friedrich, G.: The cricothyroid joint - functional aspects with regard to different types of its structure. J. Voice, **24**(2), 140–145 (2008). https://doi.org/10.1016/j.jvoice.2008.07.001
16. Alku, P., et al.: OPENGLOT-An open environment for the evaluation of glottal inverse filtering. Speech Commun. **107**, 38–47 (2019). https://doi.org/10.1016/j.specom.2019.01.005
17. Gómez-Vilda, P., et al.: Glottal source biometrical signature for voice pathology detection. Speech Commun. **51**(9), 759–781 (2009). https://doi.org/10.1016/j.specom.2008.09.005
18. Cover, T.M., Thomas, J.A.: Elements of Information Theory. John Wiley and Sons, Hoboken, NJ, USA (2012)

Personalization of Child-Robot Interaction Through Reinforcement Learning and User Classification

Anniek Jansen(✉) [ID], Konstantinos Tsiakas [ID], and Emilia I. Barakova [ID]

Eindhoven University of Technology, Eindhoven, The Netherlands
a.jansen@tue.nl

Abstract. Social robots offer promising avenues for personalized interactions, particularly in aiding children undergoing minimally invasive
surgery who often experience pain, fear, and anxiety. While distraction
methods like cartoons have shown an effect, they are not adaptive and
lack personalization to each child's needs. We propose an approach that
combines reinforcement learning (for learning a set of baseline policies for different types of users) with user modeling and classification to
create personalized and adaptive interactions for social robots with the
aim to provide higher engagement and adequate distraction from pain
in children. In the proposed approach, first a fixed policy is employed
during an assessment phase, collecting data on child-robot interactions
for a new user. Next, this data is compared to a set of user models,
in order to classify the new user into one of these models and its corresponding policy. The selected baseline policy is used during the next
interaction which should take place post-surgery. We conducted experiments to test this approach with simulated user models and our results
show that baseline policies perform best with their corresponding user
model but also achieve good results for unseen models of users who will
interact similarly within the interaction framework. Finally, we discuss
how these results can inform future research and how they can be used
for real-world implementations.

Keywords: Socially assistive robots · Adaptive personalization ·
Reinforcement learning with user classification · Child-robot
interaction · Pain management

1 Introduction

Social robots have emerged as a promising tool for personalized one-on-one interactions with various target groups. One specific target group that can greatly
benefit from this technology is children undergoing minimally invasive surgery
[6,18]. Before, during, and after such a procedure children might experience pain
as well as feel fear or anxiety which can increase the perception of pain [4]. Previous research suggests that by implementing distractions, such as engaging them

J. M. Ferrández Vicente et al. (Eds.): IWINAC 2024, LNCS 14674, pp. 310–321, 2024.
https://doi.org/10.1007/978-3-031-61140-7_30

with cartoons, children's pain tolerance can be increased, leading to a reduction in their pain experience [11].

While effective, the approach presented by James [11] fails to track the engagement of the child. Social Robots can in addition to providing distraction, respond to the way they respond to the robot, i.e. provide an active distraction and also can give insides into their state of pain, fear, or a combination of both. There have been several projects where social robots have been used in pain management [1,6,12,13,18,21], however in these cases the robot had pre-programmed interactions [12,16] or was teleoperated [1,13,21]. Our far-reaching goal is to study if a tailored engagement in which the robot adjusts to each child's interaction style might improve pain distraction.

To achieve this overarching goal, in the current study proposes an RL-based approach to design personalized and adaptive interactions between a social robot and a child. Our approach combines RL with user modeling and classification in order to tackle the "cold start" problem while deploying RL agents woth new users - unseen environments [19]. More specifically, our approach includes an assessment phase, during the child's first visit (pre-surgery), where the robot adheres to a fixed policy (behavior) exploring various emotions and records child interactions. This data is then utilized to build and classify a user model for the new user, subsequently determining the baseline policy for a personalized interaction (post-surgery). We report our preliminary results to demonstrate our approach and discuss its limitations and ways to address them towards a real-world personalized child-robot interaction.

2 Related Work

2.1 Distracting Children Using Social Robots

Social robots can provide cognitive support in different healthcare settings through social interactions with children [2]. One of the scenarios in which the social robot can provide support is before, during or after medical procedures by distracting the child and reducing stress, anxiety, and pain [2]. For instance, social robots have been used to reduce anxiety and pain in children during dental procedures [21], or during vaccination [1,12,16].

This distraction has been done for example by Rossi et al. [16] by having a humanoid robot interact with children just before and during their vaccination. The robot had different preprogrammed distraction strategies, including dialogues, songs, and dances, which were selected based on the anxiety level gauged by nurses. These distraction strategies reduced fear and anxiety and also decreased the perceived pain when compared to a condition without a robot. Similar research by Beran et al. [1], revealed that distracting the child with a robot had a positive effect - the children smiled more often, but their crying time did not decrease. The researchers used a cognitive-behavioral strategy for distraction, where the robot would give children commands to blow.

Most of these studies used a Wizard-of-Oz type of experiment where a robot would be teleoperated [2]. Other studies used preprogrammed behavior, for example in Jibb et al. [12] the robot would introduce itself and make a fixed set of dance movements while singing. These studies show that social robots can distract children and provide cognitive support in healthcare settings. In this paper, we aim to design the robot behavior through a Reinforcement Learning (RL) that can learn to personalize to a new user. At this stage we run the RL and user classification experiments on simulated user models. Our goal is to develop a set of user models and RL policies which will be be implemented on Miro-E robot to test whether it can provide personalized support to children.

2.2   RL-Based Personalization Approaches

A main challenge while designing and implementing Human-Robot Interaction (HRI) systems is the development of an efficient personalization mechanism that can enable a robot to meet the needs and/or preferences of an individual user [7]. RL has been successfully applied in human-machine interaction, including HRI, since it provides an appropriate computational framework to enable systems to dynamically adjust their behavior to make the interaction more relevant to individual users [5]. In the domain of social robots, RL has been applied to enable *affective personalization* for a language learning scenario with children [9]. More specifically, the robot which was an RL agent learned how to adjust its affective behavior, expressed as the valence and arousal of robot's voice, considering the child's affective state during the interaction. The results of this research study indicate that affective personalization using RL can improve both affective and learning outcomes. RL methods have also been used for the long-

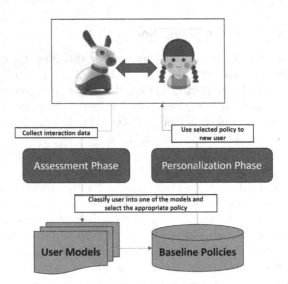

Fig. 1. The proposed approach includes an assessment phase where interaction data is collected and classified into one of the existing user models to select the most appropriate baseline policy which is deployed to provide a personalized interaction.

term personalization of socially assistive robotics (SAR) systems [14]. A long-term study has demonstrated that a fully autonomous SAR system was able to personalize its instruction and feedback over time to each child's proficiency [3].

The main challenge of RL-based personalization methods is that learning a near-optimal policy is often slow or infeasible, especially if the experiment involves real-world subjects [8]. To resolve this challenge, several approaches aim to combine RL with other methods, including user modeling. For example, cluster-based RL can learn personalized policies for different types (clusters) of users [10,19]. The goal of such approaches is to facilitate personalization by utilizing existing policies and user models (clusters). In this paper, we propose a personalization approach that combines RL with user modeling to ensure fast but efficient personalization (Fig. 1).

3   Proposed Approach

In this section, we present the real-world child-robot interaction scenario and our proposed approach on how to design personalized interactions. For the child-robot interaction, we use the Miro-E robot which has been used to provide comfort and distraction from post-operative pain and distress in children [6]. Miro-E is an animal-like social robot that can perform actions by moving its head, ears, tail, LED colors, and expressive movements. By combining these behaviors, the robot can display different emotions such as contentment, anger, and happiness. The emotions included in this work are limited to *neutral/none, content, happy, surprised, sad* and *angry* which have been already designed and tested in [6]. The robot can detect touch interactions and if it is being shaken. In the envisioned scenario, the robot would be available for interaction when children visit the hospital once before the surgery. During this first visit, they will have around 30 min to interact with the robot. After surgery, the robot will again be available for the children to interact for an undetermined amount of time, expected to be around 30 min. The goal of the robot is to engage the child by displaying the appropriate emotions during their interaction.

Based on the intended real-life scenario, to enable a personalized child-robot interaction, our approach utilizes the assessment phase to collect interaction data, based on which the robot can estimate a new user model. During this *assessment* phase, the robot follows a fixed behavior (policy) which aims to explore whether the child interacts with the robot when it enacts different emotions. During the *personalization phase*, the interaction data is used to make an estimation of the user's model and classify them into one of the existing user models from past interactions with different users. Based on this classification, the corresponding baseline policy will be selected for the robot when the child interacts after the surgery.

3.1   The RL Agent

The goal of the RL agent is to learn an optimal policy (robot behavior) that can enable the robot to select the appropriate *action* for each *state* based on a given *reward* signal, as shown in Figure 2. The robot will display a behavior and the child can interact with the robot.

The problem for the RL agent is formulated as a Markov Decision Process (MDP). An MDP is described with the *state space S, action space A, transition model $T(s, a, s')$, reward function $R(s, a, s')$ and a discount factor (γ)*. The state features are: *Current Action and Previous action= {0:Neutral, 1: Content, 2: Happy, 3: Surprised, 4: Sad, 5: Happy} and Previous Success ={0: no interaction, 1: interaction}*. Based on the current state, the robot will select one of the available behaviors as the next action. The reward is calculated by first checking if the child interacts with the robot (score = 1) or not (score = -1). Next, in order to discourage switching between behaviors when there is an interaction, the score will be increased by +1 (score = 2) if the previous action equals the current action (no behavior switching). To discourage staying in the same behavior while there is no interaction, the score will be −2. The total score is used as a reward {−2, −1, 1, 2}. Each state lasts for 10 s, resulting in 180 interactions in 30 min.

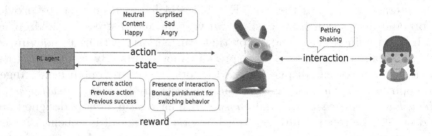

Fig. 2. Overview of the child-robot interaction. An RL agent is used to learns personalized policies, which dictate which action the robot should take based on the current state in order to maximize the reward.

The goal of the RL agent is to learn the best policy based on a given reward function (simulated user models). The best policy is the one which maximizes the expected total return $E[R]$, where $R = \sum_{i=0}^{N} \gamma^i r_i$ is the discounted sum of rewards for each episode. In interaction terms, an optimal policy maximizes the amount of child-robot interactions while avoiding meaningless robot behavior switching.

3.2   Simulated User Models

For the experiment, we used four different simulated user models (UMs) to train the baseline policies and one UM for validation (new user). These UMs were designed to represent four different types of potential users, as there was no real-world data available. The first UM simulates a child who is medium likely to interact and has a preference to interact when the robot displays happy or sad behavior and disfavors angry behavior (UM1). UM2 simulated a child who is very likely to interact with a slight preference for happy and content behavior (UM2). The third UM represents a child that is not likely to interact but slightly more likely when the robot displays happy behavior (UM3). UM4 is similar to UM1 but with different preferences, namely most likely to interact with content and less likely to interact with sad behavior but more likely with angry behavior. Furthermore, we defined another user model to be used for evaluation, UM5, which represents a child that is moderately likely to interact with surprise, sad, and happy behavior and not likely when the robot displays angry behavior. Table 1 shows the probabilities of interaction for each user model. For all UMs, the probability of interacting increases when the previous action (independent of which action) was a success and the probability will decrease if the previous action was not a success and the *same* action is selected again. In this case, the probability of interacting decreases by 80%.

Table 1. The probabilities for each user model to interact with the robot given a certain action and if the previous action was a success (P.S.) or not (no P.S.). The probability for each UM decreases by 80% if the same action is selected again while it was not a previous success

User Model	Neutral		Content		Happy		Surprise		Sad		Angry	
	P.S.	No P.S.	P.S.	No P.S.	P.S.	No P.S.	P.S.	No P.S.	P.S.	No P.S.	P.S.	No P.S.
1	0.6	0.1	0.7	0.2	0.9	0.6	0.55	0.3	0.8	0.65	0.2	0.1
2	0.7	0.5	0.8	0.7	0.9	0.7	0.75	0.8	0.6	0.5	0.6	0.4
3	0.5	0.1	0.6	0.1	0.4	0.4	0.4	0.2	0.1	0.05	0.3	0.1
4	0.6	0.05	0.8	0.15	0.55	0.45	0.45	0.2	0.6	0.35	0.5	0.4
5	0.4	0.2	0.5	0.3	0.6	0.4	0.7	0.5	0.8	0.6	0.3	0.1

4   Experiments

In this section, we present the experiments conducted to test the proposed approach. Our experiments consist of the following parts: (a) learning baseline policies, (b) testing the baseline policies with different user models, and (c) classifying a new user and selecting an appropriate baseline policy.

4.1   Learn Baseline Policies

Our first step is to learn the baseline policies (BP). To do so, we apply the SARSA algorithm to learn five different policies (Q-table); each one using a different simulated user model (environment). More specifically, each policy is trained for $E = 30000$ episodes – where an episode includes $N = 180$ interactions, using a constant learning rate ($\alpha = 0.25$). We apply an ϵ-greedy exploration with a high initial exploration rate ($\epsilon = 0.99$) gradually decreasing (95% per 250 episodes), in order to ensure an efficient exploration of the state-action space. Figure 3 visualizes the total return for each episode for the different UMs. Additionally, we visualize the success rate as the percentage of successful interactions during the episode.

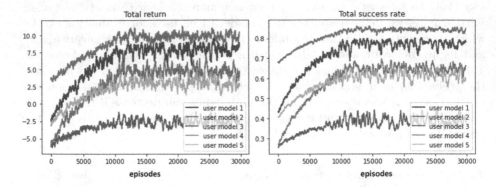

Fig. 3. We learn five policies; one baseline policy for each simulated user model. Each policy results in different expected total returns and interaction rates.

Based on the learning curves, we can observe that RL learns a different behavior for each UM resulting in different amounts of expected returns and interaction success rates. For example, baseline policy BP2 has learned how to interact with a user who is highly likely to interact with the robot, leading to the highest total return and success rate. On the contrary, baseline policy BP3 indicates a user not likely to interact, i.e., UM3. We can also observe that BPs for "similar" user models, e.g., UM1 and UM2, show similarities in terms of expected return and success rate, compared to "not similar" user models, e.g., UM3. Our basic assumption is that each baseline policy can maximize the expected return (and success rate) for its corresponding user model [20]. Furthermore, an additional assumption is that for a new user, e.g., UM5, a baseline policy which is trained on a similar UM will be more appropriate compared to a not similar one or an empty policy.

4.2   Evaluate Baseline Policies

Based on the learned baseline policies, the goal is to evaluate how these policies perform for the different simulated user models. We follow the assumption that a baseline policy will be the best policy for the corresponding user model. Our goal is to explore how each BP can perform in different environments (UM), including its training environment. To do so, we run the baseline policies (learned Q-tables) for each user model for $E = 5000$ episodes (episode = 180 interactions), with small learning ($\alpha = 0.1$) and exploration ($\epsilon = 0.1$) rates. We compare the total returns and (interaction) success rates for each pair of user model (UM) and baseline policy (BP). Figure 4 visualizes the learning curves for each UM and Table 2 includes the average total return and success rate.

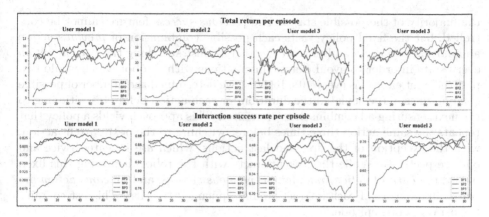

Fig. 4. Applying the baseline policies (BP) on the different user models (UM). The results show that each BP performs best for its corresponding UM.

Based on the results, we can observe that the baseline policies perform better on their own training environments (user models). Another observation is that the baseline policies can also perform well with new environment similar to their own. For example, BP1 is the best policy for UM1, but it is also a good policy for UM2, which is a "similar" user model.

4.3   Assessment Policy

Next, to find the best starting policy for a new user, interaction data is collected during the assessment phase. During this assessment phase, the robot acts according to a fixed policy. The actions for the fixed policy are preprogrammed and are independent on user interactions. Each episode consists of 180 interactions, based on the available 30 min, with each state transition occurring every 10 s. The goal of the assessment policy is to collect interaction data for

Table 2. Average return and success rates for the UMs and BPs. The values in bold indicate the highest return and success rate for each UM, demonstrating the optimal BP for each UM. For UM5, BP5 has the highest value but the second highest among the other four BPs is also highlighted.

	BP1		BP2		BP3		BP4		BP5	
	return	success	return	success	return	success	return	success	return	success
UM1	**9.63**	**0.82**	8.51	0.81	7.22	0.75	8.25	0.75	–	–
UM2	11.36	0.87	**11.64**	**0.87**	7.53	0.81	11.10	0.86	–	–
UM3	−2.09	0.39	−3.15	0.35	**−1.92**	**0.39**	−3.01	0.37	–	–
UM4	5.99	0.70	5.91	0.69	3.81	0.64	**7.10**	**0.7**	–	–
UM5	**5.33**	**0.66**	4.42	0.66	3.75	0.62	3.07	0.62	*5.34*	*0.67*

the majority of the possible states. The *previous success* feature cannot be controlled, but the fixed policy visits each possible combination of *previous action* and *current action*. In addition, we decided against switching the *current action* every state in order to avoid chaotic interactions with a robot which would display different emotions every 10 s. Instead, we determined the number of possible combinations and calculated the duration for each action before transitioning to the next, ensuring all combinations are visited. This approach yields a policy that repeats the same action three times before switching to the next current action, with the exception of the first and last actions, which are repeated twice and once respectively. While the user interacts with the robot displaying this fixed policy, the *current action, interaction, previous success,* and *previous action* are stored in an array of each interaction and appended to a list. This list contains the arrays of one episode.

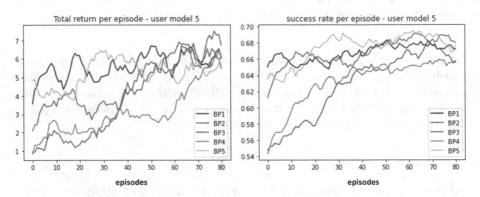

Fig. 5. Visualization of total returns and interaction success rates for the different BPs on UM5. Apart from BP5 which is the baseline policy for UM5, BP1 performs the best amongst the baseline policies.

4.4   Classification and Policy Selection

The interaction data from a new user during the assessment phase are used to classify the user to the UM that is most similar. For this purpose, a classification model was trained on the interaction data based on the four user models and used to classify a new user, (UM5), into one of the four existing UMs. More specifically, we collected training data by running the fixed assessment policy with the four simulated UMs for 1000 episodes, resulting in a total of 4000 data points. As each episode is the result of the same fixed assessment policy, each episode was stored as one instance and the list of arrays was split into 720 features. Each feature represents either the current action, the previous action, the current success or the previous success, but this was not specified in the model. As the current and previous action are fixed by the policy, the model would learn how likely each user model is to interact in for each combination of *previous action, current action* and *previous success*. For training and evaluating, a train-test split of 80%-20% was used. Using sklearn a KNN, random forest, Naive Bayes and SVM with different kernels were trained and evaluated. The parameters of the best performing models were optimized using a cross-validated grid search. An SVM with a polynomial kernel function gave the best results (accuracy = 96.50%). The trained classifier was used to classify a new UM (UM5) into one of the four existing UMs. UM5 was classified as UM1 with a confidence score of 95.17% by the SVM model.

Following our assumption that baseline policies can also perform well with similar user models, we test how the baseline policies perform with the new user model. More specifically, we ran N = 100 episodes with zero learning and exploration rates, in order to get an estimation of the expected total returns and success rates for UM5 using the different BPs. We also apply BP5 to ensure that it is an optimal policy for UM5 (Fig. 5). Apart from BP5 being the best policy for UM5, we observe that BP1 performs the best compared to the other BPs, which supports our assumption that BPs can perform well for similar UMs.

5 Discussion and Limitations

The main contribution of this paper is a domain-specific approach for personalization of a robot's behavior towards a new user, based on a classification of a set of learned user models and their corresponding baseline policies. We demonstrate our approach with simulate data in order to get insights for its applicability in realistic human-robot interactions. Our results indicate that the learned baseline policies can perform best on the user models they have been trained, but they can also perform well with models of users with similar behaviors. In the provided test example, simulated user models (UMs) correspond to users with different interaction styles. Each of the four simulated UMs represented different potential users: a child with different likelihood to interact (from low to high) and preferences for the robot emotions they interact with (e.g. happy or sad behavior for UM1, happy and content behavior for UM2). Another user model UM5, used for evaluation, represents a child with a previously unseen profile - i.e. a child who is moderately likely to interact with surprise, sad, and happy behavior, but unlikely with angry behavior. The results showed that classifying a new user into one of the existing models to select an appropriate baseline policy can be used as personalization approach. Similar approaches have been used by [15], where personalization takes place through reinforcement learning for longer-term interaction, while our approach focuses on how to generalize to unseen users (UM5) based on existing data (user models and policies) from past short-term interactions. One of the main limitations of our approach is that it aims towards a real-world deployment, but uses simulated data. However, the interaction has been carefully designed with respect to real-life clinical conditions and naturally overcomes well-known problems of RL such as the "cold start" problem. Our ongoing work includes the collection of real interaction data, towards a set of user models and their corresponding policies [19]. To do so, we need to explore and develop more advanced methods for user modeling and personalization [17], as well as for policy learning to enable online learning for interactive personalization [3,10,14].

6 Conclusion

We proposed a personalization approach which can enable a social robot to select an appropriate behavior for a new user during human-robot interaction. More specifically, the approach includes an assessment phase which classifies a new user into one of the existing user models based on interaction data and a set of existing baseline policies, determined via reinforcement learning. Our results indicate that BPs perform the best with their corresponding UM, but can also perform well for similar UMs. Limitations of this work include the use of simulated data and baseline approaches for user modeling and RL. Ongoing work includes the collection of interaction data from real users in order to build a more realistic collection of user models and their corresponding policies.

References

1. Beran, T.N., Ramirez-Serrano, A., Vanderkooi, O.G., Kuhn, S.: Humanoid robotics in health care: an exploration of children's and parents' emotional reactions. J. Health Psychol. **20**(7), 984–989 (2015)
2. Cifuentes, C.A., Pinto, M.J., Céspedes, N., Múnera, M.: Social robots in therapy and care. Curr. Robot. Rep. **1**, 59–74 (2020)
3. Clabaugh, C., et al.: Long-term personalization of an in-home socially assistive robot for children with autism spectrum disorders. Front. Robot. AI **6**, 110 (2019)
4. Cummings, E.A., Reid, G.J., Finley, G.A., McGrath, P.J., Ritchie, J.A.: Prevalence and source of pain in pediatric inpatients. Pain **68**(1), 25–31 (1996)
5. Den Hengst, F., Grua, E.M., el Hassouni, A., Hoogendoorn, M.: Reinforcement learning for personalization: a systematic literature review. Data Sci. **3**(2), 107–147 (2020)
6. Ferrari, O.I., Zhang, F., Braam, A.A., van Gurp, J.A.M., Broz, F., Barakova, E.I.: Design of child-robot interactions for comfort and distraction from post-operative pain and distress. In: Companion of the 2023 ACM/IEEE International Conference on Human-Robot Interaction. p. 686-690. HRI 2023, Association for Computing Machinery, New York, NY, USA (2023). https://doi.org/10.1145/3568294.3580174, https://doi.org/10.1145/3568294.3580174
7. Gasteiger, N., Hellou, M., Ahn, H.S.: Factors for personalization and localization to optimize human-robot interaction: a literature review. Int. J. Soc. Robot. **15**(4), 689–701 (2023)
8. Gönül, S., Namlı, T., Coşar, A., Toroslu, İH.: A reinforcement learning based algorithm for personalization of digital, just-in-time, adaptive interventions. Artif. Intell. Med. **115**, 102062 (2021)
9. Gordon, G., et al.: Affective personalization of a social robot tutor for children's second language skills. In: Proceedings of the AAAI Conference on Artificial Intelligence, vol. 30 (2016)

10. Hassouni, A., Hoogendoorn, M., van Otterlo, M., Barbaro, E.: Personalization of health interventions using cluster-based reinforcement learning. In: Miller, T., Oren, N., Sakurai, Y., Noda, I., Savarimuthu, B.T.R., Cao Son, T. (eds.) PRIMA 2018. LNCS (LNAI), vol. 11224, pp. 467–475. Springer, Cham (2018). https://doi.org/10.1007/978-3-030-03098-8_31
11. James, J., Ghai, S., Rao, K., Sharma, N.: Effectiveness of "animated cartoons" as a distraction strategy on behavioural response to pain perception among children undergoing venipuncture. Nurs. Midwifery Res. J. 8(3), 198–209 (2012)
12. Jibb, L.A., et al.: Using the mediport humanoid robot to reduce procedural pain and distress in children with cancer: a pilot randomized controlled trial. Pediatr. Blood Cancer 65(9), e27242 (2018)
13. Logan, D.E., et al.: Social robots for hospitalized children. Pediatrics 144(1), e20181511 (2019)
14. Moro, C., Nejat, G., Mihailidis, A.: Learning and personalizing socially assistive robot behaviors to aid with activities of daily living. ACM Trans. Hum.-Robot Interact. (THRI) 7(2), 1–25 (2018)
15. Park, H.W., Grover, I., Spaulding, S., Gomez, L., Breazeal, C.: A model-free affective reinforcement learning approach to personalization of an autonomous social robot companion for early literacy education. In: Proceedings of the AAAI Conference on Artificial Intelligence, vol. 33, pp. 687–694 (2019)
16. Rossi, S., Larafa, M., Ruocco, M.: Emotional and behavioural distraction by a social robot for children anxiety reduction during vaccination. Int. J. Soc. Robot. 12, 765–777 (2020)
17. Spaulding, S.L.: Lifelong Personalization for Social Robot Learning Companions: Interactive Student Modeling Across Tasks and Over Time. Ph.D. thesis, Massachusetts Institute of Technology (2022)
18. Trost, M.J., Ford, A.R., Kysh, L., Gold, J.I., Mataric, M.: Socially assistive robots for helping pediatric distress and pain: a review of current evidence and recommendations for future research and practice. Clin. J. Pain 35(5), 451–458 (2019)
19. Tsiakas, K., Abujelala, M., Makedon, F.: Task engagement as personalization feedback for socially-assistive robots and cognitive training. Technologies 6(2), 49 (2018)
20. Tsiakas, Konstantinos, Dagioglou, Maria, Karkaletsis, Vangelis, Makedon, Fillia: Adaptive robot assisted therapy using interactive reinforcement learning. In: Agah, Arvin, Cabibihan, John-John., Howard, Ayanna M.., Salichs, Miguel A.., He, Hongsheng (eds.) ICSR 2016. LNCS (LNAI), vol. 9979, pp. 11–21. Springer, Cham (2016). https://doi.org/10.1007/978-3-319-47437-3_2
21. Yasemin, M., Kasımoğlu, Y., Kocaaydın, S., Karslı, E., İnce, E.B.T., İnce, G.: Management of dental anxiety in children using robots. In: 2016 24th Signal Processing and Communication Application Conference (SIU), pp. 237–240. IEEE (2016)

EGG: AI-Based Interactive Design Object for Managing Post-operative Pain in Children

Jing Li[(✉)][iD], Kuankuan Chen[iD], Liuyiyi Yang[iD], Milou Mutsaers[iD], and Emilia Barakova[iD]

Eindhoven University of Technology, Eindhoven 5612AZ, The Netherlands
{j.li2,e.i.barakova}@tue.nl,
{k.chen2,l.yang,m.m.e.mutsaers}@student.tue.nl

Abstract. The anticipation and effective management of pain in pediatric patients is an essential component of healthcare. AI-based interactive technologies can enhance postoperative pain management by objectively measuring pain and providing an effective distraction for children. This paper presents EGG, an AI-based interactive toy designed to estimate individual pain levels and subsequently engage the children through an immersive experience utilizing visual, tactile, and audio stimuli. An exploratory study involving 16 university students was conducted to assess EGG's capability to distract users from stressful situations. The findings indicate that EGG serves as an effective tool for shifting attention away from stressful tasks and towards interactions with the device. This study explores and demonstrates an approach to utilizing AI in the design of smart interactive products for pain measurement and management.

Keywords: Pain management · Machine Learning · Interactive toy

1 Introduction

Adequate postoperative pain assessment and management in pediatric patients can significantly improve their comfort and quality of life [18]. Postoperative pain can lead to distress and anxiety among children, which may prolong their recovery and hospitalization [18]. However, effectively evaluating and addressing pain in pediatric populations during the postoperative phase poses a significant challenge, as pain is subjective and varies from one individual to another [18]. Therefore, it is essential to utilize pain assessment tools that allow for an objective assessment of pain severity [18].

Numerous strategies have been explored to address the stress experienced by children following postoperative procedures. Alongside pharmacological interventions, a range of non-pharmacological solutions, such as music therapy [11], tactile toys [13], and robot interventions [21] have been validated in hospitals

---

J. Li and K. Chen—Both authors contributed equally to this research.

J. M. Ferrández Vicente et al. (Eds.): IWINAC 2024, LNCS 14674, pp. 322–331, 2024.
https://doi.org/10.1007/978-3-031-61140-7_31

for pain management. Biofeedback has gained growing popularity [19] since it provides users with real-time feedback, based on active sensing. Nonetheless, the efficacy of most biofeedback applications in managing severe pain among pediatric patients is constrained by their limited distraction capabilities [19]. While social robots, connected to wearables for measuring stress-related physiological signals have been deployed [21] this approach is also constrained because the robot may not always be near the child, particularly when the child is confined to bed following surgery.

We designed EGG to monitor and manage postoperative pain in children, employing AI for pain detection and assessment, alongside interactive strategies for diverting children's attention away from their discomfort. The design features an intelligent and interactive EGG model, depicted in Fig. 1a accompanied by a wearable brace as illustrated in Fig. 1b. We conducted an exploratory experiment with university students to evaluate if EGG can distract users during stressful events. Data collected from 16 participants were analyzed, and the findings underscore EGG's effectiveness in both diverting attention and engaging users during stressful situations.

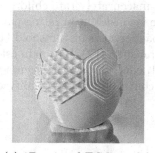

(a) 3D printed EGG model.   (b) Interaction between EGG and the brace.

Fig. 1. Prototype of EGG model and the wearable brace.

2 Related Works

2.1 Interactive Therapies for Pain Management in Children

Music therapy has been recognized for its substantial impact on pain management in children [9]. It has been shown to offer significant benefits for child patients experiencing pain, providing both physical comfort and a sense of inner peace [9]. Center et al. [10] highlighted that music therapy also can positively affect children. Engaging with music through melody, rhythm, harmony, pitch, and various other musical elements can aid individuals in pain, fostering both physical and emotional well-being [11]. Thus, interactive music devices have the potential to become a solution to pain relief.

The use of distraction as a method for alleviating acute pain in children has gained notable attention. Specifically, tactile stimulation has emerged as a key strategy in diverting children's attention away from their pain, thereby extending their pain tolerance duration [14]. Tactile toys, which cater to children's sensory needs [12], have been observed to hold children's engagement significantly longer than other types of toys. Moreover, the research conducted by Hong et al. [12] revealed that children's experience of discomfort diminished when they interacted with tactile objects. Overall, Song et al. [15] suggest that incorporating natural therapy through auditory, tactile, and visual means can ease stress.

2.2 Pain Assessment Through Heart Rate Variability (HRV) Detection and Machine Learning

HRV can indicate heart activity and overall autonomic health [2]. HRV is impacted by stress used for an objective assessment of psychological health and stress [2]. A higher HRV is indicative of good overall health and low-stress levels, whereas a lower HRV is indicative of stress, fatigue, and pain [3].

Demyttenaere et al. [4] studied pain treatment thresholds for children after major surgery. They found that parents and nurses inaccurately rate children's pain treatment thresholds. Furthermore, nurses were inconsistent in rating pain, and parents frequently overestimated their child's pain treatment threshold [4]. ML as an alternative solution has been applied to translate HRV into pain estimation in many studies [16]. Hence, integrating ML can enhance the accuracy of detecting each individual's pain and, therefore, contribute to the quality of healthcare.

3 Method

We adopted a research-through-design methodology [17], to explore how to design for managing pain in children. We designed an interactive toy called EGG, to facilitate exploration into attention diversion strategies aimed at mitigating postoperative pain among children. Recognizing the vulnerability inherent to our intended demographic, a pilot study involving 16 university students was conducted and is reported in this paper. It aimed to evaluate the usability and effectiveness of EGG as a distraction tool, and the results of this exploratory study lay the groundwork for future research, emphasizing the use of connected devices and ML technologies to improve interactive experiences in targeted scenarios.

3.1 EGG Design

EGG includes two parts: An egg-shaped model and a wearable finger brace. The EGG model is illustrated in Fig. 2a. The upper part is covered with plush material, offering a tactile experience that is both comfortable and soothing for children, designed to capture their attention and alleviate stress. The middle part consists of seven tactile pads adorned with three-dimensional textures inspired by elements of nature, such as waves and flowers, to enrich the sensory experience. The EGG is embedded with a vibrator at the top and a speaker positioned centrally. Each of the seven tactile pads is equipped with an LED light and a magnetic switch, which are activated by a magnet embedded within the wearable finger brace, as illustrated in Fig. 2b. Activation of the magnet triggers the vibrator, producing a gentle vibration around the plush part while the speaker emits distinct sound frequencies. Each pad is associated with a unique sound frequency, adding auditory diversity to the tactile engagement. Moreover, the LED lights enhance the visual appeal by illuminating the tactile pads. To further augment its interactive potential, the EGG is designed with a tumbler base, enhancing its playfulness. The wearable finger brace covers the middle finger and allows children to freely explore tactile surfaces with their other fingers, maintaining sensory engagement. The wrist area of the brace is embedded with Photoplethysmogram (PPG) sensor for measuring heart rate signals, especially heartbeats' time intervals that are used to calculate HRV [1]. Collected data is transmitted to a cloud-based ML model via Bluetooth for pain prediction. Moreover, a magnet embedded in the fingertip of the brace enables dynamic interactions with the EGG model. Depending on the assessed pain intensity, an interaction with EGG is initiated, primarily focusing on distraction. Should the algorithm detect an absence of pain, EGG remains inactive, ensuring its activation is both timely and relevant to the child's needs.

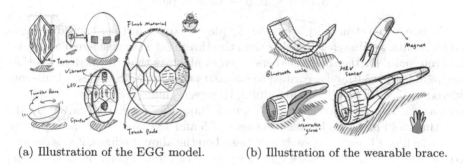

(a) Illustration of the EGG model.   (b) Illustration of the wearable brace.

Fig. 2. Sketches of EGG model and wearable brace.

Interaction Scenario. Post-operation, children are equipped with the brace, which facilitates the collection of HRV data. This data is then analyzed by the ML model to assess the children's pain levels in real-time. When a high level of pain is detected, one of the EGG's touchpads illuminates, serving to capture and divert the children's attention away from their discomfort. As the children engage with the illuminated pad, the magnet embedded in their brace triggers the emission of musical sounds and vibrations specific to that pad. Concurrently, the initially lit pad dims, and another pad lights up, guiding the child to the next interaction point. This sequence of touching the illuminated pads produces a soothing melody, designed to provide a calming effect.

3.2 Learning Algorithm

This section introduces how the learning algorithm will be integrated into the overall design of the EGG. The integration was not completed when the described research took place, which does not influence the reported results.

To predict the pain level using HRV, a dataset that contains one or more features describing HRV values is required. The ML model is trained on an acquired dataset annotated with labels, subsequently to forecast the pain level from novel, unlabeled HRV data collected via the wearable sensor. Since wrongly classifying for pain/no pain has the same loss, whereas predicting on a scale of 0–10 has a high loss, a regression model is selected. To decide on the exact, fine-tuned supervised regression model, an iteration would be executed over several options for optimal performance and for prevention of overfitting. So, if the prediction is a pain level on a scale from 0.0 to 10.0, an inference of the prediction should be applied. This inference translates the new data point's prediction to retrieve a final prediction of whether the child is in pain or not. To retrieve the prediction, the following rule has been constructed Eq. 1:

Say x represents the predicted pain level, then inference results in:

$$0.0 \leq x \leq 3.3 \rightarrow \text{Label: "no pain"} \tag{1}$$
$$3.3 < x \leq 10.0 \rightarrow \text{Label: "pain"}$$

Gerbershagen et al. [5] identified NRS equal to 4 to be the tolerable pain threshold for adults; a value that is higher than the threshold was considered moderate-to-severe pain. Furthermore, Gerbershagen et al. state that the median satisfactory pain level is 3.0, and according to Boonstra et al. [6] NRS values ≤ 5 are considered to be mild pain levels for adults. However, children are more sensitive to pain, as was found by Saxena et al. [7]. In addition, Haslam [8] concluded that the pain threshold increases between the ages of 5 and 18 years; hence, pain perception is declining from a very early age. Based on the above findings, it was decided to place the inference boundary value for pain in children slightly below the found NRS thresholds for adults, i.e., the cut-off was set at 3.3. The principle of the model described in the above paragraphs is illustrated in Fig. 3.

Following the evaluation and testing of the model, we can determine its suitability for addressing the specific problem of this project. Essentially, this process allows us to assess whether the model delivers consistent performance across various data subsets, indicating its potential for generalization and robustness. In the next iteration, the EGG will explicate why the learning algorithm concludes if the child is in pain or not, to improve the explainability of the system [20].

3.3 Experiment Design

The aim of this study was to evaluate the effectiveness of EGG in diverting attention from experiences akin to postoperative pain. Thus, the physiological data collection and ML model were not implemented in this preliminary experiment. Given

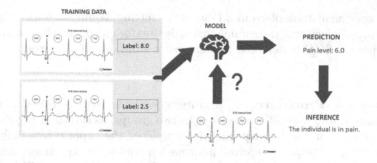

Fig. 3. The supervised learning model, with training data and a new, unlabeled HRV value as input, a prediction on the pain NRS scale as output, and an output translation to the label "pain" or "no pain".

the sensitivity and vulnerability surrounding post-operative children, We conducted an exploratory experiment with university students to investigate EGG's potential to distract users from stressful events. Pain and stress induce comparable physiological arousal [3]. Thus, we experimented on stressful events that induced a similar physiological response from participants as in pain experiences. Participants were required to complete games in a specific timeframe to provoke stress. Two distinct games were designed that require different types of attention from participants: "Spot the Difference(S-T-D)" where participants need to find all the differences in two alike photos in a 15-minute timeframe, and "Puzzles" where participants need to move puzzle pieces to form an image in a 5-minute timeframe; both facilitated through a digital platform. Participants were randomly assigned to one of two groups in a controlled experiment setup, ensuring each group engaged in the same games, either with or without the EGG distraction, to facilitate a between-subjects comparison. Additionally, a within-subjects study was conducted within the groups to further refine our understanding. This approach aims to reduce variability in the data analysis attributable to individual differences among participants, such as gaming proficiency, attention span, and levels of fatigue. The design of the experiment is depicted in Fig. 4a.

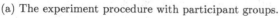

(a) The experiment procedure with participant groups.   (b) The setup with EGG.

Fig. 4. Overview of the experiment design.

The experiment took place in a laboratory setting, equipped with a table, a chair, a laptop to facilitate the gaming tasks, devices for video recording, and EGG. The setup with EGG is depicted in a snapshot from one of the experiments in Fig. 4b.

Participants & Procedure. 16 university students were recruited and randomly assigned into four different setups in two groups, as shown in Fig. 4a. Participants from each group independently completed the experiment. Before the experiment, all participants received information about the experiment and data policy from the instructor and signed a consent form. At the onset of Phase 2, the instructor initiated the video recording, activated the gaming tasks, and set the time countdown. Participants in the 'without EGG' groups were tasked with completing each game round within a specified timeframe. Similarly, participants in the 'with EGG' groups embarked on the initial game round without EGG within the same timeframe. Subsequently, the instructor came into the room to set EGG on the table, assisting participants in donning the brace. After the instructor exited the room, the participant commenced the second round of the game task as the previous round. Following Phase 2, the research team carried out interviews with the 'with EGG' group participants. These discussions focused on gathering insights into each participant's user experience, particularly their interactions with the EGG and its effectiveness as a distraction tool.

3.4   Data Analysis

The analysis of this experiment encompasses both quantitative and qualitative data, including time records, video recordings, observational notes, and interviews. Quantitative data were derived from the time and video records, while qualitative insights were extracted from the observational and interview records.

For participants in the 'without EGG' group, recorded data encompassed the duration of both the first and second game rounds. For those in the 'with EGG' group, recorded metrics included the duration of the first and second game rounds, the frequency and total duration of gaze directed towards the EGG, and the frequency and total duration of interactions with the EGG. We evaluated the difference in time between the two game rounds for each participant, calculating the time ratio (percentage) of the second round relative to the first. This time ratio formula is given in Eq. 2. This approach aimed to mitigate the influence of confounding factors such as diminished attention or fatigue, which could affect performance across consecutive game rounds. By comparing the time ratios between the two groups in two different games, we assessed EGG's effectiveness in diverting attention from the game tasks. The metrics related to the frequency and duration of gaze and interaction with EGG were analyzed in conjunction with the game-time ratios to evaluate how EGG influenced and distracted participants.

$$\text{Time Ratio} = \frac{T_2}{T_1} \times 100\%$$

(2)

T_1 = time taken in 1st game round, T_2 = time taken in 2nd game round

4 Results

We calculated the time ratio of two rounds of game tasks for each participant and compared the data between group 1 and group 2. The calculated time ratios for each participant are represented in Fig. 5. It is important to note that, among the eight participants in group 2 of the 'with EGG' experiment for round 2, one in Puzzle game and one in S-T-D game were unable to finish the task within the allocated timeframe. The time ratio of every participant in the 'with EGG' groups were higher than those in the 'without EGG' groups for the same game task. This indicates that participants spent more time accomplishing games when they were distracted by EGG.

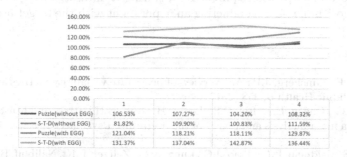

	1	2	3	4
Puzzle(without EGG)	106.53%	107.27%	104.20%	108.32%
S-T-D(without EGG)	81.82%	109.90%	100.83%	111.59%
Puzzle(with EGG)	121.04%	118.21%	118.11%	129.87%
S-T-D(with EGG)	131.37%	137.04%	142.87%	136.44%

Fig. 5. The overview of the time ratio of all participants from two groups.

We observed that all participants from group 2 looked at EGG multiple times when EGG illuminated. The average duration of observation on EGG is 4 s in Puzzle game, and 3 s in S-T-D game. Two of the participants in group 2 interacted with EGG during Puzzle game, and three of the participants interacted with EGG during S-T-D game. The average duration of interaction with EGG is 9.5 s in Puzzle game, and 5.7 s in S-T-D game. Combining the results from interview records, "light" was mentioned by all interviewees as the main distracting factor during the experiment, and "musical sound" was the main factor that attracted them to interact with EGG.

5 Discussion and Conclusion

This study aims to explore the use of intelligent and interactive techniques to manage postoperative pain in children. Through initial desk research and design exploration, EGG was developed and utilized in an exploratory experiment. Analysis of

the data gathered suggests that EGG was feasible in offering users a degree of interaction and distraction during stressful situations. Nonetheless, the study has several limitations, which warrant further attention. Additionally, there are avenues
for future research and design exploration that subsequent researchers and designers can pursue.

First, HRV detection was not implemented in the experiment, which means
EGG could not gauge participants' pain levels or stress indices. Instead, EGG was
programmed to light up one of its touchpads every 1.5 s to attract the participant's
attention. Observations and participant self-reports indicated that stress was not
evident in the experiment for a few participants. Thus, the efficacy of EGG's distraction effect in mitigating postoperative pain in children remains unconfirmed.
Secondly, the ML model has not yet been implemented or thoroughly assessed. To
properly evaluate the ML model, an experiment involving medical staff, parents,
pediatric patients, and researchers should be established. Within this framework,
various means of interactions should be conducted to evaluate the effective EGG-
child interaction strategies for diverting children's attention from their discomfort.

To summarize, for EGG to fully realize its potential and efficacy in pain management, several steps are required: 1) acquiring a dataset, 2) implementing a
learning algorithm, and 3) conducting an experiment with the target user group.

References

1. Shaffer, F., Ginsberg, J.P.: An overview of heart rate variability metrics and norms.
   Front. Public Health 5, 258 (2017)
2. Kim, H.G., Cheon, E.J., Bai, D.S., Lee, Y.H., Koo, B.H.: Stress and heart rate variability: a meta-analysis and review of the literature. Psychiatry Investig. 15(3), 235
   (2018)
3. Evans, S., Seidman, L.C., Tsao, J.C., Lung, K.C., Zeltzer, L.K., Naliboff, B.D.: Heart
   rate variability as a biomarker for autonomic nervous system response differences
   between children with chronic pain and healthy control children. J. Pain Res., 449–
   457 (2013)
4. Demyttenaere, S., Finley, G.A., Johnston, C.C., McGrath, P.J.: Pain treatment
   thresholds in children after major surgery. Clin. J. Pain 17(2), 173–177 (2001)
5. Gerbershagen, H.J., Rothaug, J., Kalkman, C.J., Meissner, W.: Determination of
   moderate-to-severe postoperative pain on the numeric rating scale: a cut-off point
   analysis applying four different methods. Br. J. Anaesth. 107(4), 619–626 (2011)
6. Boonstra, A.M., et al.: Cut-off points for mild, moderate, and severe pain on the
   numeric rating scale for pain in patients with chronic musculoskeletal pain: variability and influence of sex and catastrophizing. Front. Psychol. 7, 1466 (2016)
7. Saxena, I., Kumar, M., Barath, A.S., Verma, A., Garg, S.: Effect of age on response
   to experimental pain in normal Indian males. J. Clin. Diagn. Res. JCDR 9(9), CC05
   (2015)
8. Haslam, D.R.: Age and the perception of pain. Psychonomic Sci. 15(2), 86–87 (1969)
9. Aydin, D., Sahiner, N.: Effects of music therapy and distraction cards on pain relief
   during phlebotomy in children. Appl. Nurs. Res. 33, 164–168 (2017)
10. Center, E., Center, C., Center, P.: Music therapy (2013)
11. Bailey, L.: Music therapy in pain management. J. Pain Symptom Manage. 1, 25–28
    (1986)

12. Hong, K.: Tactile Toys: Therapy for tactile dysfunction. Int. J. Technol. Inclusive Educ. (IJTIE) **7**, 1295–1297 (2018)
13. Mary-Ellen, H., Janet, P., Karen, W., Rebecca Pillai, R., Joel, K., Taddio, A.: A randomized-controlled trial of parent-led tactile stimulation to reduce pain during infant immunization injections The Clin. J. Pain **30**(3), 259–265 (2014)
14. Karafotias, G., Korres, G., Teranishi, A., Park, W., Eid, M.: Mid-air tactile stimulation for pain distraction. IEEE Trans. Haptics **11**, 185–191 (2017)
15. Song, C., Ikei, H., Miyazaki, Y.: Physiological effects of nature therapy: a review of the research in Japan. Int. J. Environ. Res. Public Health **13**, 781 (2016)
16. Werner, P., Lopez-Martinez, D., Walter, S., Al-Hamadi, A., Gruss, S., Picard, R.: Automatic recognition methods supporting pain assessment: a survey. IEEE Trans. Affect. Comput. **13**, 530–552 (2019)
17. Koskinen, I., Zimmerman, J., Binder, T., Redstrom, J., Wensveen, S.: Design research through practice: From the lab, field, and showroom. IEEE Trans. Prof. Commun. **56**, 262–263 (2013)
18. Zieliński, J., Morawska-Kochman, M., Zatoński, T.: Pain assessment and management in children in the postoperative period: a review of the most commonly used postoperative pain assessment tools, new diagnostic methods and the latest guidelines for postoperative pain therapy in children. Adv. Clin. Exp. Med. **29**, 365–74 (2020)
19. Gatchel, R., Robinson, R., Pulliam, C., Maddrey, A.: Biofeedback with pain patients: evidence for its effectiveness. Semin. Pain Med. **1**, 55–66 (2003)
20. Górriz, J., Illán, I.: Others Computational approaches to Explainable artificial intelligence: advances in theory, applications and trends. Inform. Fusion **100**, 101945 (2023)
21. Ferrari, O., Zhang, F., Braam, A., Van Gurp, J., Broz, F.,Barakova, E.: Design of Child-robot Interactions for Comfort and Distraction from Post-operative Pain and Distress. In: Companion Of The 2023 ACM/IEEE International Conference On Human-Robot Interaction, pp. 686–690 (2023)

Cepstral Space Projection
on the Evaluation of Autistic Speech:
A Pilot Study

Andrés Gómez-Rodellar[1] , Marina Jodra-Chuan[2,3] ,
José Manuel Ferrández-Vicente[4] , and Pedro Gómez-Vilda[5(✉)]

[1] Usher Institute, Faculty of Medicine, University of Edinburgh, Edinburgh, UK
a.gomezrodellar@ed.ac.uk
[2] Department of Personality, Assessment and Clinical Psychology,
Faculty of Education, Complutense University of Madrid, C/ Rector Royo Villanova
1, 28040 Madrid, Spain
majodra@ucm.es
[3] Asociación Nuevo Horizonte, Comunidad de Madrid 43, Las Rozas de Madrid,
Madrid 28231, Spain
[4] Campus Muralla del Mar, Universidad Politécnica de Cartagena, Pza. Hospital 1,
30202 Cartagena, Spain
jm.ferrandez@upct.es
[5] NeuSpeLab, CTB, Universidad Politécnica de Madrid, 28220 Pozuelo de Alarcón,
Madrid, Spain
pedro.gomezv@upm.es

Abstract. The objective of the present study is to define potential
biomarkers from the phonation of people with Autistic Spectrum Disorder (ASD), for a better description of the syndrome functional behavior regarding stress when performing phonation tests, in sight of developing specific rehabilitation protocols to improve their communication
skills. The study included sustained vowel utterances from three male
and three female participants with ASD and intellectual disability to
be compared with normative participants by gender, associated with
neurological stress in performing vocalization tests. A methodology for
visualizing and interpreting clustering plots of mel-frequency cepstral
2-dimensional representations of phonation has been proposed. The projection technique used shows a clear differentiated behavior between ASD
and normative phonation descriptions.

Keywords: Autistic Spectrum Disorder · Speech Acoustic Analysis ·
Mel-Frequency Cepstral Coefficients · Explainability

This research has been possible thanks to a doctoral scholarship under grant number:
MR/N013166/1, funded by the MRC and CMVM, U. of Edinburgh. The authors wish
to thank Asociación Nuevo Horizonte participants for their most valuable support.

J. M. Ferrández Vicente et al. (Eds.): IWINAC 2024, LNCS 14674, pp. 332–341, 2024.
https://doi.org/10.1007/978-3-031-61140-7_32

1 Introduction

Autistic Spectrum Disorders (ASD) are a heterogeneous group of behavioral alterations that originate from neurobiological factors and manifest during childhood. Approximately 2% of the population is affected by ASD [1]. These disorders impact social communication, featuring patterns of restricted and repetitive behavior. Additionally, they often co-occur with other disorders or difficulties, such as motor deficits, intellectual disability, or other comorbidities [2]. These disorders persist throughout an individual's life, and unlike other medical conditions, there is no specific biological test for diagnosing ASD. Instead, diagnosis primarily relies on clinical evaluation. Detecting ASD early and implementing intervention programs across different environments where the child resides can lead to improvements in autistic symptoms, cognitive abilities, and overall functional adaptation. One of the greatest difficulties in early diagnosing ASD is the lack of biomarker tests, so one of the major challenges is finding markers that enable early diagnoses, classify the severity of symptoms, or assess the effectiveness of interventions. There are some scientific studies that discuss the possibility of defining biomarkers from the phonation of individuals with ASD [3], but the methodologies employed are highly varied, and most of them are based on prosody, so individuals without fully developed verbal language, but still able of phonating are excluded from the studies. Speech and voice convey significant information about emotional activation and neurological impairments (cognitive or neuromotor). Individuals with ASD exhibit emotional and neurological alterations, thus their voice and speech seem to be good candidates for searching for disorder-related biomarkers [4]. Another current challenge is accompanying this population in their aging process. ASD was first included in diagnostic manuals in 1980 (APA, 1980), so the first diagnoses receiving specialized interventions belong to individuals who are currently between 45 and 55 years old. Currently, there isn't much research on this topic, but an early aging of the population is being observed, likely caused by variables such as increased comorbidity or medical issues, use of psychotropic drugs, and risky behaviors or self-injury. The risk of mortality in individuals with ASD is higher than the rest of the population [2]. There are studies in the literature that relate voice and aging, and although they are not conclusive, they provide some indicators that may be useful for monitoring and quantifying physiological changes with age. In the case of individuals with ASD, no work has been identified in the literature until the beginning of this pioneering project, which has already been able to provide some scientific evidence [4–6]. From what has been exposed, it seems that the characteristics of ASD phonation has not been deeply studied. There is not even known evidence on a common behavior pattern of people with ASD as far as phonation and speech are concerned. Therefore, the present study is intended to offer some preliminary insights on this issue using phenomenologic descriptions from specific participants from Asociación Nuevo Horizonte, to serve as potential behavioral biomarkers for developing more intensive and extensive experimental designs to grab ASD characteristics and progress through inexpensive and ubiquitous speech analyses. The paper is organized as follows: A description of the fundamentals supporting the study is provided in Sect. 2. The materials and methods proposed are presented in Sect. 3. Section 4 presents the main characteristics of a recording from a specific person with ASD, and the results from confronting six persons with ASD regarding six normative participants. Section 5 offers a brief discussion of the results. Conclusions and final remarks are provided in Sect. 6.

2   Fundamentals

People with neurological disorders may manifest functional altered patterns in speech and phonation, as in fluency and prosody with slow and difficult language, in dysarthrias manifested as dyskinetic facial, jaw, or lingual movements, or as dysphonias, showing perturbations in the fundamental frequency. ASD manifests some features in common with neurological disorders, therefore it is expected that speech alterations may appear as a consequence. The compilation work by Fusaroli [3] explaining on whether speech might become a marker of ASD offers a wide overview and points to the fact that most of the studies of voice in people with ASD stand mainly on the description of prosody. The characteristics analyzed in the works reviewed are the mean and the variance of the fundamental frequency, and the intensity profile of the phonation, as well as fluency features, such as syllable and word duration, pauses, speech rate, and voice quality in terms of simple perturbation features (jitter and shimmer). The main conclusion of Fusaroli's work is that there is no enough evidence of acoustic markers capable of predicting clinical characteristics of the syndrome.

Autistic speech refers to patterns of disfluent speech observed in individuals with autism. These speech patterns exhibit deviations in continuity, fluidity, ease of rate, and effort. Here are several different types of disfluency commonly associated with autistic speech:

- Stuttering: it occurs when a person knows the words they want to utter but physically struggles to produce them. Characteristics of stuttering include repetition of sounds (e.g., "s-s-s-speech"), repetition of syllables (e.g., "ru-ru-running"), prolongation of sounds (e.g., "sssspeech," "whaaat", or becoming "stuck" (blocked) on a sound (e.g., "s——speech"). During a stuttering block, the word may take time to be produced, and there may be struggled attempts at sound production or silence.
- Cluttering: it occurs when a person speaks too rapidly for their speech production system to handle. Characteristics of cluttering include fast speech rate, excessive repetitions of phrases, revisions of ideas, use of filler words like "um" or "uh", or over-coarticulation (sounds in words running together, syllables being deleted).
- Atypical disfluency: it occurs when the speaker has easy repetitions or prolongations of sounds at the ends of words (e.g., "speech-eech," "light-t," "misssss"). Sometimes, the repetitions occur after the speaker has completed the word. The length of pauses between repetitions varies, and additional thoughts may be inserted during the pause.

Some of the characteristics of ASD phonation when required to produce sustained vowel emissions are the utterance of too short and compulsive vowels (e.g., "ah-ah-ah"), or soft, asthenic or whispering utterances (e.g. "ᵃhhh").

The present approach is intended to capitalize on a mel-frequency cepstral description (MFCD) of autistic phonation. The main reason behind expressing speech and phonation in terms of MFCDs is due to the property of these descriptions to provide compact and highly relevant representations of the spectral and temporal patterns present in phonation and articulation [10].

3   Experimental Framework

3.1   Materials

This research is part of a project on the longitudinal study of six persons with ASD (three males and three females), speakers of Spanish, between 43 and 54 years old, suffering from ASD and intellectual disability. It is being conducted on the association *Nuevo Horizonte* in the municipality of Las Rozas de Madrid, Spain. A first study on the emotional stress under simple tests was already published using actigraphy ([4,6]). This new study is intended to extend the former one with an eye on speech and phonation.

The demographical data of participants is presented in Tables 1 and 2, giving the gender, age, and co-morbidities present in each ASD participant, as well as the Childhood Autism Rating Scale (CARS) ([7,8]) and Dysexecutive Questionnaire (DEX) scores [9]. The association *Nuevo Horizonte* authorized the signed consent for the experimental recordings in alignment of Helsinki Declaration Ethical Reccommendations.

Table 1. ASD Participants demographical data. M-: male participants; F-: female participants; CARS: Childhood Autism Rating Scale; DEX: Dysexecutive Questionnaire; SID: Severe Intellectual Disability; PE: Psychotic Episodes; E: Epilepsy; OCD: Obsesive-Compulsive Disorders; D: Dysthymia

Code	Gender	Age	Co-morbidities	CARS	DEX
A2	F	50	SID	41	51
A3	F	48	SID	41	35
A5	F	50	SID	45	45
A1	M	51	SID, PE, E	40	29
A4	M	43	SID, PE, E	41	44
A6	M	54	SID, OCD, D	42	32

The ASD participants in the study show a certain degree of intellectual disability, and sometimes have difficulty understanding the instructions on how to perform the tests (what sounds they must utter and how they have to). This

Table 2. Normative Participants; demographical data. M-: male participants; F-: female participants

Code	Gender	Age
N1	F	46
N2	F	51
N3	F	48
N4	M	49
N5	M	52
N6	M	50

prevents using complicated voice tests, therefore the voice recording protocol has been made very simple, and consists of uttering the vowel [a:] for more than one second in a sustained manner.

3.2 Recording Speech

The recordings were taken using a Sennheiser SK 300 G2A wireless cardioid Lavalier microphone, located 15 cm from the mouth, a Sennheiser EM 300 G2 receiver, and a Motu Traveller audio acquisition board connected to a portable PC. Speech was sampled at 44.1 kHz and encoded at 16-bit resolution in uncompressed .wav format. Recordings were taken in a relaxing environment within a quiet and homey room (no soundproof to avoid stressing ambience), where participants could feel comfortable at. The recording sessions extended over three to four minutes per ASD participant; longer durations were not advisable, because the participants might show signs of fatigue, stress, and anxiety. Original recordings had to be cleaned up for undesirable interfering sounds, as caregivers' speech, noise, screaming, laughter, etc. About 30% of total phonations have to be discarded for being too short to support robust biomarker estimation. Most vowel emissions were shorter than 2 s. The assistance of caregivers becomes essential to improve recording speed and quality, as they are used to daily interaction with ASD participants, in order to ensure their cooperation, coordinate instructions, make sure they are well understood, and transmit a sense of confidence and relax.

3.3 Methods

Several options are at hand when characterizing ASD speech, among them the modelling of the spectral behavior of sustained vowel phonation by means of mel-frequency cepstral contents, because MFCCs are known to be quite responsive to minor phonation and articulation perturbations [10], and constitute compact and accurate descriptors of spectral and temporal speech patterns. Several clustering and classification techniques could be applied to MFCC descriptions, having in mind that an important aspect to be preserved is that of explainability.

Visual representations as scatter plots are of crucial importance in this respect. The problem must be expressed thence as one of projection of a 14-dimensional space to a 2 or 3-dimensional one. A possibility to be explored was to create compressed representations preserving the distances of each element to be considered (from a MFCC vector sample) with respect to a normative database centroid or groups of centroids organized by participant and by gender datasets. Each distance would be characterized by a difference vector in module and angle. For such, each phonation of sustained emissions of a target vowel (commonly an [a:] due to its generalized use) will appear represented as a cloud of sample points for each MFCC estimation in the interval of study. Following this proposition, a selected vowel segment i from utterance j $\mathbf{s}_{i,j}$ in consecutive sliding windows with a duration of 30 ms each at a sampling frequency of 44,100 Hz was processed to produce 13 mel-frequency cepstral coefficients (MFCCs vector) plus the logarithm of the signal energy within an overlap of 20 ms resulting in a 14-dimensional feature vector $\mathbf{x}_{i,j} \in \Re^{1 \times 14}$.

Assuming that $\bar{\mathbf{x}}_j$ is the average centroid of utterance j, each i-th sample mfcc vector $\mathbf{x}_{i,j}$ will define a plane with respect to that average $\bar{\mathbf{x}}_j$. The difference between these two vectors will be given by $\mathbf{d}_{i,j} = \mathbf{x}_{i,j} - \bar{\mathbf{x}}_j$. A compact representation of each sample relative to the sample set average may be defined by the module of $\mathbf{d}_{i,j}$ and the relative angle with respect to $\bar{\mathbf{x}}_j$ as:

$$\beta_{i,j} = \arccos\left(\frac{\langle \mathbf{d}_{i,j}, \bar{\mathbf{x}}_j \rangle}{\|\mathbf{d}_{i,j}\|\|\bar{\mathbf{x}}_j\|}\right) \tag{1}$$

where $\langle \cdot, \cdot \rangle$ is the inner product between any two vectors. The fact that this approach is agnostic of the second and third quadrant display between the two vectors becomes an inconvenience, for which, to overcome it a complementary angle is also estimated:

$$\gamma_{i,j} = \arccos\left(\frac{\langle \mathbf{d}_{i,j}, \bar{\mathbf{y}}_j \rangle}{\|\mathbf{d}_{i,j}\|\|\bar{\mathbf{y}}_j\|}\right) \tag{2}$$

where the average reference $\bar{\mathbf{y}}_{i,j}$ is a new vector orthogonal to $\bar{\mathbf{x}}_{i,j}$, built on the following orthogonalization premises:

$$\bar{\mathbf{y}}_j = \bar{\mathbf{x}}_{i,j}\bar{\mathbf{x}}_{i,j}^T \mathbf{v} - \mathbf{v}\bar{\mathbf{x}}_{i,j}^T \bar{\mathbf{x}}_{i,j} \tag{3}$$

where $\mathbf{v}$ may be any arbitrary vector not parallel to $\bar{\mathbf{x}}_{i,j}$ such as: $\langle \bar{\mathbf{x}}_{i,j}, \mathbf{v} \rangle \neq 0$. Now, depending on the value of $\gamma_{i,j}$ the following decision on the sign of the angle between $\mathbf{d}_{i,j}$ and $\bar{\mathbf{x}}_{i,j}$ will be:

$$\alpha_{i,j} = \begin{cases} -\beta_{i,j} & \text{if } \gamma_{i,j} > \pi/2 \\ \beta_{i,j} & \text{otherwise} \end{cases} \tag{4}$$

4 Results

As it was mentioned in the introduction, the characteristics of ASD phonation have been only shallowly studied. There is not even known evidence on a common behavior pattern of people with ASD as far as phonation and speech are concerned. Therefore, the present study is intended to offer some preliminary insights on this issue using phenomenologic descriptions from specific participants from *Asociación Nuevo Horizonte*, which cannot be generalizable. As a first sample, the EEG-band description of phonation from participant A3 following the methodology described in [11] is given in Fig. 1.

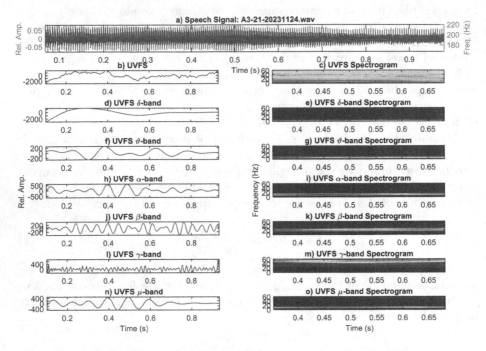

Fig. 1. An example of a maintained vowel [a:] utterance by a female ASD participant: (a) speech signal (blue) and fundamental frequency (red); (b) Vocal Fold Body Stress (VFBS); (c) Spectrogram of VFBS; (d) VFBS δ-band; (e) Spectrogram of δ-VFBS; (f) VFBS θ-band; (g) Spectrogram of θ-VFBS; (h) VFBS α-band; (i) Spectrogram of α-VFBS; (j) VFBS β-band; (k) Spectrogram of β-VFBS; (l) VFBS γ-band; (m) Spectrogram of γ-VFBS; (n) VFBS μ-band; (o) Spectrogram of μ-VFBS; (Color figure online)

Besides, the utterances of each participant by gender have been projected on a 2-dimensional subspace for easy graphical representation, as discussed in Subsect. 3.3. The MFCC datasets from each participant by gender are plotted in Fig. 2. Each circle in the plots corresponds to the projection of the 14-dimensional difference vector modulus $\|\mathbf{d}_{i,j}\|$ and angle $\alpha_{i,j}$ from each estimation window on the 2-dimensional visualization subspace, referred to each gender normative subset average vector $\mathbf{x}_{MR,FR} = mean\{\bar{\mathbf{x}}_j\}_{\forall j \in MR,FR}$, where MR and FR are the respective male and female normative subsets.

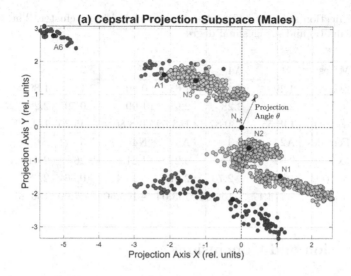

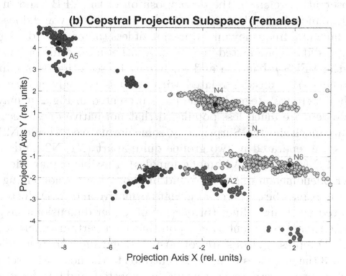

Fig. 2. Scatter plots on the MFCD vectors with respect to the correspondent normative average positions (N_M for $\mathbf{x}_M$ and N_F for $\mathbf{x}_F$). Normative samples by subject are plotted in yellow, green, and cyan. ASD samples are plotted by subject in deep blue, purple, and red. (Color figure online)

The modulus of each difference vector $\|\mathbf{d}_{i,j}\|$ gives the Euclidean distance to the reference centroid with respect to the normative subset $\mathbf{x}_{M,F}$. Similarly, the sample angles $\alpha_{i,j}$ with respect to the reference vector $\mathbf{x}_{M,F}$ point in different directions over the four quadrants. The moduli and angles for the subset difference averages $\bar{\mathbf{d}}_{jM,F}$ are given in Table 3.

Table 3. Projection samples and centroids for each subject's cluster. The angles are given in radians (r) and sexagesimal degrees (d).

Males:	A1	A4	A6	N1	N2	N3
$\|\bar{x}_{i,j}\|$:	4.29	2.44	7.68	0.80	2.14	1.89
$\alpha_{i,j}(r)$:	2.59	2.28	2.68	1.90	−0.79	2.29
$\alpha_{i,j}(d)$:	148.55	130.87	153.59	108.86	−45.25	131.29
Females:	A2	A3	A5	N4	N5	N6
$\|\bar{x}_{i,j}\|$:	2.54	5.14	9.27	1.21	2.26	2.01
$\alpha_{i,j}(r)$:	−1.99	−2.73	2.67	−1.84	−0.66	2.38
$\alpha_{i,j}(d)$:	−114.17	−156.54	153.04	−105.60	−37.99	136.26

5   Discussion and Conclusions

The first observation refers to the decomposition of the VFBS shown in Fig. 1 into EEG-like bands. It may be seen that the emission of the vowel does not show a stable fundamental frequency on a duration of less than a second, aligned with what was expected as commented in Sect. 2. Another interesting observation has to see with the VFBS μ-band (n and o). It may be seen that this band, which some researchers [12] consider related with ASD is strongly activated in the middle of the utterance. Regarding the plots presented in Fig. 2 it may be seen that ASD clusters are much less populated that normative ones, because ASD phonations are much shorter. Surprisingly, some normative (N1 and N2) and one ASD clusters are separated in two groups quite apart (N1, N2, and A1 among males, and N4, N6, A2, and A3 among females). Possible explanations for this intra-speaker phenomenon might be found in phonation tension changes during each utterance. It may be observed also that normative and ASD clusters may be easily separated by straight lines (projection of higher dimensional hyperplanes on the 2-dimensional representation), pointing to a certain different behavior as far as MFCD representations are concerned. Regarding the average distances given in Table 3 the distances from ASD centroids to the normative reference are larger than normative averages, as it would be expected, and besides, the angular distributions point mainly well into the second quadrant, whereas the normative ones distribute around their average. This observation abounds on what it is being plotted in Fig. 2, confirming the possibility of establishing a clear boundary between ASD and normative clusters. Needless to say, these results lack any statistical relevance, as they come from the small size participant datasets studied. Of course, new results would open a wider perspective to analyze neurological alterations due to emotional changes during tests. A pending study would include MFCD with VFBS-EEG-band descriptions to expose a wider perspective of ASD speech and phonation, especially regarding the μ-band, It is expected that the study results may open new possibilities for designing more sensitive protocols in the stimulation and speech rehabilitation of people with ASD. It might be said as a conclusion that the MFCC description of sustained vowel utterances from six ASD participants is shown to convey some kind of differentiation capability with respect to normative ones, always under the limitations affecting the study.

References

1. Maenner, M.J., Shaw, K.A., Baio, J., et al.: Prevalence of autism spectrum disorder among children aged 8 years- autism and developmental disabilities monitoring network, 11 Sites, US, 2016. MMWR Surveill. Summ, **69**(SS-4), 1–12 (2020)
2. American Psychiatric Association: Diagnostic and Statistical Manual of Mental Disorders, Fifth edn. text revision). Washington (2022)
3. Fusaroli, R., Lambrechts, A., Bang, D., et al.: Is voice a marker for autism spectrum disorder? A systematic review and meta-analysis. Autism Res. **10**(3), 384–407 (2017)
4. Jodra-Chuan, M., Maestro-Domingo, P., Rodellar-Biarge, V.: Anxiety Monitoring in Autistic Disabled People During Voice Recording Sessions. In: International Work-Conference on the Interplay Between Natural and Artificial Computation, vol. 13258, pp. 291–300. Springer International Publishing, Cham (2022). https://doi.org/10.1007/978-3-031-06242-1_29
5. Górriz, J.M., et al.: Computational approaches to explainable artificial intelligence: advances in theory, applications and trends. Inform. Fusion **100**, 101945 (2023). https://doi.org/10.1016/j.inffus.2023.101945
6. Rodellar-Biarge, V., Jodra-Chuan, M.: A longitudinal study of voice tremor in intellectually impaired autistic persons. In: Models and Analysis of Vocal Emissions for Biomedical Applications: 12th International Workshop, 14-16 December 2021, 67–70 (2021). https://doi.org/10.36253/978-88-5518-449-6
7. Schopler, E., Reichler, R.J., DeVellis, R.F., Daly, K.: Toward objective classification of childhood autism: Childhood Autism Rating Scale (CARS). J. Autism Dev. Disorders **10**(1), 91–103 (1980). https://doi.org/10.1007/BF02408436
8. Pedrero-Pérez, E.J., Ruiz-Sánchez-de-León, J.M., Winpenny-Tejedor, C.: Dysexecutive Questionnaire (DEX): unrestricted structural analysis in large clinical and non-clinical samples. Neuropsychol. Rehabil. **25**(6), 879–894 (2015). https://doi.org/10.1080/09602011.2014.993659
9. García-Villamisar, D., Muela, C.: Psychometric properties of the Childhood Autism Rating Scale (CARS) as a diagnostic tool for autistic adults in the workplace. Rev. Psicol. Gen. Apl. **53**, 515–521 (2000)
10. Abdul, Z.K., Al-Talabani, A.K.: Mel Frequency Cepstral Coefficient and its applications: a review. IEEE Access **10**, 122136 (2022). https://doi.org/10.1109/ACCESS.2022.3223444
11. Gómez-Rodellar, A., Mekyska, J., Gómez-Vilda, P., Brabenec, L., Šimko, P., Rektorová, I.: A pilot study on the functional stability of phonation in EEG bands after repetitive transcranial magnetic stimulation in Parkinson's disease. Int. J. Neural Syst. **33**(06), 2350028 (2023). https://doi.org/10.1142/S0129065723500284
12. Strang, C.C., Harris, A., Moody, E.J., Reed, C.L.: Peak frequency of the sensorimotor mu rhythm varies with autism-spectrum traits. Front. Neurosci. **16**, 950539 (2022). https://doi.org/10.3389/fnins.2022.950539, https://doi.org/10.1016/j.brainres.2014.08.035

Unravelling the Robot Gestures Interpretation by Children with Autism Spectrum Disorder During Human-Robot Interaction

Gema Benedicto[1,2](✉)[iD], Carlos G. Juan[1,2](✉)[iD],
Antonio Fernández-Caballero[3](✉)[iD], Eduardo Fernandez[2,4](✉)[iD],
and Jose Manuel Ferrández[1](✉)[iD]

[1] Universidad Politécnica de Cartagena, 30202 Murcia, Spain
benedicto.gema@gmail.com, jm.ferrandez@upct.es
[2] Instituto de Bioingeniería, Universidad de Miguel Hernández,
03202 Elche (Alicante), Spain
{carlos.juan01,e.fernandez}@umh.es
[3] Universidad de Castilla-La Mancha, 02071 Albacete (Castilla-La Mancha), Spain
antonio.fdez@uclm.es
[4] CIBER BBN, 03202 Elche (Alicante), Spain

Abstract. The ability to interpret and respond to nonverbal signals is crucial in human-robot interaction. This enables the establishment of effective communication and a meaningful relationship between the robot and the user. Understanding the importance of nonverbal communication is a fundamental aspect in the design of therapeutic and technological interventions for individuals with Autism Spectrum Disorder (ASD).

This study investigates how children with Autism Spectrum Disorder (ASD) interpret and respond to gestures made by robots, particularly focusing on the humanoid robot Pepper and the use of tablets, with the aim of enhancing human-robot interactions for the development of more effective therapies for ASD. Participants, both with and without ASD, engaged in sessions involving nonverbal and verbal communication scenarios with the robot and instructor. Results indicate significant differences in gesture recognition between children with ASD and neurotypical children, especially in conditions involving verbal communication. This approach aids in improving interventions, increasingly individualized and effective. Further research with larger samples and improved robot autonomy is warranted to enhance therapeutic outcomes and address limitations encountered in this study.

Keywords: Nonverbal communication · Human-robot interaction · Autism Spectrum Disorder (ASD) · Gesture recognition

1   Introduction

1.1   Social Robotics and Its Impact on Society

Social robotics is experiencing an exponential growth and it is becoming a real necessity in our daily lives. Human-robot interaction, powered by Natural Language Processing (NLP) models, adds innovation and modernity to the user experience. These interactions enhance the value of cultural centers as spaces for learning and discovery, becoming alluring for the new generations and bringing authenticity to the cultural experience [28].

Robotics is becoming increasingly established as an indispensable resource in everyday life, with continued expected use in the coming years [32]. In particular, educational robotics has become a reality in preschool education. However, despite its widespread use in extracurricular activities, it has not been yet significantly integrated into curricular activities or ordinary classes. This can be attributed to the lack of resources in schools, deficiencies in teacher training, the need to align technology with didactics and pedagogy, and the need to have a school digital plan that combines these educational practices [26].

The growth of robotics has had a significant impact on a wide range of domains, such as medicine, finance, and technology. The capabilities of the robot are used for classification, detection, and recognition tasks, among others. For these tasks to be carried out in an autonomous and even unsupervised manner, in addition to the hardware, sophisticated algorithms and data processing techniques are required [13]. Therefore, the importance of Artificial Intelligence (AI) in robotics lies in its potential to automate the tasks to be performed, which saves time and increases efficiency in the industry or daily activities in which they are involved [15].

1.2   Importance of Nonverbal Communication in Human-Robot Interaction

Communication is deemed the main structure on which social interaction lies, i.e., the fundamental key to building life in society and establishing human relationships. This interaction takes place through the transmission of messages, considered as codes learned in that social group, whether from one person to another or one community to another, always in an organized way. This is how behavioral schemes/social behaviors are formed [30].

Communication constitutes a social process influenced by the phenomenon of sharing; that is, establishing links between people. Due to this reason, on certain occasions, there are situations in which people have a mutual impact on or affect the behavior of other interlocutors [23].

The elements involved in the communication process are the sender, receiver, message, channel, context, noise or feedback, and the code [13]. Within them, the code is one of the most interesting elements to study, since it is not limited only to signals that have been genetically inherited but is the product of a meaningful socio-cultural transmission, whether conventional or invented. To use it, it must be learned through participation in the life of a social group. This approach, featuring a more cultural focus, not only emphasizes the autonomy of the human person but also responds to conceptual stimuli according to their previous cultural conditioning, based on their knowledge, ideas, and cultural norms [22].

In addition, there are two types of codes: linguistic (oral or written) and non-linguistic (visual, gestural, or acoustic) [12]. So that the receiver can correctly interpret the received messages, the sender encodes the idea, perception, or experiences that they have in their mind through a process of linguistic construction of the message, into a symbolic representation for the receiver. Then, for a proper participation in the process, the receiver must decode the sender's message in order to understand it, interpret it, and respond accordingly [25].

In the realm of nonverbal communication there is a set of complex signs with greater content or meaning than in the case of verbal communication. Indeed, roughly 30% of the information is usually transmitted verbally, whilst up to 70% is conveyed through nonverbal communication [12]. Non-linguistic codes, specifically gestural codes are of utmost importance for feedback in communication because they entail a bidirectional exchange between the both parties involved in the process [17].

Gestures are considered body movements made primarily with the hands, arms and head. Through them we can express emotions, sensations and thoughts (in the classification of gestures, these are called "gestures that express emotional states") [12]. Additionally, adaptive gestures are used to modulate compromised emotions in the form of adaptation to a situation. To put it in a nutshell, when social interaction is not compatible with the mood of an interlocutor, an uncomfortable situation may happen, which can be controlled [19].

Moreover, gestures provide us with a greater universality level [21], which facilitates effective interactions whether on a robot-robot or a human-robot basis. The case of human-robot interaction (HRI) occurs through the use of a social robot, which interacts with and communicates to the people in the vicinity. The robot is intended to act so in a way resembling the human behavior, even adhering to the established social rules [29]. Due to this reason, the robot is expected to show a social, natural behavior. To that aim, control algorithms put a special emphasis on the personal space. There are several social elements and situations that have an influence on the use of this space, including as well certain sets of psychological and physical aspects often included in the shared space. In general, it is mandatory for these robotic devices to set communication protocols or mechanisms with the purpose of reaching a more sophisticated understanding and accurate interpretation of what the human is indeed willing to convey to the robot [9].

One of the overarching conditions to be met for truly effective HRI is that the communication needs to be properly adapted and suited to the context, including verbal and nonverbal dimensions, and even implicit level [2, 29]. It should be remarked that verbal communication may be sprinkled with ambiguities on occasions, since only 7% of the information is ascribed to the words, while 38% is related to voice. Consequently, body language plays a crucial role by transmitting most of the information during the communication, reaching up to 55% of this information in certain interactions [21]. This is an all-important aspect to bear in mind when designing the robots in order to attain more natural interactions with humans, albeit always limited by practical constraints such as the physical implementation of the joints that hinders certain movements [6]. As a matter of fact, it was proven that body information, dynamic and static characteristics of the position and body gestures can successfully transmit the emotional behavior [29].

This HRI might find interesting applications and benefits in certain contexts. For instance, currently, an increasing number of interventions are emerging, with robots focusing on emotion-related skills for children with Autism Spectrum Disorders (ASD). In 2021, a study that included 892 participants, from which 570 were diagnosed with ASD, performed a meta-analysis of studies carried out with robotics and ASD based on emotion recognition. It was found that NAO and ZECA were the most used robots, while just happiness, sadness, fear, and anger were the most studied emotions. Among the skills taught using different types of robots, the most studied ones were social interactions in general and the recognition and expression of emotions in humans. However, very few studies have been conducted on robots in these two areas [5].

ASD garner a set of neurodevelopmental disorders, the main features of which are difficulty in communication and social interaction, as well as repetitive and reiterative behaviors. These disorders appear at around 18 months of age and are chiefly related to nonverbal communication. They feature low interaction and attention towards other people, little use of gestures, limited imitation capacity, and production of vocalizations [3]. Due to this reason, the importance of early attention must be highlighted, and practices and strategies implemented (such as use of gestures, visual support, and voice generators) that promote communication in different environments that guarantee greater social inclusion in the future. Boys and girls with this diagnosis [2].

2   Objetives

Social skills are defined as the skills that give human beings the ability to efficiently relate with other individuals in the environment. Thanks to these skills, humans express their desires, opinions, and feelings, respecting the behavior of others and offering attention to alleviate problems [12]. In 2000, three types of elements that make up social skills were proposed: behavioral (nonverbal, paralinguistic, and verbal communication), cognitive (perceptions about the communication environment and cognitive variables of the individual), and physiological components.

Bering this in mind, the objective of this study is deepening into the understanding of the robot gestures interpretation by individuals with ASD during HRI. Thus, the main objective of this experiment is to better understand how children with ASD interpret and respond to the gestures made by robots in order to use this information for the development and improvement of more efficient interactions between humans and robots, thereby paving the way for more sophisticated robot-based therapies for ASD.

3   Materials

In this study, a variety of technologies were used to facilitate interactions between children and a humanoid robot called Pepper. Pepper is known for their ability to communicate emotionally, adapting their behavior to the mood of the interlocutor. Pepper uses both verbal and nonverbal language and shows emotions through audio-visual information on the tablet on his chest [2].

Furthermore, a tablet is used for gesture recognition. During the study, the children indicated on the tablet, through a questionnaire with images, what gestures they thought the robot had made. This method takes advantage of the children's affinity for electronic devices, which has been shown in prior studies to improve motor, social interaction, and cognitive skills [1]. The Choregraphe software was used to master Pepper and a facial recognition was achieved by means of a webcam. Gaze estimation, which has important applications in healthcare, behavioral analysis, and communication skills, was performed using unmodified cameras, which arise as a cheap and ubiquitous option for obtaining information on human gaze coordinates [4].

4   Participants

This study is intended for children diagnosed with ASD who are involved in a study of human-robot interaction in emotional psychoeducational interventions. They met the established DSM-V (Diagnostic and Statistical Manual of Mental Disorders) criteria, with some requirements established for the main study, listed next:

1. Main diagnosis of Autism Spectrum Disorder (ASD) in the presence of comorbidities.
2. Updated clinical diagnosis
3. A similar level of affection among the participants.
4. Ability to pronounce at least one word accompanied by an expression.
5. Did not receive prior critical response training (PRT).
6. Age from 5 to 12 years.
7. IQ equal to or greater than 70 points.

Due to the low number of participants in this study, the sample was expanded to include other people who did not meet requirements 3, 4, 5, 6, and 7, since only observation is necessary and it can indicate the interpreted answer, obtaining 24 participants in total (15 with ASD diagnosis and 9 without ASD diagnosis) from 5 to 21 years.

5   Procedure

After having met the admission requirements, the participants were deemed apt to participate in gesture-recognition studies. Informed consent was obtained from parents to authorize participation when the participants were under 22 years of age. Before a participant arrived at the laboratory, the security cameras and all the setup were arranged as in Fig. 1. The participant was seated in front of Pepper robot with the wristband switched on and the instructor offered them the tablet and explained what was going to appear on the screen. At the moment the start signal was activated, the participant could begin to see the robot's gestures and select the interpreted gestures on the tablet. An instructor led all the sessions, checking that all the steps were followed appropriately, also having active participation when required.

Fig. 1. Study setup. The security cameras are located at the top left and right of the green door. The individuals take a seat and stay in front of the robot in the whitish area. (Color figure online)

The structure of the sessions in this study is composed of two parts: nonverbal communication (Part 1) and nonverbal communication complemented by verbal communication (Part 2). The gestures by the robot include emoticons that indicate affirmation, denial, question, and exclamation (in Part 1), and moods such as happy, excited, thinking, curious, bored, and kisses. As depicted in Fig. 2, the nonverbal communication (which makes the whole Part 1 and appears in Part 2 as well) comprises two steps, including also two possible senders. Indeed, the gestures were performed by Pepper robot sometimes and by the instructor some other times. The first step is composed of three affirmative, three negative, three interrogative, and three exclamatory movements/gestures. The second step consists of gestures that denote emotions, such as happiness, excitement, thinking, curiosity, boredom, and kisses. All the gestures were implemented thanks to Choregraphe software.

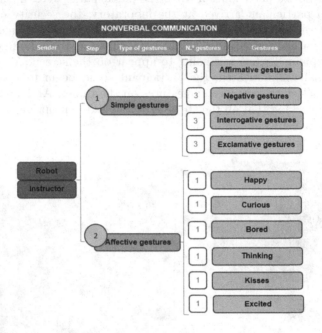

Fig. 2. Scheme of the nonverbal communication involved in this study, including the two steps and the type of gestures carried out by the robot and the instructor.

Part 2, including nonverbal communication accompanied by verbal communication, consists of the same steps as in Fig. 2 as for the nonverbal communication, with the difference that each gesture is accompanied by an oral sentence. The approximate duration of each part of the study was 15 min. Also, in each session the individual carries out one part, but in no case both parts during the same session. At the end of all stages of the study, participants completed a satisfaction questionnaire.

6   Results

The data obtained from the participants were as follows:

Conditions	Total participants	ASD participants	NT participants
Robot recognition part 1 nonverbal communication	24	15	9
Robot recognition part 1 nonverbal and verbal communication	14	9	5
Robot recognition part 2 nonverbal communication	23	15	9
Robot recognition part 2 nonverbal and verbal communication	15	9	6
Instructor recognition part 1 nonverbal communication	15	11	4
Instructor recognition part 1 nonverbal and verbal communication	3	2	1
Instructor recognition part 2 nonverbal communication	14	10	4
Instructor recognition part 2 nonverbal and verbal communication	3	2	1

Fig. 3. Number of participants for each experimental condition, divided by ASD diagnosis and neurotypical.

It is a descriptive and comparative analysis that allows us to understand the distribution of the data, central tendency, dispersion, and determine whether there are significant differences between the groups being compared. The analysis consisted of two parts: in the first, as shown in Fig. 3, the percentages of correctness of each of the gestures in each condition were extracted, and from the set of percentages, it was possible to visualize the different histograms that represent the evolution of the interpretation of the communication (Fig. 4).

In the case of "robot recognition part 1 with and without verbal communication" it can be seen that after calculating a weighted average of all the correct answers in children with autism (ASD) and in neurotypical children (NT), a variability is observed in these data, with a smaller difference in children with autism with 32.304% correct answers in the case of non-verbal communication and 33.993% of the neurotypical children, and a greater difference in the data obtained for non-verbal and verbal communication, with 47.528% in ASD, while the neurotypical children showed a weighted average of correct answers of 88.889%.

In the case of part 2, the non-verbal communication condition shows 28.89% correct answers in children with autism and 59.257% correct answers in neurotypical children. However, in the non-verbal and verbal communication condition, the percentage in autism is 37.021%, and in neurotypical children it is 83.333%.

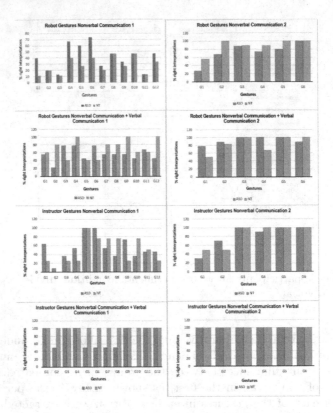

Fig. 4. Histogram of the different study conditions. Data extracted from the percentages of successes of each gesture.

Regarding the percentage of correct answers in the recognition of the instructor's gestures, the average of correct answers in non-verbal communication part 1 in autism is 59.838%, while neurotypical children obtained a weighted average of correct answers of 143.75%. In the non-verbal and verbal communication condition, the average of correct answers is 425%, and in neurotypical children it is 1200%.

Finally, for part 2 of the instructor's non-verbal communication, 49% correct answers are obtained in autism and 125% in neurotypical children. However, in the non-verbal and verbal communication condition, children with autism demonstrated a weighted average of correct answers of 300% and in neurotypical children it is 600%.

The second part of the analysis (Table 1) consisted of the evaluation of measurements such as the mean, median, standard deviation, and p-value, extracted from the Student's T test for each of the two conditions, to check if there was a significant difference between the groups.

Table 1. Statistical analysis under different conditions. The mean, median, standard deviation, and p-values were calculated

Condition	Mean	Median	Standard Deviation	p-value
Robot Gestures NVC 1 ASD	40.56833333	43.35	19.99665783	0.082615861
Robot Gestures NVC 1 NT	27.97333333	26.7	13.25591966	
Robot Gestures NVC + VC 1 ASD	56.47583333	55.55	16.72101696	0.117118335
Robot Gestures NVC + VC 1 NT	70	70	23.35496832	
Robot Gestures NVC 2 ASD	72.225	76.665	26.092574	0.209569784
Robot Gestures NVC 2 NT	88.885	94.44	17.21541141	
Robot Gestures NVC + VC 2 ASD	92.58833333	94.44	9.076176324	0.346536403
Robot Gestures NVC + VC 2 NT	83.33166667	91.665	21.08290532	
Instructor Gestures NVC 1 ASD	54.54166667	49.995	26.57555193	0.579783703
Instructor Gestures NVC 1 NT	47.91666667	37.5	31.00281023	
Instructor Gestures NVC + VC 1 ASD	70.83333333	75	33.42789617	0.006259021
Instructor Gestures NVC + VC 1 NT	100	100	0	
Instructor Gestures NVC 2 ASD	81.66666667	95	27.86873995	0.916550579
Instructor Gestures NVC 2 NT	83.33333333	100	25.81988897	
Instructor Gestures NVC + VC 2 ASD	100	100	0	
Robot Gestures NVC + VC 2 NT	100	100	0	

The data obtained in the conditions 'Robot Gestures Nonverbal Communication Part 1' in ASD and NT', 'Robot Gestures Nonverbal and Verbal Communication in ASD and NT', 'Instructor Gestures Nonverbal and Verbal Communication Part 1 in ASD and NT' and 'Instructor Gestures Nonverbal Communication Part 2', indicate that the differences observed between children with autism (ASD) and neurotypical children (NT) are statistically significant (p value <0.05). On the contrary, in the conditions 'Robot Gestures Nonverbal Communication Part 2 in ASD and NT', 'Robot Gestures Nonverbal Communication and Verbal Communication Part 2 in ASD and NT' and 'Instructor Gestures Nonverbal Communication Part 1 in ASD and NT', the data obtained suggest that there are unlikely to be significant differences between children with autism (ASD) and neurotypical children (NT).

7 Discussion

In this study, three positive expressions, two neutral and one negative were used, since the main objective was to analyze the interpretations in order to design richer and more contextual interactions between the robot and the users. Thus, when the robot interacts with a child, it can use more cheerful and active gestures to maintain their attention throughout the therapy and encourage participation, as well as in more reflective situations in which more calm is needed, neutral gestures are more appropriate.

For this reason, it is of great importance to provide the necessary educational tools in social skills (as a complement to cognitive development) from an early age, such as: the development of emotional intelligence, an adequate relationship with those around you and ideal problem resolution. , and acquisition of social and coexistence norms. This makes possible the development and evolution of interpersonal relationships and an increase in self-esteem and self-concept [12].

In general, robots can be used for educational or entertainment purposes, differentiating themselves from other more traditional methods since they have a unique physical appearance [10]. However, in the case of the most common neurodevelopmental disorder, such as autism, it has different functions. , since autistic children play differently without using elements of imagination since they present difficulties in acquiring new playing skills [20].

This can be observed in the distribution of the data obtained from the participants in which significant differences are revealed in the recognition of non-verbal communications between children with Autism Spectrum Disorder (ASD) and neurotypical children (NT) in various experimental conditions, as they are:

In the first part of the study, the results show that in general, that is, in both robot and instructor gesture recognition, accuracy is lower in children with ASD, especially evident in conditions involving verbal communication. In contrast, in the second part of the study, although the differences between both groups of participants continue to be evident, the differences are minor, especially in the addition of nonverbal communication with verbal communication.

Although these findings coincide with the previous literature mentioned in the 'Introduction' section, which states the difficulties that autistic children have in interpreting nonverbal signals and understanding subtleties, the importance of the communicative context is highlighted. The influence of verbal communication on the understanding of nonverbal signals can be seen in both groups.

However, through Choregraphe the pepper robot has been used on multiple occasions as a companion or tutor in schools, in clinical therapy, as a mediator and as an interviewer. Thus, after these interventions, improvements were observed in eye contact, joint attention, imitation, commitment, social skills [10] and symbolic play also with choregraphe and NAO [20]. This is due to the sympathy and motivation that it produces in users, in addition to repeating over and over again the action to be performed, as many times as required, establishing contact as natural as possible [18].

In addition, the Choregraphe software is very useful, as it can be easily customized and has been used from interactive psychosocial interventions assisted by the pepper robot for auditory rehabilitation (intensive sound stimulation), as a parent assistant through meaningful interactions [20], to assistant for physical rehabilitation of the hand, repeating instructions, recounting the exercises correctly performed [16] or playing the role of cultural mediator, understanding the expectations and lived experiences of children who return to a new country in which they must learning a language through all its modalities, the gestures of human communication being the most essential [19].

8   Conclusion

In conclusion, it is relevant to personalize and adapt intervention programs, and consequently robots, to the specific needs of each child with autism spectrum disorder (ASD). To this end, it is vitally important to develop intervention strategies that address difficulties in recognizing nonverbal signals, taking into account the fundamental role of verbal communication in the interpretation of social interactions.

Furthermore, long-term studies with a larger number of participants are needed to better understand the differences in non-verbal communication between children with ASD and neurotypical (NT) children, in order to improve the socio-emotional and communicative development of children with ASD.

However, it is important to recognize the limitations of this study, including the technical problems of the Pepper robot and the choregraphe software, the small sample size, and the duration of the experiments. To address these limitations, continuation of this study is currently underway. In addition, the autonomy of the robot will be improved, thus reducing the need for intervention by a technician, and obtaining a more consistent therapy for children with ASD.

In future research, we plan to continue exploring the impact of robot gestures on functional play and compare generalization results with human professionals who also perform those gestures with and without facial expression. This will assist in understanding the use of robots effectively in improving communication and social understanding skills in autistic children, as well as developing new interventions more focused on children's individual needs.

Acknowledgement. This project has received funding by grant PID2020-115220RB-C22 funded by MCIN/AEI/ 10.13039/501100011033 and, as appropriate, by "ERDF A way of making Europe", by the "European Union" or by the "European Union NextGenerationEU/PRTR", and was funded in part by grants DTS19/00175 and PDC2022-133952-100 from the Spanish "Ministerio de Ciencia, Innovación y Universidades" and by the European Union's Horizon 2020 Research and Innovation Programme under Grant Agreement No. 899287 (NeuraViPeR). Carlos G. Juan's work was funded in part by the Conselleria d'Innovació, Universitats, Ciència i Societat Digital of the Generalitat Valenciana (Government of the Valencian Community) and the European Social Fund, and partly by the State Research Agency (AEI) (Spanish State Research Agency), Ministry of Science, Innovation and Universities (Government of Spain), and the European Social Fund Plus through the APOSTD Program (ref. CIA-POS/2021/267) and through the Ramón y Cajal Program (ref. RYC2022-036257-I), respectively, as well as the "Premio Tecnologías Accesibles de Indra y Universia Fundación".

References

1. Aguilar Velázquez, R.: Aplicación Web para el desarrollo del potencial de lectoescritura en niños con autismo (2021)
2. Álvarez Guerrero, M.: Expresión emocional mediante sonidos no verbales en robots sociales [Bachelor's thesis] (2016)

3. Ávila, J.A.S.: Una revisión narrativa sobre las estrategias para la intervención de la comunicación en niños y niñas con alto riesgo de trastorno del espectro del autismo. UCMaule **63**, 81–95 (2022)
4. Ansari, M.F., Kasprowski, P., Obetkal, M.: Gaze tracking using an unmodified web camera and convolutional neural network. Appl. Sci. **11**(19), 9068 (2021)
5. Bartl-Pokorny, K.D., et al.: Robot-based intervention for children with autism spectrum disorder: a systematic literature review. IEEE Access **9**, 165433–165450 (2021)
6. Bonarini, A.: Communication in human-robot interaction. Curr. Robot. Rep. **1**, 279–285 (2020)
7. Choregraphe overview-NAO Software 1.14.5 documentation. (s. f.). Recuperado 20 de febrero de 2024. http://doc.aldebaran.com/1-14/software/choregraphe/choregraphe_overview.html
8. De Carolis, B., D'Errico, F., Macchiarulo, N., Palestra, G.: Socially inclusive robots: learning culture-related gestures by playing with pepper. In: IUI Workshops (2021)
9. Eldridge, B.D., Maciejewski, A.A.: Using genetic algorithms to optimize social robot behavior for improved pedestrian flow. In: 2005 IEEE International Conference on Systems, Man and Cybernetics, vol. 1, pp. 524–529. IEEE (2005)
10. Feidakis, M., Gkolompia, I., Mamelaki, A., Marathaki, K., Emmanouilidou, S., Agrianiti, E.: NAO robot, an educational assistant in training, educational and therapeutic sessions. In: 2023 IEEE Global Engineering Education Conference (EDUCON), pp. 1–6. IEEE (2023)
11. García, M.R.: Comunicación e interacción social. Aportes de la comunicología al estudio de la ciudad, la identidad y la inmigración. Glob. Media J. México, **1**(2), 0 (2004)
12. Gómez, F.S.J.: La comunicación. Salus **20**(3), 5–6 (2016)
13. Górriz, et al.: Computational approaches to Explainable Artificial Intelligence: advances in theory, applications and trends. Inform. Fusion **100**, 101945 (2023)
14. Granados-Ramos, D.E., Altamirano-Díaz, P.A., Sanabria-Barradas, B.: Interacciones mediante el juego en diadas madre-hijo con Trastorno del Espectro Autista (TEA). Interdisciplinaria, **40**(3) (2023)
15. Hermosilla Díaz, J.E.: Una estrategia cortés para interacciones humano-robot locales (2023)
16. Hrabar, I., Ćelan, B., Matić, D., Jerković, N., Kovačić, Z.: Towards supervised robot-assisted physical therapy after hand fractures. In: 2021 International Conference on Software, Telecommunications and Computer Networks (SoftCOM), pp. 1–6. IEEE (2021)
17. Khatin-Zadeh, O., Farsani, D., Banaruee, H.: A study of the use of iconic and metaphoric gestures with motion-based, static space-based, static object-based, and static event-based statements. Behav. Sci. **12**(7), 239 (2022)
18. Lekova, A.K., Tsvetkova, P.T.: Toward robot-assisted psychosocial techniques for sound stimulation of children born with hearing loss. In: 2021 International Conference on Information Technologies (InfoTech), pp. 1–4. IEEE (2021)
19. Liu, H., et al.: BEAT: a large-scale semantic and emotional multi-modal dataset for conversational gestures synthesis. In: European Conference on Computer Vision, pp. 612–630. Springer Nature, Cham (2022). https://doi.org/10.1007/978-3-031-20071-7_36
20. Marathaki, K., Feidakis, M., Patrikakis, C., Agrianiti, E.: Deploy social assistive robot to develop symbolic play and imitation skills in students with autism spectrum disorder. In: 2022 IEEE Global Engineering Education Conference (EDUCON), pp. 547–552. IEEE (2022)

21. Montesdeoca, J.C., Toibero, J.M., Carelli, R.: Human-robot interaction, evolution, advances and new challenges. In: 2017 XVII Workshop on Information Processing and Control (RPIC), pp. 1–4. IEEE (2017)
22. Rodríguez Cruz, M.D.P.: La comunicación e interacción humana y su incidencia en el contexto escolar. El Guiniguada (1985)
23. Rizo García, M.: La interacción y la comunicación desde los enfoques de la psicología social y la sociología fenomenológica. Breve exploración teórica. Análisi: Quaderns de comunicació i cultura, (33), 045–62 (2006)
24. Schuurmans, A.A., et al.: Validity of the Empatica E4 wristband to measure heart rate variability (HRV) parameters: a comparison to electrocardiography (ECG). J. Med. Syst. **44**, 1–11 (2020)
25. Shi, G., Xiao, Y., Li, Y., Xie, X.: From semantic communication to semantic-aware networking: Model, architecture, and open problems. IEEE Commun. Mag. **59**(8), 44–50 (2021)
26. Serrano, J.L., Sánchez Vera, M.M., Solano, I.M.: Robótica y currículum. Monográfico ERW. Una primera mirada hacia el pensamiento computacional en el currículo educativo de Infantil y Primaria en España. HipaRob (2021)
27. Sosa Medina, R., Hunting, A., Moradi, P.: Recomendaciones para el Diseño de Robots para el Acompañamiento Artificial, Robots y Adultos Mayores en la Vida Cotidiana (2022)
28. Sodre, H., et al.: Aplicacion de Robots Humanoides como Guias Interactivos en Museos: Una Simulacion con el Robot NAO. arXiv preprint arXiv:2310.17060(2023)
29. Stoeva, D., Gelautz, M.: Body language in affective human-robot interaction. In: Companion of the 2020 ACM/IEEE International Conference on Human-Robot Interaction, pp. 606–608 (2020)
30. Tomasello, M.: A Natural History of Human Thinking. Harvard University Press (2014)
31. Tölgyessy, M., Dekan, M., Chovanec, Ľ.: Skeleton tracking accuracy and precision evaluation of Kinect V1, Kinect V2, and the azure Kinect. Appl. Sci. **11**(12), 5756 (2021)
32. Zorrilla-Puerto, J., Lores-Gómez, B., Martínez-Requejo, S., & Ruiz-Lázaro, J.: El papel de la robótica en Educación Infantil: revisión sistemática para el desarrollo de habilidades. RiiTE Revista Interuniversitaria de Investigación en Tecnología Educativa, 188–194 (2023)

Real-Time Emotion Detection System's Impact on Pivotal Response Training Protocol

Gema Benedicto[1,2]([✉])(iD), Félix de la Paz[3]([✉])(iD),
Antonio Fernández-Caballero[4]([✉])(iD), and Eduardo Fernandez[2,5]([✉])(iD)

[1] Universidad Politécnica de Cartagena, Murcia 30202, Spain
benedicto.gema@gmail.com
[2] Instituto de Bioingeniería, Universidad de Miguel Hernández de Elche,
Alicante 03202, Spain
e.fernandez@umh.es
[3] Universidad Nacional de Educación a Distancia (UNED), Madrid 28015, Spain
delapaz@dia.uned.es
[4] Universidad de Castilla-La Mancha, 02071 Ciudad Real, Spain
antonio.fdez@uclm.es
[5] CIBER BBN, Elche (Alicante) 03202, Spain

Abstract. In recent years, there has been a growing emphasis on Autism Spectrum Disorder (ASD), marked by evolving classifications and increasing global prevalence. Early intervention is underscored as crucial for effective management of ASD, given that emotional dysregulation is a prominent characteristic, leading to challenges in regulating and expressing emotions in a typical manner. This study aims to propose the utilization of Empatica E4 (at the physiological level) and Face tracking (at the behavioral level) as a real-time emotion detection system, exploring its potential impact on interventions based on the Pivotal Response Treatment method (PRT) for children with autism. The goal is to enhance understanding of the child's emotions, facilitate communication, strengthen emotional connections during interventions, and promote strategies for managing intense emotions.

Integrating a real-time emotion detection system into PRT interventions holds promise for significantly enhancing the therapeutic process. By providing valuable insights into the child's emotional state, this approach offers a promising avenue to tailor treatments to individual needs and provide greater emotional support and social development for children with ASD.

Keywords: emotion detection · systems · Autism Spectrum Disorder(ASD) · real time

1 Introduction

In recent years, there has been greater evolution and focus on the term Autism Spectrum Disorder (ASD), with constantly changing classifications and increas-

J. M. Ferrández Vicente et al. (Eds.): IWINAC 2024, LNCS 14674, pp. 356–367, 2024.
https://doi.org/10.1007/978-3-031-61140-7_34

ing global prevalence [28], and although it varies between different countries, the Prevalence is higher in boys than in girls in general [11]. In countries such as the United States [36] and Germany there is an increase in ASD diagnoses, while low-income countries, including Mexico and Brazil, have reported lower numbers of diagnoses [1]. The diagnosis of autism relies on clinical evaluation by health professionals due to the absence of biological markers associated with the disorder. ASD has a complex and multifactorial etiology [19].

The most apparent signs of ASD typically emerge between 18 and 36 months of age, emphasizing the importance of early intervention for effective management [19]. Diagnostic tools such as the Diagnostic and Statistical Manual of Mental Disorders (DSM-5) are used by health professionals to identify specific criteria for ASD, including social communication deficits and repetitive behaviors. The DSM-5 categorizes ASD into three levels of impairment [22].

Autism Spectrum Disorders encompass a range of disorders with diverse etiology and clinical presentations. Most individuals with ASD have normal intellectual capacity, although intellectual disability is more prevalent in girls than in boys. The characteristics of ASD vary in severity and affect areas such as language and intellectual development differently in each individual. The appearance of these disorders occurs very early in the individual's life, beginning in childhood and continuing throughout life, always with varying degrees of impact on functioning [37].

Due to the variability in the prevalence of ASD, the need to carry out more research on the possible causes and implications is highlighted. Thus, it is crucial to offer more effective interventions and emotional support to family members affected by the disorder [1].

Through the recognition of different emotions (from facial expressions to body gestures), social communication occurs [13]. It is carried out naturally and with greater precision in neurotypical people than in children with ASD, who present a set of difficulties in recognizing emotions. Individuals with ASD present deficits in social cognition and the empathy process. This causes alterations in communication and theory of mind [6].

Furthermore, not only self-awareness and recognition of other people's emotions are affected, but also the control and modulation of emotions [35], joint attention [23] and imitative, imaginative and symbolic play, along with the planning and execution of behavior [17]. This emotional dysregulation occurs when emotions are regulated in an inadequate way and is reflected in irritability or frustration, and high sensory and emotional sensitivity [4].

Among the most used types of social skills intervention are interventions based on applied behavioral analysis (ABA), based on the principles of operant conditioning and with extensive experience in the field of ASD research [3]. Despite the cost in time and effort that this method entails, due to repeated exposure to the stimulus, being a highly structured technique and inducing learned helplessness and lack of motivation, it has been shown to be effective in improving social functioning and reduction of behaviors considered clinically "inappropriate" [16].

More recently, interventions based on ABA but with a naturalistic approach have emerged, such as Pivotal Response Treatment (PRT) developed by Robert I. Koegel, L.K. Koegel and L. Shreibman. It is characterized by the ability to be used in multiple environments and be focused on pivotal areas such as motivation, self-initiation, self-management (Lei, 2017) and response to multiple signals [34].

It is defined by the increase in the child's motivation and self-initiations through knowledge of his or her tastes and interests. The motivational procedures to teach essential behaviors that are used in the PRT are:

2. Gain their attention.
3. Offer clear opportunities (shared control and turn taking are included).
4. Child's choice.
5. Maintenance and acquisition tasks.
6. Natural and contingent rewards.
7. Reward attempts and target skill reinforcement [34].

PRT has been used in order to improve language, play and social behavior skills in minor patients with ASD, by using natural reinforcements related to the behavior being taught, and offering a reward when they try despite not carrying it out perfectly, except in case of showing no effort or getting it right by chance [18]. The development of PRT focuses on specific areas that in turn produce generalized positive improvements, in addition to creating opportunities in their natural environment such as providing a response timeout, initiative phrases, dosing the reward and breaking habituation, alternating different levels of complexity [32].

Although, after conducting a review of studies that have applied PRT, 43.6% of the studies indicated evidence of improvements with this type of intervention, and 56.4% of the studies had a set of limitations that leave in view of the fact that the evidence of collateral improvements in behavior remains scarce [34].

Not only do therapeutic interventions help us obtain more information about the psychological and emotional responses in people with ASD, but there are a series of emotion detection tools, that is, accurately capturing the emotional state of the individual, based on sensors with in order to carry out autonomous monitoring and alert in real time in a non-intrusive way [27].

For this reason, the main objective of this study is to propose the use of the Empatica E4 and Face Tracking as real-time emotion detection systems in view of its impact on an intervention with children with Autism Spectrum Disorder based on the Pivotal Response Treatment (PRT) method.

2   Research Proposal

The structure of these monitoring tools is simple, as it only consists of three main elements, such as data collection, emotion monitoring, and finally, intervention. Until now, wearable devices have been used such as bracelets (including

Empatica E4), hand gloves, headbands or chest sensors, even microphones and facial thermal images.

These detect movement signals and a range of physiological signals: heart rate, respiratory rate, skin temperature and electrodermal activity (known as EDA) and can be combined with each other to improve the emotion prediction models developed [2].

As the prediction models developed were done offline, various algorithms and collected data are used to train deep or machine learning models. These include short-term memory, convolutional neural networks (CNN) or logistic regression. In turn, among these models, there are decision trees (DT) and supervised learning algorithms such as nearest neighbor (KNN). These models demonstrate high effectiveness in predicting emotional dysregulation [9].

The ways to develop real-time systems can include machine learning models, such as:

Decision Trees (DT): Classify data based on simple rules, although less effectively when handling more complex data. In this way, they can detect patterns indicative of emotional dysregulation.

k-Nearest Neighbors (kNN): through the proximity between data points, the class to which a new point belongs can be predicted and thus identify emotional dysregulation.

Support Vector Machines (SVM): By aiming to identify the hyperplane that best separates classes in a multidimensional space, it can discern boundaries between different emotional states.

Convolutional Neural Networks (CNN): Extract spatial features from images or sequences, allowing them to identify visual patterns associated with emotions [33].

Long short-term memory (LSTM): Capture long-term dependencies in sequential data. The contribution to the field of emotions is through the analysis of temporal patterns in emotional evolution.

These machine-learning models are powerful tools that, when properly trained with relevant data, can be used to predict emotional dysregulation with a high degree of accuracy and contribute to effective early warning systems [25]. However, the importance doesn't solely lie in the model itself, but also in the selection of sensor types and attention strategies tailored to personalized information. Among these are chest sensors that monitor heart rate and breathing, which prove useful in regulating emotions, particularly in autistic children, aiding in managing periods of stress and anxiety. Additionally, headwear such as hats or headbands equipped with electroencephalography (EEG) sensors can provide insights into the mental and emotional states of autistic children. This assists in identifying patterns of brain activity associated with stress or sensory crises.

Some children with this diagnosis may experience specific sensory sensitivities, such as tactile hypersensitivity or hyposensitivity. Hand gloves equipped with pressure and temperature sensors can aid in understanding how the child responds to touch and temperature. Consequently, they can be useful in adapting the child's environment and minimizing aspects of situations that may induce sensory discomfort.

Furthermore, in order to identify stimuli or activities that align with the child's interests, it is important to comprehend their behavior and preferences. This information can be gleaned from body movement sensors and gestures [10, 21, 26]. While the selection of sensors should be tailored to the child's needs and preferences, it is also essential to choose those most appropriate for the study at hand.

User involvement in the design of the detection system is important to ensure it aligns with their needs, increasing the overall effectiveness of the system. This is the case with the Empatica E4, which not only features a user-friendly design but also ensures the security and privacy of users' physiological data collected, especially in the context of autism. Although the responsibility also lies with users to understand how data is collected, stored, and analyzed, Empatica implements transparent security measures and privacy policies that maintain user trust and comply with ethical standards [7].

Another real-time emotion detection system is based on a DL CNN model utilizing facial images. It poses a consistent challenge due to the diverse characteristics of faces, the potential display of varied emotions, and/or the overlapping of emotions. Additionally, it entails the identification and extraction of facial features, categorization, proposing an emotion classification system, and constructing the architecture of the deep convolutional neural network (DCNN) for recognizing different emotions. This architecture comprises three layers: cloud, fog, and IoT layers. However, it faces limitations in terms of data availability, as real data is not readily accessible [30].

In contrast to these methods, the Empatica E4 bracelet incorporates sensors specifically engineered to capture a comprehensive set of high-quality physiological signals in real-time. Capable of concurrently measuring the activity of the sympathetic nervous system via electrodermal activity (EDA) and heart rate (PPG), it also facilitates event labeling and correlation with physiological signals.

To date, numerous studies have showcased the precision and utility of this bracelet across various applications, ranging from stress detection to emotion classification based on the collected physiological data. With an internal memory capacity of up to 60 h and synchronization resolution every 5 s, it proves advantageous for longitudinal investigations. Of particular interest is its ability to display physiological data in real-time, rendering it an effective tool for emotion recognition in diverse scenarios [24].

An exemplary illustration of the benefits of the Empatica E4 bracelet and its potential application in tandem with human-robot interaction is elucidated in the article "Investigation of Physiological Features by Age Groups in Children with Autism. This study delves into the computerized analysis of physiological signals gathered from children with autism across different age cohorts in four countries, employing the KASPAR robot as a means of interaction.

The Empatica E4 plays a fundamental role in this study by recording key physiological data during the interaction between children and the robot, allowing the analysis of significant differences between age groups through signals such as BVP, EDA and ST. This device provides valuable information to understand the physiological responses of children with autism during interactions with assistive technologies, which may be crucial for future studies on emotions and stress in this population [31],.

Furthermore, the combination of Empatica e4 with a social robot allows facial expression data to be collected through a video camera that the robot has, whose data can be synchronized with those obtained from the bracelet and analyze the characteristics extracted from the physiological signals, such as: tonic (SCL) and phasic (SCR) component of the EDA signal, average value of the EDA signal in one stage (MEAN EDA), standard deviation of EDA (STD GSR), harmonic sum of EDA (SUM H GSR), number of SCR events in each of the different stages (EVE SCR) or the frequency of SCR appearance in a stage (FRC SCR), among others. These data can thus provide us with information about the impact of robotic therapy and allow us to successfully separate physiological signals related to pleasant, neutral and unpleasant emotions [5].

Among the signals that offer insights into observable symptoms of emotional states utilized for emotion recognition, various modalities exist, including facial expressions, skin conductance, body posture, and even eye fixation areas.

While employing eye-tracking technologies with children with autism presents challenges-requiring participants to remain seated and as calm or motionless as possible during calibration and data collection processes [15]-a tracking system termed "Face tracking" can be developed using a deep learning neural network ("Deep Learning"). This system aims to analyze facial muscle movements to track facial features, eyes, and pupils. This data can be extracted from real-time video recordings captured by a participant's webcam, enabling analysis of attention levels, focus areas, and task engagement, with a particular focus on facial expressions to gain deeper insights into emotions. This enables tailoring intervention sessions to individual participant situations. The program can operate in two modes:

– Real-time data analysis.
– Analysis of previously recorded videos. In both cases, frame-by-frame analysis is conducted.

For face and eye detection, the 'haarcascade' library is utilized, while a library named "gaze_tracking" is employed for pupil detection (Fig. 1).

In the provided image, you can visually observe the functioning of the system as follows:

The left side displays the collected data along with the coordinates for each item. The green grids represent the eye positions. The blue grid indicates the face position. The two crosses indicate the pupil positions. Every time the program runs, the data is stored in a folder with the corresponding date in the format: "(DATA COLLECTED)(date)(hour.minute)". Each file is assigned a creation date for better organization.

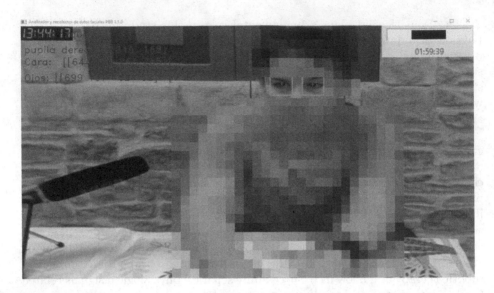

Fig. 1. Operation of the facial feature, eye, and pupil detection system in an 11-year-old boy diagnosed with ASD.

3   Impact on Pivotal Response Treatment (PRT)

The integration of a real-time emotion detection system into interventions utilizing PRT can significantly enhance the therapeutic process by offering valuable insights into the child's emotional state. This enables better comprehension of non-verbal cues, facilitates communication, and fosters a stronger emotional connection during the intervention. Additionally, it helps in identifying situations that evoke intense emotional responses, thereby promoting self-control by teaching strategies for emotional regulation.

Some of the ways in which such a system could affect the PRT intervention are in the personalization and individualization of treatment. Until now, programs have been used that are based on principles of behavioral analysis applied in a general way, in addition to the use of visual cues, developmental models, and other strategies that provide them with the necessary help to function, unlike other programs that use. fully structured environments. However, both have given positive results, or a combination of different therapies, because due to the heterogeneity of the disorder and its constant evolution of the traits that characterize it, there are children who, with one type of method, obtain a very positive response, as opposed to. to other children who progress at slower rates.

The problem lies in the difficulties in individualizing existing treatment protocols or in finding the methodology to determine what type of intervention would be most beneficial for each of the children since each part has its advantages and disadvantages. In the case of a combination of both methods, can lead to confusion among children and lower fidelity when administering the method.

On the other hand, the exclusive use of one of the methods can ignore important aspects for that individual such as emotional, communicative, or social development. Although, it has been studied that there are a low number of studies that demonstrate the effectiveness of the combination of eclectic therapies. This indicates that the most ideal would be to carry out a set of different interventions with the same approach for an individual but varying the time dedicated to each of them and depending on the abilities and characteristics of the child (degree of impairment, age, and level of development), as well as integrating strategies between different activities and within each of them.

These aspects are what must be taken into account when choosing the interventions that best fit the child and to do so, all influencing factors must be examined, such as data on the child's emotional responses during PRT sessions. Thus, the emotion detection system is capable of identifying that a child responds positively to specific emotional stimuli, which therapists and researchers can subsequently incorporate more frequently in activities with PRT to improve attention, motivation, and commitment of the child throughout the intervention [12,14,20,29].

To improve the effectiveness of the PRT protocol, the immediate feedback provided by the emotion detection system should also be examined. One study analyzed the impact of instructive feedback on teaching touch through play in children diagnosed with ASD, comparing it to tactile training without instructive feedback. The results show that instructive feedback leads to a greater frequency of playing behaviors and tactile relationships both at the table and in the play area, without hindering the proposed objectives. This indicates that the effectiveness of feedback promotes significant adaptive behaviors [9].

Even feedback alone can be conditionally reinforcing for some people, and goal setting acts as a stimulant or driver of the feedback, producing an improvement in the individual's performance. That is, goal setting together with prior learning influences behavior positively, although the combination of feedback and modeling improves behavior more in some interventions. However, it is not clear which components are the most efficient in each context [16].

Additionally, an automated emotion detection system can help objectively assess the child's emotional responses during PRT interventions. This could assist therapists in identifying long-term emotional patterns and adjusting their intervention strategies based on the child's current needs. For instance, if the system detects an increase in galvanic skin response (which may indicate anxiety or stress) during certain activities or social interactions, the therapist or researcher can adapt the environment or activities to reduce the child's stress and promote more effective participation in therapy [15].

Similarly, this system can gather data on the child's emotional responses over time, enabling a more comprehensive analysis of their evolution and progress in the intervention, as well as the identification of potential emotional patterns. It can aid therapists in facilitating the generalization of learned skills to various contexts and situations [8].

4 Conclusions

Throughout this study, the importance of adapting therapeutic treatments for children with Autism Spectrum Disorder (ASD) to their individual abilities is emphasized, enabling them to make significant advancements. The potential occurrence of crises during therapeutic sessions due to sensory or emotional overload is underscored, highlighting the necessity of preemptive measures to identify emotional fluctuations in real-time. While acknowledging the effectiveness of Pivotal Response Treatment (PRT) in addressing autism, particularly in communication and repetitive behaviors, it is noted that the dearth of current studies substantiating these findings is acknowledged. Consequently, there is a call for more robust and transparent research, prompting the proposal for utilizing real-time emotion detection systems such as Empatica E4 sensors to monitor physiological responses and enhance the customization of PRT therapies. Additionally, the integration of facial and eye-tracking systems is suggested.

Despite encountering challenges such as difficulties in fitting the Empatica E4 bracelet on children with autism, which may impede data collection and introduce movement artifacts, valuable physiological signals are gathered to comprehend emotional and stress responses during interactions with assistive technologies. Furthermore, hurdles arise when analyzing facial expressions in video recordings and categorizing them based on the child's condition and configuration. While these obstacles encompass atypical movements during interventions, children's resistance, or technical limitations such as improperly positioned cameras, some challenges are inherent in emotion recognition, and this technology is notable for its remarkable adaptability to children and tailored interventions, contrary to previous experiences.

Furthermore, these investigations aim to delve into the understanding of emotional dysregulation in autism and construct reliable predictive models to aid caregivers and enhance the quality of life. A technological intervention is sought to facilitate the development of systems addressing these health challenges, fostering technological advancements for ASD patients, mitigating costs associated with therapy-related emotional crises, and preventing setbacks in progress achieved.

Acknowledgements. This project has received funding by grant PID2020-115220RB-C22 funded by MCIN/AEI/ 10.13039/501100011033 and, as appropriate, by "ERDF A way of making Europe", by the "European Union" or by the "European Union NextGenerationEU/PRTR", and was funded in part by grants DTS19/00175 and PDC2022-133952-100 from the Spanish "Ministerio de Ciencia, Innovación y Universidades" and by the European Union's Horizon 2020 Research and Innovation Programme under Grant Agreement No. 899287 (NeuraViPeR), as well as the "Premio Tecnologías Accesibles de Indra y Universia Fundación".

References

1. André, T.G., Montero, C.V., Félix, R.E.O., Medina, M.E.G.: Prevalencia del trastorno del espectro autista: una revisión de la literatura. Jóvenes en la ciencia, **7** (2020)
2. Boateng, E., Otoo, J., Abaye, D.: Basic tenets of classification algorithms k-nearest-neighbor, support vector machine, random forest and neural network: a review. J. Data Anal. Inform. Process. **8**, 341–357 (2020)
3. Boudreau, A.M., Lucyshyn, J.M., Corkum, P., Meko, K., Smith, I.M.: Peer-mediated pivotal response treatment at school for children with autism spectrum disorder. Can. J. Sch. Psychol. **36**(1), 34–50 (2021)
4. Cai, R.Y., Richdale, A.L., Uljarević, M., Dissanayake, C., Samson, A.C.: Emotion regulation in autism spectrum disorder: where we are and where we need to go. Autism Res. **11**(7), 962–978 (2018)
5. Cosoli, G., Poli, A., Scalise, L., Spinsante, S.: Measurement of multimodal physiological signals for stimulation detection by wearable devices. Measurement **184**, 109966 (2021)
6. Drimalla, H., Baskow, I., Behnia, B., Roepke, S., Dziobek, I.: Imitation and recognition of facial emotions in autism: a computer vision approach. Mol. autism **12**, 1–15 (2021)
7. E4 connect. (s. f.). Recuperado 7 de marzo de 2024. https://e4.empatica.com/connect/privacy.php
8. Flynn, M., et al.: Assessing the effectiveness of automated emotion recognition in adults and children for clinical investigation. Front. Hum. Neurosci. **14**, 70 (2020)
9. Górriz, et al.: Computational approaches to Explainable Artificial Intelligence: advances in theory, applications and trends. Inform. Fusion **100**, 101945 (2023)
10. Grow, L.L., Kodak, T., Clements, A.: An evaluation of instructive feedback to teach play behavior to a child with autism spectrum disorder. Behav. Anal. Pract. **10**, 313–317 (2017)
11. Hazen, E.P., Stornelli, J.L., O'Rourke, J.A., Koesterer, K., McDougle, C.J.: Sensory symptoms in autism spectrum disorders. Harv. Rev. Psychiatry **22**(2), 112–124 (2014)
12. Herrera-Del Aguila, D.: Trastorno del espectro autista: la historia. Diagnóstico **60**(3), 131–133 (2021)
13. Kasari, C., Gulsrud, A., Paparella, T., Hellemann, G., Berry, K.: Randomized comparative efficacy study of parent-mediated interventions for toddlers with autism. J. Consult. Clin. Psychol. **83**(3), 554–563 (2015)
14. Keluskar, J., Reicher, D., Gorecki, A., Mazefsky, C., Crowell, J.A.: Understanding, assessing, and intervening with emotion dysregulation in autism spectrum disorder: a developmental perspective. Child Adolesc. Psychiatr. Clin. **30**(2), 335–348 (2021)
15. Koegel, R.L., Koegel, L.K., Ashbaugh, K., Bradshaw, J.: The Importance of early identification and intervention for children with or at risk for autism spectrum disorders. Int. J. Speech Lang. Pathol. **16**(1), 50–56 (2014)
16. Landowska, A., et al.: Automatic emotion recognition in children with autism: a systematic literature review. Sensors **22**(4), 1649 (2022)
17. Lei, J., Ventola, P.: Pivotal response treatment for autism spectrum disorder: current perspectives. Neuropsychiatr. Dis. Treat. **20**, 1613–1626 (2017)
18. Ojea Rúa, M.: El espectro autista: intervención psicoeducativa. Aljibe, Archidona (Málaga) (2004)

19. Ona, H.N., Larsen, K., Nordheim, L.V., Brurberg, K.G.: Effects of pivotal response treatment (PRT) for children with autism spectrum disorders (ASD): a systematic review. Rev. J. AutismDev. Disord. **7**, 78–90 (2020)
20. Pérez, M.D.L.L.A., Pérez, R.B.: Alternativas de tratamiento en los trastornos del espectro autista: una revisión bibliográfica entre 2000 y 2016. Revista de psicología clínica con niños y adolescentes **5**(1), 22–31 (2018)
21. Pickles, A., et al.: Parent-mediated social communication therapy for young children with autism (PACT): long-term follow-up of a randomised controlled trial. Lancet **388**(10059), 2501–2509 (2016)
22. Qadeib Alban, A., et al.:. Detection of challenging behaviours of children with autism using wearable sensors during interactions with social robots. In: 2021 30th IEEE International Conference on Robot and Human Interactive Communication (RO-MAN), pp. 852–859 (2021)
23. Regier, D.A., Kuhl, E.A., El Kupfer, D.J.: DSM-5: cambios en la clasificación y los criterios. Revista Oficial De La Asociación Mundial De Psiquiatría (Wpa) **12**, 92–98 (2009)
24. Rivière, Á.: Autismo: Orientaciones para la intervención educativa. Trotta, Madrid (2001)
25. Saganowski, S., Komoszyńska, J., Behnke, M., et al.: Emognition dataset: emotion recognition with self-reports, facial expressions, and physiology using wearables. Sci. Data **9**, 158 (2022)
26. Sandhu, M., et al.: Empowering Caregivers of Autism Spectrum Disorder through Sensor-Based Emotional Dysregulation Monitoring. (s. f.)
27. Schonewille, C.: Sensory processing in autism spectrum disorder (Doctoral dissertation) (2018)
28. Akansha, S., Surbhi, D.: AutisMitr: emotion recognition assistive tool for autistic children. Open Comput. Sci. **10**(1), 259–269 (2020)
29. Sosa-Piñeiro, K., Rodríguez-Padrón, Y., Romo-Morfa, A.: El Autismo. Evolución de su dimensión teórica/Autism. Theoretical considerations. Educación y sociedad **15**, 15–25 (2017)
30. Stahmer, A.C., Schreibman, L., Cunningham, A.B.: Toward a technology of treatment individualization for young children with autism spectrum disorders. Brain Res. **1380**, 229–239 (2011)
31. Talaat, F.M.: Real-time facial emotion recognition system among children with autism based on deep learning and IoT. Neural Comput. Appl. **35**, 12717–12728 (2023)
32. Toprak, E., Bilgin Aktas, S.N., Coşkun, B., Uluer, P., Kose, H., Barkana, D.E.: Investigation of physiological features by age groups in children with autism. In: 2023 IEEE 36th International Symposium on Computer-Based Medical Systems (CBMS), pp. 287–292. L'Aquila, Italy (2023)
33. Uljarević, M., Billingham, W., Cooper, M.N., Condron, P., Hardan, A.Y.: Examining effectiveness and predictors of treatment response of pivotal response treatment in autism: an umbrella review and a meta-analysis. Front. Psych. **12**, 766150 (2022)
34. Varghese, D.: Comparative study on classic machine learning algorithms. Accessed 28 July 2021 (2018)

35. Verschuur, R., Didden, R., Lang, R., Sigafoos, J., Huskens, B.: Pivotal response treatment for children with autism spectrum disorders: a systematic review. Rev. J. Autism Dev. Disord. **1**, 34–61 (2014)
36. Widen, S.C., Russell, J.A.: Young children's understanding of other's emotions. Handb. emotions **3**, 348–363 (2008)
37. Zúñiga, A.H., Balmaña, N., Salgado, M.: Los trastornos del espectro autista (TEA). Pediatría integral **21**(2), 92–108 (2017)

Intelligent Systems for Assessment, Treatment, and Assistance in Early Stages of Alzheimer's Disease and Other Dementias

Assessing the Interplay of Attributes in Dementia Prediction Through the Integration of Graph Embeddings and Unsupervised Learning

Pablo Zubasti⬤, Antonio Berlanga⬤, Miguel A. Patricio⁽✉⁾⬤,
and José M. Molina⬤

Grupo de Inteligencia Artificial Aplicada. Universidad Carlos III de Madrid, Getafe,
Spain
mpatrici@inf.uc3m.es

Abstract. Explainable Artificial Intelligence (XAI) stands as an evolving domain within modern AI methodologies. It centers on the exploration of relationships between variables, dimensionality reduction (directly associated with importance), and the explanation of model decisions. This paper introduces a methodology rooted in Graph Embeddings and unsupervised learning, specifically applied to the prediction of dementia. The focus is on elucidating the significance of prevalent clinical tests utilized in dementia diagnosis, discerning the achievable accuracy of classification models without incorporating these variable groups, and assessing the consequential impact in terms of medical cost and time efficiency.

Keywords: Explainable Artificial Intelligence · Graph Embedding ·
Dementia prediction · Artificial Intelligence in Medicine · Unsupervised
Machine Learning

1 Introduction

The global population is consistently undergoing the aging process. As indicated in the findings published in [16], the increase in the number of years correlates with a decrease in birth rates, resulting in a notable expansion of the demographic that comprises individuals 65 years and older. This demographic shift is attributed to advancements in the quality of life and extended life expectancy.

The challenge of forecasting cognitive decline and the subsequent probability that a patient develops dementia has been addressed through diverse approaches, including traditional medical methodologies and the field of medical informatics. In the latter domain, predictive modeling employs data analysis and artificial intelligence techniques to assess the probability of a patient developing dementia in the future [1, 7, 12].

J. M. Ferrández Vicente et al. (Eds.): IWINAC 2024, LNCS 14674, pp. 371–380, 2024.
https://doi.org/10.1007/978-3-031-61140-7_35

In the realm of Artificial Intelligence (AI), and particularly in Machine Learning (ML), there exists a pronounced interest in enhancing the explainability of models. Explainable Artificial Intelligence (XAI) encompasses a suite of processes and methodologies designed to enable users to comprehend and trust the results generated by ML models. As computational capabilities have advanced, more sophisticated models have emerged. However, with these models, it becomes challenging for individuals to comprehend and trace the decision-making process leading to a specific result. These models are often referred to as "black-box" models, since they are constructed purely from data. In the context of highly reliable, yet opaque models, data scientists struggle to decipher or elucidate the rationale behind specific ML model outcomes.

In healthcare, interpretability is a significant concern, as decisions must be easily understandable [15]. A doctor cannot rely on a decision that they cannot explain, and a patient cannot trust an expert who makes decisions based on computational methods without clear justification. This paper outlines a methodology grounded in Graph Embeddings and unsupervised learning for the prediction of dementia. The construction of a graph is used to delineate the relationships among variables within a classification model. Subsequently, this graph is represented through embeddings, denoted as Graph Embeddings. These embeddings can be visually portrayed in a two-dimensional map, allowing for the formation of clusters that group attributes with akin relationships. Distances between embeddings serve as quantifiers of the strength of relationships between predictor variables and the dependent variable. This methodology facilitates a nuanced analysis of variable groups closely associated with the dependent variable. Armed with this information, specialists can discern the importance of different tests. In our experimentation, we demonstrate the interdependence of clusters, elucidating the significance of prevalent clinical tests currently used in dementia diagnosis. The study also explores the accuracy attainable by classification models in the absence of these variable groups, highlighting their pivotal role in terms of cost and medical time considerations.

2   Dataset

This section delineates the dataset employed in our experiment, sourced from the OASIS (Open Access Series of Imaging Studies) initiative. Specifically, we are utilizing the OASIS-2 dataset: Longitudinal MRI Data in Nondemented and Demented Older Adults [10].

The dataset, as described in [10], comprises 373 visitor entries involving 150 patients aged between 60 to 96 years. Each visit is separated by at least one year, and each patient has a minimum of two recorded visits. Patients are classified into three groups: Demented, Non-Demented, and Converted, signifying individuals who were initially non-demented but later transitioned into a demented state. Among visits, 190 patients were classified as demented, 146 as non-demented, and 37 as converted. In total, there are 72 non-demented, 64 demented, and 14 converted cases. The study involved the participation of 62 men and 88 women. Table 1 describes the attributes of the aforementioned dataset.

Table 1. Description of the attributes of the OASIS-2 dataset.

No	Information	Attribute	Description
1	Generic	Subject ID	Unique identifier for each patient
2		MRI ID	Identifier for each patient's MRI image
3		Group	The classification given to the patient (demented, non-demented and converted)
4		Visit	The number of the visit where the data were collected
5		MR Delay	The time delay between the excitation of the hydrogen nuclei in the brain tissue sample and the acquisition of the corresponding magnetic resonance imaging (MRI) signal
6	Demographic	Gender	Gender (M or F)
7		Hand	The predominant hand of the patients. In all patients it was the right hand
8		Age	Patient's Age
9		EDUC	Years of education
10		SES	Socio-economic status (SES) ranked according to the Hollingshead Index of social status, which gives a value of 1 for the highest and 5 for the lowest.
11	Clinic	MMSE	Mini Mental State Examination (MMSE)[13]. This is the score obtained by patients in the Mini Mental State Examination. The severe condition is up to 9 points and includes 2 cases of the total number of patients analysed. For mild cognition it ranges from 10 to 18 points and contains 12 cases. Moderate cognition ranges from 19 points to 23 points and contains 39 cases. The remaining cases have values between 24 and 30 points
12		CDR	The Clinical Dementia Rating (CDR) [3] is a 5-point scale employed to assess functional performance and cognitive domains relevant to Alzheimer's disease and related dementias. The six domains evaluated are Memory, Orientation, Judgement and Problem Solving, Community Affairs, Home and Hobbies, and Self-Care. The scale assigns values as follows: 0 denotes no dementia, 0.5 indicates mild Alzheimer's dementia (AD), 1 signifies moderate AD, 2 reflects moderate-to-severe AD, and 3 represents severe AD.
13	Derived anatomical volumes	eTIV	The estimated total intracranial volume (eTIV) in cubic millimeters, as detailed in [11], serves as a crucial covariate in volumetric evaluations of the brain and its regions. This parameter is particularly pertinent in the examination of neurodegenerative diseases, offering insight into the maximal premorbid brain volume. It is noteworthy that males exhibit an eTIV approximately 12% greater than females
14		nWBV	Normalized whole-brain volume (nWBV)[4] is quantified as a percentage of pixels in the atlas and is classified based on tissue segmentation into white or grey matter
15		ASF	The atlas scaling factor (ASF) is a metric employed in neuroimaging studies to gauge the extent of brain atrophy in an individual. Calculated as the ratio of the grey matter volume to the white matter volume, the ASF is adjusted to account for the overall size of the brain

3   Graph Embedding Background

Graph analysis has been a very developed topic in the Machine Learning field, and more precisely, graph embedding techniques have become the cornerstone of preprocessing graphs projecting them into a $\delta - dimensional$ space where classification, regression and clustering algorithms can be applied with ease.

Several approaches have been used in the task of computing embeddings, but the main ones are described in this graph embedding techniques survey [5], and they are based on factorization, Random Walks or Deep Learning foundations. Our research focuses on using the first category of these techniques, the ones based on factorization methods, looking for applications in the field of medicine and XAI.

The first graph embedding algorithms (based on factorization) were developed in the 2000's and their aim was to generate a vector for each node of the graph trying to achieve dimensionality reduction. Local Linear Embedding (LLE) [17] was one of the mentioned algorithms that used a quadratic objective function derived from a neighborhood graph and was solved by computing its eigenvectors.

Laplacian Eigenmaps [6] were succesful in treating large distances between pairs of vectors because the quadratic expression mentioned before emphasized more those distances that were significant rather than those that were smaller. This false notion of *local topology preserving* was explained by Luo & et al., 2011 where they proposed a new version of the Laplacian Eigenmaps algorithm where the optimization function was modified so that short distances in the embedding space were also significant and *local topology preserving* was really accomplished.

They proposed a new algorithm named Cauchy Graph Embedding [8]. The authors of the original paper defined an iterative algorithm that converges with the embedding solution after a few iterations.

4   Cauchy Graph Embedding Algorithm Applied to OASIS-2 Dataset

4.1   Methodology Explained

With the above-mentioned Graph Embedding algorithm, we now aim to apply this technique to the OASIS-2 dataset explained before. The main idea behind this methodology is to create XAI models that help us find and understand relationships between attributes, so that the reduction in dimensionality, interaction of attributes, and importance ranking can be further obtained with the corresponding results.

Supervised and unsupervised models can also be used with the resulting embeddings, for solving classification, regression, and clustering problems. In our research we used a unsupervised clustering approach to study groups of variables that behave similar in terms of linear and non-linear correlations. The methodology consists in applying the Cauchy Graph Embedding algorithm to the correlation matrix.

The non-diagonal terms of the matrix are computed with the Pearson's Correlation formula, but we can extend this matrix and compute for each of those elements the Spearman's Correlation formula, which allows us to discover non-linear relationships between pairs of variables:

$$\rho = 1 - \frac{6\sum_{i=1}^{n} d_i^2}{n(n^2 - 1)} \tag{1}$$

where d is the difference between ranks and n the number of samples.

Since we are using two correlation matrices (linear and non-linear) that have values defined in the interval $[-1, 1]$, we need to merge these two matrices into a new one. This can be done in several (probably infinite) ways, but we decided to merge this two matrices by adding them together and multiplying the result by $1/2$. Then we square the resulting matrix to obtain a matrix whose elements are defined in the interval $[0, 1]$.

Mathematically, we compute the merged matrix as:

$$M = \left[\frac{1}{2}(P_{CM} + S_{CM})\right]^2 = \frac{1}{4}(P_{CM} + S_{CM})^2 \tag{2}$$

where P_{CM} is the Pearson Correlation Matrix (linear) and S_{CM} is the Spearman Correlation Matrix (non-linear). Note that the final matrix is computed by squaring each element, not by performing $M' = MM$.

With the merged matrix we can define a non-directed graph $G = (\mathcal{V}, \mathcal{E})$ where $\mathcal{V}$ is the set of vertices where $\mathcal{E}$ is the set of edges connecting vertices and the weights associated to the edges are stored in the adjacency matrix (merged matrix). Ultimately, we have that for a given edge e_{ij}, a weight w_{ij} is associated. Simplifying: $e_{ij} = M_{ij}$.

It is important to note that the adjacency matrix derived the correlations, leaves us with a complete graph, denoted as $\mathbb{K}_n$, where $n = |\mathcal{V}|$. In $\mathbb{K}_n$ graphs each node has $n - 1$ edges connecting with the rest of the nodes, so the number of edges can be inferred with the *handshaking lemma* as $|\mathcal{E}| = \binom{|\mathcal{V}|}{2} = \frac{1}{2}n(n-1)$. Some of these edges could have an associated weight of zero, so this is treated as equivalent to the absence of that edge.

With the adjacency matrix we can now apply the Cauchy Graph Embedding algorithm so that the whole process can be summarized as follows:

1. For a given dataset D, compute two correlation matrices (Pearson and Spearman).
2. Merge those two matrices with the formula defined in Eq. (2).
3. Build a nondirected graph $G = (\mathcal{V}, \mathcal{E})$ where the edges are related to the weights stored in the merged matrix.
4. Apply the Cauchy Graph Embedding (CGE) to the graph so that the resulting embedding $R = (\vec{r_1}, \vec{r_2}, ..., \vec{r_n}) \mid R \in \mathbb{R}^{\delta \times n}$.
5. (Optional) Use Machine Learning techniques to process the resulting embedding information. In our research, we solved a clustering problem (using *k-means* algorithm [9]) trying to find groups of attributes that correlate similarly with each other.

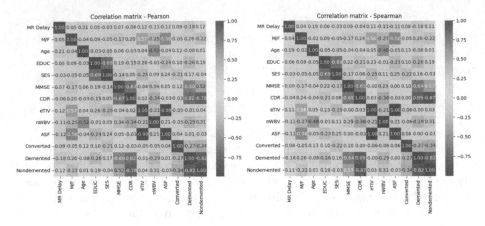

Fig. 1. The correlation matrices for Pearson's and Spearman's methods (respectively).

5   Experimental Results

The OASIS-2 dataset requires a few pre-processing layers that take care of the non-necessary attributes. Some attributes have been initially discarded because they do not provide relevant information in the context of the problem. Those attributes were *Subject ID*, *MRI ID* and *Visit*. It is also recommended to remove *Hand* since it is not statistically significant [14].

The first step in the experiments is to compute the correlation matrices explained in this paper. The results are shown in Fig. 1.

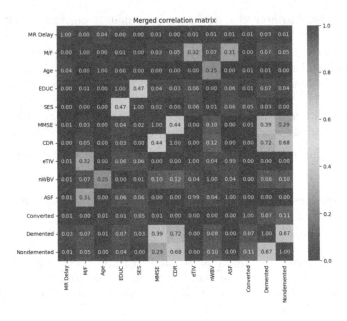

Fig. 2. Merged correlation matrix.

Then, the merged matrix is computed as shown in the Eq. (2) and the results for the OASIS-2 variables are displayed in Fig. 2.

The merged matrix, depicted in Fig. 2, can also be translated into a graph, where the associated weights are stored in the respective cells of the matrix. In theory, the maximum density achievable by the graph is defined by the corresponding $\mathbb{K}_n$ complete graph. However, in our specific case, we begin with a graph that is not fully connected (e.g., AGE and SES are not connected).

Applying the Cauchy Graph Embedding to the graph, we get the following 2D-embedding displayed on Fig. 3a. After computing the embedding, an additional clustering process was applied using k-$means$ algorithm and the $Calinski$-$Harabasz$ [2] cluster metric to calculate the optimal number of clusters, which ended up being five.

The embedding illustrates a two-dimensional distribution of OASIS-2 attributes, predicated on the precomputed relationships (see Fig. 3a).

A $Random$ $Forest$ classifier and a $Gradient$ $Boosting$ $Trees$ classifier were used to assess the efficacy of the models. These were then compared with analogous models, albeit with an augmented number of attributes derived from the groups computed by k-$means$ from the embedding. The results are detailed in Table 2.

The order in which the groups of attributes are inserted into the model is based on a ranking calculated with Eq. (3).

$$R_k = \frac{1}{n \cdot |C_k|} \sum_{i=1}^{|C_k|} \sum_{j=1}^{n} d(e_i, t_j) \tag{3}$$

where R_k is the score that a particular attribute gets for the ranking, C_k is the $kth - cluster$, n represents the number of targets (three for our embedding), and $d(e_i, t_j)$ represents the Euclidean distance, which can be computed with Eq. (4).

$$d(x_i, x_j) = \sqrt{\sum_{k=1}^{\delta} (x_{ik} - x_{jk})^2} \tag{4}$$

Table 2. Model degeneration in terms of accuracy and f1-score.

Attribute IDs	Random Forest		Gradient Boosting Trees	
	Accuracy	f1-score	Accuracy	f1-score
1, 2	80%	78%	84%	77%
1, 2, 3, 4	80%	77%	82.6%	77%
1, 2, 3, 4, 5, 6	85.3%	82%	85.3%	80%
1, 2, 3, 4, 5, 6, 7, 8, 9	86.7%	83%	85.3%	80%
1, 2, 3, 4, 5, 6, 7, 8, 9, 10	89.3%	88%	85.3%	82%

Attribute name	CDR	MMSE	nWBV	Age	EDUC	SES	M/F	ASF	eTIV	MR Delay
Attribute ID	1	2	3	4	5	6	7	8	9	10

Figure 3b depicts the accuracy obtained as groups of the attributes referenced in Table 2 are added. The overall information that the clustered embedding provides is a set of groups where correlations and transitive correlations are well defined inside each one of them. Medical experts and researchers can focus on particular groups adding new layers of explainability that improves the quality of prediction models and clinical tests. As mentioned above, eliminating attributes and ranking them with this methodology would reduce the average cost associated with diagnosing dementia.

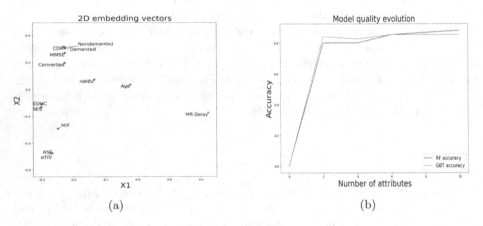

(a)   (b)

Fig. 3. (a) Resulting 2-dimensional embedding already clustered by *k-means* algorithm; (b) Evolution of model quality measured by accuracy increase.

6   Conclusions

This paper examines the efficacy of graph embedding techniques in representing relationships between attributes within a machine learning context. This representation facilitates a visual interpretation of the associations between both dependent and predictor attributes. The application chosen to demonstrate the utility of this approach is the prediction of dementia, with attribute relationships characterized by the correlation between each pair of attributes. The methodology reveals clusters of attributes strongly correlated with each other, providing valuable insights for clinicians in the analysis of related diagnostic tests. It also offers the potential to eliminate costly tests that contribute minimally to the diagnostic process. The proposed methodology imposes a few but highly adaptable constraints on the construction of the adjacency matrix for the application of the Cauchy Graph Embedding algorithm to attribute-based graphs. The results obtained from the OASIS-2 dataset indicate that only a limited number of attributes are genuinely correlated with the target variables (dementia classes). Through validation with advanced classification models, it is established that the degeneracy of the models in terms of accuracy is not substantial. The ultimate inference is that this methodology facilitates the prioritization of various tests and measurements, thus improving the efficiency and cost-effectiveness of the diagnostic process.

Acknowledgment. This study was funded by the Spanish company Grupo Mas-Movil; the public research projects of the Spanish Ministry of Science and Innovation PID2020-118249RB-C22 and PDC2021-121567-C22 - AEI/10.13039/501100011033 and the project under the call PEICTI 2021–2023 with identifier TED2021-131520B-C22

References

1. Alvi, A.M., Siuly, S., Wang, H.: A long short-term memory based framework for early detection of mild cognitive impairment from EEG signals. IEEE Trans. Emerg. Topics Comput. Intell. **7**(2) (2023). https://doi.org/10.1109/TETCI.2022. 3186180

2. Caliñski, T., Harabasz, J.: A Dendrite method foe cluster analysis. Commun. Stat. **3**(1) (1974). https://doi.org/10.1080/03610927408827101

3. Cummings, J., et al.: Exploring the relationship between patient-relevant outcomes and Alzheimer's disease progression assessed using the clinical dementia rating scale: a systematic literature review (2023). https://doi.org/10.3389/fneur.2023. 1208802

4. Fotenos, A.F., Snyder, A.Z., Girton, L.E., Morris, J.C., Buckner, R.L.: Normative estimates of cross-sectional and longitudinal brain volume decline in aging and AD. Neurology **64**(6) (2005). https://doi.org/10.1212/01.WNL.0000154530.72969.11

5. Goyal, P., Ferrara, E.: Graph embedding techniques, applications, and performance: a survey. Knowl.-Based Syst. **151** (2018). https://doi.org/10.1016/j.knosys. 2018.03.022

6. Hall, K.M.: An R-dimensional quadratic placement algorithm. Manag. Sci. **17**(3) (1970). https://doi.org/10.1287/mnsc.17.3.219

7. Javeed, A., Dallora, A.L., Berglund, J.S., Ali, A., Ali, L., Anderberg, P.: Machine learning for dementia prediction: a systematic review and future research directions. J. Med. Syst. **47**(1) (2023). https://doi.org/10.1007/s10916-023-01906-7

8. Luo, D., Ding, C., Nie, F., Huang, H.: Cauchy graph embedding. In: Proceedings of the 28th International Conference on Machine Learning, ICML 2011 (2011)

9. MacQueen, J.: Some methods for classification and analysis of multivariate observations. In: Proceedings of the fifth Berkeley Symposium on Mathematical Statistics and Probability, vol. 1 (1967)

10. Marcus, D.S., Fotenos, A.F., Csernansky, J.G., Morris, J.C., Buckner, R.L.: Open access series of imaging studies: longitudinal MRI data in nondemented and demented older adults. J. Cognit. Neurosci. **22**(12) (2010). https://doi.org/10. 1162/jocn.2009.21407

11. Marcus, D.S., Wang, T.H., Parker, J., Csernansky, J.G., Morris, J.C., Buckner, R.L.: Open Access Series of Imaging Studies (OASIS): cross-sectional MRI data in young, middle aged, nondemented, and demented older adults. J. Cognit. Neurosci. **19**(9) (2007). https://doi.org/10.1162/jocn.2007.19.9.1498

12. Sharda Y.S., Mahesh S.C.: Performance study of machine learning algorithms used for Alzheimer's disease detection. J. Pharm. Negative Results (2023). https://doi.org/10.47750/pnr.2023.14.s01.108
13. Nasreddine, Z.S., et al..: The Montreal Cognitive Assessment, MoCA: a brief screening tool for mild cognitive impairment. J. Am. Geriatr. Soc. **53**(4) (2005). https://doi.org/10.1111/j.1532-5415.2005.53221.x
14. Naugle, R.I., Cullum, C.M., Bigler, E.D., Massman, P.J.: Handedness and dementia. Percept. Motor Skills **65**(1) (1987). https://doi.org/10.2466/pms.1987.65.1.207
15. Rasheed, K., Qayyum, A., Ghaly, M., Al-Fuqaha, A., Razi, A., Qadir, J.: Explainable, trustworthy, and ethical machine learning for healthcare: a survey (2022). https://doi.org/10.1016/j.compbiomed.2022.106043
16. Roser, M., Ritchie, H.: Age Structure - Our World in Data (2019)
17. Roweis, S.T., Saul, L.K.: Nonlinear dimensionality reduction by locally linear embedding. Science **290**(5500) (2000). https://doi.org/10.1126/science.290.5500.2323

Bayesian Network Structures for Early Diagnosis of MCI Using Semantic Fluency Tests

Alba Gómez-Valadés[✉] [ID], Rafael Martínez-Tomás[ID], and Mariano Rincón[ID]

Universidad Nacional de Educación a Distancia, Madrid 28040, Spain
albagvb@dia.uned.es

Abstract. The early detection of MCI has become one of the main focuses in research since it allows early treatment to improve patient quality of life. Currently, several studies seek to combine tests with machine learning systems to increase the efficiency of diagnostics. Bayesian Networks (BN) have the advantage over other machine learning systems of being explainable. However, there is little information on how different network structures affect BN performance in the clinical setting. In this study, we used semantic fluency tests, one of the most widely used neuropsychological tests, to compare the performance of three models: Naive Bayes, BN with the variables grouped by semantic category (BN_{Test}), and BN with the variables grouped by type of variables (BN_{Var}). The models were compared on three decision thresholds: the standard 0.5, the one that maximizes the model performance, and the one that optimizes the false negatives. The results show that the best conformation of the network corresponds to (BN_{Var}) in the three thresholds selected, while (BN_{Test}) scores the worst results. This study shows that a proper structure improves the results of the BN concerning the simpler model of Naive Bayes.

Keywords: Bayesian Network · semantic fluency · MCI · neuropsychological tests · machine learning

1 Introduction

Mild cognitive impairment (MCI) is an intermediate state between normal aging and Alzheimer's disease (AD) [1]. Therefore, in a world where the incidence of AD is expected to increase as the population ages, early detection of MCI has become the subject of several studies [1–4] Neuropsychological tests are widely used for early detection of MCI due to their ease and speed of administration, lack of specialized equipment, making them more economical than alternatives, and good diagnostic utility [5,6].

Within them, semantic fluency tests stand out as one of the most consolidated tests in the neuropsychological test batteries [2,6]. This is because language and semantic memory are among the first areas affected by MCI, and

© The Author(s), under exclusive license to Springer Nature Switzerland AG 2024
J. M. Ferrández Vicente et al. (Eds.): IWINAC 2024, LNCS 14674, pp. 381–389, 2024.
https://doi.org/10.1007/978-3-031-61140-7_36

those tests are able to effectively capture these alterations [7,8]. The traditional scoring method is the count of terms within that semantic category, excluding intrusions (out-of-category terms) and perseverations (duplications) [7,9]. However, several studies have highlighted that the diagnostic utility of the test can be increased by considering the spontaneous tendency of subjects to generate successive items within a semantic subcategory and then switch to another during verbal production [7,10,11]. To quantify such information, the variables of *switching* and *clustering* have been proposed, where *switching* is the number of jumps between semantic subcategories, and *clustering* is the average size of successive groupings of words within the same semantic subcategory [11]. It has been reported that these variables can increase the effectiveness of these tests [2,7].

For the study of semantic fluency tests and associated variables, more and more research groups are employing machine learning techniques. One of the objectives pursued is the analysis of their effectiveness, either alone [6–8] or in combination with other diagnostic tests [9,12]. Another common goal is the creation of decision-support systems using machine learning techniques [7,10,13]. However, the machine learning systems used in most studies operate as a black box, making it difficult or impossible to know the logical steps followed by the system when issuing a classification [10,14]. Bayesian networks (BN) are based on probabilistic reasoning, so they can predict the value's probability of one or several variables from the values observed in other variables [15]. BNs are suitable for representing uncertainty and causality, characteristics present in the clinical domain [16], allowing to know the reasoning followed by the BN when making a diagnosis [10,14], and performing analysis on hypothetical scenarios [17]. Because of this, BNs have been employed with satisfactory results in several studies focused on the diagnosis of MCI and/or AD [10,14–17].

Using semantic fluency tests, in this study we propose and compare two BN structures with each other and regarding Naive Bayes (the simplest BN structure). The three models were compared using the default threshold of 0.5, the threshold at which each network is most efficient, and the most efficient threshold assuming a diagnostic scenario, in which the interest is to detect the maximum number of MCI subjects. The rest of the paper goes as detailed next: Sect. 2 describes the database and the methodology followed, Sect. 3 presents the results, and finally, Sect. 4 presents the conclusions.

2   Methodology

2.1   Database

We used an anonymized database from a large ongoing longitudinal study on the prevalence of MCI in the Autonomous Community of Madrid (Spain) [4]. Subjects with a previous diagnosis of neurodegenerative disease, disabling chronic disease, psychiatric disorders such as major depression, established neurological abnormality, severe sensory impairment, diabetes, stroke, and loss of consciousness were already excluded from the database. The cognitive and emotional status of the subjects was assessed using the Spanish version of the Mini-Mental State Examination [18] and the Geriatric Depression Scale [19]. The diagnosis of MCI was established based on the Petersen criteria, considering tests that evaluated different cognitive abilities [4]. The database consisted of a total of 591 monolingual Spanish subjects, with ages between 58 and 93 years and with an educational level between 0 and 22 years of study. A summary of the sociodemographic data is presented in Table 1.

Table 1. Sociodemographic summary of the subjects .

	Nº of subjects	Men/Women	Age (Mean/Std)	Education (Mean/Std)	MMSE (Mean/Std)
Healthy	328	92/236	70.16/5.92	11.63/5.42	32.87/2.17
MCI	263	64/199	72.77/6.66	8.09/6.25	30.13/3.35

2.2 Test Description

Four semantic categories or semantic fluency tests were used in this study: *animals*, *clothes*, *plants*, and *vehicles*. For each semantic category, four variables were extracted: *corrects* (count of valid terms excluding perseverations and intrusions), *switching* (number of changes between semantic subcategories), *clustering* (average size of clusters by semantic subcategories), and *total clusters* (a new variable, which refers to the total number of different semantic subcategories that have appeared during verbal production). The subsemantic categories were defined from the database according to the instructions provided in (Troyer, 2000).

2.3 Bayesian Network Structure

Three structures were compared: Naive Bayes, and two conformations of the BN: one with the variables grouped by test (BN_{Test}), and another with the variables grouped by variable type (BN_{Var}).

Description of the Bayesian Network Nodes. In both causal models there are four types of variables:

– Sociodemographic variables (V_{SD}): there has been established an association of *age*, *sex*, and educational level (*education*) with the risk of developing AD [20,21]. We established the range of the age variable between "less than 65 years", "65 to 75 years" and "more than 75 years". *Education* can take the values of "less than 8 years" (without complete primary education), "from 8 to 16 years" (with complete primary education, but not secondary education), and "more than 16 years" (with complete secondary education, and possible university education). The *sex* variable was originally discretized into "female" and "male". However, due to the relatively low percentage of male participants in the study and their distribution across *age* and *education*, we found that in the conditional probabilistic tables, many probabilities associated with men remained at the default value (0.5). The solutions evaluated here were either to reduce the discretization of the *age* and/or *education* variables or to eliminate the *sex* variable. We chose the second option because both *age* and *education* variables have an important influence on subjects' test performance [20,22,23], while the influence of *sex* is more diffuse and, for the specific case of semantic fluency tests, recent studies have not found a significant correlation between *sex* and performance [20,21,24].

- Informative variables (V_{Inf}): variables that directly score the performance of the subject in the semantic fluency tests. They correspond to *corrects, switching, clustering*, and *total clusters* (*TotalClust* in the BN). *Corrects* and *clustering* can take values from 0 to 3, while TotalClust takes the values from 0 to 2. *Switching* can take values from 0 to 3 for *animals* and *clothes*, and from 0 to 2 for *plants* and *vehicles* since people tend to make a greater number of semantic jumps in the first two semantic categories. To identify which semantic category each score comes from, a letter precedes the names of each V_{Inf}, with "A" corresponding to *animals*, "C" to *clothing*, "P" to *plants*, and "V" to *vehicles*. Therefore, *ACorrects* refers to the variable *corrects* on the semantic category *animals*.

- Latent variables (V_{Lat}): intermediate variables between V_{Inf} and the diagnosis. These variables cannot be obtained directly, but they increase the expressivity of the network. Therefore, they can contribute to improving the BN result by better capturing the relationships between other variables. For our study, these variables are the semantic fluency categories of *FSAnimals*, *FSClothes*, *FSPlants*, and *FSVehicles* for the BN_{Test}, thus grouping the V_{Inf} according to semantic category or test, or *Corrects, Switching, Clustering*, and *TotalClust*, for the BN_{Var}, grouping V_{Inf} according to variable type.

- Cognitive State variable (V_{CS}): variable of interest, for which we want to obtain the "a posteriori" probabilities from the evidence provided by the VS and V_{Inf}.

Description of the Relationships Between Nodes. Causal relationships were established with abductive reasoning for all semantic variables (V_{Inf} and V_{Lat}). In this way, the conditional probability tables are simpler and more manageable than with deductive reasoning, in which it would have been necessary to adjust tables of 3^4 for all V_{Lat} and 2^6 for V_{CS}. V_{SD} presents a deductive relationship concerning V_{CS} since they are risk factors that are not possible to modify.

Figure 1 shows the structure of the BN_{Test}. This architecture is based on organizing the V_{Inf} according to the test that originated them. In this way, each V_{Lat} (e.g., *FSAnimals*) integrates the information of the different metrics in the "animals" semantic fluency test (all V_{Inf} associated (*ACorrections, ASwitching, AClustering*, and *ATotalClust*).

On the other hand, Fig. 2 shows the structure of the BN_{Var} with the V_{Inf} organized according to the type of score. Thus, the performance of each V_{Lat} (e.g., *Corrects*) would integrate the information on the different V_{Inf} it groups (*ACorrects, PCorrects, CCorrects, VCorrects*).

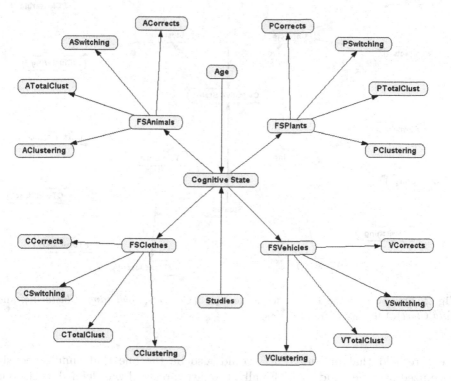

Fig. 1. Structure of the BN_{Test}, with the V_{Lat} (*FSAnimals, FSClothes, FSPlants*, and *FSVehicles*), the V_{Inf}, V_{SD}, and V_{CS}.

2.4   Implementation and Evaluation Methodology

CausalNex [25], a Python API, was used for the automatic obtention of the conditional probability tables for all variables. The performance evaluation of both BNs was performed in OpenMarkov [26], exporting the networks and the conditional probability tables and introducing the corresponding evidence. Naive Bayes results were obtained from Scikit Learn [27].

Using the MCI as the target class, the performance of the three models was compared for three thresholds. The first is the default 0.5 threshold as a control. The second is the threshold at which each model optimizes its performance, for which we choose the threshold maximizing *F1*. *F1* is the harmonic mean between *recall* and *precision* and is robust to unbalanced data sets. Therefore,

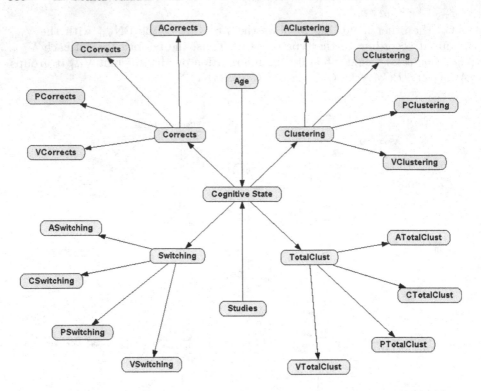

Fig. 2. Structure of the BN$_{Var}$, with the V$_{Lat}$ (*Corrects, Switching, Clustering,* and *TotalClust*), the V$_{Inf}$, V$_{SD}$, and V$_{CS}$.

the threshold that optimized *F1* would also be the one that simultaneously optimized *precision* and *recall*. Finally, the last threshold was defined as the one that optimizes the number of *false negatives*, as from a clinical point of view, the goal is to correctly identify positive (MCI) cases. However, since directly optimizing *recall* could turn the system trivial by classifying all subjects as positive, the threshold that optimized for *F2* (the ratio between *precision* and *recall* in which *recall* is given more weight) was established.

3   Results

Table 2 shows the comparative performance of the results obtained for the Naive-Bayes, BN$_{Var}$ and BN$_{Test}$ at the different thresholds. The best results correspond to the BN$_{Var}$ structure for both *F1* = 0.708 and *F2* = 0.705 followed by Naive-Bayes (*F1* = 0.695; *F2* = 0.701). The results of the BN$_{Test}$ were significantly worse (*F1* = 0.663, *F2* = 0.672). For the comparison using the threshold that gives them the best overall performance, the relationship between the three models is maintained, with BN$_{Var}$ *F1* = 0.744, NaiveBayes *F1* = 0.793, and BN$_{Test}$ *F1* = 0.710. Finally, when using the threshold that most reduces *false negatives* in each system the BN_{Var} still has the best results with F2 = 0.848. However, here NaiveBayes ($F1$ = 0.814) and BN_{Test} ($F1$ = 0.830) invert their positions, having the worst score NaiveBayes.

It is noteworthy the low performance of the BN_{Test} regarding both BN_{Var} and NaiveBayes, except for the comparison for threshold optimized to reduce the *false negatives* (F2), where the BN_{Test} has a better score than NaiveBayes. However, given the high *recall* and low *precision* of both BN, for that threshold, the number of *false* negatives has been reduced to almost zero, in exchange for a great increment of the number of *false positives*.

Table 2. Results obtained on the comparison between the three models.

	NaiveBayes			BN_{Test}			BN_{Var}		
Threshold	0.5	0.12 best F1	0.04 best F2	0.5	0.29 best F1	0.05 best F2	0.5	0.29 best F1	0.04 best F2
Accuracy	0.719	0,730	0.691	0.685	0.697	0.534	0.736	0.742	0.635
Precision	0,687	0,660	0,610	0,647	0,629	0,494	0,713	0,677	0,556
Recall	0,704	0,839	0,889	0,679	0,815	1.000	0,704	0,827	0,975
F1	0,695	0,739	0,724	0,663	0,710	0,661	0,708	0,744	0,709
F2	0,701	0,796	0,814	0,672	0,769	0,830	0,705	0,792	0,848
Roc-Auc	0,718	0,739	0,707	0,663	0,722	0,747	0,708	0,752	0,766

4 Conclusions

In this study, we obtained that the BN_{Var} (BN with the V_{Inf} organized according to variable type) is the best structure for evaluating semantic fluency tests that include several semantic categories and variables.

It is highlighted that, while an appropriate structure and setting of the latent variables increase the performance of the system (BN_{Var}), a no-optimal grouping of the variables could decrease the performance of the model concerning the basic conformation of NaiveBayes (BN_{Test}).

Acknowledgments. We would like to thanks the UNED for the grant *"Ayuda de la UNED para contrato predoctoral para la formación de personal investigador"* to A.G.-V. which help with the research presented in this paper, and to Sara García-Herranz y a M. Carmen Díaz-Mardomingo for allowing us to use their database for this project.

Disclosure of Interests. The authors have no competing interests to declare that are relevant to the content of this article.

References

1. Jitsuishi, T., Yamaguchi, A.: Searching for optimal machine learning model to classify mild cognitive impairment (MCI) subtypes using multimodal MRI data. Sci. Rep. **14**(1), 4284 (2022)
2. Bertola, L., Cunha Lima, M.L., Romano-Silva, M.A., de Moraes, E.N., Diniz, B.S., Malloy-Diniz, L.F.: Impaired generation of new subcategories and switching in a semantic verbal fluency test in older adults with mild cognitive impairment. Front. Aging Neurosci. **6** (2014)
3. Chasles, M.-J., et al.: An examination of semantic impairment in amnestic MCI and AD: what can we learn from verbal fluency? Arch. Clin. Neuropsychol. **35**, 22–30 (2020). https://doi.org/10.1093/arclin/acz018
4. Díaz-Mardomingo, M., García-Herranz, S., Rodríguez-Fernández, R., Venero, C., Peraita, H.: Problems in classifying mild cognitive impairment (MCI): one or multiple syndromes? Brain Sci. **7**, 111 (2017). https://doi.org/10.3390/brainsci7090111
5. Gurevich, P., Stuke, H., Kastrup, A., Stuke, H., Hildebrandt, H.: Neuropsychological testing and machine learning distinguish Alzheimer's disease from other causes for cognitive impairment. Front. Aging Neurosci. **9** (2017). https://doi.org/10.3389/fnagi.2017.00114
6. Zhao, Q., Guo, Q.-H., Hong, Z.: Clustering and switching during a semantic verbal fluency contribute to differential diagnosis of cognitive impairment. Neurosci. Bullet. **29**, 75–82 (2013). https://doi.org/10.1007/s12264-013-1301-7
7. Kim, N., Kim, J.-H., Wolters, M.K., MacPherson, S.E., Park, J.C.: Automatic scoring of semantic fluency. Front. Psychol. **10** (2019)
8. López-de-Ipiña, K., et al.: On the analysis of speech and disfluencies for automatic detection of mild cognitive impairment. Neural Comput. Appl. **32**, 15761–15769 (2018). https://doi.org/10.1007/s00521-018-3494-1
9. Clark, D.G., et al.: Novel verbal fluency scores and structural brain imaging for prediction of cognitive outcome in mild cognitive impairment. Alzheimer's Dementia: Diagnos. Assessm. Dis. Monitor. **2**, 113–122 (2016). https://doi.org/10.1016/j.dadm.2016.02.001
10. Guerrero, J.M., Martínez-Tomás, R., Rincón, M., Peraita, H.: Diagnosis of cognitive impairment compatible with early diagnosis of Alzheimer's disease. A Bayesian network model based on the analysis of oral definitions of semantic categories. Methods Inf. Med. **55**, 42–49 (2016). https://doi.org/10.3414/ME14-01-0071
11. Troyer, A.K.: Normative data for clustering and switching on verbal fluency tasks. J. Clin. Exp. Neuropsychol. **22**, 370–378 (2000). https://doi.org/10.1076/1380-3395(200006)22:3;1-V;FT370
12. Gupta, A., Kahali, B.: Machine learning-based cognitive impairment classification with optimal combination of neuropsychological tests. Alzheimer's & Dementia: Transl. Res. Clin. Intervent. **6**, e12049 (2020). https://doi.org/10.1002/trc2.12049
13. Bertola, L., et al.: Graph analysis of verbal fluency test discriminate between patients with Alzheimer's disease, mild cognitive impairment and normal elderly controls. Front. Aging Neurosci. **6** (2014). https://doi.org/10.3389/fnagi.2014.00185
14. Jin, Y., Su, Y., Zhou, X.-H., Huang, S., The Alzheimer's disease neuroimaging initiative: heterogeneous multimodal biomarkers analysis for Alzheimer's disease via Bayesian network. EURASIP J. Bioinform. Syst. Biol. **12** (2016). https://doi.org/10.1186/s13637-016-0046-9

15. Sun, Y., Tang, Y., Ding, S., Lv, S., Cui, Y.: Diagnose the mild cognitive impairment by constructing Bayesian network with missing data. Expert Syst. Appl. **38**, 442–449 (2011). https://doi.org/10.1016/j.eswa.2010.06.084

16. Seixas, F.L., Zadrozny, B., Laks, J., Conci, A., Muchaluat Saade, D.C.: A Bayesian network decision model for supporting the diagnosis of dementia, Alzheimer's disease and mild cognitive impairment. Comput. Biol. Med. **51**, 140–158 (2014). https://doi.org/10.1016/j.compbiomed.2014.04.010

17. Bate St Cliere, A.-R., Fenton, N.: Bayesian network modelling for the clinical diagnosis of Alzheimer's disease (preprint). In: Health Systems and Quality Improvement (2024). https://doi.org/10.1101/2023.12.30.23300452

18. Lobo, A., Ezquerra, J., Gómez Burgada, F., Sala, J.M., Seva Díaz, A.: Cognocitive mini-test (a simple practical test to detect intellectual changes in medical patients. Actas Luso-Espanolas Neurol. Psiquiatr. Ciencias Afines **7**, 189–202 (1979)

19. Yesavage, J.A., et al.: Development and validation of a geriatric depression screening scale: a preliminary report. J. Psychiat. Res. **17**, 37–49 https://doi.org/10.1016/0022-3956(82)90033-4

20. Chadjikyprianou, A., Hadjivassiliou, M., Papacostas, S., Constantinidou, F.: The neurocognitive study for the aging: longitudinal analysis on the contribution of sex, age, education and APOE E4 on cognitive performance. Front. Genet. **12** (2021)

21. García-Herranz, S., et al.: Normative data for verbal fluency, trail making, and rey-osterrieth complex figure tests on monolingual Spanish-speaking older adults. Archiv. Clin. Neuropsychol.: Off. J. Natl. Acad. Neuropsychol. **37**, 952–969 (2022). https://doi.org/10.1093/arclin/acab094

22. Godinho, F., Maruta, C., Borbinha, C., Pavão Martins, I.: Effect of education on cognitive performance in patients with mild cognitive impairment. Appl. Neuropsychol. Adult **29**, 1440–1449 (2022). https://doi.org/10.1080/23279095.2021.1887191

23. Jansen, M.G., et al.: Positive effects of education on cognitive functioning depend on clinical status and neuropathological severity. Front. Hum. Neurosci. **15** (2021)

24. Karstens, A.J., Maynard, T.R., Tremont, G.: Sex-specific differences in neuropsychological profiles of mild cognitive impairment in a hospital-based clinical sample. J. Int. Neuropsychol. Soc. **29**, 821–830 (2023). https://doi.org/10.1017/S1355617723000085

25. Beaumont, P., et al.: CausalNex (2021). https://github.com/mckinsey/causalnex. Accessed 28 Feb 2024

26. Arias, M., Pérez Martín, J., Luque, M., Díez, F.: OpenMarkov, an open-source tool for probabilistic graphical models. In: Kraus, S. (ed.) Twenty-Eighth International Joint Conference on Artificial Intelligence, pp. 6485–6487. International Joint Conferences on Artificial Intelligence (2019). https://doi.org/10.24963/ijcai.2019/931

27. Pedregosa, F., et al.: Scikit-learn: machine learning in Python. J. Mach. Learn. Res. **12**, 2825–2830 (2011)

Connectivity Patterns in Alzheimer Disease and Frontotemporal Dementia Patients Using Graph Theory

María Paula Bonomini[1,2](✉), Eduardo Ghiglioni[1,3], and Noelia Belén Rios[1,3]

[1] Instituto Argentino de Matemática "Alberto P. Calderón" (IAM), CONICET,
Buenos Aires, Argentina
paulabonomini@gmail.com
[2] Grupo Inteligencia Artificial - Universidad Tecnológica Nacional (UTN),
Facultad Regional Haedo, Haedo, Bs. As., Buenos Aires, Argentina
[3] Centro de Matemática La Plata (CMaLP) - Facultad de Cs. Exactas,
Universidad de La Plata, Buenos Aires, Argentina

Abstract. Alzheimers's Disease (AD) analisis is a high relevant topic in neuroscience nowadays. Stamm et al. studied for the first time functional connectivity in Alzheimer's Disease (AD) throughtout graph theoretical analysis. After that, a large number of scientists have studied AD using graph theory. Different indexes were computed such as Path Length, Clustering Coefficient, Small World, Global and Local Efficiency, etc. In this study, we focus in certain indexes trying to identify the differences in physiological connections among AD patients, Frontotemporal dementia (FTD) patients, and healthy controls using graph theoretical analysis. Our primary objective is to discern whether certain cortical areas exhibit differential connectivity patterns across the three groups, thereby providing valuable insights into the unique neuropathological signatures of each condition.

Keywords: Graph Theory · EEG · Alzheimer disease

1 Introduction

Alzheimer's disease (AD) is a progressive neurodegenerative disorder that is the leading cause of dementia worldwide. It is characterized by the accumulation of amyloid-β plaques and neurofibrillary tangles of hyperphosphorylated tau protein in the brain, leading to neuronal and synaptic loss and cognitive decline.
Key insights from the research studies include:

- AD diagnosis is currently supported by clinical criteria, including memory and cognitive impairment, with the exclusion of other causes of dementia through laboratory tests and neuropsychological assessments [10].
- Biomarkers for AD include *amyloid* plaques and *taurelated* neurodegeneration, detectable via imaging measures and cerebrospinal fluid analytes, which can precede clinical symptoms by years [8].

© The Author(s), under exclusive license to Springer Nature Switzerland AG 2024
J. M. Ferrández Vicente et al. (Eds.): IWINAC 2024, LNCS 14674, pp. 390–397, 2024.
https://doi.org/10.1007/978-3-031-61140-7_37

- Genetic studies have identified multiple causes of AD, with the discovery of new susceptibility genes offering insights into disease mechanisms and potential therapeutic targets [3,5,7].
- Research is moving towards understanding the earliest phase of AD, with preclinical AD defined as biomarker evidence of Alzheimer's pathological changes in cognitively healthy individuals [13].
- Artificial Intelligence (AI) has also been used to detect AD from medical images [6] or explanaible AI (xAI) can be used, as well for analizing physiological signals [9].
- Current treatments for AD are symptomatic, with drugs targeting cholinesterase enzymes and NMDA receptors; however, research is focusing on disease-modifying therapeutics that address various aspects of AD pathology6 [15].
- There is a growing emphasis on personalized medicine and the combination of lifestyle interventions with specific anti-Alzheimer's therapy to combat the disease [2,13].

The analysis of Alzheimer's disease today involves a multifaceted approach that includes clinical diagnosis supported by neuropsychological testing and biomarker analysis, genetic research to understand disease mechanisms, and the development of both symptomatic and disease-modifying treatments. The field is also exploring the potential of personalized medicine and lifestyle changes to improve outcomes for individuals with AD.

Alzheimer's disease (AD) and Frontotemporal dementia (FTD) represent two distinct neurodegenerative disorders, each characterized by unique clinical manifestations and neuropathological profiles. While AD is predominantly associated with memory impairment and cognitive decline, FTD typically manifests with changes in behavior, personality, and language abilities. Despite their differing clinical presentations, both conditions share commonalities in terms of cortical pathology and disrupted brain connectivity.

One key aspect of understanding the underlying neuropathology of these diseases lies in deciphering the intricate network of connections within the brain. The human brain is a complex system composed of various regions that interact through an intricate web of physiological connections. These connections, often referred to as the connectome, play a crucial role in orchestrating normal brain function and information processing. There were early attempts to describe AD disorder by means of graph theory. Stamm, in 2007 investigated whether functional brain networks were abnormally organized in Alzheimer's disease (AD). To this end, graph theoretical analysis was applied to matrices of functional connectivity of beta band-filtered electroencephalography (EEG) channels, finding differences in the shortest path of both groups [14].

In this study, we investigated the differences in physiological connections among AD patients, FTD patients, and healthy controls using graph theoretical analysis. Our primary objective was to discern whether certain cortical areas exhibit differential connectivity patterns across the three groups, thereby providing valuable insights into the unique neuropathological signatures of each condition.

2   Materials and Methods

Dataset Description. The data used in this study were obtained from the OpenNeuro repository (https://openneuro.org/), specifically from the dataset labeled DS004504. This dataset comprises EEG records from individuals diagnosed with Alzheimer's disease (AD), Frontotemporal dementia (FTD), and age-matched healthy controls [11].

DS004504 includes a total of 88 subjects, divided into three groups: AD patients (n=37), FTD patients (n=22), and healthy controls (n=29). The participants were matched for age, sex, and other demographic variables to minimize potential confounding effects. Clinical diagnosis of AD and FTD was established based on standardized diagnostic criteria, including comprehensive neuropsychological assessments and clinical evaluations by experienced clinicians.

2.1   Laplacian, Degree Matrices and Connectivity Measures

The Laplacian matrix was constructed over the beta-filtered EEG covariance matrix. This is, a correlation coefficient was computed on every pair of EEG electrodes bandpassed on the 13–30 Hz band (beta band) and thresholded. All those elements exceeding threshold were then binarized, and conformed the adjacency matrix. For beta filtering, a 4th order Butterworth filter between 13 and 30 Hz was accomplished. Afterwards, the degree matrix was computed, a diagonal matrix with the number of connections per channel, and the laplacian was obtained as the difference between the adjacency and the degree matrix.

In order to evaluate connectivity patterns across the different group of patients, several metrics were compared, such as *Density*, *Amount of Edges* (#*Edges*), the first non-null eigenvalue λ_{01}, the trace of the Degree matrix $\sum \lambda_i$, the standard deviation of the Degree matrix std(λ) and *Transitivity*. Metrics were implemented from graph-tool [12].

Over the laplacian matrix, the eigenvalues were calculated and the following metrics were obtained: the first non-null eigenvalue λ_{01}, the sum of all eigenvalues $\sum \lambda_i$ (trace of the degree matrix) and the standard deviation of all of the eigenvalues $std(\lambda)$.

In addition, the *Density* was computed as a ratio between the amount of edges E and the number of nodes N:

$$Density = \frac{2 * E}{N * (N - 1)} \tag{1}$$

Density refers to the ratio between the number of connections an actual graph has with respect to the maximum number of connections a graph can have. Moreover, the global clustering coefficient, also known as transitivity was computed as follows:

$$Transitivity = \frac{1}{N} \sum_v C(v) \qquad (2)$$

where N is the total number of nodes in the graph and $C(v)$ is the clustering coefficient of a node v:

$$C(v) = \frac{2 * T(v)}{deg(v) * (deg(v) - 1)} \qquad (3)$$

where $T(v)$ is the number of triangles that include node v.

3   Results

Table 1 depicts the above mentioned metrics for a particular case where the Laplacian for every patient was constructed over the beta-filtered EEG channels, for a threshold of 0.5. Table 1 shows the different parameters obtained for the 3 groups analized, Alzheimers's Disease patients (P_A), Control patients (P_C) and Frontotemporal Dementia patients (P_F) It is worth mentioning that *Density* was increasingly ordered from A to C, and then to F group, consistently with *#Edges* and the trace of the Degree matrix ($\sum \lambda_i$). Finally, note that *Transitivity* was lower for the C group as for the A and F groups.

Table 1. Connectivity measures for every patient group

	P_A	P_C	P_F
Density	0.0292	0.0643	0.0965
# Edges	5.0	11.0	16.5
λ_{01}	0.6426	0.5523	1.4592
$\sum \lambda_i$	10.0	22.0	33.0
std(λ)	1.1583	1.7264	1.9860
Transitivity	0.5556	0.4167	0.6464

Figure 1, on the other hand, shows the boxplots of the Degree matrix for every beta-filtered EEG channel accounting for every group. This matrix was constructed after thresholding the EEG covariance matrix with 0.5. Note that Alzheimers' (A) and Control (C) groups do not show connections in the F_z and F_4 channels, while the Frontotemporal Dementia (F) group does. Moreover, the F group shows an exacerbated connection pattern all over the EEG electrodes.

This pattern is recurrent when analyzing the Graph distribution among groups, which is statistically represented in Fig. 2. Notice that The Alzheimers' (A) group contains in proportion the highest amount of non-connected graphs while the Frontotemporal Dementia (F) group shows the highest amount of fully-connected graphs (or dense graphs). Here, the Control (C) group stands as the

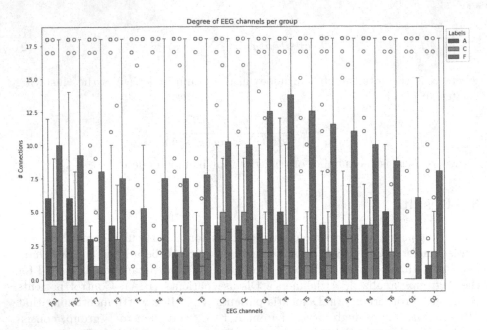

Fig. 1. Number of conections accounting for every beta-filtered EEG electrode for a threshold of 0.5. F group contained the most connected electrodes, followed by A or C groups, indistinctly.

group with the highest amount of non-dense graphs, suggesting an equilibrium between metabolic spence and functional connectivity.

In order to test whether this behaviour held for different strengths of connections, different thresholds in the EEG covariance matrix were swept from 0.3 to 0.7 in order to select increasingly stronger correlations among EEG channels. Figure 3 shows the *density* across connection strength for the three groups. Consistently, the Frontotemporal Dementia (brown) group sustained an increased density for all thresholds, while the Alzheimers' (blue) group showed a slightly higher density for small thresholds and decreased below the Contro (green) group levels when stronger correlations were accounted for.

4   Discussion and Conclusions

In this piece of work, the Control group showed, in proportion, the largest population with moderately connected graphs (non dense graphs), the Alzheimer's Disease group appeared as the group with the highest number of disconnected graphs and the Frontotemporal Dementia group the one populated with fully connected (dense) graphs mostly. Metrics such as density support this observation, which holds for Frontotemporal Dementia patients independently of correlation strength among EEG channels and for Alzheimers' patients, particularly for strongly correlated EEG channels (threshold above 0.4).

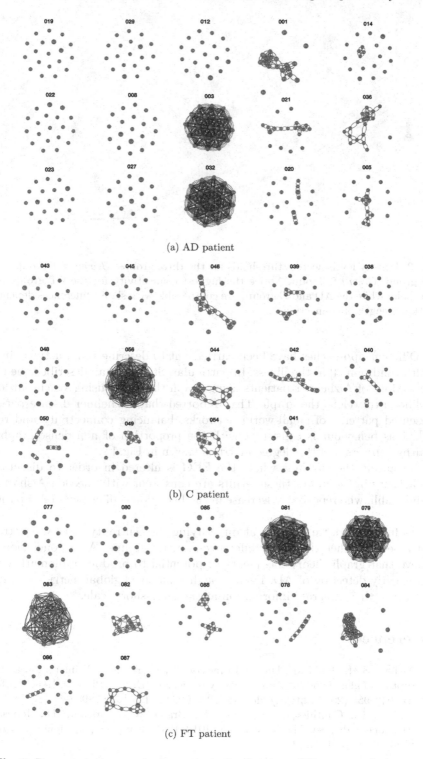

(a) AD patient

(b) C patient

(c) FT patient

Fig. 2. Representative graphs for patients for the three different populations.

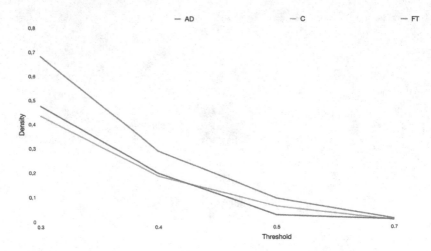

Fig. 3. Density levels accross thresholds for the three groups. *Brown)* FT group. *Blue)* AD group. *Green)* C group. Notice the highest connectivity for the FT group at all threshold, while the AD and C groups are comparable with slight differences depending on the strength of connections.

Different approaches have been carried out to describe brain activity in the health condition [4] or the illness. In particular, Stamm et al. described the EEG connections of Alzheimer patients using graph theory by using synchronization likelihood to weight the graph. They reported that Alzheimer disease patients presented patterns of small-world networks, balancing connectivity and reach [14]. This behaviour is consistent with the proportion of non dense graphs in healthy subjects and the degree matrices shown in Fig. 1.

Regarding the rhythms where the EEG is filtered in order to disentangle the activity in the brain, these results are consistent with Saeedeh Afshari and Mahdi Jalili, who reported a decrease in the beta global efficiency in AD patients [1].

As future work we can aim at quantifying the centrality of EEG electrodes and assess whether there are differences among groups. As a conclusion, we believe that graph theory has plenty of potential to produce a biomarker that allows early detection of AD. Even though some local-global metrics should be developed, that integrate information at the large-short scale.

References

1. Afshari, S.M., Jalili, M.: Directed functional networks in alzheimer's disease: disruption of global and local connectivity measures. IEEE J. Biomed. Health Inform. **21**, 949–955 (2017). https://doi.org/10.1109/JBHI.2016.2578954
2. Ballard, C., Gauthier, S., Corbett, A., Brayne, C., Aarsland, D., Jones, E.: Alzheimer's disease. The Lancet **377**, 1019–1031 (2011). https://doi.org/10.1016/S0140-6736(10)61349-9

3. Bettens, K., Sleegers, K., Broeckhoven, C.V.: Genetic insights in alzheimer's disease. Lancet Neurol. **12**, 92–104 (2013). https://doi.org/10.1016/S1474-4422(12)70259-4

4. Bonomini, M., Calvo, M., Morcillo, A., Segovia, F., Vicente, J., Fernandez-Jover, E.: The effect of breath pacing on task switching and working memory. Int. J. Neural Syst. **30**, 2050028 (2020)

5. Escott-Price, V., et al.: Gene-wide analysis detects two new susceptibility genes for Alzheimer's disease. PLoS ONE **9**, e9466 (2014). https://doi.org/10.1371/journal.pone.0094661

6. Górriz, J., et al.: Computational approaches to explainable artificial intelligence: advances in theory, applications and trends. Inf. Fusion **100**, 101945 (2023). https://doi.org/10.1016/j.inffus.2023.101945

7. Huang, Y., Mucke, L.: Alzheimer mechanisms and therapeutic strategies. Cell **148**, 1204–1222 (2012). https://doi.org/10.1016/j.cell.2012.02.040

8. Jack, C., Holtzman, D.: Biomarker modeling of Alzheimer's disease. Neuron **80**, 1347–1358 (2013). https://doi.org/10.1016/j.neuron.2013.12.003

9. Macas Ordónez, B.d.C., Garrigós, F.J., Martínez, J.J., Ferrández, J.M., Bonomini, M.P.: An explainable machine learning system for left bundle branch block detection and classification. Integr. Comput. Aided Eng. **31**(1), 43–58 (2024)

10. Mckhann, G., Drachman, D., Folstein, M., Katzman, R., Price, D., Stadlan, E.: Clinical diagnosis of Alzheimer's disease. Neurology **34**, 939–939 (1984). https://doi.org/10.1212/WNL.34.7.939

11. Miltiadous, A., et al.: A dataset of EEG recordings from: Alzheimer's disease, frontotemporal dementia and healthy subjects (2024). https://doi.org/10.18112/openneuro.ds004504.v1.0.7

12. Peixoto, T.P.: The *graph – tool* python library. figshare (2014). http://figshare.com/articles/graph_tool/1164194

13. Scheltens, P., et al.: Alzheimer's disease. The Lancet **388**, 505–517 (2016). https://doi.org/10.1016/S0140-6736(15)01124-1

14. Stam, C.J., Jones, B.F., Nolte, G., Breakspear, M., Scheltens, P.: Small-world networks and functional connectivity in Alzheimer's disease. Cereb. Cortex **17**(1), 92–99 (2007)

15. Weller, J., Budson, A.: Current understanding of alzheimer's disease diagnosis and treatment. F1000Research **7**, 1161 (2018). https://doi.org/10.12688/f1000research.14506.1

Socio-Cognitive, Affective and Physiological Computing

Binary Classification Methods for Movement Analysis from Functional Near-Infrared Spectroscopy Signals

Daniel Sánchez-Reolid[1], Roberto Sánchez-Reolid[1,2], José L. Gómez-Sirvent[1,2], Alejandro L. Borja[3], José M. Ferrández[4], and Antonio Fernández-Caballero[1,2,5(✉)]

[1] Neurocognition and Emotion Unit, Instituto de Investigación en Informática de Albacete, Albacete, Spain
antonio.fdez@uclm.es
[2] Departamento de Sistemas Informáticos, Universidad de Castilla-La Mancha, Albacete, Spain
[3] Departamento de Ingeniería Eléctrica, Electrónica, Automática y Comunicaciones, Universidad de Castilla-La Mancha, Albacete, Spain
[4] Departamento de Electrónica, Tecnología de Computadores y Proyectos, Universidad Politécnica de Cartagena, Cartagena, Spain
[5] Biomedical Research Networking Center in Mental Health, Instituto de Salud Carlos III (CIBERSAM-ISCIII), Madrid, Spain

Abstract. This paper investigates different techniques for binary classification in a multi-participant setting, with a focus on complex movement tasks. It uses statistical methods to extract features from pre-processed biosignals acquired by functional near-infrared spectroscopy (fNIRS) from real participants, obtained from the validated finger-tapping dataset. Unique approaches are used to process the fNIRS signals, including attenuation of short channel contributions and various filtering and other pre-processing techniques. For this investigation, a number of algorithms are used to optimise hyperparameters and model topologies in six different models: four conventional machine learning methods and two artificial neural networks. Among these models, the support vector machine classifier emerges as the top performer, achieving the highest average accuracy, precision, recall and F1-score (89.17%, 91.44%, 86.67% and 88.92%, respectively). However, the multi-layer perceptron classifier shows superior performance in terms of area under the ROC curve (92.56%), closely followed by the convolutional neural network classifier (91.70%), suggesting their slightly better ability to discriminate between classes. This study highlights the potential of using different classification methods to improve the accuracy of biosignal analysis obtained from fNIRS devices.

Keywords: Motor cortex · finger-tapping · functional near-infrared spectroscopy · machine learning · signal processing · classification

J. M. Ferrández Vicente et al. (Eds.): IWINAC 2024, LNCS 14674, pp. 401–410, 2024.
https://doi.org/10.1007/978-3-031-61140-7_38

1   Introduction

In our increasingly digital world, the integration of affective and movement computing holds great promise for enhancing user experiences and improving human-computer interactions [25]. From sentiment analysis in social media to adaptive virtual assistants that respond to users' emotional states, the rise of affective computing underscores the growing recognition of emotional intelligence in technology [18, 23, 24].

In this sense, it is necessary to understand the processes that take place in the different parts of the human body. In our case, it is necessary to study the nervous system and its main organ, the brain [7]. Functional near-infrared spectroscopy (fNIRS) is a cutting-edge technology that is revolutionising the neuroimaging landscape [13]. Using near-infrared light to measure changes in blood oxygen levels in the brain, fNIRS provides a non-invasive and real-time method of monitoring brain activity [11]. This innovative technique has gained prominence in fields ranging from neuroscience research to clinical applications and human-computer interaction studies [22]. Its portability and versatility open new avenues for understanding cognitive processes, improving brain-computer interfaces and contributing to advances in personalised healthcare [16, 17, 19].

The detection of movement using fNIRS signals has emerged as an innovative approach to scientific research. Unlike other technologies, fNIRS offers a unique combination of high temporal and spatial resolution. This facilitates the precise identification of brain regions involved in movement detection and processing. This advance has significant applications in neuroscience, biomedical engineering and assistive technologies, providing new insights into understanding and improving human movement perception and execution [2].

The application of machine learning (ML) and artificial intelligence (AI) to signal processing has ushered in a transformative era [9]. Advanced ML algorithms harness the ability to efficiently analyse and interpret signals ranging from audio and image data to biomedical information. In addition, by exploiting the adaptability of AI models, signal processing applications can improve accuracy, automate complex tasks, and discover patterns in vast datasets that may elude traditional methods [20].

This paper presents a set of methods for the detection and classification of fNIRS signals for the analysis of movement. The aim is to determine activation states in the motor system. For this purpose, information from a finger-tapping dataset is used [12]. To this end, innovative methods based on AI and ML will be investigated.

2   Material and Methods

2.1   The fNIRS Dataset

Five participants performed a task in which they were instructed to tap their fingers with their thumbs when they heard an auditory cue [12] in order to set up this study. If the auditory cue came from the left earphone, participants tapped with their left hand. Conversely, when the auditory cue came from the right earphone, participants tapped with their right hand. The tapping action, performed with the thumb on the fingers, coincided with the 5-second duration of the auditory stimulus. In particular, each experimental block required participants to use a single hand. Both conditions - right and left hand tapping - were randomly presented 30 times each, with the inter-stimulus interval randomly varied between 15 and 30 s. The final condition served as a control, with no motor task.

Optodes were positioned over the motor cortex for data acquisition. The setup included a total of 20 source-detector pairs, characterised by an approximate separation of 30 mm, referred to as long-range channels. In addition, the recording apparatus contained 8 additional source-detector pairs with a separation of 8 mm, referred to as short-range channels. These shorter channels were specifically designed to detect extra-cerebral changes in oxygenated and deoxygenated haemoglobin levels.

Although the finger-tapping database contains three different conditions, this article will only focus on the binary classification of the left and right hand tapping tasks, since this is a complex classification task due to the similarity of the haemodynamic response, as can be seen in Fig. 1.

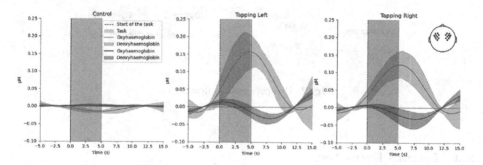

Fig. 1. Representation of the standard fNIRS response image for the conditions and region of interest of the dataset. An epoch-averaged waveform is generated for each condition. The waveform for oxygenated haemoglobin (red) and deoxygenated haemoglobin (blue) are shown. The duration of the task is shown in grey. (Color figure online)

2.2 Pre-processing

To improve the quality of the raw fNIRS signals by minimising artefacts and noise, pre-processing was performed using the MNE Python 1.4.2 package [8] in accordance with established guidelines [26] (see Fig. 2). First, the raw signals were transformed into optical density (OD) signals. Since we have short channels, we applied extracerebral systemic activity correction [21] to improve the quality of the signal. Next, we assessed the quality of the scalp-optic coupling using the scalp coupling index (SCI) [15]. Channels with an SCI below 0.8 were considered erroneous and removed, with any gaps filled by interpolation based on nearby channels.

Motion artefacts were then removed using temporal derivative distribution repair (TDDR) [6] applied to the OD signal. TDDR effectively removes spike artefacts without the need for user-specified parameters. The processed OD data were then converted to oxyhaemoglobin (HbO_2) and deoxyhaemoglobin (HbR) concentrations using the modified Beer-Lambert law [5] with a partial pathlength factor of 6. A Finite Impulse Response (FIR) bandpass filter (0.01–0.08 Hz) was used in the final pre-processing step. The low-pass component (0.08 Hz) targeted physiological noise, such as heartbeat signals, while the high-pass component (0.01 Hz) removed slow drifts. Finally, the data were segmented into epochs, with each epoch consisting of a 15-s post-stimulus segment and a preceding 5-s baseline interval for baseline correction.

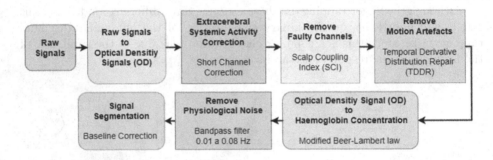

Fig. 2. Pre-processing flowchart.

2.3   Feature Extraction

Standard feature extraction procedures were used to generate vectorised representations of the data within each epoch. First, the 15 s epochs were segmented into three 5-s windows and the mean of each window was calculated for each channel. Subsequently, the means of the HbR channels were eliminated due to the strong dependence between HbO_2 and HbR channels, with HbO_2 channels typically showing a more robust response [4]. The means from all windows and HbO_2 channels were then concatenated, resulting in a feature vector of 60 features (3 time windows × 20 HbO_2 channels) for each epoch. Finally, the feature vectors, labelled X, were normalised using normalisation by Z-score:

$$X_{\text{scaled}} = \frac{X - \mu}{\sigma}$$

where X_{scaled} is the scaled version of the original data X, μ is the mean of each feature in the dataset, and σ is the standard deviation of each feature in the dataset.

2.4 Machine Learning Algorithm Selection

Python 3.10 and the libraries Scikit-learn [14], Tensorflow [1] and Keras [3] were used to implement different classifiers in the research. The hyperparameters of each model mentioned were obtained by performing a grid search process to avoid overfitting and underfitting. Default parameters were used for the remaining parameters that were not defined during the grid search. In the training process, the dataset was divided into 80% for training and validation and 20% for testing, using stratified k-fold cross-validation with 5 splits. In addition, the training process was run with 100 epochs and early stopping conditions were added to avoid using more time than necessary.

The research used six supervised classifiers from different categories. Specifically, from the classical methods, Gaussian naive Bayes (GNB), k-nearest neighbour (kNN), random forest (RF) and support vector machine (SVM) were chosen (see Table 1). Conversely, Fig. 3 shows two configurations of artificial neural networks (ANN) selected: a convolutional neural network (CNN) and a multilayer perceptron (MLP). The classifiers and their respective hyperparameters and topologies are shown in Table 1.

Table 1. Machine Learning Models and Hyperparameters

	Models	Type	Hyperparameters
Classical	GNB		Default
	kNN	Minkowski	9 neighbours
	RF		Estimators = 100 Maximum depth = 10 Minimum samples split = 5 Criterion = Gini
	SVM	Linear	$C = 0.1$ γ = Scale
ANNs	CNN		Filters in Conv1D = 32 Kernel size in Conv1D = 7 Pool size = 2 Neurons in Dense-3 = 128 Activation Dense-3 = ReLU
	MLP		Neurons in Dense-1 = 128 Activation Dense-1 = eLU Value in Dropout = 0.5 Neurons in Dense-2 = 128 Activation Dense-2 = eLU
	CNN/MLP		Neurons in Out = 1 Activation Out = Sigmoid Value of Learning Rate = 0.001 Best optimiser = Adam

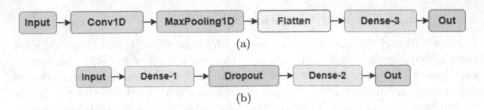

Fig. 3. (a) CNN model. (b) MLP model.

2.5 Performance Metrics

In a binary classification scenario, it is important to assess whether the models are working as intended. Several metrics were used to evaluate the performance of the models. Following the prediction made by each classifier, four types of results were observed: true positives (TP), true negatives (TN), false positives (FP) and false negatives (FN). TP and TN indicate the correct classification of an element into its respective category. Conversely, FP and FN occur when an element is classified in a class other than its actual category. The various metrics used to measure performance are as follows:

- **Accuracy (ACR)** is the degree of closeness to the true value. It is calculated by dividing the sum of TP and TN by the total number of predictions.
- **Precision (P)** is the proportion of successful positive predictions. It's calculated by dividing TP by the sum of TP and FP.
- **Recall (R)** is the proportion of relevant instances retrieved. It's calculated by dividing TP by the sum of TP and FN.
- **F1-score** is the harmonic mean of precision and recall. It provides a single value that balances both precision and recall.
- **Area under the ROC curve (AUC)** and **Receiver Operating Characteristics (ROC) curve** are metrics for classification models that assess performance across different threshold settings. The ROC curve plots the TP rate against the FP rate, and AUC represents the area under this curve, indicating the discriminative ability of the model.
- **Confusion matrix** is a table summarising the performance of a classification algorithm, showing the number of TPs, TNs, FPs and FNs.

3 Results and Discussion

3.1 Classifier Results

Table 2 presents various statistical metrics including accuracy, precision, recall, F1-score and AUC for the six classifiers. The classifiers were configured with the best hyperparameters and these results were derived from 100 rounds of stratified k-fold cross-validation with 5 splits. The dataset was split into 80% for training and validation and 20% for testing. Means and standard deviations are given for each statistical metric.

Table 2. Mean and standard deviation of the evaluation metrics of the different classifiers (in %).

Model	Accuracy	Precision	Recall	F1-Score	AUC
CNN	85.67 (7.68)	86.22 (8.55)	85.67 (6.84)	85.79 (7.09)	91.7 (7.02)
GNB	66.0 (6.72)	63.2 (5.25)	76.33 (8.88)	69.07 (6.52)	66.0 (6.72)
kNN	72.0 (5.15)	72.26 (5.72)	72.0 (7.02)	71.94 (5.17)	72.0 (5.15)
RF	79.17 (5.28)	80.15 (5.9)	78.0 (8.46)	78.8 (5.61)	79.17 (5.28)
MLP	86.83 (6.34)	87.97 (6.2)	85.33 (7.63)	86.57 (6.54)	**92.56 (7.33)**
SVM	**89.17 (4.73)**	**91.44 (5.99)**	**86.67 (4.71)**	**88.92 (4.73)**	89.17 (4.73)

Based on the results, the best classifier is the SVM classifier, which achieves the highest mean values for accuracy (89.17%), precision (91.44%), recall (86.67%) and F1-score (88.92%). This indicates its effectiveness in terms of performance in predicting the classification labels. The MLP classifier has the second highest mean accuracy (86.83%), precision (87.97%) and F1-score (86.57%). The MLP classifier only outperforms the SVM classifier in the AUC metric (92.56%). The CNN classifier has a slightly higher recall (85.67%) than the MLP model (85.33%), but both models do not show significant differences in the results. The GNB classifier has the lowest mean values for all metrics, and the kNN and RF classifiers are in the middle range.

The AUC metric also provides valuable insight into the performance of each classifier. The proposed MLP classifier achieves the highest AUC, indicating its ability to effectively discriminate between classes (see Fig. 4). The proposed CNN classifier obtains the second highest AUC, indicating its usefulness in classifying the data. In this comparison, the GNB classifier shows the lowest AUC, indicating its limitations in discriminating between classes.

In order to better contextualise these results, it is important to compare them with similar studies. For example, a previous study used learning algorithms similar to those presented in this paper [10]. It was found that the average classification accuracies achieved in that study were 59% for the SVM model and 75% for the kNN and RF models. This leads us to believe that the results obtained in this study are in line with those obtained in previous studies, even observing an improvement in our results. This increase in performance could be due to several reasons, such as the optimisation of the parameters, the quality of the data used or the implementation of more advanced pre-processing techniques.

4 Conclusions

In this paper, we compared different classification methods using statistical feature extraction on pre-processed fNIRS biosignals belonging to the validated finger-tapping dataset [12]. Novel methods have been used to process the fNIRS signal, including the suppression of the contribution of the short channels in the signal, as well as various filters and other pre-processing techniques.

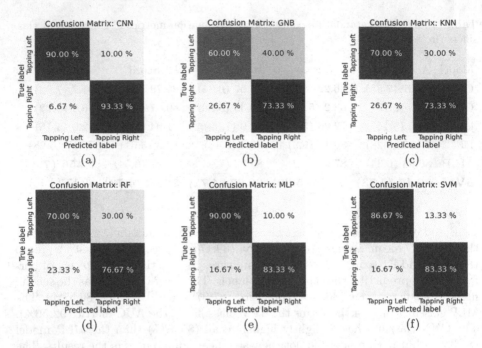

Fig. 4. Confusion matrices for the six models extracted from the 100 iterations. (a) CNN, (b) GNB, (c) kNN, (d) RF, (e) MLP and (f) SVM

In order to carry out this study, different algorithms were used to correctly dimension the hyperparameters and the different topologies of the neural networks used. The SVM classifier outperformed the others with the highest average values for accuracy, precision, recall and F1 score (89.17%, 91.44%, 86.67% and 88.92%, respectively). The MLP classifier excels in AUC (92.56%), followed by the CNN classifier (91.70%), indicating their slightly better ability to discriminate between classes.

By experimenting with networks containing different numbers of hidden layers, we have shown that deeper networks do not provide superior performance in this particular task. A likely explanation for this phenomenon is the constraint of limited training data. Deep neural networks typically require large training data sets to learn patterns effectively.

Note that advancing the field will require the incorporation of new signal modalities, larger and more diverse datasets, and machine learning methods that allow for comparison and integration of results with previous research.

These preliminary results represent a major step forward in our research efforts. The aim is to delve further into the temporal and spatial domain to improve our understanding of the underlying signals. Increasing classification accuracy promises to be a major step forward in deciphering fNIRS signals.

Acknowledgements. Grants PID2023-149753OB-C21 and PID2023-149753OB-C22 funded by Spanish MCIU/AEI/10.13039/501100011033/ERDF, EU. Grants PID2020-115220 RB-C21 and PID2020-115220RB-C22 funded by Spanish MCIN/AEI/10.13039/ 501100011033 and by "ERDF A way to make Europe". Grant BES-2021-097834 funded by MCIN/AEI/ 10.13039/501100011033 and by "ESF Investing in your future". Grant 2022-GRIN-34436 funded by Universidad de Castilla-La Mancha and by "ERDF A way of making Europe". This work has also been partially supported by Junta de Comunidades de Castilla-La Mancha/ESF (grant no. SBPLY/21/180501/000030) and by CIBERSAM, Instituto de Salud Carlos III, Ministerio de Ciencia, Innovación y Universidades.

References

1. Abadi, M., et al.: TensorFlow: Large-Scale Machine Learning on Heterogeneous Systems (2015). https://www.tensorflow.org/
2. Brigadoi, S., et al.: Motion artifacts in functional near-infrared spectroscopy: a comparison of motion correction techniques applied to real cognitive data. Neuroimage **85**, 181–191 (2014)
3. Chollet, F.: Deep Learning with Python, 2nd edn. Manning (2021)
4. Cui, X., Bray, S., Reiss, A.L.: Functional near infrared spectroscopy (NIRS) signal improvement based on negative correlation between oxygenated and deoxygenated hemoglobin dynamics. Neuroimage **49**(4), 3039–3046 (2010)
5. Delpy, D.T., Cope, M., van der Zee, P., Arridge, S., Wray, S., Wyatt, J.: Estimation of optical pathlength through tissue from direct time of flight measurement. Phys. Med. Biol. **33**(12), 1433 (1988)
6. Fishburn, F.A., Ludlum, R.S., Vaidya, C.J., Medvedev, A.V.: Temporal derivative distribution repair (TDDR): a motion correction method for fNIRS. Neuroimage **184**, 171–179 (2019)
7. García-Martínez, B., Fernández-Caballero, A., Martínez-Rodrigo, A., Alcaraz, R., Novais, P.: Evaluation of brain functional connectivity from electroencephalographic signals under different emotional states. Int. J. Neural Syst. **32**(10), 2250026 (2022)
8. Gramfort, A., et al.: MEG and EEG data analysis with MNE-Python. Front. Neurosci. **7**(267), 1–13 (2013)
9. Górriz, J., et al.: Computational approaches to explainable artificial intelligence: advances in theory, applications and trends. Inf. Fusion **100**, 101945 (2023)
10. Khan, H., Noori, F.M., Yazidi, A., Uddin, M.Z., Khan, M.N.A., Mirtaheri, P.: Classification of individual finger movements from right hand using fNIRS signals. Sensors **21**(23), 7943 (2021)
11. Lisboa, I.C., Queirós, S., Miguel, H., Sampaio, A., Santos, J.A., Pereira, A.F.: Infants' cortical processing of biological motion configuration-a fNIRS study. Infant Behav. Dev. **60**, 101450 (2020)
12. Luke, R., McAlpine, D.: fNIRS Finger Tapping Data in BIDS Format (2022). https://doi.org/10.5281/zenodo.6575155
13. Patashov, D., Menahem, Y., Gurevitch, G., Kameda, Y., Goldstein, D., Balberg, M.: fNIRS: non-stationary preprocessing methods. Biomed. Signal Process. Control **79**, 104110 (2023)
14. Pedregosa, F., et al.: Scikit-Learn: Machine Learning in Python. J. Mach. Learn. Res. **12**, 2825–2830 (2011)

15. Pollonini, L., Olds, C., Abaya, L., Bortfeld, H., Beauchamp, M.S., Oghalai, J.S.: Phoebe: a method for real time mapping of optodes-scalp coupling in functional near-infrared spectroscopy. Biomed. Opt. Express **7**(12), 5104–5119 (2016)

16. Sánchez-Reolid, D., Sánchez-Reolid, R., Fernández-Caballero, A., Borja, A.L.: Pleasure and displeasure identification from fNIRS signals. In: Novais, P., et al. (eds.) Ambient Intelligence—Software and Applications—14th International Symposium on Ambient Intelligence, pp. 209–219. Springer, Cham (2023). https://doi.org/10.1007/978-3-031-43461-7_21

17. Sánchez-Reolid, R., et al.: Artificial neural networks to assess emotional states from brain-computer interface. Electronics **7**(12), 384 (2018)

18. Sánchez-Reolid, R., Martínez-Rodrigo, A., López, M.T., Fernández-Caballero, A.: Deep support vector machines for the identification of stress condition from electrodermal activity. Int. J. Neural Syst. **30**(7), 2050031 (2020)

19. Sánchez-Reolid, R., et al.: Emotion classification from EEG with a low-cost BCI versus a high-end equipment. Int. J. Neural Syst. **32**(10), 2250041 (2022)

20. Sánchez-Reolid, R., et al.: Machine learning techniques for arousal classification from electrodermal activity: a systematic review. Sensors **22**, 8886 (2022)

21. Scholkmann, F., Metz, A.J., Wolf, M.: Measuring tissue hemodynamics and oxygenation by continuous-wave functional near-infrared spectroscopy-how robust are the different calculation methods against movement artifacts? Physiol. Meas. **35**(4), 717 (2014)

22. Shibu, C.J., Sreedharan, S., Arun, K., Kesavadas, C., Sitaram, R.: Explainable artificial intelligence model to predict brain states from fNIRS signals. Front. Hum. Neurosci. **16** (2023).https://doi.org/10.3389/fnhum.2022.1029784

23. Vicente-Querol, M.A., et al.: Effect of action units, viewpoint and immersion on emotion recognition using dynamic virtual faces. Int. J. Neural Syst. **33**(10), 2350053 (2023)

24. Vicente-Querol, M.A., et al.: Facial affect recognition in immersive virtual reality: where is the participant looking? Int. J. Neural Syst. **32**(10), 2250029 (2022)

25. Wang, Y., et al.: A systematic review on affective computing: emotion models, databases, and recent advances. Inf. Fusion **83–84**, 19–52 (2022)

26. Yücel, M.A., et al.: Best practices for fNIRS publications. Neurophotonics **8**(1), 012101 (2021)

Heart Attack Detection Using Body Posture and Facial Expression of Pain

Gabriel Rojas-Albarracín[1], Antonio Fernández-Caballero[1,2(✉)],
António Pereira[3,4], and María T. López[1,2]

[1] Instituto de Investigación en Informática de Albacete, Universidad de Castilla-La Mancha, Calle de la Investigación 2, Albacete, Spain
antonio.fdez@uclm.es
[2] Departamento de Sistemas Informáticos, Universidad de Castilla-La Mancha, Avenida de España s/n, Albacete, Spain
[3] Polytechnic Institute of Leiria, Computer Science and Communications Research Centre, School of Technology and Management, Leiria, Portugal
[4] INOV INESC INOVAÇÃO, Institute of New Technologies-Leiria Office, Leiria, Portugal

Abstract. It is not uncommon for a person to be alone when they have a heart attack. Getting help quickly can mean the difference between life and death. The pain a person feels during a heart attack may prevent them from seeking help in time, so automated methods are needed to detect and alert to such events. This article presents a proposal based on machine vision and deep learning to identify possible heart attacks. First, a typical human posture of a possible heart attack is identified using the upper body joints from skeletal studies. As similar non-infarct postures are possible, the posture analysis is integrated with the facial expression of pain to reduce the number of false positives. The proposed method has achieved 93.33% accuracy in detecting myocardial infarction.

Keywords: Human activity recognition · image analysis · heart attack detection · geometrical features · facial expression · pain detection

1 Introduction

According to studies by the World Health Organization (WHO), heart attacks have become one of the leading causes of death in developed countries [20]. This may be due to several factors, including an increase in the average age of the population [3,17]. In addition, the dynamics of today's world have made it common for people over 65 to be alone for most of the day, whether due to social, cultural or economic factors. The combination of increasing age and isolation among the elderly has made the problem of dying alone increasingly common, with heart attacks being one of the biggest contributors to this situation.

When a person has a heart attack, they experience severe chest pain [11,12]. This may mean that the person is unable to call for help themselves and if

© The Author(s), under exclusive license to Springer Nature Switzerland AG 2024
J. M. Ferrández Vicente et al. (Eds.): IWINAC 2024, LNCS 14674, pp. 411–420, 2024.
https://doi.org/10.1007/978-3-031-61140-7_39

they are not accompanied they may not receive help in time. Considering only economic factors, the cost of having a person constantly monitoring the condition of an elderly person may not be affordable for families or governments. For all the above reasons, it may be good to have automated tools to detect life-threatening situations such as heart attacks. Recognising that a person is experiencing chest pain and that it could be related to a heart attack is something that humans can easily do. But it is still a big challenge for an automated system.

Proposals for identifying adverse events can be categorised as invasive or non-invasive, depending on how the data to be analysed is obtained. Invasive methods tend to provide a high level of accuracy. However, they require the person to wear personal devices at all times [10,13–15], which for some people may require assistance from others. In this line, the use of accelerometers and gyroscopes is noteworthy [6]. The second class is based on non-invasive methods, mainly cameras [8,9,16]. Although this type of approach often requires more processing power to achieve rates similar to those of invasive systems, they have the advantage of being able to be used for several people at the same time. Moreover, the development of powerful artificial intelligence algorithms, especially of convolutional neural networks (CNNs), has allowed the use of less specialised devices, such as webcams [5,7].

This article proposes a non-invasive method to detect possible myocardial infarction. To this end, an analysis in two main steps is outlined. First, the body posture is identified and then the facial expression of pain is determined. This work includes the creation of a set of images of people simulating heart attack conditions. The proposed system is designed to be incorporated into larger applications such as healthy intelligent environments [4] and companion robots [19], enriching their ability to detect human activity [1].

2   Identification of a Potential Heart Attack

When a person is having a heart attack, two facets of their body manifest themselves: a posture in which one or both hands are held mainly to the chest, and an expression of pain on the face. This work uses these two patterns to identify people who may be having a heart attack. Figure 1 shows the steps taken to incorporate the two facts outlined above and how each process is integrated to identify a possible heart attack. On the one hand, the skeleton is analysed to identify a pose that represents a possible heart attack, and on the other hand, the face is examined to look for an expression of pain; by combining both analyses, the false positives of each are reduced.

2.1   Data Adjustment

Detection of the Joints. There are two contributions to the classification scheme of this proposal. Firstly, the coordinates of the main joints of the upper body are used, and secondly, a segment of the image containing the person's face is included. The necessary coordinates are obtained using some algorithms

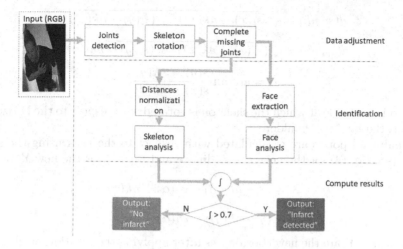

Fig. 1. Identification process of a potential heart attack in images.

that exist in the literature, such as a work that generates the main joints of the person [2]. Since the identification of a possible heart attack is represented by a posture with the hands on the chest, it is sufficient to analyse the 8 points shown in Table 1. Similarly, from the coordinates of the shoulders, it is possible to generate a bounding box containing the face of the person.

Table 1. Key points considered to identify a person's posture.

Nomenclature	Joint	Nomenclature	Joint
ns	P0: Nose	w_r	P4: Right wrist
nk	P1: Neck	s_l	P5: Left shoulder
s_r	P2: Right shoulder	e_l	P6: Left elbow
e_r	P3: Right elbow	w_l	P7: Left wrist

Rotation of the Skeleton. Often, both the posture of the person and the angle of the camera to the person change the data to be analysed, especially when the analysis is based on the absolute location of the points. In order to analyse the data obtained when generating the points (previous step) and to minimise the effect of the angle of the person in relation to the camera, it is necessary to perform a rotation of the skeleton, taking the neck of the person as the central point. First, the rotation is performed by calculating the distance between the neck and each shoulder using Eq. (1) and Eq. (2). Then take the line through the neck and the furthest shoulder to get the angle (see Eq. (3)) that will be used to rotate each joint.

$$d(s_l, nk) = \sqrt{(s_l(x) - nk(x))^2 + (s_l(y) - nk(y))^2} \tag{1}$$

$$d(s_r, nk) = \sqrt{(s_r(x) - nk(x))^2 + (s_r(y) - nk(y))^2} \tag{2}$$

$$\alpha = \arctan \frac{s(y) - nk(y)}{s(x) - nk(x)} \tag{3}$$

where α is the angle at which the skeleton is rotated with respect to the horizontal and s is the farthest shoulder.

Finally, all points are recalculated with respect to the neck using the angle *alpha* (see Eq. (4) for the new X coordinate and Eq. (5) for the new Y value).

$$X = (x - nk(x)) \cdot \cos(\alpha) + nk(x) \tag{4}$$

$$Y = (y - nk(y)) \cdot sin(\alpha) + nk(y) \tag{5}$$

where X and Y are the new coordinates after applying the rotation, while x and y are the coordinates of any point before the rotation.

Completion of the Joints. It is important to note that some of the points (corresponding to joints) may not have been detected due to various factors such as occlusion. This paper proposes to infer the location of a body part (which has not been detected) from its lateral equivalent or from neighbouring joints. For example, if the right shoulder (s_r), right elbow (e_r) or right wrist (w_r) is occluded or not present in the image, but its lateral equivalent is present, the Eqs. (6), (7) and (8) are used. The left side of the body can be inferred.

$$s_r(X, Y) = (nk(X) - s_l(X), s_l(Y)) \tag{6}$$

$$e_r(X, Y) = (nk(X) - e_l(X), e_l(Y)) \tag{7}$$

$$w_r(X, Y) = (nk(X) - w_l(X), w_l(Y)) \tag{8}$$

If the lateral equivalent joint is not available, the elbow and wrist are calculated using the Eqs. (9) and (10).

$$e_r(X, Y) = (s_r(X), s_r(Y) + d(s, nk) \tag{9}$$

$$w_r(X, Y) = (e_r(X), e_r(Y) + d(s, nk) \tag{10}$$

where $d(s, nk)$ is the distance from the neck to the farthest shoulder.

Normalisation of the Distances. To prevent the relative size of the person in the image from affecting the subsequent calculation of posture, it is necessary to normalise the distance between the points to a common distance. The normalisation of the points is done by calculating the ratio of the distance between the neck and each of the joints to the distance between the neck and the farthest shoulder (see Eq. (11) and Eq. (12)). This process projects all points onto a Cartesian plane where the coordinate $(0, 0)$ corresponds to the neck.

$$\hat{X} = \frac{X - nk(X)}{d(s, nk)} \tag{11}$$

$$\hat{Y} = \frac{Y - nk(Y)}{d(s, nk)} \tag{12}$$

where (X, Y) are the coordinates of the points to be normalised, nk is the point in the plane of the neck, $d(s, nk)$ is the distance between the neck and the farthest shoulder, and $(\hat{X}, \hat{Y})$ are the coordinates of the normalised points projected onto the plane with the vertex at the neck.

At the end of the normalisation process, a projection of the points is obtained.

Extraction of the Face. Using the points generated when the skeleton was obtained, a segment of the image corresponding to a photograph in which the person's face is found was extracted. In this case, three different distances were calculated, starting from the central point of the face (the nose) to the neck, to the left shoulder and to the right shoulder, then a square is drawn whose sides are twice the largest of these distances, and the centre of the square will be the coordinate of the nose. Finally, the resulting frame is scaled to a size of 64 × 64 pixels.

2.2   Heart Attack Posture Detection

Once the key points have been extracted and adjusted, the next step is to see if the detected position coincides with a possible heart attack. In this article, two methods have been chosen for this purpose. The first, geometric, is based on the direct location of the joints in the plane. The second, more sophisticated, uses a trained CNN to identify posture.

Geometric Identification of the Heart Attack Posture. Identifying posture through geometric analysis of the skeleton (sk-Geometric) is based on the fact that chest pain is common during a heart attack. It is therefore reasonable to assume that a person will bring one or both hands to this area. On the other hand, we have assumed that the person's chest is an imaginary quadrilateral between the shoulders and elbows. Taking this into account, it is sufficient to calculate whether the points of at least one of the two hands (or wrists) lie within the imaginary quadrilateral to identify a possible infarct pose.

Heart Attack Posture Identification Using a CNN. As mentioned above, the points detected may be out of place, mainly due to the angle of the person in relation to the camera. On the other hand, in some extreme cases, the above-mentioned corrections may not have been entirely satisfactory. For this reason, a CNN (shown in Fig. 2) has been implemented that receives the input points and provides a ratio that indicates the possibility that the given points correspond to a potential heart attack posture; this method has been named sk-CNN.

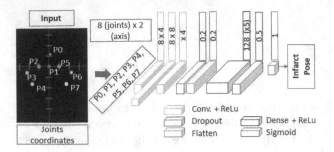

Fig. 2. Network architecture to identify a heart attack posture from a skeleton.

The sk-CNN method receives the coordinates of the points where the joints are located to identify the posture. The previously adjusted and normalised values are processed by a convolution layer. A dropout layer then removes 20% of the generated joints to reduce overtraining. The data then changes shape from 2D to 1D to be delivered in five dense layers, which are also followed by a dropout layer that removes 50% of the connections. Finally, a softmax function allows you to assess whether a received point configuration belongs to a posture that resembles a possible heart attack.

2.3 Detection of Pain in Facial Expression

Regardless of the method used to identify posture (geometric or CNN), the mere identification of a hand on the chest is not sufficient to indicate a possible heart attack. There are situations in which the person adopts similar positions, such as crossing their arms. For this reason, an analysis of the face has been added to look for patterns that indicate pain. This, together with the detection of at least one hand on the chest, should increase the certainty of detecting a heart attack in the images.

Therefore, another CNN (see Fig. 3) has been implemented to identify whether a human face shows an expression of pain (PainExpression method). This CNN receives images scaled to a size of 64 × 64 pixels and returns a ratio that indicates the likelihood that a given image corresponds to a face with a pain expression. At the entry of the CNN, the proposed design has two convolutional layers. After each convolutional layer, a max pooling layer is provided to keep the number of variables of the CNN low, thus maintaining a size that is easy to compute. In the middle of the network, just after the convolutional layers, there is a dropout layer to prevent the generated model from overfitting. This is followed by a flattening layer, which allows the 2D design of the convolutional layers to be changed to a vectorial one, so that the values generated in the previous layers are transferred to the traditional neural layers. At the end of the network, two blocks of three dense layers of 32 neurons and a dropout were added, which feeds the result of the forward propagation to a softmax function with two outputs. These classify whether or not a face has an expression of pain.

2.4   Combined Use of Posture and Pain Detection

As mentioned above, posture detection alone can lead to possible false positives in heart attack detection. Similarly, the detection of pain in the face alone is not a guarantee of a heart attack. However, if both a heart attack pose and a facial expression of pain are detected, it is reasonable to consider it a possible heart attack. In this case, the accuracy rate of both analyses is averaged, and if the value exceeds a threshold that was experimentally set at 0.7, it is identified as a heart attack.

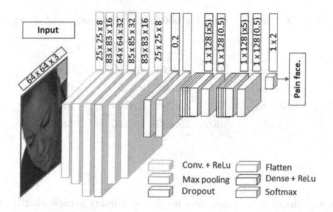

Fig. 3. Network architecture to identify pain in facial expression.

2.5   Training

The first step in conducting the training and testing is to prepare a data set of people in a possible heart attack state. This is a set of 1,400 images with a single person in each image (50% images containing a heart attack; 50% showing some other activity other than a heart attack). Some of the images in the data set were downloaded from several random sources on the internet, and others were created by us.

The number of images in the data set was then increased using the data augmentation strategy to further improve the prediction rate. Specifically, a combination of transformations (rotation, increase or decrease in width and/or height, zoom, horizontal flip, brightness and grey scale modification) was applied to each image, resulting in a total of 30,800 images. The subsets of "Heart attack" and "No heart attack", separately, were divided into three parts, namely 70% for training, 15% for validation and 15% for testing (see Table 2). This is a typical distribution in many other neural network based applications [18].

3   Results

After coding and training, all methods were tested. First, the two methods for detecting myocardial infarction from posture, the method for geometrically identifying the skeleton (sk-Geometric) and the method for identifying the skeleton with CNN (sk-CNN) were tested. Next, the method for detecting pain expression on the face (PainExpression) was tested. Finally, the combinations of PainExpression with sk-Geometric and with sk-CNN were tested. The results obtained are shown in Table 3.

Table 2. Data set used for training, validation and testing.

		Infarct	No infarct	Total
Training	70%	10,780	10,780	21,560
Validation	15%	2,310	2,310	4,620
Testing	15%	2,310	2,310	4,620
Total	100%	15,400	15,400	30,800

Table 3. Comparison among our methods of heart attack identification.

Type	Accuracy	Sensitivity	Specificity	Time
sk-Geometric	81.90	98.10	65.71	0.11 s
sk-CNN	94.29	96.19	92.38	9.48 s
PainExpression	83.81	92.38	75.24	7.40 s
sk-Geometric + PainExpression	91.43	90.48	92.38	7.63 s
sk-CNN + PainExpression	93.33	89.52	97.14	10.46 s

In the first row of Table 3 you can see that the sensitivity of the sk-Geometric method is the highest of all. This could be interpreted as a good ability to identify the correct cases of myocardial infarction. However, the rate of correct classification of cases without myocardial infarction is also the worst of all the methods, and therefore its accuracy. It should be noted that the computation times are extremely low compared to the others, which would help a system to operate in real time. On the other hand, the sk-CNN method gives more stable results because there is less difference between sensitivity and specificity. It also has a high success rate. However, as is to be expected with machine learning methods, the processing time increases significantly.

The PainExpression method alone combines the two worst aspects of the previous algorithms, as it has a high processing time but a low accuracy rate. This is understandable, as the expression of pain on the face alone cannot be an indicator of a heart attack, as quoted above. It is important to note that some of the images in the set were deliberately chosen to show people with facial expressions of pain, but in situations other than a heart attack.

As mentioned above, the main proposal of this work is not to analyse two independent ways of detecting a possible heart attack, but to combine them in order to obtain more accurate results. Table 3 presents the results of the combination of the two methods of posture identification with the method of pain expression detection in the face. The combination of PainExpression and sk-Geometric showed a remarkable improvement in precision compared to the results obtained with PainExpression alone. This was mainly due to a reduction in false positives. On the other hand, when comparing the combination with the results of PainExpression alone, a significant improvement in precision was observed, although sensitivity was negatively affected.

4   Conclusions

This article has presented a procedure for detecting a possible heart attack by analysing facial expressions and posture together, in an attempt to reduce false positives. In our experiments, we achieved 93.33% accuracy in detecting heart attacks. Therefore, we believe that this method is good enough to be implemented in smart and healthy environments or in assistance robots. This is particularly important for people who live alone, in order to prevent possible deaths. In fact, this approach would make it possible to automatically alert medical services or relatives who can provide assistance in a timely manner.

Future work will extend the dataset and build other neural network architectures applied to machine vision. We also intend to extend the proposal to other types of problems that affect people's well-being and health.

Acknowledgements. Grant PID2023-149753OB-C21 funded by Spanish MCIU/ AEI/ 10.13039/5011 00011033/ERDF, EU. Grant PID2020-115220RB-C21 funded by Spanish MCIN/ AEI/ 10.13039/ 501100011033 and by "ERDF A way to make Europe". Grant 2022-GRIN-34436 funded by Universidad de Castilla-La Mancha and by "ERDF A way of making Europe".

References

1. Bustamante, A., Belmonte, L.M., Pereira, A., González, P., Fernández-Caballero, A., Morales, R.: Vision-based human posture detection from a virtual home-care unmanned aerial vehicle. In: Ferrández Vicente, J.M., Álvarez-Sánchez, J.R., de la Paz López, F., Adeli, H. (eds.) IWINAC 2022. LNCS, vol. 13259, pp. 482–491. Springer, Cham (2022). https://doi.org/10.1007/978-3-031-06527-9_48
2. Cao, Z., Simon, T., Wei, S.E., Sheikh, Y.: Realtime multi-person 2d pose estimation using part affinity fields. In: Proceedings of the IEEE Conference on Computer Vision and Pattern Recognition, pp. 7291–7299 (2017)
3. Castillo, J.C., et al.: Software architecture for smart emotion recognition and regulation of the ageing adult. Cogn. Comput. 8(2), 357–367 (2016)

4. Fernández-Caballero, A., et al.: Smart environment architecture for emotion detection and regulation. J. Biomed. Inf. **64**, 55–73 (2016)
5. Górriz, J., et al.: Computational approaches to explainable artificial intelligence: advances in theory, applications and trends. Inf. Fusion **100**, 101945 (2023)
6. Hur, T., Bang, J., Huynh-The, T., Lee, J., Kim, J.I., Lee, S.: Iss2Image: a novel signal-encoding technique for CNN-based human activity recognition. Sensors **18**(11), 3910 (2018)
7. Lie, W.N., Le, A.T., Lin, G.H.: Human fall-down event detection based on 2D skeletons and deep learning approach. In: International Workshop on Advanced Image Technology, pp. 1–4. IEEE (2018)
8. Lozano-Monasor, E., López, M.T., Vigo-Bustos, F., Fernández-Caballero, A.: Facial expression recognition in ageing adults: from lab to ambient assisted living. J. Ambient. Intell. Humaniz. Comput. **8**(4), 567–578 (2017)
9. López, M.T., Fernández-Caballero, A., Fernández, M.A., Mira, J., Delgado, A.E.: Motion features to enhance scene segmentation in active visual attention. Pattern Recogn. Lett. **27**(5), 469–478 (2006)
10. Martínez-Rodrigo, A., García-Martínez, B., Alcaraz, R., González, P., Fernández-Caballero, A.: Multiscale entropy analysis for recognition of visually elicited negative stress from EEG recordings. Int. J. Neural Syst. **29**(2), 1850038 (2019)
11. Patel, A., Fang, J., Gillespie, C., Odom, E., Luncheon, C., Ayala, C.: Awareness of heart attack signs and symptoms and calling 9-1-1 among U.S. adults. J. Am. Coll. Cardiol. **71**(7), 808–809 (2018)
12. Rojas-Albarracín, G., Chaves, M.A., Fernández-Caballero, A., López, M.T.: Heart attack detection in colour images using convolutional neural networks. Appl. Sci. **9**(23), 5065 (2019)
13. Sánchez-Reolid, R., et al.: Artificial neural networks to assess emotional states from brain-computer interface. Electronics **7**(12), 384 (2018)
14. Sánchez-Reolid, R., Martínez-Rodrigo, A., López, M.T., Fernández-Caballero, A.: Deep support vector machines for the identification of stress condition from electrodermal activity. Int. J. Neural Syst. **30**(7), 2050031 (2020)
15. Sánchez-Reolid, R., et al.: Emotion classification from EEG with a low-cost BCI versus a high-end equipment. Int. J. Neural Syst. **32**(10), 2250041 (2022)
16. Sokolova, M.V., Serrano-Cuerda, J., Castillo, J.C., Fernández-Caballero, A.: A fuzzy model for human fall detection in infrared video. J. Intell. Fuzzy Syst. **24**(2), 215–228 (2013)
17. The World Bank: Population Ages 65 and Above (% of Total) (2017). https://data.worldbank.org/indicator/SP.POP.65UP.TO.ZS
18. Turabieh, H., Mafarja, M., Li, X.: Iterated feature selection algorithms with layered recurrent neural network for software fault prediction. Expert Syst. Appl. **122**, 27–42 (2019)
19. Wilson, G., et al.: Robot-enabled support of daily activities in smart home environments. Cogn. Syst. Res. **54**, 258–272 (2019)
20. World Health Organization: The Top 10 Causes of Death (2018). https://www.who.int/news-room/fact-sheets/detail/the-top-10-causes-of-death

Non-intrusive and Easy-to-Use IOT Solution to Improve Elderly's Quality of Life

Luís Correia[1] , Nuno Costa[1] , Antonio Fernández-Caballero[3,4] ,
and António Pereira[1,2(✉)]

[1] School of Technology and Management, Computer Science and Communication
Research Centre, Polytechnic Institute of Leiria, 2411-901 Leiria, Portugal
{apereira,luis.correia,nuno.costa}@ipleiria.pt
[2] INOV INESC Inovação, Institute of New Technologies, Leiria Office,
2411-901 Leiria, Portugal
[3] Instituto de Investigación en Informática de Albacete, 02071 Albacete, Spain
[4] Departamento de Sistemas Informáticos, Universidad de Castilla-La Mancha, 02071
Albacete, Spain

Abstract. Currently, derived from several factors the world population
is ageing at an increasing rate. Where a large part of elderly people,
who live in social isolation, tend not to have access to technology, thus
being highly info excluded. All these factors reinforce the feeling of insecurity and loneliness. It becomes a challenge to improve the quality of
life of those who still have some autonomy and are still able to live in
their homes. The Internet of Things presents itself as one of the technological paradigms with the greatest potential to enable technological
solutions to solve these problems, mainly because its main feature is the
ability to integrate information technology with physical objects present
in everyday life. The proposed solution allows the creation of intelligent
environments, in common dwellings, which monitor and control various
parameters of the residence, as well as the elderly themselves, from their
physical activity to vital parameters. As this is a non-intrusive system,
one of its main advantages is that it does not require technological knowledge on the part of senior users. The proposed solution was tested, in real
environment, where the results obtained were quite satisfactory, allowing us to conclude that besides increasing the quality of life and allowing
greater autonomy to the elderly, it gives caregivers and family members
a sense of security and permanent monitoring.

Keywords: Internet of Things · Ambient Assisted Living · Elderly
Assistance and Monitoring · Wearables

1 Introduction

Currently, the world's population is ageing due to increased life expectancy [1]
[2]. United Nations data indicate 1 in 11 people aged 65 or older in 2019. By

J. M. Ferrández Vicente et al. (Eds.): IWINAC 2024, LNCS 14674, pp. 421–430, 2024.
https://doi.org/10.1007/978-3-031-61140-7_40

2035, this group will exceed 1.1 billion, about 13% of the world [3,4]. Portugal mirrors global trends; 2021 statistics show over 2.4 million aged 65+, 23.4% of the population, with an aging index of 182:100 compared to 2011, with an average age of 45.4 [5]. Lack of services exacerbates loneliness and insecurity, compounded by technological illiteracy [6]. Addressing this challenge involves leveraging IoT to enhance elderly living conditions. Low-cost IoT solutions offer real-time monitoring, aiding caregivers and notifying them when assistance is needed. The aim is to extend elderly independence while reinforcing the sense of security of caregivers and family [7,8].

This research investigates how an IoT-based Ambient Assisted Living (AAL) system can enhance elderly quality of life. The central question is: "How can IoT-based solutions enhance elderly quality of life?" This work contributes by proposing and validating a low-cost AAL solution, collecting and monitoring real-time data without requiring user interaction [8].

The article structure is as follows: Sect. 2 provides related work, Sect. 3 outlines the proposed architecture, Sect. 4 details the prototype, Sect. 5 evaluates the system, and Sect. 6 concludes.

2   Background

This section showcases several IoT solutions tailored to enhance the daily lives of senior citizens.

In [9], researchers developed a system tailored for monitoring elderly individuals with cognitive impairments, utilizing various data collection methods such as sensors, wearables, and beacons, with data processing done on the elder's smartphone. However, the requirement for the user to carry a smartphone may raise privacy concerns. On a different note, the eWALL project detailed in [10] introduces a comprehensive solution utilizing an interactive device embedded within the user's home wall. This device provides an array of intelligent support services spanning risk management, home security, eHealth, and healthy lifestyle management. Despite its comprehensiveness, this solution lacks the capability for real-time indoor location tracking, which could limit its effectiveness. Similarly, the NOAH project discussed in [11] strives to provide aid to independent elderly individuals by integrating with existing caregiver practices. Although this project offers valuable features through its cloud-based architecture and accompanying Android applications, it falls short in monitoring vital data, physical activity, and indoor location tracking, presenting notable limitations. Meanwhile, the HABITAT project elaborated in [12] integrates a multitude of technologies, such as RFID, wearable devices, and wireless sensor networks, to create an AAL platform aimed at enhancing the daily lives of seniors. However, despite its comprehensive approach in monitoring physical activity, this solution lacks habitat monitoring and the monitoring of vital data, potentially limiting its effectiveness. Similarly, the pilot project AnAbEL proposed in [13] introduces an intelligent system targeting individuals with early symptoms of dementia through activity recognition and indoor location tracking. Nonetheless, this solution overlooks vital data monitoring and house context tracking, posing potential limitations. Lastly, [14] presents a novel framework based on Machine Learning (ML) to analyze the behavior of elderly individuals in everyday life using data from smart devices. Despite its promising results, this approach might face challenges in real-world implementation.

In conclusion, the proposed approach prioritizes discreet, low-cost systems, ensuring seniors' independence while keeping caregivers informed about their well-being. Through the adoption of unobtrusive technologies such as smart-bands, seniors can go about their daily routines without feeling excessively monitored, fostering a sense of autonomy and confidence among both seniors and their caregivers.

3   Proposed Architecture

The proposed system adheres to a conventional IoT architecture structured across four layers: Perception, Network, Data Processing, and Application, as illustrated in Fig. 1. Each module's operational mode will be elaborated upon in detail.

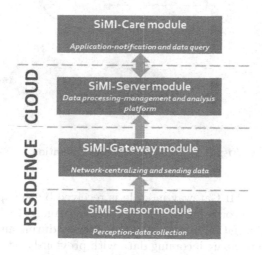

Fig. 1. Layered architecture

The SiMI-Sensor module is a crucial component of the system architecture, installed in every room of the house to gather data from environmental conditions and elderly occupants. Equipped with sensors monitoring temperature, light, humidity, movement, and door status, the module is connected to a Single Board Computer via a GPIO board. Monitoring the health and activity of the elderly involves the use of smart bands. Upon detecting movement, the module checks for smart bands and verifies their presence via BLE. If confirmed, location data is sent to the SiMI-Gateway, and measurements are requested from the smart band. Data on heart rate, step count, and battery status are then forwarded to the SiMI-Gateway. The architecture supports multi-user functionality, allowing monitoring of multiple elderly individuals with designated smart bands communicating with various SiMI-Sensor modules.

The SiMI-Gateway module serves as a central and singular device within the household, tasked with receiving messages from all SiMI-Sensor devices within the network and transmitting them via the Internet to the SiMI-Server module. Importantly, this module shares identical hardware capabilities with the SiMI-Sensor module and can gather the same range of information. Its operation is entirely self-sufficient, requiring no user interaction. Moreover, in the event of a power outage, the entire software layer is designed to initiate automatically, eliminating the need for any additional intervention.

The SiMI-Server module, depicted in Fig. 2, operates within the framework of Cloud Computing and assumes responsibility for managing, analyzing, and storing all data collected from the aforementioned modules.   Initially, data

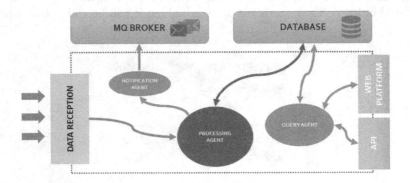

Fig. 2. SiMI-Server Module Operation

transmitted by the SiMI-Gateway module is received by the application server. These data undergo processing by the "Processing Agent", which may require accessing stored information from the database server during analysis. The "Processing Agent" can compare incoming data with previously established patterns. Upon detecting potential risk scenarios that could endanger the well-being of the elderly person, the SiMI-Engine sends alerts to caregivers/relatives via the MQ Broker (Message Queue). Subsequently, once the analysis is completed, the processed information is appropriately stored in the database. Additionally, this module offers a web platform enabling service administrators to configure details related to homes, elderly individuals, and caregivers/relatives. Through the module's API, requests from the SiMI-Care module can be addressed.

The SiMI-Care module comprises a mobile application designed for caregivers or family members, enabling remote access to comprehensive information about the elderly person's physical activity, health status, statistics, and real-time monitoring of each room in the house. Accessible from any location with internet connectivity, the application facilitates seamless retrieval of new data by making requests through the SiMI-Server module's API. In instances where unusual behaviors or parameters are detected, the module promptly receives alerts via notifications sent through the MQ Broker.

4   Implementation

This section outlines the implementation process of the architecture proposed in Sect. 3, which centers around an IoT-based system designed for non-intrusive monitoring of the daily activities of elderly individuals and environmental parameters within their homes.

The hardware selection prioritizes creating elderly-friendly environments with ubiquitous computing while ensuring an economically accessible solution. Key components include the Raspberry Pi Zero W, a compact Single Board Computer with a Linux-based OS and BLE for smart band communication. Environmental parameters are monitored using compatible sensors such as the TSL2561 brightness sensor, DHT22 temperature/humidity sensor, magnetic sensors, and HC-SR501 motion sensor. The Xiaomi Mi Band 3 smartband is chosen for monitoring elderly data, while a desktop computer serves as the server for the SiMI-Server module, and the HUAWEI Mate 20 Lite smartphone is utilized for the caregiver equipment with the SiMI-Care module.

The implementation of each module of the architecture is described below.

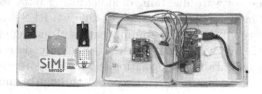

Fig. 3. SiMI-Sensor module prototype

The SiMI-Sensor module, running on a Raspberry Pi Zero W IoT device, integrates the sensors indicated above. Each component was selected for its cost-effectiveness, with an approximate cost of 38.00€per module (Fig. 3). The software layer consists of Python scripts, facilitating concurrent execution of different modules and ensuring efficient data reception. The module is programmed for automatic startup, even during power failures. The software diagram, shown in Fig. 4, includes the crucial simi-sensor.py module, responsible for detecting elderly presence, gathering data from smart bands and remaining sensors, and transmitting information to the gateway module via Wi-Fi. The SiMI-Gateway module serves as a central hub, receiving messages from various equipment and transmitting them to the SiMI-Server module. It operates independently and automatically, even during power failures.

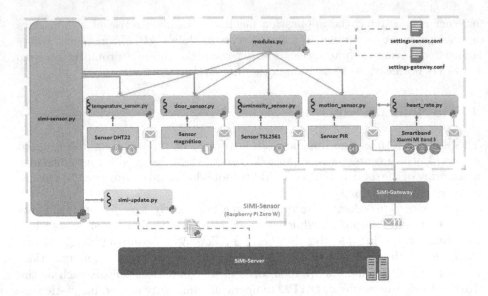

Fig. 4. SiMI-Sensor module software diagram

The SiMI-Server, located in the cloud, receives, processes, manages, and stores system information. The application layer, developed in C# language using Microsoft's ASP.NET platform, facilitates seamless data management. Figure 5 depicts the software diagram, demonstrating data exchange between the SiMI-Gateway module and SiMI-Care module via REST web services. The server also offers a web platform for administrators to manage residence details, elderly individuals, caregivers, and rules. An anomaly detection component, SiMI-Engine, analyzes database information to identify potential risks to elderly well-being.   The SiMI-Care module, executed through a mobile application,

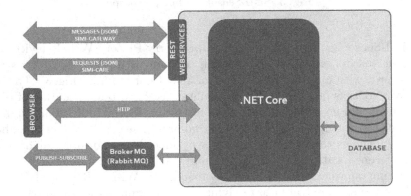

Fig. 5. SiMI-Server software diagram

provides real-time access to information regarding the elderly person and their home environment. Users are notified of harmful situations detected by consuming information from other modules. Figure 6 showcase the graphical interface of the mobile application.

Fig. 6. Chart with elderly's heartbeats

5   Evaluation

Tests were conducted to validate the developed prototype in a real environment, focusing on acceptance and robustness. The tests involved installing a test scenario in the home of an elderly individual.

- Acceptance: the acceptance of smart bands among senior users was previously validated in a study involving 11 elderly individuals aged between 65 and 78 years, with an average age of 68.9 years, comprising 63.6% females and 36.4% males [15]. Throughout the 5-day tests, participants were instructed to wear the smart bands continuously while performing daily tasks. Following each test, their satisfaction levels were evaluated through a questionnaire. Results showed that none of the respondents experienced pain while using the device, with 90.9% reporting no discomfort and the remaining 9.1% indicating some discomfort. In terms of weight, 54.6% found the bracelet very light, 36.4% considered it light, and only 9% perceived it as slightly light, with a small 9.1% finding it annoying. Additionally, 18.2% removed the smart band during tasks such as showering or washing dishes due to concerns about water damage. Notably, 91% expressed willingness to incorporate the device into their daily lives, suggesting that the majority did not find the smart band intrusive, even considering regular use.
- Robustness: To evaluate the prototype's performance and robustness, three types of tests were conducted: indoor detection time, indoor location, and

smart band data retrieval. Robustness tests involved two elderly individuals and a caregiver for 7 days. The tests monitored various house divisions with SiMI-Sensor modules: kitchen, bedroom, living room, hall, and dining room. The aim was to assess the solution's ability to monitor multiple seniors simultaneously. Elderly A (male, 84 years old) used Xiaomi Mi Band 3, while Elderly B (female, 75 years old) used Xiaomi Mi Band 2. Both had the same caregiver using the SiMI-Care module. Before the tests, rules were defined with the caregiver regarding housing and each elderly person's routines.

- Indoor location detection time: to determine the average time it takes for the system to detect the presence of an elderly person in a room, each elderly individual entered each room of the house ten times. The time from entering the room until the specific detection of the elderly person was recorded for each sample. Analysis of the results revealed that the mean detection time for the 100 samples was 13.13 s, with a standard deviation of 3.35 s. The minimum recorded detection time was 5.86 s, while the maximum was 34.14 s. Specifically, for elderly A wearing the Mi Band 3 smart band, the average detection time was 13.14 s, with a standard deviation of 4.19 s, and for elderly B with the Mi Band 2 smart band, the mean detection time was 13.13 s, with a standard deviation of 2.21 s. Notably, the detection time for both seniors and their respective smart bands was identical. Additionally, detection was found to be faster on average in the kitchen (12.22 s) and slower in the bedroom (14.70 s).

- Indoor location accuracy: in order to assess the precision and associated false negatives in the indoor positioning system, each elderly individual was instructed to move around within the household. Their positions were observed, recorded, and cross-referenced with the system's detected locations. Instances where the observed and detected locations did not match resulted in false negatives. The accuracy rates for both Elderly A and Elderly B, along with their respective smart bands (Mi Band 3 and Mi Band 2), are notably similar, with Elderly A achieving 96% accuracy and Elderly B 94%. The living room and bedroom are the primary locations where false negatives are prevalent. None of the sections within the household exhibit a location accuracy lower than 90%. On average, the accuracy for home location stands at 95%.

- Get data from smartband: The performance of data retrieval from the smart bands was assessed through a sequence of 100 data requests. Potential reasons for failure included connection errors and poor BLE signal quality. The test involved the SiMI-Sensor module in the living room, situated approximately 1.50 m from the smart bands worn by the elderly on the couch. Two series of 50 requests were made for each smart band (Mi Band 2 and 3). Both sequences exhibited similar performance, with a global success rate of 95% in reading data from the smart bands.

Currently, an interface is being developed to be added to the project, aiming to display the elderly person's activity over time and in different areas of the home.

Subsequently, the testing environment will be expanded to include 24 individuals in a real-world setting. The results will be presented in a future publication.

6 Conclusion

This work presents a cost-effective solution for supporting and monitoring elderly individuals and their homes, utilizing a network of sensors and IoT devices. The system enables elderly individuals to remain in their homes longer, autonomously and safely. Through real environment tests assessing acceptance and robustness, the system was found to accurately detect the indoor location of the elderly, monitor their activity/vital parameters, and trigger notifications for caregivers or family members. The proposed approach offers several advantages: caregivers or family members can access real-time information about the elderly person's physical condition and receive notifications about any concerning situations, even when not physically present. Moreover, the system operates non-intrusively, requiring no interaction from the elderly individual, thereby bridging the gap between technology and elderly users. Continuous monitoring provides a sense of security and confidence to the elderly, potentially prolonging their ability to live independently at home. These results suggest that the system can be extended to other user groups, such as individuals with neurodegenerative conditions or disorders, in the near future.

Funding Information. This work was supported by national funds through the Portuguese Foundation for Science and Technology (FCT), I.P., under the project UIDB/04524/2020.

References

1. Khan, H.T.: Population ageing in a globalized world: Risks and dilemmas? J. Eval. Clin. Pract. **25**, 754–760 (2018). https://doi.org/10.1111/jep.13071. ISSN: 13652753
2. Astell, A.J., et al.: Developing a pragmatic evaluation of ICTs for older adults with cognitive impairment at scale: the IN LIFE experience. Univ. Access Inf. Soc. **21**(1), 1–19 (2022). https://doi.org/10.1007/s10209-021-00849-5. ISSN: 16155297
3. Chen, X., Huang, B., Li, S.: Population ageing and inequality: evidence from China. World Econ. **41**(8), 1976–2000 (2018). https://doi.org/10.1111/twec.12551. ISSN: 14679701
4. Zhou, J., Tan, R., Lin, H.C.: Development of an integrated conceptual path model for a smart elderly care information system. Univ. Access Inf. Soc. 0123456789 (2022). https://doi.org/10.1007/s10209-022-00879-7. ISSN: 16155297
5. Instituto Nacional de Estatística. Censos - Resultados definitivos - 2021 (2022). https://www.ine.pt/xportal/xmain?xpid=INE&xpgid=ine_publicacoes& PUBLICACOESpub_boui=65586079&PUBLICACOESmodo=2&xlang=pt. Accessed 12 Dec 2022
6. Sudore, R.L., et al.: Limited literacy and mortality in the elderly: the health, aging, and body composition study. J. Gener. Internal Med. **21**(8), 806–812 (2006). https://doi.org/10.1111/j.1525-1497.2006.00539.x. ISSN: 08848734

7. Sinabell, I., Ammenwerth, E.: Challenges and recommendations for eHealth usability evaluation with elderly users: systematic review and case study. Univ. Access Inf. Soc. 0123456789 (2022). https://doi.org/10.1007/s10209-022-00949-w. ISSN: 16155297

8. de Podestá Gaspar, R., et al.: Toward improved co-designing home care solutions based on personas and design thinking with older users. Univ. Access Inf. Soc. (2022). https://doi.org/10.1007/s10209-022-00940-5. ISSN: 1615–5289

9. Berrocal, J., et al.: Rich contextual information for monitoring the elderly in an early stage of cognitive impairment. Perv. Mobile Comput. **34**, 106–125 (2017). https://doi.org/10.1016/j.pmcj.2016.05.001. ISSN: 15741192

10. Mihovska, A., Kyriazakos, S.A., Prasad, R.: eWall for active long living: assistive ICT services for chronically ill and elderly citizens. In: Conference Proceedings - IEEE International Conference on Systems, Man and Cybernetics 2014-Janua, pp. 2204–2209 (2014). https://doi.org/10.1109/smc.2014.6974251. ISSN: 1062922X

11. Kristaly, D.M., et al.: A solution for mobile computing in a cloud environment for ambient assisted living. In: MED 2018 - 26th Mediterranean Conference on Control and Automation, pp. 944–949 (2018). https://doi.org/10.1109/MED.2018.8442649.

12. Borelli, E., et al.: HABITAT: an IoT solution for independent elderly. Sensors (Switzerland) **19**(5) (2019). https://doi.org/10.3390/s19051258. ISSN: 14248220

13. J. Ginés , Manuel, G., Augusto, J.C., Stewart, J.: An- AbEL: towards empowering people living with dementia in ambient assisted living. Univ. Access Inf. Soc. **21**(2), 457–476 (2022). https://doi.org/10.1007/s10209-020-00760-5. ISSN: 16155297

14. Qian, K., et al.: Can appliances understand the behavior of elderly via machine learning? a feasibility study. IEEE Internet Things J. **8**(10), 8343–8355 (2021). https://doi.org/10.1109/JIOT.2020.3045009'

15. Correia, L., et al.: Usability of smartbands by the elderly population in the context of ambient assisted living applications. Electronics **10**(14), 1617 (2021). https://doi.org/10.3390/electronics10141617. issn: 2079–9292

Human-Computer Interaction Approach with Empathic Conversational Agent and Computer Vision

Rafael Pereira[1], Carla Mendes[1], Nuno Costa[1], Luis Frazão[1], Antonio Fernández-Caballero[2], and António Pereira[1,3(✉)]

[1] Computer Science and Communications Research Centre, School of Technology and Management, Polytechnic of Leiria, 2411-901 Leiria, Portugal
{rafael.m.pereira,carla.c.mendes,nunorod,jose.ribeiro, apereira}@ipleiria.pt
[2] Instituto de Investigación en Informática de Albacete, Universidad de Castilla-La Mancha, 02071 Albacete, Spain
antonio.fdez@uclm.es
[3] INOV INESC Inovação, Institute of New Technologies, Leiria Office, 2411-901 Leiria, Portugal

Abstract. The integration of empathy in Human-Computer Interaction (HCI) is essential for enhancing user experiences. Current HCI systems often overlook users' emotional states, limiting interaction quality. This research examines the integration of Multimodal Emotion Recognition (MER) into empathic generative-based conversational agents, encompassing facial, body, and speech emotion recognition, along with sentiment analysis. These elements are fused and incorporated into Large Language Models (LLMs) to continuously comprehend and respond to users empathically. This paper highlights the advantages of this multimodal approach over traditional unimodal systems in recognizing complex human emotions. Additionally, it provides a well-structured background on the addressed topics. The findings include an overview of deep learning in HCI, a review of methods used for emotion recognition and conversational agents, and the proposal of an HCI architecture that integrates facial, body, and speech emotion recognition and sentiment analysis into a fusion model that is fed into an LLM making an empathic conversational agent. This research contributes to the field of HCI by providing an architecture to guide the development of more realistic and meaningful HCIs through MER and a conversational agent.

Keywords: Human-Computer Interaction · Multimodal Emotion Recognition · Fusion methods · Empathic Conversational Agents

1 Introduction

The concept of empathy consists of comprehending and sharing others' emotions to forge emotional connections, which is vital for human relationships. Similarly, in HCI, empathy is crucial in ensuring more realistic, improved, convenient and meaningful interactions. However, the typical HCI, aimed at tailoring computer systems to meet the specific needs and preferences of individuals, still lacks the users' emotional state, therefore losing crucial information during these interactions [1]. Recent Artificial Intelligence (AI) techniques, such as emotion recognition and empathic conversational agents, when integrated with HCI allow for continuous understanding of the user's emotions throughout interactions and empathically responding [2].

AI encompasses several techniques and methodologies aimed at enabling machines to perform tasks that typically require human intelligence, whereas deep learning stands out as an approach to processing unstructured data (including images, voice, videos, and text, among others) relying on Artificial Neural Networks (ANNs). Emotion recognition, being a recent application of deep learning, involves detecting human emotions, generally through singular modalities such as facial features, gestures, poses, speech, and text captured through continuous interactions with the user [3]. On the other hand, generative-based conversational agents are designed to simulate human-like conversation and engage in interactions with users through natural language using several techniques, including Natural Language Processing (NLP), and deep learning with the recent advances in LLMs, to understand user input, interpret context, and generate appropriate responses.

Due to the advances of MER and conversational agents, individually, and the benefits provided when integrated with HCI, this study offers a guide covering emotion recognition modalities and key design and functionality aspects of a conversational agent. Lastly, proposing an HCI approach to ensure more realistic and meaningful interactions by leveraging HCI in conjunction with an emotion-branched fusion technique and an empathic conversational agent.

The main contributions of this study can be summarized as follows:

- Detailed guide on how deep learning impacts HCI nowadays;
- Performed a background review regarding emotion recognition, fusion methods, and conversational agents. Presented related works and described how our solution contributes to the area;
- Proposal of an HCI architecture approach aided with MER, through facial, body, and speech emotion recognition, sentiment analysis fused into an emphatic conversational agent powered with a LLM.

This research is divided into four other sections. Section 2 presents the main concepts behind deep learning, emotion recognition, and conversational agents. Section 3 presents related works and compare them with the proposed solution. Section 4 shows the architecture, features, and characteristics of the proposed solution for HCI aided with emotion recognition fed into an empathic conversational agent. Lastly, Sect. 5 introduces the challenges and directions for future work and the conclusions.

2   Background

The evolution of technology in HCI has been significantly influenced by deep learning, a subset of machine learning. Deep learning has shown performance improvements in domains such as speech recognition and object detection, with a focus on supervised learning. Supervised learning involves training a system with a labeled dataset to map inputs to outputs, which the quality of training data is crucial for model efficacy, and techniques like data augmentation help in improving data diversity for better training outcomes [4,5].

Being a type of NN in the deep learning context, Convolutional Neural Networks (CNNs) are widely used for image-based tasks in HCI, such as facial emotion recognition. These networks, with their structure of convolutional and pooling layers, process multi-array data like images efficiently. CNNs not only enhance computational efficiency but also improve the robustness of the features extracted. This NN may need high processing power and may take some time to train, which transfer learning techniques can facilitate knowledge transfer from large datasets to specific tasks and reduce the need for extensive data and computational resources [6].

Emotion recognition, related to analyzing human expressions and classifying them into emotions, is often studied individually and encounters challenges in real-life scenarios. This paper addresses these challenges through a multi-modal approach to emotion detection, aiming to mitigate problems associated with individual analysis methods. In computer vision, it includes facial movements and body language analysis from images and videos. On the other hand, linguistic contexts imply the usage of vocal nuances and text analysis to detect emotions [7].

To aggregate emotions from four contexts, fusion methods integrate modalities into a single vector, classified as early, late, and cross-modality fusion [8]. Early fusion combines all data before learning models are applied, useful when modalities are closely associated. Late fusion, applied after model processing, merges model outputs for final classification, suited for scenarios requiring modality-specific training and facing volatility. Cross-modality fusion allows for data exchange between modalities at any learning stage, enhancing predictive performance by leveraging shared contexts. The proposed solution employs late fusion, optimizing for scenarios with diverse training needs and volatile data sources [8].

Conversational agents in HCI, interacting via voice or text, vary from domain-specific to general-purpose, with their effectiveness dependent on response mechanisms like rule-based, retrieval-based, and generative approaches [9]. Large Language Models (LLMs) are generative agents that mimic human language through unsupervised learning and advanced algorithms, including Variational Autoencoders (VAEs) and Generative Adversarial Networks (GANs). Despite their computational demands, techniques like QLoRA and LoRa have been developed to optimize LLMs like LLaMA and GPT-3, significantly reducing memory and computational requirements [10,11].

3   Related Works

This section presents a summary of previous research on emphatic conversational agents designed to provide nuanced and contextually appropriate responses that recognize and adapt to the emotional states of users.

The authors in [12] created a dialogue system powered by a language model capable of generating empathic responses to text-based messages trained with an empathic conversation and additional emotional information. Hence, proposing a benchmark bot, and an empathic bot along with an emotion classifier (the fine-tuned DeepMoji model) to predict emotions conveyed in the text. Both chatbots were evaluated in quantitative studies and compared with human responses in qualitative studies involving human judges. In these tests, the empathic chatbot outperformed both the benchmark chatbot and the human-generated responses regarding perceived empathy and obtained state-of-the-art results regarding response quality. Furthermore, reaching a final F1-score of 0.81 in six basic emotions in the emotional classifier.

Daher et al. [13] proposed two chatbots to comprehend if there are any advantages to incorporating empathy in medical physical health chatbots and how to convey empathy from short-term text conversations to aid in the diagnosis of physical health problems. The first chatbot possessed no empathy and therefore only asked questions related to the diagnosis and provided the user with advice. The second chatbot, on the other hand, provided supportive, appropriate, and empathic responses through the analysis of the user's emotional state with the Empath tool. Tests involving the RoPE scale concluded that the majority of the participants preferred the empathic chatbot compared to the advice-only variant.

Zhou et al. [14] introduce a conversational agent designed to generate emotionally consistent responses in dialogue systems. It integrates emotion by using three mechanisms: embedding emotion categories, capturing changes in implicit internal emotion states, and utilizing an external emotion vocabulary for explicit emotion expressions. This approach showed that could generate responses that are not only relevant and grammatically correct but also emotionally consistent, outperforming traditional sequence-to-sequence models in both content and emotion accuracy.

Deneche et al. [15] proposes a mental health chatbot designed to aid individuals in regulating their emotions through cognitive behavior therapy techniques. It utilizes natural language processing and a lexicon-based approach to automatically identify a user's basic emotions from their input. This chatbot aims to offer personalized activities, mindfulness exercises, and an emotion diary feature to assist users in handling their emotions.

4   Proposed Solution

Empathy is a fundamental trait in ensuring realistic, natural, and meaningful interactions, therefore in the context of HCI, the goal is to provide authentic and engaging interactions through the use of empathic conversational agents. The architecture proposed in this paper, as depicted in Fig. 1, is an integrated system designed to enhance these interactions. The proposed architecture addresses the complexity of verbal and non-verbal cues in emotion detection with a dual-component system: a conversational agent module that receives emotional feedback from a MER module aiming to maintain an ongoing empathetic interaction with the user. This latter module employs deep learning algorithms to analyze multiple data streams (textual, auditory, and visual), in unison, improving the accuracy and robustness of emotion detection. The fusion model within this system synergizes the different modalities, enhancing the strengths and balancing the limitations of each. Therefore, an implementation of this architecture tries to achieve a more nuanced, empathic conversational experience that aligns closely with human communication, which inherently weaves together speech, text, and visual information.

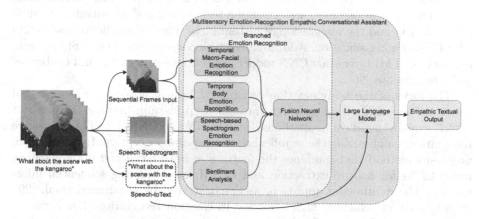

Fig. 1. Schematic representation of the proposed HCI approach architecture. Illustrates the flow from multimodal input through sequential frames, speech spectrograms, and text to the empathic conversational agent. The process integrates temporal macro-facial and body emotion recognition through computer vision, speech-based spectrogram emotion recognition, and sentiment analysis, leading to an empathic textual output generated by the fusion neural network and LLM.

As previously detailed, the system is designed to predict emotions across various contexts, either in real-time or from video recordings. This encompasses sentiment analysis from text, emotion recognition from speech spectrograms, and analysis of facial and body expressions. The following paragraphs will present potential methodologies for processing each data type within the MER module.

The analysis of textual data through a sentiment analysis model to determine the sentiment of the textual input [16]. This process involves first extracting the features from the given textual input using n-grams (consecutive n terms in text), part-of-speech tagging, stemming, removal of stop words, conjunction and negation handling as proposed by Kaur et al. [17], or even word embeddings (who represent words in a vector space by clustering words with similar meanings together) e.g. Word2vec or GloVe as described by Wankhade et al. [18]. Afterward, performing the sentiment classification, for example, using a 1D CNN classifier [19].

In the context of speech emotion recognition, possible approaches are preprocessing data through frame overlapping and windowing techniques to apply a hamming window to speech frames, thus minimizing discontinuities [20,21]. Additionally, feature normalization is recommended to standardize features via z-score normalization. For the classification phase, the employment of models such as CNNs and support vector machines is considered for the analysis of speech patterns [22].

Possible approaches for the facial emotion recognition branch are, to utilize methods like R-CNN for region of interest detection and CNN for classification, as proposed by Zaman et al. [23]. Another method could be the use of transformers [24], to tackle challenges like low light conditions and variable head poses. The application of feature extraction techniques, as demonstrated by Siva-iah et al. [25], and the integration of histogram of oriented gradients descriptors with CNNs for classification. Additionally, the incorporation of Long Short-Term memory (LSTM) layers in a CNN model is essential for the temporal context of facial expressions [26].

The focus of the body emotion recognition branch is to analyze nonverbal cues such as posture and gestures through deep learning methods. Romeo et al. [27] explore classification methods like 3D CNN and CNN + LSTM for gesture recognition, emphasizing the significance of temporal perception. Ilyas et al. [28] propose a method that combines the features of both facial and body gestures, using CNNs for feature extraction and LSTM for processing sequential information. The multimodal approach, as demonstrated by Hiranmayi et al. [29], is significant in achieving high accuracy in emotion recognition. Furthermore, the integration of a pre-trained vision transformers for gesture detection with a Resnet-34 model for facial macro-expression recognition, as done by Prakash et al. [30].

The final stage to obtain the final emotion prediction involves employing a late fusion model (using a neural network followed by a softmax layer as the final classifier), where the outputs (an array of emotion predictions) of the previously described models are combined, leveraging the strengths of each modality while compensating for their weaknesses. Hence, in some instances prioritizing certain modality data over the others. Late fusion models are advantageous over single modality models, which often struggle to generalize across different scenarios and may be sensitive to modality-specific noise. In contrast, late fusion models increase robustness to noise and variability, expecting a more reliable emotion recognition result across situations and improved performance [8,31]. Therefore, the fusion model's output would consist of a single emotion resulting from the aggregation of the four context-based emotions obtained from each of the models. This approach benefits from the ability to train each modality with a specific algorithm and may make it easier to add or exchange different modalities in the future, but lacks the sharing of cross-modality data, which could hinder learning the relationships between modalities [8].

Upon the capture of interaction with the user, the textual input obtained from a chat section (although if obtained as speech from the microphone it must be first converted to text using an automatic speech recognition algorithm aided with the speech spectrogram) is passed on to the NLP stage, where the input goes to some pre-processing stages such as segmentation, tokenization, lemmatization, and part-of-speech tagging. Then, the processed data is passed through the Natural Language Understanding (NLU) stage, to extract the intents and entities while turning the pre-processed data into a structured representation. Afterward, the data is passed on to the dialogue management stage, which aims to maintain and incorporate the context of the current and past conversations [32]. LLMs can both understand and be enhanced by emotional intelligence, and achieve better performance, truthfulness, and responsibility [33]. Therefore, by analyzing the user's textual input and the emotion obtained from the fusion model, the LLM, such as LLama 2 open source model using QLoRA finetuning approach [34], can analyze the textual prompt and use the detected emotion to provide an accurate and emphatic response which is converted into a user-readable format and presented back to the user.

This solution designs empathic conversational agents by integrating MER with a nuanced comprehension of human communication. Based on related work, such as empathic dialogue systems integrated with emotion classifiers and the use of multi-modal data for emotion detection, this methodology is set to improve the depth and precision of emotion recognition. The inclusion of textual, auditory, and visual data enables a thorough analysis of the user's emotional state, overcoming the constraints of previous systems that were limited to textual analysis or basic sentiment classification. Through a fusion model that combines these modalities, the system aims to more effectively understand and respond to human emotions. The architecture's framework, featuring distinct modules for each data type and a late fusion model for integrating these analyses, aims for a comprehensive perception of the user's emotional condition, facilitating more contextually relevant and empathetic responses.

The usage of deep learning techniques for the analysis and processing of multi-modal inputs is informed by recent progress in NLP and emotion recognition research. The efficacy of similar methodologies in related works, where deep learning algorithms have outperformed traditional methods in terms of accuracy and efficiency, underpins the anticipated positive outcomes from this proposal. The adoption of a late fusion model for the consolidation and interpretation of emotions detected across several modalities addresses the complexity of accurately capturing human emotions, which are often communicated through a mix of verbal cues, vocal tone, and facial expressions. As such, this integrated approach aims to improve the empathic responses of conversational agents and also seeks to enrich the field of HCI by proposing a more detailed and comprehensive strategy for understanding and responding to human emotions.

5 Future Work and Conclusions

This research explores the integration of MER into empathic conversational agents. The study contributes to HCI by proposing an architecture that aggregates multiple modalities, namely, textual, auditory, and visual; To detect user emotions accurately and respond empathically. The proposed solution aims to provide robustness in emotion detection compared to traditional unimodal approaches by fusion of diverse data streams.

Future work should focus on implementing the proposed architecture, focusing on the fusion accuracy of emotion detection in several contexts. Additionally, exploring the integration of an emphatic source in a generative-based conversational agent. Further research could also investigate the ethical implications and privacy concerns associated with emotion recognition technologies.

Acknowledgments. This work was supported by national funds through the Portuguese Foundation for Science and Technology (FCT), I.P., under the project UIDB/04524/2020 and was partially supported by Portuguese National funds through FITEC-Programa Interface with reference CIT "INOV-INESC Inovação-Financiamento Base"

Disclosure of Interests. The authors have no competing interests.

References

1. Jaiswal, A., Krishnama Raju, A., Deb, S.: Facial emotion detection using deep learning. In: 2020 International Conference for Emerging Technology (INCET), pp. 1–5 (2020). https://ieeexplore.ieee.org/document/9154121
2. Santos, B.S., Júnior, M.C., Nunes, M.A.S.N.: Approaches for generating empathy: a systematic mapping. In: Latifi, S. (ed.) Information Technology - New Generations. Advances in Intelligent Systems and Computing, vol. 558, pp. 715–722. Springer, Cham (2018). https://doi.org/10.1007/978-3-319-54978-1_89
3. Alrowais, F., et al.: Modified earthworm optimization with deep learning assisted emotion recognition for human computer interface. IEEE Access **11**, 35089–35096 (2023). https://ieeexplore.ieee.org/document/10091537/
4. Lecun, Y., Bengio, Y., Hinton, G.: Deep learning. Nature **521**, 7553 436–444 (2015). https://www.nature.com/articles/nature14539
5. Alrowais, F., et al.: Modified earthworm optimization with deep learning assisted emotion recognition for human computer interface. IEEE Access **11**, 35089–35096 (2023)
6. Khan, A., Sohail, A., Zahoora, U., Qureshi, A.S.: A survey of the recent architectures of deep convolutional neural networks. Artif. Intell. Rev. **53**(8), 5455–5516 (2020). https://link.springer.com/article/10.1007/s10462-020-09825-6
7. Chul, B., Id, K.: A brief review of facial emotion recognition based on visual information. Sensors **18**, 401 (2018). https://www.mdpi.com/1424-8220/18/2/401/html
8. Sleeman, W.C., Kapoor, R., Ghosh, P.: Multimodal classification: current landscape, taxonomy and future directions. ACM Comput. Surv. **55**(7), 150:1–150:31 (2022). https://dl.acm.org/doi/10.1145/3543848

9. Fernandes, S., Gawas, R., Alvares, P., Femandes, M., Kale, D., Aswale, S.: Survey on various conversational systems. In: 2020 International Conference on Emerging Trends in Information Technology and Engineering (ic-ETITE), pp. 1–8 (2020)

10. Dettmers, T., Pagnoni, A., Holtzman, A., Zettlemoyer, L.: QLoRA: efficient fine-tuning of quantized LLMs (2023). http://arxiv.org/abs/2305.14314

11. Hu, E.J., et al.: LoRA: low-rank adaptation of large language models (2021). http://arxiv.org/abs/2106.09685

12. Casas, J., Spring, T., Daher, K., Mugellini, E., Khaled, O.A., Cudré-Mauroux, P.: enhancing conversational agents with empathic abilities. In: Proceedings of the 21st ACM International Conference on Intelligent Virtual Agents, IVA 2021, pp. 41 – 47 (2021). iSBN: 9781450386197

13. Daher, K., Casas, J., Khaled, O.A., Mugellini, E.: Empathic chatbot response for medical assistance. In: Proceedings of the 20th ACM International Conference on Intelligent Virtual Agents, IVA 2020 (2020). iSBN: 9781450375863

14. Zhou, H., Huang, M., Zhang, T., Zhu, X., Liu, B.: Emotional chatting machine: emotional conversation generation with internal and external memory. In: 32nd AAAI Conference on Artificial Intelligence, AAAI 2018, pp. 730 – 738 (2018)

15. Denecke, K., Vaaheesan, S., Arulnathan, A.: A mental health chatbot for regulating emotions (sermo) - concept and usability test. IEEE Trans. Emerg. Topics Comput. **9**, 1170–1182 (2021)

16. Hajek, P., Barushka, A., Munk, M.: Neural networks with emotion associations, topic modeling and supervised term weighting for sentiment analysis. Int. J. Neural Syst. **31**(10), 2150013 (2021)

17. Kaur, H., Mangat, V. N.: A survey of sentiment analysis techniques. In: 2017 International Conference on I-SMAC (IoT in Social, Mobile, Analytics and Cloud) (I-SMAC), pp. 921–925 (2017)

18. Wankhade, M., Rao, A.C.S., Kulkarni, C.: A survey on sentiment analysis methods, applications, and challenges. Artif. Intell. Rev. **55**(7), 5731–5780 (2022). https://doi.org/10.1007/s10462-022-10144-1

19. Hung, L.P., Alias, S.: Beyond sentiment analysis: a review of recent trends in text based sentiment analysis and emotion detection. J. Adv. Comput. Intell. Intell. Inf. **27**(1), 84–95 (2023). https://www.fujipress.jp/jaciii/jc/jacii002700010084

20. Ayadi, M.E., Kamel, M.S., Karray, F.: Survey on speech emotion recognition: features, classification schemes, and databases. Pattern Recogn. **44**, 572–587 (2011)

21. De Lope, J., Graña, M.: A hybrid time-distributed deep neural architecture for speech emotion recognition. Int. J. Neural Syst. **32**(6), 2250024 (2022)

22. Badshah, A.M., Ahmad, J., Rahim, N., Baik, S.W.: Speech emotion recognition from spectrograms with deep convolutional neural network. In: 2017 International Conference on Platform Technology and Service, PlatCon 2017 - Proceedings (2017)

23. Zaman, K., Zhaoyun, S., Shah, S.M., Shoaib, M., Lili, P., Hussain, A.: Driver emotions recognition based on improved faster r-cnn and neural architectural search network. Symmetry **14**, 687 (2022)

24. Yao, H., Yang, X., Chen, D., Wang, Z., Tian, Y.: Facial expression recognition based on fine-tuned channel-spatial attention transformer. Sensors **23**, 6799 (2023). https://www.mdpi.com/1424-8220/23/15/6799/htm

25. Bellamkonda, S., Gopalan, N.P.: An enhanced facial expression recognition model using local feature fusion of gabor wavelets and local directionality patterns. Int. J. Ambient Comput. Intell. **11**, 48–70 (2020)

26. Mukhiddinov, M., Djuraev, O., Akhmedov, F., Mukhamadiyev, A., Cho, J.: Masked face emotion recognition based on facial landmarks and deep learning approaches for visually impaired people. Sensors **23**, 1080 (2023). https://www.mdpi.com/1424-8220/23/3/1080/htm

27. Romeo, M., García, D.H., Han, T., Cangelosi, A., Jokinen, K.: Predicting apparent personality from body language: benchmarking deep learning architectures for adaptive social human-robot interaction. Adv. Robot. **35**, 1167–1179 (2021)

28. Ilyas, C.M.A., Nunes, R., Nasrollahi, K., Rehm, M., Moeslund, T.B.: Deep emotion recognition through upper body movements and facial expression. In: VISIGRAPP 2021 - Proceedings of the 16th International Joint Conference on Computer Vision, Imaging and Computer Graphics Theory and Applications, vol. 5, pp. 669–679 (2021)

29. Ranganathan, H., Chakraborty, S., Panchanathan, S.: Multimodal emotion recognition using deep learning architectures. In: 2016 IEEE Winter Conference on Applications of Computer Vision, WACV 2016 (2016)

30. Prakash, V.G., et al.: Computer vision-based assessment of autistic children: analyzing interactions, emotions, human pose, and life skills. IEEE Access **11**, 47907–47929 (2023)

31. Zhu, L., Zhu, Z., Zhang, C., Xu, Y., Kong, X.: Multimodal sentiment analysis based on fusion methods: a survey. Inf. Fusion **95**, 306–325 (2023). https://www.sciencedirect.com/science/article/pii/S156625352300074X

32. Rizou, S., Paflioti, A., Theofilatos, A., Vakali, A., Sarigiannidis, G., Chatzisavvas, K.C.: Multilingual name entity recognition and intent classification employing deep learning architectures. Simul. Model. Pract. Theory **120**, 102620 (2022). https://www.sciencedirect.com/science/article/pii/S1569190X22000995

33. Li, C., et al.: Large language models understand and can be enhanced by emotional stimuli (2023). http://arxiv.org/abs/2307.11760

34. Dettmers, T., Pagnoni, A., Holtzman, A., Zettlemoyer, L.: Qlora: efficient finetuning of quantized llms (2023). https://arxiv.org/abs/2305.14314v1

Using Touch to Improve Emotion Recognition: Proposed System and Expert Validation

Luisa Merino Ramírez[1], José P. Molina[1,2] (ID), Álvaro Lanchas López[1,2], Félix de la Paz[3] (ID), Antonio Fernández-Caballero[1,2,4] (ID), and Arturo S. García[1,2(✉)] (ID)

[1] Instituto de Investigación en Informática, Unidad de Neurocognición y Emoción, 02071 Albacete, Spain
arturosimon.garcia@uclm.es
[2] Departamento de Sistemas Informáticos, Universidad de Castilla-La Mancha, 02071 Albacete, Spain
[3] Department of Artificial Intelligence, Universidad Nacional de Educación a Distancia, 28040 Madrid, Spain
[4] Biomedical Research Networking Centre in Mental Health (CIBERSAM), 28029 Madrid, Spain

Abstract. This paper explores the relationship between facial expressions of emotions and the sense of touch, with the future aim of investigating their impact on emotion recognition deficits in individuals with neurological disorders. The developed application involves a two-part system: a test designer for experts and a training simulator for patients. Using a haptic device, patients assess emotions, textures, and sensations through a survey. The system employs a client-server architecture, allowing remote monitoring by experts and promoting patient expression. The application gathers subjective and objective data for subsequent analysis. To validate the system, a study was conducted with two psychologists to identify potential usability issues prior to testing with end users.

Keywords: Emotion recognition · Haptics · Expert evaluation

1 Introduction

Often relegated to a secondary role behind vision, touch has been the subject of study in recent decades, revealing a complexity and richness that make it a fundamental tool for interaction with the world around us [15]. Vision provides insights into structural properties of objects such as shape or size, referred as macrostructure [9]. However, touch plays a crucial role in understanding an object's microstructure, which encompasses properties like hardness, texture, roughness, or temperature. While vision offers a general overview of an object's form, touch delves deeper, revealing intricate details that contribute significantly to our comprehensive perception of the object. This expanded understanding is

© The Author(s), under exclusive license to Springer Nature Switzerland AG 2024
J. M. Ferrández Vicente et al. (Eds.): IWINAC 2024, LNCS 14674, pp. 441–451, 2024.
https://doi.org/10.1007/978-3-031-61140-7_42

facilitated by haptic perception, which combines tactile and kinesthetic perceptions. Haptic perception involves the integration of sensory information from the skin (cutaneous and thermal receptors) and from the muscles and tendons (proprioception) [11]. However, haptic perception requires more time to obtain similar information compared to other senses like vision [14] since touch processes information successively, leading to increased time and memory load.

Haptic interfaces allow users to interact with virtual objects through the sense of touch. Communication with these interfaces takes place via a haptic device through which the user interacts with the virtual environment [12]. Haptic interfaces provide bi-directional communication, i.e. the user applies a force to a location within the virtual environment and the response of the haptic interface can be presented in the form of force, vibration, etc., depending on the device being used. This leads to the following categorization of haptic interfaces:

- Tactile interfaces employ various methods to stimulate the skin, such as vibration, pressure, and temperature changes. They can produce a broad range of sensations, from simple textures to complex tactile experiences, such as smoothness, bumpiness, and roughness.
- Kinesthetic or force interfaces use sensors to measure the user's movements and apply forces in response [4]. This allows users to feel the weight and resistance of objects in the virtual environment. These interfaces are often used for training and simulation applications, such as surgical simulators and flight simulators. Examples include the Phantom family of devices [1] and the Novint Falcon [7].

1.1   Emotion Recognition

The recognition and differentiation of emotions is paramount in everyday life [17]. Emotion recognition has been extensively studied due to its impact on social relationships and communication. During the 1970s, Ekman et al. identified the six basic universal emotions that can be perceived through facial expressions [5]: anger, disgust, fear, joy, sadness, and surprise. This study was a significant milestone that triggered extensive research into the intricacies of human emotions. This led to further investigations into the underlying mechanisms and expressions of emotions. Building on this foundation, a 2017 study used facial mapping techniques to investigate the role of different facial regions in emotion recognition [21]. They found that the lower face is more important for recognizing emotions of happiness, disgust, and surprise, while the eyes and eyebrows are more important for recognizing anger, fear, and sadness.

Deficits in emotion recognition, caused by brain damage or neuronal degeneration, have been observed in various disorders including schizophrenia, attention deficit disorder, and autism spectrum disorders. The use of new technologies, particularly virtual reality (VR), has recently emerged as a promising tool for treating emotion recognition disorders, offering innovative ways for further research and potential therapeutic applications [6]. These applications could improve the social and emotional well-being of people affected by these disorders [16]. A different, interesting but also challenging, research approach to emotion and face

Fig. 1. Stylus and thimble end-effectors built for the Falcon device.

recognition is haptics (tactile and force-feedback) [8]; recent studies confirm the link between touch and emotions even virtually [3]. In the next sections, we propose and detail the implementation of a system for studying this link.

2   Development of the Proposed System

For the development of the work described in this article, we have used Unity [19], an editor and engine which is very popular not only for the creation of video games, but also for the creation of 3D applications for research and other professional software. Specifically, in this work, two applications have been created with this tool, a client and a server. As it will be seen in the following sections, the client has a haptic interface formed by a Novint Falcon device [7] and the Touchable Universe plugin for Unity [18]. In addition, another tool, Adobe Fuse [2], has also been used to create the 3D models.

2.1   Haptic Interface of the Client Application

For our application we have chosen the Novint Falcon haptic device [7] on the hardware side and the Touchable Universe plugin for Unity [18] on the software side. The Falcon is a force-feedback device created by the company Novint Technologies, originally designed to be used in video games, but it has also attracted the interest of many researchers because it offers interesting features at a comparatively low cost [10]. The Falcon is a delta robot-type device, with three articulated arms that start from the body of the device and join together at the end-effector grasped by the user. This design provides 3 degrees of freedom, i.e. the user can move the effector in all three dimensions of space, but not rotate it. The working volume is $4 \times 4 \times 4$ inches (approx. 10 cm per dimension), its maximum force is 8.9 N, and its ideal sampling rate is 1 KHz, although it fluctuates between that value and 800 Hz. In addition, the maximum value of its elastic constant k measured in our laboratory is 1.8 N/mm. The Falcon's end-effector is replaceable, available in the shape of a ball or pistol grip. For this work we also have two more end-effectors, developed in our laboratory, one in the shape of a thimble and one in the shape of a pencil (Fig. 1), with which we expand the options and possibilities of the user experience.

As for the software, in addition to the Falcon's own drivers, we also used the Touchable Universe plugin [18], which facilitates the use of this device in the Unity development tool. This is a software that we have already used in other works and, although it is currently discontinued and no longer available in the Asset Store, it is still a practical and quick solution for integrating the Falcon into an application. In particular, this plugin provides the following two components:

- Haptic Camera: This script is added to the main camera and allows configuring the properties of the 3D pointer/cursor of the Falcon device.
- Haptic Mesh: This other script is added to objects (GameObjects in Unity) that are meant to be able to be touched with the Falcon device, which in our case will be 3D models representing the facial expressions associated with different emotions.

This last component allows the selection, from a drop-down list, the material or haptic texture of the object to which it is added. The available materials are: ice, stone, glass, rubber, marshmallow, wet paint, plastic, wood and steel. As it will be seen, from this list we focused at two materials in particular: marshmallow, because it provides a similar feel to that of human skin; and stone, because of the hardness and roughness that could be expected from a sculpture or statue. In addition, the component also allows for the addition of a normal map, which has been useful for adding more detail to the surface of the models when touched with the Falcon device.

2.2   Creation of the 3D Models

For the purpose of this work it was necessary to obtain or create 3D models of faces showing the different facial expressions described by Ekman for each of the six basic emotions. To this end, the software Adobe Fuse was used. Adobe Fuse is a free 3D character modeling software initially created by Mixamo and later purchased by Adobe, which can be obtained through the Steam platform [13]. Fuse facilitates the task of creating the characters thanks to its user-friendly interface and its library of models, where the user can choose one as a starting point and then modify its characteristics, such as sex, height, muscle mass, skin color, eyes or hair, and what interests us most, which is its facial expression. As a first model, it was decided to choose a female face in her 20 s, with very short hair so that the hair does not hide any of the facial features (Fig. 2, left). Starting from this model, Fuse allowed us to add any of the predefined expressions in our application (angry, awkward, cocky, confused, goofy, happy, worried), some of which fitted Ekman's description, while others had to be modified manually to make it that way. With the models created, they were imported into the Unity editor, where they were first added to the scene as GameObjects, and after some adjustments they were converted into prefabs, i.e. Unity templates that could be instantiated again as objects in the scene when the application requires it [20]. In particular, the following components were added to each of the models so that they could not only be seen, but also touched with the haptic device:

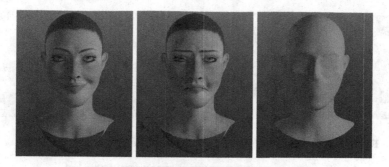

Fig. 2. Left: 3D model for emotion "joy". Center: 3D model for emotion "sadness". Right: Expressionless mannequin for hidden mode.

- Mesh renderer: Used to apply a graphical texture to the models, specified in the Material property.
- Mesh collider: Consists of a mesh composed of small triangles overlaying the 3D model, used for accurate detection of collisions with the model geometry.
- Haptic mesh: This script allows to choose the haptic texture of the model, that is, the response that the user will get when touching the model with the Falcon device. One of the limitations of this component is that it is only possible to choose from a list of predefined materials. Fortunately, there were two that suited our interests, marshmallow and stone, to represent a soft texture - more like human skin - and a hard texture - more like the feel of a sculpture - respectively. Another limitation is that it is not possible to change the material at runtime, which was solved by doubling the number of prefabs to be created, to have one set with a soft texture and another set with a hard texture.

Finally, it was also intended to include a touch-only exploration mode, in which the user could touch the face but not see it, with the aim of also studying the recognition of facial expressions through touch. Initially, this hidden mode would simply hide the graphic model, leaving only the collision mesh and the haptic texture. However, after some tests, it was observed that it was very difficult to carry out the exploration in this mode, so it was considered to facilitate it by showing a face without facial expressions as a reference (Fig. 2, right). Thus, in this hidden mode, the user is shown an expressionless mannequin on the screen, but the collision mesh and the haptic texture of the face with the expression of the specific emotion is superimposed on it.

In total, 15 prefabs were then created, representing Ekman's six basic emotions plus the neutral one, doubled for the haptic textures - marshmallow and stone - and also adding the expressionless mannequin model.

2.3   Client and Server Applications

The application has been designed and implemented following a client/server architecture that would allow the specialist to prepare, launch and follow the

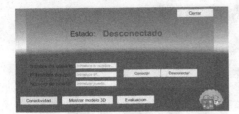

Fig. 3. Connection interfaces for the client (left) and server (right).

Fig. 4. Test setup starts by selecting one of the six basic emotions.

test from a computer different from the PC of the person who is going to perform the test. For the connectivity between client and server, the TCP/IP protocol was used, establishing a data flow through which the server communicates the test parameters to the client and the client sends the progress data and the final evaluation to the server. The 3D models (the prefabs with different emotions and haptic textures) are not sent from one computer to another, but are already included in the two programs, so that what the server sends to the client is a string including the model to be loaded, and the client opens and displays it. In particular, for the Unity implementation, TcpListener and TcpClient classes were used, which provide methods for connecting, sending and receiving data over the network in synchronous blocking mode. On the server side, a button on the interface opens a window in which the user enters the port number and then waits for the client connection (Fig. 3, right). Similarly, on the client side, a window also opens in which the user must enter his name, and the IP address and port of the server (Fig. 3, left). The name entered in the client will be the one that will be saved in the server along with the rest of the test data generated.

Server: Test Setup. Once the connection between client and server has been established, the health professional can configure the test via the interface presented by the server (Fig. 4). This interface allows, in particular, to set the type of emotion represented by the 3D model, the haptic texture (marshmallow or stone), the camera position, the mode (visible or hidden) and the maximum observation/exploration time of the model.

The expert begins to configure the test by clicking on the "Inventory" button, which opens a window displaying the different emotions available, represented by an emoticon and a name. Once the emotion has been selected, the content of the window changes to show the possible haptic textures, represented by an icon and also a name. The next step allows the specialist to focus the camera on a specific part of the model's face, since, as explained above, the Falcon device's workspace is not sufficient to cover a whole adult face. The interface facilitates this task with three preset positions: eyes, mouth and face. The first two focus on the top and bottom of the face, respectively, while the last position serves as a starting point for the user to adjust the camera to his or her discretion, using the WASD or cursor keys. After that, the expert can decide which presentation mode will be used for the test: visible, the user will be shown the model representing the emotion on the screen and can touch the same model through the haptic interface; hidden, if the visual model is replaced by a mannequin without expressive features, but the user can use the haptic interface to touch the model that is superimposed on the mannequin, invisible, and that represents the emotion. Finally, the professional can set a maximum time for the test, which by default is 5 min. Once this is done, the server then sends the client a string resulting from the concatenation of model + mode + time, all separated by the ';' character. The haptic texture is not explicitly indicated because the model name already refers to the one with the desired texture.

Client: Performing the Test. Before connecting to the server and starting a test, the user has the opportunity to practice with the available models in front of the client program and to get used to the haptic device and the stimuli obtained through it. This is the learning mode which is accessed by pressing a button in the lower right corner of the client interface, and in doing so displays a random model among all the existing ones. As mentioned above, the connection to the server is initiated through a window where the user's name, server address and port are entered. Before starting a test, the interface asks the user how he/she feels in that previous moment, information that is collected to send it to the server so that the specialist can contrast the before condition with the after one. The test starts after the client program receives the string sent by the server indicating the model to be displayed, the mode and the time. The model is not only displayed on the client, but also on the server, so that the expert can see the same thing as the other person. Using the haptic device, that person in front of the client PC can explore and touch the 3D model, in visible or hidden mode, and while doing so the position of the haptic cursor - a bright yellow sphere - is also transmitted to the expert's computer so that it can follow his or her movements. In addition, to facilitate this tracking, the cursor leaves behind it a trail of past positions that disappear after 2 s. When the time set by the professional ends, the client interface changes and a window appears with a questionnaire. The user can also terminate the observation/exploration task and access the questionnaire without waiting for the time to expire by pressing the button on the interface, which also causes the time spent to be recorded. The

Fig. 5. After finishing the test, a questionnaire is shown in the client (left), and responses are sent and shown in the server (right).

questionnaire includes the following questions, which are displayed one after the other as they are answered:

1. What emotion do you think it is represented?
2. What texture do you think it is represented?
3. How do you feel after the exploration?

For example, the first question has the following possible answers: joy, anger, fear, surprise, anger, disgust, from which the user must select the one he/she considers most in line with the emotion conveyed by the 3D model (Fig. 5, left). The responses are sent to the server application through the established communication channel, where the specialist can read them (Fig. 5, right).

Test Recording. In addition to following live from the server side the exploration of the model that is performed on the client side, we have included the functionality to record the entire test in video as the specialist sees it on his computer, for later viewing and analysis. For this purpose, we have used the free plugin called "vr Capture", developed by the company rockVR and available in the Unity Asset Store. This plugin can capture both video and audio, although in this work only video is recorded. At the end of the test, all the data collected is saved in a CSV file on the server computer, except for the video, which, if captured, is saved in a media file. In particular, the data saved in the CSV file are the following:

3   Preliminary Evaluation

A preliminary evaluation was conducted with two expert therapists with the main aim of gathering their feedback on the system's functionality, identify potential usability problems, and ensure the application meets the needs of the target population before testing with end-users. The evaluation took place in the Instituto de Investigación en Informática de Albacete (Spain). Two male psychologists, aged 34 and 23, participated in the study. Two laptops were used, one for the therapist's application and another one for the patient's application, which used a Novint Falcon device. Both computers were placed in such a way that the participant could see them simultaneously to observe the entire testing process (both the therapist's and the patient's side).

The procedure was the same for both participants and the evaluation was conducted individually. First, the workflow and each parameter of the therapist interface were explained. Then, the evaluation phase began, which consisted of the expert running different tests on a member of the research team acting as the patient. Once the tests were completed, the experts gave their opinion on the system and its functionality. Finally, they were asked for their general opinion on the usefulness of the tool within their professional context and how it might enhance their therapeutic approach.

Both participants reported a positive experience with the system and provided valuable feedback to enhance the user experience and functionality:

- Improved Visual Cues: The participants recommended adding a color change to the "Show 3D Model" button in the patient interface whenever a new test arrives. This visual cue would help patients easily identify and initiate the next assessment within the simulation environment.
- Enhanced Data Collection: While the system currently records the minute the patient questionnaire is completed, the participants suggested extending data collection to capture the individual completion time for each test within the larger assessment. This additional information could provide valuable insights into the efficiency and complexity of each test for future analysis.
- Consistency in Feedback Mechanism: The participants pointed out the absence of the haptic cursor in the expert interface when in hidden mode, which is present in the visible mode. It was suggested that the remote cursor function should be enabled in both modes to provide consistent and clear feedback for users, regardless of the chosen test environment.
- Minimize Distractions: To further optimize the patient experience and minimize potential distractions during the exploration phase, the participants suggested hiding the "Connectivity" and "Show 3D Model" buttons at the start of each test. Temporarily hiding them would allow patients to focus solely on the assessment task without unnecessary visual distractions.
- Automated Testing: Looking towards future applications, the participants proposed the development of an automated testing feature that would involve sending patients a predefined list of tests they need to complete. This automation has the potential to eliminate the need for the therapist to be present during the entire exploration process.

Finally, the participants acknowledged the potential of the application positively. However, they emphasized the importance of real-world testing to fully understand the system's effectiveness and draw conclusive findings. They recognized that the true impact and potential benefits of the application would only be revealed through controlled user testing with real patients.

4   Conclusions

In this paper, we proposed, implemented and validated a system for supporting therapies aimed at people with emotion recognition deficits. The system incorporates haptic feedback to aid in the emotion recognition. Valuable feedback from the expert validation included the implementation of improved visual cues, better data collection for further analysis and the inclusion of automated testing mechanisms, among others improvements. This feedback will be useful for improving our tool. The ultimate goal of this research is to determine whether the combination of touch and sight improves emotion recognition in those people, which could provide valuable insights into the design of tailored therapies.

Acknowledgments. Grants PID2020-115220RB-C21 and PID2023-149753OB-C21, funded by MCIN/AEI/10.13039/501100011033, and 2022-GRIN-34436, funded by UCLM, all also funded by "ERDF: A way to make Europe".

References

1. 3D Systems: Phantom Premium (2024). https://www.3dsystems.com/haptics-devices/3d-systems-phantom-premium
2. Adobe: Fuse (2024). https://www.adobe.com/es/products/fuse.htmlIn
3. Ahmed, I., Harjunen, V.J., Jacucci, G., Ravaja, N., Ruotsalo, T., Spapé, M.M.: Touching virtual humans: haptic responses reveal the emotional impact of affective agents. IEEE Trans. Affect. Comput. **14**(1), 331–342 (2020)
4. Burdea, G.C., Coiffet, P.: Virtual Reality Technology. John Wiley & Sons, Hoboken (2017)
5. Ekman, P., Friesen, W.V.: Unmasking the face: a guide to recognizing emotions from facial clues. Ishk (1975)
6. Fernández-Sotos, P., García, A.S., Vicente-Querol, M.A., Lahera, G., Rodriguez-Jimenez, R., Fernandez-Caballero, A.: Validation of dynamic virtual faces for facial affect recognition. PLoS ONE **16**(1), e0246001 (2021). https://doi.org/10.1371/journal.pone.0246001
7. Haptics House: Novint's Falcon Haptic Device (2024). https://hapticshouse.com/pages/novints-falcon-haptic-device/
8. Jamil, M.H., Park, W., Eid, M.: Emotional responses to watching and touching 3d emotional face in a virtual environment. Virt. Real. **25**(2), 553–564 (2021)
9. Katz, D., Krueger, L.E.: The World of Touch. Psychology press, Abingdon (1986)
10. Martin, S., Hillier, N.: Characterisation of the novint falcon haptic device for application as a robot manipulator. In: Australasian Conference on Robotics and Automation (ACRA), pp. 291–292. Citeseer (2009)
11. Martínez, J., García, A.S., Oliver, M., González, P., Molina, J.P.: The sense of touch as the last frontier in virtual reality technology. In: Virtual Reality Designs, pp. 218–246. CRC Press (2020)
12. Martínez, J., Martínez, D., Molina, J.P., González, P., García, A.S.: Comparison of force and vibrotactile feedback with direct stimulation for texture recognition. In: 2011 International Conference on Cyberworlds, pp. 62–68 (2011) https://doi.org/10.1109/CW.2011.23
13. Mixamo: Fuse (2024). https://store.steampowered.com/app/257400/Fuse/

14. Révész, G.: Psychology and art of the blind (1950)
15. Robles-De-La-Torre, G.: The importance of the sense of touch in virtual and real environments. IEEE Multimedia **13**(3), 24–30 (2006). https://doi.org/10.1109/MMUL.2006.69
16. Rus-Calafell, M., Gutiérrez-Maldonado, J., Ribas-Sabaté, J.: A virtual reality-integrated program for improving social skills in patients with schizophrenia: a pilot study. J. Behav. Ther. Exp. Psychiat. **45**(1), 81–89 (2014). https://doi.org/10.1016/j.jbtep.2013.09.002
17. Sachs, G., et al.: Training of affect recognition (TAR) in schizophrenia-impact on functional outcome. Schizophr. Res. **138**(2–3), 262–267 (2012). https://doi.org/10.1016/j.schres.2012.03.005
18. Touchable Universe: 3D Haptics for Novint Falcon (2021). https://assetstore.unity.com/packages/tools/physics/3d-haptics-for-novint-falcon-119281/
19. Unity Technologies: Unity Real-Time Development Platform (2024). https://unity.com/
20. Unity Technologies: Unity User Manual: Prefabs (2024). https://docs.unity3d.com/Manual/Prefabs.html
21. Wegrzyn, M., Vogt, M., Kireclioglu, B., Schneider, J., Kissler, J.: Mapping the emotional face: how individual face parts contribute to successful emotion recognition. PloS one **12**(5), e0177239 (2017). https://doi.org/10.1371/journal.pone.0177239

Affective Computing and Context Awareness in Ambient Intelligence

Human-in-the-Loop for Personality Dynamics: Proposal of a New Research Approach

Krzysztof Kutt[1]([✉])[ID], Marzena Kutt[2][ID], Bartosz Kawa[1][ID],
and Grzegorz J. Nalepa[1][ID]

[1] Jagiellonian Human-Centered AI Lab, Mark Kac Center for Complex Systems Research, Institute of Applied Computer Science, Faculty of Physics, Astronomy and Applied Computer Science, Jagiellonian University, Kraków, Poland
krzysztof.kutt@uj.edu.pl, gjn@gjn.re
[2] Institute of Psychology, University of the National Education Commission, Kraków, Poland
marzena.kutt@up.krakow.pl

Abstract. In recent years, one can observe an increasing interest in dynamic models in the personality psychology research. Opposed to the traditional paradigm—in which personality is recognized as a set of several permanent dispositions called traits—dynamic approaches treat it as a complex system based on feedback loops between individual and the environment. The growing attention to dynamic models entails the need for appropriate modelling tools. In this conceptual paper we address this demand by proposing a new approach called personality-in-the-loop, which combines state-of-the-art psychological models with the human-in-the-loop approach used in the design of intelligent systems. This new approach has a potential to open new research directions including the development of new experimental frameworks for research in personality psychology, based on simulations and methods used in the design of intelligent systems. It will also enable the development of new dynamic models of personality in silico. Finally, the proposed approach extends the field of intelligent systems design with new possibilities for processing personality-related data in these systems.

Keywords: Personality · Psychology · Human-in-the-loop · Intelligent assistants · Affective loop

1 Introduction and Motivation

The concept of personality describes a psychological construct that moderates our behavior. We find it consistent with our intuitive understanding, which allows us to distinguish between, e.g., people we describe as "the party animals" and those we describe as "the nerdy geeks" [12]. These intuitions have been extended and structured in a range of trait models emerging with the deepening understanding of personality in psychology, along with the best-known Big Five model.

© The Author(s), under exclusive license to Springer Nature Switzerland AG 2024
J. M. Ferrández Vicente et al. (Eds.): IWINAC 2024, LNCS 14674, pp. 455–464, 2024.
https://doi.org/10.1007/978-3-031-61140-7_43

Importantly, besides these models that characterize personality with a set of permanent dispositions, there are also studies that explore the dynamics of personality [23] which have been gaining increasing interest among researchers in recent years. Many of them have been summarized in the dynamics of personality approach (DPA) [20]. The key idea is the capability of self-regulation in the feedback loop.

The perception of personality has thus changed from a set of various factors in the traditional approach to a complex system that requires appropriate modelling tools. It currently relies on various statistical models used extensively in the social sciences (e.g., [15]). We argue that personality science can benefit significantly from incorporating solutions developed in data science and computer science into its portfolio of methods.

The fusion of psychological theories with theories from computer science has a long tradition (e.g., [3]), which, on the one hand, has allowed the development of a number of models of mental processes (e.g., [6]), with a particularly rich body of research on cognition models (e.g., [1,8,27]), and, on the other hand, has allowed, for example, the improvement of human-computer interaction using cognitive theories (e.g., [24]). However, to the best of our knowledge, advanced modeling and experimental tools have not yet been developed in the field of personality psychology.

In this conceptual paper, we address this idea by highlighting the similarities between the DPA approach and the human-in-the-loop (HiTL) approach used to design intelligent assistants [18,25]. In the latter, the system adapts its actions to changing user characteristics, measured by a range of sensors, to achieve the goal assumed in the chosen interaction model. In fact, the DPA and the HiTL approaches could be considered as two perspectives on the similar self-regulation problem. This will lead us to a discussion on using the HiTL approach as a robust research toolkit for DPA resulting in the proposal of the personality-in-the-loop approach.

The rest of paper is organized as follows. The personality models are summarized in Sect. 2. Then, in Sect. 3, the human-in-the-loop approach used as a basis for designing personalized systems is presented. The proposed personality-in-the-loop approach is outlined in Sect. 4. It is followed by a discussion of possible applications in Sect. 5. The paper is concluded in Sect. 6.

2   Models of Personality

The definition of personality has evolved with the development of psychology. Even today, there is no agreement on how to understand this concept. Mayer [13] attempted to identify a universal definition of the phenomenon. He concludes that according to the definitions he analyzed, personality is: (1) a psychological system, (2) composed of specific parts, (3) these parts interact with each other, (4) develop, and (5) influence behavioral expression in a systematic way [13].

Among personality theories, the so-called trait theories form a significant group. According to them, personality consists of relatively stable properties (traits). They can be defined as "dimensions of individual differences in tendencies to show consistent patterns of thoughts, feelings, and actions" [14]. Some of the most notable trait theories include [12]: Allport's Trait Theory, Cattell's 16 Factor Personality, Eysenck's Three Dimensions of Personality and the Myers-Briggs Type Indicator.

The most widely used personality model in research and scientific literature is the Big Five model [5] in which openness to experience, conscientiousness, extroversion, agreeableness, and neuroticism were identified as independent traits [2]. According to research, the model has cross-cultural stability and test-retest reliability [5], which confirms its value as a personality taxonomy. While its popularity continues unabated, it is important to note the existence of its limitations [5], in particular its insufficient power to describe, predict and explain behavior and psychological processes [15].

Besides this traditional structural-functional paradigm of personality description—in which personality traits are generally recognized as permanent dispositions—which dominates in empirical research, there is also an opposing approach that postulates personality is constantly changing [9]. The source of such a change is supposed to lie in the individual's interactions with the environment. This complex dynamic personality structure is addressed by the numerous process-oriented personality theories developed in recent years [23]. The assumption underlying them is referred to as the dynamics of personality approach (DPA) [20].

The DPA is based on systems theory also called control theory or cybernetic theory [28]. According to it, the system interacts with its environment by receiving information (inputs) that trigger internal operations and by producing outputs, i.e., behaviors, that alter the environment [21]. The underlying foundation of the DPA is a process of self-regulation through negative feedback control. The system autonomously attempts to adapt the current state to a target state, thereby aiming to achieve a goal. This in turn requires feedback on the state of the system. Within the DPA, four phases were distinguished: (1) the goal selection phase, (2) the planning phase, (3) the action phase, and (4) the evaluation phase [20] (see Fig. 1).

3   Human-in-the-Loop Approach

The outlined perspective on personality as a feedback loop corresponds to feedback loops used to personalize intelligent systems based on the growing number of "smart devices" forming the Internet of Things (IoT) [18]. From smartphones and watches to fridges, variety of devices are now equipped with sensors capable of collecting and sharing data via Internet. It creates a rich source of heterogeneous information that can be employed to serve and anticipate users' needs. In fact, leveraging the abundance of unobtrusive, wearable devices, attempts are made to create human-centered applications that try to model human mental states with an aim to deliver a personalized experience [25]. To achieve that, the human should play an active role in the system, providing feedback that adjusts

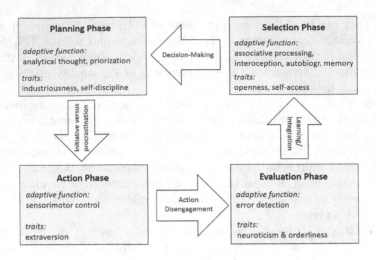

Fig. 1. Phases of the dynamics of personality approach [20].

the model since tasks of modelling human agents exhibit complexity arching beyond current capabilities of algorithms alone [26]. Approaches aiming to solve problems that include human feedback as a part of a system can be subsumed under an umbrella term of human-in-the-loop (HiTL) [18].

The HiTL application design can be considered as a three-step process (see Fig. 2 (left)) consisting of:

1. *Data acquisition.* This may consist of physiological data indirectly describing central nervous system activity, information about the person's current activity, and a description of the external environment [16].
2. *State inference.* The two parts are involved: insights into human nature, based on domain knowledge and previously collected experimental data, and algorithms suitable to process gathered data.
3. *Actuation.* When a knowledge has been distilled from the gathered data, a system should decide on action to be taken. It can produce a recommendation, actively change a state of an environment, or explicitly ask for feedback.

An instance of a feedback loop in the HiTL paradigm is the affective loop. The entire flow of the affective loop is framed by the HiTL loop and begins with the collection of relevant data. This can include psychophysiological signals, face pictures, the stream of messages from social media [4]. Based on this data, the system tries to infer the user's current affective state and then attempts to modify it (see Fig. 2 (right)), so we can call this approach emotion-in-the-loop.

4   Personality-in-the-Loop Approach Proposal

Both the weak predictive and explanatory power of existing trait models and the growing interest in dynamic models that treat personality as a feedback loop

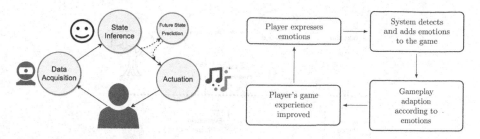

Fig. 2. The human-in-the-loop approach process (left; adapted from [18]) and the affective gaming loop [11] as an instance of the HiTL approach (right).

(Sect. 2) requires a major shift in the research paradigm. We should definitely "be flexible to how, and if at all, we aggregate variables" [15] to avoid oversimplifying the problem by treating the various underlying mechanisms as a single variable (as trait models do). We should also use repeated measures designs to collect time-series data, which will capture personality dynamics and allow us to create models that predict the state at *t+1* based on values at time *t* [15]. Approaches exploring these directions are already being studied in personality psychology (e.g., [22]) and used, for example, to distinguish between personality and psychopathology [7]. However, even if they use sophisticated statistical methods, to the best of our knowledge they do not go beyond the methodology classically used in the social sciences.

We believe that a noteworthy direction is to use the HiTL approach, which is not entirely new to the field of psychology, as it is already being used in affective computing. The affective loops developed there (emotion-in-the-loop approach; Sect. 3) address the need to model a person's internal states in a stimulus-rich environment that can dynamically induce changes in these states. This is the human-in-the-loop variant, in which the focus is not really on the whole person, but primarily on their emotions. In an analogous approach, the focus could be on personality—as its state will be inferred and altered—which justifies calling this approach personality-in-the-loop (PiTL).

By following the HiTL approach, it will be reasonable to use the methodology behind the design of intelligent agents. The result is the model shown in Fig. 3, in which the environment records data about the user and their context, makes inferences about their current state based on that data, and performs changes to induce appropriate personality adjustments. The environmental alterations are then detected by the individual, an evaluation is made, then a new goal is selected and further actions are planned to affect the environment, which closes the loop. A key step is to develop prediction models of the current internal state, which will require appropriately designed experiments and collection of sufficient data. As this is an emerging method, it will also be important to propose and evaluate methods of the environmental change that will actually produce an interaction between the environment and the personality. When these issues are addressed, the proposed PiTL approach will offer a rich set of data related to participants' self-regulatory processes, facilitating their explanation.

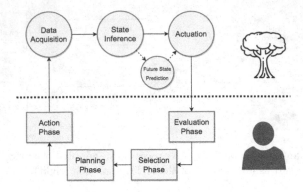

Fig. 3. Personality-in-the-loop approach overview.

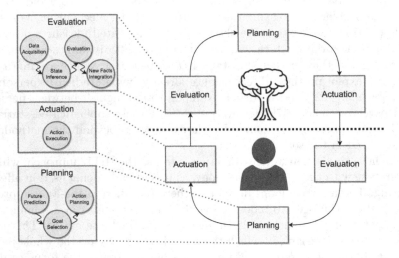

Fig. 4. Personality-in-the-loop as an interaction between two identical loops.

Further examination of the relationship between the DPA approach in personality psychology and HiTL in the creation of intelligent assistants leads to the observation of a number of similarities between these two loops. In essence, the differences between them are limited to an emphasis on other elements of the process and a flipped perspective – in the first loop, the interaction occurs with the environment and in the second – with the user. Therefore, the whole interaction between the personality and the environment (intelligent assistant, simulation, game) in Fig. 3 can be reduced to the interaction of two identical loops based on three main phases: Evaluation, Planning and Actuation, as summarized in Fig. 4.

The loop starts with perception, i.e., data acquisition, which allows to infer information about the current state of the user/environment. Then the inconsistency between the current and anticipated state, based on previous plans, is evaluated. As a result, new knowledge may be created and integrated accordingly, leading to an update of the interaction model, a change in behavioral scripts or a change in personality. Afterwards, the system/person selects an adequate goal based on predictions about the future—depending on the need to maintain the predicted future or to change it—and prepares a sequence of steps to achieve the goal. The final phase is the actual execution of the action so planned.

5   Discussion on Possible PiTL Applications

The PiTL approach enables to leverage the models developed within HiTL and implement them in the field of personality research. In particular, based on solutions used in research on affective loops and affective gaming, it allows to propose an experimental environment for the study of dynamic aspects of personality based on appropriately prepared games/simulations [10]. Firstly, they provide a stimulus-rich experimental environment, secondly, they offer the ability to fully control the stimuli, including the opportunity to force the dynamics within the developed protocols, and thirdly, they are capable of logging the entire context of the study, which facilitates the further analysis.

The PiTL approach can also be used for personality modeling *in silico*. Through appropriate models, it will allow the analysis of various dynamic aspects in the field of personality psychology. As a result, besides the statistical models used so far, knowledge-based models, machine learning models, etc. will be available for use in personality research. Clearly, in order for these models to provide actual value, they need to be enhanced with appropriate explainability methods to translate them and their decisions into theories of personality psychology.

The PiTL approach will also extend research on intelligent assistants. Owing to the presented analogies between the DPA and HiTL models, one can argue for a kind of dynamic personality of assistants. By elaborating this idea further, it allows to assess the personality of intelligent systems, in particular those that can evolve in a relatively autonomous way, such as Tay created by Microsoft [17]. On the other hand, it also allows to postulate the introduction of the personality of assistants into the design process of intelligent systems.

Finally, the development of PiTL approach may also lead to new methods of personality assessment, including its dynamic aspects, developed in the area of personality computing [19] – currently limited to trait theories.

6   Summary and Future Work

Dynamic models of personality, going beyond the classical paradigms treating it as a set of stable traits, present personality as a complex system built on feedback loops. Summarized in the dynamics of personality approach (DPA), they explain, on the one hand, the relative constancy of traits and, on the other hand, provide tools to explain the variability that occurs in different situations. A key aspect is to adequately model the interaction of the individual and his or her personality with the environment. The latter contains a number of similarities to the human-in-the-loop (HiTL) approach present in the design of intelligent assistants. As in DPA, the system operates in a feedback loop in interaction with the environment (the system user). The juxtaposition of these two models has led to the proposal of a new approach called personality-in-the-loop (PiTL).

We believe that such a framework may be used by both psychologists and computer scientists leading to the emergence of a promising area that requires the integration of knowledge and collaboration of specialists from two so far separate fields. The possible applications of the PiTL approach were outlined in the paper. These will form the basis for further work, which will be devoted to review existing datasets for potentially useful ones [15], developing detailed research plans and then to performing experiments that will verify the validity and usefulness of the proposed approach.

Acknowledgments. The research for this publication has been supported by a grant from the Priority Research Area DigiWorld under the Strategic Programme Excellence Initiative at Jagiellonian University. The research has been supported by a grant from the Faculty of Physics, Astronomy and Applied Computer Science under the Strategic Programme Excellence Initiative at Jagiellonian University.

Disclosure of Interests. The authors have no competing interests to declare that are relevant to the content of this article.

References

1. Cassimatis, N.L., Bello, P., Langley, P.: Ability, breadth, and parsimony in computational models of higher-order cognition. Cogn. Sci. **32**(8), 1304–1322 (2008). https://doi.org/10.1080/03640210802455175
2. Costa, P.T., McCrae, R.R.: Trait theories of personality. In: Barone, D.F., Hersen, M., Van Hasselt, V.B. (eds.) Advanced Personality, pp. 103–121. Springer, Boston (1998). https://doi.org/10.1007/978-1-4419-8580-4_5
3. Crupi, V., Nelson, J.D., Meder, B., Cevolani, G., Tentori, K.: Generalized information theory meets human cognition: introducing a unified framework to model uncertainty and information search. Cogn. Sci. **42**(5), 1410–1456 (2018). https://doi.org/10.1111/cogs.12613
4. Dzedzickis, A., Kaklauskas, A., Bucinskas, V.: Human emotion recognition: review of sensors and methods. Sensors **20**(3), 592 (2020). https://doi.org/10.3390/s20030592
5. Feher, A., Vernon, P.A.: Looking beyond the big five: a selective review of alternatives to the big five model of personality. Personality Individ. Differ. **169**, 110002 (2021). https://doi.org/10.1016/j.paid.2020.110002
6. Friedman, S., Forbus, K., Sherin, B.: Representing, running, and revising mental models: a computational model. Cogn. Sci. **42**(4), 1110–1145 (2018). https://doi.org/10.1111/cogs.12574
7. Hopwood, C.J., Wright, A.G.C., Bleidorn, W.: Person-environment transactions differentiate personality and psychopathology. Nat. Rev. Psychol. **1**(1), 55–63 (2022). https://doi.org/10.1038/s44159-021-00004-0
8. Kelly, M.A., Arora, N., West, R.L., Reitter, D.: Holographic declarative memory: distributional semantics as the architecture of memory. Cogn. Sci. **44**(11) (2020). https://doi.org/10.1111/cogs.12904

9. Kostromina, S.N., Grishina, N.V.: The dynamic personality: 'continuity amid change'. Psychol. Russia State Art **12**(2), 34–45 (2020). https://doi.org/10.11621/pir.2019.0203

10. Kutt, K., Drążyk, D., Bobek, S., Nalepa, G.J.: Personality-based affective adaptation methods for intelligent systems. Sensors **21**(1), 163 (2021). https://doi.org/10.3390/s21010163

11. Lara-Cabrera, R., Camacho, D.: A taxonomy and state of the art revision on affective games. Futur. Gener. Comput. Syst. **92**, 516–525 (2019)

12. Matz, S., Chan, Y.W.F., Kosinski, M.: Models of personality. In: Tkalcic, M., Carolis, B.D., de Gemmis, M., Odic, A., Kosir, A. (eds.) Emotions and Personality in Personalized Services - Models, Evaluation and Applications. Human-Computer Interaction Series, pp. 35–54. Springer, Heidelberg (2016). https://doi.org/10.1007/978-3-319-31413-6_3

13. Mayer, J.D.: Asserting the definition of personality. Online Newslett. Pers. Sci. (1), 1–4 (2007). http://www.personality-arp.org/html/newsletter01/page5d.html

14. McCrae, R.R., Costa, P.T.: Personality in Adulthood. Taylor & Francis, Abingdon (2003). https://doi.org/10.4324/9780203428412

15. Mõttus, R., et al.: Descriptive, predictive and explanatory personality research: different goals, different approaches, but a shared need to move beyond the big few traits. Eur. J. Pers. **34**(6), 1175–1201 (2020). https://doi.org/10.1002/per.2311

16. Nalepa, G.J., Kutt, K., Bobek, S.: Mobile platform for affective context-aware systems. Future Gener. Comput. Syst. **92**, 490–503 (2019). https://doi.org/10.1016/j.future.2018.02.033

17. Neff, G., Nagy, P.: Talking to bots: symbiotic agency and the case of tay. Int. J. Commun. **10**, 4915–4931 (2016)

18. Nunes, D.S.S., Zhang, P., Silva, J.S.: A survey on human-in-the-loop applications towards an internet of all. IEEE Commun. Surv. Tutor. **17**(2), 944–965 (2015). https://doi.org/10.1109/COMST.2015.2398816

19. Phan, L.V., Rauthmann, J.F.: Personality computing: new frontiers in personality assessment. Soc. Pers. Psychol. Compass **15**(7) (2021). https://doi.org/10.1111/spc3.12624

20. Quirin, M., et al.: The dynamics of personality approach (DPA): 20 tenets for uncovering the causal mechanisms of personality. Eur. J. Pers. **34**(6), 947–968 (2020). https://doi.org/10.1002/per.2295

21. Rauthmann, J.F.: Motivational factors in the perception of psychological situation characteristics. Soc. Pers. Psychol. Compass **10**(2), 92–108 (2016). https://doi.org/10.1111/spc3.12239

22. Rauthmann, J.F.: Capturing interactions, correlations, fits, and transactions: a person-environment relations model. In: The Handbook of Personality Dynamics and Processes, pp. 427–522. Elsevier (2021). https://doi.org/10.1016/B978-0-12-813995-0.00018-2

23. Rauthmann, J.F. (ed.): The Handbook of Personality Dynamics and Processes. Elsevier (2021). https://doi.org/10.1016/C2017-0-00935-7

24. Roads, B.D., Mozer, M.C.: Improving human-machine cooperative classification via cognitive theories of similarity. Cogn. Sci. **41**(5), 1394–1411 (2017). https://doi.org/10.1111/cogs.12400

25. Tkalcic, M., Carolis, B.D., de Gemmis, M., Odic, A., Kosir, A. (eds.): Emotions and Personality in Personalized Services - Models, Evaluation and Applications. Human-Computer Interaction Series. Springer, Heidelberg (2016). https://doi.org/10.1007/978-3-319-31413-6

26. Valdez, A.C., Ziefle, M.: Human factors in the age of algorithms. understanding the human-in-the-loop using agent-based modeling. In: Meiselwitz, G. (ed.) Social Computing and Social Media: Technologies and Analytics (Part II). LNCS, vol. 10914, pp. 357–371. Springer, Heidelberg (2018). https://doi.org/10.1007/978-3-319-91485-5_27
27. Varma, S.: Criteria for the design and evaluation of cognitive architectures. Cogn. Sci. **35**(7), 1329–1351 (2011). https://doi.org/10.1111/j.1551-6709.2011.01190.x
28. Wiener, N.: Cybernetics. Sci. Am. **179**(5), 14–19 (1948)

Emotion Prediction in Real-Life Scenarios: On the Way to the BIRAFFE3 Dataset

Krzysztof Kutt[✉][ID] and Grzegorz J. Nalepa[ID]

Jagiellonian Human-Centered AI Lab, Mark Kac Center for Complex Systems
Research, Institute of Applied Computer Science, Faculty of Physics, Astronomy
and Applied Computer Science, Jagiellonian University, Kraków, Poland
`krzysztof.kutt@uj.edu.pl, gjn@gjn.re`

Abstract. Despite over 20 years of research in affective computing,
emotion prediction models that would be useful in real-life out-of-the-
lab scenarios such as health care or intelligent assistants have still not
been developed. The identification of the fundamental problems behind
this concern led to the initiation of the BIRAFFE series of experiments,
whose main goal is to develop a set of techniques, tools and good practices
to introduce personalized context-based emotion processing modules in
intelligent systems/assistants. The aim of this work is to present the
work-in-progress concept of the third experiment in the BIRAFFE series
and discuss the results of the pilot study. After all conclusions have been
drawn up, actual study will be carried out, and then the collected data
will be processed and made available under the creative commons license
as BIRAFFE3 dataset.

Keywords: Affective computing · Personalization · Wearable devices ·
Emotion prediction · Dataset

1 Introduction and Motivation

Well-operating emotion prediction models, which will assess changes in emotional
state based on a set of diverse signals, will find extensive use in many areas of
life. The first to be mentioned is health care, where they can assist in treating
people with a variety of problems, like depression, schizophrenia, dementia or
post-traumatic stress disorder [8]. Emotion prediction models will also be able
to help assess cognitive abilities in difficult tasks such as participating in car
races [10] or with detecting malicious intent in the forensic area [1]. Such models
will also form the basis of new interaction scenarios in video games [19], along
with supporting a wide range of other scenarios not mentioned here.

The authors of this paper argue that the major concern is that currently
there are no prediction models that can handle the aforementioned real-life use
case scenarios. Models that achieve high performance metrics accomplish this at
the expense of the resolution of the recognized emotional states, e.g., instead of
predicting the full range of emotions, one predicts only whether the emotions

© The Author(s), under exclusive license to Springer Nature Switzerland AG 2024
J. M. Ferrández Vicente et al. (Eds.): IWINAC 2024, LNCS 14674, pp. 465–475, 2024.
https://doi.org/10.1007/978-3-031-61140-7_44

are positive or negative [27]. While the increase in model efficiency is real and replicable, with a prediction accuracy often exceeding 90% [6], the usefulness of such a model is minimal, since it will only detect large fluctuations, while the real changes we care about are more subtle.

The reduction of the resolution of the emotion space, however, is only a way of patching up the more fundamental problems that arise in the development of prediction models in affective computing. The most important of these include: (1) Many studies rely on data from immobile sensors, either research-grade or medical-grade professional equipment [13]. (2) Most studies focus on creating general emotion prediction model for all individuals [13]. (3) Training models on a single dataset. (4) In the case of models utilizing emotional expressions, there is the problem of training them on benchmark datasets that contain expressions played by actors [17]. (5) Most research is conducted entirely in the laboratory, and the results are often not reproducible [27]

To address these challenges, in 2018 we launched a series of BIRAFFE (Bio-Reactions and Faces for Emotion-based Personalization) studies in an attempt to solve aforementioned issues [22]:

1. *Mobile sensors.* Our first and fundamental idea was to create solutions for everyday users, so we have been using affordable mobile devices such as wristbands, smartwatches and simple sensory hardware platforms.
2. *Personalized models.* We are exploring the possibility of personalizing the models by enriching the data with personality profile assessments via psychological questionnaires. To the best of our knowledge, such approaches were not published when we started the first experiment in the BIRAFFE series. Currently, the idea of personalizing prediction models is being explored by various researchers, e.g., [21, 29].
3. *Development of open-access datasets.* Inherent in BIRAFFE are datasets created after each experiment made available to the entire research community under a creative commons license [12, 15]. This allows BIRAFFE's datasets to be combined with other datasets to create more device-agnostic models.
4. *Real-life facial expressions.* BIRAFFE's experiments include taking pictures of emotional expressions in real-life scenarios such as playing computer games.
5. *In-game studies.* Both in-lab and out-of-the-lab research involve a number of difficulties or limitations [27], so in our research we propose games as an intermediate solution that on the one hand offers a variety of stimuli (like an out-of-the-lab scenario) and on the other hand allows full control over the environment (like an in-lab scenario).

To date, the BIRAFFE series of experiments has led to, among other things, two datasets: BIRAFFE1 [12] and BIRAFFE2 [15], a series of analyses related to the use of personality to improve emotion prediction methods [13], consideration of the utility of existing models for recognizing emotions from faces [17], or the first proof-of-concept implementation of emotion recognition in an out-of-the-lab game [16]. The purpose of this paper is to present the ideas behind the third experiment and to discuss the first conclusions drawn from the results of the pilot study.

The BIRAFFE series of experiments addresses the widely investigated challenge of predicting emotions based on psychophysiological signals [6,11]. Various datasets have already been compiled in this area, both focusing on the problem of emotion prediction itself (for review, see [23]) and featuring the results of experiments combining games with the measurement of emotions/physiological signals (see review provided in [7]). Like BIRAFFE, part of the state-of-the-art research tackles the challenge of emotion prediction using wearables in attempt to provide everyday solutions [27].

The rest of paper is organized as follows. The design of the study is provided in Sect. 2. Then, in Sect. 3, the whole experimental protocol and setup are presented. Pilot study is summarized in Sect. 4. The paper is concluded in Sect. 5.

2   Study Design

The ultimate goal of the BIRAFFE series of experiments is to develop a set of techniques, tools and good practices to introduce personalized context-based emotion processing modules in intelligent systems/assistants.

In order to bypass the "cold start" problem, we propose an initial system adaptation based on personality assessment [13]. Once the personality profile is determined using the chosen personality computing method [25], the user can be served with a model more suited to them than a generic, non-personalized one.

On the other hand, our approach emphasizes the importance of the context in which emotions are experienced, as they are triggered, among other things, by specific stimuli/actions that occurred in the system. Appropriate identification of these associations will allow the system to change its operation in order to direct the user's emotions towards the state expected at a given stage of interaction.

Developing the methods and tools that will underlie the outlined approach requires collecting an appropriate set of data about the user, their interactions with the system (context), and their response to emotional stimuli. The preparation of such a dataset is the goal of the BIRAFFE3 experiment.

The study design follows the combined experimental protocol developed in the previous experiments in the BIRAFFE series [14,15] composed of three core components: (a) *user data* are gathered through a series of *questionnaires*, incl. personality assessment, (b) *contextual information* about the user's interactions with the system is collected in a *dedicated experimental environment based on a computer game*, which allows for detailed logging of both system and user actions in an "ecological manner", (c) *emotional reactions of the user* are recorded in a *"classical" experiment* based on the presentation of affective stimuli.

The research protocol was refined based on lessons learned from previous studies and expanded to include new elements covering newly defined objectives:

1. Data collection from mobile EEG was introduced. As devices such as Muse or Emotiv offer too weak signal quality which does not allow for their use in practical applications, we decided to use a headset of a slightly higher grade: g.Tec Unicorn Hybrid Black.

2. Data collection from eye tracker was introduced. The mobile Tobii Pro Nano device is used with tobii-research Python library for signal acquisition.
3. The ShroomDoom (https://github.com/JohnMeadow1/ShroomDoom) computer game was adapted to the needs of the experiment by adding the logging module and providing the synchronization mechanisms.
4. Due to various issues related to data collection and synchronization, it was decided to replace the BITalino (r)evolution kit with biosignalsplux Explorer and use the Lab Streaming Layer library (LSL) to synchronize the data.
5. The set of affective images used has been extended: in addition to the IAPS set [18], the SFIP [20] set is also used, allowing a larger area of Valence-Arousal space to be covered.

3   Methods (as Used in Pilot Study)

3.1   Questionnaires

Two paper-and-pen questionnaires were used in the study: (1) The Polish adaptation [28] of the NEO-FFI [3] questionnaire was used to measure the Big Five personality traits. (2) Our own Polish translation of the Core Module from the Game Experience Questionnaire (GEQ) [9] was used to assess participants' perception of a game-based research environment.

3.2   Stimuli Selection

In the experimental part, standardized affective sound and image sets were used: IADS [2], IAPS [18] and SFIP [20]. Each of the stimuli in these sets has assigned coordinates in Valence-Arousal space, which allowed them to be divided into 14 conditions for the experiment. Three levels were generated for Valence and Arousal (cf. Fig. 1): – (low, $[1, 4)$), 0 (medium, $(4, 6)$), + (high, $[6, 9]$). Then combined into nine conditions for pictures (V stands for Valence; A stands for Arousal): V–A–, V–A0, V–A+, V0A–, V0A0, V0A+, V+A–, V+A0, V+A+ and five conditions for sounds (there are no A– or V0A+ groups due to lack of such stimuli in IADS): V–A0, V–A+, V0A0, V+A0, V+A+.

For each subject, there are 7 stimuli in each of the 14 conditions, with a total of 98 stimuli. They are drawn from a pool of 24 stimuli pre-selected by us for each condition (see Fig. 1). They were chosen to spread as much as possible over the whole area. Pre-selection was done using K-Means algorithm from sklearn package. All conditions were mixed together during the presentation of the stimuli in the experiment.

3.3   Hardware and Software

The following setup was prepared for the study:

- Two PCs (processor: Intel Core i5-8600K, graphic card: MSI GeForce GTX 1070, 16 GB RAM) running under 64-bit Windows 10 1909 Education,

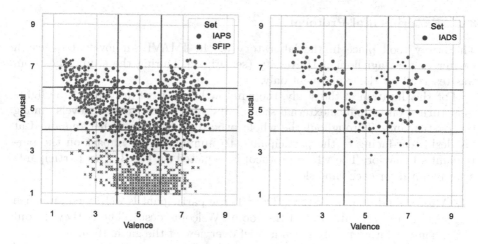

Fig. 1. Distribution of pictures (left) and sounds (right) in Valence-Arousal space. Selected stimuli are marked with larger red symbols. (Color figure online)

- Four Full HD 23" LCD screen,
- g.Tec Unicorn Hybrid Black EEG headset (24-bit ADC, 250 Hz sampling rate) with 8 gel electrodes at Fz, Cz, Pz, Oz, C3, C4, PO7, PO8 locations,
- biosignalsplux Explorer kit—the successor to BITalino (r)evolution kit used in previous BIRAFFE experiments [14,15]—with 3-leads ECG and 2-leads EDA sensors (16-bit ADC, 1 kHz sampling rate):
  - Electrocardiogram was obtained using the standard montage with electrodes placed below the collarbones (V– on the right, and reference on the left) and below the last rib on the left side of the body (V+).
  - EDA signal was gathered by 2 electrodes placed on the forehead. It is as good as classical palmar location [5], and has no side effects related to gamepad held by the subjects.
- Gamepad Sony PlayStation DualShock 4,
- External web camera Creative Live! Cam Sync 1080p V2,
- Tobii Pro Nano eye-tracker.

The protocol was running under the Python 3.8.13 and was implemented with PsychoPy 2022.1.4 library [24]. Python code controlled the execution of the stimuli presentation, photos taking, and gamepad's accelerometer signal acquisition. All of these data streams were sent to the local network via LSL.

Communication with the biosignalsplux Explorer and g.Tec Unicorn Hybrid Black was via Bluetooth, and the signals were transmitted to the local network as LSL streams using dedicated software: OpenSignals (r)evolution 2.2.1 (https://support.pluxbiosignals.com/knowledge-base/introducing-opensignals-revolution/) and Unicorn LSL (https://github.com/unicorn-bi/Unicorn-Suite-Hybrid-Black/tree/master/Unicorn.NETAPI/UnicornLSL).

All Lab Streaming Layer streams were captured with LabRecorder 1.16.2 (https://github.com/labstreaminglayer/App-LabRecorder), the default recording application for LSL.

3.4   Experimental Protocol

The study took place in the laboratory of the IMAVI Audiovisual Research Center at the Jagiellonian University (see Fig. 2). During the study, the room was reserved for the experiment only.

For the duration of the study, the window blinds were drawn and the lights were turned on to reduce external stimuli and to balance the light levels among the participants. Throughout the whole procedure, the researcher remained at his desk, rear-facing to the participants, to minimize their impact on the participant's behavior. The whole protocol is depicted on Fig. 3. Two participants were planned for each time slot:

1. After attending the study via Door 1, the participant is welcomed and then seated in a separate part of the room (Welcome desk). There, they fill out a consent form and are given a brief overview of the game (5 min).
2. When the previous subjects (from the previous time slot) have completed the stimuli session, the participants are invited to stands 3 and 4, where they are given gamepads and the first game session begins (up to 15 min).
3. When the game is finished, the participants are provided with the short information about the whole experiment. Then, they fill out the NEO-FFI inventory and gaming experience questionnaire (15 min).
4. The participants are then moved to stands 1 and 2, where they are connected to measuring devices, camera and eye tracker are calibrated, a gamepad is given and the computer protocol is started (approx. 20 min).
5. It starts with baseline signals recording (1 min).
6. Then, there is a time for on-screen instructions and training (approx. 5 min).
7. It is followed by stimuli presentation and rating session (30 min).
8. When both participants are ready and two new participants appear, a second session of the game begins (up to 15 min).

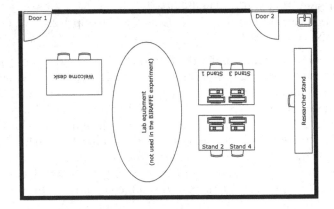

Fig. 2. Situation plan of the IMAVI laboratory

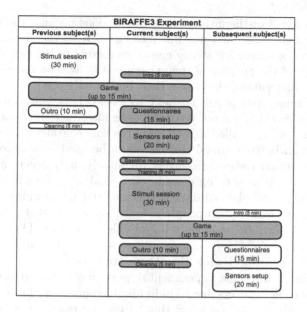

Fig. 3. Experiment protocol

9. At the end, the participants are disconnected from all of the sensors and fill out the GEQ questionnaire. Then, they leave the lab via Door 2 (10 min).
10. Finally, the devices are cleaned by researcher (5 min).

Each presentation of the stimuli lasted 6 s—as each sound in IADS set lasts 6 s—and was followed by 6 s for rating using custom affective widget [15]. Trials were separated with 6 s ISI. It resulted in 18 s between stimuli onset, which is enough for observing reactions in the ECG, EDA and EEG signals. Participants were instructed to navigate the procedure via gamepad. ECG, EDA, EEG and gamepad's accelerometer and gyroscope signals were collected continuously during the whole experiment. Facial photos were taken every 200 ms. The whole protocol lasted up to 120 min.

4   Pilot Study

The outlined experimental plan was examined in a pilot study in which 6 people participated as subjects, and additional people took part as external observers to spot potential problems. Analyses of the data collected during the pilot and all observations proposed by external observers are currently underway. Among the conclusions made so far, it is worth noting:

1. In BIRAFFE2, the entire procedure took 75 min. In BIRAFFE3 we extended it to 120 min and for the pilot subjects it was definitely too long. Therefore, in the actual experiment, we will resign from EEG measurements because putting on the EEG headset takes a lot of time.

2. The plan in Fig. 3 distinguishes two game sessions because the first one was used to learn the game and was not measured. However, during the second game, players no longer felt strong emotions related to the game, so from the point of view of the purpose of the experiment, it will be more important to measure the first game (which may then be the only one).

3. During the game, four people sit next to each other, which creates a lot of voice interactions that are not recorded. The introduction of audio recording using microphones installed in web cameras was considered. Such a recording would then be transcribed and coded to be used as additional input to emotion prediction models. However, ultimately, a complete abandonment of multi-player setup is being considered – analyzing data from such interactions requires well-planned data collection, and maintaining a schedule in which there are exactly two people in each slot (so that 4 people can play simultaneously) will be practically impossible to achieve. Therefore, we plan to use the same game, but in a simplified scenario in which one avatar is controlled by the subject while the others are bots.

4. Selected stimuli from the experimental part may cause greater emotional arousal in specific subjects due to individual experiences. The current experimental procedure does not allow this to be confirmed, therefore the introduction of the think-aloud protocol [26] is being considered.

5. Additional data about the subjects themselves and the game can be collected by extending the questionnaires to include questions about mood and life energy, previous experience with the gamepad, favorite game genres, motivation and attention during the game.

6. It is planned to use the GAPED dataset [4] as a third source of emotion-evoking images, resulting in better coverage of the Valence-Arousal space.

5   Summary and Future Work

Predicting emotions in real-life scenarios requires appropriately developed prediction models. According to our intuition, there are no such models that would be useful in various use cases yet, because the datasets that are the basis for training the models are insufficient. To address these gaps, in 2018 we initiated the BIRAFFE series of experiments.

The aim of this work was to present the work-in-progress concept of the third experiment in the BIRAFFE series. It was tested by us in a pilot study, and the most important conclusions collected so far, including various changes in the experimental protocol, are summarized in the article.

As further steps, we plan to formulate the final conclusions from the pilot and redesign the experimental procedure in an appropriate way (spring 2024), conduct the actual experiment (spring 2024), and then clean the data and publish the BIRAFFE3 dataset (summer 2024). The dataset will then form the basis for attempts to create prediction models more suitable for real-life scenarios than those available in the state-of-the-art.

Acknowledgments. The research for this publication has been supported by a grant from the Priority Research Area DigiWorld under the Strategic Programme Excellence Initiative at Jagiellonian University. The research has been supported by a grant from the Faculty of Physics, Astronomy and Applied Computer Science under the Strategic Programme Excellence Initiative at Jagiellonian University.

Disclosure of Interests. The authors have no competing interests to declare that are relevant to the content of this article.

References

1. Bhatt, P., et al.: Machine learning for cognitive behavioral analysis: datasets, methods, paradigms, and research directions. Brain Inform. **10**(1), 18 (2023). https://doi.org/10.1186/s40708-023-00196-6
2. Bradley, M.M., Lang, P.J.: The international affective digitized sounds (2nd edition; iads-2): affective ratings of sounds and instruction manual. technical report B-3. Technical report, University of Florida, Gainsville, FL (2007)
3. Costa, P., McCrae, R.: Revised NEO Personality Inventory (NEO-PI-R) and NEO Five Factor Inventory (NEO-FFI). Professional manual. Psychological Assessment Resources, Odessa, FL (1992)
4. Dan-Glauser, E.S., Scherer, K.R.: The geneva affective picture database (GAPED): a new 730-picture database focusing on valence and normative significance. Behav. Res. Methods **43**(2), 468–477 (2011). https://doi.org/10.3758/s13428-011-0064-1
5. van Dooren, M., de Vries, J.J.G., Janssen, J.H.: Emotional sweating across the body: comparing 16 different skin conductance measurement locations. Physiol. Behav. **106**(2), 298–304 (2012)
6. Dzedzickis, A., Kaklauskas, A., Bucinskas, V.: Human emotion recognition: review of sensors and methods. Sensors **20**(3), 592 (2020). https://doi.org/10.3390/s20030592
7. Fanourakis, M., Chanel, G.: AMuCS: affective multimodal counter-strike video game dataset (2024). https://doi.org/10.36227/techrxiv.170630398.84528625/v1
8. Hasnul, M.A., Aziz, N.A.B.A., Alelyani, S., Mohana, M., Aziz, A.A.: Electrocardiogram-based emotion recognition systems and their applications in healthcare - a review. Sensors **21**(15), 5015 (2021). https://doi.org/10.3390/s21155015
9. IJsselsteijn, W.A., de Kort, Y.A.W., Poels, K.: The Game Experience Questionnaire. Technische Universiteit Eindhoven (2013)
10. Katsis, C.D., Katertsidis, N.S., Ganiatsas, G., Fotiadis, D.I.: Toward emotion recognition in car-racing drivers: a biosignal processing approach. IEEE Trans. Syst. Man Cybern. Part A **38**(3), 502–512 (2008). https://doi.org/10.1109/TSMCA.2008.918624
11. Khare, S.K., Blanes-Vidal, V., Nadimi, E.S., Acharya, U.R.: Emotion recognition and artificial intelligence: a systematic review (2014–2023) and research recommendations. Inf. Fusion **102**, 102019 (2024). https://doi.org/10.1016/J.INFFUS.2023.102019
12. Kutt, K., Bobek, S., Nalepa, G.J.: BIRAFFE: bio-reactions and faces for emotion-based personalization. *Zenodo*https://doi.org/10.5281/zenodo.3442143 (2020)

13. Kutt, K., Drążyk, D., Bobek, S., Nalepa, G.J.: Personality-based affective adaptation methods for intelligent systems. Sensors **21**(1), 163 (2021). https://doi.org/10.3390/s21010163

14. Kutt, K., et al.: BIRAFFE: bio-reactions and faces for emotion-based personalization. In: AfCAI 2019. CEUR Workshop Proceedings, vol. 2609. CEUR-WS.org (2020)

15. Kutt, K., Drążyk, D., Żuchowska, L., Szelążek, M., Bobek, S., Nalepa, G.J.: BIRAFFE2, a multimodal dataset for emotion-based personalization in rich affective game environments. Sci. Data **9**, 274 (2022). https://doi.org/10.1038/s41597-022-01402-6

16. Kutt, K., Ściga, Ł., Nalepa, G.J.: Emotion-based dynamic difficulty adjustment in video games. In: DSAA 2023, pp. 1–5. IEEE (2023). https://doi.org/10.1109/DSAA60987.2023.10302578

17. Kutt, K., Sobczyk, P., Nalepa, G.J.: Evaluation of selected APIs for emotion recognition from facial expressions. In: Ferrández Vicente, J.M., Álvarez-Sánchez, J.R., de la Paz López, F., Adeli, H. (eds.) IWINAC 2022. LNCS, vol. 13259, pp. 65–74. Springer, Cham (2022). https://doi.org/10.1007/978-3-031-06527-9_7

18. Lang, P.J., Bradley, M.M., Cuthbert, B.N.: International affective picture system (IAPs): affective ratings of pictures and instruction manual. technical report B-3. Technical report, The Center for Research in Psychophysiology, University of Florida, Gainsville, FL (2008)

19. Lara-Cabrera, R., Camacho, D.: A taxonomy and state of the art revision on affective games. Futur. Gener. Comput. Syst. **92**, 516–525 (2019)

20. Michałowski, J.M., Droździel, D., Matuszewski, J., Koziejowski, W., Jednoróg, K., Marchewka, A.: The set of fear inducing pictures (SFIP): development and validation in fearful and nonfearful individuals. Behav. Res. Methods **49**(4), 1407–1419 (2017). https://doi.org/10.3758/s13428-016-0797-y

21. Milkowski, P., Saganowski, S., Gruza, M., Kazienko, P., Piasecki, M., Kocon, J.: Multitask personalized recognition of emotions evoked by textual content. In: PerCom 2022 Workshops, pp. 347–352. IEEE (2022). https://doi.org/10.1109/PerComWorkshops53856.2022.9767502

22. Nalepa, G.J., Kutt, K., Giżycka, B., Jemioło, P., Bobek, S.: Analysis and use of the emotional context with wearable devices for games and intelligent assistants. Sensors **19**(11), 2509 (2019). https://doi.org/10.3390/s19112509

23. Park, C.Y., et al.: K-EmoCon, a multimodal sensor dataset for continuous emotion recognition in naturalistic conversations. Sci. Data **7**(1), 293 (2020). https://doi.org/10.1038/s41597-020-00630-y

24. Peirce, J., et al.: Psychopy2: experiments in behavior made easy. Behav. Res. Methods **51**(1), 195–203 (2019). https://doi.org/10.3758/s13428-018-01193-y

25. Phan, L.V., Rauthmann, J.F.: Personality computing: New frontiers in personality assessment. Soc. Pers. Psychol. Compass **15**(7) (2021). https://doi.org/10.1111/spc3.12624

26. Prokop, M., Pilar, L., Tichá, I.: Impact of think-aloud on eye-tracking: a comparison of concurrent and retrospective think-aloud for research on decision-making in the game environment. Sensors **20**(10), 2750 (2020). https://doi.org/10.3390/s20102750

27. Saganowski, S., Perz, B., Polak, A.G., Kazienko, P.: Emotion recognition for everyday life using physiological signals from wearables: a systematic literature review. IEEE Trans. Affect. Comput. **12**(1), 1–21 (2021). https://doi.org/10.1109/TAFFC.2022.3176135

28. Zawadzki, B., Strelau, J., Szczepaniak, P., Śliwińska, M.: Inwentarz osobowości NEO-FFI Costy i McCrae. Adaptacja polska. Pracownia Testów Psychologicznych, Warszawa (1998)
29. Zhao, S., Gholaminejad, A., Ding, G., Gao, Y., Han, J., Keutzer, K.: Personalized emotion recognition by personality-aware high-order learning of physiological signals. ACM Trans. Multim. Comput. Commun. Appl. **15**(1s), 14:1–14:18 (2019). https://doi.org/10.1145/3233184

Towards Enhanced Emotional Interaction in the Metaverse

J. A. Rincon[1], C. Marco-Detchart[2], and V. Julian[2,3(✉)]

[1] Departamento de Digitalización, Escuela Politécnica Superior, Universidad de Burgos, 09006 Burgos, Spain
jarincon@ubu.es
[2] Valencian Research Institute for Artificial Intelligence (VRAIN), Universitat Politècnica de València (UPV), Camino de Vera s/n, 46022 Valencia, Spain
{cedmarde,vjulian}@upv.es
[3] Valencian Graduate School and Research Network of Artificial Intelligence (VALGRAI), Universitat Politècnica de València (UPV), Camino de Vera s/n, 46022 Valencia, Spain

Abstract. In the current context, as the metaverse emerges as an immersive digital space for social and professional interactions, understanding and appropriately responding to human emotions becomes critical. This paper presents an innovative approach for emotion detection and analysis in virtual environments, combining facial recognition technologies and physiological signal analysis through deep learning algorithms. Thus, this approach enhances interaction and customization in the metaverse, highlighting the importance of addressing these concerns to maximize the potential of emotional detection.

Keywords: Metaverse · Emotion detection · Deep Learning

1 Introduction

In today's context, the metaverse [1] has emerged as a rapidly expanding digital frontier, offering an immersive virtual space for both social and professional interactions. This new digital dimension promises to revolutionize how we connect, learn, and collaborate, underscoring the significance of the metaverse in modern society. As this virtual environment becomes increasingly integral to our daily lives, the importance of enhancing user interaction and experience within it cannot be overstated.

The detection of emotions in such environments is paramount for creating more engaging and personalized virtual experiences. Recognizing and responding to human emotions accurately can significantly enhance social interactions and user engagement in the metaverse. This necessity brings to light the importance of sophisticated emotion detection systems that can navigate the complexities of human emotions in virtual spaces [2].

J. M. Ferrández Vicente et al. (Eds.): IWINAC 2024, LNCS 14674, pp. 476–485, 2024.
https://doi.org/10.1007/978-3-031-61140-7_45

Focusing on the detection of emotions, camera-based systems employ facial recognition algorithms integrated with deep learning models to decode facial expressions and gestures, enabling instantaneous emotion recognition [3]. These systems scrutinize facial landmarks, expressions, and movements, delivering a visual indication of a user's emotional state within the expansive metaverse.

Simultaneously, the integration of physiological signals, such as electroencephalography (EEG), electrocardiography (ECG), or galvanic skin response (GSR), offers an additional layer of emotion detection [4]. By monitoring subtle physiological changes, these signals provide insights into emotional arousal or cognitive states, enhancing the understanding of user emotions within virtual environments. Combining camera-based vision systems and physiological signal analysis presents a holistic approach to emotion detection in the metaverse. Fusion of these modalities enables a richer comprehension of users' emotional responses, empowering virtual environments to adapt and respond dynamically to users' emotional states.

In this sense, the contribution of this paper lies in its innovative approach to emotion detection in the metaverse, utilizing a combination of facial recognition technologies and analysis of physiological signals through deep learning algorithms. By integrating these technologies, our approach significantly improves interaction and customization in virtual environments. Specifically, the proposed system demonstrates an ability to accurately capture and interpret the nuanced emotional states of users by leveraging real-time data. This facilitates more personalized and emotionally resonant interactions within the metaverse, paving the way for a new level of engagement and presence in virtual spaces.

The rest of the paper is structured as follows: Sect. 2 provides an outline of the system designed for detecting emotions and translating them into representations within the metaverse. Section 3 outlines the hardware employed for capturing various biosignals used in emotion detection. Section 4 describes the software components of the prototype, including the tools for processing biosignals and classifying emotions. Finally, Sect. 5 concludes the paper with a summary of the work and discusses future directions for research in enhancing emotional interaction within virtual environments.

2   System Description

This section aims to offer an outline of the system tasked with identifying emotions and translating them into representations within the metaverse. The system's primary objective is to capture, interpret, and portray human emotions in a virtual setting, fostering an engaging and immersive user experience. A comprehensive suite of technological elements is employed to achieve emotion detection within the metaverse. These components span from integrating sensors to processing data and converting inferred emotions into visual cues or avatars within the virtual environment.

2.1   Emotion Classification Using Biosignals

Detecting emotions through biosignals involves capturing and analysing a range of physiological cues from the human body with the aim of recognising and comprehending individuals' emotional states. These signals, referred to as biosignals, have been the focus of various research endeavours aimed at refining techniques, developing instruments, and enhancing the efficiency of emotion detection. Among these signals are heart rate (HR), electrocardiogram (ECG) representing heart electrical activity, electroencephalogram (EEG) indicating brain activity, galvanic skin response (GSR) reflecting skin conductance, respiration patterns, body temperature, and facial electromyography. Each of these signals manifests subtle changes in amplitude, offering insights into how we emotionally respond to diverse stimuli.

Among these techniques, there are varying levels of invasiveness, with some requiring specialised hardware. Certain methods can be highly invasive, causing discomfort for the user, such as EEG, which involves placing sensors directly on the scalp. Despite its widespread use, EEG can be impractical due to its intrusive nature, although it remains one of the most prevalent techniques for emotion detection.

Indeed, there are alternative signals utilised in emotion detection, including the heart's electrical activity (ECG), heart rate (HR), skin conductance level (SCL), body temperature, and facial electromyography (Facial EMG). Facial EMG specifically involves measuring the electrical activity of facial muscles. It analyses and interprets facial expressions, providing insight into various emotional states based on the muscle activity observed in different regions of the face. This technique aids in understanding the nuanced facial movements linked to different emotions. Conducting this detection involves capturing and analysing the electrical signals generated by facial muscles when an individual undergoes particular emotions. Given the close correlation between facial expressions and distinct emotional states, scrutinising patterns of muscle activity offers valuable insights into an individual's prevailing emotional state at a specific moment.

In this research, our focus has been on utilising four biosignals, all linked to the detection of emotions. To conduct this analysis, we relied on the DEAP database, a multimodal dataset for investigating human emotional states. This dataset includes electroencephalogram (EEG) recordings and peripheral physiological signals gathered from 32 participants while watching 40 one-minute music video clips. Participants rated each video based on arousal, valence, liking/dislike, dominance, and familiarity.

Among the signals captured in this dataset, we specifically concentrated on four signals, including the electromyography of the Zygomaticus muscle (depicted in Fig. 1). This particular muscle is crucial in facial expressions associated with emotions like happiness or smiling. Additionally, we explored skin conductance or GSR, commonly utilised in studies requiring emotion or stress detection, along with Plethysmograph and body temperature signals.

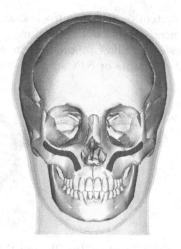

Fig. 1. Location of Zygomaticus muscle.

3   Hardware Description

This section outlines the diverse array of devices used to acquire various biosignals. Three signals were chosen for emotion detection, each requiring specific hardware to capture and amplify them.

One of the primary signals is the signal from the Zygomaticus muscle, for which we utilised an electromyography (EMG) system, as depicted in Fig. 2a.

This device is constructed using an instrumentation amplifier, which enhances the muscle signal. When the user expresses any of the emotions to be classified, the EMG system captures the electrical variations associated with muscle activity.

The photoplethysmography (PPG) signal allows us to measure volumetric changes in peripheral blood circulation. To capture this signal, we used the sensor shown in Fig. 2b, which is located in the user's right temple.

Lastly, we have the Galvanic Skin Response (GSR), also known as skin conductance or skin conductance response. It measures the skin's electrical conductivity, which varies with skin moisture and, therefore, with the level of sweat activity. This measure is often used as an indicator of emotional activity or stress. The device shown in Fig. 2c was used to capture this variation.

Once these signals have been captured and amplified, the next step was to use the ADS1256 a 24-bit analog-to-digital converter (ADC). This device digitises each one of the signals, transforming them from a continuous space to a discrete space. This ADC is connected to an ESP32, which sends the acquired data to a server. This server is used as a hosting system for trained models, which classify the emotion and send the result to the ESP32. Once the result is within the ESP32, it communicates it via Bluetooth to the glasses.

All these devices used for capturing the biosignals were integrated into a virtual reality (VR) device. The selected device was the Pico 4 (see Fig. 2d).

These sensors enable the system to capture, process, and analyse these signals, aiming to determine the user's emotional state during a session with the VR glasses. Emotion detection would allow modifying the environment or the way the user interacts with other avatars or NPCs.

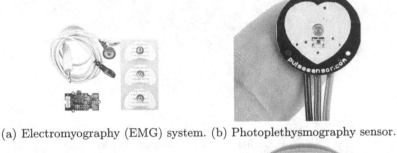

(a) Electromyography (EMG) system. (b) Photoplethysmography sensor.

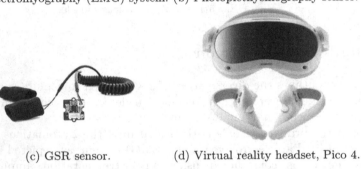

(c) GSR sensor.   (d) Virtual reality headset, Pico 4.

Fig. 2. An overview of the different elements that make up the proposed system.

4   Software Description

This section describes the software used in the prototype, which includes a set of tools that allow for the processing of different biosignals and the classification of emotions.

The emotion classification system based on biosignals is centralised on a web server created with Flask. This server processes and analyses biosignals collected from various sensors. Upon receiving the biosignals, the server employs machine learning algorithms to classify the user's emotional state based on predefined patterns and features extracted from the signals. In addition, the server facilitates real-time communication with other components of the system, such as the VR headset. The VR headset can modify the environment in which the user is situated; however, in the experiments conducted, we present the classified emotion in a text box and an associated image.

To train the model, four signals were extracted from the DEAP database: zEMG, PPG, GSR, and temperature signals. Each of these signals was divided into samples with a window size of 252 Averaging band power of 2 s, a step size of 16 (updating once every 0.125 s), and a sample rate of 128 Hz. Each signal was divided into a training group and a test group, with the training set size being 9696 × 252 and the test set size being 2425 × 252. The output of the DEAP dataset represents the emotion in a 3D space through the VAD emotional model (Valence, Arousal, Dominance), with each of these dimensions normalised between 1 and 9. For convenience and ease of handling these data, the data were normalised between 0.0 and 1.0. Therefore, the output dataset for the training data has a size of 9696 × 3, and for the test data, a size of 2425 × 3. Since the interpretation of these values to obtain the user's actual emotion can lead to confusion, it was necessary to translate this 3D space into a 2D space. To do this, the circumplex [5] model was used, which represents emotions in a space of polar coordinates. For this transformation, the circumplex model takes Valence and Arousal as references. The circumplex model was divided into 8 emotions: Happy, Excited, Afraid, Angry, Sad, Tired, Relax, Content. This transformation was carried out using fuzzy logic [6]. In this way, it was possible to transition from numerical Valence and Arousal values to discrete emotions.

A Sequential neural network model [7] was used for this purpose. The architecture of this network is shown in the following figure. The hyperparameters for this network were a batch size of 252, nclasses of 8, n epochs of 200, input shape of (252, 1), an optimiser of type adam, and a softmax in the last layer.

The following images provide a comprehensive graphical representation of the loss model for all the signals (Fig. 3). Each visualization offers valuable insights into the behavior and trends observed across the various signal datasets, aiding in a deeper understanding of the underlying patterns and dynamics within the model.

In order to represent the emotion within the Pico 4, a virtual reality environment was created. In this environment, the user could observe his emotional state at that moment in time. The environment consisted of a dialogue box, in which the user was informed of their emotional state, and at the same time, an image associated with that emotion was displayed (Fig. 4).

4.1 Emotion Aggregation

In order to perform the data fusion from the different bio-signals, we expose some basic aggregation concepts.

Definition 1 [8,9]. *A mapping $M : [0,1]^n \rightarrow [0,1]$ is an aggregation function if it is monotone non-decreasing in each of its components and satisfies $M(\mathbf{0}) = 0$ and $M(\mathbf{1}) = 1$.*

An aggregation function M is an averaging or mean if

$$\min(x_1, \ldots, x_n) \leq M(x_1, \ldots, x_n) \leq \max(x_1, \ldots, x_n).$$

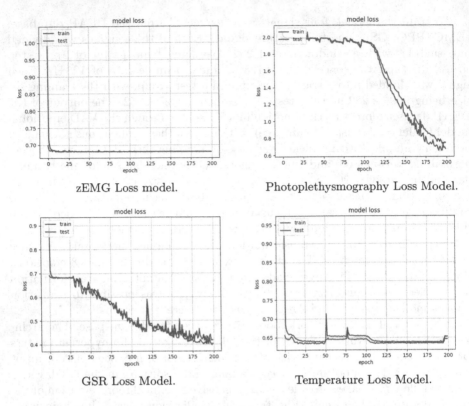

Fig. 3. Graphical representation of the loss model for all the signals.

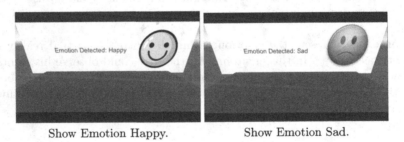

Show Emotion Happy.   Show Emotion Sad.

Fig. 4. Virtual environment for displaying user emotions.

A relevant type of aggregation function are the Ordered Weighted Averaging (OWA) operators presented by Yager [10].

Definition 2. *An OWA operator of dimension n is a mapping $\Phi : [0,1]^n \to [0,1]$ such that it exists a weighting vector $\boldsymbol{w} = (w_1, \ldots, w_n) \in [0,1]^n$ with $\sum_{i=1}^{n} w_i = 1$, and such that*

$$\Phi(x_1, \ldots, x_n) = \sum_{i=1}^{n} w_i \cdot x_{\sigma(i)},$$

where $\mathbf{x}_\sigma = (x_{\sigma(1)}, \ldots, x_{\sigma(n)})$ *is a decreasing permutation on the input* $\mathbf{x}$.

In [11] a way to compute the weighting vector is presented:

$$w_i = Q\left(\frac{i}{n}\right) - Q\left(\frac{i-1}{n}\right),$$

where Q is a fuzzy linguistic quantifier as, for instance,

$$Q(r) = \begin{cases} 0 & \text{if } 0 \leq r < a, \\ \frac{r-a}{b-a} & \text{if } a \leq r \leq b, \\ 1 & \text{if } b < r \leq 1, \end{cases} \tag{1}$$

with $a, b, r \in [0, 1]$.

For this experiment, we use the OWA operator that represents the linguistic label constructed using the parameters in Table 1.

Table 1. OWA operators representing linguistic labels along with their construction parameters

#	a	b	Linguistic label
OWA^1	0.3	0.8	*the majority of*
OWA^2	0	0.5	*at least half of*
OWA^3	0.5	1	*as much as possible*

In addition, to recover the mean aggregation, we use $\text{OWA}^4 = (\frac{1}{N}, \ldots, \frac{1}{N})$ with N being the number of elements to aggregate. Moreover, we also use $\text{OWA}^5 = (1, 0\ldots, 0)$ being the maximum and $\text{OWA}^6 = (0, 0\ldots, 1)$ to recover the minimum.

The experiment demonstrates the flexibility of OWA operators in representing various aggregation approaches through both linguistic and numerical means. This dual representation capability allows for a more tailored approach to data fusion, where the specific context or preference of the aggregation can be accurately captured. For example, *the majority of* can be used when a consensus is required among a large subset. At the same time, *at least half of* may be suitable for scenarios where a simple majority is sufficient.

The results suggest that OWA operators permit the enhancement of decision-making processes by providing a more nuanced aggregation mechanism. This is particularly relevant in complex decision-making environments where different data sources may prioritise specific outcomes over others. Linguistic labels help to articulate these priorities more clearly, enabling a more informed and consensus-driven decision-making process. This mechanism has been crucial in the integration of the different biosignals and in evaluating the relative importance of one or more signals over others.

5   Conclusions and Future Work

In this work, we have explored the detection of emotions through the analysis of biosignals, focusing on four primary signals: zygomaticus muscle electromyography (zEMG), photoplethysmography (PPG), galvanic skin response (GSR), and body temperature. This study has demonstrated the potential of integrating various biosignals to classify emotional states accurately. Using a Sequential neural network model and data fusion techniques as OWA operators, the proposal has shown promising results. Integrating these biosignals into a VR system presents a novel approach to real-time emotion recognition, potentially enhancing the user experience by dynamically adjusting content based on the user's emotional state.

Future work aims to integrate a more comprehensive set of biosignals to achieve a more detailed and nuanced understanding of emotional states, enriching the current methodology that relies on zEMG, PPG, GSR, and body temperature measurements. Furthermore, exploring a diverse range of models and approaches for emotion prediction is essential, as this will shed light on the specific impact each biosignal has on identifying emotional states. This expansion and diversification of data sources and analytical methods promises to enhance the accuracy and applicability of emotion detection systems, paving the way for more personalised and sensitive technological interactions.

Acknowledgements. This work was partially supported with grants TED2021-131295B-C32 and PID2021-123673OB-C31 funded by MCIN/AEI/10.13039/5011000 11033 and by "ERDF A way of making Europe", PROMETEO grant CIPROM/2021/077 from the Conselleria de Innovación, Universidades, Ciencia y Sociedad Digital - Generalitat Valenciana and Early Research Project grant PAID-06-23 by the Vice Rectorate Office for Research from Universitat Politècnica de València (UPV).

References

1. Mystakidis, S.: Metaverse. Encyclopedia **2**(1), 486–497 (2022)
2. Naz, A., Kopper, R., McMahan, R.P., Nadin, M.: Emotional qualities of VR space. In: 2017 IEEE Virtual Reality (VR), pp. 3–11. IEEE (2017)
3. Jaiswal, A., Raju, A.K., Deb, S.: Facial emotion detection using deep learning. In: 2020 International Conference for Emerging Technology (INCET), pp. 1–5. IEEE (2020)
4. Egger, M., Ley, M., Hanke, S.: Emotion recognition from physiological signal analysis: a review. Electron. Notes Theor. Comput. Sci. **343**, 35–55 (2019)
5. Russell, J.A.: A circumplex model of affect. J. Pers. Soc. Psychol. **39**(6), 1161 (1980)
6. Costa, A., Rincon, J.A., Carrascosa, C., Julian, V., Novais, P.: Emotions detection on an ambient intelligent system using wearable devices. Future Gener. Comput. Syst. **92**, 479–489 (2019)

7. Hutter, F., Hoos, H.H., Leyton-Brown, K.: Sequential model-based optimization for general algorithm configuration. In: Coello, C.A.C. (ed.) LION 2011. LNCS, vol. 6683, pp. 507–523. Springer, Heidelberg (2011). https://doi.org/10.1007/978-3-642-25566-3_40

8. Beliakov, G., Pradera, A., Calvo, T.: Aggregation Functions: A Guide for Practitioners, vol. 18 (2007)

9. Calvo, T., Kolesárová, A., Komorníková, M., Mesiar, R.: Aggregation operators: properties, classes and construction methods. Aggreg. Oper. New Trends Appl. **97**(1), 3–104 (2002)

10. Yager, R.R.: On ordered weighted averaging aggregation operators in multicriteria decisionmaking. IEEE Trans. Syst. Man Cybern. **18**(1), 183–190 (1988)

11. Yager, R.: Quantifier guided aggregation using OWA operators. Int. J. Intell. Syst. **11**(1), 49–73 (1996)

GOAP in Graph-Based Game Narrative Structures

Iwona Grabska-Gradzińska[ID], Ewa Grabska[ID], Paweł Węgrzyn[✉][ID],
and Leszek Nowak[ID]

Institute of Applied Computer Science, Jagiellonian University, Kraków, Poland
{iwona.grabska,ewa.grabska,pawel.wegrzyn,leszek.nowak}@uj.edu.pl

Abstract. This paper introduces a system built upon layered hierarchical graphs to depict game storylines (StoryGraph) and demonstrates its utilization in automating the generation of action sequences through the Goal-Oriented Action Planning (GOAP) technique. An advancement beyond basic action sequences relying on graph structures is the suggested semantically enriched formal model of human-computer interaction within the Story Graph. This model is designed to articulate concepts and meanings derived from the imitation of human cognition.

Keywords: game design · graph-based models · design diagrams

1 Introduction

Adventure games, a prominent genre in the game development industry, immerse players in plot events using well-established interaction methods. While the general story remains constant, each player's experience is unique. Unlike games with simple rules and predictable outcomes, adventure games have predetermined results but intricate rules that vary based on the chosen strategy. These rules impact both the narrative and gameplay, influencing player decisions. Narrative structures in computer games organize storytelling during gameplay, aiming for a coherent and engaging story within the interactive nature of games. Narrative designers in role-playing games (RPG) use diverse approaches due to the complex system formed by the game world and narrative threads. Agile Storytelling adapts narrative design to changing project conditions during game production, providing a tool that isn't universal but allows for flexibility. The selection of algorithms and techniques depends on the game type, designer preferences, and player community expectations. Combining different techniques is common to achieve an interesting storyline. Popular narrative design approaches include Narrative Branching [2,5], Emergent Storytelling [9,12], Dynamic Storytelling [2,10], and Procedural Storytelling [8]. Narrative Branching follows pre-designed structural paths, Emergent Storytelling involves unpredictable changes based on interactions, Dynamic Storytelling allows controlled narrative changes, and Procedural Storytelling uses algorithms for endless narrative diversity. AI-Driven Storytelling adapts the narrative in real-time based on player interactions and

J. M. Ferrández Vicente et al. (Eds.): IWINAC 2024, LNCS 14674, pp. 486–495, 2024.
https://doi.org/10.1007/978-3-031-61140-7_46

the game environment. Dialogue Trees provide various NPC responses, while Storygrams break down the narrative into smaller graph elements for better structure understanding. The proposed approach in this article is based on StoryGraphs, elaborate graph structures designed to enhance narrative depth and complexity.

2   StoryGraph

The narrative model of a role-playing game maps the relevant world objects, relationships and dependencies between them. The basis of the story model is a graph, hereafter referred to as the Game World State Graph (GWSG), which describes the current state of the world and is modified after each player movement and NPC action. This graph consists of vertices corresponding to the game world objects and edges representing the relationships between these objects. In terms of characteristics, we can distinguish between four types of vertices: those corresponding to locations, characters, objects and elements of narrative knowledge. Each type of node, together with the relationships between them, forms a layer. Figure 1 shows an example GWSG with the four layers indicated. The edges of this graph are directed. Their relevance to the plot is related to whether they are internal edges representing relationships between vertices from a given layer, or edges representing relationships between vertices from different layers. We consider attributes as functions defined on objects, whose codomains define a range of values depending on the property of the object the attribute describes. Different attributes are defined for different types of layer vertices.

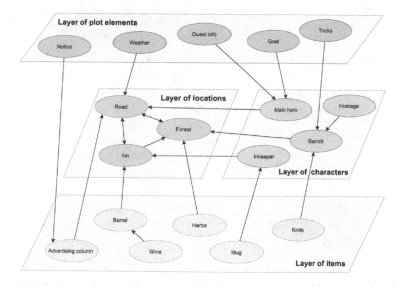

Fig. 1. Game world state graph with the four layers indicated.

2.1 Sheaf Structure

In order to optimise the execution of actions typical of video game mechanics, a new graph generation procedure has been proposed, which involves transforming graphs according to formal rules called productions. Implementing the use of productions for video games requires the use of an appropriate data structure based on the author's concept of sheaf and half-sheaf subgraphs. A sheaf-shaped subgraph is a subgraph containing one location and nodes from other layers connected to it directly or indirectly. A sheaf subgraph is a good representation of the slice of the world available to the player's current perception. A half-sheaf-shaped subgraph is a subgraph containing a node that is not a location and nodes from other layers connected to it directly or indirectly. Defining half-sheaf graphs allows a very simple implementation of the most common node operations in the game. Examples of the sheaf and half-sheaf-shaped subgraph structures distinguished in the graph are presented in Fig. 2. The whole game graph can be thought of as a forest of sheaf subgraphs embedded in the subgraph of the location layer via root-locations. All paths leaving a given location branch out to form a sheaf graph. This leads to the definition of a multi-sheaf graph. Typical world modifications resulting from game mechanics most often operate on one or more sheaves. The use of a sheaf structure consistently for a graph enables the use of a specific nested graph storage in JSON format, which stores information about the graph. The sheaf structure and the JSON notation made possible by it, which is different from typical representations of graph data structures, was designed with a view to optimising actions on the graph resulting from role-playing game mechanics.

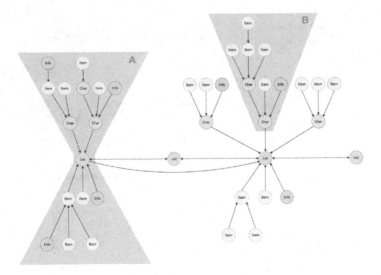

Fig. 2. Sheaf-shaped subgraph and half-sheaf-shaped subgraph in the structure of game world.

3   GOAP as a Tool for Creating Actions Sequences

In games using procedural content generation, it is possible to encounter algo-rithmically controlled NPCs. Non-playable characters (NPCs) are not controlled by the player, who can, however, sometimes interact with them. Game develop-ers try to make the actions of NPCs seem realistic. Therefore, it becomes crucial for characters to act in a logical and natural way in order to reach a tempo-rary goal. Dynamic reactions of the characters to changes in the game world are possible through various techniques of planning the actions to be performed. One of the basic techniques in this field, is the selection of actions to be per-formed through goal-directed behaviour. An understanding of this is important in the context of more advanced methods, involving the planning of a series of actions for long-term character gain. Goal-oriented behavior (GOB) encom-passes a suite of techniques facilitating the autonomous control of game char-acters. NPCs, through the application of GOB, dynamically adapt their actions to attain predefined objectives. This flexibility allows characters to concurrently pursue multiple goals of their choosing. A crucial aspect involves representing the partial or complete fulfillment of desires through unambiguous numerical val-ues, enabling the assessment of progress toward goals. Simulating the execution of available actions involves selecting the most beneficial one for the character, considering dynamically changing weights assigned to objectives that modify the character's priority hierarchy. The character, in the GOB system, prioritizes actions that maximize immediate needs without planning a predefined series leading to a goal. Certain predefined action combinations may be recognized in some GOB applications, treating them as cohesive units. For instance, know-ing that 'cook dinner' leads to 'eat dinner' satisfies the hunger need. However, the uncertainty of how the game world changes after the initial action in the known series introduces risks. Opting for momentarily profitable actions can lead to enduring negative consequences, deterring goal achievement. To address this, a distinct technique, such as the Goal-Oriented Action Planning (GOAP) method, is essential. GOAP enables characters to predict the cumulative effects of consecutive actions, facilitating the selection of the most advantageous com-bination. This paper explores the operation and implementation of the GOAP method, emphasizing its role in character decision-making for both short-term and long-term goal achievement. The GOAP technique enables character plan-ning of sequential actions. Primarily adopting a depth-first search approach, GOAP navigates a graph from the start node to the outermost vertices, back-tracking when necessary. Governed by the maximum depth of the world search, indicating the path length, the algorithm initiates with the preservation of the initial world state. The process involves selecting the first unused action, incre-menting the search depth, and simulating successive game world models until reaching the maximum search depth. Subsequently, the algorithm reverts to the last saved state and selects the next available action. The final plan comprises the series of actions performed, although the identified path may not always be opti-mal. The algorithm can terminate upon goal attainment or continue searching until all paths are explored, but exhaustive action-by-action exploration proves time-consuming. Evaluating the consequences of actions and estimating their impact on goal proximity accelerates the algorithm. This information facilitates finding the path bringing the character closest to the goal, even if unattainable, leveraging well-designed heuristic functions. However, this approach involves rejecting potential optimal action sequences. To enhance decision tree exploration efficiency, a sophisticated pathfinder algorithm like IDA* is recommended. In the StoryGraph system, the GOAP algorithm serves dual roles. Traditionally, it is employed to generate action sequences for NPC characters as they pursue predefined goals, fostering interaction with the player. A less conventional application arises during the mission design phase, where the GOAP module is utilized to enhance design diagrams. Throughout mission design, a schematic design diagram is formulated to propose a player-centric mission framework based on the defined game world. A mission, conceived as a cohesive narrative fragment, may necessitate fulfilling certain conditions, contingent on the completion of preceding missions. The conclusion of a mission is marked by achieving its final production. Mission gameplay can follow a linear or branching structure. Designers create detailed node productions based on generic productions, aligning them with appropriate game world objects and storyline attributes. Designers ensure these productions form a cause-and-effect sequence for at least one mission version. Design diagrams aid mission development by mapping critical mission passage variants and encompassing information on mission overlap, where one mission's effects become the initial conditions of another. The graph model's logic allows executing detailed productions in a different order, promoting player freedom in traversing the game. By integrating the GOAP algorithm, design diagrams focus less on detailed transitions and more on node actions (see [?]). The GOAP module facilitates determining paths for achieving intermediate sub-goals, validating their feasibility within the mission's context. This integration enhances the adaptability and narrative variety of gameplay sequences (Fig. 3).

4   Narrative Graph Model in Semantically Enriched Story Graph

This section aims to demonstrate the application of the proposed semantically enriched formal model of human-computer interaction within the Story Graph framework. It serves a dual purpose: first, to articulate concepts and meanings generated through the emulation of human cognition and, second, to introduce a novel narrative graph model. Addressing the conceptualization of adventure games, the challenge lies in capturing variations in modality and intentionality employed by players during decision-making processes [3]. Similar challenges emerge in formalizing the foundations of multimodal reasoning. A promising approach involves utilizing a family of nested graph models, encompassing a wide range of structures to partition reasoning tasks into distinct metalevel stages, as proposed in [11]. The interactive creation of the plot by the player or the novelist but also more generally the problems of multimodal reasoning where we have the ever-growing amount of knowledge and the necessity to use techniques adhering

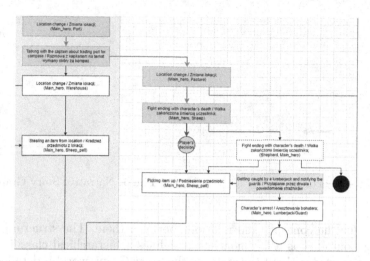

Fig. 3. Design diagram with the gamepath shown (green labels). (Color figure online)

meaning to data led researchers to search for new semantics-driven methodologies. The use of Semantic Web techniques that match meaning to data for the increasing amount of knowledge is not enough, because the system must 'understand' the data resources of knowledge that are provided to it, to organize them in the direction indicated by the system's algorithm. In other words, algorithms should model the imitation of human cognition by intelligent systems [6]. For that reason, there is a need, to develop design systems that collect data with the characteristics of the context for the next steps of generation. The closer intelligent systems get to the human cognitive process, the easier it is for them to achieve it. Therefore, a good knowledge of the principles is sought that explain how concepts are constructed with the use of human language. As a consequence, researchers propose new descriptions of models and methods of generation during the design process [7]. The Story Graph provides the basic principles for representing the states of the game world, while the proper description of the actions taken by the player is based on the technique of rewriting graphs, i.e. algorithmically creating a new graph from the one under consideration. Each action of the player is defined as a rule called production. The Story Graph is defined using the concepts and relationships between them and can be a knowledge source for computational creativity and computational ontology. Computational ontologies are understood as resources of formalized knowledge, where the degree of formalization may vary [4]. For the Story Graph, they can provide representational

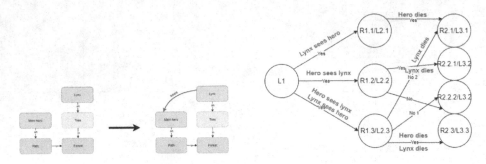

Fig. 4. Lynx sees Hero   **Fig. 5.** Narrative Story Graph

primitives for the concepts and relations between them. The structural framework of an ontology is a taxonomy that defines a hierarchical classification of concepts. Knowledge about the states of the Story Graph world is detailed based on the selected discourse domain. This means that representational classes with attributes are defined and both the relations between elements of the same class and between elements of different classes presented implicitly in the Story Graph should be defined explicitly.

There exist two types of productions in the Story Graph:

1. Generic Productions: These operate at the graph structure level, utilizing labels such as locations, characters, and items for nodes, with relations defined implicitly. This type of production enhances semantic interoperability in intelligent systems by incorporating metadata, ultimately organizing data into a controlled structure. This approach allows computer systems to exchange data efficiently by associating each piece of data with a controlled vocabulary at the computational ontology level [1].

2. Detailed Productions: Operate at the ontological level, describing a designated domain of discourse, including concepts and relations between them. So far, relations have also been described implicitly in detailed productions. We propose to specify explicit relations using their labels in detailed productions. Two types of relations are defined: the first reflects human cognition concepts, while the second mainly defines spatial or belonging relationships commonly used in semantic networks. Both are constructed using human language, and the proposed labels express axiomatic features of natural language sentences [6].

In this paper, we propose a Narrative Story Graph (NSG) with graph rewriting. There are two ways to express choices in a graph using edges or nodes. NSG is a specialized hierarchical graph in which edge labels describe choices in natural language. The proposed approach will be shown in the example describing dependencies and relations between characters. A fragment of the creation of a narrative in NSG will be illustrated, referring to the story of a meeting in the forest of two characters, the main character (Hero) and a lynx. We are starting with the following modified detailed production of the Story Graph with labeled edges. The left-hand side describes the context of the meeting of two characters with their locations. Whereas on the right-hand side of the production the edge label "sees" from the node "Lynx" to the node "Hero" is added. Using words of natural language as labels, remembering that the construction of meaning occurs in the relationship of one word with the others it makes possible to contain information in the language about game states before and after the action. For instance, the information is given in the form of label sequences of paths on the right-hand side of the production (Lynx - sees - Hero). It is a step to develop intelligent design systems, the main feature of which is context adaptability, aimed at enabling the system to capture and use information about the context of applied functions and transformations [4].

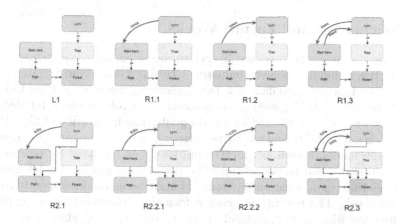

Fig. 6. Productions for Narrative Story Graph

Figure 5 shows NSG in which the node labeled L1 is the starting node. L1 is a name of the left-hand side of production shown in Fig. 4. The labels of the three edges coming from this node show choices such as lynx sees hero, lynx and hero see each other, and hero sees lynx. The target nodes of these edges in NSC contain the right-hand sides of the productions R1.1, R1.2, and R1.3 shown in Fig. 6 which differ from L1 only by adding edges with different labels showing dependencies between characters. The production R1.1 is the right-hand side of the production shown in Fig. 4. In the next steps in NRC describing the characters' actions, the target nodes for the source node L1 become source nodes for subsequent nodes and are treated as the left-hand sides L2.1, L2.2, and L2.3 of subsequent productions with the right-hand sides such as R2.1, R2.2.1, R2.2.2, and R2.3 in Fig. 6. In the number of outcoming edges of nodes containing labels L2.1, L2.2, and L2.3 is one, two, and three, respectively. These numbers represent the number of choices that are proposed regarding the actions performed for three states of the game world that differ in the dependencies between the characters. Consider for instance the node of the NSG containing the label L2.2. The content of this hierarchical node is the state of the game world in which the lynx is seen by the hero. This source node is connected by two edges to its target nodes containing two different right-hand sides of productions

R2.2.1 and R2.2.2 shown in Fig. 6. Players have a choice between killing the lynx (the game world state described in R2.2.1) or hiding the main hero in the forest (another state in R.2.2.2). It is worth noting that for node L2.3 which has three outgoing edges, its two target nodes contain the right-hand sides of productions that describe the results of actions previously considered. The proposed NSG is a model joining creating narration with creating graph productions which are used to automatically generate sequences of players' actions. Moreover, labels of all paths on the left-hand sides and right-hand sides of graph productions provide natural language information about the states of the game worlds they describe.

5   Conclusions and Future Works

The article discusses the proposed StoryGraph system for designing adventure games in the game development industry. Utilizing Game World State Graphs and a sheaf structure for efficient action execution, we use the Goal-Oriented Action Planning (GOAP) method, emphasizing its role in character decision-making for both short-term and long-term goals. The integration of GOAP aids in achieving adaptability and narrative variety in gameplay sequences. The narrative graph model, known as StoryGraph, serves as the basis for representing game world states and player actions. The use of computational ontologies and explicit relations in detailed productions enhances semantic interoperability and narrative depth. The benefits of using a formal graph structure are exploited when implementing GOAP methods both to control NPC characters and to support the quest design process. Thanks to the formalisation of structures, the same mechanisms can be used across multiple fields of operation and the effects of the algorithm can be represented and analysed within well-defined structures. Graph-based analysis tools make it possible to track and compare interactions between characters regardless of whether they are controlled by a player or an algorithm, and increase the explainability of AI-driven decisions. The proposed semantically enriched formal model aims to emulate human cognition, offering a new narrative graph model. The article concludes by presenting the Narrative Story Graph (NSG), a hierarchical graph linking narration with graph productions to generate player action sequences automatically. The NSG's labels provide natural language information about the game world states, offering a comprehensive approach to narrative design in adventure games. The study underscores the importance of context-aware design systems for effective information capture and utilization in the gaming context. The challenge for future works lies in the incorporation and support of aspects such as the need for gradual exploration of the game world and the progressive development of characters, the planning of effective information conveyance to the player, and game balancing.

Acknowledgements. The research for this publication has been supported within the Priority Research Area DigiWorld under the Strategic Programme Excellence Initiative at Jagiellonian University.

References

1. Arena, D.N.: Towards semantics-driven modelling and simulation of context-aware manufacturing systems (2019). https://api.semanticscholar.org/CorpusID: 199011503
2. Glassner, A.: Interactive Storytelling: Techniques for 21st Century Fiction. CRC Press (2017). https://books.google.pl/books?id=cWC1DwAAQBAJ
3. Grabska-Gradzińska, I., Nowak, L., Palacz, W., Grabska, E.: Application of graphs for story generation in video games. In: Proceedings of the 2021 Australasian Computer Science Week Multiconference. ACSW 2021. Association for Computing Machinery, New York (2021). https://doi.org/10.1145/3437378.3442693
4. Guarino, N., Oberle, D., Staab, S.: What is an ontology? In: Staab, S., Studer, R. (eds.) Handbook on Ontologies. International Handbooks on Information Systems, pp. 1–17. Springer, Heidelberg (2009). https://doi.org/10.1007/978-3-540-92673-3_0
5. Lebowitz, J.: Interactive Storytelling for Video Games: A Player-Centered Approach to Creating Memorable Characters and Stories. CRC Press (2017). https:// books.google.pl/books?id=bAtCAQAACAAJ
6. Monte-Serrat, D., Cattani, C.: The language conceptual formation to inspire intelligent systems. Sci 4(4) (2022). https://doi.org/10.3390/sci4040042. https://www. mdpi.com/2413-4155/4/4/42
7. Monte-Serrat, D.M., Cattani, C.: Interpretability in neural networks towards universal consistency. Int. J. Cogn. Comput. Eng. 2, 30–39 (2021). https://doi. org/10.1016/j.ijcce.2021.01.002. https://www.sciencedirect.com/science/article/ pii/S266630742100005X
8. Shaker, N., Togelius, J., Nelson, M.J.: Procedural Content Generation in Games: A Textbook and an Overview of Current Research. Springer, Cham (2016). https:// doi.org/10.1007/978-3-319-42716-4
9. Shen, E.Y.T., Lieberman, H., Davenport, G.: What's next? Emergent storytelling from video collection. In: Proceedings of the SIGCHI Conference on Human Factors in Computing Systems, CHI 2009, pp. 809–818. Association for Computing Machinery, New York (2009). https://doi.org/10.1145/1518701.1518825
10. Sicart, M.: Beyond Choices: The Design of Ethical Gameplay. The MIT Press (2013). https://books.google.pl/books?id=VNEyAgAAQBAJ
11. Sowa, J.F.: Laws, facts, and contexts: foundations for multimodal reasoning. In: Hendricks, V.F., Jorgensen, K.F., Pedersen, S.A. (eds.) Knowledge Contributors, pp. 145–184. Springer, Dordrecht (2003). https://doi.org/10.1007/978-94-007-1001-6_7
12. Steiner, K.E., Moher, T.G.: Graphic storywriter: an interactive environment for emergent storytelling. In: Proceedings of the SIGCHI Conference on Human Factors in Computing Systems, CHI 1992, pp. 357-364. Association for Computing Machinery, New York (1992). https://doi.org/10.1145/142750.142831

A Framework for Explanation-Aware Visualization and Adjudication in Object Detection: First Results and Perspectives

Arnab Ghosh Chowdhury[1], David Massanés[1], Steffen Meinert[1], and Martin Atzmueller[1,2(✉)]

[1] Semantic Information Systems Group, Osnabrück University, Osnabrück, Germany
{arnab.ghosh.chowdhury,dmassanes,steffen.meinert,
martin.atzmueller}@uos.de
[2] German Research Center for Artificial Intelligence (DFKI), Osnabrück, Germany

Abstract. Context-aware systems require context information, which essentially should rely on high-quality data. Object detection is one particular area enabling context information from the environment to be processed. Ensuring the presence of high-quality data is crucial for machine learning methods to detect objects with high precision. This paper presents a framework for explanation-aware visualization and adjudication in object detection, integrating the user into a semi-automatic verification and adjudication process, where targeted information can be transported by visualization and explanation methods. We discuss a tool for supporting such approaches and present first results and perspectives.

Keywords: Adjudication · Context-Aware Systems · Explainable AI · Human-in-the-Loop · Object Detection · Visualization

1 Introduction

Context-aware systems [1,11] exploit *context information* [6], e.g., for a better understanding in a given situation when services and functionalities are provided by the system [1]. Here, *context* in a broad sense refers to information that can be used to characterize such a situation, in particular, referring to the status of entities in the environment, like people, places, things, devices, etc. [6,11]. Therefore, it does not only refer to affective and ambient intelligence but also to sensor-based applications as well as robotics [8,30], for example, where (context) information from the environment is crucial. Here, object detection plays a pivotal role, e.g., for mobile sensing, mapping, and navigation [17,38]. For that, getting high-quality (training) data to be used in machine learning approaches is of vital importance. This paper provides a semi-automatic framework for explanation visualization, verification, and adjudication in object detection. We discuss a tool that supports the workflow of progressively verifying data annotations in

---

A. G. Chowdhury and D. Massanés—Both authors contributed equally to this work.

© The Author(s), under exclusive license to Springer Nature Switzerland AG 2024
J. M. Ferrández Vicente et al. (Eds.): IWINAC 2024, LNCS 14674, pp. 496–506, 2024.
https://doi.org/10.1007/978-3-031-61140-7_47

order to obtain a high-quality training dataset. We demonstrate the tool's usage within the context of object detection experiments we conducted.

In particular, we present VizAOD, a free, open-source web-based tool that can be useful for enabling visually assisted annotation verification and adjudication in object detection incorporating a human-in-the-loop (HITL) approach. In practice, especially in industry, it is beneficial to progressively annotate data by verifying, for example, a supervised object detection model's predictions gradually rather than trying different experiments (e.g., different architectures or loss functions), where a limited human time budget is allocated for annotation on a novel object detection dataset. The user can collectively leverage the existing open-source annotation tools such as LabelImg [36], LabelMe [37], CVAT [28] for creating object annotations together with our VizAOD tool for adjudicating the predicted labels. We present our first results working with the tool, sketching two use cases of object detection, and discuss further perspectives.

The rest of the paper is organized as follows: Sect. 2 discusses related work. Section 3 presents our proposed framework and workflow. Section 4 describes two use cases on object detection using the Global Wheat Head Detection (GWHD) [5] as well as the Lincolnbeet (LB) [26] dataset. Finally, Sect. 5 concludes the paper with a summary and interesting directions for future work.

2 Related Work

Usually, acquiring large amounts of labeled data is costly. Whenever labeled data is unavailable, skilled annotators are required to provide high-quality annotations, e.g., for object detection. In particular, adjudicating the predicted results of a deep learning neural network model is crucial, for example, for medical image analysis [12,27,33] or in the agricultural domain [16].

The Region-based convolutional neural network (R-CNN), for example, is a state-of-the-art object detection approach. Faster Region-based convolutional neural network (Faster R-CNN), a two-stage object detection architecture [25] predicts object bounds and objectness scores at each position. In contrast, You only look once (YOLO), a one-stage detector, re-frames the object detection problem as a single regression problem, directly from image pixels to bounding box coordinates and class probabilities [24]. Using a human-assisted verification process for updating object detectors and reducing the search space, in general, accelerates the rapid production of high-quality bounding-box annotations in object detection [22].

For assessing the predictions of a neural network model, different explainability techniques have been developed [7,19]. In the domain of image classification, one dominant method to highlight the importance of specific pixels for a prediction is the creation of saliency maps [29,34]. Some prominent methods to create saliency maps in the domain of object detection are called D-RISE, ODSmoothgrad, and Eigen-CAM [3,9,23]. We use Eigen-CAM, since it has the advantage that it does not depend on the backpropagation of the gradients, maximum activation locations, class relevance score, or any other form of weighting features [21]. The combination of explainability and HITL was studied recently [18,20,35], also in the domain of agriculture [32].

3   Visualization and Adjudication in Object Detection

In object detection, ensuring a high quality of the annotated dataset is crucial, specifically when iteratively annotating a novel dataset manually, compared to pseudo-label-based approaches in semi-supervised object detection [13], which might lead to incorrect labels. When predicting objects on unlabeled data using a semi-supervised object detection model, for example, assessing these predictions by approving high-quality and discarding low-quality ones is recommended [14]. VIZAOD[1] can enable such an assessment approach by incorporating a HITL approach. The general workflow for visualization, verification, and adjudication including VIZAOD consists of the steps shown in Fig. 1:

1. Using a machine learning method for object detection we can use, e.g., the initial annotations for training an (initial) object detection model.
2. Using the model, the *model inference* step predicts annotations for a subset of the unlabeled images.
3. For the predictions, the results are checked in the *interactive assessment* step using the VIZAOD tool for integrating findings of appropriate visualization and explainability methods [7,19], enabling computational sensemaking [2]. For instance, the annotation results are adjudicated via a HITL approach (*Adjudicator*) in the object detection case, either (a) *Approve*: if all bounding boxes in an image are predicted correctly, (b) *Discard*: otherwise.
4. Given *analysis* and further *annotation* phases in the HITL approach, we can refine the dataset, e.g., merge all *valid* labeled data, i.e., initial as well as approved annotations, to extend the training dataset.
5. The process is iterated, enabling further model training in order to construct and/or refine, for example, the object detection models incrementally.

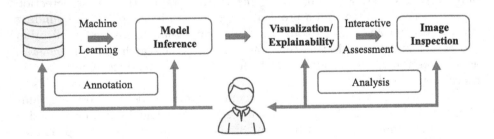

Fig. 1. An overview of the frameworks' workflow, using the VIZAOD tool.

---

[1] **VizAOD source code:** https://github.com/cslab-hub/vizaod.

For data processing VizAOD considers data annotations in CSV format. Existing open-source annotation tools typically use the PASCAL VOC (XML) or COCO (JSON) formats for annotated information. VizAOD offers conversion functionality from COCO (JSON) to CSV formatted annotations for ease of use in the explanation-aware visualization and adjudication process.

4 Exemplary Use Cases – First Results

Below, we discuss two use cases: First, we present a use case of supervised object detection initiated with partially labeled data on the GWHD dataset [5]. Afterwards, we illustrate supervised object detection on the LB dataset [26].

4.1 Object Detection Using the GWHD Dataset

We consider the GWHD benchmark dataset [5] focusing on wheat heads with consistent labeling regarding context-aware systems in the field of precision farming. To demonstrate the functionality and applicability of VizAOD, we consider the following paradigm, assuming a limited human time budget for annotation and three criteria: (1) a supervised object detection model training initiated with a partially annotated dataset, (2) verification and adjudication to *extend* the annotated dataset, and (3) further model training on an *extended annotated* dataset. For simplicity, we demonstrate model inference results for only the first two iterations on the GWHD dataset, although this is a fully annotated dataset that contains only one object type (i.e., the wheat head) in an image.

Method and Experiment. The GWHD dataset consists of a total of 3422 images (containing 147793 objects/wheat heads). We extract the relevant information from the original dataset, in particular, bounding box co-ordinates of each object in an image and other information (e.g., image width, image height, object width, object height, object area) and process the dataset for our specific experiment. The processed dataset is initially divided into 2 categories:

1. A labeled dataset, consisting of the first 500 images and corresponding object annotations (i.e., 20744 wheat heads/objects) for initial model training.
2. An unlabeled dataset, as the rest of 2922 images, discarding corresponding object annotations (i.e., 127049 wheat heads), being used for inference.

The labeled dataset is divided into a training (80%) and a validation set (20%). For the initial training, we choose the Detectron2[2] library based Faster R-CNN model [25] by leveraging a transfer learning approach[3]. We apply the same hyper-parameters as in [4] with batch size = 64. To eliminate low-scored bounding box predictions of foreground objects, the number of foreground classes

---

[2] https://github.com/facebookresearch/detectron2.
[3] https://github.com/cslab-hub/MatrixDataExtractor/tree/main/tabledetection.

and testing threshold score of Region of Interest (ROI) head of the object detection model are set to 1 and 0.5, respectively. The object detection model in this experiment usually considers two types of object classes, e.g., a *background* class (by default) and a *wheat head* class. A Resnet-101 architecture [10] integrated with a Feature Pyramid Networks (FPNs) [15] is considered as the backbone of the Faster R-CNN model. The pre-trained model weights for transfer learning and the corresponding configuration file of initial training are obtained from the *LayoutParser* approach to perform transfer learning [31].

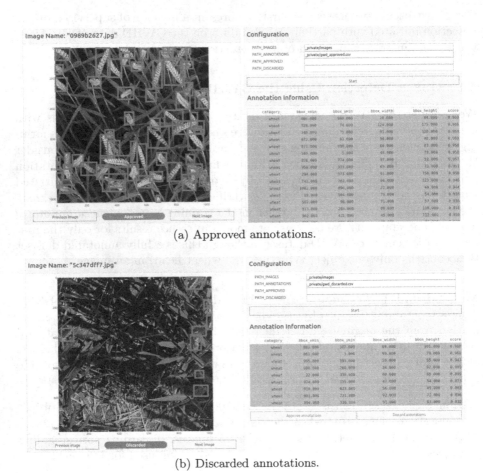

(a) Approved annotations.

(b) Discarded annotations.

Fig. 2. GWHD dataset use case: visualizing adjudicated results for object detection.

We consider a high threshold value (e.g., ≥0.7) for the objectness score of all foreground objects (i.e., wheat heads) in an image during the first inference step on the unlabeled dataset. Subsequently, we adjudicate the inferred results, adding adjudicated inferred images to the previously labeled dataset for the next training iteration. This is supported by an intuitive visualization of the image information, as shown in Fig. 2. In particular, the user can assess the images and the respective annotations and approve or discard the predicted results.

VizAOD shows the inference result (e.g., filename, object bounding box coordinates, objectness score), the colored bounding boxes of each object, and allows the user to navigate across the images. After the initial training (i.e., after iteration 1), 58 images are adjudicated among all inferred images via VizAOD. These 58 adjudicated images with annotations are included with the previously labeled dataset for the next object detection model training at iteration 2 and subsequently eliminated from the unlabeled dataset. After the second model training, 77 images are adjudicated among all inferred images. Those 77 adjudicated images with annotations are included in the labeled dataset again to increase the size of the labeled dataset and consequently removed from the unlabeled dataset. Table 1 presents the respective evaluation results (iteration = 1,2).

Table 1. GWHD dataset use case: prediction evaluation results.

Iteration	Images	Epoch	Total Class Accuracy	Foreground Class Accuracy
1	500	1000	82.42	56.25
2	558	1000	84.17	60.15

4.2 Supervised Object Detection Using the LB dataset

Another example for context-aware systems in the agricultural domain concerns automatic weed control. The LB dataset [26] is a supervised benchmark for object detection, which is designed to promote the research activities in the identification of items (e.g., sugar beet and weed) in the agricultural fields with high levels of occlusion for the improvement of object detection models in precision agriculture. To demonstrate VizAOD, we train a supervised object detection model on the LB dataset and especially review the model inference results through our VizAOD tool for further analysis.

Table 2. LB dataset use case: supervised object detection model evaluation results.

Model	Epoch	Batch Size	mAP_{50-95}	mAP_{50}	mAP_{75}	$mAP_{sugarbeet}$	mAP_{weed}
YOLOv8	300	16	54.08	76.96	58.10	70.55	37.61
YOLOv8	300	32	54.29	77.10	58.56	70.45	38.12

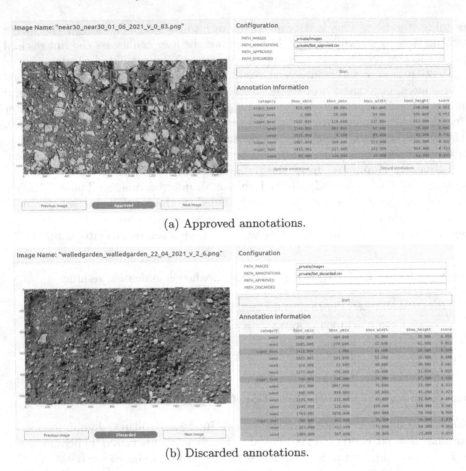

(a) Approved annotations.

(b) Discarded annotations.

Fig. 3. LB dataset use case: adjudicated results for supervised object detection.

Method and Experiment. We apply the YOLOv8[4] framework, using a transfer learning method on the LB dataset with pre-trained YOLOv8 Nano model weight to detect two types of objects (i.e., sugar beet, weed) in an image. The LB dataset is split into training (70%), validation (20%), and test (10%) sets and pre-processed for the YOLOv8 training processes. We perform two experiments considering (1) batch size = 16 and (2) batch size = 32 along with default hyperparameters; we train for three hundred epochs. Table 2 presents the evaluation results of the supervised object detection model. The evaluation metric Average Precision (AP) considers respective Intersection over Union (IoU) thresholds for computation and averaging by counting a *positive* object when a value above the threshold is observed; otherwise, a *negative* object. Two other metrics AP_{50}

---

[4] https://github.com/ultralytics/ultralytics.

and AP_{75} consider IoU thresholds 0.5 and 0.75 respectively [4]. Figure 3 shows the user's decision to approve or to discard prediction results on LB dataset.

We apply Eigen-CAM to compute and visualize the principle components of the learned features or representations from the convolutional layers [21]. This is an example of an applied explainable method for the first experiment (i.e., batch size $= 16$) shown in Fig. 4. During the model training and inference, the one-hot encoding of sugar beet and weed are denoted as 0 and 1, respectively. Figure 4a and Fig. 4b present the inference result and the result of applying Eigen-CAM. It is also possible to display the result of explanation methods like Eigen-CAM along with the inferred images, the predictions of the model, and additional information (i.e., object categories, bounding box information, objectness score of each object etc.) for verification and adjudication.

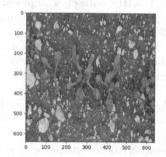
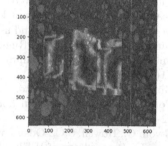

(a) Identified objects (partially correct predictions).

(b) Interpreting model's decision.

Fig. 4. LB dataset: sugar beet and weed detection with Eigen-CAM for explanation.

5   Conclusions

In this paper, we presented a framework for explanation-aware visualization and adjudication in object detection integrating our proposed VizAOD tool, which can be applied, e.g., for supervised, semi-supervised, or active learning based object detection. We discussed the respective framework and workflow in detail and described first promising results sketching two use cases using real-world benchmark data. For future work, interesting directions include extending tool's functionalities for object detection and image segmentation use cases, as well as further studies regarding explanation-aware methods for integration into the framework.

Acknowledgements. This work has been supported by the funded project *FRED*, German Federal Ministry for Economic Affairs and Climate Action (BMWK), FKZ: 01MD22003E.

References

1. Alegre, U., Augusto, J.C., Clark, T.: Engineering context-aware systems and applications: a survey. J. Syst. Softw. **117**, 55–83 (2016)
2. Atzmueller, M.: Declarative aspects in explicative data mining for computational sensemaking. In: Seipel, D., Hanus, M., Abreu, S. (eds.) Declarative Programming, pp. 97–114. Springer, Heidelberg (2018). https://doi.org/10.1007/978-3-030-00801-7_7
3. Bany Muhammad, M., Yeasin, M.: Eigen-cam: visual explanations for deep convolutional neural networks. SN Comput. Sci. **2**, 1–14 (2021)
4. Chowdhury, A.G., Schut, N., Atzmueller, M.: A hybrid information extraction approach using transfer learning on richly-structured documents. In: Proceedings of LWDA 2021 Workshops: FGWM, KDML, FGWI-BIA, and FGIR. CEUR Workshop Proceedings, vol. 2993, pp. 13–25. CEUR-WS.org (2021)
5. David, E., et al.: Global wheat head detection (GWHD) dataset: a large and diverse dataset of high-resolution RGB-labelled images to develop and benchmark wheat head detection methods. Plant Phenomics (2020)
6. Dey, A.K.: Understanding and using context. Pers. Ubiquit. Comput. **5**, 4–7 (2001)
7. Guidotti, R., Monreale, A., Ruggieri, S., Turini, F., Giannotti, F., Pedreschi, D.: A survey of methods for explaining black box models. ACM Comput. Surv. (CSUR) **51**(5) (2018)
8. Günther, M., Ruiz-Sarmiento, J., Galindo, C., González-Jiménez, J., Hertzberg, J.: Context-aware 3D object anchoring for mobile robots. Robot. Auton. Syst. **110**, 12–32 (2018)
9. Gwon, C., Howell, S.C.: Odsmoothgrad: generating saliency maps for object detectors. In: Proceedings of IEEE/CVF Conference on Computer Vision and Pattern Recognition (CVPR) Workshops, pp. 3685–3689 (2023)
10. He, K., Zhang, X., Ren, S., Sun, J.: Deep residual learning for image recognition. In: Proceedings of IEEE Conference on Computer Vision and Pattern Recognition (CVPR), pp. 770–778 (2016)
11. Hong, J.Y., Suh, E.H., Kim, S.J.: Context-aware systems: a literature review and classification. Expert Syst. Appl. **36**(4), 8509–8522 (2009)
12. Krackov, W., Sor, M., Razdan, R., Zheng, H., Kotanko, P.: Artificial intelligence methods for rapid vascular access aneurysm classification in remote or in-person settings. Blood Purif. **50**(4–5), 636–641 (2021)
13. Li, H., Wu, Z., Shrivastava, A., Davis, L.S.: Rethinking pseudo labels for semi-supervised object detection. In: Proceedings of AAAI, vol. 36, pp. 1314–1322 (2022)
14. Li, Y.F., Liang, D.M.: Safe semi-supervised learning: a brief introduction. Front. Comput. Sci. **13**, 669–676 (2019)
15. Lin, T.Y., Dollár, P., Girshick, R., He, K., Hariharan, B., Belongie, S.: Feature pyramid networks for object detection. In: Proceedings of IEEE Conference on Computer Vision and Pattern Recognition (CVPR), pp. 2117–2125 (2017)
16. Lu, Y., Young, S.: A survey of public datasets for computer vision tasks in precision agriculture. Comput. Electron. Agric. **178**, 105760 (2020)
17. Martins, R., Bersan, D., Campos, M.F., Nascimento, E.R.: Extending maps with semantic and contextual object information for robot navigation: a learning-based framework using visual and depth cues. J. Intell. Robot. Syst. **99**, 555–569 (2020)
18. Monarch, R.M.: Human-in-the-Loop Machine Learning: Active Learning and Annotation for Human-Centered AI. Simon and Schuster (2021)

19. Montavon, G., Samek, W., Müller, K.R.: Methods for interpreting and understanding deep neural networks. Digit. Signal Process. **73**, 1–15 (2018)
20. Mosqueira-Rey, E., Hernández-Pereira, E., Alonso-Ríos, D., Bobes-Bascarán, J., Fernández-Leal, Á.: Human-in-the-loop machine learning: a state of the art. Artif. Intell. Rev. **56**(4), 3005–3054 (2023)
21. Muhammad, M.B., Yeasin, M.: Eigen-cam: class activation map using principal components. In: 2020 International Joint Conference on Neural Networks (IJCNN), pp. 1–7. IEEE (2020)
22. Papadopoulos, D.P., Uijlings, J.R.R., Keller, F., Ferrari, V.: We don't need no bounding-boxes: training object class detectors using only human verification. In: Proceedings of IEEE Conference on Computer Vision and Pattern Recognition (CVPR) (2016)
23. Petsiuk, V., et al.: Black-box explanation of object detectors via saliency maps. In: Proceedings of IEEE/CVF Conference on Computer Vision and Pattern Recognition, pp. 11443–11452 (2021)
24. Redmon, J., Divvala, S., Girshick, R., Farhadi, A.: You only look once: unified, real-time object detection. In: Proceedings of IEEE Conference on Computer Vision and Pattern Recognition (CVPR), pp. 779–788 (2016)
25. Ren, S., He, K., Girshick, R., Sun, J.: Faster R-CNN: towards real-time object detection with region proposal networks. In: Advances in Neural Information Processing Systems, vol. 28 (2015)
26. Salazar-Gomez, A., Darbyshire, M., Gao, J., Sklar, E.I., Parsons, S.: Towards practical object detection for weed spraying in precision agriculture. arXiv preprint arXiv:2109.11048 (2021)
27. Sarkar, S., Majumder, S., Koehler, J.L., Landman, S.R.: An ensemble of features based deep learning neural network for reduction of inappropriate atrial fibrillation detection in implantable cardiac monitors. Heart Rhythm O2 **4**(1), 51–58 (2023)
28. Sekachev, B., et al.: opencv/cvat: v1.1.0 (2020). https://doi.org/10.5281/zenodo.4009388
29. Selvaraju, R.R., Cogswell, M., Das, A., Vedantam, R., Parikh, D., Batra, D.: Grad-cam: visual explanations from deep networks via gradient-based localization. In: Proceedings of IEEE International Conference on Computer Vision, pp. 618–626 (2017)
30. Shafti, A., Orlov, P., Faisal, A.A.: Gaze-based, context-aware robotic system for assisted reaching and grasping. In: 2019 International Conference on Robotics and Automation (ICRA), pp. 863–869. IEEE (2019)
31. Shen, Z., Zhang, R., Dell, M., Lee, B.C.G., Carlson, J., Li, W.: Layoutparser: a unified toolkit for deep learning based document image analysis. In: Llados, J., Lopresti, D., Uchida, S. (eds.) ICDAR 2021. LNCS, vol. 12821, pp. 131–146. Springer, Cham (2021). https://doi.org/10.1007/978-3-030-86549-8_9
32. Sreeram, M., Nof, S.Y.: Human-in-the-loop: role in cyber physical agricultural systems. Int. J. Comput. Commun. Control **16**(2) (2021)
33. Stidham, R.W., et al.: Performance of a deep learning model vs human reviewers in grading endoscopic disease severity of patients with ulcerative colitis. JAMA Netw. Open **2**(5), e193963–e193963 (2019)
34. Sundararajan, M., Taly, A., Yan, Q.: Axiomatic attribution for deep networks. In: International Conference on Machine Learning, pp. 3319–3328. PMLR (2017)
35. Tsiakas, K., Murray-Rust, D.: Using human-in-the-loop and explainable AI to envisage new future work practices. In: Proceedings of the 15th International Conference on PErvasive Technologies Related to Assistive Environments, pp. 588–594 (2022)

36. Tzutalin: Labelimg. Free Software: MIT License (2015). https://github.com/tzutalin/labelImg
37. Wada, K.: labelme: Image Polygonal Annotation with Python (2016). https://github.com/wkentaro/labelme
38. Yürür, Ö., Liu, C.H., Sheng, Z., Leung, V.C., Moreno, W., Leung, K.K.: Context-awareness for mobile sensing: a survey and future directions. IEEE Commun. Surv. Tutor. **18**(1), 68–93 (2014)

Learning Tools to Lecture

Optimizing Didactic Sequences with Artificial Intelligence: Integrating Bloom's Taxonomy and Emotion in the Selection of Educational Technologies

Pedro Salcedo-Lagos[1]([✉]), Pedro Pinacho-Davidson[2],
M. Angélica Pinninghoff J.[2], Ricardo Contreras A.[3], Karina Fuentes-Riffo[1],
and Miguel Friz Carrillo[4]

[1] MIIE, Facultad de Educación, Universidad de Concepción, Concepción, Chile
psalcedo@udec.cl
[2] DIICC, Facultad de Ingeniería, Universidad de Concepción, Concepción, Chile
[3] Faculty of Sciences and Engineering, Universidad Adolfo Ibáñez, Santiago, Chile
[4] DCE, Facultad de Educación, Universidad del Biobío, Concepción, Chile

Abstract. This paper presents an innovative evolution of the 'Adaptive Competence System for Technologies Integration in Education' (SACITED) tool. SACITED stands for the spanish name: Sistema Adaptativo de Competencias para la Integración de Tecnologías en Educación. SACITED now incorporates the OpenAI GPT API for the generation of didactic sequences. The tool was originally focused on mathematics but has since expanded to multiple disciplines, including Education, Engineering, and Science. This integration enables the generation of learning sequences in a more efficient and adaptive manner, significantly improving the quality and relevance of education across a broad spectrum of content. The article explains how SACITED facilitates the assessment and training of ICT (Information Communication Technologies) competencies in teachers from different disciplines, using the TPACK model and Bloom's Digital Taxonomy. The incorporation of a GPT model presents a new opportunity for unparalleled customization and adaptability in generating educational content. Initial findings indicate significant potential for enhancing ICT integration in both the classroom and teacher training, emphasizing the importance of personalized and adaptive tools in modern education.

Keywords: Digital education · digital Bloom's taxonomy · TPACK model · generation of didactic sequences · integration of LLMs in education

1 Introduction

The integration of Information and Communication Technologies (ICT) in the classroom is a crucial element for the evolution of educational methods.

© The Author(s), under exclusive license to Springer Nature Switzerland AG 2024
J. M. Ferrández Vicente et al. (Eds.): IWINAC 2024, LNCS 14674, pp. 509–517, 2024.
https://doi.org/10.1007/978-3-031-61140-7_48

This paradigm shift requires a re-evaluation of didactic strategies to improve interaction and learning in various academic disciplines. The tool 'Adaptive System of Competencies for the Integration of ICT in Education' [5], initially presented in Salcedo et al. [6,7], represents a significant advancement in this direction. Originally designed for mathematics, SACITED has expanded to include Education, Engineering, Science, and other disciplines. This expansion is a milestone in the development of adaptive and personalized educational tools.

SACITED's initial approach, which focuses on the TPACK (Technological Pedagogical and Content Knowledge) model and the Bloom Digital Taxonomy [6,7], has been effective in creating didactic sequences that promote both knowledge acquisition and competence in the use of ICT by educators. These conceptual frameworks, which are essential in instructional design, have facilitated the assessment and training of ICT competencies. They provide a solid basis for the development of relevant and effective educational content.

The incorporation of the OpenAI GPT API (hereinafter referred to as "GPT") into the SACITED framework marks a substantial advancement in the tool's evolution. By incorporating GPT's natural language processing and generation abilities, SACITED has improved its functionality in generating learning sequences. This new feature allows for better adaptation to the specific needs of different areas of knowledge, facilitating the creation of didactic sequences that are both relevant and emotionally resonant with students. Additionally, GPT's versatility in working with diverse educational content and contexts significantly broadens the scope and usefulness of SACITED across various academic disciplines.

This article presents an enhanced version of SACITED, emphasizing how the integration of GPT enhances the tool, enabling a more dynamic and contextualized generation of learning sequences. This section discusses how the integration of GPT's artificial intelligence expands the scope of SACITED beyond mathematics and improves its effectiveness in training and assessing ICT competencies in educators. Examples and case analyses demonstrate how SACITED, with the reinforcement of GPT's AI, is an essential tool in the digital education landscape of the 21st century.

The article follows a logical progression, beginning with a review of the theoretical underpinnings of SACITED. This is followed by a detailed explanation of GPT's integration and its impact on the generation of didactic sequences. Subsequently, case studies are presented to illustrate the practical application of SACITED in different disciplines, highlighting the benefits and challenges encountered. Finally, this tool's future implications for continuously improving teaching and learning methods, as well as training competent educators in using ICT in the classroom, will be discussed. In conclusion, SACITED now offers an advanced and versatile solution for the design of adaptive learning sequences. This represents a significant step towards the realization of a more integrated, interactive, and emotionally connected education. The functionality of GPT has enriched SACITED, making it even more powerful.

This article is structured as follows; first section consists of the current introduction. Second section describes the theoretical frame supporting the work. Third section is devoted to the Bloom digital taxonomy. Fourth section is to describe the evolution of the model. Fifth section shows the result of the evolution of the model. Next section focuses on testing issues and results. Finally, section seven presents the conclusions and a short description of the future work.

2   Theoretical Foundations

The design and development of educational tools in the digital age require a deep understanding of how technology interacts with and improves teaching and learning processes [2, 3].

In this context, the theoretical foundations of the 'Adaptive System of Competencies for the Integration of ICT in Education' (SACITED) are mainly based on two key concepts: the TPACK (Technological Pedagogical and Content Knowledge) model and the Bloom Digital Taxonomy. These conceptual frameworks provide a strong foundation for designing adaptive and effective didactic sequences, which are crucial for integrating ICT into various areas of knowledge.

The TPACK model, developed by Mishra and Koehler, is a framework that describes the types of knowledge educators need to effectively integrate technology into their teaching [4]. This model emphasizes the intersection of three types of knowledge: The interaction of Pedagogical Knowledge (PK), Content Knowledge (CK) and Technological Knowledge (TK) forms Content Technology Pedagogical Knowledge (TPCK). This enables educators to design and deliver content more effectively using technology. At SACITED, we use the TPACK model to guide the selection and application of technological tools and pedagogical strategies adapted to the specific content of each discipline.

3   Bloom Digital Taxonomy

The Bloom Digital Taxonomy is an adaptation of the classic Bloom Taxonomy that provides a framework for categorizing educational goals and skills, particularly in digital learning environments [1]. This modernized version includes cognitive processes and skills that are relevant to the digital environment, such as creating, evaluating and analyzing. SACITED utilizes this taxonomy to create educational sequences that not only impart knowledge but also cultivate critical thinking and problem-solving abilities in digital environments. The taxonomy acts as a framework to guarantee that learning activities cover a wide range of cognitive skills.

SACITED's comprehensive approach, which merges the TPACK model and the Bloom Digital Taxonomy, establishes a strong basis for the creation of learning sequences. The integration of these theoretical frameworks ensures that educational activities are not only technologically and content-appropriate, but also pedagogically sound. Additionally, these frameworks facilitate the adaptation of learning sequences to the changing and diverse needs of students in different disciplines. In summary, the theoretical foundations of SACITED represent a step forward in the integration of ICT in education. The SACITED tool is positioned as innovative for generating adaptive and relevant didactic sequences in the 21st century, from basic education to advanced levels in various areas of knowledge. This is achieved through the application of the TPACK model and the Bloom Digital Taxonomy.

4   Evolution of the SACITED Model

After incorporating GPT into the original model, SACITED has significantly improved its functionalities, as shown in Figs. 1 and 2.

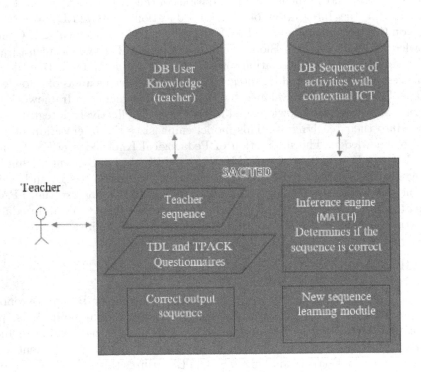

Fig. 1. The original model

Figure 1 displays the main databases and functionalities of SACITED. The system measures the ICT knowledge of the teacher through a pair of questionnaires (TPACK and TDL) and then prompts them for the content they want to learn in mathematics. The inference engine determines the most appropriate sequence from the database filled with sata acquired from semi-structured interviews with validated specialists in mathematics didactics.

The system delivers these sequences to the user, which can aid in teaching or training future teachers. The last functional block, *Module for learning new sequences*, is important as it allows for the acquisition of new sequences that can improve the database. This is determined by assessing the level of expertise of the user in the discipline.

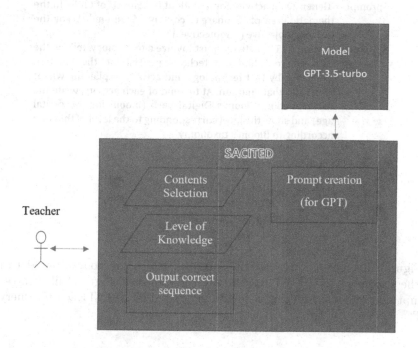

Fig. 2. The evolved model

5 Evolved Model

Figure 2 shows the evolved model, by changing two important functionalities of the system, through an API connection provided by the OpenAI to the GPT model (gpt-3.5-turbo). This allows to improve several features of the system and to improve its performance significantly.

The didactic sequences, originally obtained through semi-structured interviews with experts, are now acquired through GPT's trainng based on similar cases. This enables the generation of teaching sequences that incorporates activities, technologies and emotions in any area of knowledge.

However, it is feasible to substitute the inference and learning module with GPT's mechanisms for this purpose.

The following PHP code shows the connection through the API to GPT, so that the gpt-3.5-turbo model can provide the didactic sequence. This is then delivered to the user.

```php
<?php
// Process the request when the form is sent
$api_key = '********************************';
$endpoint = 'https://api.openai.com/v1/chat/completions';

// Concatenates the values selected in the request to the API
$prompt = 'Generate an activity for a student to '.$nivel.' of Chile. In the
           thematic area of '.$subarea.', content '.$contenido.'. For the
           learning objective ('. $objective.')';
$prompt = $prompt.'. The activity must involve a technology, tell me the
           URL where I find the technology. Tell me the emotion
           generated by that technology and activity, explaining why it
           generates that emotion. At the end of each activity, write the
           corresponding Bloom's Digital verb (bloom for the digital
           age) and show the level corresponding to the level of thinking
           according to Bloom's taxonomy. ';

// Create the body of the request
$data = [
  'model' => 'gpt-3.5-turbo', // Model name
  'messages' => [
     ['role' => 'user', 'content' => $prompt]
  ]
];
```

Figure 3 displays the for entering options, which are concatenated to create the Prompt sent to GPT to generate the sequence. Figure 4 illustrates the Prompt sent and the resulting sequence generated by SACITED after querying GPT.

6 SACITED Testing

The system was tested with a sample of 23 future mathematics teachers in their fourth year of pedagogy. The focus of the test was mainly in functionalities and error detection in the generation of sequences. The evaluation included checking for pedagogical errors of the activities, ensuring correct association of emotions with the activities, and verifying the existence of technologies and URLs at the time of creation.

The results indicate that, after each of the 23 students was asked to generate five sequences of activities for SACITED, it was found that 15% of them were not appropiate for achieving the learning objectives, according to the evaluation of the future teachers themselves. Additionally, 20% of the technologies either did not exist or had non-operational URLs. Furthermore, in 15% of the cases where SACITED determined that certain emotions would generate activities or technologies, the students did not agree with this assessment.

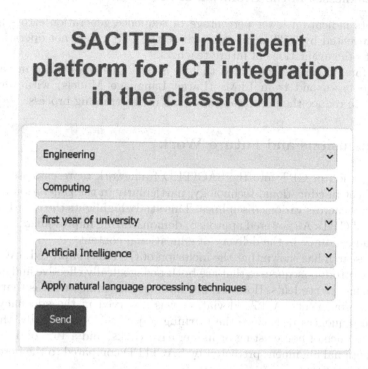

Fig. 3. Area, Content and Target Selection Screen

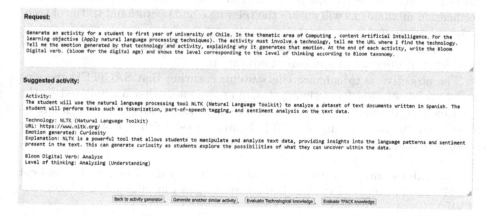

Fig. 4. Didactic Sequence Generation Screen

6.1   Weaknesses in the Evolution of SACITED

The results indicate a lower percentage of sequence generation errors in technologies invented by GPT or in cases where the URLs were not operational, in contrast to the evaluations of future teachers.

Therefore, it can be concluded that it is desirable to advance in validated knowledge bases and train LLMs (Large Language Models) with their own databases to reduce the percentage of errors in the training process.

7   Conclusions and Future Work

The integration of GPT into the SACITED framework represents a significant advancement in educational technology, particularly in the generation of didactic sequences across various disciplines. This study highlights the transformative potential of GPTs AI-powered approach, demonstrating improvements in adaptability and accuracy in the delivery of educational content.

Our research has shown that the inclusion of GPT has improved SACITED's capacity to produce sequences that are both pedagogically effective and emotionally engaging for students. However, our findings also indicate areas that require further improvements. A 15% deviation was observed in the adequacy of the generated sequences to achieve the learning objectives. Additionally, there was a 20% incidence of non-existing or inoperative URLs, and a 15% of discrepance in the emotional alignment predicted by SACITED compared to the perceptions of future educators.

These discrepancies suggest an urgent need for continuous validation of knowledge databases and refinement of training large language models with domain-specific data to minimize errors. To address this, future work will focus on developing validated knowledge bases and improving GPT's training with specialized datasets to reduce the margin of error. Additionally, integrating real-time data verification mechanisms will ensure the relevance and operational status of technological resources.

Looking to the future, SACITED's continued evolution promises to reinforce its role as an essential tool in digital education.

The objective is to enhance the system, ensuring that SACITED remains an advanced solution for designing learning sequences that are tailored to the dynamic and diverse needs of 21st-century education. With continuous improvements and rigurous testing, SACITED aims to establish a new standard for personalized and adaptive educational technologies.

Acknowledgement. This study has been partially supported by Project Fondecyt 1201572, and Project Fondecyt 1231788, National Agency for Research and Innovation (ANID).

References

1. Anderson, L.W., Krathwohl, D.R. (eds.) A Taxonomy for Learning, Teaching, and Assessing: A Revision of Bloom's Taxonomy of Educational Objectives. Longman (2001)
2. Górriz, J.M., et al.: Artificial intelligence within the interplay between natural and artificial computation: advances in data science, trends and applications. Neurocomputing **410**, 237–270 (2020)
3. Górriz, J.M., et al.: Computational approaches to explainable artificial intelligence: advances in theory, applications and trends. Inf. Fusion **100**, 101945 (2023)
4. Mishra, P., Koehler, M.J.: Technological pedagogical content knowledge: a framework for teacher knowledge. Teach. Coll. Rec. **108**(6), 1017–1054 (2006)
5. Salcedo-Lagos, P.: Adaptive System of Competencies for the Integration of ICT in Education (2024). http://www.sacited.com/robot-en
6. Salcedo-Lagos, P., Valdivia, J., López, O., Friz, M.: SACITED. Prototipo de un sistema inteligente que permite automatizar la integración de las tecnologías en el aula de clases. In Spanish. In La Tecnología Educativa Hoy. Uma Editorial (2021)
7. Salcedo-Lagos, P., Valdivia, J., López, O.: Propuesta de un sistema inteligente para determinar las mejores secuencias de aprendizaje en la integración de TIC en la enseñanza de las matemáticas. In Spanish. In La Tecnología Educativa Hoy. Uma Editorial (2021)

Contrastive Learning of Multivariate Gaussian Distributions of Incremental Classes for Continual Learning

Hyung-Jun Moon and Sung-Bae Cho[✉]

Department of Computer Science, Yonsei University, Seoul 03722, Korea
axtabio@yonsei.ac.kr, sbcho@yonsel.ac.kr

Abstract. Recent advancements in deep learning algorithms have shown remarkable performance on trained tasks, yet they struggle with "catastrophic forgetting" when faced with new tasks, highlighting the need for Continual Learning (CL) methods that update models efficiently without losing prior knowledge. CL models, constrained by limited visibility of the dataset for each task, develop a significant dependency on past tasks, complicating the integration of new information and maintaining robustness against future tasks. This paper proposes a novel CL method that leverages contrastive learning to secure a latent space for future data representation, reducing the dependency on past tasks and enhancing model adaptability. By distinguishing class spaces in the latent domain and re-representing these as sets of means and variances, our method effectively preserves past knowledge while ensuring future robustness. Experimental results show our method surpasses existing CL methods by a significant margin, proving its efficacy in handling information across past, present, and future tasks, thus establishing a robust solution for the challenges of catastrophic forgetting and task dependency in CL.

Keywords: Contrastive learning · Continual learning · Multivariate Gaussian distribution

1 Introduction

Recent deep learning algorithms have demonstrated impressive performance on the tasks they are trained for. However, as time progresses and new tasks frequently emerge, these models often face distribution shifts, leading to a degradation in performance. This phenomenon, known as "catastrophic forgetting," has led the focus of Continual Learning (CL) research to be on updating models in the most efficient way possible without losing previously acquired knowledge [1,2].

Unlike conventional deep learning methods, CL models face a constraint where only a fraction of the entire dataset is observable for each task. This limitation induces a significant dependency on the current or previous tasks, while

© The Author(s), under exclusive license to Springer Nature Switzerland AG 2024
J. M. Ferrández Vicente et al. (Eds.): IWINAC 2024, LNCS 14674, pp. 518–527, 2024.
https://doi.org/10.1007/978-3-031-61140-7_49

the unpredictability of future tasks complicates the ability to proactively address the robustness requirements for new samples during the testing phase [3]. Such dependency on past tasks presents a considerable challenge within CL, necessitating the development of methods to reduce these dependencies. For instance, consider a model that has formed a latent space suitable for past tasks, creating this space without knowledge of future data inputs. However, when actual information for a new task is introduced, conventional CL methods proceed by acquiring new knowledge while relying on the past latent space to avoid losing previous knowledge. This approach can lead to the repetition of past learning errors or complicate the setting of space for new data [4].

To mitigate the dependency issues arising from past tasks, it is essential to explore strategies that enhance model adaptability. In this context, this paper proposes a method that secures a latent space for future allocation based on contrastive learning, alongside newly trained classifiers for each task, thereby addressing the constraints of CL. By utilizing contrastive learning to reduce the relative distance between classes within the same category in the latent space, not only can we distinguish the space allocated by each class, but we can also re-represent this as a set of means and variances, storing it in memory. Reconstructing the representation of data for new tasks, the proposed method effectively preserves past knowledge while additionally ensuring robustness for future tasks.

Experiments demonstrate that our proposed method outperforms other CL approaches by more than 8 %p, particularly showing increased robustness as the number of tasks grows. Additionally, by verifying that the distributed representation memory clearly extracts the distribution of actual data, we prove that our method is effective in storing information from the past, present, and future, thereby validating it as a robust CL method.

2   Related Work

Prabhu et al. [5] introduced a method adaptable to both class and task incremental situations, where data is greedily sampled and stored in memory, to be relearned as a new model, inspiring numerous rehearsal-based methods. Despite the apparent simplicity and effectiveness of this rehearsal approach in CL contexts, it is not without its limitations. Sampling methods, while valuable for filtering relevant data for renewable memory [6,7], fall short in accurately capturing class representations [8], often leading to overfitting of the stored data.

Existing attempts to employ representation for solving CL, such as Rebuffi et al. [9] who utilized distillation to maintain representations, and Javed and White [10] who introduced OML for robust learning presentations to combat catastrophic forgetting (CF), primarily rely on data representation and meta-learning techniques. Gupta et al. [11] and Gallardo et al. [12] further explored these dimensions, with the former proposing La-MAML, a meta-learning algorithm for fast optimization, and the latter applying self-supervised learning for more generalized data representation in CL scenarios.

Moreover, efforts to employ mean and variance (prototype) for more effective representation in CL have been noted. Zhang et al. [13] introduced Variational Prototype Replays, showcasing enhanced memory efficiency through matching new data with previous data's mean and variance. Another approach by Zhang et al. [14] involves converting stabilized model layers' values into mean and variance, mirroring human memory processes for improved CL. However, these methods, grounded in the Gaussian distribution of class data, are susceptible to outliers and class overlap, due to mean location and covariance size, raising concerns about variance representation uncertainty and misclassification risks, thereby undermining stability.

The foundational regularization technique, EWC [15], restricts changes to the model's critical parameters, with subsequent gradient optimization strategies, such as Orthogonal Weight Modification (OWM) [16], promoting weight gradient orthogonality to input data to maintain output vector consistency. OWM, in particular, estimates the orthogonal projector to the null space of the input space, underscoring the significance of orthogonal regularization in safeguarding learned knowledge.

However, despite providing valuable insights into CL, these reference studies [5–16] fail to address the dependency on previous tasks, encounter constraints that necessitate omitting parts of previous tasks for the acquisition of new knowledge, or face issues in allocating space for new knowledge.

3   Proposed Method

3.1   Proposed Idea

This paper introduces a CL method designed to reduce dependency on the past and efficiently learn new spaces. Initially, we apply a data representation learning method based on contrastive learning to structure the latent space where data is represented. This approach prevents classes from being overly dispersed within the latent space and maintains a distance from other classes, creating space for new data representations to emerge as a key strength.

Once representation learning is complete, we transform these representations into Gaussian models for storage in memory. Unlike conventional CL replay-based methods, our approach eliminates the need to erase parts of previous knowledge to learn new information, thereby preserving as much knowledge as possible in memory. By leveraging these stored representations for new tasks, we implicitly regenerate representations, thus preventing new knowledge from encroaching upon prior knowledge.

3.2   Model Architecture Definition

In order to extract representations of data more efficiently, we distinguish general neural networks into Encoder and Classifier. The encoder learns the general representation of input data, which is constructed as several convolutional layers. The classifier predicts the input representations into their classes, which is

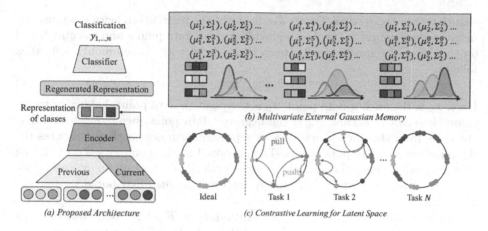

Fig. 1. (a) The overview of the proposed method. (b) The process of converting the generated class-specific representations into multivariate Gaussian distributions. (c) A schematic of the contrastive learning used to assign class representation in the latent space.

constructed as several fully connected layers. Let us denote encoder and classifier as E_k and C_k, respectively, where k represents each model after index learning of the task T_k. Task T_k consists of data x_k^i and a label y_k^i, where i represents the class. The initial task involves training the model without conducting any explicit operations on E_0 and C_0. Subsequently, we engage in preserving the model's prior knowledge gained from the preceding task. Since the previous task does not exist at $k = 0$, memory contributes nothing to learning model. Thus, the model is trained with $\mathbf{y}_0^i = C_0\left(E_0(\mathbf{x}_0^i)\right)$.

When task t_n is input, the encoder generates a data representation, which is subsequently used by the classifier for label prediction. Before proceeding to the next task, the representation transforms the expectation-maximization (EM) algorithm, converting it into a multivariate Gaussian distribution. In the subsequent task, denoted as t_{n+1}, the generative algorithm regenerates the means and variances stored in memory from tasks $t_{0\sim n}$. These regenerated representations, together with the data representation of task t_{n+1}, are then forwarded to the classifier. To ensure task-specific output representations, we employ the OWM learning mechanism, enabling the encoder to output representations in a designated space based on the task requirements. Figure 1 is a schematic diagram of the structure of the proposed method.

3.3   Learning Process

Contrastive Learning for Securing Latent Space. When task t_i is input, the encoder generates a data representation, which is subsequently used by the classifier for label prediction. Initially, we discern the classes existing within t_i and employ triplet loss to distinguish their representations from one another, ensuring their separation. Triplet loss is one of the methods to learn relationships between data points. It involves embedding given data points and learning based on the distance relationships between them. Triplet loss is commonly defined as follows:

$$L_{tri(x_a, x_p, x_n)} = max(0, d(x_a, x_p) - d(x_a, x_n) + margin) \tag{1}$$

Here, x_a is the anchor data point, x_p is the positive data point, belonging to the same class as the anchor, x_n is the negative data point, belonging to a different class from the anchor, and $d(\bullet, \bullet)$ represents a function that computes the distance between two data points. The proposed method employs the Euclidean distance. We perform the task of converting this loss term into an expression for distributed representation to facilitate integration with distributed representation memory.

Initially, the mean of the representation $R = E(x)$ is computed for data distinguished by class. This is expressed through the following equation:

$$\mu_i = 1/N_i \Sigma_{j=1}^{N_i} R(i, j) \tag{2}$$

Here, N_i represents the number of data points belonging to class i, and $R_{i,j}$ denotes the representation R for data j within class i. Computing the Covariance of Representation f. The covariance matrix of representation f signifies the interrelation between data points and is computed as follows:

$$\Sigma_i = \frac{1}{N_i - 1} m_i^T \bullet \mu_i \tag{3}$$

Utilize the mean μ and covariance Σ to construct the probability density function of the multivariate Gaussian distribution. This can be represented by the following formula:

$$f(R) = N(\mu_i, \Sigma_i) = 1/2\pi^{d/2} |\Sigma_i|^{1/2} e^{(-1/2R - \mu_i{}^T \Sigma_i^{-1} R - \mu_i))} \tag{4}$$

where d represents the dimensionality of the data. By employing the above formula, the given data representations R can be transformed into multivariate Gaussian distributions using the mean and covariance. These transformed distributions model the distribution of the given data, allowing for data analysis and learning through the characteristics of the distribution.

Since our proposed method stores knowledge in memory in the form of means and covariances to ensure both stability and plasticity, the following formula is employed to achieve this dual objective:

$$L_{KL}(f_a, f_p, f_n) = max(0, D_{KL}(N(f_a || \mu_p, \Sigma_p)) - D_{KL}(N(f_a || \mu_n, \Sigma_n)) + margin) \tag{5}$$

The KL-divergence distance measurement function:

$$D_{KL}(P||Q) = \int p(x) log \frac{p(x)}{q(x)} \tag{6}$$

Here, $D_{KL}(N(f_a || \mu_p, \Sigma_p))$ represents the KL-divergence between f_a and the mean μ_p and covariance Σ_p of class p, while $D_{KL}(N(f_a || \mu_n, \Sigma_n))$ signifies the

KL-divergence between f_a and the mean μ_n and covariance Σ_n of class n. Using KL-divergence as a distance measurement function in triplet learning entails utilizing it to measure the difference or distance between distributions of data points. This approach enables the model to learn by considering the distribution disparities between data points belonging to different classes.

Memory and Multivariate Gaussian Representation for Reproducing Past Knowledge. The reason we set the selection condition as the average of the presentation during presentation generate and data sampling is as follows:

- The objective of memory storage methods, regardless of input size, is to facilitate the storage and regeneration of data representations.
- Generating new class information for each task prevents overfitting data statically allocated to memory.
- Adjusting the encoder with raw data to obtain a more consistent data representation.

This section introduces how to convert and regenerate data with multivariate Gaussian distribution. Inspired by [17], we use multivariate Gaussian distributions and OWM (Orthogonal Weight Modification) to efficiently store and utilize previous knowledge. Every individual task, the classification is achieved by leveraging the encoder and classifier models. After training, we estimate the distribution of representations as a mixture of multivariate Gaussian distribution. Multivariate Gaussian distribution represents data with mean μ and covariance Σ as

$$N(x) = \left(\frac{1}{2\pi}\right)^{\frac{p}{2}} |\Sigma|^{-\frac{1}{2}} exp(-\frac{1}{2}(x' - \mu)^T \Sigma^{-1}(x' - \mu)) \tag{7}$$

where x' is $E(x)$. The advantage of multivariate Gaussian distribution is that the representation can be seen from multiple dimensional perspectives. Covariance shows the correlation between two variables so that multivariate Gaussian can represent the actual distribution accurately. To estimate the distribution, we use expectation-maximization (EM) algorithm to compute means and covariances. EM algorithm is a method to find the maximum log-likelihood of probability function as:

$$\mathcal{L}(X; \theta) = \ln p(X|\pi, \mu, \Sigma) = \sum_x \ln \left(\sum_{k=1}^{K} \pi_k N(x|\mu_k, \Sigma_k)\right) \tag{8}$$

where N is the number of x, K is the number of distributions, $N(\bullet)$ is the equation (2) to compute means and covariances, and π is the ratio of data in each distribution. The mean and covariance stored in memory are repeatedly used to generate data presentation, where $i > 0$. From randomly generated normal vectors S, we generate the representation $\hat{x}$ of class k as:

$$\hat{x}^k = (S * \lambda_k) \Gamma_k^T + \mu_k \tag{9}$$

$$\Sigma_k = \Gamma_k \lambda_k \Gamma_k^T \tag{10}$$

where the covariance is decomposed into an eigenvalue matrix λ_k and eigenvector matrix Γ_k. Classifier C_i performs classification through the data representation reproduced from the memory and the output of the encoder. To cope with the increase in class, a new classifier C_i is generated for each task to proceed in learning. So,

$$y_{0 \sim i} = C_i(E_i(X_i); \hat{X}_{0 \sim i-1}) \tag{11}$$

where $\hat{X}_{0 \sim i-1}$ is set of $\hat{x}$ from memory. That is, since the classifier can learn the representation of data for $T_0 \sim T_i$, the CF can be prevented.

Feature Representation with Orthogonal Regularization. To preserve the encoder's prior knowledge, we employ orthogonal weight modification, a technique that updates the model in a direction perpendicular to the gradient of the previous task, thereby preventing the loss of acquired knowledge.

Conventionally, for an FC layer the weight matrix W is updated by gradient descent algorithm and learning the k_{th} task T_k leads to the change $W^k = W^{k-1} - \lambda \Delta W_{BP}^k$ where λ is learning rate and ΔW_{BP}^k represents the gradient computed by back propagation (BP) during training T_k. To explain by using the explanation of [14], $W^{n-1}\mathbf{x}_{in}^{<n} - \lambda \Delta W_{BP}^n \neq W^{n-1}\mathbf{x}_{in}^{<n}$. The deviation accumulates across $\sim n$ out layers and causes catastrophic forgetting on previous tasks. To overcome this problem, [16] have developed OWM algorithm to restrict ΔW_{BP}^n to the orthogonal to the input of previous tasks. If $\nabla W_{n+1}^T \mathbf{x}_i = 0$, then the output will be preserve. So, we must compute an orthogonal projector matrix P that projects ∇W to the orthogonal subspace of input space. We can calculate P in an efficient as described in [16]:

$$P^k = P^{k-1} - \left(\alpha + \bar{\mathbf{x}}_k^T P^{k-1} \bar{\mathbf{x}}_k\right)^{-1} P^{k-1} \bar{\mathbf{x}}_k \bar{\mathbf{x}}_k^T P^{k-1} \tag{12}$$

where k indexes the mini-batch and x_k is the mean of the k_{th} mini-batch's inputs. Although we use FC layer to explain here, OWM can be applied to other neural networks such as convolution neural networks (CNN).

4 Experiments

4.1 Datasets and Baseline

The CIFAR-100 dataset contains 100 classes and each class has 500 train and 100 test color images. TinyImageNet consists 200 classes that include 100,000 images for training and 10,000 images for validation. We compare our method with state-of-the-art and well-established methods, including eight rehearsal based method. To facilitate comparison, we designed our experiments by drawing inspiration from the baseline employed in [18]. (ER [19], GEM [20], AGEM [6], GSS [21], FDR [22], HAL [23], ERT [24], and RM [25]), two methods leveraging Knowledge Distillation (iCaRL [9] and DER++ [26]). We further provide an upper bound (JOINT) obtained by training all tasks jointly and a lower bound simply performing SGD without any countermeasure to forgetting.

Table 1. Results (overall accuracy %) on CIFAR-100, TinyImageNet, and ImageNet-100 benchmarks, averaged over multiple runs.

Memory Buffer	Method	CIFAR100			TinyImageNet	ImageNet 100
		5 split	10 split	20 split		
-	Joint	70.21 ± 0.15	70.21 ± 0.15	71.25 ± 0.22	59.36 ± 0.19	73.82 ± 0.23
	SGD	17.27 ± 0.14	8.62 ± 0.09	4.73 ± 0.06	7.87 ± 0.24	8.72 ± 0.37
200	ER	21.94 ± 0.83	14.23 ± 0.12	9.90 ± 1.67	8.79 ± 0.21	9.58 ± 0.34
	AGEM	17.97 ± 0.26	9.44 ± 0.29	4.88 ± 0.09	8.28 ± 0.15	9.27 ± 0.08
	iCaRL	30.12 ± 2.45	22.38 ± 2.79	12.62 ± 1.43	8.64 ± 0.78	12.59 ± 0.68
	FDR	22.84 ± 1.49	14.85 ± 2.76	6.70 ± 0.79	8.77 ± 0.82	10.08 ± 0.36
	DER++	27.46 ± 1.16	21.76 ± 0.78	15.16 ± 1.53	11.16 ± 0.95	11.92 ± 0.12
	ERT	21.61 ± 0.87	12.91 ± 1.46	10.14 ± 1.96	10.85 ± 0.24	13.51 ± 1.13
	RM	32.23 ± 1.09	22.71 ± 0.93	15.15 ± 2.14	13.58 ± 1.07	16.76 ± 0.84
500	ER	27.97 ± 0.33	21.54 ± 0.29	15.36 ± 1.15	10.15 ± 0.32	11.68 ± 0.25
	AGEM	18.75 ± 0.51	9.72 ± 0.22	5.97 ± 1.13	9.67 ± 0.18	10.92 ± 0.16
	iCaRL	35.95 ± 2.16	30.25 ± 1.86	20.05 ± 1.33	10.69 ± 1.53	16.44 ± 1.35
	FDR	29.99 ± 2.23	22.81 ± 2.81	13.10 ± 3.34	10.58 ± 0.22	11.78 ± 0.40
	DER++	38.39 ± 1.57	36.15 ± 1.10	21.65 ± 1.44	19.33 ± 1.41	14.52 ± 1.86
	ERT	28.82 ± 1.83	23.00 ± 0.58	18.42 ± 1.92	12.13 ± 0.36	20.42 ± 1.13
	RM	39.47 ± 1.26	32.52 ± 1.53	23.09 ± 1.72	18.96 ± 1.34	14.56 ± 2.64
-	**Ours**	$\mathbf{41.24 \pm 8.91}$	$\mathbf{36.12 \pm 6.52}$	$\mathbf{29.12 \pm 9.23}$	$\mathbf{21.55 \pm 10.23}$	$\mathbf{24.82 \pm 3.55}$

4.2 Experimental Results

In Table 1, evaluating CIFAR-100, following the protocol by [9] for training across 5, 10, and 20 task splits, our method significantly outperformed other CL approaches, showing over 8%p improvement with 200 memory slots and 2%p with 500, highlighting its efficiency and adaptability with limited memory per class. Similarly, on the TinyImageNet and ImageNet-100 datasets, our method exceeded other Class-IL and Task-IL methods, surpassing state-of-the-art by approximately 1.2% and 4.4% in accuracy, respectively. These results demonstrate our method's consistent superiority in managing incremental learning challenges, particularly in scenarios with constrained data availability and across diverse datasets.

Figure 2 (left) presents task-specific outcomes visualized to demonstrate the decline in accuracy. Notably, the method not only exhibits the most favorable results compared to alternative methods but also demonstrates remarkable stability by retaining previous knowledge. This confirms that the proposed method adeptly addresses the dilemma of maintaining both strong performance and preventing the loss of past knowledge. The experimental results demonstrate that our method outperforms other methods on CL benchmark datasets, showing not only superior performance but also the most stable performance improvement as tasks increase, as seen in Table 1 and Fig. 2. This highlights our model's ability to pre-set the latent space for future tasks using a contrastive learning-based method, ensuring stable learning with the introduction of new tasks. Further-

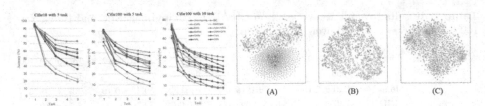

Fig. 2. (left) Task-wise accuracies (%). Joint learning shows the upper bound of the model. (right) t-SNE of actual representations and generated representations of class 0 in CIFAR100 by (A) univariate Gaussian, (B) GAN-based generator, and (C) multivariate Gaussian. Pink and blue dots represent real and generated data representations, respectively. (Color figure online)

more, Fig. 2 (right) illustrates the difference in the distribution of actual data during the restoration process from memory, indicating that our use of multivariate Gaussian distributions appropriately integrated with contrastive learning produces representations closely matching the actual data distribution. This further showcases the effectiveness of our method in utilizing regenerated representations that align with real data distributions.

5 Conclusion

This paper highlights the dependency on past tasks as a significant limitation of existing CL methods and proposes the creation of representations for CL using contrastive learning to overcome this issue. By securing the latent space for future tasks through contrastive learning and storing means and covariances in memory space, our method achieves stable performance compared to conventional CL methods.

Acknowledgements. This work was supported by the Yonsei Fellow Program funded by Lee Youn Jae, IITP grant funded by the Korea government (MSIT) (No. 2022-0-00113, Developing a Sustainable Collaborative Multi-modal Lifelong Learning Framework), and Air Force Defense Research Sciences Program funded by Air Force Office of Scientific Research.

References

1. Guo, Y., Liu, B., et al.: Online continual learning through mutual information maximization. In: ICML, pp. 8109–8126 (2022)
2. Zhao, Z., Zhang, Z., et al.: Rethinking gradient projection continual learning: stability/plasticity feature space decoupling. In: CVPR, pp. 3718–3727 (2023)
3. Buzzega, P., Boschini, M., et al.: Rethinking experience replay: a bag of tricks for continual learning. In: International Conference on Pattern Recognition, pp. 2180–2187 (2021)
4. Lomonaco, V., Maltoni, D., et al.: Rehearsal-free continual learning over small non-IID batches. In: CVPR Workshops (2020)

5. Prabhu, A., Torr, P.H.S., Dokania, P.K.: GDumb: a simple approach that questions our progress in continual learning. In: Vedaldi, A., Bischof, H., Brox, T., Frahm, J.-M. (eds.) ECCV 2020. LNCS, vol. 12347, pp. 524–540. Springer, Cham (2020). https://doi.org/10.1007/978-3-030-58536-5_31

6. Chaudhry, A., Ranzato, M.A., et al.: Efficient lifelong learning with A-GEM. arXiv preprint arXiv:1812.00420 (2018)

7. Chaudhry, A., Dokania, P.K., Ajanthan, T., Torr, P.H.S.: Riemannian walk for incremental learning: understanding forgetting and intransigence. In: Ferrari, V., Hebert, M., Sminchisescu, C., Weiss, Y. (eds.) ECCV 2018. LNCS, vol. 11215, pp. 556–572. Springer, Cham (2018). https://doi.org/10.1007/978-3-030-01252-6_33

8. Yoon, J., Madaan, D., et al.: Online coreset selection for rehearsal-based continual learning. arXiv preprint arXiv:2106.01085 (2021)

9. Rebuffi, S.A., Kolesnikov, A., et al.: iCaRL: incremental classifier and representation learning. In: CVPR, pp. 2001–2010 (2017)

10. Javed, K., White, M.: Meta-learning representations for continual learning. In: NeuRIPS, vol. 32 (2019)

11. Gupta, G., Yadav, K., et al.: Look-ahead meta learning for continual learning. In: NeuRIPS, vol. 33, pp. 11588–11598 (2020)

12. Gallardo, J., Hayes, T.L., et al.: Self-supervised training enhances online continual learning. arXiv preprint arXiv:2103.14010 (2021)

13. Zhang, M., Wang, T., et al.: Variational prototype replays for continual learning, arXiv preprint arXiv:1905.09447 (2019)

14. Zhang, B., Guo, Y., et al.: Memory recall: a simple neural network training framework against catastrophic forgetting. IEEE Trans. Neural Netw. Learn. Syst. **33**(5), 2010–2022 (2021)

15. Kirkpatrick, J., Pascanu, R., et al.: Overcoming catastrophic forgetting in neural networks. Proc. Natl. Acad. Sci. **114**(13), 3521–3526 (2017)

16. Zeng, G., Chen, Y., et al.: Continual learning of context-dependent processing in neural networks. Nat. Mach. Intell. **1**(8), 364–372 (2019)

17. Kim, T.H., Moon, H.J., et al.: Gradient regularization with multivariate distribution of previous knowledge for continual learning. In: International Conference on Intelligent Data Engineering and Automated Learning, pp. 359–368 (2022)

18. Wang, Z., Liu, L., et al.: Continual learning with lifelong vision transformer. In: CVPR, pp. 171–181 (2022)

19. Riemer, M., Cases, I., et al.: Learning to learn without forgetting by maximizing transfer and minimizing interference. arXiv preprint arXiv:1810.11910 (2018)

20. Lopez-Paz, D., Ranzato, M. A.: Gradient episodic memory for continual learning. In: NeuRIPS, vol. 30 (2017)

21. Aljundi, R., Lin, M., et al.: Gradient based sample selection for online continual learning. In: NeuRIPS, vol. 32 (2019)

22. Chen, D., Lin, Y., et al.: Measuring and relieving the over-smoothing problem for graph neural networks from the topological view. In: AAAI, vol. 34, no. 4, pp. 3438–3445 (2020)

23. Chaudhry, A., Gordo, A., et al.: Using hindsight to anchor past knowledge in continual learning. In: AAAI, vol. 35, no. 8, pp. 6993–7001 (2021)

24. Buzzega, P., Boschini, M., et al.: Rethinking experience replay: a bag of tricks for continual learning. In: CVPR, pp. 2180–2187 (2021)

25. Bang, J., Kim, H., et al.: Rainbow memory: continual learning with a memory of diverse samples. In: CVPR, pp. 8218–8227 (2021)

26. Buzzega, P., Boschini, M., et al.: Dark experience for general continual learning: a strong, simple baseline. In: NeuRIPS, vol. 33, pp. 15920–15930 (2020)

Influence of Color on Academic Performance: A Studio with Auditory Sustained Attention Within a Virtual Scenario

Gabriel Ávila-Muñoz[1][✉], Miguel A. López-Gordo[1,2][✉], and Manuel Rodríguez-Álvarez[1,3]

[1] Neuroengineering and Computation Lab, Research Centre for Information and Communication Technologies (CITIC-UGR), University of Granada, 18014 Granada, Spain
{gabriavila,malg,manolo}@ugr.es

[2] Department of Signal Theory, Telematics and Communications, Research Centre for Information and Communication Technologies (CITIC-UGR), University of Granada, 18014 Granada, Spain

[3] Department of Computer Engineering, Automation and Robotics, Research Centre for Information and Communication Technologies (CITIC-UGR), University of Granada, 18014 Granada, Spain

Abstract. It is known that colors and lighting have an influence on human physiology with potential affection to cognitive performance. Although according to some theories, cold colors (bluish) cause relaxation and concentration while warm colors (redish) cause arousal and alertness, researchers have not reached a consensus yet on the net effect that this could cause on the performance of tasks under study. The objective of the present study is to compare the academic performance under two conditions, blue and red lighting, and see if any of them could be advantageous during an auditory attentional task. Participants listened to five auditory sustained attention tests while they were exposed to either red or blue lightning, within a virtual reality environment, and the cerebral activity was recorded using EEG. Our results showed that students under the blue lighting condition achieved better and constant academic performance right after the beginning of the first test and up to the last one (68.3% vs. 60.0% median values). Also, a logistic regression model was able to classify the color condition from the Power Spectral Density of EEG bands (occipital electrodes yielding an accuracy of 84.6% (CI [57.8%–95.7%]). These results suggest that the blue color has a positive and immediate impact on the academic performance of auditory tests with noticeable differences in cerebral activity in comparison with the red color. These promising results encourage researchers to gain insights into the real influence of colors over the academic performance with immediate impact on schools and academic centers.

Keywords: Auditory sustained attention · Academic performance · EEG · VR

© The Author(s), under exclusive license to Springer Nature Switzerland AG 2024
J. M. Ferrández Vicente et al. (Eds.): IWINAC 2024, LNCS 14674, pp. 528–538, 2024.
https://doi.org/10.1007/978-3-031-61140-7_50

1   Introduction

It is thought that color could have an influence on human cognitive processes and behavior [4]. Nevertheless, in the learning and the academic spheres, there is no consensus about what color could have better academic performance (reviews [9, 12, 20]).

Results in [5] suggested that red color could have an adverse effect on task achievement. They compared different colors (red, green and three achromatic colors: gray, black and white) in different environments (laboratory and classroom) with undergraduate and high school students. Another study conducted on children [2] also showed that worse results were obtained when the color screen was red. However, another study [7] conducted different kind of tests associated to knowledge, intelligence or reasoning and reported no evidence that red could affect in a negative way to intellectual performance. Even more, a study [19] compares long-wavelength (red) light with short-wavelength light (blue) and they concluded that red light could increase alertness in the afternoon hours, especially in the post-lunch hours. Authors in [13] concluded that red is better for a simple detailed task whilst blue color is better for a complex detailed task and creative tasks, either simple or complex. It was also reported that attention, memory and preference were better with blue walls in an academic related task [15]. In another experiment [11] also concluded that blue walls are better to relax but, in terms of performance, the best scores were obtained with yellow walls, followed by red, green, blue and white. Both studies [11, 15] were made with virtual reality (VR) simulations. It is demonstrated [17, 21] the suitability of VR on color-based studies because it permits researchers to control each small detail of the experimental environment.

In general, a flaw in most of the studies is the lack of a big enough sample size to reach a high statistical power. Furthermore, the wide variety of methods and approaches (e.g., visual vs. auditory stimuli, sustained vs. selective attention, etc.) yield heterogeneous results with intrinsic difficulty to compare them and get definitive conclusions. In terms of the objective assessment of the attention, literature shows that certain cognitive tasks cause modulation of the power spectral density (PSD) of the cerebral bands: delta ($<4\,\mathrm{Hz}$), theta (4–$8\,\mathrm{Hz}$), alfa (8–$12\,\mathrm{Hz}$), beta (12–$30\,\mathrm{Hz}$) and gamma ($>30\,\mathrm{Hz}$). EEG recording is one suitable tool for measuring PSD and it is used in different studies, for instance, authors in [1] related a lower alpha PSD with an increase in the performance of an sustained attention test, meanwhile theta PSD increased. Other authors [8] pointed out that in the brain zone related to the task a decrease in the beta band precedes worse behavioral performance. In the same thought, authors in [6] presented a low-cost EEG-based system that could estimate the children's attention at class based on the beta PSD and relate it to their academic performance. They reveal that the higher the beta PSD was, the better academic performance they achieved.

The objective of the present study is to compare the academic performance under two conditions, blue and red lighting, and see if any of them could be advantageous during an auditory attentional task. We integrate two relevant technologies: on one hand, conditions will be generated and controlled and by means of a VR and, on the other hand, EEG will be recorded for the objective analysis of cerebral activity during conditions.

2   Materials and Methods

2.1   Participants and Experimental Design

Fourteen university students from the University of Granada voluntarily participated in the study (four females and ten males, age mean 20.4, std 2.4). Volunteers did not receive any benefit. The inclusion criteria was students that declared no visual or auditory impairment. The Ishihara test was applied in order to check color blindness and students with more than five errors in the plates were discarded. Only one student was discarded because he manifested fatigue and showed disapproval during the test. This study was conducted at the Research Centre for Information and Communication Technologies (CITIC-UGR). The experiment was approved by the Research Ethics Committee of the University of Granada (3702/CEIH/2023) and participants signed an informed consent document before starting.

The experiment was based on two components: *EEG device* Versatile EEG by Bitbrain (Zaragoza, Spain) was used to acquire the EEG signals during the experiment. It is equipped with 16 channels and a sampling frequency of 256 Hz. The 16 semi-dry electrodes were distributed following the 10-20 International System (AF3, AF4, F3, Fz, F4, FCz, C3, Cz, C4, P3, P4, PO7, POz, PO8, O1, O2). Ground electrode was located at AFz position meanwhile reference was located at the right ear lobe. A monitor provided real time information about the impedance of the sensor assuring they kept in the appropriate range throughout the experiment; *VR headset* Meta Quest Pro was used to immerse participants in a virtual environment programmed with Unity Engine. The whole experiment lasted about one hour and it was carried out by all subjects one at a time.

Before starting, participants were distributed randomly in two groups, each one for each of the two conditions: red environment (two females, five males, mean age 20.7 ± 3.1) and blue environment (two females, four males, mean age 20.0 ± 1.1). The different phases of the procedure are as follows (see Fig. 1).

Preparation. The experiment started with a brief introduction in which the participants were told the context and they signed the informed consent. After that, they were subjected to Ishihira test in order to discard those who had problems identifying colors. Participants sat in a comfortable chair in front of an empty desk.

Calibration. The Versatile EEG device was set up. It was adjusted until the sensors impedances were in a suitable range. Afterwards, Meta Quest Pro VR

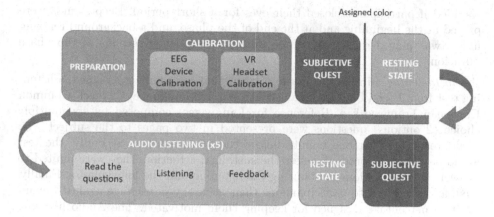

Fig. 1. Phases of the experimental procedure.

Headset was set up and hand tracking and sound were checked. The participants were instructed in how to use virtual hand interactions. Finally, EEG sensors impedances were checked again.

Subjective Test. The participants started in a white environment and they were requested to answer a subjective questionnaire in Spanish. Translated questions are shown in Table 1. This questionnaire was preceded by a reminder explanation of how to answer the questions within the VR environment. Notice that the second time (see last block in Fig. 1), the environment color was the assigned color for this subject in the experiment.

Table 1. The five questions contained in the subjective questionnaire.

Number	Subject Questions
1	What has your level of attention been so far?
2	What is your stress level right now?
3	What is your level of interest so far?
4	What has your level of mental effort exerted so far?
5	What is your level of relaxation?

Before the next phase, the color environment was changed to the assigned color for that subject (red or blue). See vertical black line in Fig. 1. This color environment will not change for the rest of the experiment.

Resting State. Participants were immersed in a virtual room without anything but the assigned color and they were asked to be relaxed without moving and staring at a fixed point located at the center of the virtual scene. A soft alarm sounded if participants closed their eyes for a short period. Beep sounds were played at the beginning and at the end of the phase, and a background relaxing music was played during the three minutes and eleven seconds of the phase duration.

Audio Listening. Firstly, within the color virtual environment assigned, a listening test from ELE (Teaching Spanish as a Foreign Language) C2 level (Common European Framework of Reference for Languages) composed by six multiple choice (2 options) questions were presented in two pages to the subject who could read them for one minute before the audio started. Secondly, the test audio is played. In order to assess the sustained attention, they were limited to answering the questions only during the listening and the following 5 s. Finally, feedback was given to participants as their accuracy percentage against a competitive percentage designed for keeping them motivated. The Audio listening phase was repeated once for each of the five chosen Spanish C2 listening exams. The order of the audios were randomized for each participant and their duration was in the range [4:46–5:03] (minutes:seconds)

2.2 Data Processing

Subject questionnaires answers were analyzed to give information about the interest, motivation and state of the participants during the experiment.

EEG data from Resting states and Audio listening phases were processed as follows. Per channel, EEG signals were divided into five-second epochs without overlapping. To each epoch, we applied a second order zero-phase shift band-pass Butterworth filter, from 1 to 40 Hz. Artifact removal was implemented by discarding epochs with absolute amplitude above 75 µV. Each epoch was then detrended and z-scored. Subsequently, we performed the spectral analysis. Per subject, the power spectral density (PSD) was calculated in different frequency bands (delta [1–4 Hz], theta [4–8 Hz], alpha [8–12 Hz], beta [12–30 Hz], and gamma [30–40 Hz], and then averaged across EEG channels. Finally, EEG channels were groups by areas and averaged: frontal (AF3, AF4, F3, Fz, F4, FCz), central (C3, Cz, C4), parietal (P3, P4) and occipital (PO7, POz, PO8, O1, O2).

A dataset was created per subject by combining the audio test questionnaires answers, the color environment and the mean of PSD of spectral bands per area. In order to see the influence of color, the academic performance was analyzed. The answers of the auditory attentional tests were splitted in two groups according to the color assigned to each participant. Due to the small sample size, the median of the scores of academic performance of both groups was analyzed. Median is a better indicator for central tendency, specially when the size of the sample is not large, and more robust against outliers [18]. Median absolute deviation was used as the uncertainty indicator [10]. Thereupon, a comparison of the cumulative evolution of correct answers was analyzed in order to assess the dynamics of the influence of color in a sustained auditory attention task. For this purpose, the cumulative scores of the academic performance per color was fitted to linear curves (one per color).

Finally, a logistic regression was implemented in order to classify the color of the environment subject from the processed EEG power bands. Leave one subject out (LOSO) cross validation was implemented due to the low samples. The overall confusion matrix was obtained from the confusion matrices that each model generated [16].

3   Results

The Fig. 2 shows the answers of participants to subjective questionnaires grouped by color environment in terms of median with median absolute deviation as uncertainty indicator. The Fig. 2a shows the absolute answers at the beginning (SQ1 = first Subject Quest) and at the end (SQ2 = second Subject Quest) of the experiment for each of the five questions (1 to 5) while the Fig. 2b represents the relative differences between the answers at the beginning and at the end for each question.

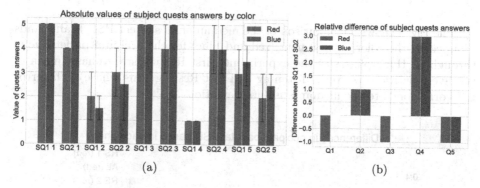

Fig. 2. Answers of participants to subjective quests grouped by color in terms of median with median absolute deviation as uncertainty indicator. (a) Absolute answers at the beginning (SQ1) and at the end (SQ2) for each question (1 to 5). (b) Relative differences between SQ1 and SQ2 for each question.

The Fig. 3a shows the color distributions (red and blue) and density curves for the percentage of correct answers of participants. The highest percentage was achieved by a red participant (90) although the blue group has a bigger median (68.3 vs 60.0).

The Fig. 3b shows a comparison of the cumulative evolution of correct answers through the five listening tests in terms of median. The error bars correspond to the median absolute deviation. Linear regression curves were calculated for all the participants data grouped by red (Eq. 1) and blue (Eq. 2) environment color.

$$y = 1.40x + 1.01 \tag{1}$$

$$y = 1.44x + 1.28 \tag{2}$$

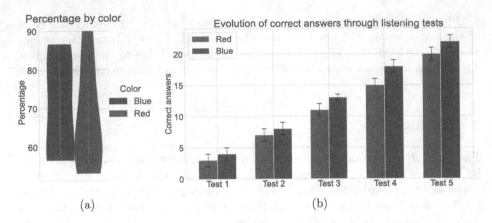

(a)   (b)

Fig. 3. Percentage of correct answers in listening tests by color. (a) Violion plot distribution. (b) Cumulative correct answers by color in terms of median. Median absolute deviation was used as the uncertain indicator. (Color figure online)

The Fig. 4 shows a comparison of the median of all subject PSD brain bands grouped by the color environment (red and blue) for the occipital-parietal zone throughout three phases of the experiment (first Resting state phase, mean of the five repetitions of Audio listening and last Resting state phase). The error bar corresponds to the median absolute deviation.

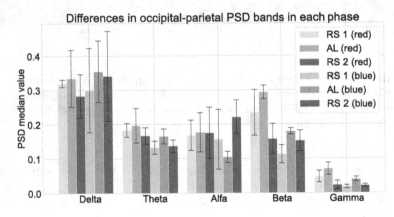

Fig. 4. Differences between color in each band in terms of median. The error bar corresponds to the median absolute deviation. (Color figure online)

The Fig. 5 represents the confusion matrix for color classification from EEG data using logistic regression. It achieved an accuracy of 84.6% (CI [57.8%–95.7%]), sensitivity of 83.3%, specificity of 85.7%, precision of 83.3% and F1 score of 0.83.

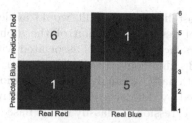

Fig. 5. Confussion matrix for color classification from PSD data using Logistic Regression.

4   Discussion

In this study a sustained auditory attention experiment was conducted within a colored blue or red virtual environment. Results suggest that the blue color has a positive and immediate impact on the academic performance of auditory tests with noticeable differences in cerebral activity in comparison with the red color.

Subjective Questionnaires. Results of subject questionnaires (see Fig. 2) show that the conditions of experiment were suitable for both red and blue groups. There is no significant difference in the answers of both groups in any of the five questions. Attention and interest remained very high and practically constant throughout the experiment whilst perceived stress increased similarly to how relaxation decreased. Finally, the mental effort increased noticeably, indicating that the experimental design was correct.

Academic Performance. The academic performance was slightly higher for the blue group in terms of median (68.3%) than for the red group (60.0%) (see Fig. 3a). This is in concordance with researchers whose results suggested that the performance of the blue environment was better than red [15]. The academic performance of the blue over the red group was obtained since the very first test and kept almost constant still the last test (see Fig. 3b). This suggests that the positive effects of immersion in blue lighting in comparison with immersion in red one, could be obtained within a really short period of a few minutes [14].

Cerebral Activity. In our study we hypothesized that blue lighting could have a positive effect on attention in comparison with the red one. In this case, that could be noticeable in the cerebral activity. The Fig. 4 shows the median of PSD across subjects for the five spectral bands under analysis registered over the occipital and occipital-parietal areas (where the visual cortex is located). It shows a remarkable enhancement of the PSD of beta and gamma bands for both groups (blue and red) during the auditory test in comparison with the Resting states phases. This is coherent with studies in literature that associate the increment of the gamma power band in the specific zone where the task is processed (occipital-parietal in visual task) [3]. However, in the alpha band, there was a noticeable difference between the blue and red group. While for the blue one alpha diminished the PSD as expected, for the red one the PSD of alpha remained almost flat. This result would evidence that blue lighting has a better capacity of desynchronization of the alpha band in comparison with red. Since alpha desynchronization is associated with visual attention and sustained attention [1,3], this could justify the better academic performance of the blue group. Additionally we analyzed if exposition to either blue or red lighting could be detected by differences in cerebral activity. With this purpose we performed a logistic regression to classify colors based on PSD of EEG bands acquired over the visual cortex (see confussion matrix in Fig. 5). It yielded a significant accuracy of 84.6% CIU[57.8%-95.7%]. That means that i) lightning causes differences in cerebral activity; ii) EEG bands convey enough information to distinguish between blue and red lightning; iii) this could justify an influence of color on academic performance.

Acknowledgements. This work was supported by grant PID2021-128529OA-I00, MCIN/AEI/10.13039/501100011033, and by ERDF A way of making Europe; grant PROYEXCEL_00084, P21_00084, Projects for Excellence Research, funded by the Council for Economic Transformation, Industry, Knowledge and Universities, Junta de Andalucía 2021. We thank the Research Support Services of the Research Centre for Information and Communication Technologies (CITIC-UGR) for the support to review this paper.

References

1. Behzadnia, A., Ghoshuni, M., Chermahini, S.A.: EEG activities and the sustained attention performance. Neurophysiology **49**(3), 226–233 (2017). https://doi.org/10.1007/s11062-017-9675-1. http://link.springer.com/10.1007/s11062-017-9675-1
2. Brooker, A., Franklin, A.: The effect of colour on children's cognitive performance. Br. J. Educ. Psychol. **86**(2), 241–255 (2016). https://doi.org/10.1111/bjep.12101
3. Clayton, M.S., Yeung, N., Cohen Kadosh, R.: The roles of cortical oscillations in sustained attention. Trends Cogn. Sci. **19**(4), 188–195 (2015). https://doi.org/10.1016/j.tics.2015.02.004.   https://linkinghub.elsevier.com/retrieve/pii/S1364661315000285
4. Elliot, A., Maier, M.: Color psychology: effects of perceiving color on psychological functioning in humans. Annu. Rev. Psychol. **65**, 95–120 (2014). https://doi.org/10.1146/annurev-psych-010213-115035
5. Elliot, A., Maier, M., Moller, A., Friedman, R., Meinhardt, J.: Color and psychological functioning: the effect of red on performance attainment. J. Exp. Psychol. Gen. **136**(1), 154–168 (2007). https://doi.org/10.1037/0096-3445.136.1.154
6. Fuentes-Martinez, V.J., Romero, S., Lopez-Gordo, M.A., Minguillon, J., Rodríguez-Álvarez, M.: Low-cost EEG multi-subject recording platform for the assessment of students' attention and the estimation of academic performance in secondary school. Sensors **23**(23), 9361 (2023). https://doi.org/10.3390/s23239361. https://www.mdpi.com/1424-8220/23/23/9361
7. Gnambs, T.: Limited evidence for the effect of red color on cognitive performance: a meta-analysis. Psychon. Bull. Rev. **27**(6), 1374–1382 (2020). https://doi.org/10.3758/s13423-020-01772-1

8. Ko, L.W., Komarov, O., Hairston, W.D., Jung, T.P., Lin, C.T.: Sustained attention in real classroom settings: an EEG study. Front. Hum. Neurosci. **11**, 388 (2017). https://doi.org/10.3389/fnhum.2017.00388. http://journal.frontiersin.org/article/10.3389/fnhum.2017.00388/full

9. Konstantzos, I., Sadeghi, S.A., Kim, M., Xiong, J., Tzempelikos, A.: The effect of lighting environment on task performance in buildings - a review. Energy Build. **226**, 110394 (2020). https://doi.org/10.1016/j.enbuild.2020.110394. https://linkinghub.elsevier.com/retrieve/pii/S0378778820318405

10. Leys, C., Ley, C., Klein, O., Bernard, P., Licata, L.: Detecting outliers: do not use standard deviation around the mean, use absolute deviation around the median. J. Exp. Soc. Psychol. **49**(4), 764–766 (2013). https://doi.org/10.1016/j.jesp.2013.03.013. https://www.sciencedirect.com/science/article/pii/S0022103113000668

11. Liu, C., Zhang, Y., Sun, L., Gao, W., Zang, Q., Li, J.: The effect of classroom wall color on learning performance: a virtual reality experiment. Build. Simul. **15**(12), 2019–2030 (2022). https://doi.org/10.1007/s12273-022-0923-y

12. Llorens-Gámez, M., Higuera-Trujillo, J.L., Omarrementeria, C.S., Llinares, C.: The impact of the design of learning spaces on attention and memory from a neuroarchitectural approach: a systematic review. Front. Archit. Res. **11**(3), 542–560 (2022). https://doi.org/10.1016/j.foar.2021.12.002. https://linkinghub.elsevier.com/retrieve/pii/S2095263521000972

13. Mehta, R., Zhu, R.: Blue or red? Exploring the effect of color on cognitive task performances. Science **323**(5918), 1226–1229 (2009). https://doi.org/10.1126/science.1169144

14. Minguillon, J., Lopez-Gordo, M.A., Renedo-Criado, D.A., Sanchez-Carrion, M.J., Pelayo, F.: Blue lighting accelerates post-stress relaxation: results of a preliminary study. PLoS ONE **12**(10), e0186399 (2017). https://doi.org/10.1371/journal.pone.0186399. https://journals.plos.org/plosone/article?id=10.1371/journal.pone.0186399

15. Nolé Fajardo, M.L., Higuera-Trujillo, J.L., Llinares, C.: Lighting, colour and geometry: which has the greatest influence on students' cognitive processes? Front. Archit. Res. **12**(4), 575–586 (2023). https://doi.org/10.1016/j.foar.2023.02.003. https://linkinghub.elsevier.com/retrieve/pii/S209526352300016X

16. Perez-Valero, E., Morillas, C., Lopez-Gordo, M.A., Minguillon, J.: Supporting the detection of early Alzheimer's disease with a four-channel EEG analysis. Int. J. Neural Syst. **33**(4), 2350021 (2023). https://doi.org/10.1142/S0129065723500211. https://www.worldscientific.com/doi/10.1142/S0129065723500211

17. Perez-Valero, E., Vaquero-Blasco, M.A., Lopez-Gordo, M.A., Morillas, C.: Quantitative assessment of stress through EEG during a virtual reality stress-relax session. Front. Comput. Neurosci. **15**, 684423 (2021). https://www.frontiersin.org/articles/10.3389/fncom.2021.684423

18. Rider, W., Witkowski, W., Kamm, J.R., Wildey, T.: Robust verification analysis. J. Comput. Phys. **307**, 146–163 (2016). https://doi.org/10.1016/j.jcp.2015.11.054. https://www.sciencedirect.com/science/article/pii/S0021999115008025

19. Sahin, L., Figueiro, M.G.: Alerting effects of short-wavelength (blue) and long-wavelength (red) lights in the afternoon. Physiol. Behav. **116-117**, 1–7 (2013). https://doi.org/10.1016/j.physbeh.2013.03.014. https://www.sciencedirect.com/science/article/pii/S0031938413000644

20. Souman, J.L., Tinga, A.M., Te Pas, S.F., Van Ee, R., Vlaskamp, B.N.: Acute alerting effects of light: a systematic literature review. Behav. Brain Res. **337**, 228–239 (2018). https://doi.org/10.1016/j.bbr.2017.09.016. https://linkinghub.elsevier.com/retrieve/pii/S0166432817311002
21. Vaquero-Blasco, M.A., Perez-Valero, E., Lopez-Gordo, M.A., Morillas, C.: Virtual reality as a portable alternative to chromotherapy rooms for stress relief: a preliminary study. Sensors **20**(21), 6211 (2020). https://doi.org/10.3390/s20216211. https://www.mdpi.com/1424-8220/20/21/6211

Author Index

A

Adorna, Henry N.   II-420
Afsar, Sezin   II-183
Alaoui, Nabih   II-461
Alinejad-Rokny, Hamid   I-98, I-139
Alinejad-Rorky, Hamid   I-150
Alizadehsani, Roohallah   I-3, I-68, I-98, I-108, I-139
Álvarez, Mauricio A.   II-451
Álvarez-Marquina, Agustín   I-282, I-300
Aravena-Cifuentes, Ana Paula   II-441
Arco, Juan E.   I-78, I-118, I-191
Argiuolo, Antonietta   II-400
Arioua, Mounir   II-461, II-474
Atashi, Alireza   I-68
Atzmueller, Martin   I-496
Ávila-Muñoz, Gabriel   I-528
Avila-Villanueva, Marina   I-191
Azorín, José M.   I-223
Azorin-Lopez, Jorge   II-75

B

Badiola-Zabala, Goizalde   II-358
Bagherzadeh, Sara   I-150
Barakova, Emilia   I-322
Barakova, Emilia I.   I-310
Barios, Juan A.   I-171
Baroni, Fabiano   I-233
Barredo, Pablo   II-173
Bdaqli, Mohammad   I-128
Beheshti, Amin   I-139, I-150
Benavent-Lledo, Manuel   II-55, II-75
Benedicto, Gema   I-342, I-356
Benítez-Rochel, Rafaela   II-3
Berenguer-Agullo, Adrian   II-95
Beristain, Andoni   II-368
Berlanga, Antonio   I-371
Berro, A.   II-246
Blanco-Ivorra, Andrea   I-171, II-65
Bologna, Guido   II-378

Bonomini, María Paula   I-245, I-390, II-495, II-504, II-511, II-518
Boquete, Damian   II-378
Borja, Alejandro L.   I-401
Bosch, Facundo   II-518
Boutay, Jean-Marc   II-378
Bueno-Crespo, Andrés   II-451

C

Caballero, Alvaro   II-262
Caballero-Martin, Daniel   II-13, II-195
Cabarle, Francis George C.   II-420
Callejas, Zoraida   I-88
Campos-Alfaro, Francella   II-105
Cano-Escalera, Guillermo   II-358
Carmona-Martínez, Pablo   II-3
Carmona-Murillo, Javier   II-33
Carnero-Pardo, Cristobal   I-191
Carreira, Karina Anahi Ojanguren   II-368
Carrillo, Miguel Friz   I-509
Castillo-Barnés, Diego   I-14, I-55, I-161, II-205
Catalán, José. M.   I-171, II-65
Chen, Kuankuan   I-322
Chen, Shuwen   II-150
Cho, Sung-Bae   I-518
Chougdali, Khalid   II-461
Chowdhury, Arnab Ghosh   I-496
Conde, Cristina   I-270
Contreras A., Ricardo   I-509
Contreras, Ricardo   II-347
Cornejo-Bueno, Laura   II-303, II-314, II-323
Correia, Luís   I-421
Costa, Nuno   I-421, I-431

D

de la Paz, Félix   I-441
de la Rosa, Francisco López   II-23
de Lope, Javier   I-261
del Ser-Quijano, Teodoro   I-191
Dios, J. R. Martínez-de   II-215

J. M. Ferrández Vicente et al. (Eds.): IWINAC 2024, LNCS 14674, pp. 539–543, 2024.
https://doi.org/10.1007/978-3-031-61140-7

Domínguez, Rocío   II-246
Domínguez-García, Jose Luis   II-246
Domínguez-Mateos, Francisco   I-282
Đurasević, Marko   II-140
Duro, Richard J.   II-105

E
Elizalde, Mariana   I-223
Eloualkadi, Ahmed   II-474
Estevez, Julian   II-13, II-195

F
Fabello, Esteban   II-368
Fernández, Eduardo   I-213, I-342, I-356,
      II-485
Fernández-Caballero, Antonio   I-342, I-356,
      I-401, I-411, I-421, I-431, I-441, II-23
Fernández-Rodríguez, Jose David   II-3,
      II-33, II-44
Fernández-Ruiz, Raúl   I-282
Ferrández, José Manuel   I-342, I-401, II-504
Ferrández-Vicente, José Manuel   I-332
Figueiredo, Patrícia   I-55
Filgueiras, Juan Luis   II-129
Fister, Dušan   II-314, II-323
Fleming, Glenda   II-368
Formoso, Marco A.   I-24, I-34, I-45, I-161
Frades-Payo, Belen   I-191
Frazão, Luis   I-431
Fuentes-Riffo, Karina   I-509, II-347

G
Galeano-Brajones, Jesús   II-33
Gallardo-Cava, Roberto   I-270
Gallego-Molina, Nicolás J.   I-14, I-24, I-34,
      I-45, I-55, I-118, I-161
Garcés, Joel Alejandro Cueva   II-485
García, Arturo S.   I-441
García-Aguilar, Iván   II-33, II-44
García-Aracil, Nicolás   I-171, II-65
García-Gutiérrez, Gabriel   II-275
García-Quismondo, Enrique   II-275
Garcia-Rodriguez, Jose   II-55, II-75, II-85,
      II-95
García-Román, Manuel Damián   II-333
García-Rubio, Irene   I-270
Garrigos, Javier   II-504

Gheoghe, Marian   II-163
Ghiglioni, Eduardo   I-390
Gigliotta, Onofrio   II-400
Gil, Miguel   II-262
Gil-Gala, Francisco J.   II-140
Giménez, Almudena   I-45
Gómez-López, María Dolores   II-461, II-474
Gómez-Orellana, Antonio Manuel   II-283,
      II-293, II-303
Gómez-Rodellar, Andrés   I-300, I-332
Gómez-Sirvent, José L.   I-401, II-23
Gómez-Valadés, Alba   I-381
Gómez-Vilda, Pedro   I-300, I-332
Gommer, Erik D.   I-203
González-Rodríguez, Inés   II-183
Goodfellow, Nicola   II-368
Górriz, Juan Manuel   I-3, I-14, I-68, I-78,
      I-98, I-108, I-118, I-128, I-139, I-150,
      I-161, I-182, I-191, II-150, II-225,
      II-246
Grabska, Ewa   I-486
Grabska-Gradzińska, Iwona   I-486
Graña, Manuel   I-261, II-13, II-195, II-358,
      II-368, II-410, II-441
Griol, David   I-88
Guerra, Barbara   II-368
Guijo-Rubio, David   II-283, II-293, II-303
Guillen-Garcia, Julio   I-270
Gutiérrez, Pedro A.   II-283, II-293

H
Haijoub, Abdelilah   II-474
Hashemi, Mohammad   I-108
Hatim, Anas   II-474
Heras, Jonathan   I-150
Hernández, Valentina   II-347
Hernández-Díaz, Alejandro M.   II-333
Herranz-Lopez, María   I-223
Hervás-Martínez, César   II-283, II-293
Hongn, Andrea   I-245, II-518
Hortal, Enrique   I-203, II-389
Hristov-Kalamov, Nikola   I-282

I
Iáñez, Eduardo   I-223
Illán, Ignacio A.   I-78
Imbernón, Baldomero   II-451

Ingallina, Fernando II-511
Ipate, Florentin II-163

J

Jafari, Mahboobeh I-139
Jafarizadeh, Ali I-3
Jansen, Anniek I-310
Janssen, Marcus L. F. I-203
Jara, Carlos II-105
Jiménez-Fernández, Silvia II-275
Jiménez-Mesa, Carmen I-78, I-191
Jiménez-Partinen, Ariadna II-116
Jodra-Chuan, Marina I-332
Joloudari, Javad Hassannataj I-68, I-98,
    I-108
Juan, Carlos G. I-342
Julian, V. I-476

K

Kably, Salaheddine II-461
Kamali, Sara I-233
Karel, Joël I-203
Karki, Suraj II-504
Kawa, Bartosz I-455
Kerexeta, Jon II-368
Khademi, Maryam I-68
Khodatars, Marjane I-150
Khoulji, Samira II-461
Komamardakhi, Seyedeh Somayeh Salehi
    I-108
Kutt, Krzysztof I-455, I-465
Kutt, Marzena I-455

L

la Paz, Félix de I-356
Ladislav, Stanke II-368
Leblanc, Quentin II-378
Leite, Gabriel M. C. II-275
Li, Jing I-322
LLamosas-Mayca, Waldemar Hugo II-333
Lledó, Luis D. II-65
López, Álvaro Lanchas I-441
López, María T. I-411
López, R. I-182
López-García, David II-225, II-246
López-Gordo, Miguel A. I-528
Lopez-Guede, Jose Manuel II-13, II-195
López-Peco, Rocío I-213
López-Pérez, Pedro J. I-118, I-161

López-Rubio, Ezequiel II-3, II-44
Lorente-Ramos, Eugenio II-333
Luna, A. I-182
Luna-Jiménez, Cristina I-88
Luna-Santamaria, J. II-215
Luna-Valero, Francisco II-33
Luongo, Maria I-253, II-400
Luque, Juan L. I-34, I-55, I-161, II-205
Luque-Baena, Rafael Marcos II-33, II-44

M

Maftoun, Mohammad I-68, I-108
Manso, Marco II-368
Marcelino, Carolina Gil II-275
Marco-Detchart, C. I-476
Martin, Cristina II-368
Martín, José Angel Sanchez II-430
Martínez, Jesica I-223
Martinez, Jose Javier II-504
Martínez-España, Raquel II-451
Martínez-Más, José II-451
Martínez-Murcia, Francisco J. I-24, I-78,
    I-161, I-182
Martínez-Pascual, David II-65
Martínez-Tomás, Rafael I-381
Martín-Noguerol, T. I-182
Massanés, David I-496
Mateo-Trujillo, J. Ignacio II-205
Maza, Ivan II-246, II-262
Meinert, Steffen I-496
Mekyska, Jiri I-300
Mendes, Carla I-431
Micol, Vicente I-223
Milano, Nicola I-253
Mitrana, Victor II-430
Molina, José M. I-371
Molina, José P. I-441
Molina-Cabello, Miguel A. II-3
Molina-Ramos, Ana I. II-116
Moon, Hyung-Jun I-518
Morais-Quilez, Igone I-261
Morales, Rafael II-23
Morales-García, Juan II-451
Moravvej, Seyed Vahid I-98
Moreno-Salvador, Lucía II-23
Moridian, Parisa I-128
Morollón Ruiz, Roberto II-485
Mulero-Pérez, David II-55, II-75
Mutsaers, Milou I-322

N

Nalepa, Grzegorz J.   I-455, I-465
Naya-Varela, Martín   II-105
Nematollahi, Mohammad Ali   I-68, I-108
Nowak, Leszek   I-486
Nuñez-Gonzalez, J. David   II-441
Núñez-Vidal, Esther   I-282

O

Ochoa, Marco Augusto Suing   II-495
Ollero, Anibal   II-215, II-246, II-262
Ordóñez, Beatriz del Cisne Macas   II-495,
    II-504, II-511
Orellana-Martín, David   II-420
Ortega-delCampo, David   I-270
Ortiz, Andrés   I-14, I-24, I-34, I-45, I-55,
    I-118, I-161, I-191, II-205
Ortiz, Mario   I-223
Ortíz-González, Ana   II-451
Ortiz-Perez, David   II-55, II-75, II-85, II-95
Orts-Escolano, Sergio   II-55

P

Palacios, Juan José   II-183
Palacios-Alonso, Daniel   I-270, I-282, I-300
Palma, Jesús   II-275
Palomo, Esteban J.   II-116
Pascual, Esperança Lladó   II-368
Patricio, Miguel A.   I-371
Paulano-Godino, F.   I-182
Păun, Mihaela   II-430
Pedrammehr, Siamak   I-3
Peinado, Alberto   II-205
Peláez-Rodríguez, C.   II-314, II-323
Pelle, Patricia   I-245
Pereira, António   I-411, I-421, I-431
Pereira, Rafael   I-431
Pérez, David   II-225, II-246
Pérez-Aracil, Jorge   II-275, II-283, II-293,
    II-303, II-314, II-323, II-333
Pérez-Jiménez, Mario J.   II-420
Pinacho-Davidson, Pedro   I-509, II-347
Pinilla, Sergio   II-275
Pinninghoff J., M. Angélica   I-509
Pinninghoff, María Angélica   II-347
Pleşsa, Mihail-Iulian   II-163
Poma, Alvaro   II-262
Ponticorvo, Michela   I-253, II-400
Porlan-Ferrando, Lucia   II-441

Pouyani, Mozhde Firoozi   I-128
Prado, Lara Eleonora   I-245, II-518
Prieto, Inmaculada   II-246
Prodanovic, Milan   II-275
Puente, Jorge   II-173, II-183

Q

Quesada, Jesús   II-140

R

Rajebi, Saman   I-3
Ramínez, Luisa Merino   I-441
Ramírez, Javier   I-78, I-118, I-161, I-182,
    I-191, II-225, II-246
Ramírez-de-Arellano, Antonio   II-420
Razi, Murat   II-410
Rincon, J. A.   I-476
Rincón, Mariano   I-381
Rios, Noelia Belén   I-390
Rodríguez, I. G.   II-215
Rodríguez-Álvarez, Manuel   I-528
Rodríguez-Capitán, Jorge   II-116
Rodriguez-Juan, Javier   II-85, II-95
Rodríguez-Rivero, Jacob   II-225, II-246
Rodríguez-Rodríguez, Ignacio   I-14, I-34,
    I-45, II-205
Rojas-Albarracín, Gabriel   I-411
Roman-Escorza, Francisco Javier   II-262
Romero, Alejandro   II-105, II-246
Roshanzamir, Mohamad   I-98
Rosique-Egea, Daniel   II-451

S

Sadeghi, Delaram   I-128, I-139
Sala, Pietro   I-108
Salcedo, Pedro   II-347
Salcedo-Lagos, Pedro   I-509
Salcedo-Sanz, Sancho   II-275, II-283, II-293,
    II-303, II-314, II-323, II-333
Sánchez-Gómez, Auxiliadora   II-205
Sánchez-Reolid, Daniel   I-401
Sánchez-Reolid, Roberto   I-401, II-23
Santos, José   II-129
Scott, Michael   II-368
Segovia, Fermín   I-182, II-225, II-246
Selga, Albert Gili   II-246
Serrano, Raúl   II-225, II-246
Shalbaf, Ahmad   I-128
Shoeibi, Afshin   I-128, I-139, I-150

Sierra, María R.   II-140
Sijstermans, Ryan   II-389
Silva, Tatiana   II-368
Sistaninezhad, Masoud   I-3
Solà, Pol Paradell   II-246
Soo, Leili   II-485
Soto-Sánchez, Cristina   I-213
Stabile, Pietro   I-55
Sun, Chang   II-389

T
Thurnhofer-Hemsi, Karl   II-116
Tomás, David   II-85
Tomáš, Vohralík   II-368
Tsiakas, Konstantinos   I-310

V
Val-Calvo, Mikel   I-213
Valenti-Soler, Meritxell   I-191
Vales, Yolanda   I-171
Varela, Ramiro   II-140
Vargas, Víctor M.   II-283, II-293
Varona, Pablo   I-233
Vázquez-García, Cristóbal   I-78

Vega-Bayo, Marta   II-303
Vela, Camino R.   II-183
Villavicencio, Diego Vinicio Orellana
      II-495, II-511
Vossen, Catherine J.   I-203

W
Wang, Jiaji   II-150
Wang, Shuihua   II-150
Węgrzyn, Paweł   I-486
Woo, Wai Lok   I-24
Wu, Meng   II-150

Y
Yang, Liuyiyi   I-322
Yozkan, Elif   I-203
Yun, Víctor Manuel Vargas   II-303

Z
Zare, Omid   I-68, I-108
Zavoiko, Rostyslav   II-44
Zea-Sevilla, Maria A.   I-191
Zhang, Yudong   II-150
Zubasti, Pablo   I-371